Indigenous and Cultural Psychology

Understanding People in Context

International and Cultural Psychology Series

Series Editor: **Anthony Marsella**, *University of Hawaii, Honolulu, Hawaii*

A Continuation Order Plan is available for this series. A continuation order will bring delivery of each new volume immediately upon publication. Volumes are billed only upon actual shipment. For further information please contact the publisher.

Indigenous and Cultural Psychology
Understanding People in Context

Edited by

Uichol Kim
Inha University
Incheon, Korea

Kuo-Shu Yang
Academic Sinica and National Taiwan University
Taipei, Taiwan

Kwang-Kuo Hwang
National Taiwan University
Taipei, Taiwan

 Springer

Library of Congress Control Number: 2005932042

ISBN-10: 0-387-28661-6   eISBN 0-387-28662-4
ISBN-13: 0-978-387-28661-7

Printed on acid-free paper

Printed in the United States of America.   (SPI/MP)

9 8 7 6 5 4 3 2 1

springer.com

Contributors

John G. Adair is Professor Emeritus of Psychology at the University of Manitoba, Winnipeg, Canada. He received his Ph.D. degree (1965) in Social Psychology from the University of Iowa. He is a former member of the Executive Committees of the International Union of Psychological Science and of the International Association of Applied Psychology and for a number of years was Coordinator of their joint program of Advanced Research and Training Seminars (ARTS). He is the author/editor of three books, three special issues of journals, and numerous articles and chapters in books. Dr. Adair's research and writing has focused on social studies of the science of psychology, addressing such topics as the social nature of human research methodology, ethics of research with human subjects, social science research policy, indigenization and development of the discipline in developing countries, and the internationalization of psychology. E-mail: *adair@Ms.UManitoba.CA*.

Yukari Ariizumi is a doctoral student at the Department of Social Psychology, University of Tokyo, Japan, where she received her M.A. in social psychology. Her dissertation is concerned with the psychological function of the gender-differentiated Japanese expressions. Her research interests include the effect of the Japanese sentence endings on person perception, self-identification, interpersonal relationship, and the gender stereotype particularly in Japanese culture.

Vibeke Grover Aukrust is Professor of Educational Psychology at the Institute for Educational Research at the University of Oslo. She has been doing cross-cultural research on language socialization and parental beliefs in Norway and the US and is currently directing a study of language and literacy development in Turkish minority children in Norway. She is the author of articles and chapters on socialization of childhood language, speech genres in parent-child conversation, and cultural differences in parental ideas about children's talk, for example, Aukrust, V. G. & Snow, C. E. (1998), "Narratives and explanations during mealtime conversations in Norway and the U.S.," *Language in Society, 27*, 221 – 246, and Aukrust (2001), "Agency and appropriation of voice — cultural differences in parental ideas about young children's talk," in *Human Development, 44*, 235–249. Address correspondence to Institute for Educational Research, University of Oslo, Pb 1092, Blindern, N-0317 Oslo, Norway; E-mail: *v.g.aukrust@ped.uio.no*.

Zeynep Aycan is an Associate Professor of Industrial and Organizational Psychology at Koç University. She completed her Ph.D. at Queen's University under the supervision of John W. Berry. She conducted Post-Doctoral studies at Faculty of Management, McGill University, where she worked with Rabindra N. Kanungo. Trained as a cross-cultural psychologist, her research focuses on the impact of culture on various aspects of organizational processes, including leadership, human resource management, and women's career development. She has published three books: *Expatriate Management: Theory and Research* (JAI Press, 1997), *Leadership, Management, Human Resource Practices in Turkey* (Turkish Psychological Association, 2000); *Frontiers of Cross-Cultural Organizational Behavior* (with Michele Gelfand & Miriam Erez; Sage, forthcoming), and more than 35 articles and book chapters. She is the co-founder of the *International Journal of Cross-Cultural Management* (Sage). She was elected as the President (2006-2008) of the International Society for the Study of Work and Organizational Values. She also served as a consultant or trainer to companies including Bechtel-Enka, Phillip-Morris, Migros, Alcatel, Efes/Pfizer, Finansbank, and GlaxoSmithKlein. She is the recipient of Recognition Award and Outstanding Young Scholar award from the Turkish Academy of Sciences for her contributions to management sciences at the national and international levels. Address correspondence to Koç University, Istanbul, Turkey. Tel: 90-212 338 1353, Fax: 90-212 338 3760. E-mail: *zaycan@ku.edu.tr*.

Pawel Boski is a Professor of Psychology at the Polish Academy of Sciences. He is also director of the Institute for Psychology of Intercultural Relations at the Warsaw School of Social Psychology. His interests include: culture psychological dimensions (especially humanism-materialism, femininity, and uncertainty avoidance); acculturation and identity; culture competence and training. Within all these research domains he advocates cultural and intercultural, rather than cross-cultural approaches. This entails a research methodology based on studies of cultural meaning (scripts, artefacts) rather than the use of culture-free scales. Address correspondence to Institute of Psychology, Polish Academy of Sciences, Warsaw, Poland. E-mail: *boskip@psychpan.waw.pl*.

Sang-Chin Choi is a Professor of Psychology at Chung-Ang University, Seoul, Korea. He received his Ph.D. from the University of Hawaii. He is currently the president of the Korean Cultural Psychological Association. He has also served as president of the Asian Association of Social Psychology and the Korean Psychological Association. He has published *Korean Psychology* (2000, Chung-Ang University Press) and co-edited *Psychology of the Korean People* (Dong-a Publisher, 1995) and *Individualism and Collectivism* (Sage, 1994). He has devoted himself to developing Korean indigenous psychology for the past twenty years. Address correspondence to Sang-Chin Choi, Department of Psychology, Chung-Ang University, Seoul 156-756, Korea. E-mail: *choi@cau.edu.kr.*

Rolando Diaz-Loving is Professor, Department of Psychology, Universidad Nacional Autonoma de Mexico, Mexico. He received his Ph.D. in Social Psychology from the University of Texas at Austin in 1981. He has been a visiting professor at the University of Manitoba and at the University of Texas. His research has focused on cross-cultural psychology, personal relationships, ethno-psychology and health. He has been the editor of the *Revista de Psicologia Social y Personalidad* and has served on editorial boards, including the *Journal of Cross-Cultural Psychology, Personal Relationships* and the *Inter American Journal of Psychology.* He has received many awards for his contributions, such as the National Award for Research in the Social Sciences from the Mexican Academy of Sciences, the Inter American Psychologist awards from the Inter American Society of Psychology, the National Psychology Award from the Mexican National Council for Teaching and Research in Psychology and the Social Sciences Research Award from the National Autonomous University of Mexico. E-mail: *loving@servidor.unam.mx.*

Lutz H. Eckensberger received his Diploma degree in psychology in 1964. He finished his doctorate in 1970, and after his Habilitation in 1973 he became a professor at the University of the Saarland (Saarbrücken), where he has been a full time professor since 1976. In 1996 he moved to Frankfurt/Main where he was director of the German Institute for International Educational Research from 1998 to 2004. He is head of the section Culture and Development in that institute, and he has a chair of Psychology at the Johann Wolfgang Goethe University in Frankfurt. In 1985–1986 he was fellow of the Center for Advanced Studies in Berlin. Besides his focus on methods and methodology, his main interest is in the field of moral development under a cultural and action theory perspective. He is also interested in the contextualization of morality in cancer and environmental issues, which implies the analysis of the relation between facts and norms, cognition and affects control and risk taking, as well self and solidarity with others. He has published over 90 articles in books and journals and edited 15 books. E-mail: *Eckensberger@dipf.de.*

Carolyn Pope Edwards is Willa Cather Professor of Psychology and Family and Consumer Sciences at the University of Nebraska, with interests in early childhood education, cross-cultural studies of socialization, and moral/social development processes within family and school settings. She is an author or editor of *Ngecha: A Kenyan Village in a Time of Rapid Social Change* (University of Nebraska Press, 2004), *Moral Motivation* (University of Nebraska Press, 2005), *Children of Different Worlds: The Emergence of Social Behavior* (Harvard University Press, 1988), *The Hundred Languages of Children: The Reggio Emilia Approach, Advanced Reflections* (Ablex, 1998), and *Bambini: The Italian Approach to Infant/Toddler Care* (Teacher College, 2001), as well as articles and chapters. She has held visiting research professor positions at universities in Kenya, Italy, and Norway. Address correspondence to Burnett Hall 322, University of Nebraska, Lincoln, NE 68588-0308, USA. E-mail: *cedwards1@unl.edu.*

Heidi Fung is an associate research fellow of the Institute of Ethnology at Academia Sinica, Taipei, Taiwan. She received her doctoral training from the Committee on Human Development at the University of Chicago. After teaching at the Department of Psychology at the Chinese University of Hong Kong for four years, she returned to her native Taiwan in 1996 to assume her current post. From 2000 to 2001, she was visiting scholar at the Yenching Institute and the Graduate School of Education at Harvard University. She has long been interested in understanding how culture and self constitute each other. Her research involves the socialization of emotion, disciplinary practices, and moral training at home with young Taiwanese children, parental child-rearing beliefs across cultures, and the methodological issues of situating human development in cultural context. Address correspondence to Institute of Ethnology, Academia Sinica, Taipei, Taiwan. E-mail: *hfung@sinica.edu.tw.*

James Georgas is Professor Emeritus of Psychology of the University of Athens, Athens, Greece; Member of the Board of Directors, International Association of Applied Psychology; President-Elect of the International Association for Cross-Cultural Psychology; Member of the Executive Committee, International Union of Psychological Science; Member of the Aristotle Prize Committee, European Federation of Psychologists Associations; Member of the Wilhelm Wundt-William James Award Committee, European Federation of Psychologists Associations and American Psychological Association; Member of the Steering Committee of the European Values Study; Partner for Greece, Leonardo Program, European Diploma in Psychology; Member of the Scholarship Committee, Alexander S. Onassis Public Benefit Foundation. His current cross-cultural research interests are on the relationships between structure and function of the family and psychological variables across cultures, theory and methodology in cross-cultural research, cross-cultural measure of intelligence, construction of psychometric tests, and attitudes and values. E-mail: *dgeorgas@psych.uoa.gr*.

Kwang-Kuo Hwang obtained his Ph.D. in social psychology at the University of Hawaii. He is currently a National Chair Professor awarded by Taiwan's Ministry of Education at National Taiwan University. He has endeavored to promote the indigenization movement of psychology and social science in Chinese society since the early 1980s, and has published eight books and more than 100 articles on related issues in both Chinese and English. He is currently President of the Asian Association of Social Psychology. E-mail: *kkhwang@ntu.edu.tw*.

Martin J. Jandl studied philosophy, history of art, and psychology at the University of Vienna. In his book entitled *Kritische Psycholopgie and Postmoderne (Critical Psychology and Postmodernism)*, published in German in 1999, he examines procedures of philosophical reflection in psychological theories. He is critical of defining human beings using cognitivism as the starting point and emphasizes the need to examine linguistic and praxeological approaches in psychology. His research interests include philosophy of psychology, philosophy of language, action theory, and philosophy of mind. Jandl lives and works as a free scientist in Vienna. E-mail: *mj.jandl@aon.at*.

Kibum Kim obtained his Ph.D. degree from Chung-Ang University in 2002. His research interests include the relationship between culture and emotion, interpersonal relationships, and self-concept in Korea. He is currently an adjunct professor at Sungkyunkwan University, Seoul, Korea.

Misuk Kim is an associate professor in the Department of Child Welfare at Chung-Ang University, Seoul, Korea. She earned her doctorate in education from the University of Massachusetts-Amherst. With strong interests in early childhood education and the Reggio Emilia approach to education, she has been an invited scholar at the University of Vermont and the Stockholm Institute of Education at the Department of Child and Youth Studies in Sweden. She has published articles concerning children's conceptual understanding and community learning, and she is now working on ethnography of a toddler classroom. Address correspondence to Department of Child Welfare Study, Chung-Ang University, 221 Huksuk-dong Dongjak-ku, Seoul, 156-756, Korea. E-mail: *kmisukch@yahoo.co.kr*.

Uichol Kim is Inha Fellow Professor at the College of Business Administration, Inha University, Incheon, Korea. He has taught at Chung-Ang University and the University of Hawaii at Manoa (1988-1994). He has specialized in the area of indigenous and cultural psychology and published over 100 articles and 12 books. His publications include *Indigenous Psychologies* (Sage, 1993), *Individualism and Collectivism* (Sage, 1994), *Progress in Asian Social Psychology* (Wiley, 1997), *Good Government* (NIAS Press, 2002) and *Democracy, Human Rights and Islam in Modern Iran* (Fagbokforlaget, 2003). He has conducted research in the area of family and parent-child relationship, educational attainment and school violence, organizational culture and change, health and subjective well-being, and democracy, human rights, and political culture. He has taught at University of Tokyo, Japan, the University of Stockholm, Sweden, the Nordic Institute for Asian Studies, Denmark, the University of Konstanz, Germany, Warsaw School of Advanced Social Psychology, Poland, and the University of Bergen, Norway. He has provided consulting services for governmental agencies and multi-national companies in Canada, Denmark, Hong Kong, India, Korea, Malaysia, Singapore, Thailand, and the United States. He is the founding editor of *Asian Journal of Social Psychology* and currently the president of Division of Psychology and National Development, International Association of Applied Psychology. E-mail: *uicholk@chol.com*.

Lisa Knoche is an applied developmental scientist and is currently the Project Director of the Getting Ready Project at the University of Nebraska-Lincoln, a five-year study of parent engagement and child learning. Her primary research interests include community based-research with disadvantaged populations and early childhood education, particularly factors related to child care quality. Her dissertation research, directed by Dr. Carolyn Edwards, focuses on social awareness, as it relates to child care quality and measures of school readiness. Lisa is interested in developing and evaluating interventions and research methodologies for use with at-risk populations in an effort to inform community-based programs and agencies. Address correspondence to 238 Teachers College Hall, UNL, Lincoln, NE 68506, USA. E-mail: *lknoche2@unl.edu*.

Asiye Kumru is Assistant Professor of Developmental Psychology at Abant Izzet Baysal University, Bolu, Turkey. She received her Ph.D. degree in 2002 in Developmental Psychology from University of Nebraska-Lincoln. She is currently the project director of a five-year longitudinal study of children's cognitive, emotional and prosocial development supported by the TUBITAK Carrrier Program, Turkey. Her research interests focus on identity, prosocial and moral development in children and adolescents, young children's socioemotional development, and gender socialization. She is the author of many chapters and articles, such as "Relational, cultural, cognitive, and affective predictors of prosocial behaviors" [*Olumlu sosyal davranislarin iliskisel, kültürel, bilissel ve duyussal bazi degiskenlerle iliskisi*], published in the *Turkish Journal of Psychology*,

2004, *19*, 109-128. Address correspondence to the Department of Psychology, Faculty of Arts and Sciences, Abant Izzet Baysal University, Golkoy/Bolu 14280, Turkey. E-mail: *kumru_a@ibu.edu.tr*.

Ramesh C. Mishra is Professor of Psychology at Banaras Hindu University. A D. Phil. from Allahabad University, he has been Post-doctoral Research Fellow, Shastri Research Fellow and Visiting Professor at Queen's University, Canada. He has also been Visiting Professor at University of Geneva and Jean Piaget Archives, Switzerland. His principal interest is in cultural influence on human development, and he has contributed numerous articles to professional journals, both in India and abroad, in the fields of cognition, acculturation, schooling, and cross-cultural studies. He has extensively contributed chapters to books, including the *Handbook of Cross-Cultural Psychology* and *the Handbook of Culture and Psychology*. He is the co-author (with J. W. Berry and D. Sinha) *of Ecology, Acculturation and Psychological Adaptation: A Study of Adivasis in Bihar*, and co-editor (with J. W. Berry and R. C. Tripathi) of *Psychology in Human and Social Development: Lessons from Diverse Cultures*. E-mail: *rcmishra_2000@yahoo.com*.

Kostas Mylonas, M.Sc., Ph.D., is a lecturer on Research Methods and Statistics in Psychology, Department of Psychology, University of Athens, Greece. His research interests include assessment and bias analysis, cross-cultural applications of factor analysis, emotional bonds and contact among family members, and multivariate methods and analysis. His recent publications include, *Factor Analysis for the HELLENIC WISC-III: Domains of Cognitive Development* (2004); two chapters in Georgas, Weiss, van de Vijver, Saklofske (Eds.), *Culture and Children's Intelligence: Cross-Cultural Analysis of the WISC-III.* Greece (2003); *Methodology of Combining the WISC-III Datasets* (2003); "Families and Values in Europe" (2004), in Arts Halman (Eds.), *European Values at the Turn of the Millennium* (2004); and "Families in Greece," in Roopnarine & Gielen (Eds.), *Families in Global Perspective* (2005). E-mail: *kmylonas@psych.uoa.gr.*

Zhong Nian graduated from the Department of Psychology of Peking University in 1983, and was a lecturer in psychology at the Institute of Anthropology at Hubei University before being promoted to the rank of Associate Professor in Psychology at Wuhan University in Wuhan, the capital city of Hubei Province in central China. He now teaches psychology at Wuhan University, and has written over 100 books and articles on Chinese culture and psychology.

Young-Shin Park is Professor of Education, Inha University, Incheon, South Korea. She was the Vice-Dean of the College of Education, Inha University, Incheon, South Korea. Her research interests include parent-child relationship, adolescent development, self-efficacy, school violence, trust, and subjective well-being. She has been conducting a longitudinal study of adolescent development in Korea for the past eight years. Her publications include *Parent-child relationship in Korea* (2004), *Adolescent Culture and Parent-Child Relationship in Korea* (2004) and *Adolescent Culture of Korea* (1997). She has been selected as the top research professor in Education, Humanities and Social Sciences at Inha University in 1999 and 2004. She is currently the editor-in-chief of *Korean Journal of Psychological and Social Issues*, consulting editor of *Asian Journal of Social Psychology*, and editor of *Korean Journal of Educational Psychology*. Address correspondence to Department of Education, Inha University, 253 Yonghyeon-dong, Nam-ku, Inchon, 402-751, South Korea. FAX: 8232-874-0535. E-mail: *yspark@inha.ac.kr*.

Rogelia Pe-Pua is a Senior Lecturer at the School of Social Science and Policy at the University of New South Wales. She taught at the Department of Psychology at the University of the Philippines for 15 years before emigrating to Australia in 1992. She is a strong force in the indigenization movement in the Philippines, known for her contribution in the development of indigenous research methodology. Her research and publications have focused on indigenous psychology and migration psychology. She has conducted several research on acculturation, cultural diversity and cross-cultural issues in Australia during the last ten years. Among these are research that involve examining the experiences of international students in Australian universities, street-frequenting ethnic youth, refugee families, Hong Kong immigrants in Australia, and the legal needs of ethnic residents in western Sydney. She has also worked collaboratively with international researchers such as international research looking at comparing ethnocultural youth identity and acculturation in 13 countries, and research on culture and trait involving 4 countries. E-mail: *R.Pe-Pua@unsw.edu.au*.

Kaiping Peng was a lecturer in psychology at Peking University's Psychology Department of China before coming to the United State in 1989. He received his Ph.D. in social psychology from the University of Michigan in Ann Arbor in 1997, and joined the faculty of the Department of Psychology of the University of California at Berkeley in the same year. He is currently an Associate Professor in Psychology and the head of the social/personality psychology program at Berkeley. He directs the culture and cognition lab at UC-Berkeley and has published four books and many articles on culture and psychology. E-mail: *kppeng@socrates. berkeley.edu*.

Julie Spencer-Rodgers is currently a post-doctoral researcher at the Department of Psychology, at the University of California, Berkeley. She received her Ph.D. degree from Berkeley in 2004. Her dissertation on culture and dialectical well-being won the prestigious Otto Klineberg

Intercultural and International Relations Award by the Society for the Psychological Study of Social Issues in 2004.

Fritz G. Wallner was born in Weiten, Austria. He studied several disciplines (philosophy, classical literatures, education). After graduation he became a teacher of high school in Wiener Neustadt. In 1981, he returned to Vienna University as senior lecturer. Since the seventies he worked intensively on Wittgenstein's Philosophy and published 40 essays and two books on this topic. In 1983 he became chairman of the International Karl Popper Symposium in Vienna and invited Karl Popper to Vienna University. In 1983, he became reader at the Department for Theoretical Physics. In the eighties and in the nineties he worked for the Ministry of Education teaching seminars for advanced education for teachers. In 1987, he became professor for Philosophie of Science. He developed a new philosophy of science, Constructive Realism, and lectured in 60 countries. In the last ten years his specific interest is focused on the relation between science and culture in this field and he analyzed the structure of Traditional Chinese Medicine and worked on the structure of indigenous knowledge systems. He wrote over 150 essays and 10 books including: *Die Grenzen der Sprache und der Erkenntnis*, 1983; Constructive Realism, 1994; *Ocho Lecciones sobre el Realismo Constructivo*, 1994; *How to deal with science if you care for other cultures*, 1997; and *Culture and Science*, 2002. E-mail: *friedrich.wallner@univie.ac.at*.

Susumu Yamaguchi is a professor at the Department of Social Psychology, the Graduate School of Humanities and Sociology, the University of Tokyo. He has been on the faculty of the University of Tokyo since 1987. His research interests include individualism-collectivism, control orientations, indigenous concept of *amae*, and implicit and explicit self-esteem across cultures. The overall aim of his research is to promote intercultural understandings by advancing scientific knowledge about human beings in various cultural contests. He believes that indigenous perspectives are essential for a better understanding of human beings in cultural contexts, although he never denies *etic* aspects of psychological processes. He is one of the founders and a former president of the Asian Association of Social Psychology. He is currently the president of the Japanese Group Dynamics Association. Address correspondence to Department of Social Psychology, Graduate School of Humanities and Sociology, University of Tokyo, Hongo 7-3-1, Bunkyo-ku, Tokyo 113-0033, Japan. E-mail: *susumy@L.u-tokyo.ac.jp*.

Chung-Fang Yang obtained her Ph.D. in Social Psychology from the University of Chicago. She had worked for Leo Burnett Advertising Co. in Chicago and taught in the Marketing Department of the University of

Washington, the University of Southern California, and the Chinese University of Hong Kong before returning to the Psychology Department at the University of Hong Kong in 1984. Since then, she has adopted the indigenous approach to the study of the psychology of the Chinese people. She is now teaching at the Department of Psychology, Sun-Yat-Sen University, in Guangzhou, people's Republic of China. Her research interests are in the areas of the Chinese self and self-presentation, interpersonal relationships (關係) and human affection (人情), and the zhong-yung (中庸) thinking style. She is now teaching at the Department of Psychology, Sun-Yat-Sen University, in Guangzhou, People's Republic of China. E-mail: *yangxhongfang@hotmail.com*

Kuo-Shu Yang is currently the Chair Professor at the Department of Psychology at Fu Guang College of Humanities and Social Sciences. He received his Ph.D. in personality and social psychology from the University of Illinois in Urbana, after which he became an Associate and then Full Professor at the Department of Psychology at National Taiwan University and was jointly appointed as Associate Research Fellow and Research Fellow at the Research Institute of Ethnology, Academia Sinica (AS) in Taiwan. He went on to serve as the Vice President of AS for four years. His research interests include the indigenized, systematic study of Chinese personality and social behavior and their changes due to societal modernization, especially Chinese familism, filial piety, psychological traditionality and modernity, individual- and social-oriented achievement motivation, and individual- and social-oriented self. He has orchestrated a group of Chinese psychologists in Taiwan, Hong Kong, and mainland China to promote an academic movement for the indigenization of psychological research in Chinese societies. He has authored and edited more than 20 books and published more than 150 academic papers in Chinese and English. He was elected as an Academician in the 1998 biennial meeting of domestic and overseas academicians of Academia Sinica. Address correspondence to Department of Psychology, National Taiwan University, Taipei, Taiwan. Fax: (886-2) 2362-9909. E-mail: *kuoshu@ntu.edu.tw.*

Zhi-Xue Zhang is an Associate Professor of Organizational Behavior at the Department of Organization Management, Guanghua School of Management, Peking University. He received his Ph.D. degree in social psychology from the University of Hong Kong. His current research interests include leadership and organizational culture, psychological factors in managerial decision making, conflict resolution and negotiation. Address correspondence to Guanghua School of Management, Peking University, Beijing, 100871, China. Fax: 86-10-62751463. E-mail: *zxzhang@gsm.pku.edu.cn.*

Preface

The development of indigenous psychology as a field has a short history. Its emergence has been stimulated by leading psychologists in various parts of the world. Virgilio Enriquez was a charismatic leader, championing *Sikolohiyang Pilipino* (Filipino psychology), which became a national movement in the Philippines (Enriquez, 1992; Pe-pua, Chapter 5, this volume). Durgan and Sinha was critical of "carbon copying" Western psychology and was a vocal advocate of indigenizing psychology. There were other scholars who stressed the importance of indigenous knowledge: Yoshi Kashima in Australia; Bame Nsamenang in Cameroon; John Berry and John Adair in Canada; Reuben Ardila in Columbia; Denise Jodelet in France; James Georgas in Greece; Michael Bond, Fanny Cheung, David Ho, Henry Kao, Kwok Leung, and Chung-Fang Yang in Hong Kong; R. K. Naidu, J. B. P. Sinha, R. C. Tripathi, Ramesh Mishra, and Girishwar Misra in India; Hiroshi Azuma, Akira Hoshino, and Susumu Yamaguchi in Japan; Sang-Chin Choi, Uichol Kim, and Young-Shin Park in Korea; Rogelio Diaz-Guerrero and Rolando Diaz-Loving in Mexico; Michael Durojaiye in Nigeria; Alfred Lagmay and Rogelia Pe-pua in the Philippines; Leo Marai of Papua New Guinea; Pawel Boski in Poland; Boris Lomov in Russia; Carl Martin Allwood in Sweden; Pierre Dasen in Switzerland; Kuo-Shu Yang and Kwang-Kuo Hwang in Taiwan; Cigdem Kâğitçibaşi in Turkey; Padmal de Silva and Rom Harré in the United Kingdom; Fathali Moghaddam, Carolyn Pope, and Joseph Trimble in the United States; and José Miguel Salazar in Venezuela. They represented individual voices, with differing perspective and emphasis.

In 1993, Kim and Berry edited a volume entitled, *Indigenous Psychologies: Research and Experience in Cultural Context*, which articulated the background, need, and direction for the development of indigenous psychologies. Kim and Berry (1993) reviewed the scientific foundation and background of indigenous psychology and differentiated it from related areas: cultural anthropology (Heelas & Locke, 1991), ethnoscience (Holland & Quinn, 1987), and cross-cultural psychology (Berry, Poortinga, Segall, & Dasen, 2002). Since the publication of Kim and Berry's (1993) volume, scientific advances in indigenous psychology have been made largely outside of the Western context (i.e., North America and Europe); as a result, many are unaware of the scientific contributions that have been made during the past decade. The current volume brings together scholars from around the world to document these advances.

Prior to the publication of Kim and Berry's (1993) volume, indigenous psychology was a relatively unknown area that was collectively labeled as indigenous psychologies. Since 1993, indigenous psychology as a field began to receive greater attention. In 1999, John G. Adair and Rolando Diaz Loving published a special issue entitled, "Indigenous Psychologies: The Meaning of the Concepts and Its Assessment," in *Applied Psychology: An International Review*. In 2000, Chung-Fang Yang and Kwang-Kuo Hwang edited a special issue of *Asian Journal of Social Psychology,* comparing indigenous, cultural, and cross-cultural approaches. Recently, the *Asian Journal of Social Psychology* published a special issue entitled "Responses to Epistemological Challenges to Indigenous Psychologies," edited by Manfusa Sham and Kwang-Kuo Hwang (2005). Carl Martin Allwood and John W. Berry edited a special issue entitled "Origins and Development of Indigenous Psychologies: An International Analysis," which will appear in the *International Journal of Psychology* (2006).

Indigenous psychology is also being recognized as an emerging field in applied, social, cultural, and cross-cultural psychology. In recent handbooks, a chapter has been devoted to indigenous psychology in the *Handbook of Cultural Psychology* (Kim, 2001) and in *Handbook of Cross-Cultural Psychology* (Sinha, 1997). In the *Encyclopedia of Applied Psychology*, development of indigenous psychologies has been reviewed (Kim & Park, 2004). In textbooks, such as *Cross-Cultural Psychology: Research and Applications* (Berry et al., 2002) and *Social Psychology across Cultures* (Smith & Bond, 1999), developments in indigenous psychology are reviewed.

Even with the publication of the Kim and Berry (1993) volume, there are still misconceptions, erroneous interpretations, and unwarranted criticisms (e.g., Adamopoulos & Lonner, 2001; Herman & Kempen, 1998; Poortinga, 1999; Triandis, 2000). These erroneous conclusions are drawn since the authors are unaware of scientific advances that are made outside the Western context. Contrary to these misconceptions, indigenous psychology is a part of a scientific tradition advocates multiple *perspectives*, but not multiple *psychologies*. As such, the current volume uses the singular form of indigenous psychology rather than the plural form. Second, indigenous psychology recognizes the importance of examining culture as providing important content and context of psychological research.

To bring together diverse viewpoints, approaches, and perspectives in indigenous psychology around the world, an international workshop entitled *Scientific Advances in Indigenous Psychologies: Philosophical, Cultural and Empirical Contributions* was held in Taipei, Taiwan, October 29-November 1, 2001. The purpose of the three-day workshop was to bring together leading scholars to document the scientific advances in indigenous psychology and to discuss possible integration of the field. The workshop provided an opportunity for participants to present their views and findings and to discuss the basis for integration and collaboration.

If we had to identify a weakness in the present volume, it is the lack of representation of psychologists representing indigenous peoples. The volume focuses on modern nations, and we could not fully represent scholarly work on indigenous peoples. We hope that a volume that focuses on the indigenous psychology of indigenous peoples will be published in the near future.

For the publication of this volume, we would like to express our sincere gratitude to the Central office of the Academia Sinica, Taipei, Taiwan for providing the financial support enabling the workshop to take place. Academia Sinica provided full funding covering airfare, accommodations, meals, and a tour of Taipei. We also express our gratitude to the Research Institute of Ethnology, Academia Sinica, and Director Dr. Ying-Kuei Huang for allowing us to use their conference rooms and facilities. We would especially like to thank the staff and personnel at the Institute of Ethnology, who ensured that the workshop was completed efficiently and successfully. We would also like to thank the Office of Research in Chinese Indigenous Psychology, National Taiwan University, in helping to organize the workshop.

Based on the workshop, the present volume has been prepared. We would like to thank Dr. Olwen Bedford for proofreading all the chapters in the volume. The task of editing all the manuscripts was accomplished with the support of a grant from National Science Council, Republic of China, NSC 93-2752-H-002-001-PAE. We would like to thank the Specialization Project, Department of Psychology, Chung-Ang University, for providing administrative and financial support. We would also like to thank Anthony J. Marsella for including the current volume in the *International and Cultural Psychology Book Series*. Finally, we would like to thank Sharon Panulla, Anna Tobias, and Herman Makler at Springer who helped to finalize the publication of this volume.

UICHOL KIM
KUO-SHU YANG
KWANG-KUO HWANG

REFERENCES

Adair, J., G., & Diaz Loving, R. (1999). Indigenous psychologies: The meaning of the concepts and its assessment. *Applied Psychology: An International Review, 48*(4), Special Issue.

Allwood, C. M., & Berry, J. W. (in press). Origins and development of indigenous psychologies: An international analysis *International Journal of Psychology*, Special Issue.

Adamopoulos, J., & Lonner, W. (2001). Culture and psychology at a crossroad: Historical perspective and theoretical analysis. In D. Matsumoto (Ed.), *Handbook of culture and psychology* (pp. 11-34). Oxford: Oxford University Press.

Berry, J. W., Poortinga, Y. H., Segall, M. H., & Dasen, P. R. (2002). *Cross-cultural psychology: Research and applications, Second Edition.* Cambridge, MA: Cambridge University.

Enriquez, V.G. (1992). *From colonial to liberation psychology: The Philippine experience.* Quezon City: University of the Philippines Press.

Heelas, P., & Lock, A. (1981). *Indigenous psychologies: The anthropology of the self.* London: Academic Press.

Hermans, J. M., & Kempen, J. G. (1998). Moving cultures: The perilous problem of cultural dichotomy in a globalized society. *American Psychologist, 53*, 1111-1120.

Holland, D., & Quinn, N. (Eds.) (1987). *Cultural models in language and thought.* Cambridge: Cambridge University Press.

Kim, U. (2001). Culture, science and indigenous psychologies: An integrated analysis. In D. Matsumoto (Ed.), *Handbook of culture and psychology* (pp.51-76). Oxford: Oxford University Press.

Kim, U., & Park, Y. S. (2004). Indigenous psychologies. In C. Spielberger (Ed.), *Encyclopedia of applied psychology* (pp. 263-269). Oxford: Elsevier Academic Press.

Poortinga, Y. H. (1999). Do differences in behavior imply a need for different psychologies? *Applied Psychology: An International Review, 48*, 419-432.

Sinha, D. (1997). Indigenizing psychology. In J.W. Berry, Y.H. Poortinga, & J. Pandey (Eds.), *Handbook of cross-cultural psychology* (pp. 130-169). Boston: Allyn & Bacon.

Smith, P. B., & Bond, M. H. (1999). *Social psychology across cultures, Second Edition.* New York: Allyn & Bacon.

Triandis, H. C. (2000). Dialectics between cultural and cross-cultural psychology. *Asian Journal of Social Psychology, 3*, 185-196.

Shams, M. & Hwang, K. K. (2005). Responses to Epistemological Challenges to Indigenous Psychologies . *Asian Journal of Social Psychology, 8*(1), Special Issue.

Hwang, K. K. & Yang, C. F., (2000). Indigenous, cultural, and cross-cultural psychologies. *Asian Journal of Social Psychology, 3*(3), Special Issue.

Contents

II. FAMILY AND SOCIALIZATION

III. COGNITIVE PROCESSES

IV. SELF AND PERSONALITY

V. APPLICATION

Part I

Theoretical and Methodological Issues

Chapter **1**

Contributions to Indigenous and Cultural Psychology
Understanding People in Context

Uichol Kim, Kuo-Shu Yang,
and Kwang-Kuo Hwang

Indigenous psychology is an emerging field in psychology. It attempts to extend the boundary and substance of general psychology. Although both indigenous and general psychology seeks to discover universal facts, principles, and laws of human behavior, the starting point of research is different. General psychology seeks to discover decontextualized, mechanical, and universal principles and it assumes that current psychological theories are universal (Koch & Leary, 1985). Indigenous psychology, however, questions the universality of existing psychological theories and attempts to discover psychological universals in social, cultural and ecological context (Kim & Berry, 1993; Yang, 2000). Indigenous psychology represents an approach in which the content (i.e., meaning, values, and beliefs) context (i.e., family, social, cultural, and ecological) are explicitly incorporated into research design.

In science, universal theories, principles, and laws must be theoretically and empirically verified rather than assumed *a priori*. General psychology has attempted to develop objective, decontextualized and universal theories of human behavior by excluding the subjective aspects of human functioning (i.e., consciousness, agency, meaning, and goals). Although concepts of agency and consciousness were central to early psychologists (e.g., Wilhelm Wundt and William James), they have been expunged with the adoption of behaviorism (Kim & Park, Chapter 2; Koch & Leary, 1985). In science, Holten (1973) noted that objective and subjective aspects are interdependent and complementary, and they are not mutually exclusive. Albert Einstein noted that "science as an existing, finished [corpus of knowledge] is the most objective, most unpersonal [thing] human beings know, [but] science as something coming into being, as aim, is just as subjective and psychologically conditioned as any other of man's efforts" (cited in Holten, 1973, p. 6–7).

Indigenous psychology advocates examining knowledge, skills, and beliefs people have about themselves and how they function in their familial, social, cultural, and ecological context. It emphasizes obtaining a descriptive understanding of human functioning in a cultural context. With the theoretical, conceptual and empirical description, ideas are developed and tested to explain the observed regularities. It is "an evolving system of psychological knowledge based on scientific research that is sufficiently compatible with the studied phenomena and their ecological, economic, social, cultural, and historical context" (Yang, 2000, p. 245). The goal is to create a more rigorous, systematic, and universal science that can be theoretically and empirically verified.

If general psychology is universal, then indigenous psychology would not be necessary. In natural sciences, scholars do not question the scientific validity of their discipline, nor do they call for indigenization. In psychology, however, psychological theories have been regarded as culture-bound, value-laden, and with limited validity (Enriquez, 1993; Kim & Berry, 1993; Koch & Leary, 1985; Shweder, 1991). From the late 1960's, many scholars recognized the limited scientific validity, generalizability, and applicability of psychological theories (Gibson, 1985; Koch & Leary, 1985; Marsella, 1998).

There has a worldwide calls for indigenization and the development of psychology that is socially and culturally valid: Africa (Durojaiye, 1993; Cameroon, Nsamenang, 1995; Zambia, Serpell, 1984), Americas (Canada, Berry, 1974; Latin America, Ardila, 1982; Mexico, Diaz-Guerrero, 1977; United States, Cronbach, 1975, Smith, 1973; Venezuela, Salazar, 1984), Asia (China, Ching, 1984; Hong Kong, Ho, 1982; India, Sinha, 1984; Japan, Azuma, 1984; Korea, Kwon, 1979; the Philippines, Enriquez, 1977; Taiwan, Yang, 1986), Europe (France, Moocovici, 1972; Germany, Graumann, 1972; Scandinavia, Smedsland, 1984), the Middle East (Iran, Moghaddam, 1987; Turkey, Kagitcibasi, 1984), and Oceania (Fiji, Samy, 1978). Nsamenang (1995) points out that "psychology is ethnocentric science, cultivated mainly in the developed world and then exported to sub-Saharan Africa (p. 729). In Canada, Berry (1974) is critical of the culture-bound and culture-blind nature of psychology and argues for the development of psychology that is relevant to Canada. In France, Moscovici (1972) points out that American psychologists adopted "for its themes of research and for the contents of its theories, the issues of *its own* society" (p.19). Azuma (1984) points out that the development of universal theories is limited since American psychologists cannot understand phenomena found outside of the United States (abbreviated as U.S.): "When a psychologist looks at a non-Western culture through Western glasses, he may fail to notice important aspects of the non-Western culture since the schemata for recognizing them are not provided by his science" (p. 49). Even American psychologists recognize that theories in general psychology reflect the cultural values of the U.S. (Murphy & Kovach, 1972; Sampson, 1977; Shweder, 1991).

The most vocal critique of general psychology came from psychologists who have been trained in the West. When they return to their country and attempted to establish psychology in their own country, they encountered numerous difficulties and began to question the validity, universality and applicability of psychological theories (e.g., Hiroshi Azuma in Japan, Sang-Chin Choi in Korea, Michael Durojaiye in Nigeria, Virgilio Enriquez and Alfred Lagmay in the Philippines, David Ho and Chung-Fang Yang in Hong Kong, Bame Nsamenang in Cameroon, José Miguel Salazar in Venezuela, Durganand Sinha and Jai B. P. Sinha in India and Kuo-Shu Yang and Kwang-Kuo Hwang in Taiwan). These scholars point out that each culture should be understood from its own frame of reference, including its own ecological, historical, philosophical, and religious context.

The worldwide call for indigenization was preceded by the paradigmic crisis in psychology experienced from the late 1960's. Elms (1975) noted that "whether they are experiencing an identity crisis, a paradigmatic crisis, or a crisis in confidence, most seem to agree that a crisis is at hand" (p. 967). Smith (1973) pointed out that "our best scientists are floundering in the search for a viable paradigm" and "it is hard to tell the blind alleys from the salients of advance" (p. 464). Although call for indigenization has been frequently equated with rejection of neo-colonial influence, the basic problem of general psychology has been identified as the inappropriate emulation of the natural sciences approach (Bandura, 1999; Cronbach, 1975; Gibson, 1985; Kim, 1999; Kim & Berry, 1993; Shweder, 1991).

Existing psychological theories are not universal since they have eliminated the very qualities that allow people to understand, predict, and control their environment. Bandura (1999) points out that "it is ironic that a science of human functioning should strip people of the very capabilities that make them unique in their power to shape their environment and their own destiny" (p. 21). As such, "psychology has undergone wrenching paradigm shifts" and "in these transformations, the theorists and their followers think, argue, and act agentically, but their theories about how other people function grant them little, if any, agentic capabilities" (p. 21). Contributors to the present volume agree that psychological phenomena must be understood in its ecological, historical, philosophical, religious and cultural context.

INDIGENOUS PSYCHOLOGY

Kim and Berry (1993) define indigenous psychology "the scientific study of human behavior or mind that is native, that is not transported from other regions, and that is designed for its people" (p. 2). Indigenous psychology advocates examining knowledge, skills, and beliefs people have about themselves and studying these aspects in their natural contexts. Theories, concepts, and methods are developed to correspond with psychological phenomena. It advocates examining explicitly the content and context of research. The goal is to create a more rigorous, systematic, universal science that can be theoretically and empirically verified. Ten characteristics of indigenous psychology can be identified.

First, indigenous psychology emphasizes examining of psychological phenomena in context: Familial (Edwards, Lisa Knoche, Aukrust, Kumru, & Kim, Chapter 6; Fung, Chapter 8; Park & Kim, Chapter 19), social (Zhang, Chapter 19), political (Pe-pua, Chapter 5), philosophical (Hwang, Chapter 4; Peng, Chapter 11; Wallner & Jandl, Chapter 3;), historical (Diaz Loving, Chapter 14), religious (Boski, Chapter 17; Eckensberger, Chapter 10; Mishra, Chapter 12), cultural (Adair, Chapter 21; Aycan, Chapter 20; Choi & Kim, Chapter 16; Yamaguchi & Ariizumi, Chapter 7; Yang, Chapter 15; Yang, Chapter 13) and ecological (Georgas & Mylonas, Chapter 9) context. Yang (2000) reviews the various definitions of indigenous psychology and concludes that "no matter how these psychologists define indigenous psychology, the definitions all express the same basic goal of developing scientific knowledge system that effectively reflects, describes, explains, or understands the psychological and behavioral activities in their native contexts in terms of culturally relevant frame of reference and culturally derived categories and theories" (p. 245–246). It emphasizes the discovery and use of natural taxonomies in search of regularities, general principles and universal laws. It examines how people view themselves, relate to others and manage their environment.

Second, contrary to popular misconception, indigenous psychologies are not the studies of Native peoples, ethnic groups, or people living in Third World countries. Indigenous researches have often been equated with anthropological studies of "exotic" people living in distant lands. Indigenous psychology is needed for all cultural, native, and ethnic groups, including economically developing countries (Mishra, Chapter 12; Pe-pua, Chapter 5; Zhang, Chapter 18), newly industrialized countries (Choi et al., Chapter 16; Kim & Park, Chapter 2; Yang, Chapter 13) and economically developed countries (Adair, Chapter 21; Edwards, et al., Chapter 6; Yamaguchi et al., Chapter 7).

Third, indigenous does not affirm or preclude the use of a particular method. Indigenous psychology is a part of the scientific tradition where an important aspect of the scientific endeavor is the discovery of appropriate methods for the phenomenon under investigation. Boulding (1980) notes that, "within the scientific community there is a great variety of methods, and one of the problems which science still has to face is the development of appropriate methods corresponding to different epistemological fields" (p. 833). Indigenous psychology advocates the use of various methodologies: Qualitative (Edwards et al., Chapter 6; Pe-pua, Chapter 5; Yang, Chapter 15), quantitative (Fung, Chapter 8; Yang, Chapter 13), experimental (Boski, Chapter 17; Yamaguchi et al., Chapter 7; Zhang, Chapter 18), comparative (Aycan, Chapter 20; Georgas et al., Chapter 8; Yamaguchi et al., Chapter 7), multiple methods (Kim et al., Chapter 2; Pe-pua, Chapter 5; Park et al., Chapter 19) and philosophical analysis (Hwang, Chapter 4; Peng et al., Chapter 11; Wallner & Jandl, Chapter 3). Results from multiple methods should be integrated to provide a more comprehensive understanding of psychological phenomena.

Fourth, it has been assumed that only natives or insiders of a culture could understand indigenous and cultural phenomena and that an outsider can only have a limited understanding. Although a person who has been born and raised in a particular community may have insights into indigenous phenomena, this may not always be the case. As Wirth (1946) observes, "the most important thing ...that we can know about a person is what he [or she] takes for granted, and the most elemental and important facts about a society are those things that are seldom debated and generally regarded as settled" (p. xxiv). An outsider, with an external point of view, can call to attention what is assumed to be natural to be actually cultural. He or she may point out peculiarities, inconsistencies, and blind spots that insiders may have overlooked (Kleinman, 1980). Both internal and external points of view are necessary in providing a comprehensive and integrated understanding of psychological phenomena (Wallner et al., Chapter 3).

Fifth, indigenous psychology is different from Heider's (1958) naive psychology. Heider (1958) noted that in the area of interpersonal behavior, "the ordinary person has a great and profound understanding of himself and of other people which, though unformulated or vaguely conceived, enables him to interact in more or less adaptive ways" (p. 2). Based on Heider's work, attribution theory and locus of control have been developed. These theories are, however, far removed from people's conception and they possess low internal and external validity (Bandura, 1997; Park & Kim, 2004). These theories have eliminated the influence of context and agency, which are central to understanding people's conception of control and belief system (Bandura, 1997; Park & Kim, 2004).

People have a complex and sophisticated understanding of themselves and their social world. They have practical and episodic understanding, but they may not have the analytical ability to describe the underlying structure or process. As will be described in the section below, episodic and analytic knowledge are two different types of knowledge. General psychology represents psychologists' analytic conceptions, interpretations, and explanations rather than an accurate representation of human psychology. In other words, the current psychological knowledge can be described as the psychology of psychologists (Harré, 2000; Kim, Park, & Park, 2000). In indigenous psychology, it is the role of researchers to translate episodic knowledge into analytic forms so that they could tested and verified.

Sixth, indigenous concepts have been analyzed as examples of indigenous psychologies. The concepts of *philotimo* in Greece (a person who is "polite, virtuous, reliable, proud," Triandis, 1972), *anasakti* in India ("non-detachment," Pande & Naidu, 1992), *amae* in Japan ("indulgent dependence," Doi, 1973), *kapwa* in the Philippines ("shared identity with other," Enriquez, 1993), and *jung* in Korea ("deep attachment and affection," Choi, Kim & Choi, 1993) have been analyzed and various culture-bound syndromes have been introduced (Yap, 1974). Although these concepts are interesting, they have limited communicative value to people who do not understand language. Second, it is difficult to ascertain whether these conceptualizations are accurate. Third, it is difficult to assess the scientific merit of these indigenous analyses since they are not supported by empirical evidence. The descriptive analysis is a starting point of research in indigenous psychologies, but they cannot be the endpoint. If so, they are examples of superficial research that do not contribute to the advancement of scientific knowledge.

The concept of *amae* has been the focus of attention as a culture-specific phenomenon with the first publication by Doi (1973). Yamaguchi et al., (Chapter 7) points out Japanese and U.S. researchers erroneously conceptualized *amae* as an example of dependence (Doi, 1973; Johnson, 1993; Lebra, 1976; Rothbaum, Weisz, Pott, Miyake, & Morelli, 2000). These researchers made claims about Japanese people without a clear descriptive understanding of *amae* and empirical evidence to support their view. They are examples of poor research and not of indigenous psychology.

Kim and Yamaguchi (1995) launched an empirical study using an open-ended questionnaire exploring various facets of *amae*. A total of 841 respondents living in various parts of Japan completed a questionnaire: 237 middle school students, 224 high school students, 243 university students, and 137 adults. The results indicate that *amae* involves an episode between two people: One person requests a specific favor that is often unreasonable and the other person grants the request. *Amae* episode occurs in close relationships, usually between parent and children or between close friends. The special request, which is often demanding and unreasonable, is granted because of the motivation to maintain the close relationship.

Yamaguchi et al. (Chapter 7) conducted a series of experiments to analyze different facets of *amae*. They define *amae* as the "presumed acceptance of one's inappropriate behavior or request." They found two underlying motivational factors: Japanese respondents engage in an *amae* episode in order to obtain a specific benefit and to verify the close relationship. The method of obtaining the desired goal is through *proxy* control (Bandura,

1997). They conclude that *amae* cannot be equated with dependence since Japanese respondents actively engage in *amae* to obtain a specific benefit through proxy control. They developed scenarios containing examples of *amae* episodes and conducted a series of experiments in Japan, Taiwan, and the U.S. They have found that American and Taiwanese respondents are more likely than Japanese respondents to engage in *amae* episode. They conclude that contrary to previous theorists, *amae* is not a culture specific phenomenon. Although it is an indigenous Japanese word, the psychological aspects of *amae* can be found in other cultures. Thus, the series of empirical studies have helped to clarify the confusion created by both Japanese and American scholars.

These empirical studies show that it is inappropriate to equate poor research with indigenous psychology. It is erroneous to equate indigenous psychology with cultural relativism, parochialism or ethnocentrism. General and cross-cultural psychologists have criticized indigenous psychology for accumulation of idiosyncratic data, fragmentation, cultural relativism, reverse ethnocentrism, moving against the trend of globalization, and questioned its scientific merit (Adamopoulos & Lonner, 2001; Herman & Kempen, 1998; Poortinga, 1999; Triandis, 2000). These are unwarranted criticisms that reflect a lack of understanding of indigenous psychology and scientific advances that have been made in the recent years.

Contrary to these misconceptions, indigenous psychology is part of a scientific tradition that advocates multiple *perspectives*, but not multiple *psychologies*. The current volume uses the singular form of indigenous psychology rather than the plural form. Indigenous psychology is a part of scientific tradition in search of psychological knowledge rooted in cultural context. This knowledge can become the basis of the discovery of psychological universals and can contribute to the advancement of psychology and science.

Seventh, many indigenous psychologists search philosophical and religious texts to explain indigenous phenomena. They use philosophical treatises (such as the Confucian Classics) or religious text (Koran or Vedas) as an explanation of psychological phenomena. We need to distinguish indigenous knowledge, philosophies and religions from indigenous psychology. Philosophical and religious texts are developed for a specific purpose several thousand years. In order to utilize these texts, we need to translate these ideas into psychological concepts and empirically verify their validity. We cannot assume that because a person is Chinese, he/she will automatically follow the Confucian way, or Hindu Dharma can explain the behavior of an individual because he/she is an Indian. Psychologists have used these texts to develop psychological concepts (Paranjpe, 1998), but these analyses are speculative philosophy and they have yet to be supported by empirical evidence. Although they provide a wealth of information and the basis of development of formal theories, they need to be empirical tested and validated.

Eighth, indigenous psychology is identified as a part of the cultural sciences tradition (Kim & Berry, 1993). Unlike physical and biological sciences, people do not merely react or adapt to the environment, but they are able to understand and change their environment, other people, and themselves (Bandura, 1997; Kim & Berry, 1993). Since we are the agents of change, we are both the subject and the object of investigation. We have insights into our world and we communicate our understanding to others. In psychology, although the objective third person point of view is *necessary*, it is not *sufficient*. We need to supplement it with the first person perspective (i.e., incorporating agency, meaning, and intention, Bandura, 1997) and the second person analysis (e.g., communication, dialogue, and discourse analysis, Harré & Gillet, 1994). We need to obtain an integrated understanding of the first-person, second-person, and third-person perspectives in order to obtain a complete picture of human functioning.

Ninth, indigenous psychology advocates a linkage of humanities (e.g., philosophy, history, religion, and literature, which focus on human experience) with social sciences (which focus on analytical knowledge, empirical analysis and verification). In addition to theoretical and empirical analysis of psychological theories, ideas from philosophy (Hwang, Chapter 4; Peng et al., Chapter 11; Wallner et al., Chapter 3), history (Diaz Loving, Chapter 14), and religion (Boski, Chapter 17; Eckensberger, Chapter 10; Mishra, Chapter 12) can provide valuable knowledge and insight.

Tenth, Enriquez (1993) identified two starting points of research in indigenous psychology: *indigenization from without* and *indigenization from within*. Indigenization from without involves taking existing psychological theories, concepts, and methods and modifying them to fit the local cultural context. The derived *etic* approach in cross-cultural psychology (e.g., Berry, Poortinga, Segall & Dasen, 2002), researches in cultural psychology (e.g., Greenfield, 2000; Shweder, 1991) and indigenization (Sinha, 1997) are examples of indigenization from without. In this approach, rather than assuming that a particular theory is universal *a priori*, researchers modify and adapt psychological theories to integrate them with the local cultural knowledge. Those aspects that can be verified across cultures are retained as possible cultural universals. Existing theories in cognitive, developmental, social and organizational psychology have been modified and extended by indigenous research (Sinha, 1997).

In the indigenization from within, theories, concepts and methods are developed internally, and indigenous information is considered to be a primary source of knowledge (Enriquez, 1993). For example, one of the core values and assumptions that psychologists from East Asia are questioning is the emphasis on individualism (Edwards et al., Chapter 6; Ho, 1982; Kim, 2001). In the East Asia, the relatedness of a person to another is considered to be fundamental (Choi et al., Chapter 16; Yang, Chapter 15). In East Asia, the word for human being can be literally translated as "human between"

(人間). In other words, it is what happens between individuals that make us human. In Chinese culture, the concept of *guanxi* (關係, "relationship") occupies the center stage defining interactions in family, school, companies, and society (Hwang, Chapter 4; Peng et al., Chapter 11; Yang, Chapter 15; Zhang, Chapter 18). In Japan, the concept of *amae* helps to define and maintain close interpersonal relationships (Yamaguchi et al., Chapter 7). In Korea, the concept of *jung* (情, "deep affection and attachment" Choi et al., Chapter 16) is a central emotion that binds family, friends, and colleagues together. Both cross-sectional and longitudinal studies yielded results that confirm the importance of close relationships in Korea which are highly reliable, valid and applicable (Kim & Park, Chapter 2; Park & Kim, Chapter 19).

CULTURE

In cross-cultural psychology, culture has been described as a fuzzy set since there is a lack of agreement in the definition, conceptualization, and operationalization (Rohner, 1984; Triandis, 1980). The word culture originates from the Latin word *cultura*, which means to till or cultivate. Tylor (1871) defined culture as "that complex whole which includes knowledge, beliefs, arts, morals, laws, customs and any other capabilities and habits acquired as a member of society" (cited in Berry et al., 2002). Herkovits (1955) suggested that "culture is the man-made part of the human environment" (p. 17). Triandis (1994) defines it as the "unstated assumptions, standard operating procedures, ways of doing things that have been internalized to such an extent that people do not argue about them" (p. 16). These definitions focus on products of culture and do not address the complexity and dynamics of culture.

Culture has been studied as a quasi-independent variable, category, point in a dimension, or a mere sum of individual characteristics. For cross-cultural comparisons, a researcher typically selects cultures using the Human Relations Area Files (HRAF), or using cultural dimensions (e.g., Hofstede, 1991). Culture has been treated as a quasi-independent variable, since researchers cannot control culture, and researchers are interested in examining its influence on behavior (Berry, 1980). These cultural dimensions and categories are statistical transformation of attitude, values, and belief obtained at the individual level. It is questionable whether these statistical summaries can accurately represent the complexity of culture.

Culture is an emergent property of individuals interacting with, managing, and changing their environment (Kim, 2001). Culture represents *the collective utilization of natural and human resources to achieve desired outcomes*; this is the process definition of culture (Kim, 2001). Differences in cultures can exist if people pursue different goals, utilize different methods and resources to realize the goals, and attach different meaning and values on them. Cultural similarities can exist if people pursue similar goals, utilize similar methods and resources to attain the goal, and attach similar meaning and values on them. Collective goals, human and natural resources, method of achieving the goals, and meaning and values attached to them are integrated to form a meaningful and coherent whole. Culture represents *a rubric of patterned variables* (Kim, 2001).

Although human beings have not changed biologically and genetically during the past 7,000 years, cultures have undergone dramatic transformations (Bandura, 1997; Kim, Helgesen, & Ahn 2002; Kim, Aasen, & Ebadi, 2003). It is our ability to understand the world and to share the knowledge with others that became the basis of our survival. Our physiology provides us with the basis, but culture helps us to use our physiology to achieve desired outcomes. To use an analogy, computers consist of hardware and software. Our physiology is the like the hardware and culture is like the software (Hofstede, 1991). A computer operates differently depending of the type of software that is downloaded. The socialization experiences of children affect their attitudes, values and behavior and they will differ from another child who grew up in another cultural environment (Edwards et al, Chapter 6; Fung, Chapter 8; Park & Kim, Chapter 19). When children are born, although they have the potential to learn any language, they usually learn one language. As adults, their native language feels natural and other languages sound alien. Language and culture provide people with ways to organize their thoughts, communicate with others and manage the world.

People possess self-reflectiveness and creativity that computers do not possess (Bandura, 1997). Computers have to be programmed to run and they operate based on the program. Human beings have the capability of examining their values, beliefs and skills and the capability to change themselves, other people and their culture (Bandura, 1997). Without culture, human beings would be like other animals, reduced to basic instincts. Without culture, people would not be able to think, feel, or behave the way they do. Culture allows people to know who they are, define what is meaningful, communicate with others and manage our environment (Kim et al., Chapter 2; Yang, Chapter 15). It is *through* culture that we think, feel, behave and manage with our reality (Shweder, 1991). Just as we use our eyes to see the world, we use our culture to understand our world. Because we think *through* our culture, it is difficult to recognize our own culture (Shweder, 1991). For a person born and raised in a particular culture, his/her own culture is feels supremely natural.

Existing psychological theories have difficulties explaining the indigenous concepts such as *amae* and academic achievement of East Asian students (Park et al., Chapter 19). This is the case since psychological theories are based on individualistic values that reflect Western cultures (Kim, Triandis, Kăğitçibaşi, Choi & Yoon, 1994). In developmental psychology, Freudian, Piagetian, behaviorist, and humanist theories largely ignore the important role played parents and culture. In East Asia, parents play a central role in child development by defining the goals of socialization, teaching the necessary cognitive, linguistic, relational, and social skills, and providing a supportive family environment (Fung, Chapter 8; Park & Kim, Chapter 19).

Concept such as guilt has a very different connotation and utility in East Asia (Azuma, 1988; Park & Kim, 2004). In Western psychoanalytic and psychological theories, guilt is presumed to be based on irrational beliefs, unrealistic fear, or forbidden wishes. Extensive use of guilt is believed to cause later developmental problems in adolescence. In East Asia, it is considered appropriate that children feel guilty or indebted toward their parents for all the devotion, indulgence, sacrifice, and love that they receive from their parents (Azuma, 1988; Ho, 1986; Park & Kim, Chapter 19). Children feel indebted since they cannot return the love and care that they received from parents. Guilt in East Asia is viewed as an important interpersonal emotion that promotes filial piety, achievement motivation, and relational closeness.

OUTLINE OF CHAPTERS

The volume is divided into five parts: I. Theoretical and Methodological issues; II. Family and Socialization; III. Cognitive Processes; IV. Self and Personality; and IV. Application. Five articles are included in the first section.

In Chapter 2, *The Scientific Foundation of Indigenous and Cultural Psychology: The Transactional Model of Science,* Kim and Park outline the scientific foundation of indigenous and cultural psychology. The authors review the scientific foundation of general and cross-cultural psychology and compare them with indigenous psychology. Indigenous psychology represents the transactional model of science in which human beings are viewed as agents of their own action. The authors note that differences in cultures exist due to different goals that cultures pursue, methods people use to attain the goals, and the differential use of natural and human resources. The author provides the East Asian perspective in which relation, rather than individuals, are viewed as the unit of analysis and provides a review of empirical studies that support this view.

In Chapter 3, *The Importance of Constructive Realism for the Indigenous Psychologies Approach,* Wallner and Jandl note that a deeper understanding of science can only be achieved by considering the following two aspects: (1) the necessity of regulating scientists' practical activities; and (2) science must lead to knowledge, or else lose its importance and become simply instrumental. The authors point out that in the traditional philosophy of science both aspects have been accepted, but the traditional philosophy of science turned out to be an inappropriate means by which to understand science. Constructivistic approaches in philosophy of science usually accepts of the first aspect, but rule out the second aspect, which means giving up the idea of science that emerged in the 16th century. To relinquish one or even both aspects can lead to relativism in science, and such relativism is dangerous. In contrast, constructive realism integrates both aspects, rejects the idea of traditional philosophy of science (i.e., the view that science is a description of the world) and avoids this dangerous relativism. Hence, the authors point out the rise of constructive realism and then argue that traditional philosophy of science and constructivistic approaches failed because they either subscribed to the view that science describes the world or because they have ruled out the necessity of a regulative instance or the necessity of interpretation. Second, the authors sketch the ontology of constructive realism. It postulates a clear distinction between a world working without human impact, but influencing and constraining humans (*wirklichkeit*), the world of the scientific constructions (*realität*) and the world of different cultures (*lebenswelt* or life-world). Constructive realism presents itself as a philosophy of science that avoids the errors of traditional philosophy of science and of the older constructivistic philosophy of science. Third, the authors discuss the method of constructive realism, called *strangification*, and explain the constructive realistic view of scientific knowledge. Fourth, the authors outline the problems of psychology pertaining to the uncertainty of the psychological subject, and then sketches aspects of the indigenous psychologies approach, a rather new discipline in psychology that reflects on the subject of psychology more appropriately than mainstream psychology. Finally, this chapter discusses the idea of a universal psychology presented by Kim and Berry (1993) and emphasizes the importance of strangification and constructive realistic ontology for the indigenous psychologies approach.

In Chapter 4, *Constructive Realism and Confucian Relationalism: An Epistemological Strategy for the Development of Indigenous Psychology*, Hwang notes the dramatic changes in ontology, epistemology, and methodology with the shift from positivism to post-positivism. The author points out that indigenous psychologists are unable to attain the goal of constructing a global psychology by adopting a bottom-up approach that emphasizes inductive methods. In order to achieve a global psychology, indigenous psychologists must make three levels of breakthroughs, namely, philosophical reflection, theoretical construction, and empirical research. With respect to philosophical reflection, constructive realism is used to illustrate the difference between significant features of the microworlds constructed by scientists and knowledge used by people in their lifeworlds. The significance of modernization for non-Western countries is also explained in terms of this philosophy. At the level of theoretical construction, indigenous psychologists should construct formal theories on the mechanisms of universal mind that are applicable to various cultures, and then use these theories to analyze the specific mentalities of people in a given culture. A series of theoretical models of Confucian Relationalism is cited to illustrate these arguments.

In the article, *From Decolonizing Psychology to the Development of a Cross-indigenous Perspective in Methodology: The Philippine Experience*, Pe-pua (Chapter 5) traces the development of indigenous research methods as it began as a part of a movement known as *Sikolohiyang Pilipino* (Filipino psychology) that calls for the use of a Filipino perspective or orientation in understanding Filipino thought and experience. The author points out that with the introduction of a paradigm shift, an indigenous approach to participant observation, interview, focus group discussion and psychological testing were developed. This approach gives importance to participant-researcher interaction, participant welfare, appropriateness of the method, and language of the participants. Features of the indigenous approach relate to the informal culture, formal structure and technological procedures. The debates on the value of indigenous methods revolve around the language issue, uniqueness of methods, insider/outsider issue, planning, and ethics. The cross-indigenous perspective calls for the full use of the indigenous approach, leading to the coming together of indigenous psychologies and contributing to cross-cultural knowledge.

In the second section, four articles examine the role of family, socialization and close relationship. In the article by Edwards, Knoche, Aukrust, Kumru, and Kim (Chapter 6) entitled, *Parental Ethnotheories of Child Development: Looking Beyond Independence and Inividualism in American Belief Systems*, the authors point out that parents, preschools, and schools in different cultures vary greatly in the extent to which children are encouraged to develop long-term relationships with peers and teachers outside the family circle. In contemporary societies, parents face complex choices as they bridge children's transitions to a wider world. The authors explore the contradictions and complications of contemporary American values around independence/interdependence and individualism/collectivism. Findings are presented from a collaborative international research study that used a newly developed questionnaire, the *Parental Concerns for Preschool Children Survey*, to assess parental beliefs, values, and judgments. The results suggest that the sample of parents from Lincoln, Nebraska wanted their children to get along with diverse people and to be able to attach quickly and readily to new caregivers as a basis for secure learning at preschool. In thinking about their own child's needs and selecting what makes a preschool or child care center "high quality," they rated most highly a "sense of belonging in the preschool" (*viz.*, getting along well with peers and not being excluded or left out), getting enough individual attention from teachers, and having activities that respond to their own interests in an environment with plenty of teachers and space. The findings are consistent with a review of literature that finds that parental ethnotheories represent configurations of values, beliefs, assumptions, conflicts, and tensions about how to relate to others and function with respect to them. Adaptive function involves being able to modify values and beliefs in the face of changing circumstances and behaving resourcefully as occasions and situations demand. The parental ethnotheories of a sample of American parents in Lincoln, Nebraska reflected a complex combination of orientations toward individual autonomy and toward community roots and group belonging.

Yamaguchi and Ariizumi (Chapter 7) point out in their article entitled, *Close Interpersonal Relationships among Japanese: Amae as Distinguished from Attachment and Dependence*, that Japanese have an indigenous concept of *amae* that describes a behavioral pattern typically found in mother-child relationship. The authors note that this concept has become known internationally after the publication of a seminal book by a Japanese psychoanalyst, Doi (1973), who claimed that *amae* is a key concept for understand Japanese mentality. Despite numerous researches inspired by Doi's work, the concept of *amae* has remained vague and consensus among researchers has not been achieved. Misunderstandings have been prevalent among Japanese and international scholars who claim that *amae* is similar to dependence and unique to Japanese, implying that Japanese (as compared to Westerners) are uniquely dependent in interpersonal relationship. However, the uniqueness of the indigenous concept does not warrant the uniqueness of Japanese behavioral pattern that the concept describes. The authors clarify the meaning of *amae* by distinguishing it from dependence and insecure attachment, both of which are often confused with *amae*. The authors review a series of empirical studies and discuss the possible *etic* nature of *amae*.

Fung (Chapter 8) in the article entitled, *Affect and Early Moral Socialization: Some Insights and Contributions from Indigenous Psychological Studies in Taiwan*, reviews the work of Martin Hoffman's influential theory of moral development which asserts the importance of affect in disciplinary encounters. The author points out that the appropriate arousal of emotion when inducing rules would effectively motivate the child to move from short-term compliance to long-term internalization. The affective experience Hoffman refers to is the highly appraised empathy, the early form of guilt and conscience. The author has found that indigenous studies on everyday moral socialization practices at home with young Taiwanese children have found similar and yet strikingly different phenomena. Corroborating Hoffman's theory, these studies find that affect indeed plays an important role in Taiwanese parents' discipline. However, instead of empathy or guilt, shame is the most frequently invoked affect. Although, on the surface, shaming practices involve abandonment and ostracism, they also have a strong group concern - to teach the youngster how to be accepted by other cultural members. The author points out that self-examination, confession, and repentance are the ultimate objectives; all pointing to internalizing rules for a better self. The motivational, prosocial, and moral nature of these routinely occurring events serves similar functions as those of empathy in Euro-American families as suggested by Hoffman. The author concludes that a valid account of the meaning of affect in disciplinary practices has to be derived from and understood within much broader contexts rooted in its own historical and cultural tradition - in this case, a tradition heavily influenced by Confucian values.

Georgas and Mylonas (Chapter 9) describe in the article entitled, *Cultures are Like All Other Cultures, Like Some Other Cultures, Like No Other Culture*, the relationship between cross-cultural psychology and indigenous psychology and a methodological approach which clarifies issues related to each. The authors outline hierarchical levels of universal traits, taxonomies of traits, and traits of the individual. The authors note that the upper two levels also refer to nomothetic methods, while the lowest level refers to the idiographic method. The authors conclude that all cultures share universal features, as well as universal psychological variables. Some cultures (e.g., Western cultures) share cultural dimensions and psychological dimensions. Each culture has distinct and possibly unique features and meanings embedded in their language, myths, and history. The question the authors raise is the degree to which psychological variables are so unique in one culture that they do not appear in any other culture. Thus, the cross-cultural comparative approach and the indigenous approach are seen as complementary. The authors discuss a methodology, with data from a 30-nation family study, which proposes classifying psychological phenomena into clusters of cultures as a complementary methodology in seeking cultural universals. The authors note that the indigenous psychological in-depth study of unique psychological concepts and their relationship to cultural factors in a country is an important goal in cross-cultural psychology, but it is highly possible that at another level, the taxonomic level, a number of countries will have common cultural elements and psychological similarities, forming a common cultural cluster.

In the third section, three articles examine cognitive processes. Eckensberger (Chapter 10) in his article entitled, *The Mutual Relevance of Indigenous Psychology and Morality*, examines the relationship of morality to indigenous psychology from four different viewpoints. First, the topic of morality is dealt with on a content level. The author points out that since morality is a central normative framework for behavior in a culture, it turns out to be the core of indigenous psychology. The author discusses the crucial question of whether or not morality is culture specific or universal. Second, the role of morality in the emergence of indigenous psychologies is treated on a science of science level and discussed by relating indigenous psychologies to cultural psychology and cross-cultural psychology. In this context, the author points out that conceptualization of various indigenous psychologies is regarded as a special case of a specific paradigm in psychology. The third argument is based on the fact that the concepts of culture used in psychology are not only analytical (asking what culture is), but also treat culture as a characteristic of a group (asking what particular culture defines a given cultural group); the author points out that this is particularly true of indigenous psychologies. The author argues that these conceptualizations of culture also have moral implications. Finally, the author discusses the basic methodological implications. The author postulates that the general research strategy proposed in cross-cultural psychology has to be complemented by heeding moral argument, and that often discussions of the distinction between qualitative and quantitative research are too superficial. Although they are sometimes seen as two alternative methodological approaches either of which may be applied, the author claims that basic research and data gathering strategies also have moral implications.

Peng, Spencer-Rodgers and Nian (Chapter 11), *Naïve Dialecticism and the Tao of Chinese Thought*, point out that people from China are naive Taoists in spirit and that Chinese thinking and reasoning are guided by a folk version of Taoism, or *naïve dialecticism*. The authors point out that this set of implicit theories of knowing is fundamentally different from the commonly known Hegelian dialectics and the Western dialectical thinking in developmental and cognitive psychology. The authors review ethnographic evidence supporting the existence of the folk version of Taoism in Chinese culture and the lives of Chinese people, and draw parallels between folk conceptions of Taoism and psychological laboratory findings suggesting that Chinese reasoning and thinking are more contextual, flexible, holistic, and dialectical as compared with typical North American thinking and reasoning. The authors conclude with a discussion of an indigenous Taoist view of cultural differences in cognition.

Mishra (Chapter 12), *Indian perspectives on cognition*, examines Indian perspectives on cognition to show how cognition is conceptualized in traditional Indian systems of thought. The author points out parallels between Indian and Western conceptualizations of cognition. The author examines the way in which traditional Indian interpretations of cognition can be integrated with current thinking about cognition in general, and cognitive processes and their development in particular.

Four articles in the third section examine the conception of self and personality. Kuo-Shu Yang (Chapter 13), *Indigenous Personality Research: The Chinese Case*, provides a systematic, critical review of empirical studies on Chinese personality from an indigenous perspective. The author reviews the area with a four-level scheme for the classification of personality constructs based upon individual orientation and social orientation. The author points out that the scheme includes four categories of personality constructs: personal-, relationship-, collective-, and other-oriented. The author points out that while the first may be considered individual-oriented; the remaining three are collectively called social-oriented. The author notes that studies on personal-oriented constructs tend to be less indigenous and those on social-oriented ones are more indigenous. Social-oriented constructs tend to be composed of two or more factorial components more or less correlated with each other, with each forming a multidimensional psychological syndrome. The author notes that in individualist cultures personal-oriented traits are more developed, differentiated, and influential in everyday life than social-oriented ones, and they should be studied more than social-oriented traits in such a culture. In contrast, in collectivist cultures social-oriented traits are more developed, differentiated, and influential than personal-oriented ones, and they should be studied more than personal-oriented traits in such a culture. Finally, the author argues that the four-level classificatory scheme incorporates both the individualistic and collectivistic conceptions of personality, and as a general model it may therefore be applicable to indigenous research in both individualist and collectivist cultures.

Diaz Loving (Chapter 14), *An Historic-Psycho-Socio-Cultural Look at the Self in Mexico*, points out that the relevance of psychological constructs cannot be evaluated if the validity, reliability and cultural sensitivity of the concepts are not established. The author notes that individual attributes and social behaviors stem from a life long dialectic between cultural norms and settings and every individual's bio-psychological tendencies. In the chapter, the historical and cultural foundations of Mexican identity are first presented, followed by an examination of the universal conceptualization of the self, and ending with an ethnopsychological study conducted to depict and understand the components that express, and the processes responsible for the evolution, development, and consolidation of the concept of self among Mexican people.

Chung-Fang Yang (Chapter 15), *The Chinese conception of the Self: Towards a Person-making Perspective*, reviews the indigenous approach that she has adopted for the past 15 years. This approach entails understanding the psychology of a people within their cultural, social, and historical context. Based on local materials and observations, the author has derived a set of commonly shared meaning systems with which the people under investigation make sense of their lives and their experiences, and give out and derive meanings while interacting with others. The author notes that this set of systems also helps indigenous researchers to understand and interpret the behaviors manifested by those people. The author outlines three goals: (1) to find a local thinking framework with which to develop an alternative perspective to the Western one in order to discover new dimensions for future studies of the self, or at least for studies of the Chinese self; (2) to explore the concept of the Chinese self at its formative stage, during the pre-Qin (先秦) period in Chinese history, and to use this deep-rooted conception to study the evolution of self-concept in the Chinese context and better understand the behaviors of modern Chinese people; (3) and, to suggest an alternative approach to the study of the self.

Choi and Kim (Chapter 16), *Naïve Psychology of Koreans' Interpersonal Mind and Behavior in Close Relationships,* note that it is often mentioned that Koreans are emotional rather than rational people. The authors point out that emotionality of Koreans in interpersonal relationships is not exactly the same as what is meant by the term in the West. Unlike the emotion as distinct and separated from the cognitive-oriented rational mind, the authors note that the Koreans' emotion in the interpersonal context is often manifested as a composite whole of emotionality and self-involved cognitive reasons connected to the emotionality aroused. At the discourse level, the nature of emotionality and its cognitive counterpart are not differentiated from each other, but fused together with one another. The authors point out that the Korean word *shimjung* (心情) refers to the state of inner experience where the particular quality of feeling is aroused in relation to particular contents of thoughts. *Shimcheong* is likely to be touched and aroused in close, long-term relationships. In the close relationship, individuality disappears and social standards of behavior such as justice, impartiality, lawfulness, objectivity and rationality are overridden by or reinterpreted *jung* (情, "affection"), *uiri* (義理, the rule of loyalty and benevolence) and ingroup favoritism. In Korea, the authors points out the existence of two types of thinking: The private *shimjung* psychology and the public social-normative psychology co-exist in delicate harmony and tension, having their own respective niches and functional values.

In the fifth section, five articles are included. Boski (Chapter 17), *Humanism - Materialism: Century-long Polish Cultural Origins and Twenty Years of Research in Cultural Psychology,* points out that cultural dimensions can be conceived of in a specific, indigenous way, or as general, theory-driven concepts. The author offers both approaches, which converge with the construct of humanism-materialism. The author starts with an analysis of main themes of Polish history and culture to provide a profile of the dominant mentality. The author points out that humanism and anti-materialism were the products of the Catholic, noble-agrarian way of life, underdeveloped urbanism, and the market economy in the hands of non-Polish ethnic groups. The author points out that weak state structures and centuries of existence under dominance of external powers added a particular preoccupation with family and nation rather than the building of civil society. The author defines humanism as a pro-social concern with the well-being of close others and the quality of interpersonal relations, which can also be derived from de-confounding two conceptual aspects present in individualism/collectivism: 1) agency (I-as-subject vs. I-as-object), and 2) orientation (self vs. social). The author notes that humanism exists when agency meets social orientation. The author presents several empirical studies to explore the nature of humanism within Polish culture and cross-culturally. The author has found that humanism is distinct from scales of either individualism or collectivism. The author notes that it is particularly strong among groups who work with and for other people; it predicts endorsement of political democracy but not of market economy. The author concludes that humanism remains strong as a Polish cultural ideal during the decade of transformation and offers a significant contrast with North American as well as with West European cultures.

Zhang (Chapter 18), *Chinese Conception of Justice and Reward Allocation*, points out that few empirical studies on distributive justice or reward allocation have been conducted in China. The author notes that reward allocation decisions are interpersonal acts. How an allocator distributes a reward is influenced by factors in the social interaction, such as the relationship between the partners and their interaction, as well as the social norms governing their behavior. The author reviews studies that have been conducted to examine the influence of social interactional factors on Chinese individuals' allocation decisions in hypothetical settings. The author reviews empirical findings on Chinese reward allocation and previous theoretical works on Chinese justice. The author concludes that both *guanxi* (interpersonal relationship) and *renqing* (affection) have an effect on Chinese reward allocation decisions, which relates to the Chinese conception of justice.

Park and Kim (Chapter 19), *Family, Parent-Child Relationship and Educational Achievement in Korea: Indigenous, Cultural, and Psychological Analysis*, examine the role that family and parent-child relationship play in influencing the academic achievement of Korean adolescents. The authors first trace the changes in the traditional parent-child relationship in modern Korea. Although the structural features of the family has changed from extended to nuclear, the basic features of parent-child relationship that emphasize sacrifice, devotion and educational aspirations for their children have not changed. The authors point out that such socialization practices instill a sense of indebtedness, respect, and emotional closeness in their children. The authors review a series of empirical studies that used indigenous methodology to examine the relationship between parent-child relationship and academic achievement. The authors review results from matched samples of parents and children, from cross-sectional samples, and from longitudinal analysis which reveal a pattern of results that explain the high level of academic achievement of Korean adolescents. These results challenge traditional psychological and educational theories that emphasize biology (i.e., innate ability, intelligence), individualistic values (e.g., intrinsic motivation, ability attribution and self-esteem) and structural features (e.g., high educational spending, small class size and individualized instruction). The authors conclude that indigenous psychology can provide a more powerful and rigorous analysis of parent-child relationship and academic achievement in Korea.

Aycan (Chapter 20), *Paternalism: Towards Conceptual Refinement and Operationalization*, focuses on the conceptualization and operationalization of one of the most prevalent cultural and managerial characteristics in Asian, Middle-Eastern and Latin American cultures - paternalism. The author notes that although paternalism has negative connotations in the economically developed nations, it has positive implications in cultures where it is rooted in indigenous psychologies including Confucianism and familialism. The author presents an analytical overview of the ways in which paternalism is construed differently in various cultural contexts and concurs that it's meaning and functions cannot be constructed without taking the cultural context into consideration. The author proposes on the basis of two dimensions (i.e., behavioral manifestations and underlying intentions), a conceptual framework to distinguish among four types of leadership approaches: benevolent paternalism, exploitative paternalism, authoritarian approach, and authoritative approach. The author demonstrates that paternalism is not a unified construct, and that it is not equal to authoritarianism. The author concludes by describing three distinct empirical studies that test the conceptual model as well as the development and validation of the measure to assess paternalism.

The final chapter by Adair (Chapter 21), *Creating Indigenous Psychologies: Insights from Empirical Social Studies of the Science of Psychology*, reviews insights derived from empirical social studies of the science of psychology that have specifically addressed the process of indigenization in three countries at different stages of discipline development: Bangladesh, India, and Canada. The author focuses on the larger discipline of psychology within the country rather than on that subset devoted exclusively to culturally-unique research. The author points out that the extent of indigenization required and the nature of the indigenization strategies followed differ across regions and between countries. The author suggests a model of the indigenization process as passing through four stages: importation, implantation, indigenization and autochthonization. The author points out that this model is helpful for viewing the progress made within each country, and for identifying factors influencing the indigenization process. The author concludes by addressing specific issues that must be confronted in the creation of indigenous psychologies.

REFERENCES

Adamopoulos, J., & Lonner, W. (2001). Culture and psychology at a crossroad: Historical perspective and theoretical analysis. In D. Matsumoto (Ed.), *Handbook of culture and psychology* (pp. 11–34). Oxford: Oxford University Press.

Ardila, R. (1982). Psychology in Latin America today. *Annual Review of Psychology, 33,* 103–122.

Azuma, H. (1984). Psychology in a non-Western country. *International Journal of Psychology, 19,* 145–155.

Azuma, H. (1988). Are Japanese really that different? The concept of development as a key for transformation. Invited address at the 24th International Congress of Psychology, Sydney, Australia, August 28-Sept. 2, 1988.

Bandura, A. (1997). *Self-efficacy: The exercise of control.* New York: Freeman.

Bandura, A. (1999). Social cognitive theory: An agentic perspective. *Asian Journal of Social Psychology, 2,* 21–42.

Berry, J. W. (1974). Canadian psychology: Some social and applied emphasis. *Canadian Psychologist, 15,* 132–139.

Berry, J. W. (1980). Introduction to methodology. In H. C. Triandis, & W. W. Lambert (Eds.), *Handbook of cross-cultural psychology: Methodology, Volume 2* (p. 1–29). Boston: Allyn and Bacon.

Berry, J. W., Poortinga, Y. H., Segall, M. H., & Dasen, P. R. (2002). *Cross-cultural psychology: Research and applications, Second Edition.* Cambridge, MA: Cambridge University.

Boulding, K. (1980). Science: Our common heritage. *Science, 207,* 831–826.

Choi, S. C., Kim, U., & Choi, S. H. (1993). Korean culture and collective representation. In Kim, U., & Berry, J. W. (Eds.), *Indigenous psychologies: Experience and research in cultural context* (pp. 193–210). Newbury Park, CA: Sage.

Cronbach, L. J. (1975). The two disciplines of scientific psychology. *American Psychologist, 12,* 671–684.

Diaz-Guerrero, R. (1977). A Mexican psychology. *American Psychologist, 32,* 934–944.

Enriquez, V. G. (1977). Toward cross-cultural knowledge through cross-indigenous methods and perspectives. *Philippine Journal of Psychology, 12,* 9–16.

Doi, T. (1973). *The anatomy of dependence.* Tokyo: Kodansha.

Durojaiye, M. O. A. (1993). Indigenous psychology in Africa: The search for meaning. In U. Kim, & J. W. Berry (Eds.), *Indigenous psychologies: Research and experience in cultural context* (pp. 211–220). Newbury Park, CA: Sage.

Elms, A. C. (1975). The crisis in confidence in social psychology. *American Psychologist, 30,* 967–976.

Enriquez, V. G. (1993). Developing a Filipino psychology. In U. Kim, & J. W. Berry (Eds.), *Indigenous psychologies: Research and experience in cultural context* (pp. 152–169). Newbury Park, CA: Sage.

Gibson, J. J. (1985). Conclusions from a century of research on sense perception. In S. Koch, & D. E. Leary (Eds.), *A century of psychology as science* (pp. 224–230). New York: McGraw Hill.

Graumann, C. F. (1972). The state of psychology, I. *International Journal of Psychology, 7,* 123–134.

Greenfield, P. M. (2000). Three approaches to the psychology of culture: Where do they come from? Where can they go? *Asian Journal of Social Psychology, 3,* 223–240.

Heider, F. (1958). *The psychology of interpersonal relations.* New York: Wiley.

Harré, R. (1999). The rediscovery of the human mind: The discursive approach. *Asian Journal of Social Psychology, 2,* 43–62.

Harré, R., & Gillet, G (1994). *The discursive mind.* Thousand Oaks, CA: Sage.

Hermans, J. M., & Kempen, J. G. (1998). Moving cultures: The perilous problem of cultural dichotomy in a globalized society. *American Psychologist, 53,* 1111–1120.

Herskovits, M. (1955). *Cultural anthropology.* New York: Knopf.

Ho, D. Y. F. (1982). Asian concepts in behavioral science. *Psychologia, 25*, 228–235.

Hofstede, G. (1991). *Cultures and organizations: Software of the mind.* New York: McGraw-Hill Book.

Holten, G. (1973). *Thematic origins of scientific thought: From Kepler to Einstein.* Cambridge, MA: Harvard University.

Johnson, F. A. (1993). *Dependency and Japanese socialization.* New York: New York University Press.

Kâğitçibaşi, C. (1984). Socialization in traditional society: A challenge to psychology. *International Journal of Psychology, 19*, 145–157.

Kim, U. (1999). After the "crisis" in social psychology: Development of the transactional model of science. *Asian Journal of Social Psychology, 2*, 1–19.

Kim, U. (2000). Indigenous, cultural, and cross-cultural psychology: Theoretical, philosophical, and epistemological analysis. *Asian Journal of Social Psychology, 3*, 265–287.

Kim, U. (2001). Culture, science and indigenous psychologies: An integrated analysis. In D. Matsumoto (Ed.), *Handbook of culture and psychology* (pp. 51–76). Oxford: Oxford University Press.

Kim, U., Aasen, H. S., & Ebadi, S. (2003). *Democracy, human rights, and Islam in modern Iran: Psychological, social and cultural perspectives.* Bergen: Fagbokforlaget.

Kim, U., & Berry, J. W. (1993). *Indigenous psychologies: Experience and research in cultural context.* Newbury Park, CA: Sage.

Kim, U., Helgesen, G., & Ahn, B. M. (2002). Democracy, trust, and political efficacy: Comparative analysis of Danish and Korean political culture. *Applied Psychology: An International Review, 51*, 317–352.

Kim, U., & Park, Y. S. (2004). Understanding the world of possibilities, illusions, and realities: Unraveling the complexities of individual and collective creativity and action. State-of the-art address presented at the XXVIII International Congress of Psychology, Beijing, August 8–13.

Kim, U., Park, Y. S., & Park, D. H. (1999). The challenge of cross-cultural psychology: The role of indigenous psychologies. *Journal of Cross-Cultural Psychology, 31(1)*, 63–75.

Kim, U., Triandis, H. C., Choi, S. C., Kâğitçibaşi, C., & Yoon, G. (Eds.) (1994). *Individualism and Collectivism: Theory, Method, and Application.* Thousand Oaks, CA: Sage.

Kim, U., & Yamaguchi, S. (1995). Conceptual and empirical analysis of *amae*: Exploration into Japanese psycho-social space. *Proceedings of the 43rd Annual Conference of the Japanese Group Dynamics Association*, pp. 158–159. Tokyo: Japanese Group Dynamics Association.

Kleinman, A. (1980). *Patients and healers in context of culture.* Berkeley: University of California Press.

Koch, S. (1985). The nature and limits of psychological knowledge: Lessons of a century qua "science." In S. Koch, & D. E. Leary (Eds.), *A century of psychology as science* (pp. 75–99). New York: McGraw Hill.

Koch, S., & Leary, D. E. (1985). *A century of psychology as science.* New York: McGraw Hill.

Kwon, T. H. (1979). Seminar on Koreanizing Western approaches to social science. *Korea Journal, 19*, 20–25.

Lebra, T. S. (1976). *Japanese patterns of behavior.* Honolulu: East-West Center.

Marsella, A. J. (1998). Toward a "global-community psychology:" Meeting the needs of a changing world. *American Psychologist, 53*, 1282–1291.

Moghaddam, F. M. (1987). Psychology in the three worlds: As reflected by the crisis in social psychology and the move toward indigenous Third World psychology. *American Psychologist, 35*, 912–920.

Moscovici, S. (1972). Society and theory in social psychology. In J. Israel and H. Tajfel (Eds.), *The context of social psychology.* London: Academic.

Murphy, G., & Kovach, J. K. (1972). *Historical introduction to modern psychology, Third Edition.* New York: Harcourt, Brace, Jovanovich.

Nsamenang, A. B. (1995). Factors influencing the development of psychology in Sub-Saharan Africa. *International Journal of Psychology, 30*, 729–738.

Pande, N., & Naidu, R. K. (1992). Anasakti and health: A study of non-attachment. *Psychology and Developing Societies, 4*, 91–104.

Park, Y. S., & Kim, U., (2004). *Adolescent culture and parent-child relationship in Korea: Indigenous psychological analysis* (in Korean). Seoul: Kyoyook Kwahaksa.

Rohner, R. P. (1986). Toward a conception of culture for cross-cultural psychology. *Journal of Cross-Cultural Psychology, 15*, 111–138.

Rothbaum, F., Weisz, J., Pott, M., Miyake, K., & Morelli, G. (2000). Attachment and culture: Security in the United States and Japan. *American Psychologist, 55*, 1093–1104.

Salazar, J. M. (1984). The use and impact of psychology in Venezuela. *International Journal of Psychology, 19*, 113–122.

Samy, J. (1978). Development and research for the Pacific, and session on theory and methods. In A. Marmak, & G. Mc Call (Eds.), *Paradise postponed: Essays on research and development in the South Pacific*. Rushcutters Bay, NSW: Pergamon.

Sampson, E. E. (1977). Psychology and the American ideal. *Journal of Personality and Social Psychology, 35*, 767–782.

Serpell, R. C. (1984). Commentary on the impact of psychology on Third World development. *International Journal of Psychology, 19*, 179–192.

Shweder, R. A. (1991). *Thinking through cultures—Expeditions in cultural psychology*. Cambridge: Harvard University Press.

Smith, M. B. (1973). Is psychology relevant to new priorities? *American Psychologist, 28*, 463–471.

Sinha, D. (1984). Psychology in the context of Third World development. *International Journal of Psychology, 19*, 17–29.

Sinha, D. (1997). Indigenizing psychology. In J. W. Berry, Y. H. Poortinga, & J. Pandey (Eds.), *Handbook of cross-cultural psychology: Theory and method, Volume 1* (pp. 25–410). Boston: Allyn and Bacon.

Smedslund, J. (1984). The invisible obvious: culture in psychology. In Lagerspetz K. M. J., & P. Niemi (Eds.), *Psychology in the 1990's*. Amsterdam: North-Holland.

Triandis, H. (1972). *The analysis of subjective culture*. New York: Wiley.

Triandis, H. (Ed.) (1980). *Handbook of cross-cultural psychology*. Boston: Allyn & Bacon.

Triandis, H. (1994). *Culture and social behavior*. New York: McGraw-Hill.

Wirth, L. (1946). Preface to K. Manheim, *Ideology and utopia: An introduction to sociology of knowledge*. New York: Harcourt, Brace and Company.

Yang, K. S. (1986). Chinese personality and its change. In M. H. Bond (Ed.), *The psychology of the Chinese people*. Hong Kong: Oxford University.

Yang, K. S. (2000). Monocultural and cross-cultural indigenous approaches: The royal road to the development of balanced global psychology *Asian Journal of Social Psychology, 3*, 241–263.

Yap, P. W. (1974). *Comparative psychiatry: A theoretical framework*. Toronto: University of Toronto.

Chapter **2**

The Scientific Foundation of Indigenous and Cultural Psychology
The Transactional Approach

Uichol Kim and Young-Shin Park

Science provides an accurate and verifiable understanding of the complex world. The physical sciences (astronomy, chemistry, and physics) were first to develop with Newtonian physics providing a simple, elegant, and mechanical explanation of the natural world. Chemists discovered the basic elements and these elements served as the building blocks for understanding the structure and formation of complex objects. Biological sciences emerged next by providing a physiological blueprint and an understanding of diverse life forms. Quantum physics extended the boundary of science by providing a probabilistic understanding of phenomena that are dynamic and fluid. These scientific understandings of the natural world and technologies have been used to control and shape the environment.

Psychology emerged as an independent discipline in 1879 when Wilhelm Wundt established a psychology laboratory in Leipzig (Boring, 1921). Within a short period, psychology began to flourish as a discipline and became very successful in terms of the number of students, faculty members, research projects, funding, and professional organizations. In terms of its scientific status, however, psychology experienced a crisis of confidence in the late 1960's (Cronbach, 1975; Lachenmeyer, 1970; Levine, 1974). Elms (1975) noted that "whether they are experiencing an identity crisis, a paradigmatic crisis, or a crisis in confidence, most seem agreed that a crisis is at hand" (p. 967). During this time, scholars around the world reacted against unjustified claims of universality and called for the development of indigenous psychologies (Kim & Berry, 1993; Sinha, 1997). The criticism of general psychology can be divided into those who questioned its external validity and those who questioned its internal validity (Kim & Berry, 1993).

Many scholars have pointed out that psychological theories reflect the values, goals, and issues of the United States (abbreviated as U.S.) and that they are not generalizable to other societies (Kim & Berry, 1993). In Canada, Berry (1974) has been critical of the culture-bound and culture-blind nature of psychology and argued for the development of psychology that is relevant to Canada. In France, Moscovici (1972) pointed out that American psychologists adopted "for its themes of research and for the contents of its theories, the issues of *its own* society" (p.19). Nsamenang (1995) pointed out that "psychology is ethnocentric science, cultivated mainly in the developed world and then exported to sub-Saharan Africa" (p. 729). Azuma (1984) noted that the development of a truly universal discipline is limited due to errors of omission: "When a psychologist looks at a non-Western culture through Western glasses, he may fail to notice important aspects of the non-Western culture since the schemata for recognizing them are not provided by his science" (p. 49). Even U.S. psychologists recognize that theories in general psychology reflect the cultural values and goals of the U.S. (Brandt, 1970; Cartwright, 1979; Koch & Leary, 1985; Sampson, 1977).

Others scholars question the internal validity of general psychology (Bandura, 1997, 1999; Cronbach, 1975; Gibson, 1985; Harré, 1999; Kim, 1999; Sampson, 1978). Modeling after Newtonian physics, general psychology attempted to develop objective, abstract, and universal theories by excluding the subjective aspects of human functioning (i.e., consciousness, agency, meaning, and beliefs). Although the concepts of agency and consciousness were central in the theories developed by Wilhelm Wundt and William James, subsequent theorists have expunged them. Koch (1985) pointed out that behaviorism "marks the transition in American psychology between indigenous *color* and indigenous *substance*" (p. 25). Although psychology was founded and developed in Europe, it became indigenized and institutionalized in the U.S.

GENERAL AND CROSS-CULTURAL PSYCHOLOGY

In general psychology, the goal is to discover a linear, objective, and lawful relationship between an independent variable (e.g., stimulus, reinforcement, or information) and the dependent variable (i.e., response or behavior) (see Figure 1). Subjective aspects that are not directly observable (e.g., consciousness, agency, intentions, and beliefs) are considered to be noise and eliminated from the research design. Unobservable concepts are linked to the independent and dependent variables as intervening

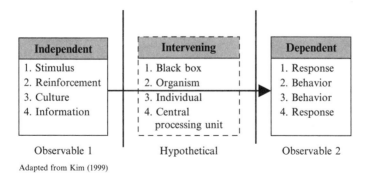

Figure 1. Linear model of causality

variables (Kimble, 1985). The mind is considered to be a black box and individuals are organisms with a brain that stores a history of reinforcement: "Brains are merely repositories for past stimuli inputs and conduits for external stimulations, but they can add nothing to their performance" (Bandura, 1999, p. 22).

With the advent of the computer, the central processor replaced the generic black box. The human brain and neural network is viewed as a digital computer that performs multiple, complex, and dynamics operations using preordained rules (Bandura, 1999). Shweder (1991) pointed out that "epistemologically speaking, knowledge-seeking in general psychology is the attempt to get a look at the central processing mechanism untainted by content and context" (p. 80). Knowledge is hierarchically organized and accessed, combined, and integrated without individuals' awareness (Harré, 1999).

Computer simulations can provide useful information as to how people perceive, process information, and make inferences. Computers, however, lack agency, consciousness, and phenomenology that human beings possess in "thinking about events, planning, constructing courses of action, and reflecting on the adequacy of one's thinking and actions" (Bandura, 1999, p. 22). Computers operate like human beings because they are programmed to mimic human thought processes. Computers are like mirrors that reflect human thought processes, but they cannot explain them. Since computers lack agency, phenomenology, and generative capabilities, they can only simulate human psychology, but they cannot explain it.

In cross-cultural psychology, researchers have adopted a linar model of causality by arguing that culture is a quasi-independent variable and behavior is the dependent variable (Berry, 1980; Triandis, 1980). Cross-cultural psychologists have defined the field by its comparative methodology and avoided defining and articulating the substance of the discipline (Berry, 1980; Triandis, 1980). They have been interested in examining how a culture (as a quasi-independent variable) affects the behavior of individuals. For cross-cultural comparisons, researchers typically select cultures using the Human Relations Area File or Hofstede's (1991) cultural dimensions. These categories or dimensions are, however, mere aggregations and permutations of behavioral and psychological data. Researchers fall into a tautological trap if these cultural categories or dimensions are then used to explain individual differences. In other words, the psychological and behavioral data that are used to categorize cultures cannot be used to explain individual differences. Cross-cultural psychology cannot avoid the problem of circularity as long as it adheres to the linear model of causality.

Indigenous and cultural psychologists attempt to examine, articulate, and analyze the substantive aspects of culture. General and cross-cultural psychologists, however, criticize the development of indigenous psychologies for accumulation of idiosyncratic data, fragmentation, reverse ethnocentrism, moving against the trend of globalization, and violating the law of parsimony (Adamopoulos & Lonner, 2001; Herman & Kempen, 1998; Poortinga, 1999; Triandis, 2000). In general and cross-cultural psychology, new phenomena from different cultures create problems since the field adheres to positivism, tautological conceptualization, and lacks a coherent understanding of culture (Kim & Park, 2005). Since cross-cultural psychology is defined by its comparative method and not by content (Berry, 1980; Triandis, 1980), it has difficulty integrating new, challenging, and diverse information. In mature sciences, such as biology, biological diversity is welcomed and scholars are constantly searching for new species to challenge, expand, and revise existing theories.

Poortinga (1999) criticized the development of indigenous psychologies since the development of multiple psychologies contradicts the scientific requirement of the law of parsimony. This criticism reflects a basic misunderstanding of the requirement of science. The law of parsimony suggests that when there are competing theories, a simple explanation should be chosen over more complex ones. For example, Copernican theory provides a mathematically elegant and more parsimonious explanation than Aristotle's geocentric view. However, it was empirical evidence that verified Copernican theory and refuted Aristotle's cosmology. Kepler's Three Laws of Planetary Motion, the appearance of Haley's comet, the trajectory of cannon balls, and Galileo's experiments supported the Copernican view and they led to the discovery of Newton's Law of Gravitational Attraction. In philosophy, ideas may be equally plausible, but in science empirical evidence is used to verify the most valid position (i.e., empirical evidence and not the law of parsimony is used to validate or refute a particular position).

Although Newton's theory provides an elegant and universal explanation of mechanical physics, the theory cannot explain the properties of light, electromagnetic radiation, and nuclear fission. Albert Einstein proposed a more complex and elaborate Theory of Relativity and $E = mc^2$

to explain phenomena at the nuclear level that Newtonian physics could not. However, Einstein's theory breaks down at the quantum level. When Einstein was confronted with the probabilistic causal explanations of quantum physics, he rejected the approach and held steadfast to the deterministic view of science: "I shall never believe that God plays dice with the world" (Musser, 2004). Although it is more parsimonious to accept the deterministic view, results from quantum physics suggest that Einstein's deterministic view is erroneous (Musser, 2004). In other words, a theory may be parsimonious but wrong. General psychology and cross-cultural psychology may provide parsimonious view of human psychology, but they are not accurate nor universal.

THE SCIENTIFIC FOUNDATION OF INDIGENOUS PSYCHOLOGY

Existing psychological theories are not universal since they have eliminated the very qualities that allow people to understand, predict, and control their environment. Bandura (1999) pointed out that "it is ironic that a science of human functioning should strip people of the very capabilities that make them unique in their power to shape their environment and their own destiny" (p. 21). As such, "psychology has undergone wrenching paradigm shifts" and "in these transformations, the theorists and their followers think, argue, and act agentically, but their theories about how other people function grant them little, if any, agentic capabilities" (p. 21). He asserted that, "the human mind is generative, creative, proactive, and self-reflective and not just reactive" (p. 22).

In the transaction model, human behavior can be explained in terms of the goals people set for themselves, the skills that they develop, the belief that their behavior can affect the outcome, and the outcome that shapes their actions (Bandura, 1997, 1999; Kim, 2000). People are agents motivated to control their lives and to attain desirable goals and avoid undesirable consequences: "The striving for control over life circumstances permeates almost everything people do throughout the life course because it provides innumerable personal and social benefits" and "unless people believe that they can produce desired efforts by their actions, they have little incentive to act" (Bandura, 1997, p. 1).

Bandura (1999) outlined the social cognitive theory that focuses on people's capabilities for self-development, adaptation, and change, and identified four features of human agency: intentionality, forethought, self-reactiveness, and self-reflectiveness. He pointed out that people "construct thoughts about future courses of action to suit ever-changing situations, assess their likely functional values, organize and deploy strategically selected options, evaluate the adequacy of their thinking based on the effects which their actions produce and whatever changes may be necessary" (p. 23). People's thoughts, emotions, and actions are emergent properties of brain activities not reducible to physiological mechanisms. Although all behavior has a biological and neurological basis, the body and brain do not determine behavior. They are used to control the environment and to realize our goals (Bandura, 1999; Harré & Gillet, 1994). Bandura (1999) noted that "people are agentic operators in their life course, not just onlooking hosts of brain mechanisms orchestrated by environment" (p. 22). The method by which people can exert control over the environment can be direct or indirect and exerted by an individual or in concert with other people.

Two types of direct control over the environment can be identified: *primary control* and *collective control* (Bandura, 1997). If a person exerts direct control over the environment, it is an example of primary control (Bandura, 1997). If people work together in concert to manage their environment, it is an example collective control (e.g., democracy). Two types of indirect control can be identified: *secondary control* and *proxy control* (Bandura, 1997). If a person obtains assistance from another person in managing the environment, it is an example of proxy control. If a person adjusts to a given environment and self-regulates to adapt to the environment, it is an example of secondary control. The effectiveness of each type of control depends on the context, individual, organization, and culture.

In the transactional model, subjective qualities (e.g., agency, intention, meaning, beliefs, and goals) are the causal link that connects the environment with behavior (Bandura, 1997; Kim, 1999). In this model, it is important to examine how an individual perceives or interprets a particular event or situation (Causal linkage 1). This information can be obtained through self-report (Bandura, 1997). The second step involves assessing how this perception affects, motivates, and directs individuals' behavior (Causal linkage 2) (see Figure 2).

In a study of management effectiveness, Bandura (1997) told one group that they did much better than average (positive feedback) and

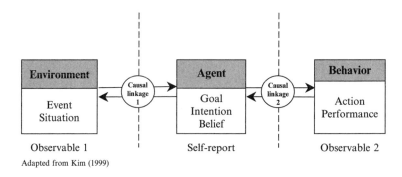

Figure 2. Transactional model

another group that they did much worse (negative feedback). He measured their self-efficacy after they received the predetermined feedback. He found that the positive feedback increased self-efficacy and negative feedback decreased self-efficacy (Causal linkage 1). In the second phase, he measured individuals' analytical ability and their actual performance on management effectiveness. Those participants with high self-efficacy were more likely to use efficient analytical ability, to perform well, and to be satisfied with their level of performance (Causal linkage 2). The reverse was true for those participants who received negative feedback.

Successful performance can increase self-efficacy, which can motivate individuals to seek more challenging goals (Bandura, 1997). The opposite pattern of results has been found for failure experiences. Successful mastery experiences can also lead to *transformative* changes in other aspects of a person's life. In a series of studies of over 400 snake phobics who were tormented for 20 to 30 years, Bandura (2004) was able to treat them in a matter of few hours by increasing their self-efficacy through modeling. He found that the mastery of snake phobia transformed their lives and improved areas unrelated to snake phobia (e.g., reducing their social timidity, becoming self-expressive, and increasing their desire to overcome other fears). Nine large-scale meta-analyses across diverse milieus that used multiple methods, analytical strategies, and experiments were conducted to examine the causal linkage between efficacy beliefs and human functioning. They confirmed the predictive generality of social cognitive theory (Bandura, 2004).

Bandura (1997, 2002, 2004) applied his theory to help people take control of their lives. His theory has been used to teach diabetic children to manage their health, employees to reduce cholesterol levels, patients with coronary artery disease in implementing lifestyle changes, patients with arthritis to manage their pain, and employees, students, and athletes to become higher achievers. The model has also been used to develop radio and television dramas to foster society-wide changes in health promotion and AIDS prevention in Tanzania, India, and Mexico and to reduce fertility rates and elevate the rights of women in China.

INDIGENOUS PSYCHOLOGY

Indigenous psychology represents the transactional scientific paradigm in which individuals are viewed as agents of their action and collective agents through their culture (Kim, 1999, 2000, 2001). In human sciences, people are both the subject and the object of investigation. Although the objective third-person perspective is *necessary* in psychology, it is not *sufficient*. We need to supplement it with the first-person experiential perspective (i.e., agency, meaning, beliefs and intention) and the second-person analysis (e.g., discourse analysis, Harré & Gillet, 1994). We need to obtain an integrated understanding of the first-person, second-person, and third-person perspectives in order to obtain a complete picture of human functioning.

In everyday life people have phenomenological, episodic, and procedural knowledge of how to manage their environment but they may not have the analytical skills to describe how it is done. Since most people do not possess the analytical skills, it is the role of the researcher to help participants articulate their actions analytically. For example, adult native English speakers can freely express their thoughts in English (i.e., procedural knowledge), but they may not know the grammatical syntax or structure (i.e., semantic knowledge). As Wittgenstein points out that, "a description of the grammar of a word is of no use in everyday life; only rarely do we pick up the use of a word by having its use described to us; and although we are trained or encouraged to master the use of the word, we are not taught to describe it" (Budd, 1989, p. 4–5). In human life, both experiential knowledge (e.g., a football player describing his experiences playing a game) and analytical knowledge (e.g., sport commentator providing a play-by-play analysis) are useful information that need to be integrated (e.g., a coach planning strategies for the next game).

Indigenous psychology advocates examining the knowledge, skills, and beliefs people have about themselves, and studying these aspects in their natural contexts. It represents a descriptive approach in which the goal of psychology is to first understand how people function in their natural contexts. It advocates a transactional model of human functioning that recognizes the importance of agency, meaning, intention, and goals. It recognizes that human psychology is complex, dynamic, and generative. Epistemology, theories, concepts, and methods must be developed to correspond to psychological phenomena. The goal is not to abandon science, objectivity, experimental method, and a search for universals, but to create a science that is firmly grounded in the descriptive understanding of human beings. The goal is to create a more rigorous, systematic, universal science that can be theoretically and empirically verified.

CULTURE

Culture is not a variable, quasi-independent variable, or a mere sum of individual characteristics. Culture is an emergent property of individuals interacting with, managing, and changing their environment. Culture represents *the collective utilization of natural and human resources to achieve desired outcomes* (Kim, 2001). Culture is defined as *a rubric of patterned variables*. Differences in cultures can exist if people set different collective goals, utilize different methods and resources to realize the goal, and attach different meaning and values on them.

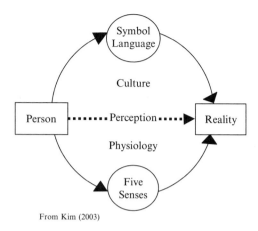

From Kim (2003)

Figure 3. Perception of reality

Contrary to popular belief, we do not perceive reality directly or objectively. When we see a tree, the image of the tree is projected in the retina. The three-dimensional tree becomes an inverted two-dimension image. The image is then sent to our brain through neurotransmission. We do not perceive tree directly or objectively, but it is reconstructed in our brain to be perceived as a tree. We perceive reality through our sense organs and also through symbols and language (see Figure 3). Culture provides human beings with symbolic knowledge to know who we are, define what is meaningful, communicate with others, and to manage the environment. This symbolic knowledge has been transformed into a digital computer language that is able to control machines and to create a new reality known as cyberspace.

Culture is as basic as our physiology. Without culture, human beings would be like other animals, reduced to basic instincts. Without culture, human beings would not be able to think, feel, or behave the way we do. It is *through* culture that we think, feel, behave, and manage our reality (Shweder, 1991). Just as we use our eyes to see the world, we use our culture to understand our world. Because we think *through* our culture, it is difficult to recognize our own culture. For a person born and raised in a particular culture, that culture feels supremely natural.

If the focus is on physiology, human limitations are evident. For example, Helen Keller was blind, deaf, and mute. Because of her disabilities, she was trapped in her body, unable to relate to the world and communicate with others. But when she discovered that she could communicate by using sign language, the whole world opened up to her. She was no longer trapped in her body, limited by her disabilities. She learned about the world using sign language and Braille, and she was

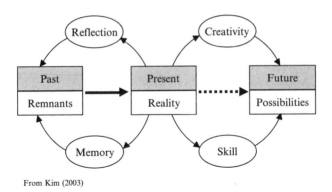

From Kim (2003)

Figure 4. Cultural change

able to teach others with disabilities. She lived in a cultural world where she had access to symbols and technology that allowed her to function and contribute to society. Similarly, Stephen Hawkings is able to contribute to theoretical physics although he suffers from severe physical disabilities. The symbolic understanding is a powerful tool that allows human beings to understand, predict, and manage our environment.

To understand a person, it is necessary to know his or her past. A person with amnesia (i.e., without a past) cannot have a sense of personal identity. A person without a future (e.g., imprisoned for life) will have difficulties living in the present. In order to understand a person, we need to know his or her past, present, and future aspirations. Similarly, in order to understand a culture, we need to understand its history, and the present and future aspirations of its people (see Figure 4).

Culture is usually associated with the study of the past (e.g., history, philosophy, art, literature, language, and crafts). The products of culture represent the past, but not the whole of culture. The most important aspect of culture is the people who have created these products. Based on the understanding of the past and the present, people infer what is possible in the future. People work individually and collectively in realizing this possibility by using the available resources and skills.

The culture that people have built for themselves can have a different meaning for their children. If the culture that is created by and for adults is imposed on their children, then it can be perceived as a prison. If the culture that adults have created is incompatible with the aspirations of their children, then their children may modify the culture. Generational conflicts arise since adults use the past to understand the present and use the past to shape the future (Kim et al., 2000). Adolescents, on the other hand, do not share the same past as their parents. Since the younger generation is not bound by the past, they can explore the future more freely and creatively.

CULTURAL TRANSFORMATIONS

In general psychology, behaviorism became the dominant paradigm in psychology emphasizing biology as the basis of all behavior. In psychiatry, Freudian theory has traditionally dominated the conceptualization and treatment of the mentally ill. Experimental psychologists criticize Freudian and neo-Freudian theories for lacking objective methods, verifiable results, and therapeutic rigor. However, both behaviorists and psychiatrists agree that biology is the basis of human psychology. In the third camp, humanists criticize behaviorists and Freudians for their negative portrayal of human beings and for not giving enough attention to human potential. However, in Maslow's hierarchy of needs, physiological needs are viewed as basic, and the other needs (e.g., self, emotional, relational and social needs) are pursued only once physiological needs are met. The three pillars of psychology assume that biology is basic to human psychology.

Many social scientists have accepted Darwin's Theory of Evolution and applied the theory to explain psychological, social, and cultural variations. Darwinian Theory assumes that human beings have evolved and survived as a species because we were able adapt to the ecology. The theory is partly right in showing that our adaptive capabilities contributed to our survival. However, human beings were able to adapt and survive not because of physiology and natural instinct, but because we were able to *overcome* our instincts (Kim, 2003).

Although human beings have not changed biologically and genetically during the past 7,000 years, cultural changes have been rather dramatic. Biology cannot explain cultural developments that are recorded outside of the body and any given individual. Cultural transformations during the last seven millennia have changed the way people understand and manage the environment (Bandura, 1997; Kim, Helgesen, & Ahn, 2002). Modern nations did not evolve in a logical, sequential, or evolutionary manner, but through clash of ideas. People were able to integrate these ideas into new cultural forms (Kim, Aasen, & Ebadi, 2003).

Cultures have undergone significant transformations, from the early Stone Age to the current Information Age. As a physically weak species, human beings were at a constant mercy of predators. We found aids in nature to protect us from predators. Although it is our natural instinct to fear fire, we were able to harness the power of fire and used it for protection and survival. We learned to cook food over the fire, which increased the kind and type of food that we could consume. Fire gave us power to transform formless clay and iron into cups, utensils, houses, and weapons. How could human beings use formless clay to make something that did not exist in nature? We were able to make these things because we had reflective and generative capabilities.

We have learned to domesticate cows, pigs, and chickens as a means of storing and producing food. We have managed to transform the instinct of predators and they are now our pets, guides, and protectors. We cultivate wild rice, wheat, or vegetables to produce food from the land. With the increased agricultural efficiency, irrigation, and storage, enough food could be produced to support a sedentary lifestyle. With an increased number of people, social, legal, and political institutions were created to manage the people who lived in close proximity.

With each succeeding generation, new knowledge accumulated and it was recorded and passed on to the next generation in oral and written form. Industrialization, commerce, and science and technology transformed subsistence economies into modern societies. Currently, democracy and the rule of law protect the right of individuals in which people enjoy a freedom and quality of life unparalleled in human history.

The developments of contraceptive methods and abortion challenge the very assumption of Darwinian Theory and biological determinism. For all animals, except human beings, mating behavior is determined by a fixed-action pattern and innate releasing mechanisms (Tinbergen, 1965).

The propagation and survival of a species is ensured by pleasure derived during the mating process. Human beings, however, have invented contraceptive methods to derive pleasure from sexual intercourse while avoiding pregnancy. In most countries, a woman can legally choose to abort the fetus during the first trimester. Even the most fervent advocate of biological influence, Dawkins (1989), acknowledges that the use of contraception, abortion, and the decrease in fertility rates in economically developed countries cannot be explained by evolutionary biology.

EAST ASIAN PERSPECTIVE

In contrast to the Western emphasis on the individuated self, Confucianism focuses on emotions that bind individuals and family members together. The Chinese, Japanese, and Korean word for human being is 人間, which can be translated literally as "human between." It is not what happens within an individual, but between individuals that makes us human (Kim, 2001). Mencius stated that: "If you see a child drowning and you don't feel compassion, then you are not human being." It is compassion that helps us to relate to the child and propels us to take the necessary action to save the child. The human essence is basically relational and can be defined in terms of the emotions people feel for one another. The love, care, and devotion that parents provide to their children are viewed as necessary and essential for a newborn child to become human.

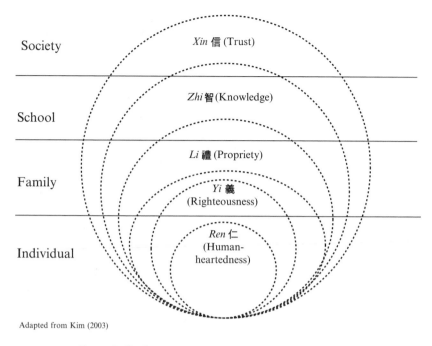

Society

Family

School

Individual

Xin 信 (Trust)

Zhi 智 (Knowledge)

Li 禮 (Propriety)

Yi 義 (Righteousness)

Ren 仁 (Human-heartedness)

Adapted from Kim (2003)

Figure 5. Confucian conception and development of the self

Confucius (551–479 BC) saw the universe and all living things in it as a manifestation of a unifying force called the *dao* (道, Truth, Unity, or the Way). In humans, *dao* is manifested in human through the virtues of *ren* (仁, human-heartedness), *yi* (義, righteousness), *li* (禮, propriety), *zhi* (智, knowledge), and *xin* (信, trust) (see Figure 5). Human-heartedness is essentially relational and individuals experience it through the love, sacrifice, and devotion of their parents. Individuals are born into a particular family, with a particular status defined by *yi* (righteousness). Righteousness requires that individuals must perform and fulfill their duties as defined by their particular status and role.

Human-heartedness and righteousness are considered two sides of the same coin. A father fulfils his duties because he loves his son, and he loves his son because he is the father. The primary relationship is the parent-child relationship as defined by *xiao dao* (孝道, filial piety). Parents demand love, reverence, obedience, and respect from their children. Children expect love, wisdom, and benevolence from their parents. The past, present, and future are not abstract entities, but embodied in relationships. Parents and ancestors represent the past and children represent the future.

Confucius considered society to be hierarchically ordered and that each person has *fen* (分, portion or place) in life. Each *fen* had attached roles, and each person must fulfill these roles. The duties and obligations of each *fen* are prescribed by *li* (propriety). Propriety articulates expectations and duties of each individual according to status and role. Social order and harmony are preserved when people observe their place in society and fulfill required obligations and duties.

The fourth virtue is *zhi* (knowledge). Knowledge is obtained through the socialization of parents and through formal education. The four concepts of human-heartedness, righteousness, propriety, and knowledge are like the two arms and two legs that people are born with; we need to cultivate and develop them in order to know how to use them. Finally, as children mature they need to interact with a wider range of people, including strangers. As such, they need to develop the virtue of *xin* (trust).

Confucian philosophy provides as rich a context for developing theories about human nature and behavior in East Asia as Greek philosophy has provided in the West. Although it is important to examine indigenous text as a source of information, researchers should not automatically assume that Chinese will follow the Confucian way, or that Hindu Dharma will automatically explain the behavior of Indians. These indigenous texts were developed within a particular culture, and they represent the interests of a particular religious group (e.g., Brahman caste in India) or social class (e.g., the ruling elite in East Asia). In order to use these texts, researchers need to translate them into psychological concepts and theories and empirically verify how they influence how people think, feel, and behave.

It is tempting to use philosophical and religious texts to explain the behavior of the Asians, but researchers must be cautious of their limitations. First, these texts could be used as a formal descriptive model, but they may not be suitable as an explanatory model. Philosophical or religious ideas are used as general guidelines, but very few people follow these guidelines meticulously. Second, within a particular culture, there are competing philosophies, religions, and worldviews. For example, Buddhism outlines a universal conception of self, relations, and society in East Asia. In addition, native religions such as Shamanism in Korea, Shintoism in Japan, and Daoism in China have influenced both Buddhism and Confucianism. These three epistemologies have mutually influenced each another and have been integrated and blended into a synthetic form (Kim, 1998).

Third, there are biases and blind spots in religious and philosophical traditions. In Confucianism, the father-son relationship is considered primary relationship and the prototype for all relationships. If we examine developmental research in East Asia, the father-son relationship turns out to be secondary, while the mother-child relationship is primary. In traditional East Asian societies, fathers participate in socialization of children after the age of three or four, which is after mothers have socialized children with basic linguistic and social skills. If the father-son relationship is primary, it is difficult to explain how Confucius and Mencius became the most renowned philosophers even though their father was not alive when they were growing up. It was their mothers who played a primary role in educating them and helping them to succeed.

Fourth, cultures change and religious and philosophical ideas also change with time and social conditions (Kim, Aasen, & Ebadi, 2003). The emphasis on paternalism and sex-role differentiation may have been functional in traditional agrarian societies, but in modern East Asian societies, egalitarian values are replacing traditional values (Kim, 1998; Park & Kim, 2004). In traditional East Asian societies, women were excluded from obtaining an education and participating in society, but this is no longer the case. In Korea, the inheritance laws, divorce laws, and family registry have changed so that women have equal rights with men (Park & Kim, Chapter 19)

Confucian philosophy can be used as a starting point for research, but not as the end point. These philosophical concepts are learned in school as a part of formal education, but they are not psychological or indigenous concepts used in everyday life. It is necessary to translate these philosophical concepts into psychological constructs. In Korea, the concept of *jung* (情, deep affection and attachment for a person, place, or thing) can be considered a functional equivalent of human-heartedness that is indigenous and used in everyday language (Choi & Kim, Chapter 15; Kim & Park, 2004a). In Japan, *amae* defined as the act of asking and receiving special favors in close relationships) could also be a psychological equivalent (Kim & Park, 2004a; Kim & Yamaguchi, 1995; Yamaguchi, Chapter 6). Although *jung* and *amae* have very different denotations, psychological analysis reveals a similar pattern of results, capturing the essence of human-heartedness.

Filial piety can be interpreted as an example of righteousness (Park & Kim, 2004). In Korea, the filial piety of taking care of parents in their old age is not only a moral imperative, but also a legal obligation that everyone must fulfill. The East Asian concepts of loyalty and duty (*giri* 義理 in Japanese and *dori* 道理 in Korean) capture the essence of righteousness. Finally, the concept of maintaining one's face (體面) is an example of propriety (Choi, Kim, & Kim, 1997).

EMPIRICAL ANALYSIS

Philosophy can provide researchers with formal theories that could explain people's actions. In psychology, empirical analysis is necessary to verify whether philosophical or indigenous ideas actually influence the way people think, feel, and behave. An empirical study was conducted in Korea to examine the basis of trust in interpersonal relationship. In the Confucian model outlined above, trust is based on human-heartedness, righteousness, propriety, and knowledge.

A total of 1,737 matched-sample of adolescents and their parents (274 middle school students, 305 high school students, and 579 mothers and 579 fathers) completed a questionnaire developed by the authors (Kim & Park, 2004b). Adolescents were first asked to rate how much they trust their mother, father, teachers, and friends on a 5-point scale (ranging from highly distrust to highly trust). Parents were asked how much they trust their children, spouse, and teachers. They were then asked to write down why they trusted the target person in an open-ended format. A similar study was conducted with 251 high school students and 268 adolescents on probation (Park, Kim & Tak, 2004).

The first striking result is that majority of Korean adolescents reported trusting their parents much more than themselves (Park et al., 2004). When they were asked the question (*Who do you trust the most?*), they gave the following response: *parents* (high school students = 62%, adolescents on probation = 63%), *myself* (high school students = 19%, adolescents on probation = 8%), *friends* (high school students = 9%, adolescents on probation = 15%), and *other family member* (high school students = 7%, adolescents on probation = 10%). These results indicate the important role that parents play. Secondly, adolescents on probation were less likely to trust themselves and more likely to trust their parents and friends as compared to high school students.

The results from the open-ended results revealed the following pattern of results. The most frequent response for adolescents is that they trusted their parents because of *sacrifice* (mother = 31%, father = 30%); followed by *consanguinity* or blood relationship (mother = 21%, father = 20%); *respect* (mother = 15%, father = 13%); *dependability* (mother = 11%, father = 16%); *mutual trust* (mother = 13%, father = 11%); and *guidance* (mother = 10%, father = 10%).

When the parents were asked why they trusted their children, they gave answers that were complementary to those of their children. The most frequent response for both mothers and fathers was *sincerity* (mothers = 32%, fathers = 31%), followed by *honesty* (mother = 31%, father = 30%), *consanguinity* (mother = 16%, father = 16%), *expectation* (mother = 9%, father = 8%), *obedience* (mother = 6%, father = 9%), and *studiousness* (mother = 3%, father = 5%). A similar pattern of results was obtained from high school students and adolescents on probation (Park et al., 2004).

These results empirically verify the Confucian idea that human-heartedness, as represented by sacrifice on the part of the parents, is the basis of trust on the part of children. The second most important basis of trust is righteousness, as reflected by the emphasis on consanguinity. The concept of propriety is reflected in the adolescents' response of *dependable* and parent's response of *expectation* and *obedience* on the part of the children. The concept of knowledge is reflected in the adolescents' response of *respect* for their parents and parents' response of *studiousness* of their children.

The emphasis on relationship contrasts with Western theories that view trust as individualistic "encapsulated interests" (Hardin, 1998). In addition, national surveys conducted in Denmark, Japan, Korea, and Sweden provide evidence that trust in relational cultures is different from the trust that develops in individualistic, rights-based cultures (Helgesen & Kim, 2002; Kim & Park, 2005).

DISCUSSION

Indigenous psychology represents the transaction model of science in which agency, meaning, intentions, beliefs, and goals are incorporated into research design. It advocates examining the knowledge, skills, and beliefs people have about themselves and how people work together with others in their cultural context. The first step is to provide a descriptive understanding of human functioning. The second steps involves developing theories and concepts that could explain the observed regularities. The goal is to create a more rigorous, systematic and universal science that can be theoretically and empirically verified.

In indigenous psychology, it is important to recognize external impositions that may distort the understanding of psychological phenomena. First, psychologists imposed the natural sciences model to study human beings. In an effort to become an independent branch of science, early psychologists tailored the discipline to fit the natural science paradigm. Although psychologists were able to achieve a modest degree of methodological sophistication, psychological knowledge became distorted. Psychologists have discarded central constructs of agency, consciousness, meaning, and intentions in order to create an objective science.

The second imposition is the assumption of the universality of psychological theories. With very little development, testing, and data, psychological theories are assumed to be universal. This assumption is particularly problematic since most theories are developed in the U.S. and tested mainly on university students in a laboratory setting.

Third, experts or professionals have imposed their views on the lay public. Heider (1958) suggested, "the ordinary person has a great and profound understanding of himself and of other people which, though unformulated or vaguely conceived, enables him to interact in more or less adaptive ways" (p. 2). Based on Heider's preliminary work, Julian Rotter developed his theory of locus of control and Bernard Weiner developed his attribution theory. These theories are, however, far removed from people's conceptions of attribution and control and, more important, they possess low internal and external validity (Bandura, 1997; Kim & Park, 2003).

Fourth, indigenous concepts have been analyzed as examples of indigenous psychology. The concept of *philotimo* in Greece (a characteristic of a person who is "polite, virtuous, reliable, proud," Triandis, 1972), *anasakti* in India (non-detachment, Pande & Naidu, 1992), *amae* in Japan (indulgent dependence, Doi, 1973), *kapwa* in the Philippines (shared identity with other, Enriquez, 1993), and *jung* in Korea (deep attachment and affection, Choi & Kim, Chapter 16) have been analyzed and various culture-bound syndromes have been introduced (Yap, 1974). Although these concepts are interesting, they have limited communicative value to scholars who do not understand language or know the phenomena first-hand. Also, it is difficult to ascertain whether these conceptualizations are accurate and to assess the scientific merit of these indigenous concepts since very little empirical evidence exists to support their claims.

The concept of *amae* has been the focus of attention with the first publication by Doi (1973). Yamaguchi and Ariizumi (Chapter 6) points out that the concept of *amae* has been erroneously interpreted as an example of dependence by both Japanese and U.S. researchers (Doi, 1973; Johnson, 1993; Lebra, 1976; Rothbaum, Weisz, Pott, Miyake, & Morelli, 2000). This assertion has been made without a clear definition of *amae* and empirical evidence to support their views. These are examples of bad research and not of indigenous psychology.

Kim and Yamaguchi (1995) launched an empirical study using an open-ended questionnaire exploring various facets of *amae*. They administered the questionnaire to a total of 841 respondents living in various parts of Japan: 237 middle school students, 224 high school students, 243 university students, and 137 adults. The results indicated that *amae* involves an episode between two people: One person requests a specific favor and the other person grants the request. An *amae* episode occurs in close relationships, usually between a parent and child and between close friends. The special request, which is often demanding and unreasonable, is granted because of the desire to maintain close relationship.

Yamaguchi and Ariizumi (Chapter 6) conducted a series of experiments to analyze different facets of *amae*. They define *amae* as the "presumed acceptance of one's inappropriate behavior or request" (p. 164-165). They have found that Japanese respondents engage in an *amae* episode in order to obtain a particular benefit through the help of a powerful other (i.e., proxy control) and to verify the close relationship (since only people who are close would be willing to grant an inappropriate request). They conclude that *amae* cannot be equated with dependence since it involves proxy control. They developed scenarios containing *amae* episodes and conducted experiments with a sample of Japanese, U.S., and Taiwanese students. They found that the U.S. and Taiwanese respondents were more likely than Japanese respondents to comply with the unreasonable request. They conclude that although *amae* is an indigenous Japanese word, the psychological features of *amae* can be found in other cultures. Thus, a series of empirical studies have helped to clarify the confusion created by

Japanese and U.S. researchers. These studies also outline key features of *amae*, which could potentially challenge the attachment and developmental theories developed in the West (Yamaguchi & Ariizumi, Chapter 6).

Finally, as outlined by Tobin, Wu and Davidson (1989), indigenous psychology encourages the use of multiple perspectives, known as the multi-vocal approach. In this approach, in addition to the researchers, participants are allowed to interpret and evaluate the results. Tobin et al. (1987) found that greatest variations across cultures appeared in the way people interpreted and evaluated other people's behavior.

Indigenous psychology advocates the creation of more rigorous theories based on epistemological and scientific foundation. Indigenous psychology advocates a linkage of humanities (which focus on human experience and creativity) with social sciences (which focus on analysis and verification). In the past century, psychologists have focused most of our attention on internal or external validity and not on practical validity. In other words, do our theories help to understand, predict, and manage human behavior? Bandura (1997) has shown that scientifically valid theory can be applied to various social milieus, using various methods to affect personal change, community change, and a large-scale societal change. In this chapter and also in the chapter by Park and Kim (Chapter 19), theories, concepts and methods developed from indigenous psychology provide more rigorous, valid and verifiable results when compared to general and cross-cultural psychology.

REFERENCES

Adamopoulos, J., & Lonner, W. (2001). Culture and psychology at a crossroad: Historical perspective and theoretical analysis. In D. Matsumoto (Ed.), *Handbook of culture and psychology* (pp. 11–34). Oxford: Oxford University Press.

Azuma, H. (1984). Psychology in a non-Western country. *International Journal of Psychology, 19*, 145–155.

Bandura, A. (1997). *Self-efficacy: The exercise of control.* New York: Freeman.

Bandura, A. (1999). Social cognitive theory: An agentic perspective. *Asian Journal of Social Psychology, 2*, 21–42.

Bandura, A. (2002). Environmental sustainability by sociocognitive declereation of population growth. In P. Schmuck, & W. Schultz (Eds.), *The psychology of sustainable development,* (pp. 209–238). Dordrecht, the Netherlands: Kluwer.

Bandura, A. (2004). Swimming against the mainstream: The early years from chilly tributary to transformative mainstream. *Behavior Research and Therapy, 42*, 613–630.

Berry, J. W. (1974). Canadian psychology: Some social and applied emphasis. *Canadian Psychologist, 15*, 132–139.

Berry, J. W. (1980). Introduction to methodology. In H. C. Triandis, & J. W. Berry (Eds.), *Handbook of Cross-Cultural Psychology, Vol. 2.* Boston: Allyn & Bacon.

Boring, E. G. (1921/50). *A history of experimental psychology.* Englewood Cliffs, NJ: Printice Hall.

Brandt, L. W. (1970). American Psychology. *American Psychologist, 25*, 1091–1093.

Budd, M. (1989). *Wittgenstein's philosophy of psychology*. London: Routledge.

Cartwright, D. (1979). Contemporary social psychology in historical perspective. *Social Psychology Quarterly, 42*, 8293.

Choi, S. C., Kim, U., & Kim, D. I. (1997). Multifaceted analyses of chemyon ("social face"): An indigenous Korean perspective. In K. Leung, U. Kim, S. Yamaguchi, & Y. Kashima (Eds.), *Progress in Asian Social Psychologies* (pp. 3–22). Singapore: John Wiley & Sons.

Cronbach, L. J. (1975). The two disciplines of scientific psychology. *American Psychologist, 30*, 671–684.

Dawkins, R. (1989). *The selfish gene*. Oxford: Oxford University Press.

Doi, T. (1973). *The anatomy of dependence*. Tokyo: Kodansha.

Elms, A. C. (1975). The crisis in confidence in social psychology. *American Psychologist, 30*, 967–976.

Enriquez, V. G. (1993). Developing a Filipino psychology. In U. Kim, & J. W. Berry (Eds.), *Indigenous psychologies: Research and experience in cultural context* (pp. 152–169). Newbury Park, CA: Sage.

Gibson, J. J. (1985). Conclusions from a century of research on sense perception. In S. Koch, & D. E. Leary (Eds.), *A century of psychology as science* (pp. 224–230). New York: McGraw Hill.

Hardin, R. (1998). Trust in government. In V. Braithwaite & M. Levi (Eds.), *Trust and governance*. New York: Russell Sage Foundation.

Harré, R. (1999). The rediscovery of the human mind: The discursive approach. *Asian Journal of Social Psychology, 2*, 43–62.

Harré, R., & Gillet, G. (1994). *The discursive mind*. Thousand Oaks, CA: Sage.

Heider, F. (1958) *The psychology of interpersonal relations*. New York: Wiley.

Helgesen,G.& Kim, U. (2002). *Good government: Nordic and East Asian perspectives*. Copenhagen: Danish Institute of International Affairs.

Hermans, J. M., & Kempen, J. G. (1998). Moving cultures: The perilous problem of cultural dichotomy in a globalized society. *American Psychologist, 53*, 1111–1120.

Hofstede, G. (1991). *Cultures and organizations: Software of the mind*. New York: McGraw-Hill Book.

Johnson, F. A. (1993). *Dependency and Japanese socialization*. New York: New York University Press.

Kim, U. (1998). Understanding Korean corporate culture: Analysis of transformative human resource management. *Strategic Human Resource Development Review, 2*, 68–101. [in Korean]

Kim, U. (1999). After the crisis in social psychology: Development of the transactional model of science. *Asian Journal of Social Psychology, 2*, 1–19.

Kim, U. (2000). Indigenous, cultural, and cross-cultural psychology: Theoretical, philosophical, and epistemological analysis. *Asian Journal of Social Psychology, 3*, 265–287.

Kim, U. (2001). Culture, science and indigenous psychologies: An integrated analysis. In D. Matsumoto (Ed.), *Handbook of culture and psychology* (pp. 51–76). Oxford: Oxford University Press.

Kim, U. (2003). Science, religion, philosophy, and culture: Psychological analysis of Western, Islamic and East Asian worldviews. In U. Kim, H. S. Aasen, S. Ebadi, (Eds.). *Democracy, human rights, and Islam in modern Iran: Psychological, social, cultural perspectives* (pp. 443–496). Bergen: Fagbokforlaget.

Kim, U., Aasen, H. S., & Ebadi, S. (Eds.) (2003). *Democracy, human rights, and Islam in modern Iran: Psychological, social and cultural perspectives*. Bergen: Fagbokforlaget.

Kim, U., & Berry, J. W. (1993). *Indigenous psychologies: Experience and research in cultural Context*. Newbury Park, CA: Sage.

Kim, U., Helgesen, G., & Ahn, B. M. (2002). Democracy, trust, and political efficacy: Comparative analysis of Danish and Korean political culture. *Applied Psychology: An International Review, 51*, 317–352.

Kim, U., & Park, Y. S. (2003). An indigenous analysis of success attribution: Comparison of Korean students and adults. In K. S. Yang, K. K. Hwang, Pedersen, P.B. & I. Daibo (Eds.), *Progress in Asian social psychology: Conceptual and empirical contributions* (pp. 171–195). New York: Preager.

Kim, U., & Park, Y. S. (2004a). Indigenous psychologies. In C. Spielberger (Ed.), *Encyclopedia of applied psychology* (pp. 263–269). Oxford: Elsevier Academic Press.

Kim, U., & Park, Y. S. (2004b). The social representation and trust of Korean society and people: Indigenous psychological analysis of the perception of Korean adolescents and adults. *Korean Journal of Psychological and Social Issues 10,* 103–129 [in Korean].

Kim, U., & Park, Y. S. (2005). Trust, relationship, and civil society in Scandinavia and East Asia: Psychological, social, and cultural analysis. *Korean Journal of Psychological and Social Issues, 11, Special Issue,* 57–85.

Kim, U., Park, Y. S., Kim, M. U., Lee, K. W., & Yu, S. H. (2000). Intergenerational differences and life-satisfaction: Comparative analysis of adolescents, adults, and the elderly. *Korean Journal of Health Psychology, 5,* 119–145 [in Korean].

Kim, U., Triandis, H. C., Choi, S. C., Kâğitçibaşi, C., & Yoon, G. (1994) (Eds.). *Individualism and Collectivism: Theory, Method, and Application.* Thousand Oaks, CA: Sage.

Kim, U., & Yamaguchi, S., (1995). Conceptual and empirical analysis of amae: Exploration into Japanese psycho-social space Exploration into Japanese psychological space. In Proceedings of the 43rd Annual Conference of the Japanese Group Dynamics Association (p. 158–159). Tokyo: Japanese Group Dynamics Association.

Kimble, G. A. (1985). Conditioning and learning. In S. Koch, & Leary D. E. (Eds.), *A century of psychology as science* (pp. 284–321). New York: McGraw Hill.

Koch, S. (1985). The nature and limits of psychological knowledge: Lessons of a century qua "science." In S. Koch, & D. E. Leary (Eds.), *A century of psychology as science* (pp. 75–99). New York: McGraw Hill.

Koch, S., & Leary, D. E. (1985). *A century of psychology as science.* New York: McGraw Hill.

Lachenmeyer, C. W. (1970). Experimentation -a misunderstood methodology in psychological and social-psychological research. *American Psychologist, 25,* 617–624.

Lebra, T. S. (1976). *Japanese patterns of behavior.* Honolulu: University of Hawaii Press.

Levine, M. (1974). Scientific method and the adversary model: Some preliminary thoughts. *American Psychologist, 29,* 661–667.

Moscovici, S. (1972). Society and theory in social psychology. In J. Israel and H. Tajfel (Eds.), *The context of social psychology.* London: Academic.

Musser, G. (2004). Was Einstein right? *Scientific American, 291,* 88–91.

Nsamenang, A. B. (1995). Factors influencing the development of psychology in Sub-Saharan Africa. *International Journal of Psychology, 30,* 729–738.

Pande, N., & Naidu, R. K. (1992). Anasakti and health: A study of non-attachment. *Psychology and Developing Societies,* [in Korean] *4,* 91–104.

Park, Y. S., & Kim, U. (2004). *Parent-child relationship in Korea: Indigenous psychological analysis of self-concept and family role.* Seoul: Kyoyook Kwahaksa. [in Korean]

Park, Y. S., Kim, U., & Tak. S. Y. (2004). Indigenous psychological analysis of delinquency among Korean adolescents: Comparison of adolescents under probation and high school students. *Korean Journal of Psychological and Social Issues, Special Issue, 10,* 107–145

Poortinga, Y. H. (1999). Do differences in behavior imply a need for different psychologies? *Applied Psychology: An International Review, 48(4),* 419–432.

Rothbaum, F., Weisz, J., Pott, M., Miyake, K., & Morelli, G. (2000). Attachment and culture: Security in the United States and Japan. *American Psychologist, 55,* 1093–1104.

Sampson, E. E. (1977). Psychology and the American ideal. *Journal of Personality and Social Psychology, 35,* 767–782.

Sampson, E. E. (1978). Scientific paradigms and social values: Wanted A scientific revolution. *Journal of Personality and Social Psychology, 36,* 1332–1343.

Shweder, R. A. (1991). *Thinking Through Cultures - Expeditions in Cultural Psychology*. Cambridge: Harvard University Press.

Sinha, D. (1997). Indigenizing psychology. In J. W. Berry, Y. H. Poortinga, & J. Pandey (Eds.), *Handbook of cross-cultural psychology: Theory and method, Volume 1*. Boston: Allyn and Bacon.

Tinbergen, N. (1965). *Animal Behavior*. New York: Time-Life Books.

Triandis, H. (1972). The *analysis of subjective culture*. New York: Wiley.

Triandis, H. (Ed.) (1980). *Handbook of cross-cultural psychology*. Boston: Allyn & Bacon.

Triandis, H. C. (2000). Dialectics between cultural and cross-cultural psychology. *Asian Journal of Social Psychology, 3*, 185–196.

Tobin, J., Wu., D. Y. H.,& Davidson, D. H. (1989) Preschool in three cultures: Japan, China, and the United States. New Haven, CT: Yale University Press.

Yap, P. W. (1974). *Comparative psychiatry: A theoretical framework*. Toronto: University of Toronto.

Chapter 3

The Importance of Constructive Realism for the Indigenous Psychologies Approach

Fritz G. Wallner and Martin J. Jandl

TRADITIONAL PHILOSOPHY OF SCIENCE AND THE RISE OF CONSTRUCTIVE REALISM

In this section we recount the failings of traditional philosophy of science and the problems due to other constructivisms, such as the famous School of Erlangen. Constructive realism is a rather new approach in philosophy of science, first presented in the 1990s by the Viennese philosopher of science Fritz G. Wallner. Although it is similar to the School of Erlangen in many aspects and viewpoints–the School of Erlangen is mistaken for social constructivism or radical constructivism–the mistakes of these constructivistic approaches are different. Hence, the story we tell will not be accepted by all constructivists or by adherents to traditional philosophy of science. We suggest that there is one point in particular at issue. If we tell a story in which philosophy of science is mistaken from the point of constructive realism, then we tell a story of progress in philosophy of science.

First, it is moot if there is any progress in intellectual history. Postmodern philosophy struggles against the idea of progress, but we do not claim that progress in intellectual history leads to truth. Thus, postmodern arguments do not work here because constructive realism avoids errors of other philosophies of science–we do not insist on the notion of progress in this respect. Second, the story of the history of philosophy of science is told differently by other philosophers. For example, Popper and his scholars do not appraise constructive philosophy of science as progress, but as a danger for science claiming that constructivism destroys the commitment of science. Popper's suspicion does not apply to constructive realism.

Bearing this point in mind, it is possible to distinguish four stages in the history of philosophy of science: naive empirism, logical empirism, critical rationalism and constructivism. This classification is not perfectly elaborated, but it is perspicuous (we adopted it from Holzkamp, 1972, pp. 80–99; for a more detailed overview see Wallner, 1994, pp. 29–67).

According to naive empirism, science is an institution to gain true knowledge of nature. The basis of science is observation and experience: The process of scientific investigation starts with collecting data by observation and experience. By means of induction scientists reveal laws of nature. Laws of nature are conceptualized as being in nature, the scientists just have to seek and to find them. Hence, scientists are led by experience, they register passively what nature reveals.

One of the main metaphors of this understanding of science is that scientists "read the book of nature." This view postulates that nature is structured by laws, and that nature is a cosmos. It is the task of the scientists to reveal the structures of the cosmos by applying the methods of a certain science. A scientist is a person with objective curiosity. Nothing but nature gives direction to scientific investigation. Revealing laws of nature is a progress towards truth. In current philosophy of science there are not many individuals who subscribe to this view, but it is obvious that many scientists in the so-called hard sciences suggest that their investigations are led by nature. Not accepting a scientific law means repudiating truth because a scientific law describes the structure of nature. That is an important point: If someone neglects the importance of, for example, investigations in the field of genetics, he or she will be suspected of suppressing the revelation of truth by science -probably he or she will be labeled a fanatic who fights the laws of nature, and fighting the truth is equal to tilting at windmills. Naive empirism does not take into account the cultural embeddedness of science, and hence it is not tolerant of sciences of other, non European cultures.

However, this view is outstripped in philosophy of science. It is the merit of logical empirism to demonstrate the failures of naive empirism. The most famous philosophers of logical empirism are Schlick, Carnap, Neurath and Reichenbach who constituted the Vienna Circle. Logical empirism neglects the doctrine of the primacy of experience and therewith Mill's doctrine of induction as a principle of genesis of knowledge. Science does not start with experience because scientists first have concepts of the observable facts. Nature does not inform scientists what they have to observe, but scientists know by themselves what they want to observe. Hence, according to the view of logical empirism, laws cannot be found in nature because nature is only describable by singular judgments, but laws of nature are universal. Science is a system of propositions building up axiomatic systems–the sphere of language cannot be passed over, science consists of sentences. The problem of reference to the world emerges, and the answer of the Vienna Circle was to claim protocol sentences–sentences (or propositions) referring directly to reality. The famous criterion of "meaningful sentences" says that a sentence (a proposition) will be meaningful if it is a protocol sentence or if it is derived from a protocol sentence. It is obvious that the philosophers of the Vienna Circle struggled against metaphysics because metaphysics operate with sentences not derived from protocol sentences, but they also rule out ethics. However, the doctrine of protocol sentences is connected with the empirical verification of proposition systems. Pregnantly formulated, the scientist is sitting in a cage of propositions trying to get in touch with reality. According to our view, it is not only the merit of logical empiricism that proves the failures of naive empiricism, but also dissolving fictions about science: The members of the Vienna Circle increased these fictions to an extreme point, and thus it became obvious that science does not work in this way. Surely, this is a merit *contre cœur*.

It is noteworthy that logical empiricism is fascinated by new developments in logic. Logic traces back to Aristotle, but at the beginning of the 20th century syllogistic logic turned to a mathematical logic (by the investigations of Frege, Russell, and Whitehead). The philosophy of science of the Vienna Circle was constituted by the reference to logic. Hence, logical empiricism is a formal methodology centered on philosophy of science as the view of science as a description of the world by the doctrine of protocol sentences.

This doctrine of verification of scientific proposition systems was repudiated and refuted by Popper. He criticized the principle of induction at the bottom of the verification of hypotheses, and stated: "*Unsere Wissenschaft ist kein Wissen: ...weder Wahrheit noch Wahrscheinlichkeit kann sie erreichen.* [Our science is not knowledge: science leads neither to truth nor to probability.]" (Popper, 1966, p. 228). Popper replaced the verification of hypotheses with the doctrine of falsification arguing for classical logic. Like logical empiricism, Popper defined science as a system of sentences with different degrees of generalization, and the reference to reality was established by singular sentences, the so-called base sentences. Popper pointed out that the truth of a generalized sentence cannot be derived from a base sentence, and hence the verification of a singular sentence says nothing about the verification of generalized sentences.

The point of Popper's argument was: Generalized sentences cannot be derived from singular sentences, but generalized sentences might contradict singular sentences. In this case the proposition system is falsified. Falsification means applying the *modus tolens*. An important assumption is obviously that base sentences actually refer to reality. A base sentence will be true if it accords to the methodology of a science and if the majority of scientists agree that this base sentence is true. Thus, Popper equated philosophy of science with the methodological logic of science. There are two points at issue with Popper's critical rationalism. First, Popper subscribed to the view that science describes the world. Second, the just-mentioned reduction of philosophy of science to logic of science deprives philosophy of science of the possibility of understanding (interpreting) microworlds. Whereas the first point is replaced by constructivistic philosophies of science (e.g. by the School of Erlangen), the second point is taken into account appropriately only by constructive realism.

But, to continue the story, Popper's view is not appropriate to science. It is possible to keep up a proposition system even if a base sentence contradicts it. Scientists will not give up a theory instantly if there are data that disapprove the theory. They try to show why these data are inacceptable or, in other words, they exhaust the theory - scientists demonstrate that data contradicting the theory are derivable from interfering conditions. This method of exhaustion is due to Dingler. However, Holzkamp's view of Dingler's philosophy neither accords to the view of constructive realism nor to the view of the School of Erlangen. (Dingler plays an important role in these two philosophies of science.) According to Holzkamp, the importance of constructivism is having shown that the primacy of theory dominates science. But, he does not even mention that Dingler gave up the idea of science as an intellectual activity by replacing this idea with the doctrine of science as a practical doing. Since Holzkamp took no notice of this very important turn in philosophy of science, we repudiate his conclusion that constructivism is erroneous. On the contrary, the constructivistic approach is appropriate to science. Many aspects of scientific investigations are only comprehensive in constructivistic and not in traditional views of philosophy of science. Since Holzkamp left the constructivistic movement (to invent a new approach in psychology), it is not necessary to dwell on his conclusion.

Dingler's turn is due to the discussions of the foundation of mathematics. Dingler argued against a Platonistic foundation of geometry–against the explanation by eternal ideas. He claims that the ideal of geometrical objects derived from plain human action and from human techniques (see Dingler, 1928). Subsequently Dingler transferred this idea to the foundations of all scientific knowledge: The foundation of science is human activity. With Dingler, a new approach of understanding science emerged, namely the understanding of science as a type of doing. Constructive realism subscribes to this idea, but we rule out Dingler's doctrine of certainty. Dingler feared loss of scientific commitment if human activities were postulated as the foundation of science, and hence he plead for keeping the old European idea of certainty–Dingler himself used the notion *certism*. Certism implies the possibility of tracing back every proposition system to doing. Since there emerge great problems, e.g. leading back Einstein's general relativity theory to human doing (Dingler actually states that relativity theory is a helping science) this view of science is mistaken.

Besides the turn to an understanding of science as a practical doing, we claim that Dingler's cancelation of the absolute mind (or superobserver) in respect to sciences is a further step of progress in understanding science appropriately. Dingler's ideas were adopted by Kamlah and Lorenzen, the founder of the School of Erlangen, and developed. They gave up the doctrine of certism, and nowadays Janich, another famous proponent of the School of Erlangen, pleads for the dependence of science on culture. But, and this is the point at issue, even the School of Erlangen subscribes to the idea that every scientific construction can be traced back to everyday life. Furthermore, the School of Erlangen does not accept the necessity of interpreting science, as claimed by constructive realism. Finally, this school pleads for a type of constructivistic idealism that does not take into account that scientific constructions always cope with nature.

There are two further constructivisms to mention. First, social constructivism formulates as program (the so-called strong program) research of the social activities of scientists and group dynamics in laboratories. It is incontestable that many important insights are due to social constructivism, but sociological investigations cannot replace philosophy of science. Understanding social constructivism not as sociology of science but as philosophy of science entails the danger of destroying the commitment of science because the idea of science without commitment is a contradiction in terms. Second, radical constructivists, like Foerster or Glasersfeld, claim that all results of knowledge are intellectual constructions matching the world, or, in other words, knowledge is a viable re-presentation of the world. However, they are mistaken because they lack a regulative instance. On the other hand, the School of Erlangen postulated a regulative instance, namely the appeal to rules. But this instance does not work because a fixed set of rules, as maintained by the school of Erlangen, is not appropriate to the freedom of science.

Our story is about the failings of traditional and constructive philosophy of science until constructive realism. This debacle of philosophy of science in respect to its normative claims is a main origin of constructive realism. The ideas of Wittgenstein and the experience of interdisciplinary cooperation and research in (natural) sciences are further origins (see Wallner and Peschl, 1991, p. 30; Wallner, 1997, pp. 37–44), but it is not possible (or necessary) to dwell on them in this context.

THE ONTOLOGY OF CONSTRUCTIVE REALISM

Perhaps the reader will ask if the name *constructive realism* is not a contradiction in terms–a philosophy of science is either constructivistic or realistic. Explaining constructive realistic ontology requires an answer to this question. It has been stated that philosophy lacks epistemological reflection and philosophy of science lacks ontology. According to that point, constructive realism is an exceptional philosophy of science because it invented an ontology. In this section we point out the ontology of constructive realism.

There are three key notions in constructive realism, namely *wirklichkeit*, *realität* and *lebenswelt*. The last notion is translated as *lifeworld*, but in English there is only the term *reality* for the other two notions. This is the reason we prefer not to translate these notions and to use the German notions.

In short, *realität* is the world of scientific constructions, *wirklichkeit* is the instance that makes human life possible and constrains it in many aspects. *Wirklichkeit* is as well the human body as the environment. *Wirklichkeit* is an instance that cannot be sensibly neglected, but *wirklichkeit* will cease if it should become subject of knowledge—trying to recognize *wirklichkeit* makes it disappear. The distinction of *wirklichkeit* and *realität* is very important, but it is not a plain distinction. An example demonstrates the difference. Imagine a conference of physicists. These physicists discuss *realität* or, to be more exact, a part of the *realität*. They discuss their constructions, and these constructions are not a representation or a model of *wirklichkeit*. To claim that constructions are representations or models of *wirklichkeit* means to allege that science describes *wirklichkeit*. However, if a scientist hurts himself by stumbling and breaking his finger, then he feels *wirklichkeit*. The explanation of the fall in physical or lifeworld terms is *realität*, but the fall and the aches are *wirklichkeit*. Thus, *wirklichkeit* is always here, but it is not recognizable.

As Wallner (1997, p. 38) stated, there is no good argument that there is no "given world". But the given world (*wirklichkeit*) must have a different function in the life of human beings than (constructed) *realität*. That we are connected with the given world (*wirklichkeit*) by life, it is never doubted. For *realität*, this is not the case. While we experiment with our constructions we have some degree of freedom. If we err with *wirklichkeit*, we risk our lives. This constuctivistic realistic doctrine is definitely not plain, especially the permanent presence and withdrawal of *wirklichkeit*. A famous French author, Lacan, presented a similar idea. Lacan distinguishes the *je* (I) and the *moi* (me). The *je* is the true subject, and the *moi* is the subject that individuals believe themselves to be; it is the result of socialization: "*Je pense où je ne suis pas, donc je suis où je ne pense pas.*" (Lacan, 1991, p.43) The place of reasoning is the language, but this place cannot be taken by *moi*. The *je* is always present—it is necessarily present because it is the instance of reasoning, but it is impossible to recognize the *je*. The constructive realistic distinction refers to a quite different field and differs from Lacan's view, but both views have in common that there is an instance that cannot be recognized or doubted.

However, if *wirklichkeit* is always here, but it is impossible to be gripped intellectually, there must be another way of getting in touch with the given world. Constructive realism pleads for a pragmatic view. Humans act on *wirklichkeit*, and by acting, humans test the constructs. But a working construct supports no insight in *wirklichkeit*. Only if a construct is not working do we have an indirect insight in *wirklichkeit*. But it is not possible to know more! We will never know what *wirklichkeit* is, but we are embedded in it. We are living with or, to be more exact, in *wirklichkeit* being a part of it without knowing what *wirklichkeit* is. Traditional theory of knowledge is mistaken because it claims that the primordial division of subject and object (or individual and environment) is to be bridged by visually based intellectual operations. Constructive realism repudiates this view replacing it with the distinction between *wirklichkeit* and *realität*. *Wirklichkeit* means primordial embeddedness without knowing, *realität* means knowing without being embedded.

Hence it is necessary to sketch out the constructive realistic doctrine of *realität*. *Realität* is the sum of scientific constructs. Since Wallner invented the notion *microworld* as a functioning scientific construct, we define *realität* as the systematic togetherness of microworlds that humankind has elaborated at a specific point in history. A microworld is a scientific proposition system that fulfils tasks usually formulated in forecasts. Thus, a microworld shows a relation between specific events that are artificially abstracted entities. Construction means that scientists are arranging information by the help of a framework, which is governing the data.

> Nothing else is meant with the notion to construct a microworld. Having constructed a microworld, we are able to master a specific group of phenomena. But still there is no knowledge at this point. You have just got the ability to solve problems. (Wallner, 1997, p. 38)

An example of a microworld is Newton's classical mechanics. It is the microworld of moving things–it is the world just for movements, and it is a functioning world. No object moves exactly in this way in everyday life, but it is a wonderful ideal world, a microworld. Thus, sometimes microworlds are actually big–movement is all over the world. But reducing the world in the sense of Newton means losing a lot of movement–all movements connected with living, all movements connected with free will, and so on. Microworlds change the world according to the human necessity to cope with the given world, but microworlds are too small to be dangerous for the world. The mastering of *wirklichkeit* is possible because the data are aspects of *wirklichkeit*, aspects that are produced by means of technical tools. It is not necessary to state again that we do not know which aspects of *wirklichkeit* are at the base of our acting, but since our actions are related to *wirklichkeit*, scientific actions are related to *wirklichkeit*, too. We can't stress enough the importance of technical tools for scientific constructions in this context–just imagine physics without technology!

Lifeworlds are cultural constructions that support means of coping with the given world, like *realität*. The difference between *realität* and lifeworld is that a lifeworld is meaningful. Microworlds are not meaningful; microworlds are functioning wholes for mastering data. Thus lifeworlds support knowledge, microworlds do not. But the idea of science is that it leads to knowlegde, not that it only masters data correctly. Constructive realism postulates that knowledge is only achieved by understanding microworlds, not by constructing them. In traditional philosophy of science a theory contains knowledge because it describes reality. Hence, for holding up the idea of knowledge constructive realism has to present another doctrine since science does not describe the world.

But, we will discuss this question in the next section. At this juncture we want to mention that constructive realism pleads for relativity. There are different microworlds refering to the same data, but if science is understood as construction, this relativity will not jeopardize the commitment of science. The relativity and plurality of microworlds will jeopardize science only if it is claimed that science describes the world. Science will not lose its commitment if one adopts the constructivistic realistic point of view! Microworlds show the high degree of human freedom in coping with the world.

> The differentiation between *realität* and *wirklichkeit* does not aim at a relativism of knowledge. Nor does it aim at giving up the idea of knowledge at all. Its purpose is to avoid surrendering ourselves to the success of our constructs in the environment. *Wirklichkeit* cannot be understood. We can only master *wirklichkeit* with the help of our constructions. If they serve us well for gaining control over the *wirklichkeit*, we will keep them. If they don't, we will discard them. When it comes to knowledge, however, we can only refer to *realität*, i.e. to what we have constructed. (Wallner, 1997, pp. 38f)

The point is: Wallner invented a new idea of knowledge. The question is: How is knowledge possible if it is only derivable from *realität* and if it is not contained in microworlds?

STRANGIFICATION – INTERDISCIPLINARITY AND INTERCULTURALITY OF CONSTRUCTIVE REALISM

According to constructive realism, sciences are samples of functioning constructs on a first level. The claim of knowledge microworlds is that they are to be interpreted so as to reveal the hidden assumptions and presuppositions of microworlds. In this sense, knowledge will only be achieved if scientists reflect upon their scientific constructs, on their scientific practice. In other words, the (self) reflection of scientific construction is the condition *sine qua non* of knowledge–microworlds that are just functioning do not contain knowledge. In terms of constructive realism, the way to achieve knowledge is called *strangification*.

Strangification is a set of strategies having one point in common: Transfering one (logical) system of propositions from their original context into another context and judging this system out of this context.

> The way to get out of your scientific skin is called strangification (*verfremdung*). Strangification is the central methodological proposal of Constructive Realism. In short, strangification means to take a proposition system out of its framework and transfer it, translate it into the framework of another scientific microworld. The first success of this movement is probably confusion. In the first moment you are not able to understand what happens. Therefore you ask where this confusion comes from. At this moment you see that the confusion comes from different background information scientists have for using a language. The confusion resulting from strangification is due to the fact that language use in science is only possible if you follow a lot of rules which are not explicitly formulated. Thus, strangification gives you insight into rules another science is implicitly working with. (Wallner, 1997, p. 39)

> The process of strangification cannot be planned in advance, because there is no meta-theoretical standardization–it rather represents a game with different contexts. Changing the context a lot of times enables us to get new insights, perspectives and views in the structure of the system of propositions. The important point is that if we look at these contexts where the system of propositions gets absurd, we will notice the implicit assumptions and considerations of this system – i.e. we investigate its tacit knowledge. (Wallner, 1997, p. 44)

Constructive realism differentiates three types of strangification. First, *linguistic strangification* means excluding contexts in which a system of statements gets absurd. This type of strangification enables the revelation of (implicit) assumptions as well as showing up the domain of application of a system of statements without falling back on meta-theoretical standardization instances. Second, applying a system or a set of methods of a discipline to a very different discipline represents *ontological strangification*. Third, by *pragmatic strangification*, the social and organizational context of scientists is observed.

> We have to give up the claim of traditional European epistemologies of complete insight. The methodologies of constructive realism have another goal. On the one hand they represent the basis for the construction of knowledge, on the other hand for the indirect insights into these constructions. As an implication of this we do not need a meta-theoretical legitimation for the methodologies of constructive realism. (Wallner, 1997, p. 46)

Slunecko (1997, p. 254) states that constructive realism suggests strangification as an organizing principle to connect competing models in a more productive way than the current strategies by which models either avoid each other or follow reductionist or unificationist fantasies. Seeing that direct reflection is often too loaded with knowing-better-arguments, constructive realism introduces strangification as a means of structuring this dialogue via a principle of indirect reflection: each participant in the dialogue reflects principally upon himself rather than upon other participants, and reflects upon himself by exposing his own theory to the conditions of another system. Slunecko highlights the importance of the indirectly reflective nature of strangification by referring to a life-world experience many of us have access to, i.e. travelling abroad:

> A foreigner is likely to perceive aspects of a region domestic residents have long become unconscious of or may never have been conscious of to begin with. The traveller may not be able to communicate these aspects, and even if he were, the residents may not listen to him or care about them. Regardless, more important in the idea of strangification is the self-reflective potential, i.e., when the reflexive impulse achieves full circle and, back to my example, the traveller abroad becomes aware of conditions which govern his life back home. Just the very failing of his actions and cognitive constructions unexpectedly sheds light on structural presuppositions which had been responsible for success at home. From within a system, a cultural context or a consensual reality of a psychotherapeutic school, the constitutive assumptions are invisible. Because of the ongoing socialization these background assumptions become unconscious and are then no longer expressible; in this process, hidden metaphysics usually plays a major role. (Slunecko, 1997, p. 254–255)

Misheva points out that by the invention of strangification a new therapeutic approach in philosophy of science emerges:

> Strangification is also meant to be one of these therapies, and in this sense it should be ranked among those suggested by Freud, who wanted to heal the psychic system, or by Marx, who wanted to heal the social system, as an alienation therapy designed for the system of science. Both social and psychic therapies have had bitter experiences in the process of their practical applications and their legitimacy is now questioned. However, the therapy which Wallner suggests not only is meant for a different system level but also has one unquestionable advantage. It is a new type of therapy. The therapy of constructive realism is self-reflexive, which means that the doctor and the patient are one. The principle, then, is that one does not give medicine to a patient without being sure that he himself will suggest it as the best cure because he is his own patient. In other words, this is a method with a special morality which does not need a system to control it: we do not do to others what we do not want to be done to ourselves. Because of this self-reflexivity, it has the chance to control itself, learn from its experience of application, and even reject itself completely when it does not work. If the method of strangification does not work, we will immediately know this when we see that the ideas of constructive realism cannot be strangified within any other theoretical context. constructive realism encourages science to perform a self-healing procedure, and this type of professional behaviour is legitimized as self-conscious acts that may lead to the solution

of professional problems, the answer to which are not to be found within the limits of one's own world. Constructive realism prescribes individual actions for those who do not fear to cross boundaries and encounter different worlds because they want to enrich their own world with new perspectives. Constructive Realism, however, also offers a therapy for healing science as a whole in that science finally has a philosophy which legislates for it the rules (methods) for crossing disciplinary boundaries. In other words, Constructive realism gives legitimacy to what scientists have already been doing at their own risk. (Misheva, 1997, pp. 126f)

An overview over the wide region of sciences shows that there are, on the one hand, sciences nearly without any potential of self-reflexivity usually called *the hard sciences*, and that there are, on the other hand, sciences with a high potential of self-reflexivity called *the soft sciences*. These latter sciences usually do not construct microworlds, but offer means of interpretation. According to the view of constructive realism this division of sciences strikes the features of sciences only on the surface because it rules out the difference between the instrumental and the interpretative level of science. Since it is necessary to interpret even the so called hard sciences, the so called soft sciences get an important role.

If we compare natural sciences and *Geisteswissenschaften*, we see in natural sciences an underestimation of interpretation, because interpretation is understood in a different sense and function. Traditionally in the natural sciences it was believed that interpretation sets in only after the acquisition of knowledge. It is widely believed that knowledge is the outcrop of the solution of the puzzle, while in fact this solution of the puzzle is no more than construction at work. It is not knowledge yet. With respect to the *Geisteswissenschaften* it is agreed that interpretation is the core of these intellectual activities. At the same time, most intellectuals underestimate the importance of interpretation because, in contrast to constructed products of natural sciences, interpretation not only can, but must be revised on the strength of its definition. (Wallner, 1997, p. 50)

Generally, knowlegde is characterized by two features. First, knowledge offers explanation, not rules for functioning contexts. Second, knowledge enables humans to cope with the world. Pertaining to these general aspects of knowledge, everyday knowledge and scientific knowledge go together. The difference in these two kinds of knowledge is not, as positivism claims, that scientific knowledge is clearer and exact. This positivistic allegation implies the idea that science describes the world. We subscribe to the view that science abstracts certain aspects of the rich *wirklichkeit*–a physicist is usually not interested in psychological issues. Sciences deal with highly specified aspects of *wirklichkeit*. This specification marks a difference to everyday know-how, but since it is impossible to close the gap between *wirklichkeit* and *realität*, scientific know-how is not closer to the true nature of the world than everyday know-how.

One difference is that a feature of science is the free choice of methods, while in everyday know-how individuals are led by tools and means of society and culture. A second difference is that everyday know-how is always embedded in a lifeworld, and lifeworlds are meaningful worlds. Thus everyday know-how is a part of everyday knowledge - individuals act and they are able to tell the reasons for their actions. In contrast, microworlds are not meaningful; scientists produce know-how that is not naturally connected with knowledge on a first level. Thus it is easy to achieve everyday knowlegde, but it is hard to achieve scientific knowledge. Perhaps this is the price that scientists have to pay for the idosyncretic invention of new worlds, microworlds.

Taking the constructive realistic theory of knowledge and the method of strangification into account, it is obvious that constructive realism is an interdisciplinary philosophy of science. But, constructive realism claims that interculturality is more important than interdisciplinarity

> because interdisciplinarity is always covered, at least in Europe and in the USA, by the same conception of science because all participants are stemming from the same cultural context. Therefore, it is important to look and to go to other cultures, and so reach an understanding of what one actually does in one's own culture. ...If we cancelled or if we reduced the differences between cultures, we would, therefore, reduce the possibilities of understanding. (Wallner, 1997, p. 60)

The importance of interculturality is connected with the constructive realistic view that science is embedded in the cultural context. We do not maintain that every scientific system of propositions can be traced back to everyday life directly (as the School of Erlangen does), but it is obvious that science and culture influence mutually. The best way of demonstrating this view is applying strangification. If you strangify a microworld (or parts of a microworld) into another cultural context then this microworld becomes absurd, perhaps even ridiculous. The reason for becoming absurd is due to cultural differences. If it is not possible to formulate a microworld in the language of another culture, then the cultural assumptions of this microworld will become obvious. By the way, to do so means using strangification as negative legitimation. It is possible to show the contexts in which a scientific propositional system works by excluding all contexts in which the scientific propositional system does not work.

THE UNCERTAINTY OF GENERAL PSYCHOLOGY: THE SUBJECT AND METHODOLOGY OF PSYCHOLOGY

Many psychology textbooks state that psychology is a young science, and that is the reason why there is no unity of psychological theories and models. A short look at the history of psychology makes obvious that it is rather the uncertainty of the psychological subject that entails the lack of unification and agreement.

The disagreement was born with psychology: When Wundt set up the first experimental laboratory in 1879, experimental psychological research began. However, Wundt claimed that only physiological processes could be investigated by experiment, and that it is impossible to apply the experimental method to higher mental processes (like reasoning and language). Mental processes are subjects of the so called *völkerpsychologie*. Even the idea of an experimental social psychology is, according to Wundt, a great mistake. (Many psychologists claim that not Wundt, but James is the founding father of modern psychology. But we won't dwell on this issue.)

Wundt's scholar Bühler developed a research program of the mind by experiment. Certainly, Bühler's experiments were quite different from current experiments because Bühler's subjects were trained persons, such as his colleagues and students. In current psychology the subject is a naive person, and generalization of the results is possible only by means of statistics. The famous Wundt-Bühler debate demonstrates that the subject of psychology is moot because psychology has both a cultural science tradition and a natural science tradition.

Behaviorism focusses on the possibility of psychology as a natural science, and for this reason the mind was said to be an old and useless illusion of metaphysics. Only observable behavior is to be taken into account. The simple terminology of Behaviorism–stimulus, response, and reinforcement–fascinated two generations of psychologists, but it turned out to be reductionistic in 1960 when Miller, Galanter, and Pribram published the book *Plans and the Structure of Behavior*. After this "cognitive turn" the human mind was re-established in psychological research, but the newborn cognitive psychology did not achieve a unity of psychology. Besides this development of mainstream psychology, there has always been a *geisteswissenschaftliche* psychology that pleads for the necessity of taking into account intentionality and consciousness of the mind. But, as Kvale (1992, p. 44) stated, in psychology, behaviorism and humanism became two sides of the same modern coin–the abstraction of men from their specific culture. Cultural content is taken as the accidental and local, the psychological processes as the essential und universal. "Here appears a double abstraction -the psyche studied by modern psychology is abstracted from its cultural content as well as from its social and historical context" (Kvale, 1992, p. 44).

Of course this story is too short to grasp the complexity of the history of psychology. Besides the many approaches developed in the last century, it would be necessary to take into account social, economic, and political developments because science is, according to constructive realism, embedded in the cultural matrix. Nevertheless this story calls attention to the lack of unity of psychology and to the many contradictory approaches in psychology. In contrast to this disunion, there is one agreement in mainstream psychology - the agreement about method.

To be a good psychological result that is noticed by the community of psychologists, the data must be generated by experiment or questionnaire and analysed by statistical methods. The importance of statistics for mainstream psychology is obvious: Students are taught a lot of statistics and the statistics classes in psychology departments are quite extensive. However, it is not clear if psychology is a natural or a cultural science because the subject of psychology is indeterminate and uncertain, but ignoring this uncertainty psychologists investigate by application of experiments and statistics. It is necessary to state that applying experiments and statistics does not decide whether a science is a natural science or a cultural science. Sure, many psychologists allege that experiments and statistics are characteristics of natural sciences, but this allegation lacks good supprt. But if the subject of a science is at issue, the methods get spoiled, too (see Wallner, 1992, p. 11).

It is interesting to note Kvale's remarks on the current state of psychology because he adds an important point to our reflections:

> One may object that important exceptions to the postulate of an intellectual stagnation of psychology as a science exist. There are, thus, rapid developments in areas as computer simulation, artificial intelligence, neuropsychology, psychogenetics, psycholinguistic and cognitive science. And on the humanities side there is the current focus upon hermeneutics, narratives, scripts, discourse analysis, and so on. These active areas are, however, on the borderline of a psychology surviving parasitically on concepts and methods imported from neighbouring disciplines. Apart from psychoanalysis, there has hardly been any major export of psychological knowledge to the neighbouring disciplines. Modern psychology, whether in the naturalist or the humanist version, has become an intellectual second-hand store, displaying a variety of collections from last year's fashions of the neighbouring disciplines – you name it, we have it. (Kvale, 1992, p. 45)

Nevertheless, professional psychology has obtained a stronghold in Western societies. Psychology is expanding as a profession. Whereas academic psychology is becoming a museum of modern thought, professional psychologists encounter human beings in their current world. In other words, there is a gap between academic and professional psychology–the well known gap between theory and practice (see Kvale, 1992, p. 48).

No doubt, psychology in its scientific positioning needs support by philosophy of science, but obviously traditional philosophy of science paid too little attention to psychology. This was the reason psychologists turned off philosophy of science and discussed the subject and the state of their discipline by themselves, excluding the philosophers who only focus on the human mind, not on the problems of the psychological subject in respect to the methods. There are many psychologists who do not reflect on their discipline and who adopt the view of naive empirism, but, on the other hand, there are psychologists who try hard to work out an appropriate philosophy of science for psychology. These people do not apply the traditional philosophy of sciences because it focusses on natural science, especially on physics. But the application of solutions proposed for physical issues to psychology does not work, and hence psychologists go their own ways. As far as we can see, the indigenous psychologies approach is an example of psychologists' attitude to working out solutions for the main problems of psychology by themselves—other examples are the postmodern approach in social psychology or cultural and cross-cultural psychology. These examples show as well that the reflection on the subject of psychology by psychologists entails the development of a new approach that avoids the main mistakes of mainstream psychology.

But this situation is unsatisfactory for philosophy of science or, to speak exactly, for constructive realism. Hence reflecting psychology is an important task for constructive realism. Wallner always paid attention to issues in psychology concerning its scientific state. The School of Erlangen has also reflected on psychology. As mentioned, there is a difference between these two constructivistic approaches in philosophy of science, and we will point out these differences by discussing the ideas of two proponents of the Erlangen School (to be exact, of the Marburg School, which is a branch of the Erlangen School.)

Hartmann (1993) sketches out a view of a proto-psychology. Proto-psychology is a methodically founded psychology, which means that contradictionary approaches are traced back to their practical interests. Proto-psychology points out the practice that is supplied by psychological theories. In general, if a theory is traced back to a lifeworld, and if every step of the development of a theory out of the lifeworld is argued, then the School of Erlangen will use the notion *proto-science*. Besides proto-psychology, there exists proto-physics, proto-chemistry, and so on. Hartmann claims that clinical psychology, educational psychology, forensic psychology, neuropsychology, and so on, supply their own praxis. Hence, it is mistaken to ask if psychology is a natural science or a cultural science because, according to Hartmann (1993), psychology is both. Psychology supplies practical interests in both fields. Subsequently Hartmann discusses the statistical methods, like variance analysis, t-tests, and so on, because for psychologists it is necessary to know of problems pertaining to statistics. Reading Hartmann's book makes obvious that he will not solve one problem in psychology. First, every psychologist knows that contradictionary approaches supply different practical interests. Hartmann tells them that variety is good and that there is no need for unity through reflecting on their subject. Second, Hartmann's arguments concerning statistics are superfluous because every student of psychology already knows about them. It is nice to argue about the alpha- and beta-error in computing t-tests, but psychologists are very well-informed on this topic. Thus, Hartmann's argument does not touch the point at issue.

Janich (1996) states that it is necessary to have a look at the instructions in psychological experiments. Facing the instructions means getting an appropriate view of psychology. Psychologists do reflect on the instructions, but the problems of psychology are not solved. For example, in the well-known imagery debate Kosslyn (1981) presented data supporting the claim of an imaginal code. Pylyshyn (1981) changed the instructions keeping all other conditions the same, and the data supported the claim that there was no imaginal code. Another example of the importance of instructions known to psychologists is the current refutation of the famous "heurisitics and bias program". Kahneman and Tversky, the most famous cognitive psychologists, presented data that demonstrate that humans are not able to reason logically under the condition of uncertainty (see Kahneman, Slovic & Tversky, 1982; Kahneman & Tversky, 1996). In current cognitive psychology it is claimed that these "hard and robust" results that were replicated hundred of times during the 1970s depended only on the instructions. Gigerenzer (1996) or Gigerenzer & Hug (1992) changed the instructions keeping all the conditions the same, and the data were totally different. The famous heuristics and bias program turned out to be an artefact in current cognitive psychology. Hence, reflecting on instructions is very important, but it will not solve the main problem of psychology: the uncertainty of the psychological subject.

Besides this issue, Wallner (1999) pointed out that the usual division of theory and practice in natural sciences is erroneous in psychology. Psychology is based on the European idea of subjectivity, which emerged in the 16th century, and this base entails contradictionary approaches. If psychology loses subjectivity and becomes an objective science, psychology will lose its subject. But if psychology focusses totally on subjectivity, then it will lose its state as science. Therefore psychology requires a different structure from other sciences. Wallner (1999) claimed that differentiation of the level of microworlds and the level of interpretation must be concepted anew for psychology. In contrast to natural science, in psychology it is necessary to strangify every microworld to lifeworld. If psychological microworlds are not strangified before application, they will lose their psychological characteristics (see Wallner, 1999, p. 216).

NOTES ON THE INDIGENOUS PSYCHOLOGIES APPROACH

Like mainstream psychology, there are different approaches in indigenous psychologies. A first approach focusses on the collective representation of psychological issues. In this sense Heelas & Lock (1981, p. 3) define indigenous psychologies as "the cultural views, theories, conjectures, classifications, assumptions, and metaphors–together with notions embedded in social institutions - which bear on psychological topics." This approach reflects an anthropological emphasis, the psychological view is secondary. A second approach emphasizes psychological issues and the mutual dialectics with culture, and we will dwell on this approach presented by Kim & Berry (1993).

As mentioned above, the indigenous psychologies approach is a result of the lack of importance of cultural issues in mainstream psychology that established the natural science paradigm as the dominant framework of psychological investigations. The cultural science tradition developed theories and methods that are appropriate to humans. If mainstream psychology neglects the importance of its cultural science tradition, it will become more and more museal (to use Kvale's words discussed above). However, Kim & Berry (1993, p. 2) defined indigenous psychologies "as the scientific study of human behavior (or the mind) that is native, that is not transported from other regions, and that is designed for its people." Sure, scientific investigations of indigenous knowledge are still in their craddle, but the authors delinate six fundamental assumptions and research strategies that are shared in this indigenous psychologies approach. We sketch out these six points, and then reformulate them in terms of constructive realism.

First, the indigenous psychologies approach emphasizes understanding rooted in ecological, cultural, political, and historical contexts.

> The indigenous psychologies approach attempts to document, organize, and interpret the understanding people have about themselves and their world. It emphasizes the use of natural taxonomies as units of analysis. It examines how individuals and groups interact within their context. This information is then used as a tool for discovering psychological invariants. The second step involves explaining causes behind the observed invariants. The third step consists of comparing results across different contexts for futher refinement and extension. (Kim & Berry, 1993, p. 3)

Second, Kim and Berry (1993) stress that indigenous psychologies are not studies of exotic people in faraway places. Indigenous studies of native people are necessary, but indigenous understanding is also needed for developed countries: "The indigenous psychologies approach affirms the need for each culture to develop its own indigenous understanding" (p. 3). Third, as a consequence of point two, it is necessary to take into account that within a particular society there are many perspectives not shared by all groups. Fourth, the indigenous psychologies do not apply any one particular method; they use a multitude of methods. The reason is that "results from multiple methods could be integrated to provide a more comprehensive and robust understanding of psychological phenomena" (p. 4). Fifth, the authors stress that a particular perspective cannot be assumed to be inherently superior to another. But, the authors state that "the assumption that a person must be born and raised in a particular culture to understand it is not always valid" (p. 4) They quote Kleinman (1980) who suggested that cross-indigenous comparisons may serve as mirrors for understanding one's own culture. Sixth, according to the authors the indigenous psychologies approach aims at discovering universal facts, principles, and laws. They formulated the following: The indigenous psychologies approach

> does not, however, assume *a priori* the existence of psychological universals. If they exist, they need to be theoretically and empirically verified. The discovery process, however, differs qualitatively from that of general psychology. In the indigenous psychologies approach, individual, social, cultural, and temporal variations are incorporated into the research design, rather than eliminated or controlled. This approach advocates the use of cross-cultural and cross-indigenous investigations. (Kim & Berry, 1993, p. 4)

Formulated in terms of constructive realism, some of these six points change their meaning. The first point is one of them. When Kim and Berry (1993, p. 3) emphasized that the indigenous psychologies approach attemps to document, organize, and interpret the understanding people have about themselves and their world, we add that this understanding is a kind of strangification. We not only view the interpretation as a strangification, but even the documentation and organization, because for documentation and organization of the understanding of native people it is necessary to translate their psychological beliefs into another language (English, for example). A translation changes these beliefs inasmuch as the original meaning is taken out of its native context and is put into the context of the language used for translation. It is necessary to mind that language is connected with the social and cultural world inseparably. Hence translation is a first strangification, and documentation and organization are further ones. Even if Kim and Berry (1993) underlined the necessity to take natural taxonomies as units of analysis, the original (native or indigenous) features of these natural taxonomies get lost because they are viewed and judged from an external point of view. It is impossible to get out of one's own cultural skin. Taking the cultural impact and the importance of language for science into account, the etic/emic distinction (see Berry & Kim, 1993, p. 278) should also be reformulated.

To use a further term from constructive realism, if you formulate an indigenous psychology for the Western world (in English, Spanish, German, and so on), then you will construct a microworld. This microworld does not describe the mind; neither does the microworld of indigenous people describe their mind. Thus, when Kim and Berry (1993, p. 3) add that indigenous microworlds, translated in another language and applying scientific methods, are, second, the base to look for psychological invariants and then, third, comparing the results across different contexts for further refinement and extension, then the construction of microworlds becomes obvious. As constructive realism claims, it is not possible to describe *wirklichkeit*–humans are always constructing *realität*. Hence, the research results of the indigenous psychologies approach are *realität*, too.

The second point says that not only exotic people are the subject of indigenous psychological investigations, but it is also necessary for every culture to develop its own indigenous understanding. In terms of constructive realism, understanding is only possible by strangification, and strangification needs different contexts. Strangification within a culture is possible because there are manifold perspectives in a culture not shared by all social groups - the third point listed by Kim and Berry (1993, p. 3). The many methods in the indigenous psychologies approach cannot be reformulated in terms of constructive realism, but we agree to the claim of Kim and Berry so far as results from multiple methods could provide a more comprehensive and robust understanding of psychological phenomena. The application of different methods requires a comparison of results within the indigenous psychologies, and this comparison requires taking the results out of their original context and putting them into the context of another method (or scientific language). Obviously this is nothing other than strangification. The acceptance of multiple methods entails ways of strangification within indigenous psychologies.

The last two points listed by Kim and Berry (1993, p. 4) counter two illusions: First, the illusion that people in faraway places who are born and raised in a particular culture as well as persons of the Western culture are conscious of their cultural assumptions and that they understand their culture entirely. Second, the illusion assuming that there are *a priori* psychological universals. The example of traveling abroad discussed above shows that constructive realism agrees with Kim and Berry (1993) in the first point. But the second illusion denied by the authors must be analysed precisely because Kim and Berry (1993) neglect the *a priori* assumption that there are universal facts, universal principles, and universal laws, but probably such universals exist. It is mistaken to postulate psychological universals *a priori*, but maybe indigenous psychologies reveal universals *a posteriori*. When we reformulated the first point within the terminology of constructive realism, a difference between the ideas of indigenous psychologies approach and constructive realism concerning the view of science as a description or construction became perceptible, but now the difference is obvious. In sharp contrast to constructive realism, Kim and Berry (1993) view science as description of the investigated subject. The indigenous psychologies approach purports to describe the mind of indigenous people. It is the idea and the necessity of interculturality in indigenous psychologies that takes the edge off this view of science, and hence we will have a look at interculturality in the indigenous psychologies approach.

If psychological universals are not *a priori* assumptions, they must result from empirical investigation. Therefore the indigenous psychologies approach, investigations of indigenous people, is supplied by the cross-indigenous approach. This enlargement leads to the comparison of results from one indigenous psychology with others "in search of universal generalization" (Kim & Berry, 1993, p. 5). The authors repudiate the view that the existing psychology is a universal psychology, it is best charaterized as American psychology. However, a comparison of psychological phenomena between two cultures yields two kinds of knowledge: culture specific and culturally shared. For example, in the United States most definitions of intelligence focus on cognitive ability. As Dasen (1984) states the Baoulé culture, like American culture, views intelligence in terms of literacy, memory, and the ability to process information quickly. But this form of intelligence is regarded as meaningful only when applied for the well-being of the community. In addition to cognitive abilities, the Baoulé emphasize social intelligence. Further, Dasen reports on a unique feature of intelligence of Baloué culture that is not found in the United States or Europe, namely "to be lucky and to bring good luck." This may reflect a spiritual aspect lacking in the USA or in Europe. "By comparing intelligence in two cultures, one not only discovers culturally unique and culturally shared characteristics, but increases the total range of the measured phenomenon." (Kim & Berry, 1993, p. 7) The comparison of two cultures may yield results that do not reflect true differences, but represent research artefacts (see Kim & Berry, 1993, p. 7), but this problem can be solved within the indigenous psychologies approach. It is a problem of methods that should be discussed by scientists.

It is also possible to compare a phenomenon in three or more cultures. Kim and Berry (1993, p. 9f) discussed cross-indigenous research into the form of address. In several European languages two pronouns are used to mark social relationships. In Germany *du* represents the informal and familiar form and *sie* represents the formal form. In a typical dyadic relationship, a person of higher social standing could use the *du* form to address someone of lower standing. The person of lower standing usually uses the *sie* form. According to Brown (1965), this reflects unequal status. Further, the *du* form is used between dyads of intimate equals while the *sie* form is used between strangers. These usages reflect social distance. However, in Japanese there are no pronomial equivalents to the *du/sie* forms, the levels of formality are directly coded in the verb endings. These cross-indigenous comparisons are completed by investigations of forms of address in Chinese, Greek, and Korean nominal forms. Kim and Berry (1993, p. 10) state: "Brown's invariant norm of address has been confirmed. Thus, this norm could be considered a candidate for a true etic. Similar to the norms of address, Ho (1993) suggests that the norm of reciprocity could be considered universal." For Kim and Berry (1993) the systematic studies of indigenous psychologies across different cultures allow research of general principles and psychological universals. If this cross-indigenous approach is integrated into indigenous psychologies, the "eventual outcome can be termed a universal psychology" (Berry & Kim, 1993, p. 278).

For the purpose of our argument it is not necessary to discuss the interesting contributions of Berry (1993), Berry and Kim (1993), Enriquez (1993), or other contributions of indigenous psychologies. Up to now we have pointed out the main ideas of the indigenous psychologies approach (in the sense of Kim & Berry, 1993) pertaining to the theoretical scientific foundation of this new approach in psychology. What we will discuss next is: What does it mean to construct a universal psychology from the viewpoint of constructive realism?

The application of constructive realism to the indigenous psychologies approach shows that generalization of empirical facts is a challenge for every science. No doubt, the problem of generalization in mainstream psychology is solved by two postulates. First, the experimental generation of data and the application of statistics to these data warrant generalization. Second, there is the *a priori* assumption that the brains of humans are similar, and thus the reasoning is comparable. This second point that warrants universalization is to be found in cognitive psychology. In this discipline the brain is regarded as the hardware and reasoning as the software. Thus, mainstream psychology tries to achieve one hundred or more test subjects for an experiment because, according to textbooks of statistics, this number warrants generalization. Generalization by statistics will only be possible if the second assumption is taken into account.

This idea of generalization and universalization is repudiated by the indigenous psychologies approach. Maintaining that mainstream psychology is both culture blind and culture bound (see Berry & Kim, p. 277), this approach claims that reasoning (and feeling, and so on) is not a function of the hardware brain, but results from being embedded in different cultural matrices. In indigenous psychologies it is impossible to claim that psychological phenomena result only from the function of the brain because there are obvious differences between cultures that can be explained by assumption number two of mainstream psychology only if one culture (Western) is said to be superior. That is why the field of the investigated phenomenon has to be enlarged to all cultures.

No doubt, this idea of generalization and universalization is an illusion. First, it would be a very large-scale research program to travel across the whole globe to investigate all indigenous psychologies. Second, for a real universalization in this sense, the history and even the future of each culture must be taken into account. In contrast to the view of universalization in mainstream psychology, the view of universalization in the indigenous psychologies approach is not dangerous. The danger of adapting all cultures to the US or European culture and of depreciating what is not adaptable is a corollary of mainstream psychology's view. Maybe the way of generalization and the way to a universal psychology proposed by the indigenous psychologies approach is an illusion, maybe it is an idea in the sense of Kant. However, constructive realism claims that even this view of a universal psychology is a construct, not a description of the mind, and constructive realism emphasizes that the idea of universalization is not necessary for knowledge, and perhaps it even destroys knowledge.

As we mentioned, the theory of knowledge presented by constructive realism requires different contexts, different constructs, different languages, and different lifeworlds. If the dream of a universal psychology in the sense of Kim and Berry (1993), Berry and Kim (1993), or Berry (1993) became true, then the multiple indigenous psychologies would be formulated in one or in a few languages (in English and Spanish, for example). For example, the Korean or the Indian indigenous psychology can then be known by the community of indigenous psychologists, but it is taken out of its original context and thus loses its cultural embeddedness. But, without being embedded in their original cultural matrix, the indigenous psychologies lose the possibility of being a context of strangification. And this would be a great damage.

The indigenous psychologies approach is an impressive new approach in psychology that makes obvious the boundaries of mainstream psychology and underlines another understanding of human beings. This understanding is also traced back to European ideas (as mentioned earlier), but the understanding of humans as cultural beings allows and enables cross-cultural and indigenous investigations without depreciation of other cultures. The view that one culture is not superior becomes more important. Yes, this new view in philosophy and psychology is in conflict with globalisation and the dominance of the Western (namely the American) culture. The indigenous psychologies approach offers ways of knowledge, but not in the sense of describing all psychological phenomena in all cultures, but in the sense of strangification.

We are critical of the idea of universalization presented by the indigenous psychologies approach because constructive realism pleads for giving up the old idea of unity. The sense of unity of humankind was, is, and will be to blur or, in the worst case, to erase cultural differences. The idea of unity says that all men and women are equal, but it was Westerners who decided who is more equal" (to use Orwell's well-known formulation). This European idea does not claim that unity also includes differences. Therefore, we replace this idea with the idea of constructing *realität* and the idea of living in constructed lifeworlds. In the first case, the constructor is an individual, in the second case the constructor is a social group. In this way we hope to hold up the idea of difference.

Finally, we want to reiterate the importance of constructive realism for the indigenous psychologies approach. First, constructive realism is an intercultural philosophy of science. With its method, strangification, it presents a new and different theory of knowledge, and this is congenial to the indigenous psychologies approach. Second, if indigenous psychologies take into account the ontology of constructive realism, an appropriate formulation of its goals will be possible. Constructive realism excludes the old idea of description and pleads for the idea of construction, the idea of science as action. We believe the division of the three instances (*wirklichkeit, realität* and lifeworld) is useful for indigenous psychologies. Third, the ideas of constructive realism are not only applicable to further constructions of indigenous psychologies' microworlds, but also to those just presented. Strangification means taking a microworld or parts of a microworld and putting it or them in a different context. But strangification is not meant as a onesided means to knowledge. It is not meant that we (the American and European psychologists) use indigenous psychologies as contexts of strangification. Strangification forces a real dialogue that offers both partners a way of understanding their own constructs. Strangification focusses the process of dialogue because in this dialogue the implicit assumptions become conscious. Strangification does not focus on a goal. It is not possible to state at any point: Now we've got knowledge, let us stop strangifying our constructs.

It is obvious that constructive realism is an appropriate philosophy of science to indigenous psychologies and cross-cultural psychology. There are many people who maintain that Popper's critical rationalism is an appropriate philosophy of science for current mainstream psychology. But since mainstream psychology has become a museum of modern thoughts, critical rationalism turns out to be an old fashioned (as opposed to erroneous) philosophy of science. We hope that mainstream psychology is changable inasmuch as it will take into account humans as cultural beings, and then constructive realism will be an appropriate philosophy of science. But at this juncture, constructive realism is critical to mainstream psychology and agrees with new approaches in psychology such as the indigenous psychologies approach.

REFERENCES

Berry, J. W. (1993). Psychology in and of Canada: One small step toward a universal psychology. In U. Kim, & J. W. Berry (Eds.), *Indigenous psychologies. Research and experience in cultural context* (pp. 260–276). London: Sage Publications.

Berry, J. W., & Kim, U. (1993). The way ahead: From indigenous psychologies to a universal psychology. In U. Kim, & J. W. Berry (Eds.), *Indigenous psychologies. Research and experience in cultural context* (pp. 277–280). London: Sage Publications.

Brown, R. (1965). *Social psychology*. New York: Free Press.

Dasen, P. (1984). The cross-cultural study of intelligence: Piaget and the Baoulé. *International Journal of Psychology, 19*, 407–434.

Dingler, H. (1928). *Das Experiment. Sein Wesen und seine Geschichte*. München: Verlag Ernst Reinhardt.

Enriquez, V. G. (1993). Developing a Filipino psychology. In U. Kim, & J. W. Berry (Eds.), *Indigenous psychologies. Research and experience in cultural context* (pp. 152–169). London: Sage Publications.

Gigerenzer, G. (1996). On narrow norms and vague heuristics: A rebuttal to Kahneman and Tversky. *Psychological Review, 103*, 592–596.

Gigerenzer, G., & Hug, K. (1992). Domain-specific reasoning: Social contracts, cheating, and perspective change. *Cognition, 43*, 127–171.

Ho, David Yau-Fai (1993). Relational orientation in Asian social psychology. In U. Kim, & J. W. Berry (Eds.), *Indigenous psychologies. Research and Experience in Cultural Context* (pp. 240–259). London: Sage Publications.

Holzkamp, K. (1972). Wissenschaftstheoretische Voraussetzungen kritisch-emanzipatorischer Psychologie. In K. Holzkamp, *Kritische Psychologie. Vorbereitende Arbeiten* (pp 75–146). Frankfurt a.M.: Fischer.

Hartmann, D. (1993). *Naturwissenschaftliche Theorien: wissenschaftstheoretische Grundlagen am Beispiel der Psychologie*. Mannheim: BI-Wiss.-Verlag.

Heelas, P., & Lock, A. (Eds.) (1981). *Indigenous psychologies. The anthropology of the self*. London: Academic.

Kahneman, D., Slovic, P., & Tversky, A. (Eds.) (1982). *Judgment under uncertainty: Heuristics and biases*. Cambridge: Cambridge University Press.

Kahneman, D., & Tversky, A. (1996). On the reality of cognitive illusions. *Psychological Review, 103*, 582–591.

Kim, U., & Berry, J. W. (1993). Introduction. In U. Kim, & J. W. Berry (eds.), *Indigenous psychologies. Research and experience in cultural context* (pp. 1–29). London: Sage Publications.

Kleinman, A. (1980). *Patients and healers in context of cultures*. Berkely: University of California Press.

Janich, P. (1996). Das Experiment in der Psychologie. In P. Janich, *Konstruktivismus und Naturerkenntnis. Auf dem Weg zum Kulturalismus* (pp. 275–289). Frankfurt a.M.: Suhrkamp.

Kosslyn, S. M. (1981). The Medium and the Message in Mental Imagery: A Theory. *Psychological Review, Vol. 88, No. 1*, 46–66.

Kvale, S. (1992). Postmodern Psychology. Contradiction in Terms? In S. Kvale (Ed.), *Psychology and Postmodernism* (pp. 31–57). London: Sage Publications.

Lacan, J. (1991). Das Drängen des Buchstabens. In J. Lacan, *Schriften II* (p.15–59). Weinheim: Quadriga.

Misheva, V. (1997). Constructive realism: Towards a construction of reality. In Th. Slunecko (Hg.), *The movement of constructive realism* (pp. 109–145). Wien: Braumüller.

Popper, K. R. (1966). *Logik der Forschung* (2. Auflage). Tübingen.

Pylyshyn, Z. W. (1981). The imagery debate: Analogue media versus tacit knowledge. *Psychological Review, Vol. 88, No. 1*, 16–45.

Slunecko, Th. (1997). Simplicity and diversity in psychotherapy. In Th. Slunecko (Hg.), *The movement of constructive realism* (pp.243–262). Wien: Braumüller.

Wallner, F. (1992). Prolegomena zu einer Philosophie der Psychologie. In F. Wallner, *Konstruktion der realität* (p.11–22). Vienna: WUV.

Wallner, F. (1994). *Constructive realism. Aspects of a new epistemological movement*. Vienna: Braumüller.

Wallner, F. G. (1997). *How to deal with science if you care for other cultures. Constructive realism in the intercultural world*. Wien: Braumüller.

Wallner, F., & Peschl, M. (1991). Cognitive science -an experiment in constructive realism. Constructive science -an experiment in cognitive science. In C. V. Dijkum, and F. Wallner (ed.). *Constructive realism in discussion* (pp.30–39). Amsterdam: Sokrates Science Publisher.

Wallner, F. G. (1999). Das Bewusstsein – eine abendländische Konstruktion. In Th. Slunecko et al. (Hg.), *Psychologie des bewusstseins – bewusstsein der psychologie. Giselher Guttmann zum 65. Geburtstag* (pp.201–232). Wien: WUV.

Chapter 4

Constructive Realism and Confucian Relationalism

An Epistemological Strategy for the Development of Indigenous Psychology

Kwang-Kuo Hwang

A spirit of anti-colonialism in opposition to Westernized or Americanized psychology inspired the emergence of indigenous psychologies in many non-Western countries (e.g., Enriquez, 1981; 1982; Sinha, 1984; 1986) in the early 1980s. This work attracted interest and attention from mainstream psychologists throughout the 1990s (Shiraev & Levy, 2001), not to mention widespread skepticism over the legitimacy of the approach. Bitter debates occurred among psychologists supporting indigenous psychology and cross-cultural psychology (Hwang & Yang, 2000).

The indigenous psychology camp argued that the mission of their approach was "the study of human behavior and mental processes within a cultural context that relies on values, concepts, belief systems, methodologies, and other resources indigenous to the specific ethnic or cultural group under investigation" (Ho, 1998a, p. 94). The goal of indigenous psychologists is to develop "a psychology based on and responsive to indigenous culture and indigenous realities" (Enriquez, 1993, p.158), through "the scientific study of human behavior that is native, that is not transported from other regions, and that is designed for its people" (Kim & Berry, 1993). Indigenous psychologists advocated focus on indigenization from within (Enriquez, 1993), or "a bottom-up model building paradigm" (Kim, 2000, p. 265) that treats people "as interactive and proactive agents of their own actions" that occur in a meaningful context (Kim, Park, & Park, 2000).

Cross-cultural psychologists criticized this approach. They argued that the advantages of the indigenous approach, such as exclusive coverage of a particular culture group or the idiosyncratic approach of studying native behavior in a meaningful context is also claimed by anthropologists. Accumulating anthropological data with this approach may therefore not have direct implication for psychological research. Mainstream psychologists are interested in psychological phenomena, not in anthropology. They questioned the legitimacy of the indigenous approach as a scientific research method for psychology (Triandis, 2000). Some cross-cultural psychologists argued that the difference in behavioral repertoires across cultural populations should be understood against the background of a frame of commonalties (Poortinga, 1999), and asserted that too much emphasis on cultural uniqueness amounts to a kind of ethnocentrism in reverse (Ho, 1988; Poortinga, 1996).

In response, most indigenous psychologists have argued that the development of numerous indigenous psychologies is not their final goal. Rather, their final goal is to develop an Asian psychology (Ho, 1988), a global psychology (Enriquez, 1993; Yang, 1993), a universal psychology (Kim & Berry, 1993; Berry & Kim 1993), or a human psychology (Yang, 1993). To achieve this goal, they have proposed several research methods or approaches, including the derived *etic* approach (Berry, 1989; Berry & Kim, 1993), the metatheory method (Ho, 1998a), the cross indigenous method (Enriquez, 1977; 1993), as well as cross-cultural indigenous psychology (Yang, 1997, 1999).

The transition from indigenous psychologies to an Asian psychology, global psychology, universal psychology or a human psychology implies a significant change in philosophical assumption, which can be illustrated by an important argument proposed by Berry, Poortinga, Segall and Dasen (1992). They pointed out that there are three philosophical assumptions in cross-cultural psychology, namely, *absolutism, universalism,* and *relativism,* which correspond to three research orientations: *imposed etic, derived etic,* and *emic.* Western (American) psychology researchers ignore cultural differences and insist on the *imposed etic* approach as well as its philosophical assumption of *absolutism* by imposing Western theories and research instruments on people of non-Western societies. In contrast, indigenous psychology researchers follow the strategy of the *emic* approach, with its philosophical assumption of *relativism,* using indigenous instruments and methods of research with the expectation of developing substantial theories or models that are culturally specific to local people. However, the goal underpinning the search for a global psychology, universal psychology, or human psychology can only be obtained by changing the philosophical assumption from *relativism* to *universalism.* If researchers maintain the philosophical assumption of relativism, and insist on a bottom-up approach for constructing substantial theories through the inductive methods of positivism, it will be very difficult to achieve the goal of developing a global psychology.

My argument for the importance of universalism is supported by a distinction proposed by cultural psychologists to explain their fundamental view of human nature: one mind, many mentalities (Shweder, 1996, 2000; Shweder et. al., 1998). This phrase indicates that the psychological functioning or mechanisms of the human mind are the same all over the world, but that people may evolve various mentalities in different social and cultural environments. The goal of achieving a global psychology entails the expectation that the knowledge system constructed by indigenous psychologists should reflect not only the universal human mind, but also the particular mentality in a given culture. Differences in behavioral repertoires across various groups should be explained against the background of a broader frame of commonness (Poortinga, 1999). Indigenous psychologists should incorporate both cultural variation and cross-cultural invariance into their research schemes. This goal cannot be achieved by the inductive approach as suggested by those indigenous psychologists who insist on the philosophy of positivism. Closer examination of the terms *mind* and *mentality* reveals the reason the inductive approach is insufficient.

According to Shweder's (2000) definition, *mind* means "the totality of actual and potential conceptual contents of human cognitive process," and *mentality* denotes "the cognized and activated subset of mind" (p. 210). A *mentality* is owned or exercised by some group of particular individuals, so it can be a subject for research in cultural psychology. In contrast, *mind* refers to all the conceptual content that any human being might ever cognize and activate or represent. This universal mind cannot become the subject of research in cultural psychology. If indigenous psychologists want to achieve the goal of universalization with the inductive approach, they would have to carry out a very large-scale research program traveling around the globe to investigate all indigenous psychologies. Moreover, they would also have to take into account what has been manifested in the history and even the future of each culture (Wallner & Jandl, Chapter 3).

Obviously this is an impossible mission. So, how can indigenous psychologists solve this dilemma and achieve the goal of a global psychology? From the perspective of philosophy of science, they should abandon the inductive approach advocated by positivists, adopt the philosophical assumptions of post-positivism, construct formal theories about the psychological functioning of the human mind on the basis of previous findings using critical rationality (Popper, 1963) or creative imagination (Hempel, 1966), and then use these theories to analyze the particular mentality of a people in an indigenous culture by examining their psychology and behaviors in their lifeworlds.

Elaboration of this academic proposal is the goal of this article. First, I briefly review the dramatic change in ontology, epistemology, and methodology that occurred in the philosophy of science with switch from positivism to post-positivism. Based on the philosophy of post-positivism, I critically review various approaches as suggested by indigenous psychologists for achieving the goal of universal psychology. In order to explain the mentalities of people in non-Western societies that might develop with modernization, I adopt the philosophy of constructive realism to illustrate the difference between the knowledge constructed by scientists and the knowledge used by ordinary people in their lifeworlds. From the perspective of constructive realism, the language and knowledge developed by a cultural group during the progress of their history can be viewed as manifestations of the deep structure of that culture, which can be analyzed through the method of structuralism. In the last section of this article, I use my analysis of Confucian cultural tradition as an example to illustrate how indigenous psychologists can construct a series of theoretical models both to explain the psychological mechanisms of the universal human mind, and to interpret the particular mentality of Confucian culture.

THE DRAMATIC CHANGE IN THE PHILOSOPHY OF SCIENCE

Since mainstream philosophy of science moved from positivism to post-positivism, it has become clear that, epistemologically, scientific theory is constructed through the critical thinking of scientists, not inducted from empirical facts. It is not only methodologically impractical to verify scientific propositions in the manner suggested by positivists, but falsification is also difficult, as noted by Hempel and Lakatos. If indigenous psychology is defined as a branch of science, indigenous researchers must face this dilemma and seek its solution. Towards this end, in this section I review the dramatic changes in epistemology and methodology that occurred with the shift in the philosophy of science from positivism to post-positivism with a brief presentation of Popper's evolutionary epistemology, Hempel's logical empiricism, and Laktos' concept of scientific research program.

Positivism

The method of induction had been regarded as the main approach for acquiring knowledge through positivism. For instance, Wittgenstein (1889–1951), whose earlier works had profound influence on the Vienna Circle in the 1920's, maintained in his famous writing *Tractatus Logico-Philosophicus* that the main activity of science is to use language to describe the world. Atomic facts should be described with elementary propositions in a scientific theory that can be verified with empirical methods. Through the logical deduction of truth functions, elementary propositions can be combined into a scientific proposition. A proposition is a picture of reality, and the totality of true propositions reflects the nature science as a whole (Wittgenstein, 1922/1961).

Wittgenstein's earlier philosophy takes a position of copy theory or photo theory, insisting that a scientific proposition has to copy or to record atomic facts and their structure clearly and correctly. Elementary propositions describe atomic facts repeatedly experienced by human beings, and scientific rules are established on the basis of these repeated empirical facts. Elementary propositions, which are the fundamental components of a theoretical proposition, are induced from past experience.

Schlick (1882–1936), the organizer of the Vienna Circle, contributed much to the promotion of the ideas of logical positivism. He argued that when a person elaborates the meaning of a sentence, that person is trying to explain the conditions for the sentence to be a true proposition, which is the way to verify the sentence. As Schlick observed, the meaning of a proposition is the way to verify it (Schlick, 1936).

Popper's Evolutionary Epistemology

With active promotion by the Vienna Circle, logical positivism had an extraordinary influence on the thoughts of the scientific community from 1930–1950. When it reached the peak of academic prestige, it began receiving criticism from its academic opponents. The first challenge came from Karl Popper's (1902–1994) evolutionary epistemology. Popper (1963) argued that scientific theories are not induced from empirical facts, but deduced by scientists with critical rationality. The procedure of scientific research should begin with a problem. When a scientist finds new empirical facts that cannot be explained, or inconsistencies in preexisting theories, a tentative solution or theory may be proposed to solve the problem. Potential errors are eliminated by examining the theory against empirical facts in the world.

The deductive method Popper advocated is not the traditional deduction grounded in axiomatic premises. Popper argued that the premises of deduction for a tentative theory of scientific conjecture should be repeatedly subjected to empirical examination. This method is called *deduction with examination*. Popper (1963) suggested, "Our intellect does not draw its laws from nature, but tries-with varying degrees of success - to impose upon nature laws which it freely invents" (p. 191). According to one of Popper's analogies, the water bucket of scientific theory will not be spontaneously full so long as scientists work hard to fill it with accumulated empirical facts. Instead, theory is like a searchlight. Scientists must continuously bring up problems and make conjectures, so as to cast the light of theory on the future (Popper, 1972, p. 431-457). If a theory records only previous findings, and nothing can be deduced from it except preexisting facts, what is the use of the theory?

Popper also opposed the principle of verification as advocated by positivists. According to Popper, a theoretical proposition cannot be verified, it can only be falsified by empirical facts contradictory to the theory. Scientific theory is stated with general predications. However, empirical facts are individually experienced. No matter how many times a particular experience is repeated, it cannot verify a proposition of general prediction. For instance, no matter how many white swans have been observed, the proposition of general predication "swans are white" still cannot be verified, because our observations cannot include all swans. Therefore, scientists cannot *verify* theoretical propositions, only *falsify* them, or reserve them temporarily before they are falsified.

Hempel's Logical Empiricism

When logical positivism was criticized, Hempel, who had participated in the academic discussions of the Vienna Circle in earlier years, tried to modify its shortcomings and proposed the new idea of logical empiricism. In his *Aspects of Scientific Explanation* (Hempel, 1965), he proposed a model of covering law, which stated that scientific explanation usually contains two kinds of statements, namely, general laws, and antecedent conditions. Using these two kinds of *explanans* as the premises, a scientist can deduct a description of a phenomenon, which is called the *explanandum*.

Hempel pointed out the difficulty of falsifying a hypothetical proposition. When scientists test a hypothesis, they must propose several auxiliary hypotheses that prescribe the antecedent conditions for its occurrence. Some of these auxiliary hypotheses are related to the scientific theory itself, and some to experimental design, instrumental equipment, or research procedures. A combination of all these conditions may lead to the occurrence of the phenomenon observed.

Scientists obtaining a negative result from research, rarely give up their general laws easily. Instead, they carefully examine their research instruments, reconsider the experimental design, or even repeat the experiment. These steps imply only consideration of whether there is anything wrong with the auxiliary hypotheses, indicating that it is not easy to falsify a hypothesis.

For this reason, Hempel (1965) argued that the target to be examined in scientific activity is not a sole hypothesis, but the whole theoretical system. Moreover, Hempel (1966) also believed that theory is not obtained by induction. It was impossible for a scientist to induce theory from empirical facts. For example, Newton's law of gravity and Einstein's theory of relativity were not inducted from a collection of observed phenomena. Scientists created them through imagination to explain what was observed. "The transition from data to theory requires creative imagination. Scientific hypothesis and theories are not *derived* from observed facts, but *invented* in order to account for them. They constitute guesses at the connections that might obtain the phenomena under study, at uniformities and patterns that might underlie the occurrence" (Hempel, 1966, p. 15).

Lakatos' Scientific Research Program

Lakatos (1978), one of Popper's students, also denounced Popper's falsificationism as a "naïve falsificationism" or "dogmatic falsificationism," claiming scientists will not easily give up propositions of a scientific theory once they are falsified by empirical research as Popper predicted.

Empirical refutation cannot easily eliminate errors in theory because propositions in scientific theory usually contain conditional sentences with *ceteris partibus*. Examination of a theoretical proposition should be carried out under specific conditions, no matter whether an experiment or observation is used. When an empirical fact obtained from an experiment or observation contradicts the prediction of the theory, a researcher is unable to ascertain whether it the contradiction was caused by theoretical mistakes or by experimental or observational features. The famous *Duhem-Quine thesis* indicated that a theory can never be refuted if it is protected with *auxiliary hypotheses*. In other words, as long as a scientist is able to use imagination, *auxiliary hypotheses* may be proposed to attribute anomalies to other factors and to protect the core of the theory against falsification.

In Lakotos' (1970) view, the weakness of Popper's philosophy lies in the fact that it is unable to provide a sound basis for falsification. A scientific theory exists not in isolation, but as part of a series of theories with tight inner connections. Thus, Lakotos proposed a *sophisticated falsificationism* and advocated replacing the idea of *theory* with a *series of theories*, called a *Scientific Research Program*. He suggested that the basic unit for examination in scientific research is neither a particular scientific proposition, nor an isolated theory, but rather a series of theories or a research program.

A Critical Review of Research Strategies for Constructing a Universal Psychology

The dramatic changes in epistemology and methodology with the switch from positivism to post-positivism have significant implication for indigenous psychologists in developing a global psychology. Strictly speaking, indigenous psychologists cannot attain the goal of building theoretical models for a global psychology through an inductive approach. What they can do is use their creative imagination or critical rationality to construct a formal theory on the psychological mechanisms of the universal human mind that apply to various cultures, and then use it as a framework for analyzing the specific mentalities of given cultures. If indigenous psychologists insist on the inductive approach of positivism, which emphasizes construction of a substantial theory that can first be applied to a particular culture, and then integration of these psychologies to attain the goal of a global psychology, they will encounter several epistemological or methodological difficulties. In this section, I review and discuss the feasibility of methods for constructing a global psychology proposed by several major indigenous psychologists, including the derived *etic* approach, the cross-indigenous method, the metatheory approach, and cross-cultural indigenous psychology.

The Derived *Etic* Approach

Berry (1969, 1989) classified the research approaches of cross-cultural psychology into three categories, namely, imposed *etic*, *emic*, and derived *etic*. The imposed *etic* approach assumes that the concepts used by a researcher can be applied to all cultures. However, if concepts originate from outside the culture in which they are applied, they are very likely to be insufficient. Most indigenous psychologists advocate the emic approach, which emphasizes use of concepts and terms from the local cultural system to understand the meanings of local phenomena. The derived *etic* approach attempts to integrate the knowledge obtained by the imposed *etic* and *emic* approaches through a process of comparison. Berry and Kim (1993) regarded the derived *etic* approach as a necessary step in constructing a more universal psychology.

A crucial question to ask at this point is what the nature of the imposed theory to be used by indigenous psychologists in a derived *etic* approach for constructing a theory of global psychology should be. If it is a formal theory for interpreting psychological mechanisms of the human mind that is applicable to various cultures (though assumptions might be falsified by empirical facts), the derived *etic* approach proposed by Berry (1969, 1989) is acceptable. On the other hand, if it is a substantial theory referring to an acculturation strategy of integration "where psychology draws upon the ideas, theories, methods, and findings of both [cultures], [and] eventually all societies yield to the generalized universal psychology" (Berry, 1993, p. 272), such an advocacy implies repeated use of inductive method, and its feasibility is dubious. Following this approach, no matter how many cultures are studied, the studies contribute only "one small step toward a universal psychology" (Berry, 1993, p. 260). The final goal of attaining a global psychology would always be far away.

The Cross-Indigenous Method

Enriquez (1977, 1993) separated indigenous research strategy into *indigenization from within* and *indigenization from without*. The indigenization from without approach is very similar to the imposed *etic* approach. It advocates importing (Western) knowledge of psychology from dominant source cultures to interpret data obtained from the target culture in the third world. Enriquez strongly opposed this approach. Instead he advocated the indigenization from within approach using "the local languages and cultures as sources for theory, method, and praxis" (Enriquez, 1993, p. 163). In order to increase the generalizability of research findings in indigenous psychology, he proposed a cross-indigenous method that entailed using various cultures as the source for cross-indigenous psychology, expecting to broaden the database for building a global psychology.

The focus of Enriquez's (1977, 1993) discourse is language and culture. His cross-indigenization method is subject to the dilemma of the inductive approach if it results in a substantial theory of psychology with higher generalizability to different cultures. Though it is expected that "with the cross-indigenous approach, not only can universal regularities be discovered, but also the total range of a phenomenon investigated is increased" (Kim & Berry, 1993, p. 11), there are still some doubts about "how such an integration of knowledge derived in different cultural systems [can] actually be realized" (Poortinga, 1997, p. 361). Even Enriquez (1993) himself admitted "cross-cultural psychology will remain a promise so long as indigenous psychologies remain untapped because of language and cultural barriers" (p. 154).

Meta-Theory Approach

Indigenous psychologists argue that blindly adopting imported foreign theories may result in pitfalls of ethnocentrism, because they contain many concepts that are strange to the target culture. But, Ho (1988; 1998a) argued that relying on indigenous concepts alone might also lead to similar difficulty, and would not eliminate the fundamental predicament of culture-centrism. Ho distinguished theories along an indigenous-exotic dimension (Ho, 1998a). Indigenous theories are constructed on the basis of values and concepts of the target culture; they represent the viewpoint of insiders. In contrast, exotic theories are produced with values and concepts alien to the target culture and represent the viewpoint of outsiders. In order to eliminate the potential incongruence of various theories, Ho proposed development of a metatheory by comparing indigenous and exotic theories in terms of contents, theorists, and cultures.

His approach also implies the potential difficulty from using an inductive approach. Ho's metatheory thus constructed is just a mini-metatheory. "It may be expanded for multicultural and even holocultural studies in which the target universe includes all known cultures in the whole world" (Ho, 1998a, p. 93). Ho's proposal raises the question: To what extent should the target universe of such a mini-metatheory be expanded to include all known cultures in the whole world?

Cross-Cultural Indigenous Psychology

Yang (1993) supported the distinction between exogenous indigenization and endogenous indigenization, or indigenization from without and indigenization from within made by Enriquez (1979). He further divided indigenous psychology into monocultural indigenous psychology and cross-cultural indigenous psychology, and argued that Westernized or Americanized psychology is also a kind of monocultural indigenous psychology. The construction of regional psychological theories cannot merely rely on monocultural indigenous studies, but must integrate related knowledge from several indigenous psychologies through cross-cultural indigenous studies (Yang, 1997, 2000).

At the first glance, Yang's arguments are very similar to Enriquez's. But, Yang went on to discuss the integration procedure from the perspectives of content and approach. So far as content is concerned, he proposed two types of integration, namely, empirical and theoretical. Empirical integration "rests mainly on the common characteristics (components, processes, constructs, structures, or patterns) and functions shared by all the compared indigenous psychologies" (Yang, 2000, p. 258).

With respect to theoretical integration, Yang (2000) stated, "If a psychological theory is able to adequately understand, explain and predict psychological and behavioral phenomena in a certain domain across two or more cultures, it may be said that the theory integrates the phenomena in that domain for those cultures" (p. 258). His proposal is very similar to the derived *etic* approach advocated by Berry (1993). But the question remains, with insistence on the cross-cultural indigenous psychology approach, who would be able to construct a theory to integrate the common characters and functions shared by all the compared indigenous psychologies?

Yang (2000) also proposed three integration approaches in his cross-cultural indigenous psychology (CCI approach). To explain the integrating function of the CCI approach, Yang (2000) stated: "In each CCI study, psychological and behavioral characteristics and their functions in a certain domain can be empirically and theoretically analyzed and organized to form a meaningful miniature knowledge system" (p. 259). In order for this cross-culturally indigenous knowledge to have high external validity, Yang (2000) emphasized that "it is important to include as many diverse or heterogeneous cultures as possible" (p. 259). Perhaps he was considering the feasibility of this proposal when he cited Huntington's (1993, 1997) argument that there are three major distinctive groups of cultures— Christian, Confucian, and Muslim. Because these three groups are highly dissimilar and are composed of the largest populations in the world, he suggested using cultures representative of this triad plus Buddhist culture as subjects for future cross-cultural indigenous research.

Three Levels of Breakthroughs

Though the question of whether the cross-cultural indigenous psychology approach as proposed by Yang can be used to achieve the goal of a global psychology is still open to discussion, his suggestion for studying the main cultures of Christianity, Confucianism, Islam, and Buddhism in the contemporary world and their modernization deserves special attention from indigenous psychologists. Modernization (or Westernization) is an inevitable trend for most non-Western countries in the world. In order to make progress in indigenous psychology or social science, it is necessary for non-Western scholars to make three levels of breakthroughs: philosophical reflection, theoretical construction, and empirical research. They must assimilate the major academic performance of the West to propose a philosophy to illuminate their own historical situations. This philosophy must be able to explain not only the meaning of modernization, but also specific features of indigenous cultures in non-Western countries. It should also be able to explain why social scientists in non-Western countries should develop indigenous social science during their process of modernization.

In the context of this article there are essential differences between the knowledge systems of non-Western countries inherited from local cultural traditions and knowledge systems constructed by scientists after the industrial revolution in the 18th century. Once the "one mind, many mentalities" presumption of cultural psychology is accepted (Shweder, 1996, 2000; Shweder, et. al., 1998), it is necessary to establish a philosophy to guide researchers in what the essential differences between the two systems of knowledge are, and what the changes to people's mentalities during the process of modernization in non-Western countries might be.

Constructive realism is just such a philosophy. It meets all the requirements stated above. In the following sections, I present the main ideas of constructive realism, and use constructive realism to answer several disputes about the indigenization of psychology. After that, I use my analysis of Confucian cultural traditions as an example to illustrate my arguments.

CONSTRUCTIVE REALISM

Constructive realism is a philosophy of science proposed by the Vienna School in attempt to synthesize the previous paradigm of social science (Wallner, 1994; Wallner et al., Chapter 3). According to constructive realism there are three levels of reality, the most important of which is called the *actuality or wirklichkeit*. The actuality is the world in which we find ourselves, or the given world that all living creatures must rely on to survive. The given world may have certain structures, or may function by its own rules. However, humans have no way to recognize these structures or rules.

No matter how humans attempt to explain these structures, the explanation and therefore our comprehension is always a construction of human beings.

Lifeworlds and Microworlds

The world as constructed by human beings can be divided into two categories: lifeworlds and microworlds. Human beings construct these two worlds with different ways of thinking, which are supported by different types of rationalities. The knowledge created in each construction results in different worldviews with distinct functions. These two worlds constitute two levels of constructed reality for human beings (see Table 1).

The first constructed reality is the lifeworld in which humans live. For the individual, a *lifeworld* is a primordial world in which everything presents itself in a self-evident way. Before human beings began to develop scientific knowledge, they tried to understand their experiences in daily life, and to make various explanations, structures, and responses to their lifeworlds. These explanations and responses belonged to a domain of pre-logical, pre-technical and pre-instrumental thinking, their richness lies in individual life experiences (Husserl, 1970).

Any scientific construction can be regarded as a *microworld*. A microworld can be a theoretical model built on the basis of realism, or a theoretical interpretation of a social phenomenon provided by a social scientist from a particular perspective. Within any given microworld, the reality of the given world is replaced by a second order constructed reality that can be corroborated.

Lifeworlds are constantly sustained by a transcendental formal structure called cultural heritage. Language is the most important carrier of cultural heritage. People use language to play games as they interact in their lifeworlds. A *language game* is any kind of human practice or activity shared by people living in a given culture, which constitutes various forms of life. *Forms of life* refer to patterns of thinking that are manifest in cultural heritage, such as customs, folkways, institutions and traditional practices in a particular historical and cultural condition. Language games are inevitably rooted in these forms of life (Wittgenstein, 1945/1958).

Table 1. Two Types of Knowledge in Lifeworld and Microworld

	Lifeworld	Microworld
Constructor	Cultural group	Single scientist
Ways of thinking	Originative thinking	Technique thinking
Types of rationality	Substantive rationality	Formal rationality
Patterns of construction	Participative constructive	Dominative construction
Functions of worldview	Meaning of life	Recognition of world

Originative Thinking and Technical Thinking

People living in the same culture over a long-term period of evolution construct the natural language used in a lifeworld. In the formative years of a particular culture, people concentrate themselves on observing and contemplating the nature of every object in their lifeworld. They rid themselves of their own will and intention, and try their best to make all things manifest in the language they create to represent it. Heiderger (1966) labeled this way of thinking *originative thinking*.

The language and way of thinking scientists use to construct theoretical microworlds are completely distinct from those used by people in their lifeworlds. Scientific knowledge is not obtained by contemplating the nature of things. Instead, scientists intentionally created it to reach a specific goal, so it has a compulsory and aggressive character that demands the most gain with the least cost. Such *technical thinking* has no interest in representing things in the objective world, and making things the object of knowledge. Instead, this type of thinking attempts to exploit natural resources by every means, and to transfer them into the storage of human beings.

The scientific microworld is not the only thematic world that human beings have constructed. Guided by various themes for different needs, human beings have also constructed the microworlds of ethics, aesthetics, and religion. Because each thematic world is constructed with a particular way of thinking under the guidance of a certain theme, all phenomena irrelevant to that theme will be excluded. Therefore, each microworld bears a predetermined partiality and narrowness.

Substantive Rationality and Formal Rationality

Technical thinking uses certain ground principles as a foundation. Modern people calculate their thinking with reference to a ground principle which serves as the foundation for rational thinking. But, what is meant by *rationality*? Is the originative thinking needed by people in their lifeworlds irrational or lacking in rationality?

These questions can be answered through a consideration of Max Weber's works on comparative religion. In order to investigate the cause of the rise of industrial capitalism in the modern world, Weber (1921/1963; 1930/1992) proposed a set of contrasting concepts to highlight the unique features of Western civilization. He indicated that with the occurrence of the Renaissance in the 14th century, many west European countries experienced an expansion of rationalism in such fields as science, law, politics and religion. He noted that the unique feature of *formal rationality* characterized the rationalism manifested in Europe after the Renaissance, which was completely different from the *substantive rationality* emphasized in other civilizations. Formal rationality emphasizes the calculability of means and procedures that can be used to pursue personal goals, and pays attention only to value-natural facts. In contrast, substantive rationality refers to the value of ends or results judged from a particular position, and provides no clear-cut means and procedures for reaching goals (Brubarker, 1984).

According to Weber's conceptual framework, all microworlds constructed by scientists contain the essence of formal rationality. Such microworlds of scientific knowledge are products of construction attained by scientists who are doing research in a specific domain utilizing the Cartesian way of thinking that emerged after the European Renaissance of the 14th century. It is essentially different from the way of constructing knowledge used by non-Western people in their lifeworlds.

Participative Construction and Dominative Construction

This point can be illustrated with Levy-Bruhl's (1910/1966) anthropological study of primitive thinking. His pioneer works in this field indicated that the cultural system of any primitive people, including their mythology and religion, is constituted on a basis of the law of mystical participation (Evans-Prichard, 1964), which conceptualizes human beings as parts of an inseparable entity that can be viewed as a consciousness of cosmic holism (Taylor, 1871/1958).

In a pre-modern or primitive culture, the collective representation constituted by the law of mystical participation would seldom be refuted by empirical experience. Tradition and authority protect the culture from challenges by antagonistic information. Members of the community usually experience collective representations with shared sentiment, rather than examining them with empirical facts. People in many pre-modern cultures describe people and objects encountered in various situations with abundant vivid language. By doing so, they develop a rich lexicon in which the meanings of words are not only flexible, but can also be reshaped with the variation of experiences, people, and objects.

In pre-modern civilizations, people construct the knowledge in their lifeworlds through *participative construction* (Shen, 1994). The scientific microworlds constructed by Westerners with the philosophy of Cartesian dualism can be called *dominative construction*. Knowledge constructed in these two ways is completely different in nature and mutually incompatible.

Two Worldviews

The language games people play usually entail a particular worldview. The worldviews in the lifeworld and the microworld are essentially different. Walsh and Middleton (1984) indicated that the worldview in a given culture usually answers four broad categories of questions: Who am I? What is my situation of life? Why do I suffer? How do I find salvation? A worldview not only describes human nature but also the relationship between humans and the world, as well as one's historical situation in the world. It provides a diagnosis for problems and prescribes a recipe for their solution.

The worldview in a microworld does not have such a function. In his lexicon theory, Kuhn (1987) indicated that the scientific lexicon is composed of a set of terms with structure and content, which constitute an interrelated network. Scientists use terms in the lexicon to make propositions in a theory for describing the nature of the world. Scientific lexicons contain a particular way of seeing the world. Members of the same scientific community must master the same lexicon, understand meanings of each term, and share the same worldview in order to communicate with one another, think about the same problem and engage in related research in the same scientific community. But, the microworld worldview provides no answers to problems related to the meaning of life.

THE EVOLUTION OF SOCIETY

The evolution of social representations from the knowledge of substantive rationality constructed by originative thinking to the knowledge of formal rationality constructed by metaphysical thinking is the consequence of a series of qualitative transformations that are discontinuous in both content and cognitive structure (Hwang, 2000). As microworlds are developed, some of the language, rationality, and thinking entailed by these microworlds may penetrate and become infused into people's lifeworlds. Such transformation and penetration may result in drastic changes in people's social lives. However, the process of change may have different implications for Western and non-Western societies.

Lifeworlds and Social Systems

The general impact of such a transformation on the social lives of human beings can be understood by Habermas' (1978) theory on the differentiation of social systems from peoples' lifeworlds. Habermas pointed out that an individual's lifeworld is composed of three levels, namely, culture, society and individual. For people sharing a certain cultural heritage, intersubjective communication may determine the interpretation of cultural tradition, so they share the power of re-interpreting it. For a society, communication may help people to establish acceptable standards of behavior, identify with their community, and strengthen the integration of society. For the individual, growth and learning resulting from constant communication may enable individuals to strengthen their capacity for action and help them to shape the integrity of their personalities.

During the evolution of a society, social systems may become differentiated from people's lifeworlds, causing people to live in two completely different worlds. Such differentiated systems are not only different from people's lifeworlds, but also antagonistic to one another. The three functions of communication in an individual's lifeworld are mutual understanding, coordination of action, and socialization. These functions of communication may satisfy three kinds of social needs: cultural reproduction, social integration, and individual socialization.

In contrast, the major aim of sustaining most social systems in modern societies is material reproduction, and the criterion for evaluating system evolution is the enhancement of social control. In order to achieve this goal of material reproduction, each system must be paired with the most efficient microworld of scientific knowledge. People working in the system have to use the technical thinking entailed by the microworld to solve the problems they encounter in their tasks. Because of the replacement of originative thinking with technical thinking, money and power replace the position of language in lifeworlds, and become the media for system integration. Seeking consensus through communication and coordination may also take into consideration the one-dimensional thinking of reward and punishment. Systems in the lifeworld are liberated from regulation by social norms, and become more and more autonomous. Finally the new order of the social system begins to instrumentalize the lifeworld. This process is called *colonization* of the lifeworld by the system (Habermas, 1978).

The Development of Non-Western Countries

The process of differentiating the social system from people's lifeworlds has completely different implications for Western and non-Western countries. The modernization of Western countries developed from the interior of the civilization, while the essential elements of modernization for non-Western countries are transplanted from the exterior of their traditional cultures.

This point can be illustrated from a wider perspective. In order to explain the cultural changes in the world in terms of dependency theory, Henry (1986) argued that the patterns of cultural change in central and peripheral countries were roughly similar before the emergence of a world economic system. Religion was dominant in all cultural systems. Art, philosophy, and other practical areas of knowledge were all subordinate to its claims of truth. Religious symbols provided by priests were used to satisfy people's needs for identification.

However, with the emergence of a capitalist world system, central and peripheral countries began to develop in different directions. While central countries constructed capitalist systems of production, the new elites in these countries gradually came to control the machines of the nation. They systematically connected scientific and producing activities, and established global trading systems. Traditional pre-capitalism cultural configurations became disorganized. Mythology, etiquette, and the metaphysic worldview of religion were replaced by market rationality and instrumental rationality for systems of scientific production. The balance between the two life spheres organized by formal rationality and substantive rationality was destroyed. Sub-spheres organized by purposive-rational actions gradually overrode religious rationality, and became the dominating form of cultural change in central countries.

While the dominating form of cultural change in central countries has become the process of formal and scientific rationalization, in peripheral countries, the leading form of cultural change is a structural and symbolic adjustment process aimed at facing and legitimizing the foreign cultural hegemony that makes their societies peripheral. Since capitalist peripheral societies have accepted their particular role in the global economic system, their functions of production are usually very narrow. Instead of producing by technical innovation in response to the demands of domestic markets, they usually produce a single original equipment manufacturing product according to the demands of foreign markets. As a consequence, the economic systems of capitalist peripheral countries produce the same products in an unchanging way. They mostly produce primary industry products with little modification or scientific innovation. The necessity for scientific research is decreased, the possibility for developing a domestic scientific community is diminished, and it is difficult to institutionalize a productive research organization. All these factors may hinder the emergence of a new cultural pattern that is characterized by the rationality of formal science.

The Co-Existence of Modernity and Traditionalism

Because the production equipment and operation techniques in peripheral countries are transplanted from central countries, the technical knowledge used need not be provided by the peripheral cultural system. It is therefore unnecessary for peripheral cultural systems to rationalize their knowledge production systems scientifically. Though most peripheral countries have universities, their main task is to train technicians for maintenance and operation of their manufacturing systems, rather than to promote rationalization of their cultural systems. The co-existence of modernity and traditionalism has become apparent in many non-Western countries.

During their process of growth, children learn traditional patterns of thinking and behaving by acquisition of language in their lifeworld, which shapes their personality orientation with originative thinking.

As they grow up and attend school, they begin to learn scientific knowledge originated from the West. Knowledge from different origins with different natures becomes mixed in their cognitive systems, and helps them to deal with problems in different situations of their lifeworlds.

When adults in non-Western countries are engaged in production work in a social system, they are likely to use knowledge from a scientific microworld as well as technical thinking with formal rationality to solve the problems encountered in their tasks. When they return to their intimate society and interact with family members or acquaintances, they may switch cognitive frames (Kitayama & Markus, 1999; Hong et al, 2000), and adopt some habitual patterns of activity and substantive rationality learned during earlier socialization. When individuals encounter crisis or drastic changes in life situations in which their problems cannot be solved by scientific knowledge, they are especially likely to return to cultural traditions and seek solutions in their traditional worldview. In order to understand the psychology and behavior of non-Western people, it is necessary to develop indigenous psychologies in the various non-Western societies.

BUILDING MODELS OF INDIGENOUS PSYCHOLOGY: CONFUCIAN RELATIONALISM

The trend towards globalization facilitates intercultural communication among cultures all over the world. It would be very difficult to find any autonomous and self-contained cultural whole in the present post-colonial age (Eldridge, 1999). How can psychologists develop a new paradigm of indigenous psychology to capture such features of modern society as connectedness, cultural diffusion, and fluidity of cultural identity (Hermans & Kempem, 1998)?

From the perspective of constructive realism, to accomplish this goal psychologists should construct microworlds encompassing the major aspects of an indigenous culture using the paradigms of Western social science, which might be used as a framework for studying the psychology of people in their lifeworlds. On this point, Greenfield (2000) delivered the following statement:

> The incorporation of culture into mainstream psychology will not come from simply presenting data on group differences, no matter how exciting or dramatic these differences may be. My most important theoretical mission is to introduce the idea of a deep structure of culture. As in language, deep structure of culture generates behaviors and interpretations of human behavior in an infinite array of domains and situations. I believe that the concepts behind individualism and collectivism, independence and interdependence, a relational vs. an individual orientation and so on are all indexing a common deep structure. (p. 229)

I strongly agree with Greenfield's arguments. But, how can researchers identify the common deep structures of the human mind?

The Deep Structure of Culture

From the perspective of structuralism (Lévi-Strauss, 1976), all human activities, including cognitions as well as actions, result from simulating various relations in nature. Nature is a system with steady, unchangeable, and mutually-linked relations among its various components. As a part of nature, from generation to generation people have gradually developed various sets of customs in their lifeworlds that are congruent with the natural order. These customs, rites, and various forms of life are the consequences of routinization, crystallization, or systematization of human practices in simulation of nature. For the sake of survival and prosperity, human rationality has to handle the various events encountered in a person's lifeworld so as to adjust to the environment. The diversified social phenomena seen in a given society are manifested from an undetectable underlying structure that originated from the inherited capability of the human mind.

These structures are the unconscious models of human rationality, which are a kind of autonomous model followed by human thinking. All of the empirical facts in human social life are a result of the arrangement and combination of these models. The human capability to simulate nature is manifest in the customs and social relationships of pre-modern civilization. The more advanced the society, the more progressed the civilization, and the more complicated the social relationships. Many linkages among people depart from the natural order, which makes recognition of the original appearance of some pre-modern civilizations difficult. The goal of structuralism is to reveal the fundamental structure of cultural relations that might be very complicated in appearance.

From the perspective of structuralism, both the language games played by people in their lifeworlds and the microworlds of knowledge constructed by scientists have their own structures. But there are tremendous differences between these two kinds of structure. In terms of Piaget's (1972) genetic epistemology, the structure of scientific knowledge is a *conscious* model constructed with formal operational thinking by an individual scientist with fully developed intelligence. In contrast, the language games played by people in their lifeworlds are constituted by the rationality of a cultural group under the influence of their collective unconscious over the history of their evolution. These language games originate from the deep structure of the culture, which is an *unconscious* model. People are unaware of it directly in their daily lives, but researchers may reveal the deep structure using the methods of structuralism.

With this insight, I constructed a Face and Favor model on the basis of scientific realism (Hwang, 1987), used this model as a framework to analyze the deep structure of Chinese cultural tradition by the method of

structuralism (Hwang, 1988; 1995), and then constructed a series of theoretical models on Confucian relationalism (Hwang, 1997–8; 2000). The
Face and Favor model was constructed on the basis of social exchange
behaviors that are universal in human society. My examination of Chinese
cultural tradition used the most popular and important classics in pre-
modern East Asian civilization as materials and resulted in two levels of
analysis: social exchange behavior, and language. An isomorphic relationship between the Face and Favor model and Confucian ethics for
ordinary people is assumed.

The Face and Favor Model

In the Face and Favor model, the two parties in the interaction are defined
as the *petitioner* and the *resource allocator*. When a petitioner requests the
resource allocator to allocate the resources in his control in a manner beneficial to the petitioner, the first cognitive process of the resource allocator
is to judge the *guanxi* (degree of closeness) of the relationship. The allocator must ask, "What is the relationship between us?"

The relationship in this model is represented by the rectangular box
presented in Figure 1. The shaded area of the rectangle is called the *expressive* component, which denotes a tendency to consider the welfare of the
opposite party. The blank portion of the rectangle is the *instrumental* component, which implies an attempt to utilize the relationship to attain a
personal goal. According to the proportions of these two components,
interpersonal relationships can be classified into one of three categories:
expressive ties, mixed ties or instrumental ties.

Classification of interpersonal relationships into three categories
incorporates some important concepts of Western justice theory. For
example, Lerner (1981) classified an individual's experience of interpersonal relationships into three categories in accordance with the sequence
of one's development: in the earliest stage, an individual may share emotional responses with those of *identical* relationship, when the person
grows up, gradually increasing contacts with more kinds of people, *unit*
or *nonunit* relationships with others may be differentiated. Unit relationships are with people similar to oneself in age, sexual distinction, or residence. Nonunit relationships are with others more obviously different
from oneself.

An individual may use different standards of justice to interact with
others of different relationships. In an identical relationship when an individual cares about the development and welfare of the opposite party, a person will likely use the *need* rule to allocate resources. In a unit relationship,
in which one treats the opposite party as a human being and emphasizes the
importance of maintaining harmonious relationship, the *renqing* (affection)
rule is more likely to be applied. In nonunit relationships, as both parties of

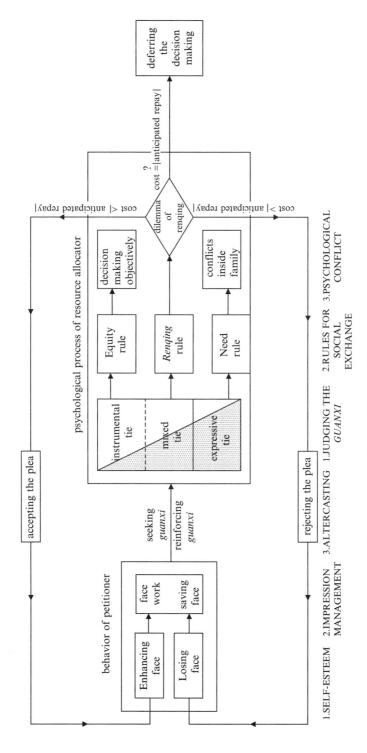

Figure 1. A theoretical model of face and favor in Chinese society (Adapted from Hwang 1987: 948)

the interaction consider only their own roles and emphasize the efficiency of work, the *equity* rule is most commonly used (Deutsch, 1975; Greenberg & Cohen, 1982; Lerner, 1975, 1977, Leventhal, 1976).

The Face and Favor model assumes that an individual may use the need rule, the *renqing* rule, or the equity rule to interact with the three kinds of people. This assumption can be viewed as a manifestation of the universal model in Chinese culture. In interacting with any of these three kinds of people, one may consider the *cost* to be paid, as well as the *repayment* that may be obtained from the other party, and then calculate the likely *outcome* of the social exchange. Because an individual expects to associate with others of expressive or mixed ties again in the future, when facing a request for a favor from a person of one of these kinds of ties, the affective ingredient of the relationship is taken into consideration. As a result, the decision may not be rational, and could result in dilemma of affection or family conflict. In contrast, when interacting with another of instrumental ties, only a rational act of calculation is necessary, so an objective decision can be made.

From the discourse above, it may seem that the Face and Favor model is constructed by integrating the core concepts of social exchange theory and justice theory on the philosophical basis of scientific realism. Formal theory constructed in this manner is universal and applicable to various cultures. An understanding of Confucian ethics for ordinary people and the five cardinal rules will illuminate the relevance of this theory to social behaviors in Chinese culture.

Confucian Ethics for Ordinary People

In my book *Knowledge and Action* (Hwang, 1995), I analyzed the deep structure of Confucianism and subdivided the ethical arrangements for interpersonal relationships proposed by the Way of Humanity into two categories: ethics for ordinary people, and ethics for scholars. The former category, which should be followed by everyone including scholars, is best described by the following propositions in The Golden Mean:

> *Benevolence is the characteristic attribute of personhood. The first priority of its expression is showing affection to those closely related to us. Righteousness means appropriateness; respecting the superior is its most important rule. Loving others according to who they are, and respecting superiors according to their ranks gives rise to the forms and distinctions of propriety (li) in social life. Unless social inequities have a true moral basis, government of the people is an impossibility.* (Chapter 20)

These statements illustrate the crucial relationship among the concepts of benevolence, righteousness, and propriety. Confucius advised that social interaction should begin with an assessment of the role relationship between oneself and others along two social dimensions: intimacy/

distance and superiority/inferiority. Behavior that favors people with whom one has a close relationship can be termed benevolence (*ren*); respecting those for whom respect is required by the relationship is called righteousness (*yi*); and acting according to previously established rites or social norms is called propriety (*li*).

In justice theory of Western social psychology, the concept of justice in human society is divided into two categories: procedural justice and distributive justice. Procedural justice refers to the types of procedures that should be used by members of a group to determine methods of resource distribution. Distributive justice is the particular method of resource distribution that is accepted by group members (Leventhal, 1976, 1980).

Confucius advocated that procedural justice in social interaction should follow the principle of respecting the superior. The person who occupies the superior position should play the role of the resource allocator. In choosing an appropriate method for distributive justice, the resource allocator should follow the principle of favoring the intimate. Furthermore, from the Confucian perspective, it is righteous to make decisions in this way.

Figure 1 diagrams the dynamics of Chinese resource allocation. Confucian ethics for ordinary people can be mapped into the model as displayed in Figure 2. In the psychological process of the resource allocator, the expressive component in the relationship (*guanxi*) corresponds to the concept of *ren*. *Yi* is to choose an appropriate rule for exchange by considering the expressive component (or affection) between the actors. After careful consideration, the final behavior should follow the social norm of politeness (*li*).

The Five Cardinal Rules of Confucianism

Emphasizing the principle of respecting the superior in procedural justice and the principle of favoring the intimate in distributive justice constitutes the formal structure of Confucian ethics for ordinary people. While this formal structure is manifest in many types of interpersonal relationships, Confucians made additional specific ethical demands on particular relationships. Confucians conceived five cardinal rules for the five major dyadic relationships, proposing that social interaction between members of each pair should proceed according to the Way of Humanity. Each of the roles in these five relationships is distinct, indicating that the core values emphasized in each are also different:

> Between father and son, there should be affection; between sovereign and subordinate, righteousness; between husband and wife, attention to their separate functions; between elder brother and younger, a proper order; and between friends, friendship. (The Works of Mencius, Chapter 3A: Duke Wen of Teng).

The Psychological Process of the Resource Allocator

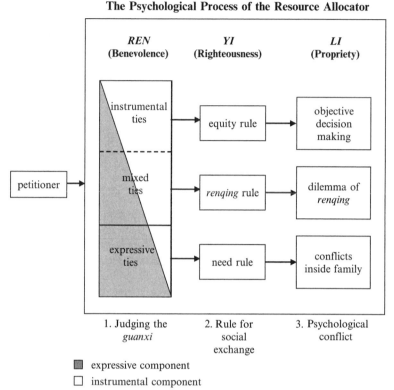

Figure 2. The Confucian ethical system of benevolence-righteousness-propriety for ordinary people (Adapted from Hwang 1995, p. 233)

Three of these rules were designed for regulating interpersonal relationships with the family (expressive ties). The other two are for mixed ties–friends and sovereign/subordinate. It should also be noted that, except for the relationship between friends, the relationships are all vertical ones between superiors and inferiors.

> *What are the things which humans consider righteous (yi)? Kindness on the part of the father, and filial duty on that of the son; gentleness on the part of the elder brother, and obedience on that of the younger; righteousness on the part of the husband, and submission on that of the wife; kindness on the part of the elders, and deference on that of juniors; benevolence on the part of the ruler, and loyalty on that of the minister. These are the ten things which humans consider being right. (Li Chi, Chapter 9: Li Yun)*

The passage above, which does not include a reference to relationships between friends, promotes the idea that social interaction should follow the principle of respecting the superior. In accordance with the idea of "the ten things of righteousness (*yi*)," persons who assume the roles of father, elder brother, husband, elders, or ruler should make decisions in line with the principles of kindness, gentleness, righteousness, kindness, and benevolence respectively. And for those who assume the roles of son, younger brother, wife, juniors, or minister, the principles of filial duty, obedience, submission, deference, loyalty and obedience to the instructions of the former group apply.

Among "the ten things of righteousness," Confucians most emphasized the importance of "kindness on the part of the father, and filial duty on that of the son." The reason the ethical arrangements between parents and child receive greatest emphasis in Confucianism is related to the Confucian ontology of life. In contemplating the origin of one's own life, Confucians do not suppose that there is a creator independently existing outside the world as Christians do. On the contrary, they recognize a simple and clear-cut fact on the basis of their cosmology. One's life is inherited from one's parents and ancestors. All Confucian ideas about filial piety are derived from this simple and indisputable fact.

The Psychosociogram

In my article "Chinese Relationalism: Theoretical Consideration and Methodological Consideration" (Hwang, 2000), I cited Ho's concept of methodological relationalism (Ho, 1991; 1998b). I also pointed out that the theoretical model of Face and Favor and the deep structure of Confucian ethics for ordinary people are constructed with the intention of depicting the person-in-relations, i.e., how a person interacts with others of different relationships. According to constructive realism, both are microworlds constructed by social scientists. In order to understand how personhood is manifested in the lifeworlds of East Asian people, social scientists must also consider all parties involved in a social event, i.e., persons-in-relation in daily life.

In that same article, I cited Hsu's (1971a) concept of the psychosociogram to illustrate how a person interacts with other persons-in-relation under the influence of Confucianism. Hsu's psychosociogram consists of seven irregular, concentric layers: unconscious, pre-conscious, unexpressed conscious, expressible conscious, intimate society and culture, operative society and culture, wider society and culture, and outer world (see Figure 3). Layer 4 in Figure 3 is labeled *expressible conscious*. It contains the feelings and ideas that individuals communicate to fellow human beings: love, hatred, greed, vision, and knowledge of the ways of doing things according to the moral, social, and technical standards of the culture. Layer 3 consists of significant others with whom the individual has intimate relationships, pets, cultural usage, and material collections. The individual's relationships with humans, animals, artifacts, and cultural rules in this layer tend to be

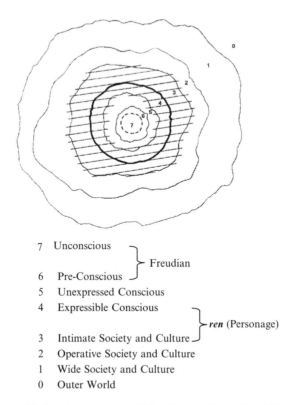

7   Unconscious ⎤
                  ⎬ Freudian
6   Pre-Conscious ⎦
5   Unexpressed Conscious
4   Expressible Conscious   ⎤
                             ⎬ *ren* (Personage)
3   Intimate Society and Culture ⎦
2   Operative Society and Culture
1   Wide Society and Culture
0   Outer World

Figure 3. The Psychosociogram of Man (Adapted from Hsu, 1971, p. 25)

"a matter of feeling rather than of usefulness" (Hsu, 1971a, p. 26). In contrast, the individual may establish only formal role relationships with those inhabiting Layer 2 by considering "their usefulness to him rather than his feeling toward them" (Hsu, 1971a, p. 26).

Hsu labeled the shaded area covering Layer 3 and 4 and partially covering Layers 2 and 5 *ren*, and roughly translated this Chinese word to English as *personage*. The Chinese conception of *ren* is based on an individual's transactions with fellow human beings. It implies that one may maintain a satisfactory level of psyche and interpersonal equilibrium within the shaded area only by endeavoring to be *ren* (*zuo ren*) and learning to be *ren* (*xue zuo ren*). Hsu defined the process of maintaining a constant state by fitting one's external behavior to the interpersonal standards of the society and culture as *psychosocial homeostasis* (Hsu, 1971a).

Comparing my analysis of Confucian cultural tradition with Hsu's works, it can be seen that the arrangement of the father-son relationship in Chinese society, i.e., the father-son axis (Hsu, 1971b), can be viewed as a manifestation of the principle of respecting the superior. The Confucian ethical system of benevolence-righteousness-propriety for ordinary people as depicted in Figure 2 corresponds to Hsu's psychosociogram in Figure 3. The shaded area of *ren* in Figure 3 signifies the expressive component between the resource allocator and others. *Usefulness* denotes the instrumental component between the dyad. The intimate society of Layer 3 consists of expressive ties and mixed ties, the operative society of Layer 2 is composed of instrumental ties. When a Chinese person interacts with others by following appropriate rules for social exchange, the phenomenology of that person's social world might be perceived in the manner described by Hsu's psychosociogram. In other words, my theoretical Face and Favor model describes the state of psychosocial homeostasis with the precise terminology of social exchange theory, and my analysis of Confucianism enables reinterpretation of the psychosociogram in terms of Confucian cultural tradition.

The Isomorphic Structures

From the viewpoint of constructive realism, the theoretical models of Face and Favor and Confucian ethics for ordinary people discussed in the previous subsections are both microworlds constructed by social scientists. Culture groups create the deep structure of their culture unconsciously with rationality, but the structure cannot be recognized intuitively through the rationality of ordinary people. The structure can only be recognized when revealed and reinterpreted by a researcher.

As soon as the unconscious model has been revealed by a social scientist, it can be reasonably assumed that the model can be applied to various cultures. For instance, in his book entitled *Structure of Social Life* Alan P. Fiske (1991) classified elementary forms of social behavior into four main categories: *Authority ranking* is an unsymmetrical relationship that is usually exhibited in the hierarchical order of status, which emphasizes the exercise of power and command as well as its accompanying respect and obedience. *Communal sharing* is a relationship of undifferentiated identity, community, group identification, or affection, which usually appears in the intimate relations between kin. *Equality matching* is a one-to-one relationship. Each party is separate but equal to one another, so emphasis is on reciprocity of equilibrium (or an eye for an eye), allocating resources equally without consideration of one's own contribution, and giving the same amount of compensation to those who occupy the same position. In the *market pricing* relationship, both parties compare merit of various goods on the basis of an intermodel metric of value, and calculate their own gains and losses to decide how to process the exchange.

A comparison between my theoretical Face and Favor model and these four modes reveals that authority ranking is implied in the relationship between petitioner and resource allocator, and the relationships of communal sharing, equality matching, and market pricing, respectively correspond to expressive ties, mixed ties, instrumental ties and their related rules of exchange in my model.

By the same token, comparing Fiske's four modes of interpersonal relationships with Confucian ethics for ordinary people, it can be seen that the procedural justice of respecting the superior corresponds to the concept of authority ranking, while the Confucian distributive justice of favoring the intimate corresponds to other modes of interpersonal relationships such as communal sharing, equality matching, and market pricing.

From the perspective of constructive realism (Wallner, 1994; Wallner & Jandl, 2001), the theoretical Face and Favor model constructed on the basis of social exchange theory can be strangified to the four elementary forms of interpersonal relationships proposed by Fiske (1991, 1992). It is applicable to other cultures as well. Using the linguistic records in Confucian scriptures to analyze the deep structure of Confucianism, it is clear that the theoretical Face and Favor model and Confucian ethics for ordinary people are isomphic to each other and can be strangified from one to another. Nevertheless, linguistic analysis reveals the specific features of interpersonal relationships in Confucian society.

MODERNIZATION OF CONFUCIAN SOCIETIES

Considering my theoretical models in the context of constructive realism, the meaning of modernization for Confucian societies is clear. The five cardinal ethics emphasized in Confucianism are derived from the deep structure of Confucian ethics for ordinary people as depicted in Figure 2. Using the psychosociogram as illustrated in Figure 3, in traditional Confucian society, individuals in daily life mainly interacts with those living in their intimate society. Social statuses are mainly determined by consanguineous relationships, and so it can be called an ascribed status. Therefore, it is very likely for individuals to interact with others in terms of Confucian ethics.

Under the impact of modernization, a variety of social systems have developed that are different from the lifeworlds of people in traditional Confucian societies. For example, individuals need to use various microworlds of knowledge to perform production work. Social status is mainly determined by a person's ability to perform work tasks or other forms of power, and is therefore labeled *achieved status*. According to modern organizational principles, individuals should follow the equity rule to interact with others of instrumental ties in such an operating society. But, under the influence of Confucian ethics for ordinary people, the principles of respecting the superior and favoring the intimate might mingle with imported organizational ideas to affect an individual's interpersonal relationships in the operating society. In the next section, an example from empirical research is used to illustrate this point, and the motivation to work in East Asian societies explored.

Work Motivation in a Confucian Society

After completing a college education, an individual may find a job within the social system and begin to use a particular microworld of knowledge to perform production tasks in the operating society. Why people will work hard under such conditions is a question frequently asked in organizational psychology. Since 1960, a series of theories on work motivation has been developed by Western psychologists, including expectancy theory (Vroom, 1964), equity theory (Adams, 1965), goal setting theory (Locke & Latham, 1990), and work characteristic theory (Hackman & Oldman, 1976).

Liu (2001) reviewed these theories and found that they reflect the profound cultural influence of Western individualism. In constructing theories on work motivation, most Western psychologists paid attention to the satisfaction of the individual's hierarchy of need, evaluation of work action, social comparison of input and outcome, achieving short-term goals, and the job design for facilitating the individual's motives. They scarcely mentioned future development of the job, emotional reactions to work conditions, or the possible influence of complicated interpersonal relationships in the work situation.

Liu (2001) therefore adopted a bottom-up research strategy and interviewed 524 employees from enterprises in Taiwan. He used the critical incident technique (Flanagan, 1954) to collect specific cases in which subjects either wanted to work hard or didn't want to work hard. He then constructed a Work Motivation Scale on the basis of the data thus collected, and administered it to 750 employees working in different types of enterprises. Responses were analyzed with factor analysis. Items with low factor loadings were deleted, and four factors were obtained.

Items on the first factor, Future Development, were related to the challenge of the task, the potential for future development, sense of achievement, sense of mission, opportunity for promotion, the possibility of realizing one's ideal, and so on. Factor 2 was labeled Horizontal Competition. It consisted of items relating to caring about one's own work performance, aggressive competition in work, unwillingness to lose to others, taking care of one's face, and willingness to work hard to obtain a promotion, an increase in salary, or to be recognized by the supervisor.

Most items on Factor 3, Vertical Identification, were related to evaluation of and attitude towards the supervisor. For example, they included whether the supervisor has to shoulder responsibility or not, whether the supervisor takes the subordinates' benefits into consideration, whether the supervisor is supported by colleagues, or whether the supervisor is worthy of trust and loyal devotion. Contents of items on Factor 4 were mostly related to feelings to the current work environment, such as frustration, being betrayed, being cheated, being in a dilemma, being indecisive, and so on. Factor 4 was labeled Work Environment.

From the perspective of Confucian relationalism, the contents of these four factors have very important meanings that require elaboration. Both Factor 1 and 4 are related to the dimension of temporality. Factor 1 implies the opportunity to develop in ones' job, and Factor 4 measures one's subjective feelings about the conditions of one's current work. Factors 2 and 3 are specialized to measure the interpersonal relationships in one's work environment: Factor 2 relates to one's horizontal relationships, while Factor 3 concentrates on vertical relationships.

Under the influence of Confusion relationalism, individuals tend to perceive the self as integrated with society; the self can not be removed from one's complicated interpersonal network (Hwang, 2000). In Chinese society, answers to the question of why people work hard are not restricted to the satisfaction of personal need, equity in resource distribution, or rational assessment of the work environment. For most people in Confucian societies, having a job means settling down in an interpersonal network both physically and psychologically. Such a state can be evaluated from temporal and social dimensions. For the temporal dimension, one should consider not only the present condition of one's work, but also the potential for future development. For the social dimension, in facing the complicated interpersonal relationships in one's work environment, one has to consider not only vertical relationship with superiors, but also horizontal relationship with colleagues (Hwang, 1997–8).

Long-Term Orientation

In another study, Liu (2001) surveyed 1111 employees from various types of enterprises to investigate the connection between the four aspects of work motivation and the intention to work hard using correlation and regression analysis. The correlation coefficients between the four motivational factors and the intention to work hard were .49, .37, .40, and .37 respectively. When the effects of intercorrelation were controlled with partial correlation, the coefficients of partial correlation became .29, .14, .33, and .14. Both sets of the aforementioned coefficients reached the statistical level of significance ($P < .01$). A regression analysis with the four motivational factors as independent variables and the intention to work hard as the dependent variable resulted in the standardized regression coefficients (β) of .30, .15, .28, .14 respectively. All reached the statistical level of significance (P < .01). The adjusted R^2 was .37. All these statistical analyses indicate that there are substantial correlations between the intention to work hard and the four motivational factors measured by Liu's instrument.

So far as the goal and performance are concerned, the temporal dimension has different meanings in Eastern and Western societies. Chinese people tend to display a long-term orientation in pursuing the achievement of their goals (Hofstede, 1993), and don't care much about short-term performance or failure. In order to pursue a long-term goal, they are willing to patiently accept long-term training or education, establish their personal relationships carefully, and accumulate wealth with the spirit of hard work and thriftiness. The resources thus accumulated can be utilized to pursue higher achievement (Hwang, 1999). When a psychologist studies work motivation in a Chinese society, it is inadequate to study only short-term goals as suggested by goal setting theory, or the satisfaction of personal needs. The Chinese style is a process of pursuing future performance and development through continuous learning and self-improvement. Frustrations and difficulties may be encountered in the process of striving for the goal. The Confucian cultural tradition emphasizes the importance of self-cultivation by purging one's desires and ambitions or by self-effacing with with modesty in such a situation. It also promotes such work values as "the more frustration, the more bravery" and "being unflinching despite repeated setbacks," rather than rational evaluation and choice among costs and benefits of various alternatives. Therefore, feelings about current conditions and future development of work may become a motive for hard work among Chinese people.

CONCLUSION

In a keynote speech delivered to the Third Conference of Asian Social Psychology, Kim (2000) pointed out several limitations of using Confucian philosophy to explain the behavior of East Asian societies. He argued that "Confucian philosophy can be used as a starting point for research, but not as the end point. Confucian ideas can be used to develop hypotheses, constructs, and theories about human development and relationships. Once these ideas are developed, researchers need to test and verify them empirically" (Kim, 2000, p. 283).

I generally agree with Kim's arguments. Nevertheless, I also believe that all theories about human development or relationships should be constructed on the grounds of a sound philosophy. The attempt to construct a theory about human relationships on the basis of Confucian ideas is no exception to this rule. Therefore, this article proposes the epistemological strategy of using constructive realism as the philosophical basis for developing indigenous psychology, and advocates that the important goals for indigenization of psychology in East Asian societies are to ascertain the deep structure of various cultural traditions, construct microworlds of scientific theory, and use these microworlds as a frame of reference for conducting empirical research on people's lifeworlds. In this article I have presented a series of models on Confucian relationalism with several examples to explain how to conduct empirical research with indigenous psychology in East Asian societies. It is hoped that such an epistemological strategy can be used as a starting point, not as the end point, for future development of East Asian indigenous psychology.

REFERENCES

Adams, J. S. (1965). Inequity in social exchange. In E. Berkowitz (Ed.), *Advances in experimental social psychology, Vol. 2* (pp. 267–299). New York: Academic Press.

Berry, J. W. (1969). On cross-cultural comparability. *International Journal of Psychology, 4*, 119–128.

Berry, J. W. (1989). Imposed *etics-emics-derived* etics: The operationalization of a compelling idea. *International Journal of Psychology, 24*, 721–735.

Berry, J. W. (1993). Psychology in and of Canada: One small step toward a universal psychology. In U. Kim & J. W. Berry (Eds.). *Indigenous psychologies: Research and experience in cultural context* (pp. 260–275). Newbury Park, CA: Sage.

Berry, J. W., & Kim, U. (1993). The way ahead: From indigenous psychologies to a universal psychology. In U. Kim & J. W. Berry (Eds.), *Indigenous psychologies: Research and experience in cultural context* (pp. 277–280). Newbury Park, CA: Sage.

Berry, J. W., Poortinga, Y. H., Segall, M. H., & Dasen, P. R. (1992). *Cross-cultural psychology: Research and applications.* Cambridge: Cambridge University Press.

Brubarker, R. (1984). *The Limits of rationality: An essay on the social and moral thought of Max Weber* (pp. 35–43). London: George Allen & Unwin.

Deutsch, M. (1975). Equity, equality, and need: What determines which value will be used as the basis of distributive justice? *Journal of Social Issues, 31*, 137–149.

Eldridge, J. (1999). Culture at work. In H. Beyan & P. Glavanis (Eds.), *Patterns of social inequality* (pp. 97–108). New York: Longman.

Enriquez, V. (1977). Filipino psychology in the Third World. *Philippine Journal of Psychology, 10*, 3–18.

Enriquez, V. G. (1979). Towards cross-cultural knowledge through cross-indigenous methods and perspectives. In J. L. M. Binnie-Dawson, G.H. Blowers, & R. Hoosain (Eds.), *Perspectives in Asian cross-cultural psychology* (pp. 29–41). Lisse: Swets & Zeitlinger, BV.

Enriquez, V. G. (1981). *Decolonizing the Filipino psyche.* Quezon City: Psychology Research and Training House.

Enriquez, V. G. (1982). *Towards a Filipino psychology.* Quezon City: Psychology Research and Training House.

Enriquez, V. (1993). Developing a Filipino psychology. In U. Kim & J. Berry, *Indigenous psychologies: Research and experience in cultural context* (pp. 152–169). Newbury Park, CA: Sage.

Evans-Pritchard, E. E. (1964). *Social anthropology and other essays.* New York: Free Press.

Fiske, A. P. (1991). *Structures of social life: The four elementary forms of human relations.* New York: The Free Press.

Fiske, A. P. (1992). The four elementary forms of society: Framework for a unified theory of social relations. *Psychological Review, 99*, 688–723.

Flanagan, J. C. (1954). The critical incident technique. *Psychological Bulletin, 51*, 327–358.

Greenberg, J. and Cohen, R. L. (1982). Why justice? Normative and instrumental interpretations. In J. Greenberg and R. L. Cohen (Eds.). *Equity and justice in social behavior* (pp. 437–467). New York: Academic Press.

Greenfield, P. M. (2000). Three approaches to the psychology of culture: Where do they come from? Where can they go? *Asian Journal of Social Psychology, 3*, 223–240.

Habermas, J. (1978). *Theory of communicative action. Vol.II, Lifeworld and system: A critique of functionalist reason.* Boston: Beacon Press.

Hackman, J. R., & Oldham, G. R. (1976). Motivation through the design of work: Test of a theory. *Organizational Behavior and Human Performance, 16*, 250–279.

Heiderger, M. (1966). *Discourse on thinking.* New York: Harper and Row.

Hempel, C. G. (1965). *Aspects of scientific explanation.* New York: Macmillan.

Hempel, C. G. (1966). *Philosophy of natural science.* Englewood Cliff, New Jersey: Prentice-Hall.

Henry, P. (1986). Indigenous religion and the transformation of peripheral society. In J. K. Hadden & A. Shupe (Eds.), *Prophetic religion and politics* (pp. 123–150). New York: Paragon House.

Hermans, J. M., & Kempen, J. G. (1998). Moving cultures: The perilous problem of cultural dichotomy in a globalized society. *American Psychologist, 53*, 1111–1120.

Ho, D. Y. F. (1988). Asian psychology: A dialogue on indigenization and beyond. In A. C. Paranjpe, D. Y. F. Ho, & R. W. Rieber (Eds.), *Asian contributions to psychology* (pp. 53–77). New York: Praeger.

Ho, D. Y. F. (1991). Relational orientation and methodological relationalism. *Bulletin of the Hong Kong Psychological Society, 26–27*, 81–95.

Ho, D.Y. F. (1998a). Indigenous psychologies: Asian perspectives. *Journal of cross-cultural psychology, 29*, 88–103.

Ho, D. Y. F. (1998b). Interpersonal relationships and relationship dominance: An analysis based on methodological relationalism. *Asian Journal of Social Psychology, 1*, 1–16.

Hofstede, G. (1993). Cultural constraints in management theories. *Academy of Management Executive, 7*, 81–94.

Hong, Y. Y., Morris, M. W., Chiu, C. Y., & Veronica, B. M. (2000). Multicultural minds: A dynamic constructivist approach to culture and cognition. *American Psychologist, 55*, 709–720.

Hsu, F. L. K. (1971a). Psychological homeostasis and *jen*: Conceptual tools for advancing psychological anthropology. *American Anthropologist, 73*, 23–44.

Hsu, F. L. K. (1971b). A hypotheses on kinship and culture. In F. L. K. Hsu (Ed.), *Kinship and culture* (pp. 3–29). Chicago: Aldine.

Huntington, S. (1993). The clash of civilizations? *Foreign Affairs, 27*, 22–49.

Huntington, S. (1997). *The clash of civilizations and the remaking of world order.* New York: Simon & Schuster.

Husserl, E. (1970). *The crisis of European sciences and transcendental phenomenology: An introduction to phenomenological philosophy* (E. Hysserl, Trans.). Evanston: Northwestern University Press.

Hwang, K. K. (1987). Face and favor: the Chinese power game. *American Journal of Sociology, 92*(4), 944–974.

Hwang, K. K. (1988). *Confucianism and East Asian modernization* (in Chinese). Taipei: Chu-Lin Book Co.

Hwang, K. K. (1995). *Knowledge and action: A social-psychological interpretation of Chinese cultural tradition* (In Chinese). Taipei: Sin-Li.

Hwang, K. K. (1997–8). *Guanxi* and *mientze*: Conflict resolution in Chinese society. *Intercultural Communication Studies, 3*, 17–37.

Hwang, K. K. (1999). Filial piety and loyalty: The types of social identification in Confucianism. *Asian Journal of Social Psychology, 2*, 129–149.

Hwang, K. K. (2000). On Chinese relationalism: Theoretical construction and methodological considerations. *Journal for the Theory of Social Behavior, 30*, 155–178.

Hwang, K. K., & Yang, C. F. (2000). Guest Editors' Preface. *Asian Journal of Social Psychology,
3*, 183.

Kim, U. (2000). Indigenous, cultural, and cross-cultural psychology: A theoretical, conceptual, and epistemological analysis. *Asian Journal of Social Psychology, 3*, 265–287.

Kim, U., & Berry, J. (1993). Introduction. In U. Kim & J. Berry (Eds.), *Indigenous cultural psychologies: Research and experience in cultural context* (pp. 1–29). Newbury Park, CA: Sage.

Kitayama, S., & Markus, H.R. (1999). Yin and yang of the Japanese self: The cultural psychology of personality coherence. In D. Cervone & Y. Shoda (Eds.), *The coherence of personality: Social cognitive bases of personality consistency, variability, and organization*
(pp.242–302). New York: Guilford Press.

Kim, U., Park, Y. S., & Park, D. (2000). The challenger of cross-cultural psychology: The role
of the indigenous psychologies. *Journal of Cross-Cultural Psychology, 31*, 63–75.

Kuhn, T. (1987). What are scientific revolutions? In L. Kruger, L. J. Datson, & M. Heidelberger
(Eds.), *The probabilistic revolution* (pp. 7–22). Cambridge, Mass.: MIT Press.

Lakatos, I. (1970). Falsification and the methodology of scientific research programmes. In
I. Lakatos & A. Musgrave (Eds.), *Criticism and the growth of knowledge* (pp. 91–196).
Cambridge: Cambridge University Press.

Lakatos, I. (1978). Popper in demarcation and induction. *The methodology of scientific research
programmes*. Cambridge University Press.

Lerner, M. J. (1975). The just motive in social behavior: introduction. *Journal of Social Issues,
31*, 1–19.

Lerner, M. J. (1977). The just motive in social behavior: Some hypotheses as to its origins and
forms. *Journal of Personality, 45*, 1–52.

Lerner, M. J. (1981). The justice motive in human relations: Some thoughts on what we know
and need to know about justice. In M. Lerner and S. C. Lerner (Ed.), *The Justice motive in
social behavior: Adapting to times of scarcity and change* (pp. 1–35). New York: Plenum
Press.

Leventhal, G. S. (1976). Fairness in social relationships. In J. Thibant, J. Spence, & R. T.
Carson (Eds.), *Contemporary topics in social psychology* (pp. 221–239). Morristown, NJ:
General Learning Press.

Leventhal, G. S. (1980). What should be done with equity theory? In K. J. Gergen, M. S.
Greenburg, & R. H Wills (Eds.), *Social exchange: Advances in theory and research* (pp.
27–55). New York: Plenum Press.

Levi-Strauss, C. (1976). *Structural anthropology.* (M. Layton, Trans.). New York: Basic Books.

Levy-Bruhl, L. (1910/1966). *How natives think,* (L. A. Clare, Trans.). New York: Washington
Square Press.

Liu, C. M. (2001). The development of an integrated model of work motivation: A bottom-
up inquiry process. *Chinese Journal of Psychology, 43*, 189–206.

Locke, E. A. & Latham, G. P. (1990). *A theory of goal setting and task performance.* Englewood
Cliffs, NJ: Prentice-Hall.

Piaget, J. (1972). *The principles of genetic epistemology.* London: Routledge & Kegan Paul.

Poortinga, Y. H. (1996). Indigenous psychology: Scientific ethnocentrism in a new guise? In
J. Pandey, D. Sinha, & D. P. S. Bhawuk (Eds.), *Asian contributions to cross-cultural psychology* (pp. 59–71). Thousand Oaks, CA: Sage Publications.

Poortinga, Y. H. (1997). Towards convergence. In J. W. Berry, Y. H. Poortinga, J. Pandey, P. R.
Dasen, T. S. Saraswathi, M. H. Segall, & C. Kagitcibasi (Eds.), *Handbook of cross-cultural
psychology, Second Edition, Vol. 1,* (pp. 347–387). Boston, MA: Allyn & Bacon.

Poortinga, Y. H. (1999). Do differences in behavior imply a need for different psychologies?
Applied Psychology: An International Review, 48, 419–432.

Popper, K.R. (1963). *Conjectures and refutations: The growth of scientific knowledge*. London: Routledge & Kegan Paul.

Popper, K.R. (1972). *Objective knowledge: An evolutionary approach*. Oxford: Oxford University Press.

Schlick, M. (1936). Meaning and verification. *The philosophical review, 45,* 339–369.

Shen, V. (1994). *Confucianism, Taoism and constructive realism*. Bruck: WUV-Universitäsverlag.

Shiraev, E. & Levy, D. (2001). *Introduction to cross-cultural psychology*. London: Allyn and Bacon.

Shweder, R. A. (1996). The "mind" of cultural psychology. In P. Baltes and U. Staudinger (Eds.), *Interactive minds: Life-span perspectives on the social foundations of cognition* (pp. 430–436). New York: Cambridge University Press.

Shweder, R. A. (2000). The psychology of practice and the practice of the three psychologies. *Asian journal of social psychology, 3,* 207–222

Shweder, R. A., Goodnow, J., Hatano, G., LeVine, R., Markus, H., & Miller, P. (1998). The cultural psychology of development: One mind, many mentalities. In W. Damon (Eds.), *Handbook of child psychology, Vol. 1,* 865–937. New York: John Wiley & Sons.

Sinha, D. (1984). Psychology in the context of Third World development. *International Journal of Psychology, 19,* 17–29.

Sinha, D. (1986). *Psychology in a Third World country*: The Indian Experience. New Delhi: Sage.

Triandis, H. C. (2000). Dialectics between cultural and cross-cultural psychology. *Asian Journal of Social Psychology, 3,* 185–195.

Taylor, E. B. (1871/1958). *Primitive culture*. London.

Vroom, V. H. (1964). *Work and motivation*. New York: Wiley.

Wallner, F. (1994). *Constructive realism: Aspects of new epistemological movement*. Wien: W. Braumuller.

Walsh, B. J., & Middleton, J. R. (1984). *The transforming vision: Shaping a Christian world view*. Downers Grove, IL: Inter-Varsity Press.

Weber, M. (1921/1963). *The sociology of religion*. Boston: Beacon Press.

Weber, M. (1930/1992). *The Protestant ethic and the spirit of capitalism*. (T. Parsons, Trans.). London: Routledge.

Wittgenstein, L. (1922/1961). *Tractatus logico-philosophicus*, (D. F. Pears & B.F. McGuinnies, Trans.). London: Routledge & Kegan Paul.

Wittgenstein, L. (1945/1958). *Philosophical investigations*. (G. E. M. Anscombe, Trans.). Oxford: Blackwell.

Yang, K. S. (1993). Why do we need to develop an indigenous Chinese psychology? *Indigenous Psychological Research in Chinese Societies, 1,* 6–88. (In Chinese).

Yang, K. S. (1997). Indigenous compatibility in psychological research and its related problems. *Indigenous Psychological Research in Chinese Societies, 8,* 75–120. (In Chinese.)

Yang, K. S. (1999). Towards an indigenous Chinese psychology: A selective review of methodological, theoretical, and empirical accomplishments. *Chinese Journal of Psychology, 41,* 181–211.

Yang, K. S. (2000). Monocultural and cross-cultural indigenous approaches: The royal road to the development of a balanced global psychology. *Asian Journal of Social Psychology, 3,* 241–263.

Chapter 5

From Decolonizing Psychology to the Development of a Cross-Indigenous Perspective in Methodology
The Philippine Experience

Rogelia Pe-Pua

It all began in 1975 when a postgraduate student at the University of the Philippines Psychology Department decided to take a different approach in her field research. Carmen Santiago (1975, 1977) was interested in studying the concept of *pagkalalaki*, a term that is difficult to translate to English but would roughly refer to maleness, manhood, manliness, machismo, or all of these. She started reviewing the literature and found that the available literature (mostly Western) was not relevant to this Filipino concept. So she ventured out into a Philippine village without a clear-cut research design or a literature review, and started interacting with the local residents. What was clear to her was a single question for the men whose views she was interested in obtaining: What is the meaning of *pagkalalaki*? In the course of her finding the best strategies for conducting this research, she discovered the *pakapa-kapa* approach, which was later defined by Torres (1982, p. 171) as "a suppositionless approach to social scientific investigations. As implied by the term itself, *pakapa-kapa* is an approach characterized by groping, searching and probing into an unsystematized mass of social data to obtain order, meaning and directions for research". *Pakapa-kapa* provided the impetus for encouraging Filipino social scientists to discover methods of research that are indigenous to Filipino participants. *Pakapa-kapa* was a turning point in Philippine social science research.

This chapter will discuss the history of the development of indigenous methods in the Philippines, including the epistemological basis for these methods. Specifically, it will explain the basis of indigenization efforts in Philippine psychology, the debate within cross-cultural psychology on the nature and value of indigenization, the application of indigenous methods, and a critique of these methods.

DECOLONIZING PHILIPPINE PSYCHOLOGY

The seeds for developing indigenous research methods in the Philippines were planted during the early years of the 1970s when Virgilio Enriquez (Carmen Santiago's professor) spearheaded a movement known as *Sikolohiyang Pilipino* (Filipino psychology) that calls for understanding Filipino thought and experience from a Filipino perspective or orientation (Enriquez, 1975). The idea of the "indigenous" then becomes relevant in relation to the Western psychology tradition (the exogenous, the colonial) that has dominated the teaching and practice of psychology in the Philippines and which has resulted in an understanding of the Filipino that has been deemed inappropriate and insignificant. For instance, Filipinos' predisposition to be indirect when they communicate was regarded as being dishonest and socially ingratiating and as reflecting a deceptive verbal description of reality (Enriquez, 1992). In reality, i.e. using a Filipino perspective, this indirectness serves a number of purposes, for example, reflecting concern for the feelings of others to avoid the other person losing face or getting embarrassed if directly confronted with negativity, conforming with the norm of humility and modesty by not directly recognizing one's own ability and achievements, and so on.

With the shift to an indigenous psychology, Enriquez and his colleagues and students were able to unravel relevant Filipino characteristics and explain them through the eyes of the native Filipino. This effort has resulted in a body of knowledge that includes indigenous concepts and methods. One such concept that unfolded was *kapwa* (shared identity), which is at the core of Filipino social psychology, and which is at the heart of the structure of Filipino values. Enriquez refuted the widely-acclaimed observation by an American researcher that the main Filipino value is *pakikisama*, or maintaining smooth interpersonal relations, which would explain why Filipinos try to go along with the group or majority decision (conformity) (Lynch, 1961, 1973). Instead, Enriquez clarified that *pakikisama* is simply a colonial/accommodative surface value, and that the core value is *pakikipagkapwa*, which means treating the other person as *kapwa* or fellow human being (Enriquez, 1978, 1994). The discovery of *kapwa* and the articulation of its structure have an implication for the way we conduct indigenous research which I will elaborate later.

The history, nature, and contribution of *Sikolohiyang Pilipino* have been synthesized in a paper by Pe-Pua and Protacio-Marcelino (2000). We outlined its different filiations or influential traditions, its major characteristics as an indigenous Asian psychology, the development of indigenous concepts and theories, its impact on the teaching of psychology, its areas of application, and the debates within *Sikolohiyang Pilipino*. Much of the strategy for discovering *Sikolohiyang Pilipino* is based on assessing historical and socio-cultural realities, understanding the local language, rediscovering the dimensions of the Filipino character and explaining psychological concepts using a Filipino perspective. These resulted in a body of knowledge that includes indigenous concepts and methods, in short, a psychology that is appropriate and significant to Filipinos. We emphasized that indigenous psychologies such as *Sikolohiyang Pilipino* are making a contribution to a truly universal psychology.

Initial work on developing *Sikolohiyang Pilipino* concentrated on a type of indigenization that is based largely on simple translation of concepts, methods, theories, and measures into Filipino. For example, psychological tests were translated into the local language and modified in content so that a Philippine-type version of the originally borrowed test was produced. On the other hand, another type of indigenization was given more emphasis after the translation attempts failed to capture or express a truly Filipino psychology. This attempt is called *indigenization from within* (as opposed to *indigenization from without*), which means looking for the indigenous psychology from within the culture itself and not just clothing a foreign body with a local dress. In fact, the word *indigenization* is erroneous here because how can you indigenize something that is already indigenous? *Cultural revalidation* is a better term (Enriquez, 1992).

FROM *PAKAPA-KAPA* TO A PARADIGM SHIFT

As mentioned above, *pakapa-kapa* was a turning point. *Pakapa-kapa* "implies an exploration into cultural, social or psychological data without the chains of overriding theoretical frameworks borrowed from observations outside the focus of investigation" (Torres, 1982, p. 171). This has some advantages.

> First, the presuppositionless approach results in putting aside, even if momentarily, so-called "universal" concepts of psychology. Instead, *pakapa-kapa* leads to discovering cultural particularities. Second, *pakapa-kapa* enables the Filipino psychologist to be more creative in his tools and data base. With this approach, he is not tied down to experimental and other similar techniques. Neither is he hampered by the use of procedures which may locally be irrelevant, difficult to apply, or costly. Instead, *pakapa-kapa* works along traditionally accepted probe procedures. (Torres, 1982, p. 173)

Pakapa-kapa paved the way for a close examination of the loopholes of Philippine social research: many of the research topics were not relevant to the needs of the people being studied, (Western) methods were inappropriate to the ways of the people, definitions were based on Western theories, and there was an overemphasis on data rather than on the process of doing research. As an alternative, Santiago and Enriquez (1976) proposed ways of making research more Filipino-oriented. The resulting methods were considered indigenous—not imported nor invented, but natural or existing patterns of behavior (not methods), discovered and developed as research methods.

INDIGENOUS METHODS

A number of indigenous methods have been written about, drawing on the Philippine experience. I will outline here some of the distinctive ones, related to the well-known participant observation, interview, focus group discussion, and personality testing methods.

The Indigenous Approach to Participant Observation

The indigenous methods developed in the Philippines have been likened to field methods more familiar to anthropologists than psychologists (Sevilla, 1985). This comparison is correct to a certain extent. The indigenous approach however gives participant observation greater precision

> from the minimum of establishing and maintaining empathy through *pag-dalaw-dalaw* ("informal visiting", "dropping in" or the more culturally idiomatic *"napadaan lang po"* in "passing by"), to a more direct interaction in the culture bearer's natural habitat *pakikisalamuha* ("interactive research"). Data quality changes from *pakikipanuluyan* ("live-in visitor") to *pakikipanira-han* ("participant dweller"), and *pagpisan* ("live-in, one of us, participant"). While they all partake of the defining characteristics of what is simply called "participant observation" in Western anthropology, be it *pakikipanirahan* or *pagpisan*, the Filipino anthropologist knows which type of data to trust on the basis of the kind of participant observation used. It is indeed a difference in kind and not just a difference in form. A higher data quality is expected, for example, from *pakikipamuhay* ("living with") as against *pakikipanuluyan*. (Enriquez, 1994, p. 58)

Let us examine some of these indigenous variants of participant observation. It must be noted that within these variants, indigenous researchers incorporate specific techniques of data gathering such as interviewing and observation.

"Nakikiugaling pagmamasid" was coined by Bennagen (1985) to describe his version of participant observation as he worked with the

Agtas (an indigenous tribe) of Isabela in northern Philippines. *Pagmamasid* means observation, and *nakikiugali* means adopting the behaviors and ways of a particular group as one's own, which was what Bennagen did because he is not an Agta. But, he added that this process of *pakikiugali* includes not just observable behavior but mental behavior as well: "It is important that one embraces not just the external ways, but becomes one in thought as well—have the readiness of the mind to understand them" (my translation) (Bennagen, 1985, p. 406). In this methodological approach, the researchers have to embrace the culture of the group they are studying as their own, at least temporarily, in order to fully understand and appreciate it. Afterwards, they will look at this culture again from a distance in order to organize the data they have obtained in a logical and reasonable process that is true to the culture they have studied.

Pagdalaw-dalaw (frequent visits) also refers to a behavior Filipinos are used to. It is expressed as *pangangapitbahay* (visiting neighbors), *pangangapitkuwarto* (visiting people in the next room), and others. Two university students used *pagdalaw-dalaw* to conduct research among the garbage scavengers of Malabon, Rizal (Gepigon & Francisco, 1978). They visited the *tambakan* (dump sites) which was the source of livelihood of these scavengers. It was impossible for them to reside there, even if they wanted to, for obvious reasons. Nor could they participate in their activities for it would mean competing with their participants for a meager source of income. The best thing to do was *pagdalaw-dalaw* which helped the participants get used to the researchers. While the initial reception was characterized by suspicion towards the researchers, the relationship between researchers and participants eventually developed into one of friendship and trust. In this study, the researchers also discovered the importance of recognizing "dress code". It was imprudent for them to come in attire similar to the scavengers (i.e., tattered t-shirts and pants) in an attempt to be accepted as one of them – to do so was to cast insult on their perceived low status. So they came in casual jeans and t-shirts and blended quite well with their research participants (*pakikibagay* or being in accord with).

The word *pakikisama* was first used in Philippine psychological literature to refer to a supposed Filipino value. Then it was identified as the highest level of social interaction under the *Ibang-Tao* category. This time, Nery (1979) used it to call the variant of participant observation which he employed in his study of "callboys" in a bar in Manila. Nery knew that if he were to use the traditional anthropological participant observation method, the risk would be very high – either that he would become a callboy himself, or a client, or a pimp at the very least. So, instead, he started out by simply frequenting the hangouts of the callboys, inviting them to sit down and drink in the bar. Then, he invited them to eat or drink outside the bar or at his residence. These were timed to coincide with free time of the callboys. However, despite the attractiveness of the *pakikisama* approach, there were some inconveniences that he had to overcome. But, it still proved to be easier to handle than the participant observation technique which would have produced some ethical problems, and entailed extremely unrealistic and serious sacrifices on the researcher's part.

Panunuluyan ("residing in the research setting") was first articulated as a method by Nicdao-Henson (1982), and then further elaborated by San Juan and Soriaga (1985). Nicdao-Henson lived in the village of Tiaong, Quezon for three months in the house of her cousin who was married and had three children. The house was located at the center of town so other parts of the village were accessible from there. By living in the community, she gained an in-depth understanding of village life, both the common activities and the unique or special occurrences. This depth is reflected in her report on the concept of time among the residents, conceptualized as much in a symbolic way as in a temporal sense.

San Juan and Soriaga (1985) define *panunuluyan* as a method where the researcher lives, sleeps in the house of, and shares food with a host who has extended hospitality to the researcher. The host can be a friend, a relative, or someone referred to the researcher by a friend or a relative. *Panunuluyan* is more in keeping with Filipino culture compared to staying in a hotel when one is traveling. San Juan and Soriaga link this behavior to a way of fulfilling one's need to connect with our fellow human beings (*kapwa*). They see it as a form of *pagdalaw* (visiting) since the stay is temporary and short-term, the host family is present, the visitor will be given a bed and food, money is usually not exchanged, and the visitor is treated as a guest. (But, this must be distinguished from Gepigon and Francisco's *pagdalaw-dalaw,* or frequent visits, which do not include living with research participants.) They also draw the line between *panunuluyan* and *paninirahan* (residing more permanently), and *pananahanan* (assuming responsibilities related to taking care of the home), and *pakikisuno* (even less short-term, such as an overnight stay). San Juan and Soriaga provided a detailed manual-like discussion of the art of *panunuluyan*, covering the following topics: perspectives of the visitor and the host and the relationship between the two parties; responsibilities and expectations related to sleeping, sharing food, and other activities; the importance of *pakikiramdam* (sensitivity to cues), and having a *tulay* ("bridge" or middle person); and the step-by-step process (preparation, the travel, observation, from *pakikisuno* to *panunuluyan*; greeting and getting to know the host; settling down and sharing responsibilities in the house; establishing rapport; getting on with data gathering; saying goodbyes and thank-you and departure); and ethical issues.

The Indigenous Interview

Pagtatanong-tanong is a Filipino word which means "asking questions." The repetition of *tanong* (question) to *tanong-tanong* indicates apparent casualness when the inquirer is truly determined to get answers to his questions. *Pagtatanong-tanong* is a behavior that Filipinos ordinarily exhibit. Filipinos are used to spending hours chatting and exchanging questions and ideas. Not many Filipinos are exposed to the interview, but definitely, all Filipinos are used to *pagtatanong-tanong* (Pe-Pua, 1985, 1989).

Pagtatanong-tanong was first documented as a research method by Gonzales (1982) although what Santiago (1975) referred to as *pakikipanayam* (interview) was actually in the tradition of *pagtatanong-tanong*. Nicdao-Henson (1982) also called one of her techniques *pagtatanong-tanong* in her study of the indigenous concept of time. Nonetheless, Gonzales was the first to write about the reasons and characteristics of this method. She detailed the goals of the method, characteristics of the person using the method, the venue, time and occasion, the respondents, and the step-by-step process of *pagtatanong-tanong*. Pe-Pua (1985, 1989) later expounded on these characteristics, explained the underlying assumptions and elevated it to the status of a cross-cultural method after trialing it with non-Filipino participants in Hawaii, USA.

Pagtatanong-tanong is sometimes interpreted as an informal interview or at best an "improvisation" that approximates the interview method, but this is not correct. Although there are some similarities, *pagtatanong-tanong* is basically different from the interview. Besides, the use of the local term *pagtatanong-tanong* highlights the importance of tapping culturally appropriate indigenous research methods without claiming exclusivity to it for the particular culture (Pe-Pua. 1985, 1989).

Pagtatanong-tanong has four major characteristics: (1) It is participatory in nature, and the participant has an input in the structure of the interaction in terms of defining its direction and in terms of time management. (2) The researcher and the participant are equal in status; both parties may ask questions for about the same length of time. (4) It is appropriate and adaptive to the conditions of the group of participants in that it conforms to existing group norms. (4) It is integrated with other indigenous research methods (Pe-Pua, 1985, 1989).

Santiago (1975) used *pagtatanong-tanong* very sensitively on a culturally sensitive topic, *pagkalalaki* (malehood, masculinity, etc.). She was aware that if she insisted on interviewing the men in the village individually, people would misinterpret this as a ploy to "seduce" the men. So she spent her first few days in the field trying to find out the best way to get the men. Based on this, she went to places where the men commonly gathered, such as the local makeshift store that would usually have some benches in the front. She also invited the men to her house, but always in a group because most Filipinos feel uncomfortable being "interviewed" alone, and much more so if this is a male respondent being interviewed by a female researcher. Santiago also avoided structured questions. She started with a single question, "What is *pagkalalaki*?" and the rest of the questions followed on from the answers of the respondent. Her justification for not having a set of standard questions is that the participants would feel like they are undergoing an interrogation. There was also a danger of word going around the small town – pretty soon, prospective respondents would know what was being asked, and might even memorize answers!

Nicdao-Henson (1982) also used *pagtatanong-tanong* within the participant observation framework in her research on the concept of time. Just like Santiago, she did not have a structured interview guide. The questions developed as the *pagtatanong-tanong* went on. She also adjusted her manner to the particular characteristics of the respondents. For example, her voice and behavior became more gentle and soft when dealing with older people compared to younger ones. She used *pagtatanong-tanong* when there were realities that she could not understand, or when she wanted to verify some data.

I used *pagtatanong-tanong* as the main method in my study of migration and return migration among Ilocanos (Filipinos from the Ilocos region in the Philippines) who have lived in Hawaii for ten years or more (called *Hawayano* upon their return to Ilocos). Since there were three of us involved in the data collection, I prepared a list of topics and sub-topics to be covered. This list was simply a guide. The wording of questions to cover these topics was left to the *nagtatanong-tanong* (the person conducting the *pagtatanong-tanong*). There was no strict sequence to follow. Not being a native speaker of the local language, I had to learn to speak Ilocano, the language of the *pagtatanong-tanong*. A level of *pakikipagpalagayang-loob* (rapport, mutual trust) was attained for all cases. The community's acceptance of the research was indicated by the openness they showed me and the two other researchers who were local residents of the areas. Another indication is when they would remark fondly every time I would be around, "Here comes the *Hawayana* (female *Hawayano*)!" A year after I carried out the study, even before I presented my dissertation to the University of the Philippines to be given a Ph.D., I returned to my research sites and presented my findings to the Hawayanos using the Ilocano language. These presentations were attended by members of the wider community as well. They remarked that this was a good gesture since they were not expecting that they would be the first to learn the results. The presentations made a lot of scientific sense as well since these were opportunities to verify the findings, to clarify points that surfaced during the data analysis that were a bit vague, leading to more confidence in the validity of the study (Pe-Pua, 1988).

The *pagtatanong-tanong* can be carried out individually or in natural clusters. Thus, a prospective participant is encouraged to bring along a friend or two if he/she does not wish to be interviewed alone. Also, participants know each other and feel comfortable in each other's company.

In some cases, the natural cluster atmosphere stimulates discussion affecting participants more effectively than the individual *pagtatanong-tanong*. *Pagtatanong-tanong* within a natural cluster works well for many Filipinos who are used to being surrounded by friends and family in every stage in their lives. When Santiago (1975) did not object to the men in her study bringing along a friend or two, she was utilizing the natural cluster to benefit her research.

The Children's Rehabilitation Center (CRC) (1990) recommended *pagtatanong-tanong* as a method for research in its training manual for dealing with children in conflict situations such as children of war and victims of abuse. They clarified the goals of *pagtatanong-tanong* as not just gathering valid information, but clarifying, confirming and verifying data collected for the sake of accurate and effective delivery of the study.

The CRC also recommended another indigenous variant of the interview, *pakikipagkuwentuhan* ("story-telling"), when dealing with topics that are not commonly discussed, for issues that people would not own up to, such as sensitive issues related to sexuality or abuse. This method allows a free flow of opinions and experiences (personal or that of a third party). But there should be safeguards against deviating too much from the topic of discussion. The method was earlier defined by a CRC staff as "an indigenous research method of collecting data from a group or individuals who express their opinions, beliefs, knowledge and experience freely and informally" (my translation) (Enriquez, 1988).

Pakikipagkuwentuhan was first described by de Vera (1976) by way of relating how she used it to study extra-marital relationships. De Vera was aware that Filipinos would not openly admit to having extra-marital affairs so the formal interview or the *pagtatanong-tanong* was out of the question as a research method. Instead, she used a popular item that Filipinos like to talk about–movies. Since extra-marital affairs were (and still are) a frequent element in Philippine movies, she used these as the stories around which she asked about opinions on the reasons people engage in these affairs, the consequences on and reactions of family, friends, and the community. De Vera observed the advantage of this method in bringing out opinions for which respondents would not feel threatened to discuss, and its ability to allow respondents to express themselves freely since the discussion was not focused directly on their experience. She observed, however, that some participants tended to simply go along with the opinions of others, that women respondents were less participative, that some participants were domineering, and sometimes the *kuwentuhan* (story-telling) deviated from the research topic.

De Vera's *pakikipagkuwentuhan* method was criticized by Orteza (1997) on the following grounds: The purpose of the research was hidden from the participants who were made to believe that she was just interested in their opinions outside the context of a research project. This trickery is a breach of the basic principle of indigenous research, that of treating the participants as equal, according them the respect that one's *kapwa* (fellow human being) deserve. The level of interaction implied in de Vera's use of *pakikipagkuwentuhan* is that of *pakikibagay* (getting along with), which is still outside the "one-of-us" category. The story-telling aspect was with the use of movie plots as stimuli for discussion, instead of weaving stories related to people's lives. There were other technical problems such as the selective screening of participants according to perceived credibility of their views, and the data analysis of ranking responses, similar to quantitative approaches.

Orteza proceeded to provide us with a better articulation of *pakikipagkuwentuhan* as a powerful method for collecting data about people's personal and collective experience and views. She compared the *pakikipagkuwentuhan* of the 1980's to that of the 1990's and corrected the mistaken notion that this is used only for sensitive and difficult topics/issues. She made the important point that one can use *pakikipagkuwentuhan* in practically any given situation in the spirit of *pakikipagkapwa* (shared identity). Thus, when people engage in *pakikipagkuwentuhan*, they would feel free to weave stories. In real-life situations, this transaction can go on with people becoming oblivious of time. Elements are added or subtracted from the stories going around the group. Even when people meet for the first time, once rapport is established, they can engage in this type of interaction. It simply cannot accommodate just *pakikibagay* (getting along with). In reality, participants also become oblivious of the level of interaction. It is assumed that *pakikipagpalagayang-loob* (being in rapport/understanding/acceptance with) exists. Otherwise, it is not the indigenous method with which Filipinos are so familiar (Orteza, 1997).

Orteza defined *pakikipagkuwentuhan* as

> an informal, free, social process of exchanging information, thoughts and knowledge that are innate in a group's everyday life. It is a form of collective research where researchers and participants share equal status. The whole process, which is guided by rules of *pakikipagkapwa* (treating each other as fellow human being), must produce a story or stories that can be analyzed (my translation) (Orteza, 1997, p. 22).

If participants are interested in the topic, they would join the *kuwentuhan* (story-telling or discussion) spontaneously. In the spirit of equality of status, the researchers would also be expected to share their views and add to the stories. Orteza also discussed the role of the researcher and the participants, the research topic, place and time, the *pakikipagkuwentuhan* session, and how to analyze the stories produced. On the last point, the grounded theory approach becomes relevant, where the resulting "theory" is grounded on data gathered directly from the participants. Therefore, the response categories are not pre-determined.

Collective Indigenous Discussion

Pakikipagkuwentuhan is a cross between the interview and the focus group discussion. The distinct characteristic of *pakikipagkuwentuhan* is the free exchange of ideas leading to *stories* that can be analyzed.

There is another indigenous method that captures the group environment of the focus group discussion. This is the collective indigenous discussion or *ginabayang talakayan*. Galvez described this method very much like a focus group discussion except for one basic element: the researcher and participants collectively decide on the topic/s of discussion and the flow of the discussion. Thus, the *ginabayang talakayan* is "a method of collective research where a group of participants engage in sharing and exchanging knowledge, experience and opinions on a topic/topics they have collectively agreed to discuss" (my translation) (Galvez, 1988).

Galvez and Enriquez (1988, cited in Enriquez, 1994, p. 73) conducted a study on understanding the Filipino male using the *ginabayang talakayan* method. They recruited their participants through existing indigenous/ community groups such as men's clubs, fraternities, *barkadas* (peer groups), sports clubs, etc. Thus, the participants were assumed to have rapport with each other, and this study focused on group opinion. The discussion groups consisted of four to six participants per group, all males, aged 16 to over 40, students and employees/workers. The sessions went from three to three-and-a-half hours.

Another study that used this method was on Filipino sexuality (Pe-Pua, Aguling-Dalisay & Sto. Domingo, 1993). Twenty *ginabayang talakayan* were conducted consisting of four to six participants per group. Before starting the discussion, we would first get their approval on a discussion guide prepared by the facilitator. They could change this guide if they felt it was insufficient, too long, or inadequate or irrelevant to their experience. This procedure somehow gave the participants a feeling of importance and control over the way the discussion would proceed. We held separate discussions for men and women. The groups were also homogenous in terms of age, marital status, and socio-ethnolinguistic group. The women's groups were led by a female facilitator, and the men's groups by a male facilitator. We used the local language or dialect. The sessions would go for one to three hours. The discussions were informal, very relaxed, animated, and interspersed with a lot of bantering and jokes. All discussions were taped.

Enriquez gave the collective indigenous discussion a special meaning when he described the way this was carried out by the Philippine Psychology Research and Training House (PPRTH). During Enriquez's time, the PPRTH used to hold the *Piling-Piling Huwebes* (Special Thursdays) that had three elements: an indigenous concept or practice, an indigenous drink or beverage, and an indigenous food–all three having the same initial letter of the alphabet. For example, the PPRTH would invite a resource person to discuss the indigenous concept of *subli* (a song form in Batangas). An indigenous drink, *salabat* (ginger ale), and an indigenous food, *suman* (a type of rice cake) would be served. Thus, this Special Thursday would be called *Salabat, Suman at Subli*. Enriquez (1994, pp. 56–57) described this type of discussion as "research cum consciousness raising" in the sense that "The encounter always goes beyond the collective discussion of research data and analysis." Starting with the indigenous expert discussing the topic and oftentimes, giving a demonstration or performance, the event would continue on with an open forum or discussion. When the audience is encouraged to be active in this discussion and sometimes experience the topic of the day it is possible to gather research data on their attitudes, while at the same time raise their consciousness and awareness of the indigenous culture and practices. Enriquez proposed that this strategy (the PPH approach) be used when dealing with research topics that are sensitive, such as AIDS, sexuality, abuse, and so on. The Piling-Piling Huwebes eventually was renamed Piling-Piling Araw (Special day) and is a tradition that is still pursued by the Philippine Psychology Research and Training House and the Pambansang Samahan sa Sikolohiyang Pilipino (National Association of Filipino Psychology).

Indigenization of Psychological Testing[1]

The area of Filipino Personality is the richest ground from which local concepts and values were discovered. Hand in hand with this is the indigenization of psychological testing in the Philippines.

Reviews on the status of Philippine psychological measurement in the 1970s and 1980s pointed out the twin problems of the inapplicability of foreign-made tests and the dearth of locally developed tests (Carlota, 1980; Guanzon, 1985; Lazo, 1977; Lazo, de Jesus & Tiglao, 1976; Ramos, 1977). Carlota (1980) noted several trends in personality measurement, citing developments in the areas of personality testing, and the measurement of abilities and aptitudes, and of deviant behavior. Guanzon (1985) decried the tendency of local test users to use foreign-made tests as it were "lock, stock, and barrel" with no attempt whatsoever to adapt these tests through item or test modification, test translation, or development of local norms.

Enriquez and his associates developed the *Panukat ng Ugali at Pagkatao* (PUP) (Measure of Character and Personality) in 1975. This test utilized dimensions of personality that are relevant to Filipinos. In the history of Philippine psychological measurement, Enriquez's PUP clearly stands out as probably the first instrument that is culturally sensitive in its assessment

---

[1] The author acknowledges the contribution of Ma. Angeles Guanzon-Lapeña in the writing of this section.

of the Filipino personality. Psychological testing may be of Western origin, however, the substance of the PUP originated from an indigenous understanding of the Filipinos. The test administration procedures of the PUP were also adapted to Filipino ways (Enriquez & Guanzon, 1985). The PUP was later followed by other indigenous personality measures.

Cipres-Ortega and Guanzon-Lapeña (1997) have given evidence of an upsurge in the development of indigenous psychological measures during the last five years. Interest has grown by leaps and bounds from the handful of tests in educational psychology, which were locally developed in the 1950s, to the interest in personality testing of the projective type in the 1960s. They further noted that

> the 1970s saw tests developed in creativity, self-perception, personality and vocational testing, and the 1980s an increased interest in personality testing, with a number of researchers doing studies on the Filipino child and the Filipino adolescent. And in the 1990s, tests were developed to measure a wide variety of Filipino characteristics—*katalinuhan* [intelligence], *pagkarelihiyoso* [religiosity], *kaasalang sekswal* [sexual behavior], *kakayahang magdala ng tensyon* [ability to handle stress], *pagkamabahala* [anxiety], *kahustuhang emosyonal* [emotional stability], *kakayahang berbal sa Filipino* [verbal ability in Filipino, Filipino management style, dementia screening, empathy, and trustworthiness, to name a few. (Cipres-Ortega & Guanzon-Lapeña, 1997, p. 7)

APPLICATION OF PHILIPPINE INDIGENOUS METHODS OUTSIDE THE PHILIPPINES

Several researchers have attempted to apply Philippine indigenous methods beyond Philippine soils and shores, and not necessarily with Filipino participants. In 1982, I talked about *pagtatanong-tanong* at the Center for Culture Learning at the East-West Center in Hawaii, USA. In a study on social situational factors in cross-cultural adjustment headed by Richard Brislin, I used *pagtatanong-tanong* among Korean, Japanese, and Hawaiian respondents and discovered that it worked; it is a cross-cultural method. It has similarities with the life history method as used by Horoiwa (1983) in her study of Japanese growing up outside Japan. The Hawaiians' "talk story" behavior is similar to the Filipino *pagtatanong-tanong* and *pakikipagkuwentuhan*.

I have also continued to use not only *pagtatanong-tanong*, but the cross-indigenous approach in researching migrant and ethnic communities in Australia. Among street-frequenting youth, the natural cluster or individual *pagtatanong-tanong* helped document the myriad issues affecting these young people who were constantly negotiating their place in a multicultural society (Pe-Pua, 1996). The *ginabayang talakayan* style was incorporated in the focus group discussions with international students in two Australian universities to understand issues such as intergroup relations, their perceptions of the learning environment, and their overall adjustment to life in Australia (Pe-Pua, 1994, 1995). Again, the *pagtatanong-tanong* and *ginabayang talakayan* approaches were very effective in our research on the "astronaut" families and "parachute" children—Hong Kong immigrants who "landed" in Australia and then one or both parents returned to Hong Kong to resume work or business, leaving the spouse and children in Australia to cope with cross-cultural adjustments, and changing roles and responsibilities (Pe-Pua, Mitchell, Iredale & Castles, 1996). The same methods were applied to our study on the legal needs of migrant groups in a Sydney local government area (Pe-Pua & Echevarria, 1998), and another with refugee and family entrant families in Australia (Iredale, Mitchell, Pe-Pua, & Pittaway, 1996). Only in a few instances were the research participants of Filipino background. The research in Australia included Macedonians, Pacific Islanders, Koreans, Serbians, Croatians, Lebanese, South Americans, Portuguese, and so on—reflecting the multicultural composition of Australian society. I also include *pakapa-kapa* (searching technique) and *pagtatanong-tanong* in teaching research methods courses in the undergraduate and postgraduate levels at the University of New South Wales in Australia.

Moving on to other shores, the Philippine indigenous methods worked effectively in my research on Filipino migrant workers in Spain and Italy. The indigenous interview and collective group discussion immediately sparked a wealth of information which the workers were so keen to share. The research situation was also an opportunity for them to put things in perspective and undertake a self-assessment of the value and success of their sojourn (Pe-Pua, 2003).

Protacio-Marcelino (1996) used *pagtatanong-tanong* and *pakikipagkuwentuhan* with second generation Filipino-American youth to examine the influence of Filipino and American cultures on their process of search, discovery, creation and development of their cultural/ethnic identity. The *pagtatanong-tanong* was aided by an interview guide, while the *pakikipagkuwentuhan* used the style of asking the participant to simply tell the story of their lives as they were growing up between two cultures.

After this snapshot of indigenous research methods, we are ready to examine the guiding principles of these methods and the features of the indigenous research approach.

GUIDING PRINCIPLES FOR INDIGENOUS METHODS

Following on from the approach of tapping indigenous psychological knowledge to discover indigenous concepts and research methods, followers of *Sikolohiyang Pilipino* transformed the core value of *kapwa* to become a pivotal concept to articulate five basic guiding principles for the use of indigenous perspective in research. *Kapwa* (shared identity, fellow human being) provides a guide for understanding the transaction between researchers and research participants.

The first guiding principle in indigenous research is that the level of interaction or relationship that exists between the researcher and the participants significantly determines the quality of the data obtained. There are two categories of *kapwa*: the *Ibang-Tao* ("outsider") and the *Hindi-Ibang-Tao* ("one-of-us"). In Filipino social interaction, one is immediately "placed" into one of these two categories; and how one is placed determines the level of interaction one engenders. For example, if one is regarded as *ibang-tao*, the interaction can range from *pakikitungo* (transaction/civility with), to *pakikisalamuha* (inter-action with), to *pakikilahok* (joining/participating), to *pakikibagay* (in-conformity with/in-accord with), and to *pakikisama* (getting along with). If one is regarded as *hindi-ibang-tao*, you can expect *pakikipag-palagayang-loob* (being in-rapport/understanding/acceptance with, mutual trust), *pakikisangkot* (getting involved), or the highest level of *pakikiisa* (being one with). In the research context, one should aim at reaching the first level under *Hindi-Ibang-Tao*, which is *pakikipagpalagayang-loob*, at the minimum, if one wants to be assured of good quality data.

The dichotomy of the "one-of-us" and the "outsider" categories reflects a value for defining membership in a group that determines the boundaries or the extent of allowable behavior for a person. Many a time the relationship between the researcher and the participants continues long after the research is over.

Second principle: Researchers should treat research participants as equal, if not superior—like a fellow human being and not like a guinea pig whose sole function is to provide data. From this principle, certain behaviors on the part of the researcher are prescribed. For example, in the method of *pagtatanong-tanong* (literally, "asking questions" in a fairly casual manner), the participants are free to ask the researcher as many questions as they want, therefore acting much like "researchers" themselves. These questions should be accorded the same respect and not avoided (Pe-Pua, 1989). In many of the research methods, participants actually have an input in the research process itself—in terms of time management, structure of the questions, and interpretation—without their being aware of it.

Third principle: We should give more importance to the welfare of the participants than to obtaining data from them. The goal of research is understanding, but not at the expense of the very people from whom this understanding will spring. The primary ethical responsibility of researchers should be to the people and not to their institution or funding agency. For example, if the publication of the research report will jeopardize the situation of the people, then it should not be continued. If the needs of the community are discovered in the course of doing research on a different topic, and it is within the researchers' capability to help, then they should help. The research, aside from being enlightening for the respondents, should also be empowering.

Fourth principle: Research methods should be chosen on the basis of appropriateness to the population (and not sophistication of the method) and it should be made to adapt to existing cultural norms. For example, having somebody else butt in in the middle of an interview session is not something to be upset over; one should go through the process of getting to know each other first informally before asking questions on topics that are not that common to people. Researchers cannot expect people to adjust to the method; the method should adjust to the people. And here is where *pakikiramdam* is most needed—in trying to figure out how the research method will work most effectively. *Pakikiramdam* is another indigenous concept discovered in Filipino psychology. It refers to a special kind of sensitivity to cues which will guide researchers in their interaction with group members, especially with Filipinos who are used to indirect and non-verbal manners of communicating and expressing thoughts, attitudes, feelings and emotions. It is through *pakikiramdam* that a researcher will know when to ask personal questions and when not to pursue them; when it is time to leave; or how to interpret a "yes" or a "no".

Fifth principle: The language of the people should be the language of the research at all times. If this is not possible, local researchers should be tapped for assistance. It is in their own mother tongue that a person can truly express their innermost sentiments, ideas, perceptions, and attitudes.

FEATURES OF THE INDIGENOUS RESEARCH APPROACH

Enriquez (1992) tried to distinguish the indigenous research approach from dominant, established approaches such as experimental research, survey research, and participatory research–in terms of informal culture, formal structure, and technological procedures (see Table 1). The indigenous research approach would seem to be closer in characteristics to the participatory research approach; but even with this, there are distinct differences.

Informal culture: In terms of values and ideologies, indigenous research recognizes knowledge as inseparable from praxis, consciousness, identity, and involvement. In terms of beliefs and theories, a multimethod, appropriate and total approach is the way to obtain valid information. In terms of norms and assumptions, the researcher seeks to be one with the group being studied, by way of his/her actions (Enriquez, 1992).

Formal structure: In terms of the division of labor, the indigenous researcher and participants work at the level of unity. The researcher uses

Table 1. A Comparison of Research Approaches in Culture, Structure and Procedures

	Experimental research	Survey research	Participatory research	Indigenous research
INFORMAL CULTURE				
Values, Ideologies	Discover causal laws; internally valid experiments	Data-based relationships; external validity	Social change; relevant knowledge; mutual influence	Knowledge as praxis, consciousness, identity and involvement
Beliefs, Theories	Valid information from experimenter objectivity and control	Valid information from sample selection and statistical control	Valid information from relationships with research participants	Valid information from a multi-method, appropriate and total approach
Norms, Assumptions	Adhere to experimental procedure	Adhere to 'contract' with participants	Negotiate issues jointly as they arise	Enhance awareness as one with-the-other
FORMAL STRUCTURE				
Division of Labor	'Experimenters' run 'subjects' in experiments	'Researchers' collect data from 'respondents"	'Researchers' and 'participants' work as colleagues	Researcher systematizes and participants reconfirm; researcher and researchee work at level of unity
Distribution of Power	Experimenters control subjects' activities	Researchers define appropriate responses	Researchers and participants negotiate activities on equal footing	Culture-bearer provides the implied and articulated limits of the research enterprise
TECHNOLOGICAL PROCEDURES				
Problem Definition	Experimenters deduce from theory	Researchers induce issues/ variables from data	Parties negotiate shared interests and define problems	Problem definition given by culture-bearers. Issues must be part of their awareness. Awareness may be created through involvement on the basis of identification with the indigenous

Continued

Table 1. (*cont.*)

	Experimental research	Survey research	Participatory research	Indigenous research
Research Design	From experimental design	From technologies for sample selection, instrument design	From pragmatic possibilities of situation	Research design as output and not as blueprint. Secondary research strategies (e.g. survey, experiments) adopted whenever appropriate
Data Collection	Run experiments and tabulate responses	Administer interview, questionnaire	Most credible party collects	Involved party collects. Quality of data as a function of critical involvement
Utilization of Findings	Disseminated to other experimenters for theory-building	Disseminated to researchers; or policy-makers	Shared with others relevant to action	Primarily for the culture-bearers; not shared with others at culture-bearers' expense

Overview of indigenous research (Enriquez, 1986). Statements on Experimental, Survey and Participatory Research are from "Organizing Participatory Research: Interfaces for Joint Inquiry and Organization Change," (Dave Brown, *Journal of Occupational Behavior*, January 1983, 4 (1), 9–19).

his/her ability to systematize things, with the participants reconfirming such efforts. In terms of distribution of power, from the virtual absolute power of the experimenter (full control of subjects' activities), to the diminished power of the survey researcher (determining scope, defining responses, sampling respondents), to the clipping of the participatory researcher's power (researchers and participants negotiate activities on equal footing), power rests not on the indigenous researcher but on the culture-bearer participants who provide and determine the scope and limits of research (Enriquez, 1992).

Technological procedures: In terms of problem definition, indigenous research does not deduce this from theory (as experimental researchers do) nor just evaluate issues from data (as survey researchers do), but actually goes beyond the participatory research approach where the problem is defined by researchers and participants together. Indigenous researchers let the community of culture-bearers define the problems and issues. There is no blueprint for a research design. Instead, the design is a result of the collective planning and decision-making of the participants, with the indigenous researcher acting as facilitator. In terms of data collection, while participatory research encourages only the most credible party to collect data, indigenous research allows only the involved party to collect data. In terms of utilization of findings, the culture-bearer participants determine how findings will be shared, or whether it should be shared at all! (Enriquez, 1992) Data collection follows what Viney (1988) described as the mutual-orientation model where "both data collector and contributor give something to, and gain something from, the data collection" (cited in Enriquez, 1994, p. 61).

We can see from the above discussion that indigenous research challenges the traditional role of researcher and participant. Enriquez (1992) argued that experimental and survey researchers wield a monopoly of power, making them "research emperors", perpetuating their own interest, preserving the status quo, sometimes at the expense of the powerless indigenous people. This power relation is modified in participatory research where researcher and participants begin to share power and status and become co-equal. Indigenous research went a step further—reversing the power role relation. Here, it is the culture bearer participants who determine the scope of the research, define the problem, lead the way to determining the appropriate method of obtaining information, collect the data, and determine its use. The participants become the indigenous researchers, and the social scientist contributes by being a facilitator, "a morale booster, networker, or at most a consultant who confers about the research problem with the community who are, in this case, the real researchers" (Enriquez, 1994, p. 59). Indigenous method is therefore not just culturally sensitive and appropriate, but it is also people-oriented (Enriquez, 1992).

The indigenous research approach therefore represents a paradigm shift, whereby facilitation research is the underpinning definition of research.

> Facilitation research in *Sikolohiyang Pilipino* operates with the knowledge that an indigenous group has its own methods of research and documentation. In majority-minority relations, facilitation research stems from a strong desire to empower the minority and immigrant peoples who used to be just a source of data. (Enriquez, 1994, pp. 58–59)

DEBATES ON THE VALUE OF USING INDIGENOUS METHODS

Indigenous methods developed out of a realization that the non-selective use of western methods has lead to a misunderstanding of Filipino psychology, a picture that was based on using western, inappropriate criteria. The pitfalls of such an approach were recognized in Philippine social science literature as early as the 1960s and 1970s (Feliciano, 1965; Espiritu, 1968; Santiago, 1975; Santiago & Enriquez, 1976).

Indigenous methods were applied and tested in various research situations. They have been reviewed by a number of writers (Sevilla, 1978, 1985; Margallo, 1982). Some of the issues raised were in relation to language, the uniqueness of the method, the insider/outsider issue, observer/investigator bias, and ethics.

The Language Issue

Full use of the native language or dialect of the indigenous group is integral to the indigenous research approach. The native language or dialect is the language through which the members can best and comfortably express their ideas, emotions, beliefs and attitudes. It is scientifically sensible to use the local language as source of theory, method, and praxis because the exclusive use of a mainstream language "can lead to the neglect of the wealth of indigenous concepts and methods embodied in a language more meaningful to the culture" (Alfonso, 1977).

Sevilla (1985) pointed out that a problem faced by Filipino indigenous research is that there has always been a strong bias toward English as medium of instruction and thinking in Philippine academe. This is based on a "colonial mentality" towards (a perception of superiority of) Western-based knowledge, theories and methods. While this observation is true, the reality speaks for an upsurge in studies conducted in the indigenous tradition with the full use of the local languages and dialects. From this emerged a wealth of indigenous concepts that are relevant to Filipinos, and which are a contribution to universal psychological knowledge. Documentation was a task that Enriquez and his colleagues took seriously. Since 1976, the *Sikolohiyang Pilipino* Resource Collection (now housed at the University of the Philippines) accumulated more than 10,000 papers written in the Filipino language on Filipino psychology, culture, history, and the arts (Enriquez, 1992). Student and professional researchers continue to contribute to this wealth of material on indigenous psychology.

How Unique Are the Indigenous Methods?

Sevilla (1985) also questioned the "uniqueness" of the indigenous methods. Somehow, the indigenous perspective seems to promise us something quite different from the traditional methods of the West, for is it not one of the reasons we "turned away from the West" to discover the indigenous? And yet, these indigenous methods are not even unique to psychology, Sevilla laments. They are very similar to techniques of participant observation known to anthropologists and sociologists.

To address this concern, we must point out that a method that is indigenous to one culture is not necessarily unique to this culture, but definitely appropriate and thus relevant to it. Also, what is indigenous in one is not necessarily applicable to another culture. Thus, the cross-indigenous perspective demands that we discover and use whatever is found to be indigenous in the particular culture–with the end view of comparing the outcomes with those emanating from other cultures using their own indigenous methods and practices. As Enriquez (1992) put it, "Indigenous psychology does not aim to create a psychology applicable only to the indigenous culture. More accurately, indigenous psychology aims to develop a psychology based on and responsive to the indigenous culture and realities" (p. 91).

The Insider/Outsider Issue

The insider or the culture-bearer researchers have an advantage in doing indigenous research. They know the language of the people. They can better appreciate their values, sentiments, beliefs and experiences. They are more likely to be readily accepted by the research participants since they are "one-of-us". Inasmuch as both the research participants and the researcher are culture-bearers, the phenomenon of "going emic on somebody else's emic" (Enriquez, 1979, 1992) can be avoided. If the researcher is not a member of the ethnic minority group nor has any close linkage with it, he/she should exert extra effort to learn the language.

Does this mean then that the outsider or non-culture-bearer researcher has no place in indigenous research?

In the end, having an outsider and an insider is the best arrangement. The expected "bias" of the insider will be balanced by the assumed "objectivity" of the outsider. The outsider can alert the insider about certain aspects of the research which the insider might be taking for granted. On the other hand, the insider can comment on the interpretation of the outsider and offer some suggestions for improvement or correction whenever possible and necessary (Brislin & Holwill, 1977).

Observer/Investigator Bias

One problem always brought out with the use of indigenous methods is the subjectivity of the participant's responses and the researcher's interpretation of the data. Subjectivity or reactivity of the participant who wishes to please the researcher can be avoided in the first place if the relationship between the two parties is one of mutual trust. Similarly, consistency of the response can be checked by repeating the question in a different way.

The problems of investigator bias and data contamination can be solved by having more than one person do the research so that more than one viewpoint is represented. This ensures reliability and validity. If the researchers are familiar with the language, cultural norms and values of the participants among other things, then accuracy and relevance of their interpretations can be optimized. They should try to approximate the status of an "insider" to minimize responses tailored to the expectations of an outsider. Threats to reliability and validity can be handled through repeated sampling from as many participants as possible, manipulating situations such that behavioral concomitants of a construct become probable, and cross-checking data with other documents unobtrusively (Torres, 1982).

Pakapa-kapa or Careful Planning?

In her review of some indigenous studies, Margallo (1982) pointed out that the indigenous research model is undoubtedly more suitable to the Filipino culture. If not carefully planned and conducted, however, it could be susceptible to confounding effects just like western methods. While appearing simple, indigenous methods are in fact very demanding in terms of the sensitivities of which one needs to be aware. Margallo's comments on the studies she examined brought to the fore the importance of clarifying what *pakapa-kapa* entails. While the approach points to "groping" and "exploration," a sense of "going with the flow", the actual execution of indigenous research must still follow the rigors of scientific research. By rigor, we do not mean standardization. Rather, we mean careful planning, flexibility in design, attention to depth, sensitivity to cues, conscientious and careful documentation, attention to individual participants' unique contribution or input, and so on.

Ethical Issues

Margallo (1982) raised another issue which she called the "ethics of manipulation" (p. 237). The indigenous research model gives importance to establishing a relationship between researcher and participants at a level of rapport and mutual trust, a minimum level for obtaining authentic data. In other words, data gathering is enhanced by winning the participants' friendship and trust.

> The friendship, then, for all intent and purposes, is a mere strategy for data gathering, a serious offence against the sacredness of personal relationships among Filipinos. Here is where the Model apparently fails to suit the nature of the people for which it was designed. (Margallo, 1982, p. 237)

This is indeed a serious issue that should be addressed. Indigenous researchers should always remember to regard the participants as fellow human beings first and foremost.

San Juan and Soriaga (1985) addressed the issue of "manipulation" directly in relation to *panunuluyan* ('living in') by pointing out that the participants have the power to decide the level of involvement and the level of interaction that they want to occur. It is up to them to extend friendship to the researcher, which more often than not, they would.

In other words, friendship is not extorted for the sake of gathering data. It is a fundamental requirement of the transaction in indigenous research. And the researcher is compelled to respect this relationship. Thus, San Juan and Soriaga (1985) proceeded to point out that when faced with a decision on how to handle the results when there is a potential harm to the participants, it should be clear that the welfare of the participants must take precedence over the researcher's responsibility to the funding agency, for example.

Mendoza (2001, ch. 4) gave a view contrary to the idea of the "ethics of manipulation". After describing how she incorporated Filipino indigenous approaches in her study of Filipino and Filipino American identities, she noted that these methods

> turn on a number of cultural value assumptions, that is, provisionality, informality, cultural sensitivity, and successful attainment of relational engagement (*pakikipagkapwa* or "being-at-one-with") as the best, if not the only, way to access cultural knowledge and to be welcomed to participate in a community's inner life. Well-documented in Filipino psychological literature, this establishing of personal contact, not only instrumentally as a prelude to the attainment of strategic ends, but as an end in itself, has been found to be normative in most Filipino (and I would presume, as well, in Filipino American) communities. (pp. 67–68)

In other words, friendship is not used as a way to ensure valid data or enhance the participants' participation or self-disclosures. Establishing a friendship-like relationship is a commonly valued goal in any social interaction, including that which transpires in the course of undertaking research.

Ethical issues cannot be ignored especially if the researcher is sincere about maintaining a status of equality between him/herself and the participant. The researcher should never treat the participant as an object of research, but as an active *participant*. The status of equality applies even at the data reporting stage which will have to involve the participants themselves. The accuracy of data interpretation and the fairness of the presentation should be confirmed by the participants. As much as possible, their consent for publication should be obtained; afterwards, they should be made aware of it. If the publication will harm the participants, then no such action should be taken.

It is also worthwhile to find out the group's reaction to the interaction. What did they get out of it? Did they enjoy it? Did they learn something new, like knowledge about some other culture or group?

The social and moral responsibility of the researcher to the indigenous group is also challenged. Now that the researcher has learned a lot about the group, what does he intend to do for them? Considering that many researchers in the past have ignored the question, it is understandable that some participants feel reluctant and inhibited towards other researchers.

FROM THE INDIGENOUS TO THE CROSS-INDIGENOUS

As principal methods of investigation, *Sikolohiyang Pilipino* encourages cross-indigenous method, multi-method, multi-language approach, appropriate field methods, and a total approach (triangulation method) (Enriquez, 1985, 1992).

The cross-indigenous perspective is shown in Figure 1. Indigenous psychologies result from tapping the culture as a source of cultural knowledge. The different indigenous psychologies are then put together in a pool called "cross-cultural knowledge". This knowledge is in contrast to the "cross-cultural" knowledge derived from a psychology that is dominated by Western theories and methods (see Figure 2) (Enriquez, 1979, 1992).

Enriquez viewed the cross-indigenous perspective in the light of Alfredo Lagmay's (another noted Filipino psychologist) total approach, Campbell and Fiske's (1964) argument for the multi-method approach, and his own argument for a multi-language/multi-culture approach based on indigenous viewpoints (Enriquez, 1975). By "total," Lagmay was referring to not just a social science method, nor just a philosophical approach. He was also referring to "the fact that while the method is objective and the bias scientific, the approach undeniably involves the total human being, including human judgment and human values" (Enriquez, 1992, p. 92).

The use of several languages is also part of the framework of the cross-indigenous perspective. The indigenous psychology is discovered through the full use of the native language(s), the language of the research participants, not that of the university-trained social scientist. Thus, in evolving "cross-indigenous" knowledge, several languages from several cultures are the media through which cross-cultural realities are presented. The way *pag-tatanong-tanong* and other indigenous methods have been used beyond the Philippine geographical boundaries, and involving people from various cultures is an evidence of the value and feasibility of cross-indigenizing.

It must be made clear that the indigenous and cross-indigenous approach do not espouse a different brand of science from what is traditionally valued in the social sciences. "While *Sikolohiyang Pilipino* dissociated itself from Anglo-American psychology by reconstructing its own history, it

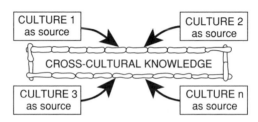

Note: The direction of arrows indicates "indigenization from within".

Figure 1. Towards a global psychology through a cross-indigenous perspective

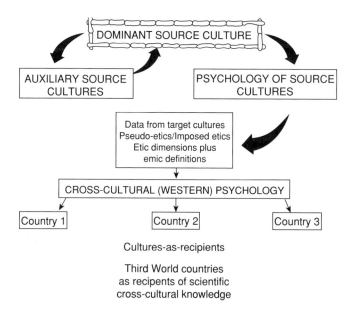

Figure 2. A schematic diagram of uni-national dominance in psychology (indigenization from without)

accepted the philosophical traditions and paradigms of science as neither Eastern nor Western but global." (Enriquez, 1994, p. 48) In fact, Enriquez believed that

> the indigenous Filipino philosophy of science is more exacting than its Anglo-American counterpart ... [and this] incorporates the demands of empirical validation from *katatagan* ("replicability and reliability"), to *katapatan* ("multiple operationism and validity") but also requires *patibay* ("certification"), *patotoo* ("affirmability and attestability") and *patunay* ("authenticity"). (Enriquez, 1994, p. 49)

For example, the validity of a statement or conclusion is enhanced if two or more sources of information corroborate it. Procedurally, this entails presenting the findings of a study to the participants for affirmation and attestation. Talisayon (1994) studied the concepts of *patotoo* (validity or "establishing the truth") among indigenous Filipino spiritual groups and discovered that this process is not limited to empirical validation but includes alternative modalities such as experiential authentication.

CONCLUSION

We have learned many social research methods from our colleagues in the west. Some of these are appropriate (which we should continue to use), and some are not (which we should give up). We need to pay more attention to those methods that are indigenous, tried and tested that are rooted in the indigenous culture.

Philippine psychology has come a long way in developing an alternative perspective in understanding Philippine realities and concepts. Proponents of *Sikolohiyang Pilipino* have done a lot in terms of documenting advances in developing indigenous concepts and methods.

The development of indigenous research methods in the Philippines gained momentum from the seminal work of Santiago and Enriquez (1976) in espousing a Filipino orientation in psychological research. This momentum has not faltered. Tapping indigenous behavior, indigenous methods were articulated, trialed, refined and exported overseas. From a basically indigenous perspective, Philippine psychology also made a bid for a cross-indigenous perspective in support of a universal psychology that takes into account the frameworks of indigenous cultures.

A "cross-cultural psychology" will continue to be only a promise for as long as the indigenous psychologies are untapped because of language and culture barriers (Enriquez, 1979). The advances of scholars in the Philippines should serve as an encouragement to look within indigenous cultures for ways of doing research that are not only appropriate and relevant within, but from which researchers in the West and East could benefit.

REFERENCES

Alfonso, A.B. (1977). *Towards developing Philippine Psychology: Language-related issues in teaching and research*. Paper prepared for the Fourth Conference of the Asian Association of National Languages, University of Malaysia, Kuala Lumpur, Malaysia.

Bennagen, P.L. (1985). Nakikiugaling pagmamasid: Pananaliksik sa kulturang Agta [Participant observation: Research on Agta culture]. In A. Aganon & M. David (Eds.), *Sikolohiyang Pilipino: Isyu, pananaw at kaalaman (New directions in indigenous psychology)* (pp. 397–415). Manila: National Book Store.

Brislin, R., & Holwill, F. (1977). Reactions of indigenous people to the writings of behavioral and social scientists. *International Journal of Intercultural Relations, 1*, 15–34.

Campbell, D.T., & Fiske, D.W. (1964). Convergent and discriminant validation by the multi-trait-multi-method matrix. *Psychology Bulletin, 56*, 81–105.

Carlota, A.J. (1980). Research trends in psychological testing. In A. Carlota & L. Lazo (Eds.), *Psychological measurement: A book of readings* (pp. 31–47). Quezon City: U.P. Psychology Foundation, 1987.

Children's Rehabilitation Center. (1990). *Gabay sa Pagsasanay* [Training Manual]. Quezon City: Author.

Cipres-Ortega, S., & Guanzon-Lapeña, M. (1997, July). *Locally Developed Psychological Tests: A Critical Review*. Paper presented at the Annual Scientific Meeting of the National Academy of Science and Technology, Manila, Philippines.

De Vera, M.G.A. (1976). Pakikipagkuwentuhan: Paano kaya pag-aaralan ang pakikiapid? [Pakikipagkuwentuhan: How do we study extra-marital affairs?]. In R. Pe-Pua (Ed.),

Sikolohiyang Pilipino: Teorya, metodo at gamit (Filipino Psychology: Theory, method and application) (pp. 187–193). Quezon City: Surian ng Sikolohiyang Pilipino. 1982.

Enriquez, V.G. (1975). Mga batayan ng Sikolohiyang Pilipino sa kultura at kasaysayan [The bases of Filipino psychology in culture and history]. *General Education Journal, 29,* 61–88.

Enriquez, V.G. (1978). *Kapwa*: A core concept in Filipino social psychology. *Philippine Social Sciences and Humanities Review, 42* (1–4).

Enriquez, V.G. (1979). Towards cross-cultural knowledge through cross-indigenous methods and perspective. *Philippine Journal of Psychology 12,* 9–15.

Enriquez, V.G. (1985). The development of psychological thought in the Philippines. In A. Aganon & M. David (Eds.), *Sikolohiyang Pilipino: Isyu, pananaw at kaalaman (New directions in indigenous psychology)* (pp. 149–176). Manila: National Book Store.

Enriquez, V.G. (1992). *From colonial to liberation psychology.* Quezon City: University of the Philippines Press.

Enriquez, V.G. (1994). *Pagbabangong-dangal: Indigenous psychology & cultural empowerment.* Quezon City: Akademya ng Kultura at Sikolohiyang Pilipino.

Enriquez, V.G., & Guanzon-Lapeña, M.C. (1985). Towards the assessment of personality and culture: The *Panukat ng Ugali at Pagkatao. Philippine Journal of Educational Measurement, 4* (1), 15–54.

Enriquez, R. (1988). Pakikipagkuwentuhan: Isang katutubong metodo ng pananaliksik [Pakikipagkuwentuhan: An indigenous research method]. In R. Pe-Pua (Ed.), *Mga piling babasahin sa panlarangang pananaliksik II* [Selected readings on field research II]. Quezon City: University of the Philippines.

Espiritu, A.C. (1968). The limits of applicability of Western concepts, values and methods in the social sciences to the concrete realities of Asian societies. In *The relevance of social sciences in contemporary Asia* (pp. 35–44). Tokyo: World Student Christian Federation.

Feliciano, G.D. (1965). The limits of Western social research methods in rural Philippines: The need for innovation, *Lipunan, 1* (1), 114–128.

Galvez, R. (1988). Ang ginabayang talakayan: Katutubong pamamaraan ng sama-samang pananaliksik [The collective discussion: An indigenous method of participatory research]. In R. Pe-Pua (Ed.), *Mga piling babasahin sa panlarangang pananaliksik II* [Selected readings on field research II]. Quezon City: University of the Philippines.

Gepigon, S.D., & Francisco, V.A. (1978). Pagdalaw at pakikipagpalagayang-loob sa mamumulot ng basura [Visiting and making friends with the garbage scavengers]. In L.F. Antonio, et. al. (Eds.), *Ulat ng Ikatlong Pambansang Kumperensya sa Sikolohiyang Pilipino [Proceedings of the Third National Conference on Filipino Psychology]* (pp. 133–146). Quezon City: Pambansang Samahan sa Sikolohiyang Pilipino.

Gonzales, L.F. (1982). Ang pagtatanung-tanong: Dahilan at katangian [Pagtatanung-tanong: Reasons and characteristics]. In R. Pe-Pua (Ed.), *Sikolohiyang Pilipino: Teorya, metodo at gamit (Filipino Psychology: Theory, method and application)* (pp. 175–186). Quezon City: Surian ng Sikolohiyang Pilipino.

Guanzon, M.C. (1985). Paggamit ng panukat sikolohikal sa Pilipinas: Kalagayan at mga isyu [Psychological measurement in the Philippines: Status and issues]. In A. Aganon & M. David (Eds.), *Sikolohiyang Pilipino: Isyu, pananaw at kaalaman (New directions in indigenous psychology)* (pp. 341–370). Manila: National Book Store.

Horoiwa, N. (1983). *Kaigai seicho Nihonjin no tekio to sentaku — Life history ni yoru kenkyu* [Adaptive strategies and identity changes of Japanese growing up abroad]. Unpublished master's thesis, Tsukuba University, Japan.

Iredale, R., Mitchell, C., Pe-Pua, R., & Pittaway, E. (1996). *Ambivalent welcome: Settlement experiences of humanitarian entrant families in Australia.* Canberra: Department of Immigration and Multicultural Affairs.

Lazo, L. (1977). Psychological testing in schools: An assessment. *Philippine Journal of Psychology, 11* (1), 23–27.

Lazo, L., Vasquez-de Jesus, L., & Edralin-Tiglao, R. (1976). A survey of psychological meas-urement practices in the Philippines: Clinical, industrial, and educational settings. In A. Carlota & L. Lazo (Eds.), *Psychological measurement: A book of readings* (pp. 2–30). Quezon City: U.P. Psychology Foundation, 1987.

Lynch, F. (1961). Social acceptance. In F. Lynch (Ed.), *Four Readings on Philippine Values* (pp. 1–21). Quezon City: Ateneo de Manila University Press.

Lynch, F. (1973). Social acceptance reconsidered. In F. Lynch & A. de Guzman II (Eds.), *IPC Papers No. 2. Four readings on Philippine values* (pp. 1–68). Quezon City: Ateneo de Manila University.

Margallo, S. (1982). The challenge of making a scientific indigenous field research: An evalu-ation of studies using *maka-Pilipinong pananaliksik* [Filipino-oriented research]. In R. Pe-Pua (Ed.), *Sikolohiyang Pilipino: Teorya, Metodo at Gamit (Filipino Psychology: Theory, Method and Application)* (pp. 233–239). Quezon City: Surian ng Sikolohiyang Pilipino, 1982.

Mendoza, S.L. (2001). *Between the home and the diaspora: The politics of theorizing Filipino and Filipino American identities (Asian Americans: Reconceptualizing Culture, History, Politics).* USA: Routledge.

Nery, L. (1979). *Pakikisama* as a method: A study of a subculture. *Philippine Journal of Psychology, 12* (1), 27–32.

Nicdao-Henson, E. (1982). Pakikipanuluyan: Tungo sa pag-unawa sa kahulugan ng panahon [Living in the community: A guide to understanding the concept of time]. In R. Pe-Pua (Ed.), *Sikolohiyang Pilipino: Teorya, metodo at gamit (Filipino Psychology: Theory, method and application)* (pp. 209–220). Quezon City: Surian ng Sikolohiyang Pilipino, 1982.

Orteza, G.O. (1997). Pakikipagkuwentuhan: Isang pamamaraan ng sama-samang pananalik-sik, pagpapatotoo, at pagtulong sa Sikolohiyang Pilipino [Pakikipagkuwentuhan: A method of collective research, establishing validity, and contributing to Filipino Psychology]. *PPRTH Occasional Papers Series No. 1.* Quezon City: Philippine Psychology Research and Training House.

Pe-Pua, R. (1985). Pagtatanong-tanong: Katutubong metodo ng pananaliksik [Pagtatanong-tanong: An indigenous research method]. In A. Aganon & M. David (Eds.), *Sikolohiyang Pilipino: Isyu, pananaw at kaalaman (New directions in indigenous psychology)* (pp. 416–432). Manila: National Book Store.

Pe-Pua, R. (1988). *Ang mga balikbayang Hawayano ng Ilocos Norte: Pandarayuhan at pagbabalik* [The Hawayano returnees of Ilocos Norte: Migration and return migration]. Unpublished doctoral dissertation, University of the Philippines, Philippines.

Pe-Pua, R. (1989). *Pagtatanong-tanong*: A cross-cultural research method. *International Journal of Intercultural Relations, 13,* 147–163.

Pe-Pua, R. (1994). *Being an Asian on campus: A look into the cross-cultural experiences of overseas students at the University of Wollongong.* Wollongong: Centre for Multicultural Studies, University of Wollongong.

Pe-Pua, R. (1995). *Being an overseas student at UNSW: Perceptions about the learning environ-ment, university services and intergroup relations.* Sydney: International Student Centre, UNSW.

Pe-Pua, R. (1996). *'We're just like other kids': Street-frequenting youth of non-English-speaking background.* Canberra: Australian Government Publishing Service.

Pe-Pua, R. (2003). Wife, mother and maid: The triple role of Filipino domestic workers in Spain and Italy. In N. Piper & M. Roces (Eds.), *Wife or Worker? Asian women and migra-tion* (pp. 157–180). Lanham: Rowman and Littlefield.

Pe-Pua, R., Aguiling-Dalisay, G., & Sto Domingo, M. (1993). Pagkababae at pagkalalaki: Tungo sa pag-unawa sa sekswalidad ng mga Pilipino [Being a woman, being a man: Towards understanding Filipino sexuality]. *Diwa, 10,* 1–4.

Pe-Pua, R., & Echevarria, A. (1998). *Cultural appropriateness, or plain customer service?: Legal needs of NESB residents in Fairfield.* Sydney: Ettinger House.

Pe-Pua, R., Mitchell, C., Iredale, R., & Castles, S. (1996). *Astronaut families and parachute children: The Cycle of migration between Hong Kong and Australia.* Canberra: Australian Government Publishing Service.

Pe-Pua, R., & Protacio-Marcelino, E. (2000). Sikolohiyang Pilipino (Filipino psychology): A legacy of Virgilio G. Enriquez. *Asian Journal of Social Psychology, 3,* 49–71.

Protacio-Marcelino, E. (1996). *Identidad at etnisidad: Pananaw at karanasan ng mga estudyanteng Filipino-Amerikano sa California* [Identity and Ethnicity: Perspectives and Experiences of Filipino-American Students in California]. Unpublished doctoral dissertation in Psychology, University of the Philippines, Quezon City, Philippines.

Ramos, E. (1977). Assessment of psychological testing in the Philippines: Focus on industries and national education. *Philippine Journal of Psychology, 11* (1), 19–22.

San Juan, J., & Soriaga, R. (1985). Panunuluyan: Mula paninimbang hanggang malalimang pakikipagpalagayang-loob [Panunuluyan: Interaction techniques and levels of relationship]. In A. Aganon & M. David (Eds.), *Sikolohiyang Pilipino: Isyu, pananaw at kaalaman (New directions in indigenous psychology)* (pp. 433–480). Manila: National Book Store.

Santiago, C.E. (1975). Ang kahulugan ng pagkalalake sa mga Pilipino [The meaning of 'masculinity' among Filipinos]. In V.G. Enriquez (Ed.), *Serye ng mga papel sa pagkataong pilipino (Series of papers in Filipino personality)* (pp. 51–70). Lunsod Quezon: Philippine Psychology Research House.

Santiago, C.E. (1977). Pakapa-kapa: Paglilinaw ng isang konsepto sa nayon [Pakapa-kapa: Clarifying a concept in a rural setting]. In R. Pe-Pua (Ed.), *Sikolohiyang Pilipino: Teorya, metodo at gamit (Filipino Psychology: Theory, method and application)* (pp. 161–170). Quezon City: Surian ng Sikolohiyang Pilipino, 1982.

Santiago, C.E., & Enriquez, V.G. (1976). Tungo sa makapilipinong pananaliksik [Towards a Filipino-oriented research]. *Sikolohiyang Pilipino: Mga Piling Papel, 1* (4), 3–10.

Sevilla, J.C. (1978). Indigenous research methods: evaluating first returns. In R. Pe-Pua (Ed.), *Sikolohiyang Pilipino: Teorya, metodo at gamit (Filipino Psychology: Theory, method and application)* (pp. 221–232). Quezon City: Surian ng Sikolohiyang Pilipino, 1982.

Sevilla, J.C. (1985). Evaluating indigenous methods: a second look. In V.G. Enriquez (Ed.), *Indigenous psychology: A book of readings* (pp. 266–274). Quezon City; Akademya ng Sikolohiyang Pilipino. 1990.

Talisayon, S.D. (1994). *Patotoo*—Concepts of validity among some Filipino spiritual groups. In T.B. Obusan & A.R. Enriquez (Eds), *Pamamaraan: Indigenous knowledge and evolving research paradigms.* Quezon City: Asian Center, University of the Philippines.

Torres, A. (1982). *"Pakapa-kapa"* as an approach in Philippine Psychology. In R. Pe-Pua (Ed.), *Sikolohiyang Pilipino: Teorya, metodo at gamit (Filipino Psychology: Theory, method and application)* (pp. 171–174). Quezon City: Surian ng Sikolohiyang Pilipino.

Part II
Family and Socialization

Chapter **6**

Parental Ethnotheories of Child Development
Looking Beyond Independence and Individualism in American Belief Systems

Carolyn Pope Edwards, Lisa Knoche,
Vibeke Aukrust, Asiye Kumru, and Misuk Kim

Over the past several decades, the topic of child development in a cultural context has received a great deal of theoretical and empirical investigation. Investigators from the fields of indigenous and cultural psychology have argued that childhood is socially and historically constructed, rather than a universal process with a standard sequence of developmental stages or descriptions. As a result, many psychologists have become doubtful that any stage theory of cognitive or social-emotional development can be found to be valid for all times and places. In placing more theoretical emphasis on contextual processes, they define culture as a complex system of common symbolic action patterns (or scripts) built up through everyday human social interaction by means of which individuals create common meanings and in terms of which they organize experience. Researchers understand culture to be organized and coherent, but not homogenous or static, and realize that the complex dynamic system of culture constantly undergoes transformation as participants (adults and children) negotiate and re-negotiate meanings through social interaction. These negotiations and transactions give rise to unceasing heterogeneity and variability in how different individuals and groups of individuals interpret values and meanings.

However, while many psychologists—both inside and outside the fields of indigenous and cultural psychology–are now willing to give up the idea of a universal path of child development and a universal story of parenting, they have not necessarily foreclosed on the possibility of discovering and describing some universal processes that underlie socialization and development-in-context. The roots of such universalities would lie in the biological aspects of child development, in the evolutionary processes of *adaptation*, and in the unique symbolic and problem-solving capacities of the human organism as a culture-bearing species. For instance, according to functionalist psychological anthropologists, shared (cultural) processes surround the developing child and promote in the long view the survival of families and groups if they are to demonstrate continuity in the face of ecological change and resource competition, (e.g. Edwards & Whiting, 2004; Gallimore, Goldenberg, & Weisner, 1993; LeVine, Dixon, LeVine, Richman, Leiderman, Keefer, & Brazelton, 1994; LeVine, Miller, & West, 1988; Weisner, 1996, 2002; Whiting & Edwards, 1988; Whiting & Whiting, 1980). As LeVine and colleagues (1994) state:

> A population tends to <u>share</u> an environment, symbol systems for <u>encoding</u> it, and organizations and codes of conduct for <u>adapting</u> to it (emphasis added). It is through the enactment of these population-specific codes of conduct in locally organized practices that human adaptation occurs. Human adaptation, in other words, is largely attributable to the operation of specific social organizations (e.g. families, communities, empires) following culturally prescribed scripts (normative models) in subsistence, reproduction, and other domains [communication and social regulation]. (p. 12)

It follows, then, that in seeking to understand child development in a cultural context, psychologists need to support collaborative and interdisciplinary developmental science that crosses international borders. Such research can advance cross-cultural psychology, cultural psychology, and indigenous psychology, understood as three sub-disciplines composed of scientists who frequently communicate and debate with one another and mutually inform one another's research programs. For example, to turn to parental belief systems, the particular topic of this chapter, it is clear that collaborative international studies are needed to support the goal of cross-cultural psychologists for findings that go beyond simply describing cultural differences in parental beliefs. Comparative researchers need to shed light on whether parental beliefs are (or are not) systematically related to differences in child outcomes; and they need meta-analyses and reviews to explore between- and within-culture variations in parental beliefs, with a focus on issues of social change (Saraswathi, 2000). Likewise, collaborative research programs can foster the goals of indigenous psychology and cultural psychology and lay out valid descriptions of individual development in their particular cultural contexts and the processes, principles, and critical concepts needed for defining, analyzing, and predicting outcomes of child development-in-context. The project described in this chapter is based on an approach that integrates elements of comparative methodology to serve the aim of describing particular scenarios of child development in unique contexts. The research team of cultural insiders and outsiders allows for a look at American belief systems based on a dialogue of multiple perspectives.

PARENTAL ETHNOTHEORIES AND THE CHILD'S LEARNING ENVIRONMENT

In every cultural community, human beings form families, raise children, and seek to pass on to them strategies that will promote their future survival and success as well as that of others in their group. Overarching parental goals provide for children the framework of an agenda for development, what Nsamenang (2000) calls the cultural "curriculum." This cultural curriculum has been described in many ways. John and Beatrice Whiting, in founding the contemporary field of comparative child development, coined the term *cultural learning environment* to refer to all of the dimensions (macro and micro) of everyday life that set the stage for child development and socialization (Whiting & Whiting, 1975). At every age period of childhood, distinctively different normative styles of companionship emerge and are influenced by the surrounding context (Whiting & Edwards, 1988). Particularly powerful and influential aspects of the cultural learning environment have been identified: gender, age, status/rank, and kinship relationships of social partners; the ongoing activities of work, play, and rest; and the basic organizing features associated with social structure (subsistence strategies, division of labor between males and females, family and household structure, residential patterns, education, media, technology, and social networks and community institutions). These factors influence what kinds and how much play and work children do, with whom they spend their time, how and where they eat and sleep, what education they receive, and what contact they have with the wider community.

Whiting (1976) argued that culture is too often treated as a "packaged variable" by social scientists, who see it as a nebulous but all pervasive explanation for variance left over and unexplained by individual variables (age, gender, social class, intelligence, and so on), and simply packaged as a black box called "ethnicity x" or "culture y." Although Whiting argued that human beings themselves may be ultimately unfathomable and incommensurable, that is not true for human culture (understood as the shared component of everyday beliefs, values, and practices). Whiting (1980) strove to define cultural dimensions that explain important normative characteristics of adult and child behavior that could be observed, measured, manipulated, and summarized by the techniques of science. The best data on the transmission of culture can be obtained using multiple methods, focusing on one domain and a limited set of hypotheses at a time. She argued that researchers need to continue to search for independent variables at the cultural level that are most powerful for explaining parent and child behavior around the world (Weisner & Edwards, 2001).

Thomas Weisner has advanced this basic perspective using the idea of the *ecocultural niche,* or *activity setting* (Gallimore, Goldenberg, & Weisner, 1993), to retain the functionalist assumption that cultural learning environments evolve continuously over time to promote adaptation to constraints imposed by external factors, changes in the subsistence base, climatic changes, and the political economies of the region. Activity settings are the routine everyday experiences that provide children with opportunities to learn and develop through modeling and interacting with others. They are the instantiation of the ecological and cultural systems surrounding the child and family, and the means by which institutions and prevailing cultural norms make themselves felt in the lives of children and influence their development.

Super and Harkness (1986), focusing on the child as a developing as well as learning organism, have put forward the term *developmental niche* which, building upon the approach of the Whitings, they define in terms of three key features: 1) organization of everyday life, that is, the physical and social settings and daily routines in which and through which the child lives, learns, grows, and develops; 2) parenting practices, that is, the culturally-regulated routines of child-care and child-training that are used by the child's caregivers; 3) cultural belief systems, the cognitive models and folk-theories, or *parental ethnotheories,* that caregivers hold regarding children, families, and themselves, and bring to their interaction with children.

Harkness and Super (1995) believe that cross-cultural studies of well-functioning families illuminate different cultural pathways to successful parenting. They focus their research on the third component, parental ethnotheories, because they believe that ethnotheories are the "nexus through which elements of the larger culture are filtered," and the source of the first two components, daily organization and parental practices (Harkness et al. 2001, p. 9). In this respect, Harkness and Super disagree with the Whitings who believed that values and beliefs (including expressive systems such as the arts and parental beliefs) are consequences that derive from material conditions and dimensions of everyday life, rather than the reverse (Whiting, 1980; Whiting et al., 1966). The Whitings put forward for empirical test the proposition that how families live is primary and predictive of parental values and beliefs, and they hypothesized that changes in parenting are brought about more by socioeconomic and population changes than by the introduction of new ideologies (cf. Goodnow, 2001). As Greenfield, Maynard, and Childs (2003) have put it, "In sum, socialization and development are not fixed but adapt, in a coordinated way, to changing ecological conditions" (p. 455).

An example of findings that are consistent with the Whiting conjecture about childrearing concerns is Kenyan village women's changing beliefs and values (Edwards, 2002). An international, multidisciplinary team of collaborators (Edwards & Whiting, editors, 2004) has recently published their case study of Ngecha, a Gikuyu community in the Central Province of Kenya undergoing rapid social change from an agrarian to a wage earning economy during a five-year period shortly after national independence (1968–1973). Village women became important protagonists and agents of social change as they experienced the various technological innovations and adjusted to the requisite modifications in their daily routines and living arrangements. As they sought their children's success in formal schooling, the most modernized mothers modified their concept of the "good child" and came to consider the constellation of "clever, inquisitive, confident, brave" more praiseworthy than the traditional Gikuyu constellation of "respectful, obedient, generous, and good-hearted." Mothers rearranged their value priorities and long-term aspirations for their children, leading to conflict between these new values and those of the Gikuyu of earlier generations. They participated in increased importance of nuclear families with more communication and closeness between young husbands and wives and greater autonomy from the authority of elder extended kin. Ngecha women also displayed a new resourcefulness in facing new opportunities to make money through cash cropping and other farming activities, going to secondary school and technical training, and making contact with the new national politics and culture. An overall theme of the volume is family adaptation, and how the change process impacted the daily lives of women and children and was seen through the eyes of the women who were important actors in the process. The volume documents the kaleidoscopic nature of culture change indicating how a change in one aspect of economy, technology, resources, or external opportunities leads to unplanned consequences in another set of cultural beliefs, values, and practices.

PARENTAL ETHNOTHEORIES IN THE UNITED STATES: INDEPENDENCE/INTERDEPENDENCE AND INDIVIDUALISM/COLLECTIVISM

Having presented the basic assumptions underlying this chapter, we now narrow the focus to one particular society and its cultural belief systems. We begin with a look at recent thinking about some domains of parental beliefs of deepest and most abiding interest to North American psychologists—that interest presumably stemming from the closeness of those domains to core values of American mainstream culture: *independence* (versus *dependence*, or versus *interdependence*) and *individualism* (versus *collectivism*) (Stewart & Bennett, 1991). Contemporary researchers have come to question these old dichotomies and have complicated the characterization of American core beliefs about independence and individualism.

The broadest possible review of literature on American parental ethnotheories about independence and individualism would conceivably draw from the great body of past research on American childrearing and socialization. However, since parental beliefs about childrearing have not been empirically linked to values and behaviors in any definitive way, this review is limited to the much smaller body of research in which investigators have looked at parental beliefs from an explicitly cultural framework and seen them as evidence of cultural socialization. This more limited body of research allows for an examination of the role of American culture in the construction of parental thinking about children's development, based on the assumption that parental ideas are culturally shared sets of meaning constructed within broader cultural belief systems (Goodnow & Collins, 1990; Lightfoot & Valsiner, 1992).

Several concepts have been used in the literature to capture parental ideas about young children. Some approaches have favored the concept of *folk theories* (Bruner, 1996) when referring to the cognitive models that parents hold regarding child development, socialization, and family interaction. Goodnow and Collins (1990) preferred the concept of *parental ideas*, questioning the extent to which parental thinking about everyday life can be regarded as a "theory." Because there is considerable overlap in usage of this terminology throughout the literature, however, we use the concepts of *parental belief systems* and *ethnotheories* interchangeably to capture the notion of parental cognitive models.

The most widely studied set of American parental beliefs concerns *independence*. For many years, the dichotomy of interest was *independence/dependence*, based on the theoretical notion that *dependency* is a learned motivational system, the manifestations of which are help-seeking, approval-seeking, and proximity-seeking behaviors, all of which serve to promote the survival of the developing child until their purpose is outgrown as the child matures toward autonomous adulthood (Gewirtz, 1972). In recent years, however, many researchers have come to believe that independence is a culturally specific goal of childrearing and that many cultures favor *interdependence* rather than independence as a developmental outcome. This debate positions both independence and interdependence as alternative endpoints of maturity. Independence and interdependence are polar opposites–either the two ends of a continuum, or else mutually exclusive categories (Raeff, 2000). Researchers such as Greenfield and Suzuki (1998) note that both independence and interdependence are manifest in a culturally diverse society such as the United States, but independence is differentially preferred by mainstream Americans while interdependence is preferred by many American minority and new immigrant populations. Along the same vein, others claim that European-American parents place greater emphasis on the fostering of individual achievement in their children than do members of many other cultures, whose people may place greater value on family or community identification and on achievement conceived of as familial or group success (Harkness, Super, and Keefer, 1992; Lynch and Hanson, 1998).

However, in recent years, more researchers are starting to criticize the independence-interdependence dichotomy as too simplistic. Moreover, they have sought to describe what may actually be a complex relationship between, on the one hand, independence/interdependence and on the other hand, *individualism/collectivism*. Individualism and collectivism are usually defined as overarching value systems that can be used to characterized groups of people at the societal level (Kim, Triandis, Kagitcibasi, Choi & Yoon, 1994). In their meta-analysis of empirical studies of individualism/collectivism outside and inside the United States, Oyserman, Coon, and Kemmelmeier (2002) suggest that individualism in all of its variations is commonly associated with valuing personal independence, with facilitating interactions with strangers and with fostering "a willingness to leave relationships that are not beneficial to the person" (p. 36). Conversely, collectivism implicates obligation and duty to an in-group and "willingness to remain permanently in relationships, even in personally costly ones" (p. 36). They concluded that even though the diverse research literature related to this topic does not lend itself to simple summary, individualism seems to promote ease of interacting with strangers while collectivity promotes in-group preferences in relationships. Individualism and collectivism are independent value dimensions, and a society can score high or low in either individualism or collectivism. Their review suggests that American samples generally score high on individualism but moderately on collectivism. Americans generally interact with more people more easily, than do the groups they were compared to, but at the same time Americans still feel obliged to certain groups–the difference being that these obligations are perceived as voluntary rather than compulsory.

Taking an extreme stand against the entire line of research, Killen and Wainryb (2000) have argued that cultural communities do not actually provide coherent and integrated systems of meanings and practices that can be characterized as either individualistic or collectivistic. Instead, Killen and Wainryb state that "individualistic concerns with independence and collectivistic concerns with interdependence coexist in Western and non-Western cultures" (Killen & Wainryb, 2000, p. 7). Individuals acquire multiple social orientations as they grow up, and cultures make available to them multiple orientations for use in different situations.

Taking a somewhat different approach, Raeff, Greenfield, and Quiroz (2000) have argued that both individualism and collectivism are complex and multifaceted value systems. In spite of being complex, however, these systems are still useful for understanding different cultural values about relationships. In their view, individualism and collectivism are value orientations at the societal or *cultural level*, while independence/interdependence are value orientations at the *individual level*. A society can be characterized as collectivistic or individualistic, but not as independent or interdependent in its value orientation. Rather, all societies, whether collectivistic or individualistic, must provide viable pathways to both independence and interdependence for their citizens, because both orientations are required for individuals to function in a mature way as part of a social group (Raeff, 1997). The European-American assumptions of freedom and equality include positive valuations of both independence and interdependence, defined in relation to each other. To support this point of view, Raeff (2000) found that American parents of toddlers defined independence in terms of separateness from others and uniqueness, and interdependence in terms of friendly engagement and prosocial behavior such as sharing, and they valued both kinds of behaviors in their babies.

Weisner (2001) also presents a complicating view of the American predilection for independence, but in a different way that centers on intrapsychic conflict. In a special issue devoted to the contributions of Beatrice Whiting to psychological anthropology, Weisner (2001) noted that Whiting liked to caricature what she saw as the American preoccupation with independence by calling it a "dependency hang-up." Whiting assumed that passionate arguments about a particular value often point to deep-seated conflicts and underlying contradictions. As evidence of a fundamental conflict about dependency underneath the American rhetoric about independence, she used data from the Six Culture Study (Whiting & Whiting, 1975). The data comparing the observed behavior of children aged 2 to 10 years showed that those from Orchard Town, New England were especially high in the dependency behaviors of seeking attention, resources and recognition from their parents. At the same time, they were frequently rewarded for a more egoistic self expression and pushed towards self-reliance in dressing, eating, toileting, sleeping, and other self-help skills (Whiting & Edwards, 1998). Weisner (2001) analyzed data from a longitudinal study of California countercultural and nonconventional families from the 1970s who were trying to challenge and counter American family practices and put new values into practice in raising their own children, including questioning the dependency conflicts they had experienced growing up. Weisner's observational data showed that these families had high levels of children seeking attention from parents, verbal negotiations, and dependency interactions, suggesting that these parents and children were reproducing the characteristic American "dependency/autonomy" conflict. This behavioral pattern occurred whether or not parents were strongly countercultural in their values. At the same time, there was significant intergenerational transmission of values from parents to children, a process revealing intergenerational as well as intrapsychic conflicts.

To conclude this section, the contemporary picture of American parents' ethnotheories has complicated considerably the characterization of American beliefs about independence/interdependence and individualism/collectivism. This viewpoint suggests the active and somewhat unpredictable role that developing individuals take in negotiating personal meanings to guide their lives. Participating in social groups that are significant to them, they co-construct complex and multifaceted belief systems that allow them to function in a dynamic and fluid society. Put more simply, people hold many ideas in mind, sometimes overlapping, sometimes contradictory, in their cultural toolkits, which they can pull out and use when needed.

However, generalized patterns can still be identified, and perhaps now is the time to move beyond the preoccupation with concepts of independence/interdependence (and individualism/collectivism) and instead study other constellations of American parental belief systems in their complexity. Looking at groups of American parents and children living in communities that interact dynamically and change over time, we can see how people's identifications, affiliations, and short- and long-term goals lead them to use their various conceptual tools in patterned and recognizable ways and to argue and act more on the basis of some belief systems rather than others. The belief systems that can be identified turn out to be configurations of ideas that cannot be described in simple dichotomies but that can still be understood as coherent and organized, and that are instantiated or grounded in their everyday social relationships and interactions with institutions.

AMERICAN PARENTAL ETHNOTHEORIES INVOLVING YOUNG CHILDREN'S BELIEFS ABOUT CHILDREN'S NEEDS FOR CLOSE RELATIONSHIPS OUTSIDE THE FAMILY

This final section of the paper draws on collaborative research (Aukrust, Edwards, Kumru, Knoche, & Kim, 2003). The original source and inspiration for this work was experience with intellectuals from European countries (especially Italy, Norway, and Scotland) who raised questions about how the social relational value priorities of their countries contrasted with the United States version of the Western mind. These Europeans raised questions about whether there is any single Westernized mentality.

In earlier research addressing the question of contrasts between U.S. and European approaches to childrearing, it was found that American and Italian parents and preschool teachers hold different assumptions about the depth and quality of close relationships that young children can form in the preschool, as well as for how important peer-peer and adult-child attachments are for learning and development (Edwards & Gandini, 1989; Edwards, Gandini, & Forman, 1993, 1998; Edwards, Gandini, & Giovannini, 1996; Gandini & Edwards, 2001). Samples of parents from both societies say that they put young children in preschool or childcare so they can make friends and develop cognitive and social skills that will get them ready for primary school. However, relative to parents from Italian samples (as well as parents from Japanese and Australian samples), parents from U.S. samples have very early expectations for their children acquiring certain kinds of verbal skills for getting along and negotiating with peers, independently of direct adult supervision and intervention. For example, these American samples are found to state that by age 4, children should have substantial capacities to take initiative, negotiate, stand up for their rights, ask questions, state their own needs, and explain their ideas—skills all clearly related to getting along in an assertive and self-directed way with one's peers at preschool (Edwards et al.; Hess et al., 1980).

Building on this work, the purpose of our project was to discover whether and how parents differ between and within cultures in their ethnotheories as related to young children's social relationships in childcare, preschool, and primary school. In contemporary societies throughout the world, parents must mediate and bridge their young children's transitions to a wider world. But how best to do so raises many questions for parents. For example, should they focus on giving children experiences that help them learn to form and maintain close ties with a few particular people? Or, instead, should they provide experiences that foster connecting in a friendly, less intimate way with a diverse succession of new people? The answers that parents construct may depend at least partly on their beliefs about what kind of preschool their child attends, as well as what kind of society their children will need to deal with as they grow older.

Our hypothesis was that some parents (perhaps those in residentially stable and culturally homogeneous societies) might expect that their children will benefit most if the children develop intimate and long-term ties with particular peers and teachers in preschools and primary schools, because these children are going to continue to live in close proximity to and interact with these same people for years to come. In contrast, other parents might expect that their children most need to develop skills for communicating and relating to people with whom they do not share a continuing relationship history, because residential or educational mobility in a mobile, fluid, diverse society is their likely destiny.

In mainstream United States culture today, relationships and communications both inside and outside the family have been found to be fostered when individuals use an *explicit* style of expression that allows their views and goals to be clearly recognized by others whether familiar or unfamiliar. This style of communication goes well with an assumption that over their lifetime, children will need to form relationships, interact, negotiate, and exchange resources with many people whom they do not know and with whom they will have only limited, short-term contact (Stewart & Bennett, 1991). Such a way of organizing relationships and communications has been found to differ from the structuring of relationships and communications in varied Asian, African, and South American cultural groups. For example, in some Asian and Latino cultures, relationships within the extended family are often prioritized over relationships outside the family (Lynch & Hanson, 1998). People are expected to fulfill implicit social obligations toward one another through unspoken emotional intimacy, based on long-term relationships and an *implicit* or indirect communication style.

Parents from four communities participated in the study. Two of these communities, Oslo (national capital of Norway) and Lincoln (state capital of Nebraska) are typical cities from Western Europe and the United States. Norway has been found to be distinctive in its emphasis on *equality* and *local belongingness* (Kiel, 1993), giving rise to a particular "egalitarian individualism" different from the more competitive American individualism. The other two communities, Ankara (national capital of Turkey) and Seoul (national capital of South Korea) provide contrasts from Middle East and Far East Asia. Compared to the communities of Lincoln and Oslo, our lead investigators from these countries (Kumru and Kim) expected parents in Ankara and Seoul to value familism and social-relational continuity with extended kin. However, because success in these societies is so dependent on educational achievement, the investigators also predicted that parental beliefs about their children's needs would reflect values favoring skills necessary for getting along in school.

The social organization of preschools and schools in these four communities differs in interesting ways. Two of them (United States and South Korea) feature preschool and primary school systems oriented toward change because every year it is usual for children to be placed with a new set of teachers and classmates (Shim & Herwig, 1997). We wondered, does this method of organizing schools serve to prepare children to succeed in a society oriented to residential and/or educational mobility and capacity to deal with newcomers and strangers? In contrast, the other two countries (Norway and Turkey) feature preschool and primary systems fostering continuity, because children stay with the same teachers and classmates for several years (Bo, 1993; Kapci & Guler; 1999). We wondered, does this way of organizing schools serve to maximize children's opportunities for developing multi-year extended relationships with peers and teachers?

We assumed that the macro features of educational organization–products of history and sociological forces–might be expected to reflect parents' ideas about how children should learn to deal with people outside the extended family. The Norwegian and Turkish school systems would seem to orient parents to focus on child experiences that help them learn to form and maintain close ties with a few particular people, and to develop a continuing relationship history. The American and South Korean school systems would seem to orient parents to focus on experiences that foster connecting with a diverse succession of new people. The full results are presented in a journal publication (Aukrust et al., 2003), but here the focus is what the findings may tell us about American parental models of close relationships for young children and sense of belonging in preschool.

The Lincoln, Nebraska, parents (n = 95, 90% mothers) were recruited through 7 preschools or childcare centers. The class sizes varied from 10–15 children, with commonly 2 teachers per classroom. Each preschool had its own curriculum and was supported mostly by parental tuition (with subsidies for some qualified children). The children did not necessarily live close to their school but were driven by parents. The mean age of the parents was 32.8 years, and their preschool child had a mean age of 4 years 3 months. Most parents (74%) were married or living together with the target child's other parent. Mean number of children in the family was 1.9. (The samples from the other communities were similar in size and parental age and social class).

Residential stability was of particular interest to the investigators because of the study focus on parental embeddedness in their local community as a predictor of their ideas and beliefs. Most Lincoln sample families (72%) lived in proximity to one or more close relatives, such as the child's grandparents, aunts, uncles, or cousins. The Lincoln sample was the most geographically mobile in our study, but perhaps not so very mobile by American standards. Lincoln is a medium-sized city of the American Midwest with many families living within driving distance of kin. Nebraska is one of the U.S. states with highest residential stability: in most counties, including Lincoln/Lancaster County, at least 60% of residents were born in-state (New York Times, September 30, 2002, p. A16). The percentage of families in our sample who had moved within the past 2 years was 51%. Parents were asked where they had grown up, and 65% had grown up in the community in which they were presently living. Asked about their plans to leave their city, 50% of the parents in the Lincoln sample reported that they would expect to move away at some point.

Findings from only two sections of our results are discussed here. The first concerns the subscale called Parental Beliefs about Social and Communication skills. It consisted of 6 paired sets of items that assessed beliefs that parents might hold concerning the communication skills their own young child needs most. One item in each set reflected preference for

Table 1. Ethnotheories of Parents in Lincoln, Nebraska, USA, Concerning Young Children's Communication Skills

The following 6 statements reflect ideas that parents may think about young children. Participants rated pairs of alternatives (1 = fully agree with A, 2 = mostly agree with A, 3 = mostly agree with B, 4 = fully agree with B), considering their own child as they answered.	N = 95
Higher scores indicate greater agreement with the second alternatives, indicating preference for intensive, long-term relationships and communication. A mean score of 2.5 indicates equal balance in parental preference for the A and B alternatives.	M (SD)
1. What young children today most need is	
—confidence to meet and communicate with new people, in new situations, *vs.* —capacity to form deep, meaningful relationships that provide security and continuity.	2.53 (.10)
2. Communication skill comes from —learning to make oneself understood to people who do not understand immediately, *vs.* —having many conversations with people the child knows well.	2.55 (.10)
3. Young children should have attachment relationships with adults —at preschool as a basis for secure learning, *vs.* —only at home, not at preschool or child care.	1.61 (.07)
4. Young children need —time together with a variety of people from different backgrounds and cultures, *vs.* —to get to know a few people well and become part of a close group.	1.60 (.08)
5. Young children need —playmates, but at this age it is not important whether they develop into close friends, *vs.* —friendships that will last and continue into the years to come.	2.33 (.09)
6. At any age, it is important and useful to —make friends quickly and easily, *vs.* —hold onto close friends and have a few people you can really trust.	2.70 (.10)

intensive, long-term relationships and communication style. The other reflected preference for more short-term, immediate relationships and communication style. Parents were asked to report their agreement with one statement or the other (using a 4-point scale).

The findings (see Table 1) show that the Lincoln parents were fairly close to the midpoint on four of the six choices (mean = 2.5). They were more likely to favor the A versus B alternative when it came to believing that young children should form attachment relationships with adults at the preschool or childcare (versus only at home). They also favored the proposal that young children need time together with a variety of people from different backgrounds and cultures (versus getting to know a few people well and become part of a close group). Thus, these parents wanted their children to get along with diverse people and to be able to attach quickly and readily to new caregivers as a basis for secure learning at preschool. In general, they put almost equal weight on both the A and B styles of communicating and relating though leaning toward the A alternative for two questions. If we return to Oyserman et al.'s (2002) definition of individualism as an orientation promoting ease of interacting with strangers while collectivism as one promoting in-group preferences in relationships, then this sample of Lincoln parents appears to not strongly favor one orientation over the other.

The second set of findings to be presented focuses on the subscale of Parental Values About Dimensions of Preschool Quality. Thirteen items allowed parental rating of dimensions along which preschool programs might vary. Parents were asked to rate the items by selecting the 4 they thought most important and the 4 to be least important, again thinking about their own child as they answered. The items addressed children's groups (e.g. "children play with the same friends every day"), curriculum (e.g. "activities build on children's expressed ideas and interests"), group size (e.g. "class group small enough so that teachers can give individual attention"), parent-teacher relationships (e.g. "parent-teacher relationships become close over time"), school reputation (e.g. "school has a history known to families and a special identity"), and administration (e.g. "school leadership is stable and provides direction, is not chaotic").

The findings show that the Lincoln parents were most likely to choose the following four variables as the most important elements of quality. These four variables seem to relate to qualities of the immediate present, the here and now of a child-centered classroom and curriculum:

Table 2. Ethnotheories of Parents in Lincoln, Nebraska, USA, Concerning Dimensions of Preschool Quality

Parents' beliefs about what dimensions of quality are most important for a preschool or childcare program. Parents selected their 4 most important dimensions, and 4 least important dimensions. For analysis, these were weighted as 3 = most important, 2 = not selected, 1 = least important.	M (SD)
1. Class groups are stable because few children come and go	1.66 (.07)
2. Class groups small enough that teachers can give individual attention	2.68 (.06)
3. Children play with same few friends every day	1.53 (.07)
4. Friendship groups stay together from one year to the next	1.52 (.07)
5. Parent-teacher relationships become close over time	2.18 (.07)
6. Children experience a sense of belonging in the classroom	2.74 (.06)
7. Parents get to know each other well and become a group	1.50 (.08)
8. School has enough teachers and space	2.29 (.07)
9. Many experienced teachers stay at school for a long time	2.20 (.07)
10. School leadership is stable and provides direction—is not chaotic	2.29 (.07)
11. Activities build on children's expressed ideas and interests	2.47 (.06)
12. Activities connect and develop into long-term projects or themes	1.97 (.08)
13. School has a history known to families and a special identity	1.51 (.07)

- ◆ Children experience a sense of belonging in the classroom
- ◆ Class groups small enough that teachers can give children individual attention
- ◆ Activities build on children's expressed ideas and interests
- ◆ School has enough teachers and space.

The Lincoln parents also rated four variables as least important. These variables seem to relate to relationships that involve continuity over time:

- ◆ Children play with the same few friends every day
- ◆ Friendship groups stay together from one year to the next
- ◆ Parents get to know one another well and become a group
- ◆ School has a history known to families and a special identity.

These findings are consistent with a prediction that a sample of American parents would put strong emphasis on their children getting along well with peers (not being excluded or left out), but at the same time, put relatively less emphasis on their children having close and enduring relationships with either adults or children in the nonfamilial setting of preschool.

Multidimensional scalings of these data were performed by Knoche (2001). This kind of analysis provides a statistical way of analyzing the

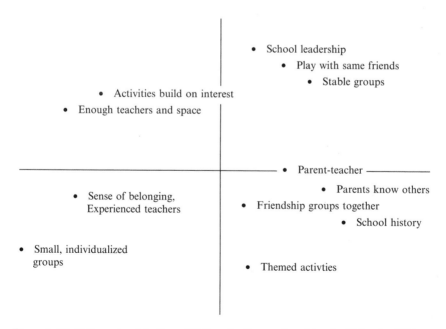

Figure 1. Multidimensional Scaling of Ratings by Parents from Lincoln, Nebraska, USA, on Dimensions of Preschool Quality

Abbreviated Label	Full Item Description
• *School Leadership*	School leadership is stable and provides direction
• *Play same friends*	Children play with same friends every day
• *Stable groups*	Class groups are stable
• *Activities build on interest*	Activities build on children's expressed interest
• *Enough teachers and space*	School has enough teachers and space
• *Parent-teacher*	Parent-teacher relationships close
• *Parents know others*	Parents get to know each other well and become a group
• *School history*	School has known history and identity to families
• *Friendship groups together*	Friendship groups stay together year to year
• *Themed activities*	Activities connect and develop into themes
• *Small, individualized groups*	Class groups are small enough for individual attention
• *Sense of belonging*	Children experience sense of belonging,
• *Experienced teachers*	Experienced teachers at school long time

configuration underlying how a set of variables relate one to another for a set of research participants. Thus, it provides a window into their underlying meaning system as they responded to the questionnaire, thinking about their own child as they answered. The Lincoln, Nebraska data were susceptible to a 2-dimensional solution with acceptable stress (.15) and explaining a high percentage of variance (.89). The visual rendering of this solution is provided in Figure 1. It is quite easy to interpret this solution as having a horizontal axis representing focus on *quality in the immediate present* versus *quality dependent on long term relationships*. The vertical dimension appears to represent *adult quality variables* versus *child and activity quality variables*

Of special interest is variable 6 "sense of belonging in the classroom." In fact, across all four samples, this was a very highly ranked variable (Aukrust et al., 2003). Figure 1 indicates that for the Lincoln parents, this variable was positioned within a little cluster off by itself along with variable 2 "class groups small enough that teachers can give individual attention." In other words, children's sense of belonging was believed by Lincoln parents to be closely related to their children being in small classroom groups where they received sufficient individualized attention from teachers. In contrast, in the multidimensional scalings for the other three communities, variable 6 "sense of belonging" took different positions in the visual configuration. In the data from Oslo, Norway (Figure 2) for example, "sense of belonging" was in a cluster with variable 2 "class groups small enough" (as in Lincoln) but also containing variable 9 "experienced teachers stay at school a long time," a variable not at all close to variable 6 for the Lincoln parents. In the data from Ankara, Turkey (Figure 3), "sense of belonging" was part of a tight cluster containing 6 other variables (variables 2, 5, 8, 9, 11, and 12), but was far from variable 3 "children play with the same few friends every day." In the data from Seoul, Korea (Figure 4), "sense of belonging" mapped closest to

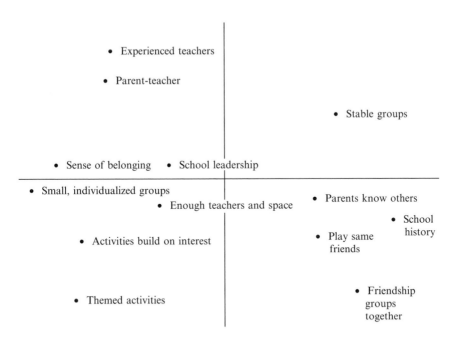

Figure 2. Multidimensional Scaling of Ratings by Parents from Oslo, Norway, on Dimensions of Preschool Quality

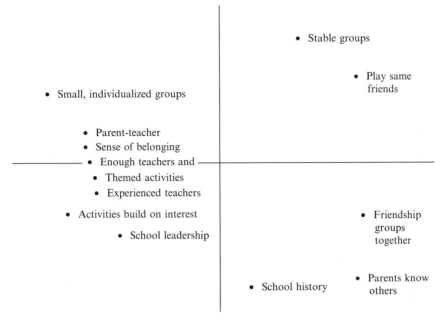

Figure 3. Multidimensional Scaling of Ratings by Parents from Ankara, Turkey, on Dimensions of Preschool Quality

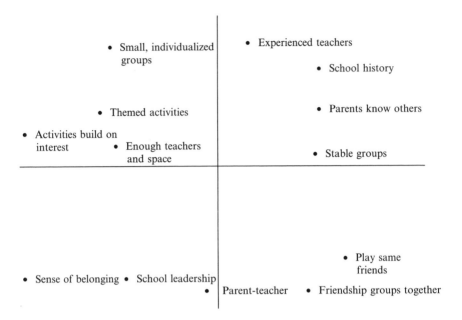

Figure 4. Multidimensional Scaling of Ratings by Parents from Seoul, Korea, on Dimensions of Preschool Quality

variable 3 "children play with the same few friends every day," and was also near to variable 10 "stable school leadership" and 5 "close parent-teacher relationships," but not close to variable 2.

If we again turn to Oyserman et al. (2002) concepts of individualism as an orientation promoting ease of interacting with strangers, and collectivism as promoting obligation to an in-group and willingness to remain permanently in relationships, even in personally costly ones, then this sample of Lincoln, Nebraska parents appears to be quite individualistic in its understanding of what constitutes a high-quality childcare or preschool experience. Indeed, the parental model goes along with the organization of the early care and education system in Nebraska (and elsewhere in the USA), where standards of quality are rated on high teacher-child ratios, daily curriculum planning, and plentiful resources, but not on teacher stability or children's social relationships with peers.

In sum, the Lincoln, Nebraska, parents have a more balanced view of the kinds of social and communication skills they value for their children's development (indicated by their responses to the Parental Beliefs about Social and Communication skills scale) than they do for the kind of preschool environment that they consider to be of high quality for their children (found on the Parental Values About Dimensions of Preschool

Quality measure). Individualism is more highly expressed in Lincoln parents' concepts about where their children should spend out-of-home time than it is in their views of what social and communication skills are desirable for children.

SUMMARY AND CONCLUSIONS

Culture is organized and coherent, but not homogeneous and static. It is a dynamic system that a group of people who share an environment use to encode and adapt to their surroundings, make a living, raise families, communicate with one another, and regulate their social behavior. Parental belief systems are part of the learning environment that enfolds developing children and embed their learning, growth, work, play, education, and participation in a shared system of meaning.

The parental ethnotheories of American parents suggest some contradictions and tensions in their configurations of beliefs about childrearing, and perhaps these match the confusions and contradictions of contemporary life as they know it. In the past, both researchers and the public have tended to discuss American childrearing ideas in a long-familiar language of independence and individualism. However, a fresh and closer look reveals that their sets of beliefs contain some tension between their goals for their children's development and for their children's daily environments.

The approach of indigenous psychology takes researchers inside the American system of parental ethnotheories and allows researchers to see how parental beliefs and goals can be set into dynamic interrelationship for parents and children. People frame issues in terms of the discourse they use everyday and the situations and routines they face in their current lives. In our four-culture project on Young Children's Close Relationships Outside of the Family, parents from Lincoln, Nebraska particularly wanted their children to quickly gain the social and communicative skills for getting along and for functioning well in a community of relative strangers, for example, being able to attach quickly and readily to new caregivers as a basis for secure learning at preschool. At the same time, they almost equally favored the social and communication skills valuable for becoming part of a close-knit group and forming lasting relationships. In thinking about their own child's needs and selecting what makes a preschool or child care center high quality, Lincoln parents looked to individualistic features related to the immediate present, such as sense of belonging (not being excluded or left out), getting enough individual attention from teachers, and having activities that respond to their own interests in an environment with plenty of teachers and space. While they wanted their children to be able to make close friends and become attached to teachers (values fostering interdependence), they did not see a high quality out-of-home experience dependent on forming intimate or relationships with either adults or children in the preschool.

In some ways, the ethnotheories of these Nebraska parents are part of a framework of expectations about the kinds of social relationships their children have at present and will meet in the future in a fairly mobile (sometimes confusing and stressful) context that values close-knit families and settled ties to Nebraska roots but at the same time provides incentives for people to change jobs, residences, schools, and friendships fairly often—where many people learn to relish change and its possibilities and opportunities while minimizing the costs of relationship turnover.

REFERENCES

Aukrust, V., Edwards, C.P., Kumru, A., Knoche, L., & Kim, M. (2003). Young children's close relationships outside of the family: Parental ethnotheories in four communities, in Norway, United States, Turkey, and Korea. *International Journal of Behavior Development, 27*, 481–494.

Bo, I. (1993). Norway. In M. Cochran (Ed.), *International handbook of child care policies and programs* (pp. 391–414). Westport, CT: Greenwood Press.

Bruner, J. (1996). *The culture of education.* Cambridge: Harvard University Press.

Edwards, C.P. (2002). Evolving questions and comparative perspectives in cultural/historical research. *Human Development, 171*, 307–312.

Edwards, C.P. & Gandini, L. (1989). Teachers' expectations about the timing of developmental skills: A cross-cultural study. *Young Children, 44*, 15–19.

Edwards, C.P., Gandini, L., & Giovannini, D. (1996). The contrasting developmental expectations of parents and early childhood teachers in two cultural communities. In S. Harkness and C. Super (Eds.), *Parents' cultural belief systems* (pp. 270–288). New York: Guilford.

Edwards, C. P. & Whiting, B. B. (2004). *Ngecha: A Kenyan village in a time of rapid social change* (Eds.). Lincoln, Nebraska: University of Nebraska Press.

Gallimore, R., Goldenberg, C.N., & Weisner, T.S. (1993). The social construction and subjective reality of activity settings: Implications for community psychology. *American Journal of Community Psychology, 21*, 537–559.

Gewirtz, J. L. (Eds.) (1972). *Attachment and dependency.* Washington, D.C.: Winston and Sons.

Goodnow, J. (2001). Commentary: culture and parenting, cross-cutting issues. *International Society for the Study of Behavioral Development Newsletter,* Number 1 Serial No. 38, 13–14.

Goodnow, J. & Collins, W. A. (1990). *Development according to parents: The nature, sources, and consequences of parents' ideas.* Hillsdale, NJ: Lawrence Erlbaum.

Greenfield, P. M., Maynard, A. E., & Childs, C. P. (2003). Historical change, cultural learning, and cognitive representation in Zinacantec Maya children. *Cognitive Development, 18*, 455–487.

Greenfield, P.M., & Suzuki, L.K. (1998). Culture and human development: Implications for parenting, education, pediatrics, and mental health. In I.E. Sigel and K.A. Renninger (Eds), *Child psychology in practice (Handbook of child psychology, ed. 5, vol. 4).* New York: John Wiley.

Harkness, S., & Super, C. (1995). Culture and parenting. In M. Bornstein (Ed.), *Handbook of parenting, volume 2. Biology and ecology of parenting* (pp. 211–234). Mahwah, NJ: Lawrence Erlbaum Associates.

Harkness, S., Super, C. M. & Keefer, C. H. (1992). Learning to be an American parent: How cultural models gain directive force. In R. G. D'Andrade and C. Strauss (Eds.), *Human motives and cultural models*. New York: Cambridge University Press.

Harkness, S., Super, C. S., Axia, V., Eliasz, A., Palacios, J., & Welles-Nystrom, B. (2001). *International Society for the Study of Behavioral Development Newsletter*, Number 1 Serial No. 38, 9–13.

Hess, R.D., Kashiwagi, K., Azuma, H., Price, G. G., & Dickson, W. P. (1980). Maternal expectations for mastery of developmental tasks in Japan and the United States. *International Journal of Psychology, 15*, 259–271.

Kapci, E. G. & Guler, D. (1999). Pre-school education in Turkey: Policies and practices in their historical context. *Early Child Development and Care, 156*, 53–62.

Kiel, A. H. (Ed.). (1993). *Continuity and change: Aspects of contemporary Norway*. Oslo: Scandinavian University Press.

Killen, M. & Wainryb, C. (2000). Independence and interdependence in diverse cultural contexts. In S. Harkness, C. Raeff, and C. Super (Eds.), *Variability in the cultural construction of the child* (pp. 5–22). San Francisco: Jossey-Bass New Directions for Child and Adolescent Development, no. 87.

Kim, U., Triandis, H. C., Kagitcibasi, C., Choi, S. C., & Yoon, G. (Eds.) (1994). *Individualism and collectivism: Theory, method and applications*. Thousand Oaks, CA: Sage Publications.

Knoche, L. (2001). Representing parental questionnaires on preschool quality by multidimensional scaling. 996 paper, Department of Psychology, University of Nebraska—Lincoln.

LeVine, R.A., Miller, P.M., & West, M.M. (Eds). (1988). *Parental behavior in diverse societies*. San Francisco, CA: Jossey Bass, New Directions for Child Development, No. 40.

LeVine, R. A., Dixon, S., LeVine, S., Richman, A., Leiderman, P.H., Keefer, C., & Brazelton, T.B. (1994). *Child care and culture: Lessons from Africa*. London: Cambridge University Press.

Lightfoot, C. & Valsiner, J. (1992). Parental belief systems under the influence: Social guidance of the construction of personal cultures *Parental belief systems: The psychological consequences for children*. In I. Sigel, A. McGillicuddy-DeLisis, & J. Goodnow (Eds.), (pp. 393–414). Hillsdale, NJ: Lawrence Erlbaum.

Lynch, E.W. & Hanson, J.M. (1998. *Developing cross-cultural competence: A guide for working with children and their families, 2nd ed*. Baltimore MD: Paul Brookes.

Munroe, R.H., & Munroe, R.L. (1984). Children's work in four cultures: Determinants and consequences. *American Anthropologist, 86*, 369–379.

Nsamenang, A.B. (2000). Issues in indigenous approaches to developmental research in sub-Saharan Africa. *International Society for the Study of Behavioral Development Newsletter*, Number 1 Serial No. 38, 1–2.

Oyserman, D., Coon, H. M., & Kemmelmeier, M. (2002). Rethinking individualism and collectivism: Evaluation of theoretical assumptions and meta-analyses. *Psychological Bulletin, 128*, 3–72.

Raeff, C. (1997). Individuals in relationships: cultural values, children's social interactions, and the development of an American individualistic self. *Developmental Review, 17*, 205–238

Raeff, C. (2000). European-American parents' ideas about their toddlers' independence and interdependence. *Journal of Applied Developmental Psychology, 21*, 183–205.

Raeff, C., Greenfield, P.M., & Quiroz, B. (2000). Conceptualizing interpersonal relationships in the cultural contexts of individualism and collectivism. In S. Harkness, C. Raeff, and C. Super (Eds.), *Variability in the cultural construction of the child* (pp. 59–74). San Francisco: Jossey-Bass New Directions for Child and Adolescent Development, no. 87.

Saraswathi, T.S. (2000). Commentary: Culture and parenting: Beyond description of alternative beliefs and practices. *International Society for the Study of Behavioral Development Newsletter*, Number 1 Serial No. 38, 14–15.

Shim, S. & Herwig, J. (1997). Korean teachers' beliefs and teaching practices in Korean early childhood education. *Early Child Development and Care, 132*, 45–55.

Super, C. & Harkness, S. (1986). The developmental niche: a conceptualization at the interface of child and culture. *International Journal of Behavioral Development, 9,* 545–569.

Stewart, E. & Bennett, M. (1991). *American cultural patterns: A cross-cultural perspective.* Yarmouth: Intercultural Press.

Weisner, T. S. (1996). The 5 to 7 transition as an ecocultural project. In A. J. Sameroff & M. M. Haith (Eds.), *The five to seven year shift: The age of reason and responsibility* (pp. 295–328). Chicago: University of Chicago Press.

Weisner, T.S. (2001). The American dependency conflict: Continuities and discontinuities in behavior and values of countercultural parents and their children. *Ethos, 29,* 271–295.

Weisner, T.S. (2002). Ecocultural understanding of children's developmental pathways. *Human Development, 45,* 275–281.

Weisner, T.S. & Edwards, C.P. (2001). Introduction to a special issue in honor of the contributions of Beatrice B. Whiting. *Ethos, 29,* 1–8.

Whiting, B.B. (1976). The problem of the packaged variable. In K.F. Riegel & J. A. Meacham (Eds.), *The developing individual in a changing world, Vol. I: Historical and cultural issues.* Netherlands: Mouton and Co.

Whiting, B.B. (1980). Culture and social behavior: A model for the development of social behavior. *Ethos, 8,* 95–116.

Whiting, B.B., & Edwards, C.P. (1988). *Children of different worlds: The formation of social behavior.* Cambridge, MA: Harvard University Press.

Whiting, B.B., & Whiting, J.W.M. (1975). *Children of six cultures: A psychocultural analysis.* Cambridge, MA: Harvard University Press.

Whiting, J.W.M., Child, I.L., Lambert, W.W., Fischer, A.M., Fischer, J.L., Nydegger, C., Nydegger, W., Maretzki, H., Maretzki, T., Minturn, L., Romney, A.K., Romney, R.. (1966). *Field guide for a study of socialization.* New York: John Wiley.

Chapter 7

Close Interpersonal Relationships among Japanese
Amae *as Distinguished from Attachment and Dependence*

Susumu Yamaguchi and Yukari Ariizumi

Japanese have an indigenous concept, *amae* (甘え), that describes a behavioral pattern typically found in mother-child relationships. This concept became known internationally after the publication of a seminal book by a Japanese psychoanalyst, Doi (1971), who claimed that *amae* is a key concept for understanding Japanese mentality. Despite the numerous studies inspired by Doi's work, the concept of *amae* has remained vague, and consensus among researchers has not yet been achieved. Many international scholars misunderstand the concept, and believe that *amae* is similar to dependence and unique to Japanese, implying that Japanese (as compared to Westerners) are uniquely dependent in their interpersonal relationships. However, the uniqueness of the indigenous concept does not necessarily imply that the Japanese behavioral pattern the concept describes is also unique. This article clarifies the meaning of *amae* by distinguishing it from dependence and insecure attachment, both of which are often confused with *amae*. The *etic* nature of *amae* is then discussed.

WHAT IS *AMAE?*

Definition controversies

Doi defined *amae* in various ways. For example, he wrote that "one may perhaps describe *amae* as, ultimately, an attempt psychologically to deny the fact of separation from the mother" (1973, p. 74). He also wrote that *amae* roughly corresponds to dependency or dependency need (Doi, 1997), whereas in yet another article *amae* is defined as depending upon another's love or basking in another's indulgence (Doi, 1992). Most recently, Doi also defined *amae* as acting on the presumption that one's counterparts favor one (Doi, 2001). According to Doi (2001), one engages in this kind of behavior automatically without awareness. *Amae* is an expression of love and also represents emotional dependence. Because Doi's definition has been broad and has fluctuated over time, researchers have criticized the ambiguity in his definitions and some have proposed their own definition of *amae* (Kumagai, 1981; Lebra, 1976; Maruta, 1992; Okonogi, 1968; Pelzel, 1977; Sofue, 1972; Taketomo, 1986). For example, Sofue (1972) defined *amae* as depending on others with the expectation that they will accept it.

Taketomo (1986), who has advanced the most systematic criticism against Doi's theory, argued that Doi ignored the rules in *amae* interactions. According to Taketomo, *amae* episodes are characterized by the following features: (a) Interactions are under a temporary suspension of some ordinary restraints. (b) The suspension is agreed upon by the interactants. In such a situation, interactants are allowed to do what they are normally expected not to do. For example, a ten-year-old boy may ask his mother to dress him, although ten-year-olds are normally expected to dress themselves. A husband can behave like a child to his wife, although he is a mature adult. In these examples, the boy and the husband engage in inappropriate behavior that is not allowed in an ordinary interpersonal relationship. Their behavior is accepted when their counterpart accepts the suspension of the ordinary restraints: a boy's managing his own clothes and a husband's behaving in a mature way.

Given the disagreements on the definition of *amae* and the lack of empirical research (except a few sporadic and unsystematic studies), Kim and Yamaguchi (1995) administered an open-ended questionnaire on *amae* to 237 junior high students, 224 senior high students, 243 college students, and 137 adults. The questionnaire tapped various aspects of *amae* in everyday interactions. The results indicated: (a) *Amae* is associated with either positive and negative emotions or feelings. (b) *Amae* is acceptable as long as it does not disrupt interpersonal relationships. (c) There are two kinds of *amae* interactions: a vertical relationship, which is typically found between mother and child, and horizontal relationship, which is typical between friends.

What *Amae* Means in Everyday Life

Extending Taketomo's (1986) argument and the results of the open-ended questionnaire, *amae* can be defined as *presumed acceptance of one's inappropriate behavior or request* (Yamaguchi, 1999a). In close relationships, one is able to presume that one's inappropriate behavior or request will be accepted due to the positive or at least non-negative attitude of one's counterpart. This definition of *amae* implies that two components, the inappropriate behavior or request and presumption of acceptance, are involved in *amae* episodes.

The two components of *amae* are the focus of the empirical examination in this study designed to test the validity of the above definition. Because *amae* is an everyday word, a folk psychology approach was adopted (Yamaguchi, 1999b). Japanese lay people experience *amae* either as the actor or the target in everyday life. In this sense, they are experts in *amae*, albeit their lay epistemology may not be systematic and thus limited scientifically. As Bruner (1990) stated, people anticipate and judge one another and draw conclusions about the worthwhileness of their lives through folk psychology. A folk psychology is also expected "to provide a system by which people organize their experience in, knowledge about, and transactions with the world" (Bruner, 1990, p. 35). Thus, a folk psychology of *amae* can provide a thorough understanding, because it reveals how people use the word in everyday life and thus allows one to grasp the *amae* phenomenon as commonly observed in everyday Japanese life. In addition, a folk psychology of *amae* guarantees the ecological validity of the definition of *amae*. The definition of a concept is ecologically valid if it is consistent with lay people's perception and judgment (Yamaguchi, 2004a).

Presumption of acceptance. In one study, participants were presented with 20 vignettes describing *amae* interactions in which the protagonist does something inappropriate (Yamaguchi., 1999b). In the presumption condition, the protagonist presumed that the inappropriate behavior or request would be accepted by the counterpart, whereas in the no-presumption condition, the protagonist did not presume that it would be accepted. In the control condition, no information regarding the presumption of acceptance was given. The participants were asked if they would label the inappropriate behavior described in the 20 scenarios as *amae*. Eighty-seven percent of the participants labeled the inappropriate behavior or request as *amae* in the presumption condition, whereas only 42 percent of the participants in the no-presumption condition and 59 percent of participants in the control condition labeled the inappropriate behavior or request as *amae*.

Ambivalent attitude toward amae requester. Because *amae* involves an inappropriate behavior or request, one might expect that the *amae* requester is disliked. We hypothesized the contrary; *amae* is at least sometimes perceived as an expression of love, as Doi (2001) and Kim and Yamguchi (1995) suggested. Thus, if one requests *amae*, one would be perceived as expressing love toward one's counterpart. In a similar vein, one who never requests *amae* can be perceived as a person who never expresses love toward anyone. This kind of person would be perceived as cold. Thus, we predicted that people would have an ambivalent attitude toward an *amae* requester, because *amae* involves both positive and negative aspects. That is, an inappropriate behavior or request and an expression of love. To test this prediction, Yamaguchi (1999b) asked participants to evaluate a person (a) who always requests *amae*, (b) who sometimes requests *amae*, or (c) who never requests *amae*, on a seven-point bipolar scale (e.g., warm-cold). The results indicated, as predicted, that the participants had an ambivalent attitude toward the three types of *amae* requesters. On the likeability dimension, they liked a person who sometimes requests *amae* best and least liked a person who never requests *amae*. On the other hand, on the fairness dimension, the person who never requests *amae* was evaluated most highly and the person who always requests *amae* was evaluated as lowest on the fairness dimension.

The data collected so far suggest that one can count on others in close relationships when one wants to behave inappropriately or when one has an inappropriate request. But, how is *amae* different from attachment and dependence? Yamaguchi (2004a) claimed that *amae* can be differentiated both from dependence and insecure attachment. In the next section, Yamaguchi's (2004a) argument is elaborated.

AMAE AND DEPENDENCE

Dependence is also a controversial concept. It has been defined in various ways because it has been studied in three domains of psychology: developmental, clinical, and social psychology (Bornstein, 1993). For example, Birtchnell (1988) proposed a definition from a developmental perspective: the dependent person is an adult behaving as though he or she were a child (p. 120). Perhaps the most important characteristic of a dependent person would be that the person is dependent on others for acceptance and approval (Birtchnell, 1988). Attempting to incorporate previous definitions, Bornstein proposed a comprehensive definition of dependence including its motivational, cognitive, affective, and behavioral components. Dependency is characterized by motivation to be guided by others, perception that others are powerful and can control the outcome of situations, a tendency to become anxious when required to function independently, and a tendency to seek approval, guidance, and to yield to others (Bornstein, p. 19).

Perhaps the most important difference between *amae* and dependence is its locus of control. In successful *amae* episodes, because the inappropriate behavior or request is accepted, the *amae* requester can control the outcome of the situation. In contrast, the dependent person cannot control the outcome. Thus, the *amae* requester can be a causal agent, whereas the dependent person has to be the puppet of someone else. This difference in terms of the agent of control is discussed in Yamaguchi (2001). *Amae* can be considered a kind of control attempt in which the agent (i.e., *amae* requester) controls the situation through another person; known as *proxy control* (Bandura, 1982). It is intriguing that in *amae* episodes, the powerful people are controlled by the less powerful who make an inappropriate request that is accepted by the powerful person, especially when they are in a close relationship.

As Bandura (1982) correctly pointed out, proxy control has the problem that individuals attempting it have to give up their direct control over the situation and thus miss the opportunity to acquire necessary skills to directly control the situation. However, individuals with sufficient interpersonal skills to persuade powerful others to work for their benefit have advantages in terms of survival: they can keep the situation under their control as long as someone who is powerful is available and willing to help them.

The second difference is the need for approval or guidance. The *amae* requester knows what they want. In this sense, the *amae* requester does not need any guidance and thus is psychologically independent. Because the *amae* requester presumes that his or her inappropriate behavior or request will be accepted by the counterpart, he or she does not need approval from the counterpart. Thus, unlike the dependent person, the *amae* requester can maintain or even bolster his or her sense of self-worth. As long as the *amae* request is accepted, *amae* requesters can be self-confident in terms of controlling the environment to their liking and also in terms of the approval of the counterpart.

One possible defect of *amae*, from a Western perspective, is the lack of direct control of the environment. *Amae* requesters cannot control the environment directly because they are less powerful or reluctant to do so directly. This problem, however, depends on the dominant cultural values. In a Western society, one is supposed to be independent and autonomous. To become an adult in a Western society means that one has acquired the requisite skills to function independently in the society. In East Asia, on the other hand, individuals are not always required to be autonomous. Rather, interdependence is emphasized (Markus & Kitayama, 1991) and proxy control is more widely accepted. Probably for this reason, *amae* episodes can be seen among adults as well as children in East Asian societies. Successful *amae* requesters are often successful in society because those who are good at *amae* (i.e., proxy control) can control the environment to a greater extent than those who never request *amae*. In Japan, children who cannot request *amae* are often seen as maladapted (Okonogi, 1968). In *amae* episodes, one can maintain and verify a close relationship and at the same time control the situation. This may be the reason people choose to request *amae* rather than attempt to directly control a situation.

AMAE AND ATTACHMENT

According to Bowlby (1969), "attachment behavior refers to seeking and maintaining proximity to another individual" (p. 241). Beyond physical proximity, attachment involves strong bonds of affection to particular others, typically one's parents in the case of infants. Bowlby hypothesized that an attachment behavioral system guides infants to be attached to their caregivers for safety and survival. Although systematic empirical research on attachment started with infants, attachment relationships have been found among adolescents and adults as well.

In laboratory settings, attachment has been systematically studied using the Strange Situation procedure (Ainsworth, Blehar, Waters, & Wall, 1978). In Strange Situation studies, securely attached children who play happily with the toys and explore a new environment in their mother's presence are considered most adaptive. However, Rothbaum, Weisz, Pott, Miyake, and Morelli (2000) advanced the argument that attachment theory is deeply rooted in Western thought and cannot be readily applied to Eastern cultures. They identified three core hypotheses of attachment theory: sensitivity hypothesis, competence hypothesis, and secure base hypothesis. Of those three hypotheses, the latter two are relevant here.

The competence hypothesis assumes that competence is a consequence of infants' successful attachment to their caregivers (Rothbaum et al., 2000). Rothbaum et al. argued that the definition of competence reflects Western values and cannot be valid in the East. Although competence includes autonomy, independence, and self-efficacy in the West, those behavioral tendencies are not necessarily valued in the East, such as Japan where interpersonal harmony is emphasized. Thus, the claimed link between the secure attachment of infants and their competence cannot be found in Japan (Rothbaum et al., 2000). As argued in the previous section, one can attempt to depend on others when one has confidence in their favorable attitude toward oneself. Thus, in terms of attachment theory, securely attached children can afford to presume the acceptance of their inappropriate behavior or request by their counterpart because they feel they are accepted.

The secure base hypothesis of attachment theory assumes that the secure base with the attachment figure is used by infants to gain the support necessary for adaptation to the outside world (Rothbaum et al., 2000). From the perspective of *amae*, one would question whether the secure base is used only to adapt to the environment. If infants can gain support from the attachment figure, they may well use the attachment figure as a proxy to obtain what they want. The goal of those infants would not be limited to adaptation to the environment. If they can gain support from the attachment figure, they may well overuse the secure base to the extent that their inappropriate needs, which are not necessary for adaptation to the environment, are fulfilled. The Western theory of attachment assumes that caregivers limit their support to what infants need to adapt to the environment. However, if caregivers are more flexible in terms of providing support, they can let infants request *amae* and accept such requests.

Rothbaum et al. (2000) related attachment to dependence in their argument, because they equated *amae* and dependence. However, because *amae* can be distinguished from dependence, the relationship between attachment and *amae* should be readdressed. In this respect, it can be argued that attachment can lead to *amae* when caregivers provide support for infants unconditionally beyond their support for infants' adaptation to the environment. Thus, from the present perspective, attachment can be a source of *amae,* but it should not be equated to *amae,* which involves an inappropriate behavior or request. As a result of attachment, infants or even adults can develop *amae* behavioral tendencies rather than independence and autonomy. Although Doi (2001) argued that Bowlby's work on attachment between child and mother is relevant to *amae* in Japan (p. 83), attachment as studied in the West and *amae* represent two different constructs.

MOTIVATIONS UNDERLYING *AMAE*

If *amae* is not equivalent to psychological dependence or insecure attachment, what motivates people to engage in *amae* behaviors or requests? So far, the need for unconditional love or favor has been emphasized by theorists. In normal situations, newborns are given unconditional love from their mother. Then they may well develop the need for unconditional love, which is similar to what Balint called primary object-love (Balint, 1956). According to Balint, infants assume that their pleasure is also their care-givers' pleasure. Infants also feel that they should be loved and satisfied by their parents without giving anything in return to the parents. This kind of love is passive and it can be distinguished from active love, which develops at a later stage of individual development.

The second need that motivates people to engage in *amae* behavior is the need for control. As discussed previously, people attempt to control the physical and social environment for their own well-being using *amae* requests.

Each of these two motivations would lead people to engage in inappropriate behavior or make inappropriate requests. In other words, *amae* can be motivated by the need for unconditional acceptance and/or the need for control. For example, when a boy requests an expensive toy, it can be motivated by the child's need for unconditional acceptance by his parents and/or his desire for the expensive toy. If the acceptance by his parents is more important for the boy, he will not insist on the expensive toy. As long as he can confirm that he is accepted by his parents, he will be happy even if he is offered a less expensive toy. In contrast, if he is more interested in the toy, he will insist on it. Once he gets the toy, he may ignore his parents because his parents' acceptance is less important in this case. This line of reasoning suggests that there are two different kinds of *amae*, which can be referred to as emotional *amae* and manipulative *amae*. Although both kinds of *amae* include inappropriate behavior with the presumption of acceptance, the goal of the *amae* request is different in each case.

Emotional Aspects of *Amae*

This is a prototype of *amae*, because the need for love/favor is most essential for infants, who cannot survive without being taken care of by adults. Even after having grown up, the sense of being accepted unconditionally is comfortable for children and even for adults. Suppose that a young girl requests her boy friend to purchase jewelry for her, even though she already has a lot. If this request, which is inappropriate in an ordinary situation, is intended to confirm that she is accepted by her boy friend, the requested jewelry is less important than confirming his unconditional love. What she is seeking is his acceptance. As such, what is requested does not matter. It can be a new dress, a car, or anything that is inappropriate for that situation. She is just eager to know that she is accepted by him to the extent that even an inappropriate request is approved.

Manipulative Aspects of *Amae*

This type of *amae* is more frequently found among older children and adults who have learned that they can obtain what they normally cannot afford by requesting *amae* of more powerful people. As described, an *amae* request can be used to control one's social and physical environment. If the need for control is dominant, what is requested is more important than being accepted by one's counterpart. In the case of the young girl who requests jewelry, if she really just wants the jewelry, once she receives it she may even leave him. In an extreme case, she would pretend that she is seeking unconditional love from her boyfriend, who is really just a tool to get what she wants. This kind of *amae* is manipulative and undesirable to the counterpart.

The two kinds of *amae* are not necessarily mutually exclusive. Both the need for unconditional love/favor and the need for control can underlie an *amae* behavior or request (Figure 1). That is, *amae* requesters may be seeking both unconditional love/favor and a specific object or goal to different degrees, depending on the situation and the target of the *amae* request. Thus, in most everyday practice of *amae*, it is very difficult for observers to know which motivation is more dominant in an *amae* requester's mind.

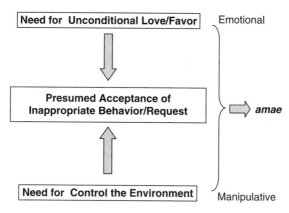

Figure 1. Motivation underlying *amae*.

The above reasoning has implication for how to deal with the undesirable aspect of *amae*, i.e., inappropriate behavior or requests in close relationships. When an inappropriate behavior or request is intolerable to the *amae* requester's counterpart, the counterpart can stop or decline the inappropriate behavior. The mere rejection of an inappropriate behavior or request, however, may be taken by the *amae*-requester as the rejection of love, which is typically underlying *amae* as long as the request is not completely manipulative. If this happens, the close relationship between the son and the mother, for example, would deteriorate to the extent that the son loses confidence in his mother's love. It is advisable, therefore, that the counterpart differentiates between the inappropriate aspect of *amae* and the emotional aspect of amae. For example, suppose a ten-year old boy asks his mother to dress him. The mother could reasonably decline his request, but in doing so she is advised to add that she loves him despite his inappropriate request.

UNIVERSALITY OF *AMAE*

Given the distinction between *amae* and closely related concepts such as dependence and attachment, readers might be ready to accept the possibility that *amae* episodes are universal rather than unique to Japanese culture. As a first step to examine this possibility, *amae* episodes in which a protagonist requests something inappropriate with the assumption that his/her counterpart will accept the request were presented to undergraduate students in the U.S. and Taiwan (Yamaguchi, 2004b). In one episode, a protagonist asked her best friend to take care of her cat for one week after she had made reservation for a one-week tour, presuming that her best friend would agree to take care of the cat. In response to being asked whether they would make such a request, U.S. and Taiwanese participants answered that they would do so to a greater extent than the Japanese subjects, indicating that Americans and Taiwanese would engage in a behavior which is labeled as *amae* by Japanese. Thus, although the research still remains explorative, the initial evidence suggests strongly that *amae* is an *etic* phenomenon.

CONCLUSION

Amae can and should be distinguished from the similar concepts of dependence and insecure attachment. Even though individuals who request *amae* may be physically or financially dependent on their counterpart, they can be independent psychologically. Those who request *amae* have their own agenda regarding how to adapt to the environment or what they want. In this sense, they are psychologically independent when they behave inappropriately or make an inappropriate request. If their counterpart keeps accepting their behavior or request, the counterpart is under their control. If successful in their *amae* request, they cannot only adapt to the environment but also get what they want, even though what they want may be inappropriate for their age, social status, or situation.

Insecure attachment is also different from *amae*. One may request *amae* of a person to whom one is securely attached, expecting of this person almost unconditional love or favor. Thus, attachment provides a basis on which one can request *amae*. When one is insecure about one's acceptance by a caregiver or more generally a powerful person, one will not be able to initiate an *amae* behavior or request. In this sense, *amae* reflects healthy and socially acceptable psychological development in East Asia, as long as its inappropriateness does not exceed a certain limit that varies with relationship. Socially adaptive East Asians are those who can be both autonomous and skillful *amae* requesters depending on the situation. As previous studies have shown, those who request *amae* sometimes are best liked. Psychologically independent and autonomous people in East Asia can in some situations request *amae* to maintain harmonious interpersonal relationships. Because the counterpart can feel valued by the *amae* requester, inappropriate behavior or an inappropriate request within limits can be useful in facilitating a close relationship.

Conceptual clarification of *amae* and related constructs such as insecure attachment, and dependence suggests that *amae* may be a universal rather than indigenous Japanese phenomenon, albeit the concept of *amae* may be unique to Japanese culture. The initial evidence indicates that people in other cultures also engage in inappropriate behavior described as *amae* by Japanese. Future studies will reveal the *etic* nature of what the indigenous Japanese concept of *amae* entails.

REFERENCES

Ainsworth, M. D. S., Blehar, M. C., Waters, E., & Wall, S. (1978). Patterns of attachment: A psychological study of the strange situation. Hillsdale, NJ: Erlbaum.

Balint, M. (1956). *Primary love and psycho-analytic technique*. New York: Liveright.

Bandura, A. (1982). Self-efficacy mechanism in human agency. *American Psychologist, 37*, 122–147.

Birtchnell, J. (1988). Defining dependence. *British Journal of Medical Psychology, 61*, 111–123.

Bornstein, R. F. (1993). *Dependent personality*. New York: Guilford.

Bowlby, J. (1969). Attachment and loss: Vol. 1. Attachment. New York: Basic Books.

Bruner, J. S. (1990). *Acts of meaning*. Cambridge, Mass.: Harvard University Press.

Doi, T. (1971). *Amae no kozo [The anatomy of dependence]*. Tokyo: Kobundo.

Doi, T. (1973). *The anatomy of dependence*. Tokyo: Kodansha.

Doi, T. (1992). On the concept of Amae. *Infant Mental Health Journal, 13*, 7–11.

Doi, T. (1997). Some reflections on the concept of Amae. Paper presented at the symposium "Amae reconsidered: Sweet indulgence, the suspension of formality, dependency, and refueling in Japan," at the 86th annual meeting of American Psychoanalytic Association, May 17, San Diego.

Doi, T. (2001). *Zoku amae no kozo [Anatomy of dependence (rev.)]*. Tokyo: Koubundo.

Kim, U., & Yamaguchi, S., (1995). Conceptual and empirical analysis of amae: Exploration into Japanese psychological space (1). In Proceedings of the 43rd Annual Conference of the Japanese Group Dynamics Association (p.158–159). Tokyo: Japanese Group Dynamics Association.

Kumagai, H. (1981). A dissection of intimacy: A study of "bipolar posturating" in Japanese social interaction. *Culture, Medicine, and Psychiatry, 5*, 249–272.

Lebra, T. S. (1976). *Japanese patterns of behavior*. Honolulu: East-West Center.

Markus, H. R., & Kitayama, S. (1991). Culture and the self: Implications for cognition, emotion, and motivation. *Psychological Review, 98*, 224–253.

Maruta, T. (1992). Does an American puppy amaeru? A comment on Dr. Doi's paper. *Infant Mental Health Journal, 13* (1), 12–17.

Okonogi, K. (1968). The personal background and theoretical problems of the "Amae" theory (Doi). *Seishin Bunseki Kenkyu, 14*, 14–19.

Pelzel, J. (1977). Book review: Japanese personality in culutre. *Culture, Medicine, and Psychiatry, I*, 299–315.

Rothbaum, F., Weisz, J., Pott, M., Miyake, K., & Morelli, G. (2000). Attachment and culture: Security in the United States and Japan. *American Psychologist, 55*, 1093–1104.

Sofue, T. (1972). Nihonjin no ishiki to kokuminsei no hensenkatei [The transition process of Japanese consciousness and nationality]. In H. Akuto, K. Tominaga & T. Sofue (Eds.), *Hendouki no nihonshakai [Japanese society in the period of instability]*. Tokyo: Nihon Housou Shuppan Kyokai.

Taketomo, Y. (1986). Amae as metalanguage: A critique of Doi's theory of Amae. *Journal of the American Academy of Psychoanalysis, 14*, 525–544.

Yamaguchi, S. (1999a). [Nichijyo-go to shiteno Amae kara kangaeru] Meaning of *amae* as an everyday word. In Kitayama, O. (Ed.), *Clinical Japanese 3: Amae and resignation (Nihongo Rinsho 3: Amae to Akirame)*. Seiwa Shoten.

Yamaguchi, S. (1999b, June). *Amae*: When people presume acceptance of their own inappropriate behavior. Paper presented at AAAS meeting, San Francisco.

Yamaguchi, S. (2001). Culture and control orientations. In D. Matsumoto (Ed.), *The handbook of culture and psychology* (pp. 223–243). New York: Oxford University Press.

Yamaguchi, S. (2004a). Further clarifications of the concept of *Amae* in relation to dependence and attachment. *Human Development, 47,* 28–33.

Yamaguchi, S. (2004b). An indigenous approach to a possibly *etic* phenomenon: A case of *Amae*. Keynote address presented at the 17th Congress of the International Association for Cross-Cultural Psychology, August 4, Xi'an, China.

Chapter 8

Affect and Early Moral Socialization: Some Insights and Contributions from Indigenous Psychological Studies in Taiwan

Heidi Fung

As reviewed by Gibbs & Schnell (1985) and Gibbs (1991a, 1991b), there are two major contemporary theories of moral development: Kohlberg's individual-oriented cognitivism and Hoffman's social-oriented emotivism. The former stresses a progressive cognitive construction of moral reasoning and judgment following a sequence of invariant stages. In contrast, in the latter approach, affect, empathy, or empathy-related guilt, plays a central role in motivating the child toward internalization. A large literature on moral development in the Taiwanese population has been developed in the Kohlbergian tradition (e.g., Cheng, 1991; Fu & Lei, 1991; Hwang, 1998; Kohlberg, 1969; Lei, 1984, 1994; Ma, 1998; also see a review in C. F. Yang, 1996, pp. 159–206). Some are supportive, others critical. By comparison, not much attention has been given to the role of affect in moral socialization until recently (Fung, 1994, 1999, 2001; Fung & Chen, 2001, 2002; Fung, Lieber, & Leung, 2003). The purpose of this paper is twofold: first, it attempts to fill this gap in the literature in the light of accumulated knowledge and findings from recent indigenous studies on moral socialization and early training in Taiwan, and secondly, with the support of significant cultural variations found in these indigenous studies, it offers a critique of the neglect of culture in Hoffman's theory.

Similar to Hoffman's argument, I shall stress the importance of affect in moral development in Chinese culture. However, instead of the empathy highlighted in American families, shame, with its culture-specific facets and characters, turned out to play a crucial role in the context of daily moral training in the observed Taiwanese families. Rather than refuting the cognitive and physiological capacities of various feeling states (including empathy, guilt, and shame) in children of either cultural group, this finding reveals that the interpretation of the emotional component highlighted in the foreground when disciplining young children may vary across cultures. The Taiwanese experience of shame in early training may challenge the common claim in the psychoanalytical and psychiatric literature that shame, in contrast to guilt, is a dangerous and destructive affect which has little to do with moral internalization. Indeed, indigenous meaning of affective experiences has to be understood and interpreted within its situated multi-layered social, historical and cultural contexts, which in turn supports the value and the necessity of adopting an indigenous approach in studying culture.

Before moving on to discuss Hoffman's theory, I would like to first say a few words about my view on cultural comparisons. In order to "globalize local knowledge" (Shweder, 1999, 2000), I believe comparisons within as well as across cultures are not only necessary but also important. However, how to make such comparison is what really matters. In the classic review essay on culture dated half a century ago, Kroeber and Kluckholn (1952) laid out some principles for cultural comparison:

> Comparisons of cultures must not be simplistic in terms of an arbitrary or preconceived universal value system, but must be multiple, with each culture first understood in terms of its own particular value system and therefore its own idiosyncratic structure. After that, comparison can with gradually increasing reliability reveal to what degree values, significances, and qualities are common to the compared cultures, and to what degree distinctive. (p. 174)

In other words, it should be a process derived from a detailed study of a specific (sub-)cultural group compared with other groups studied in equal detail. Hence, instead of adopting Hoffman's theory as a perceived universal system, the comparison begins with a thorough understanding of the indigenous affective experiences occurred in disciplinary encounters in each case.

HOFFMAN'S THEORY: AFFECT, DISCIPLINE, AND MORAL DEVELOPMENT

The overarching goal of moral socialization is internalization of rules and norms in order to transform the novice into a competent cultural member (Grusec & Goodnow, 1994; Kochanska & Aksan, 1995; Kochanska et al., 1998). In Hoffman's affect primacy theory, affect bears the key role in such a process while empathy is the determining affect (Hoffman, 1975, 1983,

1984, 1987, 1991b, 1994, 2000). Empathy here refers to "the vicarious affective response to another person," and instead of being defined in outcome terms, it is "the processes responsible for one's having a feeling more appropriate to another's situation than to one's own situation" (Hoffman, 1984, p. 103). The earliest form of empathy seems to be manifested in the contagious crying of infants. A more mature sense of empathy begins to emerge during the second year of life when the child is able to differentiate self and other and hence to develop an understanding of others as separate beings. To progress from egocentric distress to altruistic concerns, and from responses to the immediate situation to mental representations beyond the situation, the novice has to achieve advancement in cognitive abilities, including developing the concept of person permanence, person identity on the empathic experience, the linguistic ability to comprehend and express cues of affective states, as well as the ability to transform empathic into sympathetic distress and to make causal attributions in the shaping and transformation of empathy (Hoffman, 1984, 2000).

While these cognitive abilities are primarily biologically programmed, parental socializing inductions are seen as necessary and important, because "even when children have the cognitive and affective requisites of guilt, they may not actually experience it unless an external agent such as the parent is present to compel them to attend to the harm done to the victim and to their own role in the victim's plight" (Hoffman, 1982, p. 98). Although Hoffman acknowledges moral norms could also be taught in non-disciplinary encounters (such as in dinner table conversation or by setting up the adult's own actions as examples), he argues that the discipline encounter, a recurrent salient feature in the child's daily life, is most important in the course of internalization, because it provides not only the direct and explicit link between moral norms and the child's egoistic desires and behaviors, but also the earliest experience of being expected to control one's deviant actions (Hoffman, 1983). According to him, the effective discipline mainly involves the following steps:

1. The inevitable conflict: When the child transgresses or harms others, there will be conflict between the caregiver and the child inherent in the discipline encounter, because from the latter's perspective, any intervention to his/her motivated misdeed could hardly be seen as fair and reasonable. On the caregiver's side, a mixture of various techniques, such as love withdrawal, power-assertion, as well as induction, is usually deployed.
2. The emotion work: A reasonable amount of imposed fear is necessary to stop the child from misbehaving and to make the child pay attention to the information contained in the inductive component. Elicitation of empathy, concerning the consequences of the child's misdeed and the well-being of the victim, is the main message

embodied in induction and is central to the moral norm. Appropriate arousal enables the child to produce a heightened awareness of both the victim's distress and the child's role in causing it.

3. From affect to cognition: Through putting the child in the third party's perspective, parent-child conflict will be lessened. This helps the child to perceive the parent's intervention as fair and to focus on the message content instead of its source (the parent). It results in his feelings of emphatic stress and guilt, which motivate the child to gain knowledge of moral norms. Such a co-occurring synthesis of knowledge and affect, or rather, emotionally charged knowledge, is termed by Hoffman (1983, 1991b, 1994) a hot moral cognition.

4. From compliance to internalization: Over time, from countless discipline encounters as encoded in long-term memories, and owing to the child's active role in processing the information, the child will eventually be transformed from being compelled to obey due to external sanctions to autonomously experiencing the moral norm as internally deriving from the self. In the parents' absence, and even before transgressing or harming someone, the child is able to anticipate the result and the feeling of guilt. The child's egoistic motive will yield to a moral motive expanding to higher order moral principles.

What Hoffman described is an information-processing model of moral socialization and internalization. Through cues of distress from the victim as well as the caregiver's reprimand, the child has to process the informational content in inductions, the causal connection between the child's action and the victim's physical or psychological state as well as any additional information regarding dimensions of the moral norm against harming others that may be communicated. Affect, empathy, or empathy-based guilt, gives this cognitive process a motivational or obligatory quality. In order to effectively motivate the child, an optimal level of discomfort and stress needs to be aroused (Hoffman, 1982, 1983, 1984, 2000). Too little of such arousal may prompt the child to ignore the moral message, while too much may provoke excessive conflict or unnecessary negative reactions (e.g., anger, resentment, anxiety, fear). Either problem could interfere with the process of facilitating the child's internalization of moral norms.

A CRITIQUE OF HOFFMAN'S THEORY

Hoffman's theory has made important contributions, and it is also fundamentally different from Kohlberg's theories.[1] First, conceptualizations, theories, as well as empirical data regarding moral development prior to

---

[1] For his own view on how his theory differs from Kohlberg's, please see Hoffman (1991a).

Hoffman "had not viewed children as capable of moral actions and caring behaviors until they reached school age" (Zahn-Waxler & Robinson, 1995, p. 144). Hoffman not only assumed early developmental origins for morality, but also laid out the significance of early socialization in the developmental trajectory. Second, his theory incorporated the affective dimension that had long been neglected in earlier studies. Affect indeed accounts for the motivational dimension in internalizing moral norms and hence plays a major role in the socialization process. Moreover, compared to Kohlberg's inclination toward ideological individualism and rationalism (see for instance, Hogan, 1975), moral development in Hoffman's theory is much more social, relational, and interactive in nature. Besides being tuned with prosocial and altruistic concerns, affect (i.e., empathy) is also expressed in a relational context, the two-way mutually influencing interactions between caregiver and child. In addition to socialization through inductions on the parent's part, the child's increasing cognitive abilities could also enhance the sophistication or subtlety that parents are likely to exercise in their inductions.

However, Hoffman's theory completely overlooks the role of culture and the situated meaning of emotional experience in cultural contexts. He explicitly put forth his views about culture in his recent book, in which he argued for the universality of empathy and the process of its arousal on the grounds of universally shared physiological features due to a common evolutionary history (Hoffman, 2000). It is evident, for instance, that empathy has its basis in the human brain's limbic and neural systems, that all cultures presumably have language to express feelings, and that all humans attend to a victim's facial expression of distress.

To Hoffman, possible cultural differences may come from only two areas: the development of a sense of self and the role of induction in socialization. As to the former, he refuted cultural psychologists' reports that, in his words, "the Western self is more fully developed than the self in more 'collectivist' non-Western societies" (Hoffman, 2000, p. 275). According to Hoffman's reading of their theories, individuals in non-Western societies, due to the cultural goal of interdependence, develop a sense of self that is merged with others instead of being a separate and distinct entity. This lack of a distinct sense of self may cause confusion in the development from egocentric to altruistic empathy. However, based on his observations of similar cognitive structures across the species, Hoffman believed that human beings in any culture should all be aware of the continuous kinesthetic sensations and inner feelings and thoughts from their own bodies, and to mentally represent and sense their own actions. He thus concluded, "It should therefore be impossible for an adult with a normal brain to feel that his or her self is merged with others" (Hoffman, 2000, p. 276).

On the second area of possible cultural differences, Hoffman admitted that in the absence of cross-cultural data, it is hardly conclusive. Nevertheless, by associating induction with guilt and internalization, he speculated that induction may not play an important role in other communities where guilt and internalization are not emphasized. He says, "transgression guilt and moral internalization may make little sense in small, traditional, homogeneous societies in which individuals are under constant surveillance by role models and other authorities throughout life," whereas "in liberal democracies, however, without 'a cop on every corner,' and especially in the educated middle classes, induction, guilt, and moral internalization are meaningful concepts" (Hoffman, 2000, p. 282).

Hoffman's arguments reveal a rather simplistic, naïve and ethnocentric view on culture. He sees cultures only in dichotomous paradigms (Western vs. non-Western, individualistic vs. collectivistic), and each culture (or group of cultures) as a homogeneous and static whole (for instance, all non-Western cultures are collectivistic while all Western ones are individualistic). Even if the framework of interdependent vs. independent self construals is cross-culturally validated, as argued by Markus and Kitayama (1991),

> an interdependent view of self does not result in a merging of self and other, nor does it imply that one must always be in the company of others to function effectively, or that people do not have a sense of themselves as agents who are the origins of their own actions. On the contrary, it takes a high degree of self-control and agency to effectively adjust oneself to various interpersonal contingencies. (Markus & Kitayama, 1991, p. 228)

Most of all, he failed to situate emotion in its cultural context and take indigenous interpretations of affective experience into account. Therefore, we do not know, for instance, why Hoffman believed induction only works with guilt and why internalization would not be a socializing goal or outcome for members in "small and traditional" societies, who are "under constant surveillance." Indeed, in addition to the biological, physiological, and cognitive means for expressing feeling states (particularly the so-called primary emotions) that are innate, affective experience also pertains to sophisticated and complex rules and norms that are culturally labeled, regulated, constructed, and interpreted (Briggs, 1970; Rosaldo, 1984; Lutz, 1988; Lutz & White, 1986; Miller & Sperry, 1986; Shweder, 1991). As Lutz (1988) pointed out, "the biological basis of human experience, including that termed emotional, is not denied," but "the point has been to critique essentialism in the understanding of emotion and to explore the relatively neglected ways in which social and cultural forces help to give emotions their observed character" (p. 210). She argued that "emotional experience is not precultural but preeminently cultural," and that emotion "can more profitably be viewed as serving complex communicative, moral, and cultural purposes rather than simply as labels for internal states whose nature or essence is presumed to be universal" (p. 5).

Even Mencius said, "All humans have feelings of empathy (惻隱之心人皆有之 *ceyin zhixin ren jie you zhi*)." While there is little doubt that empathy is universally experienced, nevertheless, similar affective experience related to empathic stress may have different meanings in different cultural contexts, which extend far beyond facial or verbal expressions. Besides, it may not necessarily be the only salient emotion in the context of disciplinary encounters across cultures. In the following, I shall exemplify the cultural aspect of affective experience with a case study—the role of shame in early moral socialization in Taiwanese families. Before doing that, indigenous meanings of shame have to be located in the higher-order cultural and historical contexts in relation to Confucian ideologies and Taiwanese childrearing beliefs and practices.

SHAME (羞恥*XIUCHI*) IN TAIWANESE CULTURE

Despite the fact that shame has been recognized as one quintessential socio-moral affect (Barrett, 1995; Karen, 1992; Kilborne, 1995; Lewis, 1992), most works in the psychoanalytic and psychiatric literature assert that, compared to guilt, it is a much less moral, desirable, constructive, and altruistic emotion with little effect on internalization (Tangney, 1998; Tangney et al., 1995, 1992; also see reviews in Creighton, 1990; Fung, 1994; Fung et al, 2003). However, under the influence of Confucianism,[2] shame has been not only a highly elaborate or hypercognized emotion (Mascolo, Fisher, & Lin, 2003; Wang, Li, & Fischer, 2001), but also an underscored moral virtue in Chinese culture (Wilson, 1970, 1981; Schoenhals, 1993; Hu, 1944; King & Myers, 1977; Hwang, 1987; Zhai, 1995; C. L. Chu, 1972; Ho, 1976; Fung et al., 1998). As Mascolo et al. (2003) remarked,

> whereas shame in the United States carries stigmatizing connotations, shame/guilt among the Chinese offers the promise of reintegration into the family or community following reestablishment of appropriate behavior. As such, shame is not primarily a threat to self-esteem; instead, it is a vehicle for social cohesion and the development of self. (p. 395)

---

[2] Although there are concerns about over-emphasis of the dominance of Confucianism in Chinese culture, and the possible gap between abstract elite ideologies and concrete mundane life of the general public (e.g., Lau & Yeung, 1996; C. F. Yang, 1996), even with increasing globalization, the essence of Confucianism is still found to be alive and well in various aspects of contemporary Chinese lives, such as child-rearing (Ho, 1996; Wu, 1996; Chao, 1994, 1995), narrative practices (Miller et al., 1996, 1997; Fung, Miller, & Lin, 2004), leadership in organizations (Farh & Cheng, 1999, 2000), family life (Hsia, Vera, & Berardo, 1999; M. H. Yeh & K. S. Yang, 1997), interpersonal relationships (K. S. Yang, 1992; Gabrenya & Hwang, 1996), as well as achievement (Li, 2001, 2002; Yu, 1996; Ho, 1994).

The salience of shame is eminently reflected in the rich and complex variety of the lexical terms and labels for shame, humiliation, embarrassment, face, and related notions in the Chinese language (Her, 1990; Russell & Yik, 1996; Shaver et al., 1992; Wilson, 1981; Mascolo et al., 2003; Wang et al., 2001; C. R. L. Chu, 1987, 1988, 1989, Hwang, 1997). In a cross-cultural hierarchical cluster analysis of emotion categories (Shaver et al., 1992), only in the Chinese sample (but not in the U.S. and Italian samples) did shame emerge as a separately and distinctively labeled cluster, which included shame, guilt, regret, and diffidence. In a follow-up study by Wang, Li, and Fischer (2001), Chinese-speaking informants identified 113 core shame terms in Chinese, which were hierarchically organized into a complex three-level system: various common situations that can cause the self to fear losing face, the self's actual feeling state of shame after losing face, and the self's moral conscience and the associated guilt feelings. Two points are worth noting in these studies: first, the distinction between shame and guilt in Chinese is often blurred both in concept and in terminology (Wang, Li, & Fischer, 2001). Moreover, Chinese children seem to learn these concepts quite early in their lives. While only a small proportion of their American counterparts reported that their children understood "ashamed" and "embarrassed" (10% and 16.7% respectively), 95% of Chinese mothers reported that their three year olds had already understood "shame" (Shaver et al., 1992, p. 199).

In addition to the Chinese language, a significant section of Confucius' *Analects* also deals with the value of shame (C. L. Chu, 1972). Shame (羞惡之心 *xiue zhixin*), together with empathy (惻隱之心 *ceyin zhixin*), reverence (恭敬之心 *gongjing zhixin*), and conscience (是非之心 *shifei zhixin*) were termed by Mencius "the four beginnings of virtue (四端 *siduan*)," the virtues being respectively righteousness (義 *yi*), benevolence (仁 *ren*), propriety (禮 *li*), and wisdom (智 *zhi*). Likewise, another renowned ancient philosopher, Guan Zhong (管仲), also endorsed propriety (禮 *li*), righteousness (義 *yi*), honesty (廉 *lian*), and shame (恥 *chi*) as "the four ethical principles of a country (國之四維 *guo zhi siwei*)." When asked what makes a true scholar, Confucius presented three characteristics in the following order: a sense of shame, being filial and fraternal, and being sincere in what he says and carries out what he does (Chang, 1997, p. 118). According to Confucian ideology, "a false gentleman can be superior to a truly small man." The distinction between them is that since the former still wants and needs the appearance of propriety to rule, his behavior can be constrained by shame, whereas the latter does not even have a sense of shame (Liu & Liu, 2003). Even to this day, compared to European and North American cultures, shame plays a greater role in constraining the power of the ruler in Chinese societies (Hwang, 1987; Liu & Liu, 2003). Reviewing the Chinese concept of face, Zhai (1995) maintains that the essential mechanism of its operation relies on shame, and raises several points regarding shame in Confucian thought: 1) shame is greatly emphasized and valued; 2) shame is simultaneously about moral internalization and external sanctions; 3) shame is part of the fulfillment of the ideal personhood; and 4) the criteria of shame are closely related to the virtues of righteousness, benevolence, propriety, and wisdom (p. 231).

There indeed has been a long tradition of associating shame with moral socialization. In the Zhou clan's familial instructions dated from the Ching Dynasty in China, it is said that,

> What distinguishes the human being from the animal is shame. When a person does not know shame, his conscience would vanish. For such a person, parents would have no way to discipline; teachers and friends would have no way to advise. Without the will to strive upward, how could one improve? To be an official without shame is treacherous; how could he be loyal? To be a son without shame is disobedient; how could he be filial? To be a neighbor without shame is wicked; how could he be benevolent?... As one knows shame, the sense of right and wrong would be realized, and his dying conscience would have a chance to revive. (Zhai, 1995, p. 232)

Two hundred years later, in today's Taiwanese primary schools, Chinese classes still teach that "To possess the feeling of shame is to be near to courage (知恥近乎勇 *zhichi jinhu yung*)," taken from *The Doctrine of the Mean* by Confucius. The following is its explanation in a standard textbook:[3]

> When one says or does something wrong, if he is able to reflect on his own behavior and won't repeat the same mistake again, this is "having a sense of shame." When one has a sense of shame, he would know what to say and what to do, and after self-reflection, he is able to truly repent, amend his wrongdoings, and proceed towards his ideals without any fear of difficulties. Someone like this not only knows shame but also has the courage to confront hardship; he is also a courageous person... After all ordinary people are not saints or sages, so that one can hardly avoid transgressing. However, after saying or doing something wrong, if one is not willing to examine and mend his behavior, he does not seek ways to improve himself. If he is able to truly reflect and truly repent, he will have the courage to make changes and improvements, leading to the rebirth of a new person.

Although the above two passages come from different sources several generations apart and were written for different purposes for

---

[3] This is quoted from Lesson Nine in a sixth grade Chinese textbook (p. 41) published by the government National Institute for Compilation and Translation. By the academic year of 1996, the National Institute for Compilation and Translation was the only compiler and publisher for all textbooks and curricula in all primary schools on Taiwan. Since year 1996, this market has been open to private publishers and schools began to have the liberty to choose and adopt various versions of textbooks and curricula.

different readers, they carry a similar message: Shame is a tool to teach or advice right and wrong, which motivates one to repent and strive for improvement. All its elements and objectives–self-reflection, confession, repentance, and conscience–point to moral internalization. Shame is motivational, prosocial, and moral. This may explain why Schoenhals (1993) characterizes the Chinese culture as a shame-socialized culture.[4] According to Schoenhals (1993), compared to non-shame-socialized cultures, members in shame-socialized cultures are more likely to be explicitly socialized and expected to be sensitive to shame and have a greater tendency "to use negative judgments about an individual's actions–rather than about the individual himself or his status or the sum of his actions–to urge individuals to act well and appropriately" (Schoenhals, 1993, p. 194).

DISCIPLINE AND EARLY TRAINING IN CHINESE FAMILIES

Even though affect or shame has not been directly addressed, a large body of literature on Chinese socialization bears on this issue. Many describe traditional Chinese social structures as patriarchic and Chinese parenting as authoritarian, strict, or even harsh (Ho, 1986, 1996; Wu, 1981, 1985, 1996; Chao, 1994, 1995; Lay, Liang, Tang, & Wang, 1997a; Lay, Wang, Soong, & Yang, 1997b; Lin & Wang, 1995). Such a fundamental inequality between parent and child mainly comes from the traditional stress on filial obligations, particularly of sons (Wu, 1981; K. H. Yeh, 1997; K. H. Yeh & K. S. Yang, 1991; Ho, 1996). One of its salient characteristics is that "these obligations were permanent, in force not only while the son was a child, but after he grew up, and continuing even after the death of his parents" (through ancestor worship) (Schoenhals, 1993, p. 141). While some aspects of these traditions (such as the different treatment between sons and daughters, the absolute authority entitled to fathers or household heads, and cohabitation of several generations) have changed as society evolves over time, others still persist in varying degrees (Lin & Wang, 1995; Schoenhals, 1993, chap. 6).

According to Wu (1981), even to this day, there are two co-existing mechanisms that train filial piety, one of which is "the maintenance of parental authority and children's obedience through harsh discipline" (p. 151). While recognizing the wide variation within the Chinese culture, Ho (1986) concludes in his thorough review: "Chinese parents tend to be highly lenient or even indulgent in their attitudes toward the infant and young child, in sharp contrast to the strict discipline they impose on older children" (p. 35). This shift is believed to occur when the child reaches "the

---

[4] This differs from a shame culture. For criticisms of the dichotomy of guilt culture vs. shame culture, please see Chapter 8 in Schoenhals (1993) as well as other sources (e.g., Piers & Singer, 1953; Lebra, 1971, 1983; Creighton, 1990; Fung, 1994, 1999).

age of understanding (懂事 *dongshi*)" at around 4 to 6 years, and disciplinary techniques such as threatening, scolding, shaming, and physical punishment will become acceptable and are frequently applied (Ho 1986, p. 16). However, others disagree with this belief in a golden age for young children and report that parental discipline, correction, and training (管 *guan*) begin as early as when the child is able to walk, comprehend, or talk, which usually occur before the age of two or three (Wu, 1981; Miller et al., 1996, 1997; Chao, 1994; Fung et al., 1998). Through questionnaire surveys, Lay et al. (1997a, 1997b) found that the usage of negative language is a prevailing phenomenon in Taiwanese families as reported by the young generation, regardless of the age of the child (from kindergarten to college students) and the socioeconomic status of the parent. This negative or abusive language involves shaming, threatening, name-calling, and rebuking. Another cross-island survey on parental attitudes towards corporal punishment (Lin & Wang, 1995) revealed that, although most of today's Taiwan parents report that they have a peer-like relationship with their children, they still believe that parents are fully responsible for disciplining their children, particularly for their moral development. Harsh punishment (e.g., corporal punishment) is seen as necessary and effective in some situations, particularly for the sake of preventing youngsters from becoming delinquent (Lin & Wang, 1995, pp. 45–47). Indeed, the traditionally valued merit of filial piety could overemphasize parents' rights and legitimize their abusive and unreasonable behavior toward their children.

Nevertheless, there is also another mechanism in childreading: "the inducement of both physical and emotional closeness so that a lifelong bond is assured" (Wu, 1981, p. 151). Some noticeable phenomena include the physical closeness between mother and child (particularly during the first years of life), the degree to which Chinese parents are willing to sacrifice themselves for their children's schooling, and the prolonged parent-child interdependence (Chao, 1994, 1996; Wu, 1981). Even in discipline, there are safeguards against excessive punishment as well. For example, when one parent acts as the "black face (黑臉 *heilian*)" or the bad cop, another (or the elders in the family[5]) often play the "white face (白臉 *bailian*)" or the good cop. Intimidation occurs much more frequently than actual punishing, and some seemingly severe punitive methods, such as kneeling down for a period of time (often for the purpose of self-examination), "though shameful for the child and effective, appears to be less harmful in physical terms" (Wu, 1981, p. 156).

To conclude, when the two mechanisms are juxtaposed, strict discipline is carried out largely by establishing a close tie. In his observations of Chinese parents of teenagers, Schoenhals (1993) described, "in fact the parents who insisted that their children yield to them were also

---

[5] In traditional Chinese families, a child belongs not only to the parents, but also to the whole clan.

the ones I observed indulging their children's desire" (p. 152). Similarly, the intertwining of parental love, care and affection with the heavily didactic narrative practices observed in Taiwanese families may explain why the child was able to accept repeated accounts of him/her as a failed moral actor without becoming discouraged from making independent moral judgment (see extended examples in Fung, Miller, & Lin, 2004). Such a "blending of voices," in which a critical parental voice blends with a voice of loving sentiments, may be hard to appreciate from a Euro-American perspective (Miller et al., 1997, p. 566). This is also why Chao (1994) argues that although Chinese parents tended to score higher than their American counterparts on standard scales of authoritarian parenting style, applying the western concept of authoritarianism to Chinese parents may not be fair. Unlike the notion of hostility, dominance, aggression, and rejection in the Western concept of authoritarian parenting, the Chinese indigenous concept of strict discipline or training (管教 *guanjiao*) takes place in a supportive, involved, and devoted context of parent-child relationship (Chao, 1994, pp. 1116–1118).

SHAME AND EARLY MORAL SOCIALIZATION

Although not directly addressed, affect is certainly crucial in Chinese moral development. Shame, in particular, may play a central role in such a process, and its meaning has to be understood in its own terms in its situated cultural and historical contexts. In past years, my colleagues and I (Fung, 1994, 1999, 2001; Fung & Chen, 2001, 2002; Fung et al., 2003) have been examining how shame or shaming is employed and manipulated in young Taiwanese children's homes. In our ethnographic and longitudinal observations[6] of spontaneous family interactions in young children's homes when the focal child was between 2.6 and 4, "events of shame" were found to occur regularly at all age points in all families (at a rate of 2.5 events per hour). Most of these events (78%) were occasioned by the focal child's precipitating transgression, and, through various communicative resources the caregiver, consciously or unconsciously, attempted to provoke the child's feelings of shame by casting him/her in an unfavorable light in an effort to forestall or bring an end to the transgression (termed "prototypical events of shame"). The communicative channels could be linguistic (e.g., using explicit labels or makers for shame, invoking the third party's judgment, threats of abandonment or punishment, making disparaging attributions, and name callings), paralinguistic

---

[6] These systematic home observations were videotaped, verbatim transcribed, and meticulously analyzed at the discourse level. In addition to observations, several sets of audiotaped parental interviews at different stages in the study were also transcribed and analyzed (see Fung, 1994, 1999).

(e.g., emphatic stress, angry intonation, and loud or slow delivery), vocal (e.g., making disapproval sounds, and sighs), as well as nonlinguistic (e.g., displaying shame gesture, staring at the child, frowning, pursing up lips, pushing the child away, and enacting physical punitive acts).

Accompanying the elicitation of shame feelings, there was also reasoning for what and why the child had done was wrong and reminder of rules which were often emphasized as having been taught before. Yet, "bringing the transgression to an end" or immediate compliance apparently did not seem to be its uppermost purpose, because, in the majority of the events (86%), shaming and reasoning still continued even after the child had quit misbehaving. There were also events (22%) which occurred when the child was well-behaved without a precipitating transgression, in which the caregiver invoked the child's transgression or shameful experience in the distant past (termed "nonprototypical events of shame") as a way to provoke his/her shame feelings.

Moreover, one-third of both prototypical and nonprototypical events occurred as sequential events. That is, several subevents or episodes are contained within an event, one leading to another in chains (up to six in succession), and involved multiple transgressions committed by the child at different times in different places (up to four spacio-temporal worlds in succession). Most of these subevents referred to subsequent transgression in the here-and-now (60%), in which, for instance, the child's inappropriate responses to parental shaming and reprimand (e.g., crying or talking back) could be interpreted as another transgression and brought more shaming. The subsequent subevents could also involve further accounts of previously committed transgressions (31%). The temporal reference therefore dated back as recent as just before the taping session on the same day or as distant as a few months to almost three years ago during the child's infancy. The remaining sequential episodes (9%), which usually drew the whole event to an end, were marked by a noticeable shift to the future. In these future tensed subevents, instead of focusing on the committed misdeeds, the emphasis was rather the norms, as the caregiver tried to rehearse the "thou shalts" and the "thou shalt nots" with the child in the similar anticipated situations and to project a better-behaved child who would remember the rules and not transgress again.

In nearly half (46%) of these events and subevents, one or more (1.2 on the average) persons[7] were invoked as the judgmental other. These third parties could be physically present or absent during the observed period. Examples included, "Auntie (the researcher) is laughing at you," "Uncle hasn't visited us for a long time because he's scared of you," "Daddy will spank you when he comes back from work," "I'm gonna go ask your teacher and see if she would approve (of your behavior)," and

---

[7] Or category of persons, e.g., teachers and little friends (referring to peers).

"Other kids in school won't like to play with you." Of all non-present judgmental third parties, the largest category was total strangers[8] (60%), followed by father (22%), and relatives and family acquaintances (18%). Even future boyfriend or unborn sibling could be used as "shamers" (see Fung & Chen, 2001). It is worth noting that although mostly it was the mother who exercised discipline, she sometimes assigned the role of the stern "black face" to the father as if allying herself with the child. The fact that she would need extra weight from other respected or admired persons might indicate that either she was not as authoritarian or harsh as she seemed to be, or, consciously or unconsciously, she attempted to deemphasize herself as an authority figure.

The child in fact was an enthusiastic participant in the process and ranked the second highest (32%) in terms of contribution of turns at speaking, next to the caregiver (48%) and higher than siblings and the researcher. Interactions among them in these events were mostly carried out in a playful manner (62% of all events).[9] In our interview data, parents, for their part, could not escape the burden of being alert to their children's misdeeds, of keeping account of past transgressions, and of remaining vigilant for opportunities to guide and correct, if they were to discharge their responsibilities as moral educators of their children. While it was necessary to have the child feel ashamed after committing a misdeed, they also expressed concerns about the possible damage of harsh discipline and too much shame or shaming. Doing so would only make the child escape from being responsible for his/her own behavior and discourage him/her to amend and improve (see Fung, 1999). However, interestingly, achieving well-balanced shaming did not seem to be the sole responsibility of the adult. The child, in fact, was also expected to be able to appreciate the parental intention of motivating him/her and the moral message contained in the reprimand, and hence to bear and handle a reasonable amount of shame. In other words, the full effect of shaming and discipline was a joint effort accomplished by both the caregiver and the child (Fung, 1999).

To summarize, events of shame often began with a past-oriented "accusation" about the child's failure to listen and follow rules that were taught before. While most were triggered by here-and-now transgressions, the "criminal scenes" in the distant past were also reconstructed and the rules reenacted even when the child was well behaved. Charged with reasonable amount of shame, the child was expected to cognitively

---

[8] For instance, other people, other little friends, no one (in cases like "no one would like you," "no one would play with you"), and uncle policeman (referring to any police officer on the street), etc.

[9] The tone or key (see Hymes, 1972) put across in the event could be playful, neutral, or serious, as determined by the situational cues conveyed through multiple communicative channels by all participants.

respond, process, and comprehend the implicit moral message. Besides the request for compliance and confession, these events also carried strong future-oriented implications with expectations for a better self. The caregiver literally took the child on a trip through multiple temporal and spatial stages where the child had committed transgressions, and other people, real or imaginary, acquainted or unacquainted, present or absent, were ready to witness or judge the child's behavior (as being invited by the caregiver). At first sight, these disciplinary practices point to the cultivation of sensitivity to others' possible criticisms and evaluations. Nevertheless, when examined more carefully, such training also served another more important objective—to develop the ability to examine and reflect upon one's own behavior. Since the child had not yet acquired the ability to do so, caregivers assessed the child's behaviors collaboratively with him/her through explicit messages and instructions and overt connections between spacio-temporal worlds, past, present as well as future. Hence, similar moral messages could be repetitively packaged and repackaged, and similar experiences could be interpreted and reinterpreted, each time with subtle differences in its point, purpose, and/or structure. Indeed, shaming practices at home with these young children is about internalization. This explains why shaming and reasoning still proceeded even after the child's submissive compliance in the here-and-now or why they could be brought up by reenacting a past transgression.

As a consequence, although training in this manner seems too harsh to children at such young age, this developmental stage is also the only period in which I observed this type of practices at home. In my continued relationship with these families over the past decade, I have noticed that the parents have long since stopped publicly shaming and disciplining their now teen-aged children, let alone invoking the elaborative forms of sequentially chained events and invocations of judgmental third parities (Fung & Chen, 2002).

CONCLUSIONS

The findings in our studies reveal the role of shame in socializing practices with young children in Taiwanese families. These affective experiences resonate with cultural meanings of shame in the Confucian tradition and have to be understood within the context of a blend of harsh discipline and close attachment in Chinese parenting styles. These indigenous works did not start with an attempt of cultural comparison, nor did they ever apply any "Western theories or models" (including Hoffman's) to the understanding of the local phenomena. However, as shown in Table 1, the possible steps involved in these emotion-laden discursive practices may in fact look very similar to those of empathy practiced by Euro-American

Table 1. Affect and Moral Socialization – Comparisons between Empathy in Euro-American Families and Shame in Taiwanese Families

		Euro-American Families *Empathy*	Taiwanese Families *Shame*
The Inevitable Conflict	Caregiver	Perceive C's behavior as transgression Intervene C's will-/desire-driven behavior	Perceive C's behavior as transgression Intervene C's will-/desire-driven behavior Reenact C's past transgression
	Child	Perceive CG as unfair, unreasonable	Perceive CG as unfair, unreasonable
The Emotion Work	Caregiver	Arouse optimal level of discomfort and stress in C	Arouse optimal level of discomfort and stress in C
	Child	Motivated to tune into the prosocial & moral message	Motivated to tune into the prosocial & moral message
From Affect to Cognition	Caregiver	Induction & reasoning (hot cognitions) Third party's (victim) perspective > CG's	Induction, reasoning, (re)interpretation of the past (hot cognitions) Third party's perspective (judge/witness) > CG's
	Child	Help to perceive CG as fair, reasonable (source) Process the prosocial and moral message (content)	Help to perceive CG as fair, reasonable (source) Process the prosocial and moral message (content)
From Compliance to Internalization	Child	Internal motive system for anticipatory guilt Become more advanced in cognitive/moral development	Self-examination and reflection for anticipatory shame Become more acceptable by other cultural members

families as reported in Hoffman's studies. To these Taiwan families, shame is indeed motivational, prosocial, and moral. It involves the induction of the cognitive knowledge of moral norms, which is charged with an appropriate amount of affective stress. Nevertheless, unlike empathy, shame may also involve parental invocations of the child's past transgression, and therefore the norms could be reestablished through reconstructing, reliving, and reinterpreting the past. Also unlike empathy, the third party introduced by the caregiver is a judgmental witness rather than a victim. However, he may serve a similar function—the voice of another person could alleviate the inevitable parent-child conflict in discipline encounters. While with the help of external weight, the ultimate goal nevertheless is inwardly directed to internalize rules and norms and hence acquire the ability to self-examine and self-reflect upon one's own thoughts and behaviors. Moreover, in addition to an assertion of the inner attributes and abilities as is the case in Hoffman's studies, such a goal of internalization within the self in these Taiwanese families seems also to have a much stronger group concern: to be accepted by other cultural members.

Our findings from intensive observations of daily interactions in Taiwanese families support the contention for importance of affect in early moral socialization in Hoffman's theory. However, they also highlight Hoffman's neglect of culture in understanding affective experience. While the feeling states at the physical and biological level may well be universal, the meaning of affective experiences can be culture-specific and has to be interpreted in its socio-cultural context. For instance, in a narrative study with the same Taiwanese children, Miller, Sandel, Liang, & Fung (2001) found that parents' storytelling of their own personal experiences practiced in these families shared a similar function as that of their European American counterparts—forging parent-child affective bonds through the invocation of empathy. However, the difference between them lies in the presumed nature of this empathy and in the ends that it serves (Miller et al., 2001, p. 174). By citing concrete examples of admirable behavior from their lives and the hardship the previous generation(s) had endured, the Taiwanese mothers seemed to invoke the child's empathy for her; this empathy motivated the child to respect, appreciate, and emulate the mother, and hence to live up to the parent's high standards. In contrast, in the European American families, through narrating the adults' faults as a way to equalize the parent-child asymmetry, the child empathized with a fallible mother, and became more ready to admit his/her own faults.

Indeed, "it is ludicrous to imagine that the emotional functioning of people in different cultures is basically the same. It is just as ludicrous to imagine that each culture's emotional life is unique" (Shweder, 1991, p. 252). What is most challenging is to fully come to terms with the experience-near concepts and meanings (Geertz, 1984) in each (sub-)cultural group. Experience-near concepts are not always naturally noticeable or easily articulated by its native members, whether it is the researcher or the informant. This in turn supports the indigenization of psychological studies of Chinese people. As K. S. Yang (1997a) asserted, the indigenous approach should "accurately reveal, or effectively reconstruct, Chinese psychological and behavioral processes, mechanisms, and patterns closely embedded in the political, economic, cultural, and historical context of a Chinese society" (p. 71). We have to constantly pursue the highest degree of "indigenous congruousness or compatibility" (K. S. Yang, 1997a, 1997b) between the researcher, the researched topic, and the everyday life of the people we study.

REFERENCES

Barrett, K. C. (1995). A functionalist approach to shame and guilt. In J. P. Tangney & K. W. Fischer (Eds.), *Self-conscious emotions* (pp. 25–63). New York: Guildford Press.

Briggs, J. (1970). *Never in anger: Portrait of an Eskimo family.* Cambridge: Harvard University Press.

Chang, H. C. (1997). Language and words: Communication in the Analects of Confucius. *Journal of Language and Social Psychology, 16,* 107–131.

Chao, R. K. (1994). Beyond parental control and authoritarian parenting style: Understanding Chinese parenting through the cultural notion of training. *Child Development, 65,* 1111–1119.

Chao, R. K. (1995). Chinese and European American cultural models of self reflected in mothers' child-rearing beliefs. *Ethos, 23,* 328–354.

Chao, R. K. (1996). Chinese and European American mothers' beliefs about the role of parenting in children's school success. *Journal of Cross-Cultural Psychology, 27,* 403–423.

Cheng, S. W. (1991). On the cross-culturability of moral judgment development. In C. F. Yang & H. S. R. Kao (Eds.), *Chinese people, Chinese minds* (pp. 333–400). Taipei, Taiwan: Yuan Liu. (in Chinese)

Chu, C. L. (1972). On the same orientation of the Chinese from the interrelationship among society, individual, and culture. In Y. Y. Lee & K. S. Yang (Eds.), *Symposium on the character of the Chinese: An interdisciplinary approach* (pp. 85–125). Taipei, Taiwan: Institute of Ethnology, Academia Sinica. (in Chinese)

Chu, C. R. L. (1987). Chinese social interactions: The operation of face. *Chinese Journal of Sociology, 11,* 23–53. (in Chinese)

Chu, C. R. L. (1988). Face and achievement: Social-oriented motivation. *Chinese Journal of Psychology, 31,* 79–90. (in Chinese)

Chu, C. R. L. (1989). The pressure of "face" and its attributions and reactions. In K. S. Yang & K. K. Hwang (Eds.), *Chinese psychology and behaviors* (pp. 177–212). Taipei, Taiwan: Gui Guan. (in Chinese)

Creighton, M. R. (1990). Revisiting shame and guilt cultures: A forty-year pilgrimage. *Ethos, 18,* 279–307.

Farh, J. L. & Cheng, B. S. (1999). A cultural analysis of paternalistic leadership in Chinese organizations. In J. T. Li, A. S. Tsui, & E. Weldon (Eds.), *Management and organizations in the Chinese context* (pp. 84–127). London: MacMillan.

Farh, J. L. & Cheng, B. S. (2000). Paternalistic leadership in Chinese organizations: Analysis from a cultural perspective. *Indigenous Psychological Research in Chinese Societies, 13,* 127–180. (in Chinese)

Fu, B. Y. & Lei, T. (1991). The development of social thoughts in Hong Kong and Taiwan. In C. F. Yang & H. S. R. Kao (Eds.), *Chinese people, Chinese minds* (pp. 213–304). Taipei, Taiwan: Yuan Liu. (in Chinese)

Fung, H. (1994). *The socialization of shame in young Chinese children.* Unpublished doctoral dissertation, University of Chicago, Chicago.

Fung, H. (1999). Becoming a moral child: The socialization of shame among young Chinese children. *Ethos, 27,* 180–209.

Fung, H. (2001, June). *Why do Taiwanese parents "shame" their children? Understanding developing selves in socio-cultural contexts.* Paper presented at the 2nd International Social Anthropology Conference, Brunel University and the Royal Anthropological Institute, West London, United Kingdom.

Fung, H., & Chen, E. C. H. (2001). Across time and beyond skin: Self and transgression in the everyday socialization of shame among Taiwanese preschool children. *Social Development, 10,* 419–436

Fung, H., & Chen, E. C. H. (2002). Affect, culture, and moral socialization: Shame as an example. To appear in T. L. Hu, M. T. Hsu, & K. H. Yeh (Eds.), *Emotion, affect, and culture* (pp. 17–48). Taipei, Taiwan: Institute of Ethnology, Academia Sinica. (in Chinese)

Fung, H., Leung, K. W., & Yeh, Y. H. (1998, July). *Growing up the Confucian way: Child-rearing beliefs and practices in Taiwan and Hong Kong.* Poster session presented at the biennial meeting of the International Society for the Study of Behavioral Development, Bern, Switzerland.

Fung, H., Lieber, E., & Leung, P. W. L. (2003). Parental beliefs on shame and moral socialization in Taiwan, Hong Kong, and the United States. In K. S. Yang, K. K. Hwang, Pedersen, P. B. & I. Daibo (Eds.), *Progress in Asian social psychology: Conceptual and empirical contributions* (pp. 83–109). Westport, CT: Praeger.

Fung, H., Miller, P. J., & Lin, L. C. (2004). Listening is active: Lessons from the narrative practices of Taiwanese families. In M. W. Pratt & B. E. Fiese (Eds.), *Family stories and the life course: Across time and generations* (pp. 303–323). Mahwah, NJ: Lawrence Erlbaum Associates.

Gabrenya, W. K., & Hwang, K. K. (1996). Chinese social interaction: Harmony and hierarchy on the good earth. In M. H. Bond (Ed.), *Handbook of Chinese psychology* (pp. 309–321). Hong Kong: Oxford University Press.

Geertz, C. (1984). "From the native's point of view": On the nature of anthropological understanding. In R. A. Shweder & R. A. LeVine (Eds.), *Culture theory: Essays on mind, self, and emotion* (pp. 123–136). Cambridge, UK: Cambridge University Press.

Gibbs, J. C. & Schnell, S. V. (1985). Moral development "versus" socialization: A critique. *American Psychologist, 10,* 1071–1080.

Gibbs, J. C. (1991a). Toward an integration of Kohlberg's and Hoffman's moral development theories. *Human Development, 34,* 88–104.

Gibbs, J. C. (1991b). Toward an integration of Kohlberg's and Hoffman's theories of morality. In W. M. Kurtines & J. L. Gewirtz (Eds.), *Handbook of moral behavior and development, Vol. 1: Theory* (pp. 183–222). Hillsdale, NJ: Lawrence Erlbaum.

Grusec, J. E., & Goodnow, J. J. (1994). Internalization of values: Model, review, and commentaries. *Developmental Psychology, 30,* 4–19.

Her, E. H. L. (1990). *A phenomenological explication of shame in a shame culture: A cross-cultural perspective.* Unpublished doctoral dissertation, Southern Illinois University, Carbondale.

Ho, D. Y. F. (1976). On the concept of face. *American Journal of Society, 81,* 867–884.

Ho, D. Y. F. (1986). Chinese patterns of socialization: A critical review. In M. H. Bond (Ed.), *The psychology of the Chinese people* (pp. 1–37). Hong Kong: Oxford University Press.

Ho, D. Y. F. (1994). Cognitive socialization in Confucian heritage cultures. In P. M. Greenfield & R. R. Cocking (Eds.), *Cross-cultural roots of minority child development* (pp. 285–313). Hillsdale, NJ: Lawrence Erlbaum Associates.

Ho, D. Y. F. (1996). Filial piety and its psychological consequences. In M. H. Bond (Ed.), *The handbook of Chinese psychology* (pp. 155–188). Hong Kong: Oxford University Press.

Hoffman, M. L. (1975). Development synthesis of affect and cognition and its implications for altruistic motivation. *Developmental Psychology, 11,* 605–622

Hoffman, M. L. (1982). Affect and moral development. In D. Cicchetti, & P. Hesse (Eds.), *Emotional development* (New Directions for Child Development No. 16, pp. 83–103). San Francisco: Jossey-Bass.

Hoffman, M. L. (1983). Affective and cognitive processes in moral internalization. In E. T. Higgins, D. Ruble, & W. Hartup (Eds.), *Social cognition and social development: A sociocultural perspective* (pp. 236–274). New York: Cambridge University Press.

Hoffman, M. L. (1984). Interaction of affect and cognition in empathy. In C. E. Izard, J. Kagan, & R. B. Zajonc (Eds.), *Emotions, cognition, and behavior* (pp. 103–131). Cambridge, UK: Cambridge University Press.

Hoffman, M. L. (1987). The contribution of empathy to justice and moral judgment. In Eisenberg & J. Strayer (Eds.), *Empathy and its development* (pp. 47–80). New York: Cambridge University Press.

Hoffman, M. L. (1991a). Commentary. *Human Development, 34,* 105–110.

Hoffman, M. L. (1991b). Empathy, social cognition, and moral action. In W. M. Kurtines & J. L. Gewirtz (Eds.), *Handbook of moral behavior and development, Vol.1: Theory* (pp. 275–301). Hillsdale, NJ: Lawrence Erlbaum.

Hoffman, M. L. (1994). Discipline and internalization. *Developmental Psychology, 30,* 26–28.

Hoffman, M. L. (2000). *Empathy and moral development: Implications for caring and justice.* New York: Cambridge University Press.

Hogan, R. (1975). Theoretical egocentrism and the problem of compliance. *American Psychologist, 30,* 533–540.

Hsia, H. C., Vera, H., & Berardo, F. M. (1999). Prolegomena for a sociological study of the Chinese family in indigenous terms. *Journal of Family Issues, 20,* 789–806.

Hu, H. C. (1944). The Chinese concept of "face." *American Anthropologist, 46,* 45–64.

Hwang, K. K. (1987). Face and favor: The Chinese power game. *American Journal of Sociology, 92,* 944–974.

Hwang, K. K. (1997). *Guanxi* and *mientze*: Conflict resolution in Chinese society. *Intercultural Communication Studies, VII(1),* 17–42.

Hwang, K. K. (1998). Tow moralities:Reinterpreting the finding of empirical research on moral reasoning in Taiwan. *Asian Journal of Social Psychology, 1,* 211–238.

Hymes, D. (1972). Models of the interaction of language and social life. In J. J. Gumperz & D. Hymes (Eds.), *Directions in sociolinguistics: The ethnography of communication* (pp. 35–71). New York: Holt, Rinehart & Winston.

Karen, R. (1992). Shame. *Atlantic, 269,* 40–70.

Kilborne, B. (1995). Truths that cannot go naked: Shame in many forms. *Psychiatry, 58,* 278–297.

King, A. Y. C., & Myers, J. T. (1977). *Shame as an incomplete conception of Chinese culture: A study of face* (Social Research Center Occasional Paper No. 63). Hong Kong: Chinese University of Hong Kong.

Kochanska, G., & Aksan, N. (1995). Mother-child mutually positive affect, the quality of child compliance to requests and prohibitions, and maternal control as correlates of early internalization. *Child Development, 66,* 236–254.

Kochanska,G., Tjebkes, T. L., & Forman, D. R. (1998). Children's emerging regulation of conduct: Restraint, compliance, and internalization from infancy to the second year. *Child Development, 69,* 1378–1389.

Kohlberg, L. (1969). Stage and sequence: The cognitive-developmental approach to socialization. In D. A. Goslin (Ed.), *Handbook of socialization theory and research* (pp. 347–480). Chicago: Rand McNally.

Kroeber, A. L., & Kluckholn, C. (1952). *Culture: A critical review of concepts and definitions.* Cambridge, MA: Peabody Museum of American Archaeology and Ethnology, Harvard University.

Lau, S., & Yeung, P. W. (1996). Understanding Chinese child development: The role of culture in socialization. In S. Lau (Ed.), *Growing up the Chinese way: Chinese child and adolescent development* (pp. 29–44). Hong Kong: The Chinese University Press.

Lay, K. L., Liang, K. Y., Tang, C. A., & Wang, S. H. (1997a, May). *The analytical framework and prevalence of parental use of negative language: Different perspectives between parents and children*. Paper presented to the 4th Conference of Chinese Psychology and Behavioral Sciences. Academia Sinica, Taipei, Taiwan. (in Chinese)

Lay, K. L., Wang, S. H., Soong, P., & Yang, W. M. (1997b, April). *Verbal abuse in Chinese families: Its prevalence and consequences*. Paper presented at the biennial meeting of the Society for Research in Child Development, Washington, D.C.

Lebra, T. S. (1971). The social mechanism of guilt and shame: The Japanese case. *Anthropological Quarterly, 44*, 241–255.

Lebra, T. S. (1983). Shame and guilt: A psychocultural view of the Japanese self. *Ethos, 11*, 192–209.

Lei, T. (1984). A longitudinal study of moral judgment development in Taiwan: An interim report. *Proceedings of the Sixth International Symposium on Asian Studies, 6*, 49–65.

Lei, T. (1994). Being and becoming moral in a Chinese culture: Unique or universal? *Cross-Cultural Research, 28*, 58–91.

Lewis, M. (1992). *Shame: The exposed self*. New York: Free Press.

Li, J. (2001). Chinese conceptualization of learning. *Ethos, 29*, 111–137.

Li, J. (2002). A cultural model of learning: Chinese "heart and mind for wanting to learn." *Journal of Cross-Cultural Psychology, 33*, 246–267.

Lin, W. Y., & Wang, C. W. (1995). Chinese parenting: A view of strict discipline or corporal punishment? *Indigenous Psychological Research in Chinese Societies, 3*, 1–57. (in Chinese)

Liu, J. H, & Liu, S. H. (2003). The role of the social psychologist in the benevolent authority and plurality of powers: Systems of historical affordance for authority. In K. S. Yang, K. K. Hwang, Pedersen, P. B. & I. Daibo (Eds.), *Progress in Asian social psychology: Conceptual and empirical contributions* (pp. 43–64). Westport, CT: Praeger.

Lutz, C. (1988). *Unnatural emotions: Everyday sentiments on a Micronesian atoll and their challenge to Western theory*. Chicago: University of Chicago Press.

Lutz, C., & White, G. M. (1986). The anthropology of emotions. *Annual Review of Anthropology, 15*, 405–436.

Ma, H. K. (1998). Chinese affective and cognitive moral development: A seven developmental stage theory. *Indigenous Psychological Research in Chinese Societies, 7*, 166–212 (in Chinese)

Markus, H. R., & Kitayama, S. (1991). Culture and the self: Implications for cognition, emotion, and motivation. *Psychological Review, 98*, 224–253.

Mascolo, M. F., Fischer, K. W., & Li, J. (2003). Dynamic development of component systems of emotions: Pride, shame, and guilt in China and the United States. In R. Davidson, K. R. Scherer, and H. Goldsmith (Eds.), *Handbook of Affective Sciences* (pp. 375–408). Oxford, UK: Oxford University Press.

Miller, P. J., Fung, H., & Mintz, J. (1996). Self-construction through narrative practices: A Chinese and American comparison of early socialization. *Ethos, 24*, 237–280.

Miller, P. J., Sandel, T. L., Liang, C. H., & Fung, H. (2001). Narrating transgressions in Longwood: The discourses, meanings, and paradoxes of an American socializing practice. *Ethos, 29*, 159–186.

Miller, P. J., & Sperry, L. L. (1986). The socialization of anger and aggression. *Merrill-Palmer Quarterly, 33*, 1–31.

Miller, P. J., Wiley, A., Fung, H., & Liang, C. H. (1997). Personal storytelling as a medium of socialization in Chinese and American families. *Child Development, 68*, 557–568.

Piers, G., & Singer, M. B. (1953). *Shame and guilt: A psychoanalytic and a cultural study*. New York: W. W. Norton.

Rosaldo, M. (1984). Toward an anthropology of self and feeling. In R. A. Shweder & R. A. LeVine (Eds.), *Culture theory: Essays on mind, self, and emotion* (pp. 137–157). Cambridge, UK: Cambridge University Press.

Russell, J., & Yik, M. (1996). Emotion among the Chinese. In M. H. Bond (Ed.), *The Handbook of Chinese Psychology* (pp. 166–188). Hong Kong: Oxford University Press.

Schoenhals, M. (1993). *The paradox of power in a People's Republic of China middle school.* Armonk, NY: M. E. Sharpe.

Shaver, P. R., Wu, S., & Schwartz, J. C. (1992). Cross-cultural similarities and differences in emotion and its representation: A prototype approach. In M. S. Clark (Ed.), *Review of personality and social psychology* (pp. 175–212). Newbury Park, CA: Sage.

Shweder, R. A. (1991). Menstrual pollution, soul loss, and the comparative study of emotions. In R. A. Shweder, *Thinking through cultures: Expeditions in cultural psychology* (pp. 241–65). Cambridge, MA: Harvard University Press.

Shweder, R. A. (1999). Why cultural psychology? *Ethos 27*, 62–73.

Shweder, R. A. (2000). The psychology of practice and the practice of the three psychologies. *Asian Journal of Social Psychology, 3*, 207–222.

Tangney, J. P. (1998). How does guilt differ from shame? In J. Bybee (Ed.), *Guilt and children* (pp. 1–17). San Diego: Academic Press.

Tangney, J. P., Burggraf, S. A., & Wagner, P. E. (1995). Shame-proneness, guilt-proneness, and psychological symptoms. In J. P. Tangney & K. W. Fischer (Eds.), *Self-conscious emotions: They psychology of shame, guilt, embarrassment, and pride* (pp. 343–367). New York: Guilford.

Tangney, J. P., Wagner, P., Fletcher, C., & Gramzow, R. (1992). Shame into anger? The relation of shame and guilt to anger and self-reported aggression. *Journal of Personality and Social Psychology, 62*, 669–675.

Wang, L., Li, J., & Fischer, K. W. (2001). *The organization of shame in Chinese.* Manuscript submitted for publication.

Wilson, R. W. (1970). *Learning to be Chinese.* Cambridge, MA: MIT Press.

Wilson, R. W. (1981). Moral behavior in Chinese society: A theoretical perspective. In R. W. Wilson, S. L. Greenblatt, & A. A. Wilson (Eds.), *Moral behavior in Chinese society* (pp. 117–136). New York: Praeger.

Wu, David Y. H. (1981). Child abuse in Taiwan. In J. Korbin (Ed.), *Child abuse and neglect: Cross-cultural perspectives* (pp. 139–165). Berkeley, CA: University of California Press.

Wu, D. Y. H. (1985). Child training in Chinese culture. In W. S. Tsend and D. Y. H. Wu (Eds.), *Chinese culture and mental health* (pp. 113–34). Orlando, FL: Academic Press.

Wu, D. Y. H. (1996). Chinese childhood socialization. In M. H. Bond, (Ed.), *The handbook of Chinese psychology* (pp. 143–154). Hong Kong: Oxford University Press.

Yang, C. F. (1996). *How to study Chinese? Collection of essays on indigenous psychology.* Taipei, Taiwan: Guei Guan. (in Chinese)

Yang, K. S. (1992). The social orientation of Chinese. In K. S. Yang, & A. B. Yu (Eds.), *Chinese psychology and behaviors: Methods and concepts.* Taipei, Taiwan: Gui Guan. (in Chinese)

Yang, K. S. (1997a). Indigenising Westernized Chinese psychology. In M. H. Bond (Ed.), *Working at the interface of cultures: Eighteen lives in social science* (pp. 62–76). London: Routledge.

Yang, K. S. (1997b). Indigenous compatibility in psychological research and its related problems. *Indigenous Psychological Research in Chinese Societies, 8*, 75–120. (in Chinese)

Yeh. M. H., & Yang, K. S. (1997). Chinese familism: Conceptual analysis and empirical assessment. *Bulletin of the Institute of Ethnology, Academia Sinica, 83*, 169–225. (in Chinese)

Yeh, K. H. (1997). Changes in the Taiwan people's concept of filial piety. In L. Y. Chang, Y. H. Lu, & F. C. Wang (Eds.), *Taiwanese society in 1990s: Taiwan social change survey symposium series II* (pp. 171–214). Taipei, Taiwan: Institute of Sociology, Academia Sinica. (in Chinese)

Yeh, K. H., & Yang, K. S. (1991). The analysis of the cognitive structure of filial piety. In K. S. Yang & K. K. Hwang (Eds.), *Chinese psychology and behaviors* (pp. 95–133). Taipei, Taiwan: Gui Guan. (in Chinese)

Yu, A. B. (1996). Ultimate life concerns, self, and Chinese achievement motivation. In M. H. Bond (Ed.), *The handbook of Chinese psychology* (pp. 227–246). Hong Kong: Oxford University Press.

Zahn-Waxler, C., & Robinson, J. (1995). Empathy and guilt: Early origins of feelings of responsibility. In J. P. Tangney, & K. W. Fischer (Eds.), *Self-conscious emotions: The psychology of shame, guilt, embarrassment, and pride* (pp. 143–173). New York: Guilford.

Zhai, X. W. (1995). *The Chinese concepts of face.* Taipei, Taiwan: Gui Guan. (In Chinese)

Chapter 9

Cultures Are Like All Other Cultures, Like Some Other Cultures, Like No Other Culture

James Georgas and Kostas Mylonas

The theme of this chapter is the relationship between cross-cultural psychology and indigenous psychology[1] and a methodological approach that can potentially satisfy the goals of both. Indigenous psychology is an integral part of cross-cultural psychology. Whereas cultural psychology has taken the extreme stance that the essence of culture is unique in its symbols and significance so as to preclude meaningful comparisons between different cultures (Shweder, 1990), the accepted definition of cross-cultural psychology includes two basic dimensions: universal psychological phenomena across cultures and psychological phenomena specific to cultures.

---

[1] The etymology of the Greek term *indigenous psychology* might be of interest. It was generated by Adair's (1999) differentiation between *indigenous* and *autochthonous*. Three words in the Greek language are employed for this concept. One is, as Adair has written, *autochthonous*. The root *auto* in Greece has a number of meanings. In this regard it means "he," "she," "it," "they," or "those." "Chthon" is derived from the root "chthonos," which means "land." Thus, autochthonous is defined as "a resident from the onset in the land of one's family." A second word is "gegenis," derived from "ge" another word for "earth" or "land," and "genis," derived from "genos," which means "descent," "lineage," "family" and is defined as "one who has been born in a specific place, who belongs there as a native inhabitant." A third term is "ithagenis," "one who resides in one's place of birth and descent." The terms "indigenous" in English or "indigene" in French are derived from "endogenis," meaning "endo" or "internal" and again "genos," but which is defined in Greek as "that which is caused by internal processes." However, the term "indigenous" was mistakenly translated into English by social scientists in the 19th century as meaning "native." At this point the use of the term "indigenous" has been established in scientific usage, and we of course will continue to employ it.

The theme "empirical, philosophical, and cultural issues in indigenous psychology," is highly relevant to cross-cultural psychology at this stage in its development. The relationship of cross-cultural psychology to indigenous psychology and to cultural psychology has been discussed by many researchers (Berry & Dasen, 1974; Shweder, 1990; Kim & Berry, 1993; Diaz-Guerrero, 1993; Sinha, 1997; Berry, 1999; Adair & Diaz-Loving, 1999; and in the special issue of Indigenous, Cultural, and Cross-cultural psychologies, 2000).

Kim (Kim & Berry, 1993; Kim, Park, & Park, 1999) has been a protagonist in this effort to emphasize the need for psychologists from non-Western countries not to merely copy western theories and methods but to take the initiative to be creative and think about psychological concepts based on the context of their own culture, and to experiment with methods.

Cross-cultural psychology was developed as a way of detecting cultural diversity in psychology theories and research. At another stage, the awareness of the domination of American and European psychology led to the questioning of the application of western derived theories, methods, and interpretation of research results to non-western cultures. A related question was the omission of psychological phenomena observed in non-western cultures (Kim & Berry, 1993). Indigenous psychology became a legitimate branch of cross-cultural psychology when it emphasized the in-depth study of the cultural context in which psychological phenomena are embedded. This was in contrast to the conventional practice in cross-cultural research of focusing only on the level of the psychological phenomena and giving lip-service to the concept of culture by interpreting research results in terms of similarities or differences in ethnic groups, e.g., "Greeks" or the name of the country "Greece," and without specifying relationships with potential cultural level context variables. Thus, an important goal of indigenous psychology is to answer questions regarding the second dimension of the definition of cross-cultural psychology "psychological phenomena specific to cultures" by specifying culture-psychology relationships. A proposal of one way of doing this will be presented later in this paper.

The relationship of indigenous psychology to cross-cultural psychology has been discussed by Kim and Berry (1993). They specified six key aspects of indigenous psychology: 1) contextual understanding, 2) study of peoples in all cultures and also ethnic groups in polyethnic nations, 3) distinction between nations and cultures, 4) employment of multiple methods and new methodology, 5) clarification of external observer vs. internal observer bias, and 6) discovery of universal facts, principles and laws that could explain human diversity.

Berry (2000) has recently proposed a framework integrating the cultural, indigenous and comparative traditions of research, described as a symbiotic approach that could lead to the study of a "universal psychology," and not a psychology that reflects western psychological theories. Cross-cultural psychology is described as a symbiosis of the cultural or in-depth approach and the comparative approach.

Kim, Park, and Park (1999) argued that the predominant findings and methods of contemporary western psychology are not suited to other cultures. Kim delineated the key elements of the Korean approach with an emphasis on a bottom-up model-building approach. He also raised important epistemological issues of two types of knowledge—analytical, semantic, and declarative knowledge; and phenomenological, episodic, procedural knowledge—as parallel methods of investigating psychological data in different cultures and advocated more holistic and qualitative methods as an alternative paradigm for a Korean indigenous psychology approach.

Poortinga's (1999) viewpoint regarding the tendency of some psychologists to rely strictly on cultural interpretation of the uniqueness of their findings also touched on an important epistemological issue. That is, the scientific method is 1) public, meaning the researcher is obliged to describe thoroughly the method employed, and 2) replicable, meaning that other researchers must be able to apply the same method and reproduce the results. In other words, those who argue for a culturalist interpretation of the uniqueness of behavior must also show that this behavior does *not* occur in other cultures. Poortinga essentially agrees with Berry (2000) that indigenous psychology should have both a cultural and a cross-cultural dimension, and that the search for universals should be an integral part of its goals.

Adair (1999) acknowledged the growing limitations of Western models in psychology and suggested that the goal of indigenous psychology was to make psychological research more culturally sensitive and to make it more autochthonous, that is, more independent of its imported origins, and more focused on addressing local issues, customs, behaviors, and local training.

Diaz-Loving (1999) took as a starting point the lack of cultural sensitivity and the ethnocentric perspective of the "Euro-Meso-North-American" scientific psychological tradition, which has resulted in indiscriminate imposition of universal categories and findings across behavioural settings. He supported the indigenisation of psychology in general and employed the example of Mexican ethnopsychology as a potential solution. Diaz-Loving argued that autochthonous researchers are aware of the social, ecological, and cultural variables in their culture that provide a theoretical framework for interpretation of results. He also suggested that one benefit of indigenous psychology is the discovery of unique characteristics in a culture, and a second is the study of the relationships of culturally relevant variables to universal constructs.

GREECE AND INDIGENOUS PSYCHOLOGY

Coming from Greece, and having written an indigenous analysis of Greek culture (Georgas, 1993) and its effects on values and family (Georgas, 1999; Georgas, Berry, van de Vijver, Kagitçibasi & Poortinga, in press; Georgas, Mylonas, et al., 2001) it is clear that we support the indigenous psychology approach. When the first author returned to Greece in 1964 after training in psychology in the United States, his interest in cross-cultural psychology and his emerging interest of looking at psychological phenomena from the perspective of the Greek culture were stimulated by certain experiences. Although the term *indigenous psychology* was not employed at that time, this perceptual set was already established in the first author's approaches to psychology.

Over 30 years ago, in teaching courses in developmental psychology, the descriptions of the crisis of adolescents of American developmental psychology textbooks did not seem to fit the Greek adolescent or the Greek family, e.g., the rebellion of adolescents towards parents, the goals of American parents to encourage independence of their children, that young adults should live in a separate household from their families, they should be independent economically from their families, that psychological problems of adolescents and young adults were interpreted as due to their being too emotionally close to and too dependent on their parents, and the prescription proposed by many psychotherapists for children to distance themselves geographically and emotionally from their parents. Since in Greek culture at that time, the opposite was observed or prescribed, e.g., goals of parents were to encourage cooperation and interdependence of children on the family, it appeared that either the Greek family was pathological because they did not promote individualist behaviors, a position actually taken by some American trained social and behavioral scientists at that time, or perhaps these American bred psychological theories did not pertain to the Greek context.

In writing a textbook on social psychology in Greek (Georgas, 1986), the issue of American emic versus Greek culture emerged repeatedly. For example, in reviewing the literature on attitudes and behavior, situations employed in experiments were taken from the American context–with over 90 percent of the literature American–almost all examples were irrelevant to the Greek culture. The final manuscript attempted to separate the concepts and the theories which appeared to have cross-cultural invariance.

Construction of a scale of family values (Georgas, 1999) employed in a number of studies was based on examination of the Greek literature on family and on the generation of potential Greek values by Greek students.

An indigenous psychology approach was employed in Georgas (1993), in which Greek culture was analyzed employing elements of Berry's (1976) ecocultural framework and also with a historical analysis similar to the approach of Diaz-Guerrero (1993).

METHODOLOGY AND INDIGENOUS PSYCHOLOGY

An old adage in psychology has always remained tucked in a corner of the first author's mind. It has played the role of an epistemological prompter, albeit an oversimplification, in how to look at psychological phenomena. The adage is (Kluckhohn & Murray, 1950),

Man is like all other men,
like some other men,
like no other man

The three hierarchical levels of personality implied by the adage are universal traits, taxonomies of traits, and individual traits. The upper two levels also refer to nomothetic methods while the lowest level refers to idiographic methods.

The adage could also apply to cross-cultural psychology and to indigenous psychology, that is, "Cultures are like all other cultures, like some other cultures, like no other culture." Surely all cultures share universal features as well as universal psychological variables. Groups of cultures share features on psychological variables. And cultures have specific and possibly unique features and meanings, e.g., language, myths, meanings, symbols.

However, the term *culture* has a number of definitions. One refers to its constituent elements, e.g., patterns of behaviors, transmitted symbols, values, etc. Culture is also employed to designate a group of people with the same culture as defined above, or as a synonym for *ethnic group* or, as used in our discipline, as a synonym for *nation* or *country*. Anthropologists argue that if *culture* is defined strictly as referring to ethnic groups, their numbers are estimated to be in the thousands. If culture is equated with nation-state or country, the number is approximately two hundred. However, culture is also employed in taxonomies of nations or ethnic groups with similar characteristics, e.g., European culture, Arabian culture, or Francophone cultures.

Thus, in discussing the definition of a cultural group in indigenous psychology, the unit of study has usually been a nation-state, but it has also been ethnic groups within a country. The point here is that indigenous psychology may study a relatively small ethnic group or a country, but the focus can also be on clusters of countries with similar constituent cultural elements, or clusters of countries with similar psychological patterns of variables.

The predominant arguments underlying the indigenous psychology approach were presented earlier in this chapter. Among them are the search for specific psychological adaptations to cultural elements. Research generated by non-western psychologists related to indigenous concepts, and related to addressing their own cultural and social issues is highly desirable in cross-cultural psychology and in psychology in general. The Korean indigenous bottom-up model-building approach described by Kim is very positive. But the claim of uniqueness of psychological concepts in a culture begs the question, as Poortinga has stated (1989), of to what degree these cultural concepts or methods are unique to their culture. It is highly probable that there is a considerable degree of uniqueness of psychological phenomena in every culture. A psycholinguistic analysis of the semantics in any culture would reveal this uniqueness of words in any language, and indeed in the same language in different cultures. A word such as *amai*, the need for dependency, in Japanese (according to Doi, as cited in Poortinga, 1999), may have a unique semantic specification, the conceptual definition and emotional loadings shaped by historical and cultural elements. Most of us would agree, as psychoanalysis and psychology has shown us through the idiographic approach, that "man is like no other man," that the personality of every individual is unique, even in identical twins. Does this mean that psychology is composed of billions of personality theories? Most cross-cultural psychologists would agree that the manifestations of psychological processes are embedded in culture. According to Berry, et al. (1992), for example, although cognitive processes are universal across cultures, the different manifestations of cognitive processes represent different types of cognitive adaptations to the specific ecological demands and ecocultural patterns of cultures. That is, universals can be described as aptitudes, not shaped by culture, while manifestations can be described as abilities or skill levels influenced by culture. The same would apply to other psychological variables, such as emotions, in which the basic emotional types are universal, but their behavioral manifestations are shaped by the cultural context and historical development of the culture.

It is a matter of at which level psychologists want to look at phenomena. If the purpose is to look only for unique phenomena at the micro-level, then by definition, there is no comparison possible, e.g. "Culture is like no other culture." It is difficult to agree with the arguments of cultural psychologists that the psychological meanings of each cultural group are so unique to their cultural context that comparisons between cultures are not possible. We do not believe that indigenous psychology has taken or wishes to take this solipsistic path.

If we believe psychology is a science, then a basic epistemological methodology is the in-depth analysis of a phenomenon as well as the taxonomy of the phenomenon. And it is very possible that these unique psychological variables within a specific culture may be similar to those in "some other cultures," which can only be determined through cross-cultural studies. For example, Diaz-Loving reported (1999) the methodology of the Mexican Historic-Socio-Cultural Premises (Diaz-Guerrero, 1993) which led to results that indicated the importance of the family for all social behavior. Key elements of family dynamics and values in Mexico were the power and supremacy of the father, and the love and absolute and necessary sacrifice of the mother, the cardinal trait abnegation of satisfying the needs of others over self, and the central traditionalism factor of Affiliative-Obedience vs. Active Self-Affirmation (*children should always obey their parents, when parents are strict children grow up correctly, everyone should love their mother and respect their father*), hierarchical family structure based on respect towards others who are higher in the social hierarchy, particularly parents and relatives, etc. In research in Greece (Georgas, 1999), we found very similar family structure and functions, with values such as, *father should be the head of the family...handle the money in the household...the breadwinner...provide a dowry for the daughter. Mother should live for her children...accept the decisions of the father...agree with the opinions of the father...place is in the home*. These values are related to the traditional roles of the patriarchal extended family in which the father was the head of the family who acted in an authoritarian manner and controlled the finances, while the mother was a submissive, conciliatory housewife who cared for the children. Yes, it is true that the historical and social cultural contexts of Mexico and Greece are uniquely different, there are different symbols in each culture, and the Greek and Mexican languages are unique. But if one investigates the psychological concepts at the comparative level, there appears to be a degree of similarity of the family in Mexico and Greece.

Thus, we do not see a conflict between the cross-cultural comparative approach and the indigenous approach; they are complementary. We do believe that the generation of cross-cultural research by autochthonous researchers is desirable and necessary, including the employment of indigenously generated methodology. But we also believe there is another goal of indigenous psychology related to the cross-cultural or comparative approach. That is, for scientists from non-western cultures to generate concepts and methods that can then be studied cross-culturally. This is implied in point 6 of Kim and Berry (1993) that one of the goals of the indigenous psychologies approach is the discovery of universal facts, principles, and laws that could explain human diversity, or as Kim et al. (1999) have called it, a "bottom-up" approach.

CULTURAL UNIVERSALS AND CULTURAL SPECIFICS

The purpose of this paper is to present a methodology that would enhance the interaction between the indigenous psychology approach and the cross-cultural comparative approach. This proposed methodology can classify psychological phenomena into clusters of cultures as a complementary methodology to seeking cultural universals. This is consistent with the proposal discussed above, that the indigenous psychological in-depth study of unique psychological concepts and their relationship to cultural factors in a country is an important goal in cross-cultural psychology, but it is highly possible that at another level, the taxonomic level, a number of countries will have common cultural elements and psychological similarities, forming a common cultural cluster. Thus, the study of some psychological phenomena will result in cultural clusters and not psychological universals; an issue of relevance to the bottom-up approach in indigenous psychology.

In Georgas and Berry (1995) it was demonstrated that nations could be grouped into clusters based on five a-priori dimensions based on Berry's Ecocultural Framework: Ecology, Education, Economics, Mass communications and Population ecosocial indices, and Religion categorized in terms of the major religions. Kroeber (1939) grouped many cultures into broader culture areas. Forde (1934) demonstrated the existence of broad groupings of cultures in Sub-Saharan Africa.

In a recent manuscript (Georgas, van de Vijver, & Berry, 2004) nations were classified according to Affluence and Religious denominations and relationships were explored with psychological data from studies of Hofstede (1980), Inglehart (1997), Schwartz (1994), Smith, Dugan and Trompenaars (1996) on values, and of Diener (1996) on subjective well-being. The results indicated that employing the Ecocultural Framework to classify countries with similar ecological, social, and institutional patterns can lead to establishing cultural clusters with common ecosocial indices. These ecosocial indices, in turn, were shown to have systematic relationships with psychological variables.

Construct Equivalence and Psychological Universals

Construct equivalence is concerned with the equivalence of a construct across cultures. If constructs are not identical across cultures, comparisons of items on a questionnaire are not possible. Construct bias can occur if an imposed emic construct is merely compared in terms of means between different cultures without investigating for equivalence of the constructs (Poortinga, 1989). Construct equivalence can be established with different statistical techniques (Leung & Bond, 1989; van de Vijver & Leung, 1997), usually a combination of exploratory factor analysis and target rotations, together with an estimation of the degree of factorial agreement, most often Tucker's Phi. The degree of equivalence needed to establish, what is subsequently termed *factor equivalence* is a Tucker Phi above .90, while values lower than .90 indicate lack of factor equivalence across the cultures.

The process of attaining factor equivalence across cultures is dependent on selection of the items loading on these common factors, so that the degree of equivalence is above .90. Factor equivalence is often attained by deleting items which are discrepant, that are not found in the factor structure in all the cultures. In some cases, cultures that do not have an equivalent factor structure with other cultures are also deleted until the degree of factor equivalence reaches .90. It is a methodology employing these deleted items and deleted cultures that we will discuss in the next section.

Equivalence and Cultural Clusters

The purpose of the methodology of Factor Equivalence is to establish Construct Equivalence across cultures, that is, psychological universals. And it makes sense that not all the items of a questionnaire will load on these Factor Equivalent structures across all the cultures. It is possible, however, that the deleted items may show patterns that define cultural clusters on other non-equivalent factors, or may show supplementary patterns of psychological factors that define clusters of cultures, even on the construct with Factor Equivalence.

The utility of this method would be to enable the determination of constructs specific to clusters of nations with common cultural psychological phenomena. It provides a complementary method to determining psychological universals by establishing psychological constructs that may be found only in some cultures–an extension, as argued above, of the indigenous psychology approach.

THE EUROPEAN VALUES STUDY AND FAMILY VALUES

The methodology will be illustrated with data from the European Values study (Halman, 2001). Georgas, Mylonas, Gari, and Panagiotopoulou, (2004) analyzed the data related to family and values based on representative samples (n = 39,919) from 33 European countries. The mean age of the respondents was 45 years (sd = 17.18) and the range was from 16 to 99 years of age; 45.9% of the respondents were males and 54.1% were females.

The purpose was to construct a family values framework by determining cross-cultural universals and differences, with the objective of investigating the relationships between cultural variation and family values. Information was gathered *within* each culture on the relationship between cultural and family values, which represent the indigenous approach. The cross-cultural analyses presented the family values universals across all cultures, and the universal patterns of family values that characterize the family in different clusters of cultures. Thus, the findings provide a system of assessment that can be employed in studying applied issues related to psychological correlates of family values in these and other cultures, but will also employ a culture-specific approach leading to a more valid interpretation of the meaning of these variables within cultural zones.

The European Values Study contained 71 sets of questions, with sub-sets of questions from each set. The data were collected from 39,919 cases (unweighted N) from 33 European countries[2]. Fifty one questions were selected from the EVS questionnaire in the areas of family and marriage (e.g., how important is family in life), parental issues and priorities (e.g., both parents are needed for a child to grow up happily in a family), occupation related family values (e.g., being a housewife is just as fulfilling as work for pay), religion and family (e.g., importance of shared religious beliefs in marriage), and a few general value items related to family life (e.g., freedom of choice and control over life).

UNIVERSAL CONSTRUCTS AND CULTURE SPECIFIC CONSTRUCTS

The methodology was carried out in two stages. The first stage sought to determine which constructs were universal across the 33 countries. It was expected that universal construct equivalence would be found, but would not account for a large amount of variance. The second stage was based on the hypothesis that there may be universal family constructs across the countries, but there also may be culture specific constructs with items characteristic of clusters of countries. This would require a clusters of countries methodology.

CONSTRUCT EQUIVALENCE OF FAMILY VALUES

Stage 1: Universal Constructs

The purpose of the first stage was to determine universal factors of family values. The procedure for establishing factor equivalence described by van de Vijver and Leung (1997) and by van de Vijver and Poortinga (2002) was employed. The first step was the exploratory factor analysis of the overall correlation matrix based on the pooled data from all 33 countries. The second step was the exploratory factor analysis of each country. The third step was to compare the factor structure of each country with the overall factor of the pooled data by employing Tucker Phi as the criterion for factor equivalence.

---

[2] Austria (Aus), Belarus (Bls), Belgium (B), Bulgaria (Bg), Croatia (Cr), Czechia (Cz), Denmark (Dk), East Germany (EG), Estonia (Est), Finland (Fn), France (F), Greece (Gr), Hungary (Hg), Iceland (Ic), Ireland (Ire), Italy (It), Latvia (Lt), Lithuania (Ltn), Luxembourg (LXB), Malta (Mt), the Netherlands (H), Northern Ireland (NIre), Poland (Pl), Portugal (Pt), Romania (Rom), Russia (Rs), Slovakia (Slk), Slovenia (Slv), Spain (Es), Sweden (Sw), Ukraine (Ukr), United Kingdom (UK), and West Germany (WG).

Step 1. Overall Factor Analysis of the Pooled Data

Because the EVS items were at different levels of measurement, e.g., some at two levels, some at three levels, some at five levels, correlations could not be computed with Pearson *r*. Several ways of circumventing the problem were considered, including mathematical transformations for all continuous variables, and the use of Kendall Tau-b, Kendall Tau-c, and Gamma coefficients; Spearman Rho coefficients seemed the most appropriate for handling the ordinal data in the factor analyses despite the large number of tied data. Employing Spearman Rho rather than Pearson *r* in factor analysis, where there are problems with the metric scale has also been supported by Thurstone (1947), Tabachnick and Fidell

Table 1. Factor Analysis Outcomes for All 33 Countries

Factors	1	2	3	4	5	6	7
% of variance explained	12.21	7.39	5.62	3.55	3.39	2.98	2.77
attend religious services	**.79**	.04	.22	.03	−.02	.07	.09
importance of religion	**.78**	.07	.21	.05	.03	.10	.03
are you a religious person	**.74**	.02	.09	.03	.03	.04	.05
spend time in church	**.69**	.00	.21	.05	−.09	.04	.05
church and family life	**.60**	−.01	.11	.15	.02	.04	−.04
shared religious beliefs	**.48**	.11	.17	.09	.08	.02	.03
discussing problems	.02	**.73**	.00	−.08	−.04	.06	−.02
talking about mutual interests	.09	**.70**	.05	.10	.08	.11	−.03
spending time together	.08	**.66**	.10	.13	.15	.09	−.04
understanding & tolerance in marriage	−.01	**.60**	−.02	−.03	−.11	.01	.02
mutual respect and appreciation	.02	**.56**	−.01	−.05	−.13	−.02	−.01
happy sexual relationship	−.09	**.51**	−.06	.00	.30	−.02	.02
sharing household chores	.02	**.51**	.00	−.05	.23	.07	−.22
abortion justified?	.23	−.02	**.81**	.13	.10	.03	.03
approval of abortion if not wanting more children	−.24	−.05	**−.79**	.07	.05	−.02	−.10
approval of abortion if woman not married	−.22	−.03	**−.79**	.01	.03	.00	−.07
is divorce justified?	.18	−.04	**.63**	.24	.14	.03	−.01
marriage or long-term relationship is necessary for one to be happy	.07	.07	.06	**.67**	.06	.06	−.08
woman needs to have children to be fulfilled	.07	−.07	.01	**.64**	.09	.01	−.01
both parents needed in a family	.04	−.02	.10	**.62**	.03	−.03	.17
adequate income	.00	.08	.00	.12	**.71**	.01	.01
good housing	.00	.21	.00	.13	**.62**	.01	−.06
can people be trusted?	−.01	.00	−.14	−.09	**−.40**	−.01	−.13
concerned with eldery	.17	.09	.06	.05	.00	**.70**	−.04
help eldery	.15	.19	.02	−.06	−.11	**.69**	−.03
prepared to do something to improve conditions of family	−.05	.03	.00	.03	.02	**.64**	.03

Continued

Table 1. (*cont.*)

Factors	1	2	3	4	5	6	7
% of variance explained	12.21	7.39	5.62	3.55	3.39	2.98	2.77
concerned with living conditions of immediate family	.00	−.05	.05	.09	.19	**.54**	.01
working mother&children can have warm rels	.05	.00	.12	.15	−.01	.01	**.69**
fathers looking after children are well suited for doing so	.10	−.13	.01	.03	.07	−.02	**.65**
income should come from both husband and wife	.00	−.12	.04	−.30	−.08	−.05	**.56**

For Table 1, all questions with a loading of |.39| or less (not participating in any of the factors) are not reported; total variance explained = 37.9%

(1989), Kline (1993), Guilford (1956), and Graziano and Raulin (1989). Thus, Spearman Rho coefficients for all 51 questions for all 39,799 participants (weighted data) from the 33 counties in the sample were inserted into a square matrix for further exploration of the overall factor structure (Table 1).

Seven factors emerged for the overall factor solution (analyzing the pooled correlation matrix for all 33 countries). The model employed was principal component analysis with varimax rotation, and the number of factors extracted was based on the Kaiser-Guttman and the Scree test criteria. The explained variance was 37.9%. Loadings greater than |.40| were interpreted. Factor 1 was named *Religiosity and family life*. Factor 2 was named *Companionship in marriage*, and appeared to be consistent with the relationship between husband and wife or partners in which they actively share problems and interests, spend time together, have a happy sexual relationship, and have an atmosphere of equality. Factor 3 was named *Abortion, divorce, and adultery*. Factor 4 was named *Children, family life, and marriage*; this factor is most likely related to a traditional nuclear family structure. Factor 5 was named *Family security* and associates with housing and income prerequisites and mutual trust in the family. Factor 6 was named *Importance of living conditions of family and the elderly*. Factor 7 was named *Working wife and mother* and refers to working mother relationships with her children, fathers looking after children and income provision from both husband and wife.

Step 2. Factor Analysis of Each Country

For each of the 33 countries, and following the same method of factor analysis, seven-factor structures were computed. Spearman Rho correlations were also used for the factor analysis for each country separately.

Step 3. Testing for factor equivalence of each country with the overall factor structure

The next step was to compare the factor structure of each country with the overall factor structure based on the pooled data, employing Tucker Phi coefficients of at least .90 as the criterion for factor equivalence. The factor analyses of the countries resulted in a 33 by 7 matrix, with each matrix column containing 51 factor loadings (matrix rows). These 231 (that is, 33×7) vectors would then be compared for their equivalence against the seven overall factors, thus we calculated all Tucker Phi coefficients (231 vectors $\times$ 7 overall factors = 1,617 Tucker Phi indices). Maximum expected factor equivalence would yield 231 Tucker Phi coefficients greater than .90. Such a result would mean that each of the factors in each country was equivalent to one overall factor.

The Tucker Phi coefficient is somewhat tolerant of differences in factor loadings and is analogous to the number of items that take part in the analysis. That is, the Tucker Phi coefficient takes into account the information included in the proportion of items forming a factor, in comparison to the overall number of items (including those that do not take part in this factor). However, if the number of items initially analyzed is large, then it is more likely to neglect a rather large proportion of items with different loadings within the same constructs across two factor structures, which is due to the large proportion of similar loadings for this comparison. This oversight may result in Tucker Phi coefficients that do not really denote factor equivalence but merely factor similarity, although the index remains high. However, for the purpose of our analysis, it would be incompatible to employ other factor structure comparison methods[3], since the relevant literature is based on Tucker Phi indices. Thus, although the previous remarks were taken into account, we decided to examine the Tucker Phi indices for this factor equivalence testing stage.

The results of this comparison were:

- The first overall factor *Religiosity and family life* reached 100% factor equivalence; that is, the same factor was found in all 33 countries.
- The second overall factor *Companionship in marriage* reached only 48% of equivalence (16 countries with Tucker Phi coefficients greater than .90).
- The third overall factor *Abortion, divorce and adultery* reached 81% of equivalence.

---

[3] An alternative approach would be to employ the Cattell Salience coefficient (Cattell, Balcar, Horn, & Nesselroade, 1969; Tabachnick and Fidell, 2001), a coefficient that is not computed as the correlation between two factors but as a hypothesis-driven statistical criterion and is accompanied by significance levels.

- Only 6% of the countries had Tucker Phi coefficients greater than .90 for the *Children, family life, marriage* overall factor.
- Only 3% of the countries had Tucker Phi coefficients greater than .90 for the *Family security* overall factor.
- *Importance of living conditions of the family and the elderly* reached a low 36% of factor equivalence.
- Finally, *Working wife and mother* had 0% agreement.

In summary, although there was absolute agreement with each country's factor structure (33 hits) for the first overall factor, and satisfactory factor agreement for the third overall factor, it was not the case for five of the overall factors. Thus, the Tucker Phi coefficients indicated that not all country factors were identical or similar to the overall factor structure. The ratio of the observed factor equivalence to the expected overall factor equivalence for the total of the seven factors was only 39% (factor equivalence was observed for 92 Tucker coefficients for the seven factor structures elicited for each country in comparison to the overall seven factor structure).

Stage 2: Factor Equivalence between Each of the 33 Countries

In this stage, factor equivalence was tested between each of the 33 countries. This is a stricter criterion than comparison of each country's factor structure with the overall or pooled data factor structure. The method followed in this study was designed to distinguish between the items that would give factor equivalent structures among all the countries and the items that would give partial equivalence, that is, factor equivalence for some countries but not all.

Step 1: Testing for Factor Equivalence between All 33 Countries

The factor structures of the 51 items as already computed for each country separately (principal components analyses–orthogonal rotation of the axes) were implemented. Tucker Phi coefficients were calculated for the factor structures between all pairs of countries (33 countries $\times$ 32 $\div$ 2 = 528 pairs of countries) for seven-factor structures.

Step 2: Percent of Factor Equivalence for Each Factor Based on 33 Countries

Factor equivalence percentages were computed on the basis of the maximum expected number of factor equivalence hits possible (for all 528 pairs of countries in comparison for factor equivalence, the maximum number of hits would be 528 $\times$ 7 = 3,696), since for each pair of countries, maximum equivalence would mean that each factor of the first country in the pair could be equivalent to just one factor in the other country of the pair. The equivalent pairs for all pairwise comparisons were then counted (out of the 25,872 Phi coefficients calculated in all, which is $7 \times 7 = 49$ indices in each of the 528 matrices), and resulted to the percentage of equivalence for each factor. The percentage of number of hits could then be regarded as a measure of overall factor congruence among countries. It could be argued e.g., that 90% of the number of hits would mean strong factor congruence, and 40% to 60% would correspond to a low percentage of hits or partial factor congruence.

The results were that only 881 coefficients (24%) were equal to or greater than .90 in the "hit matrix". Thus, although factor equivalence was high or moderate for the first 3 factors at the country-overall structures comparison, it was low for the comparisons of all seven factors among the 33 countries.

Common Items Across Countries

After inspection of the equivalent factors among countries, it was apparent that some items were common across most of the 33 countries e.g., "discussing the problems is an important part of a successful marriage," "talking about mutual interests is an important part of a successful marriage," "is abortion justified?" On the other hand, some items were found only within some clusters of countries e.g., "faithfulness is an important part of a successful marriage," "importance of religion." Thus, we have examples of items that are a part of the overall factor equivalence by constituting such equivalent factors across countries, but we also observe patterns of items that may reflect the existence of clusters of countries with potentially culture specific items. Table 2 presents two such examples of item-patterns across the 33 countries: a homogeneous subset of items loading on a single factor across all countries and a less homogeneous subset of items loading on a second factor. The homogeneity reduction is mainly due to a small subset of items that load on this second factor just for a number of countries, possibly defining a culture specific facet for this factor. A closer inspection of these items indicated that items like these might support factor equivalence for clusters of countries, also "defining" the cluster; for example, "spending time in church," "attending religious services," and "shared religious beliefs are an important part of a successful marriage," had high loadings on the factor for specific countries (Austria, Italy, Spain, Northern Ireland, Poland, Slovakia, and Greece), although this same factor for all countries included a number of other items as well. Such family values could be the country specific part and could possibly define clusters of countries. However, the above is simply a description of the patterns of items. In the next stage, we describe the statistical technique employed to determine clusters of countries.

Table 2. An Example with Two Factors across the 33 Countries: Indications of Equivalence within Groups of Countries

Countries	F	UK	WG	EG	Aus	It	Es	Pt	H	B	DK	Sw	Fn	Ic	NIr	Ir	Est	Lt	Lth	Pl	Cz	SlK	Hg	Rom	Bg	Cr	Gr	Rs	Mt	LXB	Slv	Ukr	Bls
1) Order of factor in each country's factor structure:	1	3	1	5	3	3	2	2	1	2	2	3	3	3	2	1	2	2	2	2	2	2	2	1	1	1	2	2	2	2	2	1	1
2) Order of factor in each country's factor structure:	3	2	2	4	4	1	1	3	3	1	1	4	4	1	1	2	1	1	3	1	4	1	3	2	3	3	3	3	6	6	1	3	3
abortion justified?	X	X	X	X	X	X	+	X	X	X	X	X	X	X	X	X	X	X	+	X	X	X	X	X	X	X	X	X	+	X	X	X	X
is divorce justified?	X	X	+	+	+	+	+	+	+	X	X	+	X	x	+	+	+	X	+	X	+	+	X	X	X	X	+	X	X	X	X	X	X
approval of abortion if woman not married	X	X	X	X	X	X	X	X	X	X	X	X	X	X	X	X	X	X	X	X	X	X	X	X	X	X	+	X	X	X	X	X	X
approval of abortion if not wanting more children	X	X	X	X	X	X	X	X	X	X	X	X	X	X	X	X	x	X	X	X	X	X	X	X	+	X	x	X	X	X	X	X	X
is adultery justified?	x	x	X	+					x	+	x						X	+	+	x					X		x		x		x	x	x
woman single parent without relationship	x	x								x	x							x											x				x
one must love/respect parents despite their faults																											+				x		
importance religion				x	X	X	X					x	x		X				X	X	X	X			X	X	X						
attend religious services					X	X	X					x	x		X				X	X	X	X		X	X	X	X						
church and family life					x	x	X							+					+	+	X	X		X	X	X							
shared religious beliefs					+	x	X												x	x	X	X			X	X	X						
spend time in church					X	+	X		+	+		+		X		X									+	X	+						
parental responsibilities																								x	x		x						
importance of family in life																								X	X								
spend time with friends																		+															
children suffer with working mother																															x		
women want home and children																															+		
being a housewife is just as fulfilling as working for pay																											x						
men are less able in handling emotions																		x															
both parents needed in a family											x																						
in future, more emphasis on family life																											+						
concerned with living conditions of immediate family																								X									
concerned with elderly																											+						
help elderly																											+						
importance friends aquaintances																											x						

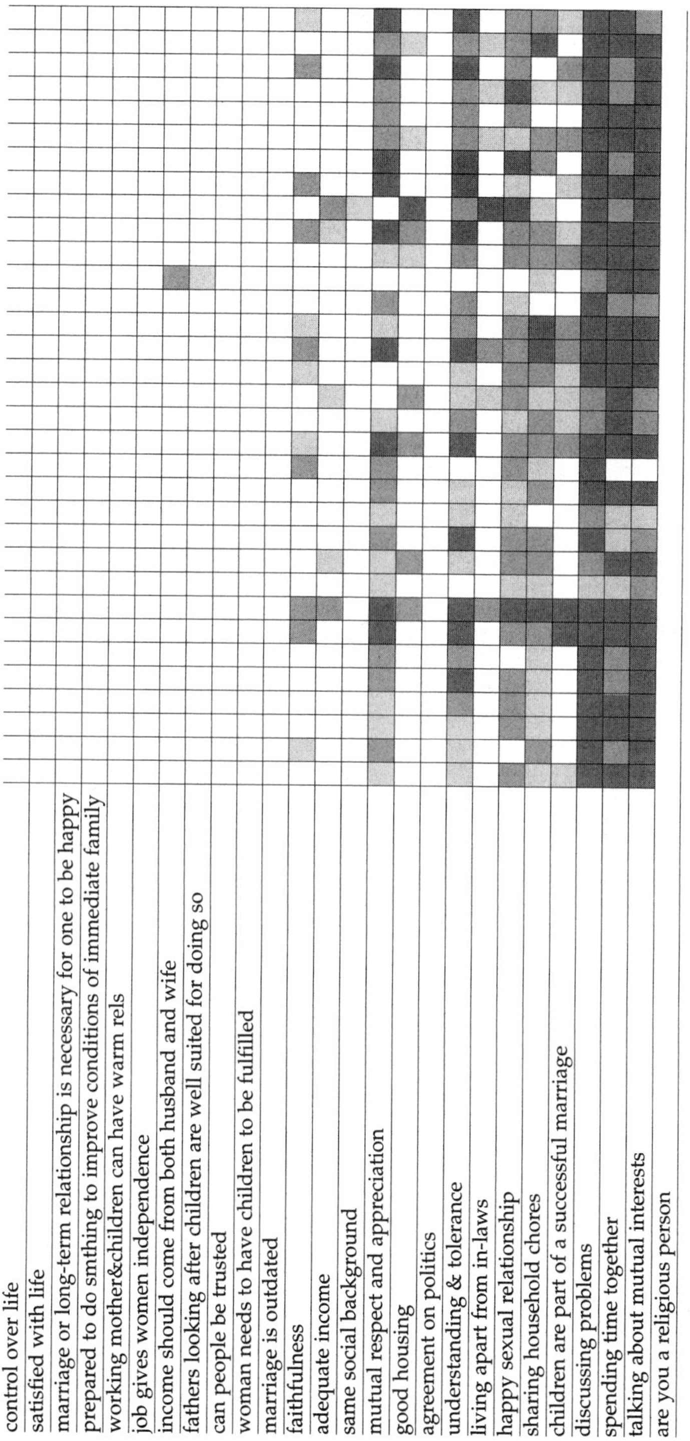

Row labels (left axis):

- control over life
- satisfied with life
- marriage or long-term relationship is necessary for one to be happy
- prepared to do smthing to improve conditions of immediate family
- working mother&children can have warm rels
- job gives women independence
- income should come from both husband and wife
- fathers looking after children are well suited for doing so
- can people be trusted
- woman needs to have children to be fulfilled
- marriage is outdated
- faithfulness
- adequate income
- same social background
- mutual respect and appreciation
- good housing
- agreement on politics
- understanding & tolerance
- living apart from in-laws
- happy sexual relationship
- sharing household chores
- children are part of a successful marriage
- discussing problems
- spending time together
- talking about mutual interests
- are you a religious person

Note: Shaded or marked blocks denote an item loading on the respective factor for each of the 33 countries, according to the following keys:

Key: Factor 1

- ▢ Loadings between |.40| and |.50|
- ▨ Loadings between |.51| and |.60|
- ▨ Loadings higher than |.60|

Key: Factor 2

- ☒ Loadings between |.40| and |.50|
- ⊞ Loadings between |.51| and |.60|
- ☒ Loadings higher than |.60|

Our decision to proceed in determining clusters of countries was also based on further consideration of the advantages and disadvantages of the methods employed up to this point. These factor equivalence testing methods assume universality, at least to some extent. The first method compared the pooled correlation matrix of the 33 countries with each country's correlation matrix. The second method compared the factor structures among all pairs of countries and also assumes that if universality exists, it should be present for *all* countries in the analysis, an unlikely event in most cases, although there are exceptions (Georgas, Weiss, van de Vijver, & Saklofske, 2003). Universality or equivalence of factor structures is sometimes achieved by excluding discrepant items or even countries from the analysis (Muthén, 1994; van de Vijver & Poortinga, 2002). Thus, the above methods provide some information on construct equivalence across countries, but do not provide information on items that might be culture specific for clusters of countries.

A CLUSTERS OF COUNTRIES METHODOLOGY

The basic hypothesis of this paradigm is that there may be some universal family value constructs across cultures, but there also may be constructs made up of items which contain both common items across countries and also items which are characteristic to groups or clusters of countries.

Instead of deleting discrepant items or countries (van de Vijver & Poortinga, 2002) in order to determine universal factors, a procedure was followed with the purpose of identifying common or universal items in each factor across clusters of countries and also items specific to the factor structure of each country cluster. The advantage of such a procedure is that it employs the information contained in the same data used for factor analysis under a different perspective. Thus, instead of relying only on the intercorrelations of the 51 items in the analysis and comparing the 33 factor structures, we should attempt a higher – aggregated – level solution, by also relying on the information of the similarities and dissimilarities among the same 51 items at the country level as measures of homogeneity among countries in their patterns of response.

Following the above rationale, a country level cluster analysis was employed with aggregates of the participants' responses, the 51 mean values for each of the 33 countries, followed by a within clusters of countries factor analysis of the raw score family values at the individual level. For the first stage of this country level analysis, the standardized transformations of the 51 item means were inserted into a 51 items by 33 countries matrix and hierarchically cluster analyzed in the attempt to form homogeneous country sets, that is, to determine clusters of countries with similar patterns of family values. Four clusters of countries were obtained:

1. Austria, Belgium, Czech Republic, France, West Germany, East Germany, Luxembourg, Slovenia, Spain, and the United Kingdom. This cluster is composed primarily of Western European Countries, seven members of the European Union, with two exceptions, the Czech Republic and Slovenia ($n = 12,861$).
2. Belarus, Bulgaria, Estonia, Hungary, Latvia, Lithuania, Romania, Russia, Slovakia, and Ukraine. This cluster is clearly composed of Eastern European and Socialist countries associated with the former Soviet Union ($n = 11,527$).
3. Croatia, Greece, Ireland, Northern Ireland, Italy, Poland, and Portugal. This cluster is also composed primarily of Western European countries, five members of the EU, with exceptions Croatia and Poland ($n = 8,358$).
4. Denmark, Finland, Iceland, the Netherlands, and Sweden. Except for the Netherlands, this cluster is composed of Scandinavian countries ($n = 5,560$).

Malta was not a part of any of the four clusters. For each cluster separately (all countries involved were collapsed for their family value scores within each cluster) correlation matrices were calculated for the raw score family values; Spearman Rho coefficients were computed for all matrices and all values and these matrices were then factor analyzed for each cluster of countries. For all items, their participation to some common factor across clusters, some partly common factor or specific factor, is presented in Table 3 along with the overall factor structure as a starting point.

A closer look to Table 3 reveals interesting differences for family values among the four clusters of countries. There are items that contribute to factor equivalence across all 33 countries (such as the "importance of religion for family life" or the answer to the question "is divorce justified"; there are also items that contribute less to the overall factor equivalence since they take part in the factor structures of two clusters of countries (such as "mutual respect and appreciation importance for a successful marriage" and the "adequate income importance for a successful marriage" value). Then, there are other items that take part in a single specific factor structure that holds for only one cluster of countries, but may very well form an overall factor in the overall factor solution. This is the case for the items forming the FU2-OVR factor present for the countries in the second cluster (Belarus . . . Ukraine) portraying the concerns about the immediate members of the family including the elderly. On the basis of such evidence, one might argue that some items form universal sets-factors for all 33 countries in their clusters, some other items form universal

Table 3. Items Participating in the Overall and Cluster Factor Structures

Items	Overall	Cluster 1	Cluster 2	Cluster 3	Cluster 4
importance of religion	A	A	A	A	A
spending time in church	A	A	A	A	A
attending religious services	A	A	A	A	A
church and family life	A	A	A	A	A
are you a religious person?	A	A	U2	E	A
shared religious beliefs (important in marriage)	B	B	B	B	B
sharing household chores (important in marriage)	B	B	B	B	B
discussing problems (important in marriage)	B	B	B	B	B
spending time together (important in marriage)	B	B	B	B	B
talking about mutual interests (important in marriage)	B	B	B	B	B
happy sexual relationship (important in marriage)	B	E	B	B	B
mutual respect and appreciation (important in marriage)	B		B	B	
understanding & tolerance (important in marriage)	B		B	B	
children are part of a successful marriage			B	B	U4a
faithfulness (important in marriage)			B	B	U4b
is abortion justified?	C	C	C	C	C
is divorce justified?	C	C	C	C	C
approval of abortion if woman not married	C	C	C	C	C
approval of abortion if not wanting more children	C	C	C	C	C
is adultery justified?		C	C		U4b
marriage or long-term relationship is necessary for one to be happy	D	D	D	D	D
both parents needed in a family	D	D	D	D	D
woman needs to have children to be fulfilled	D	D	D	D	D
woman single parent without relationship			D		D
parental responsibilities			D		
adequate income (important in marriage)	E	E		E	U4a
good housing (important in marriage)	E	E		E	U4a
can people be trusted?	E				

same social background (important in marriage)			U2	E
agreement on politics (important in marriage)			U2	E
concerned with elderly	F	FU2-OVR		
prepared to do smthg to improve conditions of immediate family	F	FU2-OVR		
help elderly	F	FU2-OVR		
concerned with living conditions of immediate family	F			U4a
working mother & children can have warm relations	G		G	G
income should come from both husband and wife	G		G	G
fathers looking after children are well suited for doing so	G		G	G
job gives women independence	G		G	G
children suffer with working mother		H	HU2U3	
women want home and children		H	HU2U3	
housewife is just as fulfilling as working for pay		H	HU2U3	
importance of family in life	U1			U4b
in future, more emphasis on family life	U1			U4b
marriage is outdated	U1			

Key: ("U" stands for factors unique in one cluster structure, OVR stands for Overall factor):

A	Religiosity and Family life
B	Companionship in marriage (similar factor: B)
C	Abortion, divorce & adultery
D	Children, family life, and marriage (similar factor: D)
E	Family security (similar factor: E)
G	Working wife and mother (similar factor: G)
FU2-OVR	Importance of living conditions of family and the elderly (cluster 2 & overall)
HU2U3	Woman's role as a housewife (clusters 2 & 3)
U1	Importance of marriage and family life (cluster 1 only)
U2	Same social, political and religious background (cluster 2 only)
U4a	Adequate income, good housing and children (cluster 4 only)
U4b	Importance or keeping the family together (cluster 4 only)

sets within some and not all clusters of countries, and finally, some items form factors for just one cluster of countries as an indication of specific properties on family values within this cluster only.

The next step was to compute the composite factor indices (as means of the standardized raw scores, expressed as T-scores) to explore for the actual support or rejection of these family value factors within each cluster of countries separately. The respective means (for the weighted data) were also calculated for the overall factors, and then analysis of variance results were computed for all possible comparisons (if the factor existed for at least two clusters of countries). Of course, the main objective of this analysis was not to explore for the possible differences among the four clusters of countries but to verify that these differences, although not extensive, due to their systematic nature and their consistent pattern are an indirect advocate of the general method employed. For example, it seems that cluster 3 countries (Greece, Ireland, Northern Ireland, Italy, Portugal, Croatia and Poland) stand more in favour of the religiosity and family life values (mean T-score of 53.97) and strongly against abortion and divorce issues (mean T-score of 47.38). Cluster 2 countries (Belarus, Bulgaria, Estonia, Hungary, Latvia, Lithuania, Romania, Russia, Slovakia, and Ukraine–all associated with the former Soviet Union) support religiosity and family life values (mean T-score of 51.45) and they also support values associated with children in family life and marriage (mean T-score of 51.78). On the other hand, cluster 4 countries (Denmark, Finland, Iceland, Sweden, The Netherlands) are strongly in favour of divorce and abortion necessity (mean T-score of 54.15) and strongly against family values that reflect the conventional family life of "children, family life and marriage" (mean T-score of 45.17). Cluster 1 countries (Austria, Belgium, France, West Germany, East Germany, Luxembourg, Spain, United Kingdom, the Czech Republic and Slovenia) consistently hold the third place next to the cluster 4 Scandinavian countries for all four factors of family values.

CONCLUSIONS

The purpose of this paper was to present a methodology that would enhance the interaction and communication between the indigenous psychology approach and the cross-cultural comparative approach. The indigenous psychology approach is extremely important in cross cultural psychology for a number of reasons. It emphasizes the study of psychological variables within the context of the culture. Because psychology has been dominated for over 100 years by western nations, many psychological concepts and findings reflect psychological issues and concepts that may not be as relevant or valid in other cultures. Cross-cultural psychology has played a key role in emphasizing this issue. Thus, another reason for the importance of indigenous psychology is to encourage psychologists from non-western cultures to creatively study psychological concepts that may be important to their cultures. However, a critical point in methodology is raised if it is claimed that the psychological variable or phenomenon is unique in that culture.

It begs the question of what is meant by *unique*. Does *unique* refer to psychological variables or phenomena, or does it refer to the manifestation of the psychological phenomenon within the context of the culture? If it means that certain psychological variables or concepts are by themselves unique in a culture, e.g., that people in one culture have genetically specific cognitive processes that differ from humans in other cultures, or that certain emotions in a culture are not found in other cultures, then we categorically disagree. However, if cognitive processes are intrinsically related to the context of a culture, e.g., people in hunting and gathering cultures do not have use for calculus, or that the type of expression of emotions is intrinsically related to context of the culture, then we agree. But even if this result is found through a bottom-up approach, the indigenous psychologist has to separate the analysis at psychological and cultural levels. That is, the indigenous psychologist should seek to determine at the psychological level if the psychological variable is also present in other cultures –the cross-cultural approach. Second, the indigenous psychologist should seek to determine the degree of similarity of the cultures–also a comparative approach. This strategy enables the indigenous psychologist to determine the degree to which the specific cultural contexts have shaped the morphology of the psychological concept or behavior in the cultures.

The paradigms discussed in this paper, "Man is like all other men, like some other men, like no other man," and "Cultures are like all other cultures, like some other cultures, like no other culture," can be helpful here. A methodology has been presented that can measure psychological phenomena at three different hierarchical levels: universal, clusters of cultures, and culture-specific. The use of the term *culture-specific* is important here because it refers to the pattern of manifestation of the psychological variable within the cultural context as unique, rather than maintaining that the psychological phenomenon by itself is unique.

From the above examples and the overall procedure, it could be argued that the findings provide a system for studying issues related to psychological variables in two ways: 1) on the basis of factor congruence, and 2) on the basis of the indigenous approach, which seems to salvage the information for country-cluster-defining items or functions that would otherwise be considered biased or simply not culture equivalent. Thus, those differences found for family values that were non-equivalent for all 33 countries, were also as important as the differences – or the similarities–described for the country equivalent values. Thus, this methodology might provide a means of determining clusters of countries with common patterns of psychological variables as well as patterns that may be culture-specific.

REFERENCES

Adair, J. G., & Diaz-Loving, R. (1999). Indigenous psychologies: The meaning of the concept and its assessment: Introduction. *Applied Psychology, 48*, 397–402.

Adair, J. G. (1999). Indigenisation of psychology: The concept and its practical implementation. *Applied Psychology, 48*, 403–418.

Berry, J. W. (1976). *Human ecology and cognitive style: Comparative studies in cultural and psychological adaptation.* New York: Sage/Halsted/Wiley.

Berry, J. W. (1999). On the unity of the field of culture and psychology. In J. Adamopoulos & Y. Kashima (Eds.), *Social psychology and cultural context* (pp. 7–15). Thousand Oaks, CA: Sage.

Berry, J. W. (2000). Cross-cultural psychology: A symbiosis of cultural and comparative approaches. *Asian Journal of Social Psychology, 3*, 197–205.

Berry, J. W., Dasen, P. (1974). Introduction. In J.W. Berry & P. Dasen (Eds.), *Culture and cognition* (pp. 1–20). London: Methuen.

Berry, J. W., Poortinga, Y. H., Segall, M. H., & Dasen, P. R. (1992). *Cross-cultural psychology: Research and applications.* Cambridge, UK: Cambridge University Press.

Cattell, R. B., Balcar, K. R., Horn, J. L., & Nesselroade, J. R. (1969). Factor matching procedures: an improvement of the s index; with tables. *Educational and Psychological Measurement, 29*, 781–792.

Diaz-Guerrero, R. (1993). Mexican Ethnopsychology. In U. Kim & J. W. Berry. (Eds.), *Indigenous psychologies: Theory, method & experience in cultural context* (pp. 44–55). Beverly Hills: Sage.

Diaz-Loving, R. (1999). The indigenisation of psychology: Birth of a new science or rekindling of an old one? *Applied Psychology, 48*, 433–449.

Diener, E. (1996). Subjective well-being in cross-cultural perspective. In H. Grad, A. Blanco, & J. Georgas (Eds.), *Key issues in cross-cultural psychology* (pp. 319–330). Lisse, the Netherlands: Swets & Zeitlinger.

Forde, D. (1934). *Habitat, economy and society.* London: Methuen.

Georgas, J. & Berry, J. W. (1995). An ecocultural taxonomy for cross-cultural psychology. *Cross-Cultural Research, 29*, 121–157.

Georgas, J. (1986) *Koinonike psychologia.* [Social Psychology]. Vol. 1 & 2. Athens: Ellinika Grammata.

Georgas, J. (1993). An ecological-social model for indigenous psychology: The example of Greece. In U. Kim & J. W. Berry. (Eds.), *Indigenous psychologies: Theory, method & experience in cultural context* (pp. 56–78). Beverly Hills: Sage.

Georgas, J. (1999). Family as a context variable in cross-cultural psychology. In J. Adamopoulos & Y. Kashima (Eds.), *Social psychology and cultural context* (pp. 163–175). Beverly Hills: Sage.

Georgas, J., Berry, J. W., van de Vijver, F., Kagitçibasi, Ç., & Poortinga, Y. H. (Eds.). (in press). *Psychological Variations in Family Structure and Function Across Cultures.* Cambridge: Cambridge University Press.

Georgas, J., van de Vijver, F. J. R., & Berry, J. W. (2004). The Ecocultural Framework, Ecosocial Indices, and Psychological Variables in Cross-Cultural Research. *Journal of Cross-Cultural Psychology, 35*(1), 74–96.

Georgas, J., Mylonas, K., Bafiti, T., Christakopoulou, S., Poortinga, Y. H., Kagitçibasi, Ç., Orung, S., Sunar, D., Kwak, K., Ataca, B., Berry, J. W., Charalambous, N., Goodwin, R., Wang, W.-Z., Angleitner, A., Stepanikova, I., Pick, S., Givaudan, M., Zhuravliova-Gionis, I., Konantambigi, R., Gelfand, M. J., Velislava, M., McBride-Chang, M., & Kodiç, Y. (2001). Functional Relationships in the nuclear and extended family: A 16 culture study. *International Journal of Psychology, 36*, 289–300.

Georgas, J., Mylonas, K., Gari, E., and Panagiotopoulou, P. (2004). European cultures, family, and values. In L. Halman & W. Arts (Eds.). *European values at the end of the millenium* (pp. 167–204). Leiden: Brill.

Georgas, J., Weiss, L.G., van de Vijver, F.J.R., & Saklofske, D.H. (Eds.) (2003). *Culture and Children's Intelligence: Cross-Cultural Analysis of the WISC-III.* CA: Academic Press.

Graziano, A.M., & Raulin, M.L. (1989). *Research Methods: A Process of Inquiry.* New York: Harper and Row Publishers, Inc.

Guilford, J.P. (1956). *Psychometric Methods.* New York: McGraw-Hill.

Halman, L. (2001). *The European values study: A third wave.* Tilburg, The Netherlands: EVS WORC Tilburg University.

Hofstede, G. (1980). *Culture's consequences.* Beverly Hills, CA: Sage.

Inglehart, R. (1997). *Modernization and postmodernization: Changing values and political styles in advanced industrial society.* Princeton, NJ: Princeton University Press.

Kim & Berry (1993): Indigenous, cultural, and cross-cultural psychologies. (2000). *Asian Journal of Social Psychology [Special issue], 3,* (3)

Kim, U., & Berry, J. W. (Eds.) (1993). *Indigenous psychologies: Theory, method & experience in cultural context.* Beverly Hills: Sage.

Kim, U., Park, Y. S., & Park, D. (1999). The Korean indigenous psychology approach: Theoretical considerations and empirical applications. *Applied Psychology, 48,* 451–464.

Kline, P. (1993). *The Handbook of Psychological Testing.* London: Routledge.

Kluckhohn, C., & Murray, H. A. (1950). Personality formation: the determinants. In C. Kluckhohn & H. A. Murray (Eds.), *Personality in nature, society and culture.* New York: Alfred A. Knopf.

Kroeber, A.L. (1939). *Cultural and natural areas of North America.* Berkeley: University of California Press.

Leung, K., & Bond, M. H. (1989). On the empirical identification of dimensions for cross-cultural comparison. *Journal of Cross-Cultural Psychology, 20,* 133–151.

Muthén, B.O. (1994). Multilevel covariance structure analysis. *Sociological Methods & Research, 22,* 376–398.

Poortinga, Y. H. (1989). Equivalence of cross-cultural data: An overview of basic issues. *International Journal of Psychology, 24,* 737–756.

Poortinga, Y.H. (1999). Do differences in behavior imply a need for different psychologies? *Applied Psychology, 48,* 419–432.

Schwartz, S. H. (1994). Beyond individualism/collectivism: New cultural dimensions of values. In U. Kim, H. C. Triandis, C. Kagitcibasi, S. C. Choi, & G. Yoon (Eds.), *Individualism and Collectivism* (pp. 85–119). Thousand Oaks, CA: Sage.

Shweder, R. A. (1990). Cultural psychology: What is it? In J.W. Stigler, R.A. Shweder, & G. Herdt (Eds.), *Cultural psychology: Essays on comparative human development* (pp. 1–4). Cambridge: Cambridge University Press.

Sinha D. (1997). Indigenizing psychology. In J. W. Berry, Y. H. Poortinga, & J. Pandey (Eds.). *Handbook of cross-cultural psychology.* Vol. 1: Theory and method (pp. 129–169). Boston: Allyn & Bacon.

Smith, P. B., Dugan, S., & Trompenaars, F. (1996). National culture and values of organizational employees. *Journal of Cross-Cultural Psychology, 27,* 231–264.

Tabachnick, B.G., & Fidell, L.S. (2001). *Using Multivariate Statistics.* 4th edition. USA: Allyn and Bacon.

Thurstone, L.L. (1947). *Multiple Factor Analysis: A development and expansion of The Vectors of Mind.* The University of Chicago Press: Chicago, Illinois.

Van de Vijver, F. & Leung, K. (1997). *Methods and data analysis for cross-cultural research.* Thousand Oaks, CA: Sage.

Van de Vijver, F. J. R., & Poortinga, Y. H. (2002). Structural equivalence in multilevel research. *Journal of Cross-Cultural Psychology, 33*(2), 141–156.

Part III

Cognitive Processes

Chapter **10**

The Mutual Relevance of Indigenous Psychology and Morality

Lutz H. Eckensberger

The relation of morality to indigenous psychology (IP) is examined from four different yet complementary viewpoints. Basically, a western meta-perspective is taken. First, the topic of morality is dealt with on a content level: If social scientists (as a first approximation) conceive of IP as a psychology that aims at understanding, explaining, and predicting people's behavior within specific cultures, then cultural rule systems, which are normative frameworks for individual behavior, can be understood as the core and the main *differentia specifica* of such a psychology. Morality is one of these rule systems, both in the tradition of cultural relativism and cultural pluralism. The crucial question of whether or not morality is culture specific (indigenous) or universal is discussed.

Second, the role of morality in the emergence of IPs is treated at the science of science level. Certainly this is not the place to add to the discussion about what the concept of IP means and how this conception differs from cross-cultural psychology (CCP) as well as cultural psychology (CP), which has become salient during the last decade. Yet, if one deals with the topic of IP, one has to define one's own position, and a moral perspective will be used to develop such a position.

Third, a slightly strange argument is developed based on the fact that particularly from an IP perspective, research on culture does not just serve an analytical function (answering the question "What is culture?"), but treats culture as a characteristic of a group. It is postulated that this conceptualization of cultures as more or less homogeneous entities has moral implications.

Finally, basic methodical implications are discussed, though they are also addressed in the previous sections. It is postulated that the general research strategy proposed in CCP must also be complemented by heeding moral arguments.

MORAL JUDGMENTS: UNIVERSAL OR CONTEXT BOUND NORMATIVE ORIENTATIONS OF HUMANS?

In this domain, Kohlberg's theory of moral development undoubtedly has had the most important and salient impact on cross-cultural research. Therefore, the following arguments are primarily based on this research[1].

In the Western tradition, moral rules concern what is considered intrinsically good or bad. Moral principles refer to human rights in general and to individual rights and obligations in particular, and they primarily concern standards of justice, general welfare, and the avoidance of harm to others. Morals develop along with the individual's increasing insight into social necessities and are therefore considered rational and objective. Positive examples are personal honesty, responsibility, and readiness to act when someone is in need of help. Examples of the absence of moral regulation are theft, murder, or dishonest behavior.

Kohlberg deserves admiration simply for claiming during the period of relativistic orientation in the fifties (Kohlberg, 1958) that morality (as the epitome of cultural relativism) is a universal phenomenon and, additionally, that it develops in a cross-culturally invariant sequence, always progressing in a non-reversible order (Kohlberg, e.g. 1976, 1986). At the empirical level a considerable amount of data supports Kohlberg's claims: Universal developmental trends exist when the material was scored by means of the latest manual (Colby et al., 1987). From a quantitative point of view, stages 2 to 5 appear to exist trans-culturally, and the trans-cultural invariance of the stages is supported within the limits of the reliability of the manual (for critical details see Eckensberger, 1986), although stage 5 is rarely found. It is important that these general trends in stage development did not reveal much of a Western bias–higher stages were also found in non-western cultures (like in Taiwan and India), though higher stages are rare even in the West (for more detailed information on stage consistency theory, A-/B-substages, developmental antecedents, etc. see Eckensberger & Zimba, 1997; Edwards, 1986; Snarey, 1985; Vine, 1986).

But from a qualitative, indigenous point of view, serious doubts still exist about the cross-cultural validity of the theory. Some critics call for modifications of Kohlberg's scheme only, others for more substantial changes in it is considered incomplete at best, or misleading and wrong at worst.

---

[1] Since Kohlberg refined his theory continuously, it is difficult to do him justice. See Eckensberger and Zimba (1997) for a discussion of the main changes in his theory.

Evidently morality in non-western cultures is duty based rather than rights based, although this contrast was probably overemphasized by American individualism rather than by western ethics in general. After all, Kant's deontic Ethic, on which much of the modern western ethics is based (Kant, 1968/1788), was also duty rather than rights based. However, this orientation towards duties is evident, for instance, in the Japanese (Confucian) principle of *giri-ninjo* (loyalty-human affection), the Indian (Hindu) ethic of duty (Miller, 1994; Shweder et al., 1987), and the Confucian principle of filial piety, which according to Hwang (1998) is a mandatory unconditional positive duty.

From a cross-cultural perspective, the status of stage 3 and 4 and stage transitions to stage 4 are opaque, because these two stages represent quite different understandings of the social world. Ma (1988) and Edwards (1986) questioned the strict definition of Kohlberg's stage 4 in terms of laws and institutions. Based on her investigations of face-to-face societies, Edwards concluded that the social perspective of an informal understanding of roles should be sufficient for scoring stage 4. On the other hand, much collective thinking based on various ideals of harmony somehow seems to resemble stage 3 thinking. But, it is quite unclear whether this relates to the stage notion or to basic moral principles. Setiono (1994), for instance, claims that the Javanese concepts of *hormat* (respect for older people) and *rukun* (harmonious social relations), resemble Kohlberg's stage 3, and thus that Javanese people showed a local adaptation, in that they had already reached an optimal moral development at stage 3. But Setiono (1994) simultaneously calls these concepts moral principles. Snarey (1983) mentions the principles of collective happiness in the Kibbutz. Lei and Cheng (1984) refer to different types of "collective conflict-solving strategies", not mentioned by Kohlberg, in some of their Taiwanese interviews, which were thus difficult to analyze. Tietjen and Walker (1984) faced similar problems in Papua New Guinea.

Ma (1998) reconstructed indigenous Chinese stages of moral thinking by first assuming what he calls "a general or master structure" and then constructing Western and Chinese sub-structures, the latter based on the norm of filial piety and social altruism, social order, and the norm of propriety. However, indigenous stages were only proposed for stage 4 and higher. Stages 1 to 3 were assumed to be identical to those in the West.

These examples also suggest that in some non-western cultures *equity* is more important than *equality*. Respect is distributed unequally. This is true for respecting older persons (*hormat*) and for the ideal of harmonious relations (*rukun*) in Java, and filial piety in Confucian cultures. Similarly, Ma (1988) pointed to the Chinese (Confucian) principle of *ren* (love, benevolence, human-heartedness, man-to-manness, sympathy, perfect virtue). In India justice is generally understood as what one deserves. But deservedness differs along various aspects: Kinship (eldest son deserves most), *Varna*

(Caste–Brahmins deserve most), gender (men deserve more). Equality only exists when all other factors have been considered (Krishnan, 1997).

The relationship of some of these principles to western ethics (the justice ethic and the ethic of responsibility and care) remains unclear in detail. Hwang (1998) elaborated that many of the Chinese concepts–which he called "Confucian ethics for ordinary people" (p. 216) like *ren*, *yi* and *li* resemble Western concepts (benevolence, respect for others, and acting according rules), although there are differences in detail. "*Yi*, for instance, is often translated as *justice*, but it is usually linked to other Chinese characters which modify its meaning" (Hwang, 1998, p. 217). The Chinese principle of *ren*, the Javanese principles of *hormat* and *rukun*, the principles of collective happiness, filial piety, collective utility, communal interconnectedness, and harmony all seem to represent principles close to Gilligan's (1982) concepts of care and responsibility, which as a whole represent moral matters encompassing the voice of the "community" (*Gemeinschaft*; Snarey & Keljo, 1991). Kohlberg himself tried to integrate both of these perspectives (justice and care) when defining the "co-ordination between justice and benevolence" as an important feature of the structure of stage 6 in one of his last papers (Kohlberg, Boyd & LeVine, 1986).

In particular, Miller's work indicated that Gilligan's concept of caring (and therefore also Kohlberg's) varies cross-culturally. She claimed that caring in Gilligan's sense is based on Western cultural views of the self and thus is culturally bound. Americans (and perhaps others from modern Western cultures) conceptualize caring as based on perceived intrinsic duties. Miller (1994) postulated an "individually oriented" interpersonal moral code in the U.S. in contrast to a "duty based" moral code in India, which gives less weight to individual discretion and choice in interpersonal responsibilities. It is also important, as Hwang (1998) clarified, that filial piety, because it is considered mandatory, leads to a specific Confucian dilemma". Following filial piety is deemed more important than other basic general principles like "do not steal".

This tension between the relation of the self to the immediate social world and the social world of humans at large is also evident in different conceptualizations of *weness* (Choi & Kim, Chapter 15). In Indonesian *Kita* and *Kami* refer to we-ness on different levels of social reality (Hassan, 2002). The *Kami*-mode refers to the level of interpersonal relations and groups based on empathy and reciprocal respect–which also implies discrimination and exclusion of others. The *Kita*-mode, however, refers to a transpersonal level of moral thinking (Eckensberger, Döring, & Breit, 2001), which implies commonality with others oriented towards basic human virtues and principles, which are true for all of humankind and not only for a particular culture.

Complementing these types of social reality, a private and a public self can be distinguished in many non-western cultures. In Hinduism, the individual role is *samanya dharma*, the societal role *varnaashram dharma*. In Hong Kong a *small I* and a *big I* are distinguished (Ma, 1998). In Japan *honne* means one's natural, real, or inner wishes, and *tatemai* is understood as the standards by which one is bound outwardly (Sugiyama-Lebra, 1976).

From here it is a small step to the notion that the relation between agency and rule systems (particularly to morality) is crucial. In the west, morality is clearly understood as being highly relevant to the self, ego, or agency (see for instance the element *upholding character* in Kohlberg's scoring system). From a cross-cultural perspective, this relationship is even more pronounced. In some cultures self-development is itself normative: In Hinduism and Buddhism self-cultivation culminates in liberating oneself from the self (Hinduism: Universal self–*Atman*, in Buddhism–*Nirvana*). Beyond this, there is the duty of self-realization through education in India (Clemens, 2004).

Apart from the fact that the distinction between personal concerns, convention, and morality as rule systems, proposed by Turiel and Nucci and their colleagues, was also found in other cultures (cf. Eckensberger & Zimba, 1997), two aspects of this approach are becoming increasingly important:

First, it is evident, particularly in cross-cultural research, that it is not the prototypical event/situation as such that defines whether or not a specific behavior/action falls into one of these rule systems, but rather the interpretation of such an event in the context of a whole indigenous cosmology. An example from Zimba (1994) may clarify this point.

The Chewa and Tumbuka of Zambia distinguish sexually hot individuals (teenagers and adults of child-bearing age) from sexually cold ones (infants, seriously sick persons, neophytes in the rites of passage, and adults who have ended their sexual involvement). They also believe that engaging in *chigololo*, that is, premarital sex by hot individuals, causes illness (the outbreak of *vumba*–a type of influenza) amongst the cold moral patients. *Chigololo* pollutes sexually hot individuals and makes them transmit the pollution to sexually cold individuals through fire, touch, salt, and air. The harm that cold individuals may suffer due to the sexual misconduct of hot individuals is real harm for the Chewa and the Tumbuka. Consequently, they interpret premarital sex as a moral issue, as opposed to American university students who understand such activity as either a personal issue or as a convention.

The causal chain of harm that the Chewa and the Tumbuka perceive is not shared at a universal level. Yet, it demonstrates that protecting moral patients from harm, regardless of how this is conceived of in a specific context, can take different forms, conceptualizations, and characteristics. Actions that do not protect moral patients from harm are morally wrong in principle, whether local or universal, whether allowed or forbidden. Harming is harming and in an African context.

Second, the most important difference in moral thinking and behavior, based on the domain specificity of rule systems, is probably due to what Vasudev (1984) highlighted in the case of India. In most Non-western cultures, religion and morality (philosophy) are not separated into philosophy or science as they have been in the West since after the Renaissance and the Enlightenment. This does not mean, however, that "ordinary people" in the West make this distinction, as can be seen in the emergence of fundamentalist Christian moral arguments during the 2004 election campaigns in the US.

In fact, most of the concepts that define the different principles of respect are rooted in religious belief systems rather than in morality, some in Islam, others in Hinduism, or Confucianism. But these roots also lead to entirely different prescriptive principles. Vasudev explained, for instance, why the Indian principle of respect for all life exists, leading to the principle of nonviolence (*ahimsa*) in Hinduism. Huebner and Garrod (1991) pointed out that in some Hindu and Buddhist cultures morality is embedded in conceptions about the nature of human existence itself. The law of karma (i.e., the adding up of good [*dharma*] and bad [*adharma*] actions, which may have been committed in earlier lives) is especially regarded as crucial because it leads to types of moral reasoning totally different from the ones defined in Kohlberg's stage theory and manual.

Ma (1998) also postulated a seventh stage, which is partially defined by "sainted altruism" rooted in Buddhism. Kohlberg (1973) wrote some "notes towards a seventh stage" (p. 201) as well, indicating clearly that this stage would deal with the question of "why be moral?" And he added, "The answer to the question 'Why be moral?' at this level entails the question 'Why live?' (and the parallel question, 'How to face death?'), so that ultimate moral maturity requires a mature solution to the question of the meaning of life. This, in turn, is hardly a moral question per se: It is an ontological or religious one" (p. 202). So, social scientists end up where they started: With a clear cut distinction of morality and religion in the West, which is simply nonexistent in many non-Western cultures.

Shweder and his colleagues have doubts concerning the domain-specificity of normative rule systems. Their Indian data suggest that the moral domain appears to be the only one available for making social judgments (Shweder et al., 1987). Shweder maintained that all socio-normative convictions are moral, but he assumed that there are different ways of talking about morality: One kind of morality concerns freedom, right, harm, and justice, which he called the *ethics of autonomy*. Another kind of morality concerns duty and the collective enterprise, which he called the *ethics of community*. A third concerns purity, sanctity, and the realization of one's spiritual nature, which he called the *ethics of divinity* (Shweder & Haidt, 1991). However, whether and in what respect this proposal is really different from the conceptions of different domains is debatable. In any case, Shweder had a much broader concept of morality.

The overall conclusion of this overview is not quite satisfactory, but it is productive: On the one hand there are quite a number of culture specific (*indigenous*) materials and ethical positions that clearly differ from the West. On the other hand, there is some communality at another, deeper level. There are similarities between ethical concepts in different cultures, pointing to some kind of common denominator or a certain universality of ethical principles, even if they are rooted in religion.

Emergence of Indigenous Psychologies from the Perspective of Morality

The emergence of IPs is a rather recent development in the history of psychology (Sinha, 1997). There are, however, several articles and chapters that deal with differences and similarities between the big three culture-based psychologies (CBPs), although unfortunately, there is no common terminology or perspective. I argue that a moral perspective can help in clarifying these concepts. Space limitations do not allow for a detailed elaboration. This will be done elsewhere.

The three approaches (CCP, CP and IP) can be distinguished with regard to many dimensions or aspects. Sometimes they are reconstructed on the basis of the practical (social-political) reasons that led to their development (Greenfield, 2000; Kim, 2000); sometimes they are distinguished by analytical dimensions, e.g. their aims, scope, and focus (Yang, 2000), by theoretical orientations (Shweder, 2000; Yang, 2000), or by methodical perspectives (Yang, 2000). The features used to define and distinguish the three psychological camps also vary to quite an extent in scope and number: just to indicate the variety - Yang (2000) used a total of 18 features, Shweder (2000) four for IP and six for CP.

If one takes a closer look at the arguments, then the three approaches are evidently not regarded as equidistant by most authors. In many cases CP and IP are considered much closer to one another than to CCP (Shweder, 2000, Yang, 2000, as well as implicitly Kim, 2000).

If one applies a Kuhnian (1970) perspective to the three culture-based approaches to psychology by looking at the underlying models of humans hidden in these approaches, then one can argue that CCP follows a paradigm different to that of CP and IP (Eckensberger, 1979, 2002): Mainstream CCP clearly stays within the natural science orientation of mainstream psychology, it follows the nomothetic science ideal (which either follows physics or biology). It complements mainstream research strategies methodically by aiming to test cultural influences on the development of behavior and examining the universality of psychological structures and functions. It is based on causality, prediction (usually by measurement), and objectivity (regarding subjects and culture as objects). Culture as content is "invisible but obvious" (Smedslund, 1984), however, because of the natural science program, it is not an explicit part of psychology. CP, on the other hand, conceives of humans as meaning creating subjects (*"homo interpretans"*, cf. Eckensberger, 1993), who not only anticipate events, but plan them intentionally and are in principle potentially aware of their activities as well as of themselves and others. Culture in the sense of symbolic meaning is assumed to be unique to humans, hence a psychology of humans cannot do without it. This paradigm or perspective is not simply another approach to CCP, rather it differs profoundly and qualitatively in many basic assumptions about humans.

In CP, cultural rules that help one to understand human actions replace or at least complement the natural laws used as a framework for explaining human behavior. This distinction is precisely what was implied when Shweder (2000) discussed the differences between humans and nature, and focused upon goals, values, and pictures as the main concern of CP.

Regarding IP from this perspective, it seems that it is difficult to distinguish from CP. Kim (1990, p. 195), for instance, regards IP as "psychological knowledge that is native, that is not transplanted from another region, and that is designed for its people." Enriquez (1982) defined IP as a system of psychological thought and practice that is rooted in a particular cultural tradition. Berry et al. (1993, p. 381) interpret IP as the psychology of a cultural group based on the day-to-day behavior of its members, for which local points of view provide the paradigms that guide the collection and interpretation of psychological information. Greenfield (2000) made an interesting point in delineating IP from CP, however, she maintained that IP goes beyond CP (which has concentrated increasingly on ethnotheories in recent years) by taking "informal folk theories of psychological functioning and formaliz[ing] them into psychological theories" (p. 225).

The viewpoint of moral development helps to elaborate this point, going even one step further by analyzing the type of folk theories IP builds upon. From this perspective, it turns out that IP emerged exactly in those cultures that do not distinguish between religion and ethics (in philosophy), and where rules of conduct are rooted either in Buddhism, Confucianism, Taoism, Hinduism, Islam, Shintoism, or tribal religious belief systems. That is, it originated in Non-western religions. This point is explicitly made by Ho, Si-qing Peng, Lai, and Chan (2001). In fact, if one looks at empirical research in various fields (need to achieve, school achievements, emotions), in most cases one of the enumerated religious systems is referred to. Developmental stages in India, for instance, are often summarized in terms of the stages distinguished in the Vedes (Saraswathi & Ganapathy, 2002; Vasudev, 1984). This also appears to be true for Latin America, where psychology is "inextricably embedded in the development of language, magic, religion, and philosophy" (Diaz-Guerrero, 1994, p. 717, cited by Sinha, 1997, p. 144). This also seems to be true for Africa. Nsamenang (1992), for instance, distinguishes three basic components of selfhood (spiritual, ancestral, and social), which include religion. Thus for many Non-Western psychologists, their own culture is visible and obvious because an explicit relationship between their religious beliefs and their cultures exists. So, from a psychological point of view, religion cannot simply be considered a system that competes with morality or even science, rather it represents one rule-system that people believe in and which therefore also governs their behavior to a considerable extent. In this respect, religion is an essential object of psychology as a cultural science, this is true for CP in general, and for IP in particular.

If one agrees with this analysis, then IP (by necessity) also follows a model of humans that is potentially self-reflective and that is the very same model as CP. This is so because the basis for (any kind of) religion is the self-reflectivity of humans. Humans not only reflect upon their existence, they also attach meaning to their life as well as to the world, and also comprehend the end of this existence: Humans know for sure that they will die, and they attach meaning to death. This is the cradle of religion (Eckensberger, 1993) and of culture (Morin, 1973).

Thus, my basic understanding is that the hidden assumptions made in the three CBPs are firstly, the distinction between a natural and cultural science orientation (CCP vs. CP and IP) and secondly, a distinction between secular cultural rules and cultural rules (CP and IP) that do not explicitly differentiate between secular and transcendental categories. This analysis illuminates the rather large similarities between CP and IP, and their shared differences from CCP.

Apart from moral and religious rules as *differentia specifica* of IP and CP, moral aspects are relevant to the interrelationship of the three culture-based psychologies in practical research. Berry (2000) argued fruitfully that the three perspectives are complementary. But, again from a Kuhnian perspective, this complementarity is not as easy to accomplish as one would wish. This is so because the two paradigms (CCP on the one hand, and CP and IP on the other) are not only different, but also basically incommensurable. They are defended, evaluated, or even devalued by the respective disciplinary matrices or scientific communities. Berry, for instance, accused cultural psychologists of just creating a new niche for some people trying to attain specific social positions at the IACCP conference in Yogyakarta (2002). If one agrees with the proposal that this incommensuralibity should actually lead to complementarity, then necessarily the various perspectives have to be mutually respected by the different communities (Eckensberger, 2002). This is not easy for CCP and CP because paradigms are defined by their methods (exemplars) to a large extent. Though methodical pluralism is increasingly propagated in meta-discussions (van de Vijver & Poortinga, 2002), when it comes to normative programs of "how to do CCP", a strictly quantitative research strategy, in which subjects and cultures are regarded as objects, following the basic strategy of classical physics (experimentation, quasi-experimentation, prediction, measurement, and control of variables, see van de Vijver & Leung, 1997), is preferred (by the same people who call for pluralism).

If this analysis is at least partially true, then the necessary mutual respect between the three CBPs is even more difficult to achieve in case of IP. This is so, because religions are rooted in existential dimensions. They are not based on knowledge, but on faith. In addition, although the goals of religion and cultural rules of conduct may be accepted as identical, their content (the mentalities in Shweder's sense) is quite different.

Theoretically, the program of how to develop tolerance for other religions (and thus also for different IPs) in order to attain mutual understanding appears to be clear: One follows Greenfield's (2000) proposal that there are "deep structures" in cultures that lead to a shared or universal CP. This means, one simply has to dig for the deep structures of religions, find the common ground, and then interpret the different manifestations of religion as metaphors for basically the same existential phenomena, thus coming to tolerate them as well. Fuad Hassan (2002), in his brilliant introductory keynote speech at the conference of the IACCP in Yokyakarta, took a similar position when he proposed that social scientists should move to the *Kita*-mode of we-ness that entails a sense of unity with others regarding basic human virtues and principles, thus enabling people to share the we-worlds of others with different religions.

Although I basically agree, there are three barriers that make realizing this plausible insight a really difficult task (Eckensberger, 1993). First, it is an extremely delicate matter for the individual person to understand or to develop the abstracted deep structure of religions because even most adults in the West do not reach the stage of principled reasoning (Eckensberger & Zimba, 1997). Second, and this is more intriguing, the content of religion can be interpreted at different levels of abstractness or directness–literally or metaphorically. At both levels different interpretations are possible. The *literal interpretation* directly implies religiously prescribed ways of behaving. Usually there are claims that the respective fundamentalist understanding represents the only truth. It seems quite plausible that tolerance towards other religions (which imply other truths) is rather unlikely. Tolerance means really accepting or respecting something or somebody. But can one accept two religions and two truths, while simultaneously claiming that there is only one?

Finally, the proposal itself could possibly lead to a serious dilemma. If religions are interpreted entirely as metaphors for the basic existential problems of humans, then their constructive quality by necessity will be discovered and consequently they could lose one of the primary functions for which they were once developed: the function of coping with death. When religion is regarded as a human construction, its basic function of reducing existential anxiety about death is no longer being fulfilled.

THE MORAL IMPLICATIONS OF TREATING CULTURES AS HOMOGENEOUS WHOLES

There is another angle from which morality constitutes an important dimension in the discussion of the emergence of IP, namely whether culture is seen as a theoretical concept that defines the unique feature of humans and therefore is common to all, or whether it is understood as a characteristic of a special group, and, if the latter is the case, whether it is seen as a dynamic "integrated constellation of common practices" or rather as a "fixed categorical property of individuals" (Rogoff & Angelillo, 2002). Usually this issue is handled in the context of methodical or methodological arguments, but it also has moral implications that are frequently not considered. A summary of the history and complexity of the concept of culture is not necessary here. However, regardless of the dimensions or logical status of the concept, it is evident that a specific culture is also formed by attribution processes, by constructions in the eye of the beholder, and this construction highlights differences more than similarities. This was stated rather vividly by Gutmann (1967) when he wrote:

> [in the same way as] we find out that we are air breathers, and 'air' only becomes an objectified datum, when we first fall into the water…cross-cultural experience…gets us out of our social skin, out of our accustomed psychosocial ecology. (p. 189)

This experience is based on subjectively interpreted superficial differences. Such cultural differences are more easily detected or experienced than similarities (the visible but non-obvious). Research on morality across cultures points to many underlying similarities of ethics/religions. The same seems to be true for the other rule systems that can be distinguished. But the argument here is that not only lay persons emphasize differences more than similarities (at least at first culture contact), we as psychologists have also more often focussed on differences than similarities, ever since the context of development has been considered important. This is particularly true for IP, almost by definition. Even when social scientists do not analyze individual cultures, the distinction between basic types of cultures, mostly individualistic and collectivistic cultures, dominates the whole field. This applies to all three camps of CBPs for different reasons. Whether we index cultures in quantitative approaches, or whether we assume shared meaning systems or practices–we demarcate cultures by doing so. In the process of globalization, of migration, and economic competition, the moral implications of treating other cultures as groups that are unique and therefore different, and consequently minimizing similarities, is not only dysfunctional but may even be dangerous. This is especially obvious in terror management theory (Greenberg et al, 1986), which is explicitly based on the existential fear of death (Becker, 1973) and the security gained by assuming or constructing shared cultural practices and meanings. There is ample empirical evidence that in the case of threats and danger, the social construction of sharing a culture and belonging to the same cultural group is not only strengthened, but goes hand in hand with a moral devaluation of other cultures, or more generally, of differing groups of people. The reaction to September 11, which led to a general devaluation of Muslims in some parts of the West, is a very recent example. Psychologists, working in the field of culture-based psychologies should therefore be particularly aware of these processes, as they bear a special responsibility for the implications of their cultural models. This is probably exactly what Fuad Hassan (2002) had in mind in the speech just mentioned.

There is a second aspect regarding the greater focus on differences. Most of the intercultural communication literature is based on the fundamental differences in the cultural standards of cultures, as represented in critical incidents (Brislin et al., 1986). Again, a moral dimension is crucial. Much of this literature seems to aim at a better understanding of a foreign culture through knowledge of its standards. But a second glance shows that many programs of intercultural communication are strategic in orientation rather than aimed at mutual understanding and respect. The goal is to gain a better understanding of another culture to do better business. This can be justified by moral reasons (improvement of living conditions in the foreign culture), but there is always the danger of exploitation that psychologists should be aware of and sensitive to.

However, to return to the central issue of whether different cultures really need different psychologies, or whether there is some common ground that will in the long run allow for one psychology for all humans: Many authors of CP and IP are not really decided on this issue, though in most cases their ultimate aim is to construct a psychology that applies to all humans but retains cultural uniqueness. Berry and Kim (1993) constructed a matrix (of topics and societies) that basically follows the same idea that Stern (1911) proposed in his early "differential psychology"–a matrix to analyze the relationship between general processes and individual cases (p. 17). Yang (2000) proposed a pyramid model. Shweder (2000) differentiated a (universal) mind and (unique) mentalities.

The general point, however, is that this tension is not just an academic issue; it has moral implications as well. Social scientists should focus on similarities more than they do. Even Brett (2000), who discussed several models of negotiation between cultures, started out by demarcating groups according to their particular cultures, yet concluded with the observation that "there is a distribution of traits within a culture. Two negotiators from cultures with distinct but overlapping distributions of cultural characteristics may find they have very similar cultural values and norms, despite the differences in their cultures" (p. 103). Sinha and Tripathi (1994) demonstrated impressively that Indian culture is characterized by its heterogeneity. They elaborated in detail the coexistence of quite different orientations within the Indian culture and even in Hinduism, in which "juxtapositions of contradictory elements are to be found where *dharma* (duty) and *moska* (salvation) coexist with pursuit of wealth (*artha*) and sexual satisfaction (*kama*) as constituents of cardinal duties" (p 127). Of course, cultures are dynamic and heterogeneous, but usually social scientists do not consider the moral implications of "forgetting about it".

THE MORALITY OF METHODS IN IP

This is probably a strange heading for those who are convinced that science is morally neutral and that methods in particular are neutral. But the opaque attitude of some researchers impels me once more to make at least a few comments on this issue.

There seems to be no clear cut consensus about the question of whether IP needs or leads to a specific method. Of course, it is agreed upon that (cultural) contents have to be retained. The issue, however, is whether IP needs or calls for different research strategies and methods of data gathering. Kim, for instance, seems to be ambivalent about this point. On the one hand he underlined the role of phenomenology (Kim, 2000), on the other hand he considered the concept of IP as methodically open (pers. communication). Others like Van Vlaenderen (1993, p. 93, as quoted by Sinha, 1997, p.142) called for "a new methodology, new research techniques, and new types of relationships between the researcher and research participants in the research effort." Yang (2000) also proposed a specific indigenous research strategy. From a CP point of view, the methods clearly have to deal with the analysis of subjective meaning, although other methods can be used additionally, depending on specific issues of concern. Again, only those dimensions that follow from a moral point of view are mentioned in short.

The most widely accepted research strategy once proposed by Berry (1969), which can be summarized as the emic, imposed *etic*, derived *etic* sequence, is in a sense imperialistic in that it starts with one (usually Western) culture. Under a CP perspective, one should, however, start with a joint (top down) discussion of the concepts one aims to study. This discourse is not only based on mutual respect among researchers and their cultural backgrounds, it also implies that one is confronted with cultural similarities and differences, which means that it can lead to a fruitful reflection of the concepts involved and the cultural prejudices one may have about the foreign as well as one's own culture. As a result of such a strategy, a consensual *etic* rather than a derived *etic* would result (Eckensberger, 1994), which also reflects the fact that the validation of theories is a social process. However, the problem of understanding (amongst researchers) remains, both because of the different languages (even if English is spoken, the connotations will certainly differ in many cases) and the different cultural backgrounds. This problem is discussed rather productively in analytical philosophy, where Quine and Davidson, for instance, touch on problems of translation. Interestingly, these problems are not formulated technically, but rather in moral terms, by proposing two preconditions (a) the use of empathy, and (b) the principle of charity, which means ascribing the maximum of truth to sentences uttered in a dialogue (or foreign language) (Quine, 1976).

At the level of data gathering, a theory based on an agency by necessity implies that the person tested is both a subject, whose own perspectives, interests, and hypotheses have to be respected, and an object of the study at the same time. So, the investigator necessarily has to adopt a bifocal attitude. As methods are oriented toward processes rather than outcomes, they are much more dialogical than methods usually are. Misra (2001, p. 16) takes a similar position by arguing "We need to move from a psychology of response to a psychology of construction. Construction (of meaning) through continuous dialog between the researcher and studied phenomenon takes place on the basis of indicators." These dialogical methods again imply a moral dimension, a performatory attitude on the side of the researcher (Habermas, 1981).

Respecting the investigated person should be a precondition of all empirical studies. Yet, it is interesting how seldom this is discussed with reference to concrete methods. Keller (1997), for instance, is one of the few developmentalists to reflect upon this problem with reference to the stranger situation in the tradition of Ainsworth, which is applied almost all over the globe. If it is true that babies experience stress in the stranger situation, then it is hard to justify placing them in a situation that could possibly change their attachment to their caretakers. This is even more problematic if this kind of experience (being alone, and then meeting a stranger) is rather unusual in a culture, such as in Japan, for instance (Miyake, Chen and Campos, 1985).

HUMAN ACTION AS A POSSIBLE UNIVERSAL FOR PSYCHOLOGY

In an early analysis (Eckensberger, 1979) the tension between the unique and the general, between the subject and culture, was used as criterion to evaluate existing psychological theories from a cross-cultural perspective.

Without repeating these early arguments, I discovered that all but one theory family allows for the possibility of defining the uniqueness of the single case (events, objects and persons) and developing a theory that contains the individual as well as the culture. This was the family of action theories based on the French tradition of Janet (Schwartz, 1951) as well as on German philosophy (from Dilthey, 1894 to Habermas, 1981) and Russian activity theory (see Eckensberger, 1995). They make use of the perspective of *homo interpretans*, a meaning-creating and potentially self-reflective agency. Action theory is not just a foundation for creating a culture-based psychology (Boesch, 1991; Eckensberger, 1996), action theories are also particularly attractive in the present context in which morality is the object of theorizing and research because the concept of morality analytically presupposes a decision made by a potentially self-reflective agency capable of deciding. Without the assumption of an agency who can be held responsible for an action and its outcome, a definition of morality is hardly possible–which is why non-human nature is considered morally neutral.

It is assumed that humans are not only influenced by culture, but also create culture, and that they use culture as the lens or medium to understand the world and as a means of coping with it instrumentally and socially. In addition a common deep structure is assumed to be fundamental to this entire dialectical process linking the agency and culture. The model assumes that every human being as an agency is capable of reflective processes and that actions can be differentiated analytically at three levels. At the first level (primary actions), all humans develop goals (intentionality), choose means, and evaluate the processes resulting from interacting with the material environment (instrumental actions) or with others (communicative actions), thereby creating their understanding of the world during ontogeny (for a detailed explication see Eckensberger, 1990, 1995, 2002). In the person, schemata about the world are constructed, and in the environment material and social consequences of actions occur that form the enabling and constraining conditions of further actions. These schemata can be shaped by exclusively child-oriented activities in the West or within co-occurring care structures in some non-western cultures (Keller & Eckensberger, 1998), yet both can be formulated within the same framework. Likewise, action controls (action oriented or secondary actions) with corresponding control beliefs and normative frameworks are developed that constitute social standards and control beliefs in the person, and conventions and laws within the culture, and which define constraints and support for further actions. They can be based on the ideal of harmony in India (Sinha, 1996), for instance, or on dominating the world in the West, yet, they can both be analyzed in terms of the same function within an action. Emotions as important processes in action regulations, like shame and guilt, can also vary in different cultures–shame, for instance, may be experienced in Japan in situations that usually elicit anger and aggressive actions in the West (Kornadt, 2002), yet the basic function of emotions as regulators of actions remains the same. They are just embedded in different meaning systems, and this is what action theory is about. Finally, the agency is interpreted on the basis of reflective processes (third order actions), though agencies may differ in the sense of being interdependent or independent (Markus and Kitayama, 1991), yet they still remain agencies. Most important, at this level the operation of contemplating existence by the agency him- or herself is the very basis for religiosity in the subject and religion in the culture. So without an agency contemplating the ultimate, it is hard to define what religion is all about.

We specifically applied this model to morality and its development in context. The results are manifold and promising. Our action theory reconstruction of moral development used action elements as a criterion of structure (goal taking instead of role taking) and resulted in stages that entail increases in the kind and number of action elements considered in a moral decision. This analysis ended up with more stages than Kohlberg proposed (Eckensberger & Reinshagen, 1980), and in four instead of three levels of moral judgment (Eckensberger, Döring, & Breit, 2001). These are generated in two social interpretation spheres, the *interpersonal sphere*, defined by concrete interactions with concrete persons, and the *transpersonal social sphere*, determined by functions and roles. According to our data and theoretical analysis, development proceeds from heteronomy to autonomy within both levels, which implies that this model is particularly suitable for defining the adequacy of moral structures in face to face societies (Edwards' problem), which constitute an interpersonal space. This conceptualization solves the problem of the transition from stage 3 to stage 4 in Kohlberg's scheme elegantly, and it fits concepts like the Indonesian concepts *Kami* and *Kita* perfectly. We have also started research on the domain specificity of rules, and proposed ways of distinguishing and interrelating different domains of rule systems (conventions, law, religion) by interpreting them as different forms of actions and co-actions (Eckensberger, Kapadia, Wagels, 2000). So, this approach seems to allow one to distinguish the general (action scheme) and the unique manifestation of meaning systems and interpretations.

CONCLUSIONS

The analysis of the concept of IP and its relationship to CCP and CP from a Kuhnian viewpoint by necessity results in the construction of cultures of psychology, which may not represent what psychologists actually do or how they think about their discipline in everyday research or counseling.

Yet, it highlights the deep structure of these scientific cultures. One of the main issues raised by the foregoing analysis is the question of the relationship between religious systems and daily life in different cultures. In an earlier study, for example, Murray Thomas (1988), not only analyzed different religions in the Orient (Hinduism, Buddhism, Confucianism, Shinto, and Islam) at a theoretical level (as they are represented in the scripts), but also popular beliefs about humans held by subjects from these different religions. This work (which he does not consider a "complete journey into the realm of Oriental theories" but "only as few steps along the way", p. 338) demonstrates that (a) these religions in fact have an enormous impact on daily life (although this impact is domain specific); that (b) of course people vary in their amount of knowledge about their religion; that (c) modernization clearly has an influence (not Christianity but Western life style)–a topic also highlighted in a recent study in India with respect to the tension between Sanscritizing psychology and the evolving new middle class structures (Säävälä, 2001); and that (d) in many societies several religions compete with one another, but do not merge.

However, the main problem of how to deal with the tension between CCP (and mainstream psychology) and various CPs will remain. What the future of IP will bring is of particular interest. It is an open question whether IP will align itself with the one rather than the other approach. From my point of view, however, IP runs the risk of losing its particular cultural content, if it turns to CCP. I also expect that the more the non-Western cultures change to a Western life style, the more closely the concept of IP will resemble CP. On the other hand, a revival of religiously based life styles and institutions is occurring in the West as well, as is particularly evident in the U.S.

REFERENCES

Becker, E. (1973). *The denial of death*. New York: Free Press.

Berry, J. W. (1969). On cross-cultural comparability. *International Journal of Psychology, 4*, 119–128.

Berry, J. W. (2000). Cross-cultural psychology: A symbiosis of cultural and comparative approaches. *Asian Journal of Social Psychology, 3*, 197–205.

Berry, J. W. & Kim, U. (1993). The way ahead: From indigenous psychologies to a universal psychology. In U. Kim & J. W. Berry (Eds.), *Indigenous psychologies: Research and experience in cultural context* (pp. 277–280). Newbury Park, CA: Sage.

Boesch, E. E. (1991). *Symbolic action theory and cultural psychology*. Berlin: Springer

Brett, J. M. (2000). Culture and negotiation. *International Journal of Psychology, 35* (2), 97–104.

Brislin, R. W. & Cushner, K. & Cherrie, C. & Yong, M. (1986). *Intercultural interactions: A practical guide*. Beverly Hills: Sage.

Clemens, Iris. (2004). Bildung – Semantik – Kultur: Subjektive Theorien über *education* im indischen Kontext. Dissertation, Frankfurt am Main.

Colby, A. & Kohlberg, L. (1987). *The measurement of moral judgment. Vol. 2: Standard issue scoring manual*. Cambridge: Cambridge University Press.

Diaz-Guerrero, R. (1994). Origin and development of psychology in Latin America. *International Journal of Psychology, 29,* 717–727.

Dilthey, W. (1894/1957). *Ideen über eine beschreibende und zergliedernde Psychologie. Sitzungsberichte der Berliner Akademie der Wissenschaften* (1894). In Gesammelte Schriften, Bd. V., S.139–240. Stuttgart.

Eckensberger, L. H. (1979). A metamethodological evaluation of psychological theories from a cross-cultural perspective. In L. H. Eckensberger, W. J. Lonner & Y. H. Poortinga (Eds.), *Cross-cultural contributions to psychology* (pp. 255–275). Amsterdam: Swets and Zeitlinger.

Eckensberger, L. H. (1986). Handlung, Konflikt und Reflexion: Zur Dialektik von Struktur und Inhalt im moralischen Urteil. In W. Edelstein & G. Nunner-Winkler (Eds.), *Zur Bestimmung der Moral. Philosophische und sozialwissenschaftliche Beiträge zur Moralforschung* (S. 409–442). Frankfurt: Suhrkamp.

Eckensberger, L. H. (1990). On the necessity of the culture concept in psychology: A view from cross-cultural psychology. In F. J. R. van de Vijver & G. J. M. Hutschemaekers (Eds.), *The investigation of culture. Current issues in cultural psychology* (pp. 153–183). Tilburg: Tilburg University Press.

Eckensberger, L. H. (1993). Zur Beziehung zwischen den Kategorien des Glaubens und der Religion in der Psychologie In T.V. Gramkrelidze (Ed.), *Brücken. Beiträge zum Dialog der Wissenschaften aus den Partneruniversitäten Praha, Saarbrücken, Sofia, Tbilissi und Warszawa* (pp. 49–104). Tbilissi, Universitätsdruck.

Eckensberger. L.H. (1994). On the social psychology of cross-cultural research. In A.-M-Bouvey, F.J.R. van de Vijver, P. Boski & P. Schmitz (Eds.), *Journeys into cross-cultural psychology* (pp. 31–40). Lisse: Zwets & Zeitlinger.

Eckensberger, L. H. (1995). Activity or action: Two different roads towards an integration of culture into psychology? *Psychology & Culture, 1,* 67–80.

Eckensberger, L. H. (1996). Agency, action and culture: Three basic concepts for psychology in general and cross-cultural psychology in specific. In J. Pandey, D. Sinha & P. S. Bhawak (Eds.), *Asian contribution to cross-cultural psychology* (pp. 72–102). New Delhi: Sage.

Eckensberger, L. H. (2002). Paradigms revisited: From incommensurability to respected complementarity. In H. Keller, Y. Poortinga & A. Schölmerich (Eds.), *Biology, culture, and development: Integrating diverse perspectives* (pp. 341–383). Cambridge: Cambridge University Press.

Eckensberger, L. H., Döring, T. & Breit. H. (2001). Moral dimensions in risk evaluation. Research in social problems and public policy. In G. Boehm, J.Nerb, T. L. McDaniels, & H. Spada (Eds.), *Special issue on environmental risks: Perception, evaluation and management* (pp. 137–163.) (Vol. 9). Oxford, UK: Elsevier Science.

Eckensberger, L. H., Kapadia, Sh., & Wagels, K. (2000). *Social Cognitive Domains of Thinking in Marriage Partner Selection*: The Indian Context. Paper of the 16th ISSBD Biennal Meeting in Beijing.

Eckensberger, L. H., & Reinshagen, H. (1980). Kohlbergs Stufentheorie der Entwicklung des Moralischen Urteils: Ein Versuch ihrer Reinterpretation im Bezugsrahmen handlungs-theoretischer Konzepte. In L. H. Eckensberger, & R. K. Silbereisen (Eds.), *Entwicklung sozialer Kognitionen: Modelle, Theorien, Methoden, Anwendung* (S. 65–131). Stuttgart. Germany: Klett-Cotta.

Eckensberger, L. H., & Zimba, R. F. (1997). The development of moral judgment. In P. Dasen, & T. S. Saraswathi (Eds.), *Handbook of cross-cultural psychology (2nd ed.): Vol. 2. Developmental Psychology* (pp. 299–338). Boston: Allyn & Bacon.

Edwards, C. P. (1986). Cross-cultural research on Kohlberg's stages: The basis for consensus. In Modgil S. & Modgil C. (Eds.), *Lawrence Kohlberg: Consensus and controversy,* (pp. 419–430). London: The Falmer Press.

Enriquez, A. (1982). *Towards a Filipino psychology*. Quezon City: Psychology Research and Training House.

Gilligan, C. (1982). *In a different voice. Psychological theory and women's development*. Cambridge, MA: Harvard University Press.

Greenberg, J., Pyszczynski, T. & Solomon, S. (1986). The causes and consequences of a need for self-esteem: A terror management theory. In R. Baumeister (Ed.), *The private and the public self* (pp. 189–212). New York: Springer.

Greenfield, P. M. (2000). Three approaches to the psychology of culture: Where do they come from? Where can they go? *Asian Journal of Social Psychology, 3*, 223–240.

Gutmann, D. (1967). On cross-cultural studies as a naturalistic approach in psychology. *Human Development, 10*, 187–198.

Habermas, J. (1981). *Theorie des kommunikativen Handelns*. 2. Bde. Frankfurt am Main: Suhrkamp.

Hassan, Fuad (2002). *Cultural diversity and the prospect of peace-building through sharing a we-world. Key note speech*. XVI Congress of the International Association for Cross-Cultural Psychology. Unity in Diversity: Enhancing a peaceful world. July 15–19, 2002 Yogyakarta, Indonesia

Ho, D., Y. F., Peng, S., Lai, A. Ch. & Chan, S. F. (2001). Indigenization and beyond: Methodological relationalism in the study of personality across cultural traditions. *Journal of Personality, 69*(6), 925–953.

Huebner, A. & Garrod, A. (1991). Moral reasoning in a karmic world. *Human Development, 34*, 341–352.

Hwang, K.-K. (1998). Two moralities: Reinterpreting the findings of empirical research on moral reasoning in Taiwan. *Asian Journal of Social Psychology, 1*, 211–238.

Kant, I. (1968/1788). Kritik der Praktischen Vernunft. In W. Weischedel (Hrsg.), *Werkausgabe in 12 Bänden*, Bd. VII. Frankfurt am Main: Suhrkamp.

Keller, H. (1997). Entwicklungspsychopathologie. In H. Keller (Hrsg.), *Handbuch der Kleinkindforschung*, 2. Auflage (S. 625–641). Bern: Huber.

Keller. H. & Eckensberger, L. H. (1998). Kultur und Entwicklung. In H. Keller (Hrsg.), *Lehrbuch. Entwicklungspsychologie* (S. 57–96). Bern: Huber.

Kim, U. (1990). Indigenous psychology: Science and applications. In R. Brislin (Ed.), *Applied cross-cultural psychology* (pp. 142–160). Newbury Park, CA: Sage.

Kim, U. (2000). Indigenous, cultural, and cross-cultural psychology: A theoretical, conceptual, and epistemological analysis. *A Journal of Social Psychology, 3*, 265–287.

Kohlberg, L. (1958). *The development of modes of moral thinking and choice in the years ten to sixteen*. Unpublished doctoral dissertation. University of Chicago.

Kohlberg, L. (1973). Continuities in childhood and adult moral development revisited. In P. Baltes & K. W. Schaie (Eds.), *Life-span developmental psychology: Personality and socialization*. (pp. 180–204). New York: Academic Press.

Kohlberg, L. (1976). Moral stages and moralization: The cognitive-developmental approach. In T. E. Licona, (Hrsg.), *Moral development and behavior. Theory research and social issues* (pp. 31–53). New York: Holt, Rinehart and Winston.

Kohlberg, L. (1986). A current statement on some theoretical issues. In Modgil S. & Modgil C. (Eds.) *Lawrence Kohlberg: Consensus and controversity*. (pp. 485–546). London, Philadelphia: The Falmer Press.

Kohlberg, L., Boyd, D., & LeVine, C. (1986). Die Wiederkehr der sechsten Stufe: Gerechtigkeit, Wohlwollen und der Standpunkt der Moral. In W. Edelstein & G. Nunner-Winkler (Eds.), *Zur Bestimmung der Moral: Philosophische und sozialwissenschaftliche Beiträge zur Moralforschung* (pp. 205–240). Frankfurt/M., Germany: Suhrkamp.

Kornadt, H-J. (2002). Biology, culture and child rearing: The development of social motives. In H. Keller, Y. Poortinga & A. Schölmerich (Eds.), *Biology, culture, and development: Integrating diverse perspectives* (pp. 191–211). Cambridge: Cambridge University Press.

Krishnan, L. (1997). Distributed justice in the Indian perspective. In H.S.K Kao & D. Sinha (eds.), *Asian perspectives on psychology, vol 19, Cross-cultural research and methodology issues* (pp. 185–200). New Delhi: Sage.

Kuhn, T. S. (1970). *The structure of scientific revolutions.* Chicago: University of Chicago Press.

Lei, T. & Cheng, S. W. (1984). *An empirical study of Kohlberg's theory and scoring system of moral judgment in Chinese society.* Unpublished manuscript, Harvard University, Cambridge, MA.

Ma, H. K. (1988). Objective moral judgment in Hong Kong, Mainland China and England. *Journal of Cross-Cultural Psychology, 19* (1), 78–95.

Ma, H. K. (1998). *The Chinese stage structure of moral development. A cross-cultural perspective.* Manuscript. Department of Education Studies. Hong Kong, Baptist University.

Markus, H. R. & Kitayama, S. (1991). Culture and the self: Implications for cognition, emotion, and motivation. *Psychological Review, 98,* 224–253.

Miller, J. G. (1994). Cultural diversity in the morality of caring: Individually-oriented versus duty-based interpersonal moral codes. *Cross-Cultural Research, 28* (1), 3–39.

Misra, G. (2001). Culture and self: Implications for psychological inquiry. *Journal of Indian Psychology, 19* (1), 1–20.

Miyake, K., Chen, S. & Campos, J. J. (1985). Infant temperament, mothers mode of interaction, and attachment in Japan. An interim report. *Monographs of the Society for Research in Child Development, 50* (1–2, Serial No. 209).

Morin, E. (1973). *Das Rätsel des Humanen* [The riddle of the humane]. Munich/Zurich: Piper.

Murray Thomas, R. (1988). *Oriental theories of human development.* New York: Lang.

Nsamenang, A. B. (1992). *Human development in cultural context. A Third World perspective.* Vol. 16. Newsbury Park: Sage.

Quine, W. v. O. (1976). *Word & Object.* Cambridge: The MIT Press.

Rogoff, B. & Angelillo, C. (2002). Investigating the Coordinated Functioning of Multifaceted Cultural Practices in Human Development. *Human Development, 45,* 211–225.

Säävälä, M. (2001). Low caste but middle-class: Some religious strategies for middle-class identification in Hyderabad. *Contributions to Indian Society, 35*(3), 295–318.

Saraswathi, T.S. & Ganapathy, H. (2002). The Hindu world view of child and human development: Reflections in contemporary parental ethnotheories. In H. Keller, Y. Poortinga & A. Schölmerich (Eds.), *Biology, culture, and development: Integrating diverse perspectives* (pp. 80–88). Cambridge: Cambridge University Press.

Schwartz, L. (1951). *Die Neurosen und die dynamische Psychologie von Pierre Janet* [Neuroses and the dynamic psychology of Pierre Janet]. Basel, Switzerland: Schwabe.

Setiono, K. (1994). *Morality from the viewpoint of Javanese tradition.* Paper presented at the Symposium "Eco-ethical thinking from a cross-cultural perspective", July 1994, Kirkel, Germany.

Shweder, R. A. (2000). The psychology of practice and the practice of the three psychologies. *Asian Journal of Social Psychology, 3,* 207–222.

Shweder, R. A. & Haidt, J. (1991). *The future of moral psychology: Truth, intuition and the pluralist way.* Manuscript prepared for Psychological Science.

Shweder, R. A., Mahapatra, M. & Miller, J. G. (1987). Culture and moral development. In J. Kagan, & S. Lamb (Eds.), *The emergence of morality in young children* (pp. 1–83). Chicago: Chicago University Press.

Sinha, D. (1996). Cross-cultural psychology: The Asian scenario. In J. Pandey, D. Sinha & D. P. S. Bhawuk (Eds.), *Asian contributions to cross-cultural psychology* (pp. 20–41). New Delhi: Sage Publications.

Sinha, D. (1997). Indigenizing psychology. In J. W. Berry, Y. H. Poortinga & J. Pandey (Eds.), *Handbook of cross-cultural psychology* (2nd ed.), vol. 1 (pp. 129–169). Boston, MA.: Allyn & Bacon.

Sinha, D., & Tripathi, R. C. (1994). Individualism in a collective culture: A case of coexistence of opposites. In U. Kim, H. C. Triandis, C. Kagitcibasi, S. Choi, & G. Yoon (Eds.),

Individualism and collectivism: Theory, method and applications, (pp.123–126). Thousand Oaks: Sage.

Smedslund, J. (1984). The invisible obvious: Culture in psychology. In K. M. J. Lagerspetz & P. Niemi (Eds.), Psychology in the 1990's. Amsterdam: North-Holland.

Snarey, J. (1983). The social and moral development of Kibbutz founders and abras: A cross-sectional and longitudinal cross-cultural study (Doctoral dissertation, Harvard University, 1982). *Dissertation Abstracts International, 43* (10), 3416b.

Snarey, J. (1985). Cross-cultural universality of socio-moral development: A critical review of Kohlbergian research. *Psychological Bulletin, 97* (2), 202–232.

Snarey, J. & Keljo, K. (1991). In a Gemeinschaft voice: The cross-cultural expansion of moral development theory. In W. M. Kurtines & J. L. Gewirtz (Eds.), *Handbook of moral behaviour and development, Vol. I: Theory,* (pp. 395–424). Hillsdale, NJ: Erlbaum.

Stern, W. (1911²) *Die Differentielle Psychologie in ihren methodischen Grundlagen.* Ed. K. Pawlik. Bern: Hans Huber. (Nachdruck 1994).

Sugiyama Lebra, T. (1976). Japanese patterns of behavior. Honolulu: University of Hawaii Press.

Tietjen, A. & Walker, L. (1984). *Moral reasoning and leadership among men in a Papua New Guinea village.* Unpublished manuscript, University of British Columbia, Vancouver, Canada.

Van de Vijver, F. & Leung, K. (1997). *Methods and data analysis for cross-cultural research.* Thousands Oaks, CA: Sage.

Van de Vijver, F. & Poortinga, Y. H. (2002). On the Study of Culture in Developmental Science. *Human Development, 45,* 246–256.

Van Vlaenderen, H. (1993). Psychological research in the process of social change: A contribution to community development. *Psychology and Developing Societies, 5,* 95–110.

Vasudev, J. (1984). Kohlberg's claim to universality. An Indian perspective. Paper for the Second Rinberg Conference, Rinberg West Germany.

Vine, I. (1986). Moral maturity in socio-cultural perspective: Are Kohlberg's stages universal? In Modgil, S. & Modgil C. (Eds.), *Lawrence Kohlberg: Consensus and controversy* (pp. 431–450). London, Philadelphia: The Falmer Press.

Yang, K. S. (2000). Monocultural and cross-cultural indigenous approaches : The royal road to the development of a balanced global psychology. *Asian Journal of Social Psychology, 3,* 241–263.

Zimba, R. F. (1994). The understanding of morality, convention, and personal preference in an African setting. Findings from Zambia. *Journal of Cross-Cultural Psychology, 25* (3), 369–393.

Chapter 11

Naïve Dialecticism and the Tao of Chinese Thought

Kaiping Peng, Julie Spencer-Rodgers, and Zhong Nian

> All of Chinese roots are in the Taoist tradition.
> LU XUN, Chinese writer, 1918.

> A Chinese thought without Taoism is like a tree without roots
> JOSEPH NEEDHAM, 1990

Recent cross-cultural work on Chinese cognition, particularly research comparing Chinese and Western (mostly American) reasoning and social judgment, has revealed substantial and fascinating differences in the ways individuals from these two cultural groups make sense of their everyday environments (see Nisbett, Peng, Choi, & Norenzayan, 2001; Peng, Ames, & Knowles, 2001 for reviews). This line of work has shed light on differences in how Chinese and Western individuals evaluate themselves (e.g., Markus & Kitayama, 1991; Spencer-Rodgers & Peng, 2004; Spencer-Rodgers, et al., 2004), attribute causes to events (e.g., Lee, Hallahan, & Herzog, 1996; Morris & Peng, 1994), interpret physical phenomena (Peng & Knowles, 2003), and make judgments and decisions (e.g., Ji, Peng & Nisbett, 2000; Peng & Nisbett, 1999; Yates, Lee, & Shinotsuka, 1996; Yates, Lee, & Bush, 1997). These empirical findings support claims frequently made by scholars in a variety of academic fields concerning the different intellectual traditions of the West and East (see reviews by Lloyd, 1990; Nakamaru, 1964; Needham, 1954), which have been characterized as contrasts between abstract and concrete (Nakamura, 1964; Northrop, 1946, 1966), analytic and holistic (Moore, 1967; Nisbett et al., 2001), linear and circular (Hang, 1966), Laplacean and fatalistic (Phillips & Wright, 1977; Wright & Phillips, 1980), person-centered and situation-centered (Hsu, 1981; Yang, 1986), dispositional and contextual (Morris & Peng, 1994), argument-constructing and argument-abhorring (Liu, 1986; Yates & Lee, 1996), synthesis-oriented and dialectical (Peng & Nisbett, 1999; Spencer-Rodgers et al., 2004), and so on.

However, explanations of the differences between the East and West have relied almost exclusively on theoretical constructs generated in Western cultural contexts, based on Western concepts, and used by Western scholars. For instance, early theories regarding Chinese reasoning have included notions of national character (Bellah, Madsen, Sullivan, Swidler, & Tipton, 1985), values (Kluckhorn & Strodtbeck, 1961; Schwartz, 1992), social systems (Parsons & Shils, 1951), morality (Shweder, 1982), religion (Bakan, 1966), ecology (Berry, 1976, 1979), child-rearing patterns (Barry, Child, & Bacon, 1959), economic development (Adelman & Morris, 1967), modernity (Berger, Berger, & Kellner, 1973; lnkeles & Smith, 1974), and, more recently, individualism-collectivism (Hofstede, 1980; Hofstede & Bond, 1984; Triandis, 1989, 1995), and independent-interdependent self construals (Markus & Kitayama, 1991). The significance of these pioneering attempts is hardly disputable: If one-fourth of the world's population is thinking and reasoning in ways different from what we have learned from current psychology (which is largely based on American samples), then our understanding of human reasoning is at best incomplete and at worst culturally biased.

Given the fact that few of the above theories were proposed by Chinese scholars or based on Chinese concepts, the question then becomes: How would the Chinese think about their own ways of thinking? In other words, would a Chinese theory of cultural differences be different from a theory centered on Western concepts?

The idea of using Chinese concepts to explain Chinese psychological phenomena is not entirely new. There have been genuine efforts in psychology, particularly by psychologists from Taiwan, Hong Kong, Singapore, and China, to develop theories and research paradigms based largely on Chinese cultural concepts, a pursuit of an *emic* approach to Eastern psychological phenomena that has been proudly labeled *indigenous psychology*. For example, Francis Hsu, a China-born and -educated American cultural anthropologist, shifted from the use of Western Freudian notions to the use of Chinese *ren* as the central theme of his theory on Chinese psychology (Hsu, 1953). In addition, two influential social psychologists in Asia, Kuo-shu Yang and Michael Bond, have used Confucian value systems to explain Chinese social behavior (Bond, 1987, 1997; Yang, 1986), and several other East Asian psychologists (such as Yang Zhong-Fang, Kwok Leung, David Ho, Huang Guang-guo, etc.) have used other indigenous Chinese concepts, such as *zhong yong, mianzi* (face), and *guanxi* (connection) to explain a variety of psychological phenomena. These efforts have made a strong impact on mainstream psychology and on the general public in the West. For instance, two Chinese concepts, *guanxi* (connection) and *mianzi* (face), have been appropriated into the English language, and have been popularly accepted as fundamental to the operation of Chinese society (e.g., Gold, 1996).

Yet one important aspect of Chinese culture has been consistently over-looked. For years, Chinese philosophers and historians have suggested that whereas Confucianism presides over Chinese *social* life, Taoism may play an equally important role in Chinese *mental* life (Lu, 1918; Needham, 1990; Zhang & Chen, 1991; Zhou, 1990). Indeed, the observation that Chinese are Confucianists in public and Taoists in private may reflect the essence of Chinese psychology (Shen, 1985). In other words, whereas Chinese sociology and, to a certain extent, social psychology, may be based on Confucian teachings (Bond, 1997), Chinese cognitive psychology, or the thinking and reasoning of Chinese lay people, may be best seen as reflecting Taoist teachings. Lu Xun, one of the most prominent Chinese writers of the 20th century, claimed that all roots of Chinese thinking are in the Taoist tradition (Lu Xun, August 8, 1918, Letter to Xu Shou-tang). He is not alone in believing that the essence of Chinese thought is Taoist. For instance, British Sinologist Joseph Needham wrote in his classic book *History of Chinese Science and Technology*, "A Chinese thought without Taoism is like a tree without roots" (Needham, 1990, p. 198). Chinese philosopher Jing Yu-ling further argued that the epistemological principle of Chinese intellectuals is to "Practice the Tao, understand the Tao, and master the Tao" (Jing, 1987, p.16). The Tao is considered to be the highest goal of intellectual life and the defining motivation for Chinese thinking and behavior. As Chinese philosopher Hsu Dao-jing claimed, "The Tao has become the core of Chinese cultures, the beliefs of Chinese people and the foundation of Chinese societies" (Hsu, 1994, p. 1).

This paper attempts to introduce the indigenous concepts of Tao into mainstream cultural psychology. We suggest that Chinese are naïve Taoists in spirit and that Chinese thinking and reasoning are guided by folk versions of Taoism, which we label *naïve dialecticism*. Such folk beliefs constitute the foundation of Chinese implicit theories of knowing. We summarize ethnographic evidence that supports the existence of a folk version of Taoism in Chinese culture and then discuss the practice of folk Taoism in the everyday lives of Chinese people. We argue that because of Taoist traditions, Chinese reasoning and thinking can be regarded as more contextual, flexible, holistic, and dialectical as compared with Western thinking and reasoning. We conclude with a Taoist view of cultural psychology and cross-cultural research on human cognition and a discussion of an indigenous Taoist view of cultural differences in reasoning and thinking.

The Essence of Taoism

Taoism is one of the three teachings–Confucianism, Taoism, and Buddhism–in Chinese culture. However, Taoism has rarely been referred to as a religion, as it deals more with the art of living. In many ways, Taoism is concerned with understanding the nature of the world, knowledge, and human life, which is, in part, what folk psychology is all about.

The Meaning of Tao

Although there can be no equivalent in English for the word *Tao* (道), loosely translated, it means "the way" or "the path." In *Tao Te Ching*, the great Lao-zi asserted that "The Tao is not the Tao" (570-490 BC/1993). That is, the term *Tao*, which is expressible in words, is not the same as the *eternal Tao*: a name that can be spoken cannot capture that which is intangible. It is nothing and everything at the same time. The word *Tao* is just a convenient way of describing a construct that is, in essence, nameless. Lao-zi compared the Tao to water: Water flows naturally, without interference, and does not attract attention. In its weak, unnoticed actions, water (in the same way as the Tao) is able to overcome the strong.

Even in contemporary Chinese, *Tao* has multiple meanings. According to a national survey of Mandarin, the term has over ten different definitions (Liu, 1990). In addition to its common meaning of "the way," *Tao* also means "rules," "patterns and laws of nature," and "an epistemologically driven means of understanding." Typical English interpretations of Chinese *Tao* include "method," "nature," "spirit," "rules," "truth," "pattern," "metaphysics," and "perspectives" (Liu, 1990, p. 1). None of these interpretations allows Western audiences to fully grasp the Chinese concept of Tao.

Basic Concepts of Taoism

It is somehow inappropriate to discuss basic concepts of Taoism, since Tao is a holistic construct that cannot be decomposed. Nevertheless, it is possible to summarize Lao-zi's essential points that inform the classic *Tao Te Ching*, including the ideas of non-duality, two poles (yin-yang), perpetual change, three treasures the five elements, and non-action.

Non-duality. The notion of non-duality refers to the belief that "matter is spirit" and that "spirit is matter." The Tao is at once the void and all matter that confronts us. If we say, "it is the void," we are claiming that it is not matter, which in fact it also is. Thus, to understand the void, we must also understand matter.

Two poles. The ontological foundation of Taoism is the concept of yin and yang. According to Taoism, the Tao operates through the interaction of yin and yang. Yin is the negative, passive, and feminine, whereas yang is the positive, active, and masculine. Neither can exist without the other, and neither is inferior to the other.

A full circle of perpetual change. The rational basis of non-duality is the notion of perpetual change. All things in the universe are seen as constantly changing in orderly cycles. Taoism teaches observation and exploration of these various cycles of change. Contemplation leads to understanding; tranquility is achieved when pain and loss become as essential as pleasure and gain.

Three treasures. Ching (essence), *chi* (vitality), and *shen* (spirit) are the three substances of energy in the Taoist view of life, and hence, the essence of Taoism. These three substances are believed to be active at all levels of being, from the tiniest organism to the vast universe itself.

Five elements (wu hsing). It is the Taoist belief that the natural interactions in the universe can be characterized into the interaction of five elements (*wu hsing*): metal, wood, water, fire, and earth.

Non-action (wu wei). The notion of non-action does not mean that people are to do nothing, but rather, they are to avoid doing anything that is not spontaneous and should always adjust to the situation. They should act effortlessly, like a tree that bends towards the sun when it needs sunshine. Upon reaching *wu wei*, people attain freedom from greed, anxiety, and other mundane troubles.

The Essence of Taoism: The Mutual Dependence of Two Opposites

One of the most fundamental of Chinese beliefs is the notion of the mutual dependency of two opposites, which is deeply rooted in the basic teachings of Taoism. *The Book of Lao Zi* (also known as *Tao Te Ching*) has a number of passages that deal with the importance of the mutual dependency of two sides of a contradiction. In Chapter 2, Lao-zi (570?-490? BCE/1993) states:

> When the people of the world all know beauty as beauty,
> There arises the recognition of ugliness.
> When they all know the good as good,
> There arises the recognition of evil.
> And so, being and nonbeing produce each other;
> Difficulty and ease complete each other;
> Long and short contrast each other;
> High and low distinguish each another;
> Sounds and tones harmonize each other;
> Front and back accompany each other.
> Thus, the sage manages affairs by non-action,
> And teaches by saying nothing. (p. 16)

Therefore, according to Taoist teaching, the two sides of any contradiction exist in active harmony; they are mutually opposed, and at the same time, mutually connected, controlling, and dependent.

FOLK TAOISM IN CHINESE CULTURES

There is a notable difference between Confucianism and Taoism in that the former is more officially sanctioned in social practice and belief systems, whereas the latter is more relevant to folk beliefs and practice

(Chen, 1996, Yang, 2001). Hence Taoist thought has in fact a broader base of appeal among lay Chinese, but has received less attention in elite philosophers' discussion of Chinese history. Chinese scholars have only recently begun to study the influence of Taoism on Chinese life and systems of thought, such as Yang's discussion of Taoist teaching methods (Yang, 1996) and the influence of Taoism among ethnic minorities in China (Deng, 2000). These authors, to a certain degree, are pioneers in introducing the concept of Taoism to the field of cross-cultural psychology. Chinese systems of thought are, of course, much more complicated, multifaceted, and obviously the result of the blending of different religious and cultural heritages. But there is a folk version of Taoism extant in Chinese thought and belief systems (*naïve dialecticism*), which can be studied through empirical psychological methods of inquiry.

One way to demonstrate the existence of a folk version of Taoism is to examine folklore, or public representations of Taoism. In our studies, we have consistently found an apparent connection between Taoist teachings and Chinese folklore, notably in Chinese proverbs. Anthropologists believe that proverbs are distilled embodiments of folk wisdom (see Arewa & Dundes, 1964). They are defined as short expressions of cultural wisdom, truth, morals, and norms that exist in a "metaphorical, fixed and memorable form" that are "handed down from generation to generation" (Mieder, 1993, p. 5). Thus, one way to see the significance of Taoism in Chinese mental life is to identify Chinese proverbs that emphasize Taoist teachings, particularly the notions of change, connection, compromise, covariation, context, and contradiction (the mutual dependency of two opposites). Empirical research has shown that such proverbs are indeed numerous. For example, in a content analysis of Chinese proverbs compiled by Lian (1964), close to 20% were found to be Taoist in nature (Peng, 1997). For example, with respect to the notion of context, Chinese believe that "even a ferocious dragon cannot beat the snake in its old haunts" and "ice three feet thick is not due to one day's cold." With respect to the notion of contradiction, Chinese believe that "a wise person can be victim of his own wisdom," "there is no sweet without bitterness," and "failure is the mother of success." Other proverbs exemplify the notion of covariation. Chinese believe that "if there is peace in one's home everything will prosper" and "there are no poor soldiers under a good general." With respect to the notion of change, Chinese suggest "one learns a lesson each time one suffers losses." Finally, Chinese warn that "when two tigers fight, one is bound to lose," exemplifying the notion of compromise. These proverbs are not just thought-provoking. Rather, they serve many of the same functions that culture does: Proverbs can summarize a situation, pass judgment on another's behavior, recommend a course of action, or serve as precedents for current action.

Naïve Dialecticism as Collective Representations of Taoism

As cultural psychologists, it is not our job simply to recount folklore or resurrect broad descriptive claims about Chinese culture made by philosophers, anthropologists, historians, and other scholars in the humanities. Rather, the role of the cultural psychologist is to answer questions concerning *how* and *why* Chinese people think and reason differently from individuals in other cultures. The first question to be addressed is whether differences in philosophical traditions between Chinese and non-Chinese are located at the broad cultural level or at the level of the individual. That is, do the differences outlined here concern cultural ideology or psychological phenomena? We argue that Taoist teachings exist both as cultural ideology and as individual, cognitive representations. We can connect the Taoist teachings with individual psychology by studying individual representations of the Tao, and by studying how these individual representations affect individual psychological processes.

If psychologists agree that cultural differences are a matter of individual psychology, the question then becomes: What sorts of mental processes or structures are the source of these cultural differences? We argue for representational differences, or differences in folk theories, as the fundamental cause of many cultural differences in reasoning. There is mounting evidence in psychology connecting cultural theories with individual psychology (see Morris, Menon, & Ames, 2001; Peng et al., 2001, for reviews). Culture-specific theories are shared mental representations among members of different cultures–theories that are part of a culture's "collective representations" (Durkheim, 1898).

What are the Chinese collective representations of Taoism? It is difficult to identify the major components of Chinese representations of Taoism precisely because they are Taoist in nature, and hence highly flexible with multiple meanings and functions. This paper takes a rather non-Taoist approach in decomposing Chinese dialectical epistemology. Nevertheless, we believe that this epistemology can be identified and summarized into distinctive principles by comparing it with central themes of Western thinking and reasoning. This approach, admittedly, is analytic and reductionistic, and fundamentally inconsistent with the spirit of Taoism. The principles identified herein may also not cover all aspects of Chinese collective representations, but only those that lend themselves most easily to abstraction and analysis in empirical studies. Because in some ways these naïve dialectical principles resemble characteristics of Hegel's dialectics (without its idealism and method of dialectics: thesis, antithesis, and synthesis), we refer to them as *naïve dialecticism*.

Principle of Change (Bian Yi Lu)

The principle of change holds that reality is a process. It does not stand still; it is in constant flux. The example of the principle of change that most readily comes to mind is the Taoist attitude towards concepts or words that reflect existence and knowledge. Because reality is dynamic and flexible, concepts that reflect reality are also active, changeable, and subjective. For instance, Zhuang-zi explicitly claimed that concepts should not be taken literally because they are not fixed. Zhuang-zi asserted, "The Tao has never known boundaries (of concepts); words have no constancy" (Zhuang-zi, 370-301 BC/1968, p. 43). That is, boundaries and distinct categories are associated with the impairment of the Tao and are foreign to the Tao. Accordingly, Zhuang-zi said that the sage does not discriminate among ideas and that "those who discriminate fail to see (the Tao)" (Zhuang-zi, 370-301 BCE/1968, p. 44).

Principle of Contradiction (Ma Dun Lu)

The principle of contradiction argues that reality, particularly the reality of life, is not precise and cut-and-dried, but rather, complex and full of contradiction. The principle of contradiction among contemporary Chinese is commonly expressed as "dividing one into two" (that are contradictory to one another). This saying has been widely misattributed to (and officially propagated by) Chairman Mao's philosophical thinking (1937/1962). However, the ideas behind this saying can be readily traced to the *Yi ling/ I-Ching* (Book of Changes), in which the principle of contradiction is clearly expressed. For example, its basic theme is that "Yin and Yang make up the way," such that the world is simply a single, integrated entity. According to the *Yi ling/I-Ching*, the differentiation and separation of things is but an expression of the interaction between opposites (yin and yang); the motivating energy for both parts of the contradictory pair of yin and yang all come from the Tao (or origin of the universe) and revert to the Tao.

Principle of Relationship or Holism (Zheng He Lu)

The principle of holism maintains that in reality, as well as in human life, nothing is isolated and independent; rather, everything is relational and connected. If psychologists really want to know anything fully, we must know all of its relations–how it affects and is affected by everything else. The Chinese holistic mode of thought is epitomized in two basic assumptions of Taoism: the two poles (yin and yang) and the five elements. The ideal state of human thinking is "the unity of heaven and humanity" (*tian ren he yi*) that considers heaven and humanity as two sides (*xiang fen*, meaning separation) of an organic whole (*he yi*, meaning unity), but not as independent parts of an integrated whole.

The straightforward translation of this principle is that our understanding of even a simple event must depend on all sorts of complex relationships, because everything in the universe is related to everything else in some way. One can understand nothing in isolated pieces. The parts are meaningful in their relations to the whole, just as individual musical instruments are to an orchestra. The whole is more than the sum of its parts. We must understand the whole to understand the parts. Anything taken in isolation is out of context, and hence distorted.

We suggest that these Taoist principles are shared mental representations of Chinese people. They are interrelated, coherent elements of naïve dialecticism. The principle of change is the logical foundation of naïve dialecticism: The notion of change leads to a belief in contradiction, and contradiction comes as a result of a belief in change (if all phenomena in the universe are constantly changing, then what is true today may not be true tomorrow). Holism, in turn, is the consequence of a belief in change and contradiction. In many ways, these three principles are somewhat at odds with the basic laws of Aristotelian logic, the building blocks of naïve Aristotelianism. These basic laws include the *law of identity* (if something is true, then it is true; thus A = A), the *law of non-contradiction* (no statement can be both true and false; thus $A \neq$ not A), and the *law of the excluded middle* (all statements are either true or false; thus $(A \lor B) \& (A \& B)$). Such fundamental differences in thinking lead to interesting and important cultural differences for psychological research.

For instance, there are various models in the psychological and anthropological literature that describe differences between Chinese and Western thinking and reasoning. Many are related to the principles of naïve dialecticism. For instance, it has been suggested that the Chinese, in contrast to Westerners, have little interest in abstract reasoning. Their way of thinking is more concrete, confined largely to the realm of the immediately apprehended (Northrop, 1946). The Chinese way of thinking is also described as utilitarian and pragmatic (Nakamura, 1960), focusing on concrete real-life problems rather than general theories or ideas. The psychological evidence for to this argument is the fact that Chinese prefer to use concrete rather than abstract traits to describe themselves. This may reflect precisely the naïve dialectical view that nothing is absolute and stable, and hence can be abstracted. Research has found that abstract self-description and concrete self-description may be two independent dimensions in East Asian cultures (Rhee, Uleman, Lee, & Roman, 1995). In other words, East Asian participants can respond abstractly or concretely to the "Who Am I?" question, depending on the context in which the question is asked (Cousins, 1989). In a recent study, we found that the Chinese not only used more concrete self-descriptions, but more changeable, contradictory, and holistic statements when describing the self (Spencer-Rodgers, Boucher, Mori, Wnag, & Peng, 2005). Chinese and European-American participants' responses on the Twenty Statements Test (TST) were coded for any type of transition (e.g., recent, ongoing, or desired change) in their personality traits, physical characteristics, goals, etc. For example, the free-response "I am someone who tries hard not to lie" represents a dynamic self-statement relative to the static self-statement "I am honest." In accordance with the principle of change, Chinese listed three times as many dynamic self-statements than did European-Americans. Consistent with the principle of contradiction, Chinese listed a greater proportion of contradictory self-statements (e.g., "I am young, yet old at the same time"), contradictory paired self-statements (e.g., "I am hardworking" listed on line 2 and "I am lazy" listed on line 8), and not-self statements (e.g., "I am not from a wealthy family"), than did European-Americans. Finally, in accordance with the principle of holism, they cited more holistic self-statements (e.g., "I am one but many") on the TST. These findings suggest that a greater amount of dialectical self-knowledge is retrieved spontaneously from memory among Chinese than European-Americans.

However, we have to point out that there is a fundamental difference between Chinese naïve dialecticism and the commonly understood dialectical thinking in Western thought. In Western intellectual domains, dialectical thinking usually refers to three levels of analysis, including dialectic dynamics at the societal level (e.g., Hegelian or Marxist dialectics), dialectical argumentation at the level of interpersonal discourse, and dialectical integration at the intrapsychic level. Importantly, Chinese naïve dialecticism is different from all three types of Western dialectical thought. Western dialectical thinking is fundamentally consistent with the laws of formal logic, and aggressive in the sense that contradiction requires synthesis rather than mere acceptance. The key difference is that Chinese naïve dialecticism does not regard contradiction as illogical and tends to accept the harmonious unity of opposites. Chinese tend to view people who don't believe the coexistence of opposites as having made a kind or error or as short sighted or narrow minded. Western dialectical thought, particularly the Marxist dialectic, treats contradiction as antagonistic. As Lenin (1961) wrote in the *Philosophical Notebooks*, the unity of opposites is only temporary, transitory, and conditional. Equilibrium and harmony are only temporary; conflict, contradiction, and the struggle of opposing tendencies are permanent (Peng & Ames, 2001; Peng & Nisbett, 2000).

Implication for Theories Concerning Cultural Differences between East and West

An important theoretical argument made here is that cultural differences between Western and Chinese people in the domains of thinking and reasoning can be attributed to differences between Western and Eastern folk epistemologies. Western folk beliefs of knowing, or understanding of the nature of the world and human life are Aristotelian in spirit, emphasizing constancy (identity), synthesis (non-contradiction), and extremes (no middle ground). In contrast, Chinese emphasize a dialectical approach that values change, contradiction, and relationships. These important cultural variation have broad implications for the ways in which psychologists understand and theorize about cultural variation in general.

As discussed at the beginning of this paper, cultural variation between the East and West has been understood in many different ways. These differences are numerous and complicated, and each of the above constructs may encompass different aspects of cultural variation. On the other hand, none of these constructs can provide a coherent story to explain all of the observed cultural variation. Even the relatively prominent theories characterizing cultural variation between Chinese and Western peoples would have difficulty explaining some specific cultural variations, or would explain them in a way that is too sweeping. For example, individualism-collectivism (or independent-interdependent selves) alone cannot explain why Chinese tolerate contradiction in their thinking and reasoning, because there are some collectivist cultures that might not embrace dialectical approaches (e.g., Mexican American culture), and some cultures that value dialectical thinking are hard to characterize as individualistic or collectivistic (e.g., Jewish American culture).

From a dialectical perspective, the common views of individualism-collectivism and independent-interdependent selves, are, by their very nature, examples of Western models of explanation, which are based on all-or-nothing dichotomies that treat individuals and collectives as two opposing entities. This perspective assumes that a culture must be *either* individualistic *or* collectivistic (or possess either independent-selves or interdependent-selves), but not both. In our opinion, this polarized dichotomy is, in itself, a reflection of Western formal logic that cannot tolerate contradiction, even at the risk of exaggerating certain aspects of a culture (e.g., individualism) or discounting other aspects of the culture (e.g., collectivism).

The Chinese model of explanation presupposes a part-whole approach. Thus parts exist only within wholes with which they have inseparable relations. As applied to people, the Chinese perspective rejects an atomistic explanation of individuals' behaviors, and instead refers to individuals' relations to some whole, such as the family, society, Tao, and so on (Hansen, 1983; Munro, 1985). Therefore Chinese explanation of cultural differences are not based on dichotomies, but rather rely on a holistic model in which each culture has a relatively differential affinity to or distance from the whole. To illustrate, a Chinese understanding of this paper would not conclude that Chinese are dialectical in dealing with contradiction and Americans are not, but that all cultures can be more or less dialectical, and the Chinese happen to be more prone to thinking dialectically than people from other cultures, because of their Taoist folk epistemology.

We admit that it is unlikely that the single concept of naïve dialecticism can explain all Eastern-Western psychological distinction, and it is not intended to do so. Naïve dialecticism instead attempts to provide an intermediate level of explanation of cultural variation, a bridge between macro-level explanations (e.g., individualism-collectivism) and micro-level explanations of cognitive differences (e.g., person-centered versus situation-centered cognition). We believe that ecological or ideological differences between East and West produce different social theories about human behavior, such as individualism-collectivism. These social differences, in turn, facilitate the growth and development of culture-specific epistemologies (e.g., naïve dialecticism) that affect people's views about the nature of existence and knowledge, as well as their understanding of logic and rationality. Culture-specific epistemologies then lead to more direct causes of cognitive variation among cultures, such as folk wisdom, education, parenting styles, and customs (micro-level variables). Thus a specific cultural difference in cognition can be explained by its direct causes, and people's culture-specific intuitive theories about the events being studied. Cultural differences in cognition can be, and in many cases have been, explained by culture-specific social theories and ecological differences. However, these explanations must be tested and proven, not assumed. A multilevel approach, we believe, is more constructive and informative than simplistic, categorical explanations of cultural variations. This approach recognizes the complexity and relativity of cultural differences and its predictions are concrete and falsifiable.

Normative Questions

So, which style of reasoning is better, the Western or the Chinese? If the indigenous line of research seeks to accomplish anything, it is a new perspective on studying cultural differences. Instead of making normative claims about which culture-specific ways of reasoning are better or worse, the indigenous approach argues for the mutual dependency and complementarity of both. The focus is on understanding the paradox of universality and culture-specificity of cognitive processes, and the new evidence that, across cultures, there are different cognitive styles that organize cognitive functions in different ways. The cultural and social implications of this research may reach beyond purely intellectual exploration. This research may provide evidence that cultural diversity has important practical advantages: The Western approach may be excellent for many purposes, and the East Asian dialectical approach, excellent for many other purposes.

Figure 1. The symbol of Tao (*yin yang tai ji tu*)

Let us close with a symbol of Chinese culture, the symbol of Tao (yin-yang *tai ji tu*), in which two famous cognates of Chinese dialectical epistemology, yin and yang, stand for opposite qualities–a symbol of harmony between two extremes (see Figure 1). It is, in our opinion, an exemplary symbol of naïve dialecticism. The wave shapes reflect continual movement, which is the essence of the principle of change. The principle of contradiction is represented by the fact that there is a white spot inside the black shape, and a black spot inside the white shape, which is natural and logical according to Chinese naïve dialecticism. The principle of holism is apparent, because the beauty of this symbol can only be appreciated holistically, as the whole generates and regulates the cycle of changes between yang and yin. If we use this symbol, in a loose way, to characterize the cultural differences found in cross-cultural research, then the reasoning style represented by Westerners would be "yang," because of its forceful, linear, and persistent style, which is optimal for scientific exploration. On the other hand, the dialectical reasoning represented by Chinese would be "yin," because of its tolerant, holistic, and flexible style, which is optimal for negotiating in complex social interactions. Therefore, the ideal state or ultimate strength of human thinking should be a combination of both yin and yang, a synthesis of many different ways of thinking.

REFERENCES

Adelman, L., & Morris, C. T. (1967). *Society, politics and economic development: A quantitative approach*. Baltimore: Johns Hopkins University Press.

Arewa, E., & Dundes, A. (1964). Proverbs and the ethnography of speaking folklore. *American Anthropologist, 66,* 70–85.

Ayalti, H. (1963). *Yiddish proverbs*. New York: Schocken Books.

Bakan, D. (1966). *The duality of human existence*. Chicago: Rand McNally.

Barry, H., Child, I., & Bacon, M. (1959). Relation of child training to subsistence economy. *American Anthropologist, 61*, 51–63.

Bellah, R. N., Madsen, R., Sullivan, W. M., Swindler, A., & Tipton, S.M. (1985). *Habits of the heart: Individualism and commitment in American life*. Berkeley: University of California Press.

Berger, P., Berger, P., & Kelner, H. (1973). *The homeless mind*. New York: Random House.

Berry, J. W. (1976). *Human ecology and cognitive style: Comparative studies in cultural and psychological adaptation*. New York: Sage/Halsted.

Berry, J. W. (1979). A cultural ecology of social behavior. In L. Berkowitz (Ed.), *Advances in experimental social psychology* (pp. 177–207). New York: Academic Press.

Bond, M. H. (1988). Finding universal dimensions of individual variation in multicultural studies of values: The Rokeach and Chinese value surveys. *Journal of Personality and Social Psychology, 55*, 1009–1015.

Bond, M. H. (1991). Beyond the Chinese face: Insights from Psychology. Oxford University Press, New York.

Cao, C. J. (1982). *Explanation of Zhung Zi*. Beijing: Zhong Hua Publish House. (In Chinese).

Caropra, F. (1975). *The tao of physics*. Berkeley: Shambala.

Dasen, P. R. (1972). Cross-cultural Piagetian research: A summary. *Journal of Cross-Cultural Psychology, 3*, 23–40

Dasen, P. R. (1977). *Piagetian psychology: Cross cultural contributions*. New York: Gardner Press.

Hang, T. C. (1966). *Chinese national character*. Taipei: Shang Wu Co. (In Chinese).

Hansen, C. (1983). *Language and logic in ancient China*. Ann Arbor: University of Michigan Press.

Hoftsted, G. (1980). *Culture's consequences: International differences in work-related values*. Beverly Hills, CA: Sage.

Hofstede, G. (1984). National cultures revisited. *Behavior Science Research, 18*, 285–305.

Hofstede, G., & Bond, M. (1984). Hofstede's culture dimensions: An independent validation using Rokeach's Value Survey. *Journal of Cross-cultural Psychology, 15*, 417–433.

Hsu, F. L. K. (1953). *Americans and Chinese: Two ways of life*. New York: H. Schuman

Hsu, F. L. K. (1981). *Americans and Chinese: Passage to differences* (3rd ed). Honolulu: University of Hawaii Press.

Inkeles, A., & Smith, D.H. (1974). *Becoming modern*. Cambridge, MA: Harvard University Press.

Ji, L., & Peng, K. & Nisbett, R. (2000). Culture, control and perception of relations in environment. *Journal of Personality and Social Psychology, 78*, 943–955.

Kluckhorn, F., & Strodbeck, F. (1961). *Variations in value orientations*. Evanston, IL: Row, Peterson.

Lao-Zi. (570?-490? BC/1993). *The book of Lao Zi*. Beijing: Foreign Language Press.

Lee, F., Hallahan, M., & Herzog, T. (1996). Explaining real-life events: How culture and domain shape attributions. *Personality and Social Psychology Bulletin, 22*, 732–741.

Li, Z. L. (1989). On the dual characters of Chinese traditional thinking modes and difficulty in changing them. *Studies on Chinese traditional philosophy and culture*. (In Chinese).

Lian, S. (1964). *Far East English-English, English-Chinese Dictionary of Idioms and Phrases*. Taipei: Far East Publish House.

Liu, S. H. (1974). The use of analogy and symbolism in tradictional Chinese philosophy. *Journal of Chinese Philosophy, 1*, 313–338.

Liu, X. G. (1988). *The philosophy of Zhung Zi and its evolution*. Beijing: The Social Science Press of China. (In Chinese).

Lloyd, G. E. R. (1990). *Demystifying mentalities*. Cambridge: Cambridge University Press.

Mao, T-T. (1937/1962). *Four essays on philosophy*. Beijing: People's Press. (In Chinese).

Markus, H. & Kitayama, S. (1991). Culture and the self: Implications for cognition, emotion, and motivation. *Psychological Review, 98*, 224–253.

Mieder, W. (1993). *Proverbs are never out of season: Popular Wisdom in the Modern Age*. Oxford: Oxford University Press.

Moore, C. A. (1967). Introduction: The humanistic Chinese mind. In Charles A. Moore (ed). *The Chinese mind: Essentials of Chinese philosophy and culture*. Honolulu, East-West Center Press.

Morris, M., & Peng, K. (1994). Culture and cause: American and Chinese Attribution of physical and social events. *Journal of Personality and Social psychology, 67*, 949–971.

Morris, M., Nisbett, R., & Peng, K. (1993). Causal understanding across domains and cultures. In D. Sperber and D. Premack (Eds.). *Causal Cognition: Multidisciplinary debates*. Oxford University Press.

Munro, D. J. (1969). *The concept of man in early China*. Stanford, CA: Stanford University Press.

Munro, D. J. (1977). *The concept of man in contemporary China*. Ann Arbor: University of Michigan Press.

Munro, D. J. (1985). *Individualism and holism: Studies in Confucian and Taoist values*. Ann Arbor: Center for Chinese Studies, University of Michigan.

Nakamura, H. (1964). *Ways of thinking of Eastern peoples: India, China, Tibet, Japan*. Honolulu: East-West Center Press.

Needham, J. (1954). *Science and civilization in China*: Volume I. Cambridge: University Press.

Needham, J. (1962). *Science and Civilization in China (Volume IV. Physics and physical technology)*. Cambridge: Cambridge University Press.

Nisbett, R., Peng, K., Choi, I., & Norenzanan, A. (2001). Culture and system of thoughts: Holistic versus analytic cognition. *Psychological Review, 108*, 291–310.

Northrop, F. S. C. (1946). *The meeting of East and West: An inquiry concerning world understanding*. New York: The Macmillan Company.

Northrop, F. S. C. (1966). *The meeting of East and West: An inquiry concerning world understanding*. New York: Collier Books.

Parson, T., & Shils, E.A. (1951). *Toward a general theory of action*. Cambridge, MA: Harvard University Press.

Peng, K. & Ames, D. (2001). Psychology of dialectical thinking. In N. Smelser & P. Baltes (Eds.). *International encyclopedia of the Social and Behavior sciences*. Oxford, England: Elsevier Science.

Peng, K., Ames, D., & Knowles, E. (2001). Culture and human inference: Perspectives from three traditions. In D. Masumoto (Ed). *Handbook of culture and psychology* (pp. 243–263) New York: Oxford University Press.

Peng, K., & Knowles, E. D. (2003). Culture, education, and the attribution of physical causality. *Personality and Social Psychology Bulletin, 29* (10), 1272–1284.

Peng, K. & Nisbett, R. (1999). Culture, dialectics, and reasoning about contradiction. *American Psychologist, 54*, 741–754.

Peng, K. & Nisbett, R. (2000). Dialectical responses to questions on dialectical thinking. *American Psychologist, 55*, 1067–1068.

Piaget, J. (1980). *Experiments in contradiction*. Chicago: University of Chicago Press.

Phillips, L. D, & Wright, G. N. (1977). Cultural differences in viewing uncertainty and assessing probabilities. In H. Jungermann and G.de Zeeuw (Eds.), *Decision making and change in human affairs*, Dordrecht: D. Reidel.

Riegel, K.F. (1973). Dialectical operations: The final period of cognitive development. *Human Development, 18*, 430–443.

Rodgers, J. & Peng, K. (2005). The dialectical self:Contradiction, change, and holism in the East Asian self concept. In RM Sorrentino, D. Cohen, JM. Olson, & MP, Zanna. (eds.). *Culture and social behaviour: The Ontario Symposium, 10*, 227–249. Mahwah, NJ, US: Lawrence Erlbaum Associatles, Publishers.

Shen, D. (1985). *Mo Jing Luo Ji Xue (The logic of Mo Jing)*. Beijing: The Social Science Press of China. (In Chinese).

Spencer-Rodgers, J., et al, (2004). Dialectical self-esteem and East-West differences in psychological well-being. *Personality and Social Psychology Bulletin*. 30, 1416–1432.

Spencer-Rodgers, J., Boucher, H. C., Mori, S., Wang, L., & Peng, K. (2005). *Culture and self-perception: Naïve dialecticism and East Asian conceptual selves*. Unpublished manuscript, University of California, Berkeley.

Shweder, R. A. (1982). *Beyond self-constructed knowledge: The study of culture and morality*. Merrill-Palmer Quarterly, 28, 41–69.

Triandis, H. C. (1989). Cross-cultural studies of individualism and collectivism. *Nebraska Symposium on Motivation*. Lincoln: University of Nebraska Press.

Triandis, H. C. (1995). *Individualism and collectivism*. Boulder: Westview Press.

Wang, M. (1987). *Studies on Daoism and Daoist religion*. Beijing: The Social Science Press of China. (In Chinese).

Wang, D. J. (1979). *The history of Chinese logical thought*. Shanghai: People's Press of Shanghai.(In Chinese).

Wright, G. N., & Phillips, L. D. (1980). Cultural variation in probabilistic thinking: Alternative ways of dealing with uncertainty. *International Journal of Psychology, 15*, 239–257.

Yang, K. S. (1986). Chinese personality and its change. In Bond, M. H. (ed). *The psychology of the Chinese people* (pp. 160–170). Hong Kong: Oxford University Press.

Yates, J. F., & Lee, J. (1996). Chinese decision-making. In M.H. Bond (Ed.), *The handbook of Chinese psychology*. Hong Kong: Oxford University Press.

Yates, J. F., Lee, J., & Shinotsuka, H. (1996). Beliefs about overconfidence, including its cross-national variation. *Organizational Behavior & Human Decision Processes, 65*, 138–147.

Yates, J. F., Lee, J., & Bush, J. (1997). General knowledge overconfidence: Cross-national variations, response style, and "reality." *Organizational behavior and human decision processes*.

Zhang, D. L. (1985). *The concept of "Tian Ren He Yi" in Chinese philosophy*. Beijing University Journal, 1, p.8. (In Chinese).

Zhang, D. L., & Chen, Z. Y. (1991). *Zhongguo Siwei Pianxiang (The orientation of Chinese thinking)*. Beijing: Social Science Press. (In Chinese).

Zhou, G. X. (1990). *Chinese traditional philosophy*. Beijing: Beijing Normal University Press (In Chinese).

Zhuang-zi. (370?-301?/1968). *The complete works of Chuang Tzu* (Translated by Watson, B.) New York: Columbia University Press.

Chapter 12

Indian Perspectives on Cognition

R. C. Mishra

This chapter examines Indian perspectives on cognition to show how cognition is conceptualized in traditional Indian systems of thought. Parallels between Indian and Western conceptualizations of cognition are pointed out. Effort is also made to examine the way in which traditional Indian interpretations of cognition can be integrated with current thinking about cognition in general, and cognitive processes and their development in particular.

HISTORICAL ROOTS

Generally speaking, cognition refers to every process by which individuals obtain and utilize knowledge (Mishra, 1997). This knowledge may be about the self or the external world, and may be real or imagined. Analysis, recognition, labeling, categorization, thinking, reasoning, and planning constitute the fundamental processes of cognition. They are implicated in several behavioral domains. Psychologists and educators have taken an interest in the study of these processes for a long time. The common questions asked are: How do people come to know about themselves and their environment? Are there some general principles of the acquisition of knowledge? Does this knowledge come mainly through biological maturity, or through the individual's interaction with the environment, or through self-reflection? Is this knowledge absolute, or is it relative to individuals' physical, social, cultural, and psychological conditions? Both Western and Indian theorists have addressed these questions in the context of cognition.

A glance at the state of affairs in this field would suggest that ancient thinkers in India (and also in the West) did not really make a distinction between different disciplines of knowledge. In recent decades divisions in the field represented only convenient arrangements for the study of a specific set of phenomena by specific groups of people. As a result, quite interesting communication and sharing among various disciplines in the previous decades is evident. This is particularly true in India where most psychology departments were nested in a department of philosophy. In later years, the desire of psychologists to move closer to the natural sciences led to communication breakdowns to the extent that psychology and philosophy were considered to devote themselves to very different goals. For example, Watson (1913) portrayed philosophy as "armchair speculation," and psychology as a science concerned primarily with the solution of practical problems through behavioral technology.

During the following decades, this line of thinking became fairly strong in the West through the work of Skinner and other behaviorists. Consequently, psychology in the West came to be widely regarded as an anti-philosophical and anti-religious discipline. It grew more along the lines of the physical sciences. Laboratories served as the ideal place, and "reductionism" as the ideal approach for the study of psychological phenomena. Problems that could not be studied in the laboratory applying the principle of reduction were dropped from the domain of mainstream psychology (Berry, Mishra, & Tripathi, 2003; Mishra, 1981). The study of cognitive phenomena in the West largely followed this lead for several decades. This trend was so strongly reflected in India that psychology here came to be regarded as "largely imitative" (Pandey, 1988). The effect was evident in the choice of western concepts, models, theories, and methods of study. As Asthana (1988) remarked, "The concerns of western psychology of yester years are the current interest of the Indian psychologists" (p. 155–156).

The sole exception is perhaps the area of consciousness studies (Rao, 2001), which has inspired at least some research worldwide based on concepts and models derived from classical Indian thought. Although it has generated a reverse flow of activities from the Indian to the western world (e.g., in research on yoga and meditation), the richness of Indian philosophy has not yet been much utilized in the development and practice of psychology either in India or in the West.

THE CONSTRUCTIONIST APPROACH

In relatively recent years, many scholars have resorted to a trend of thought, which is now referred to as "constructionist." Piaget (1954) pioneered this view of cognition in psychology in his book, *The Construction of Reality in the Child*. Gergen (1985) and Harré (1986, 1987) popularized it in psychology in relatively more recent years. This perspective stands in sharp contrast to the highly reductionism view of cognition presented by the positivistic scientific tradition in psychology.

According to the constructionist perspective, human beings cognitively construct and reconstruct a view of the world around them. All people, whether children or adults, laypeople or philosophers, religious or scientific, are involved in the task of construction, although they may represent different levels of sophistication in their efforts. Piaget's work demonstrates how infants begin to know about the world around them through their sensory (e.g., looking, listening, smelling) and motor (e.g., grasping, sucking) activities. Gradually many complex cognitive structures or capacities emerge that allow them to engage in formal thinking based on abstraction and logic. Thus, Piaget finds in children the representation of a philosopher who is seriously concerned with the discovery of causality in various events encountered in the surrounding world. In doing so, children behave much like a scientist; they engage in experimentally verifying the lawful relationships among a variety of natural events. This approach departs from mechanistic models by allowing a greater role to individuals during the formative years of their cognition.

THE INDIGENOUS PSYCHOLOGY OF INDIA

The indigenous psychology of India is deeply rooted in the philosophical and religious thoughts of the ancient sages. Diversity among philosophers in explaining cognitive phenomena has led to the emergence of several schools of thought, which present somewhat diverse views on human cognition. It would be difficult to present an account of the different views exemplified by these various schools. On the other hand, a search for broad similarities among them reveals that many seem to accept either the authority of the *Vedas* (the ancient most scriptural texts in India considered to be created by God and realized by seers), or the *Upanishads* (the philosophical treatise created towards the later phase of the long period when Vedic texts were composed, probably 1,500–600 BCE).

It is believed that even Buddha (563–483 BCE), who did not accept the authority of the Vedic scriptures, knew the teachings of many of these Upanishads, and considered them not only unorthodox, but also quite useful for humanity at large. Later, several other systems of philosophy, such as *Mimansa, Vedant, Sankhya, Yoga, Nyaya* and *Vaishesik*, emerged from attempts aimed at providing integrated theories based on interpretation of the *Upanishads*.

While these traditional sources continue to serve as treasures of psychological thinking and knowledge, several scholarly monographs dealing with the fundamental nature and scope of Indian psychology have also been produced in the last few decades. They comprise most of what seems to be relevant today for the development of psychological science, and address topics ranging from basic psychological processes (e.g., sensation, perception) to broader domains of human behavior (e.g., human happiness and health).

The most frequently quoted volumes are *Hindu Psychology: Its Meaning for the West* (Akhilanand, 1948) and *Asian Psychology* (Murphy & Murphy, 1968). Three volumes of *Indian Psychology* have been published. They constitute the richest source for discovering classical Indian psychological ideas. The first volume of this book (Sinha, 1958/1986) is wholly devoted to cognition; it covers a whole range of topics including, perception, memory, imagination, language, and thinking, with material on dreams as well as abnormal and supernormal perception. *Development of Psychological Thought in India* (Ramachandra Rao, 1962) is another important work on Indian thought. Safaya's (1975) *Indian Psychology* presents a critical analysis of psychological speculation in Indian philosophical literature, and proclaims that "Indian psychology not only exists, but surpasses Western psychology in scope, methodology, and validity of conclusions" (p. 5). Kuppuswamy (1985) published *Elements of Ancient Indian Psychology*. Paranjpe's (1984) book, *Theoretical Psychology: The Meeting of East and West* is currently one of the most frequently cited and influential publications. Another book, *Self and Identity in Modern Psychology and Indian Thought* (Paranjpe, 1998) is also equally influential. Discussion of the cognitive aspect of self in this book is highly stimulating for those who wish to understand cognition from an Indian point of view.

It may be mentioned at the outset that although all of these publications seem to be pregnant with grand ideas, conceptual schemes, and theoretical underpinnings, they have not stimulated much scientific research in psychology in general, or on cognition in particular (except for a few studies that try to apply and validate Indian concepts (e.g., Dwivedi, 1987)). Thus, while presenting Indian perspectives on cognition in this chapter, the conceptual and theoretical aspects of cognitive phenomena will surface more than empirical aspects. However, an attempt will be made to link the Indian viewpoint with those that are popular in the current scientific research on cognition.

Cognition in Indian Perspectives

Much discussion of the Indian perspective on cognition can be found in the ancient scriptures produced in Sanskrit as well as in the collections and interpretations made during the past few decades by both Indian and western scholars. First of all, there is no equivalent term in Sanskrit that can exactly capture the meaning of cognition in the sense it is used in the discipline of psychology today. The closest term is *jnana*, which is usually translated into English as "knowledge". The popular term used in textbooks written in Hindi is *sanjnana*, which literally means "appropriate knowledge". There are difficulties in accepting these meanings of cognition. For example, knowledge generally involves the notion of veridical cognition, whereas *jnana* does not necessarily imply veridicality. According to Datta (1932), the word *jnana* stands for all kinds of cognition, whether it is veridical (*yathartha*) or non-veridical (*mithya*). Then, there are several sources that produce different types of knowledge or *janana*. One form of this knowledge is scientific (e.g., knowledge of mathematics, physics, or history). Another form of knowledge is collective (e.g., knowledge of a group of people through traditions), and still another form is personal (e.g., personal experiences). While the first form of knowledge may be acceptable to scientists, the other two forms may not be acceptable as valid sources of knowledge (Krishnamurthy, 1998).

There is another word in Sanskrit, *prama*, which means valid cognition. One of its grammatical derivations is *pramatri*, which means the "knower" (i.e., the one who tries to obtain valid cognition). Another grammatical derivation, *pramana*, refers to the source that causes or brings about knowledge and validates cognition. Consciousness is regarded as the first stage of cognition. This conceptualization goes against the notion of Freud (1915) and Jung (1958), who showed how complex thought processes could occur without awareness.

Indian philosophical literature deals with the problems of consciousness in a very detailed manner. First of all, it is believed that the unconscious is not the negation of consciousness; instead, it refers to mental phenomena that are not readily available to introspection. Secondly, it presents an elaborate account of sense organs, which are held responsible for all kinds of consciousness. Buddhists recognize six types of sense organs: visual, auditory, olfactory, gustatory, tactile, and mental, each having a different basis. The cognitive faculty that apprehends objects that cannot be sensed is called *mind*. Although mind is immaterial and invisible, it is considered as a sense organ in Buddhist as well as other systems of Indian thought.

A distinction is made between the organs of knowledge (e.g., eye, ear, called *buddhindriya*) and the organs of action (e.g., hand, feet, called *karmendriya*). The former serve as instruments of knowledge; the latter serve as instruments for the expression and conduction of knowledge. This distinction is very similar to the distinction made between sensory and motor mechanisms through which organisms know about the external world and interact with it. These are called external organs or senses. The function of these senses is presided over by internal senses that include *manas* (mind), *ahamkara* (empirical ego), and *buddhi* (intellect). The external organs or senses provide an immediate impression of various objects in a discrete form. This impression is synthesized by the mind (the internal sense), and the knowledge based on it is further synthesized and validated by the other two internal senses respectively. Thus, *manas* is viewed as the chief organ in relation to the functions of the external senses; *ahamkara* is regarded as the chief organ in relation to the functions of *manas*; and *buddhi* is regarded as the chief organ in relation to the functions of *ahamkara*.

The external senses can apprehend only the present, whereas the internal senses can apprehend not only present, but also past and future. In this sense, the latter appear to be more vital organs than the former.

There is much discussion of the relationship between knowledge (*jnana*) and intellect (*buddhi*). It is argued that intellect has the capacity to utilize knowledge in order to think clearly, objectively, and understandably. It is a capacity of direct apperception. Thus, on the one hand, one finds knowledge that is always linked to the past, and to which something is always being added. On the other hand is the intellect, which is extremely sensitive, alert, and awakened. Because of these inherent qualities, intellect neither holds on to a particular decision or evaluation, nor is it conditioned with a particular place, time, or person. Sensitivity is regarded as the most significant characteristic of intellect. In the absence of sensitivity, knowledge may turn out to be extremely dangerous. For example, it can be used for all sorts of destructive purposes. Hence, the Indian systems of thought strongly aim at achieving consistency and balance between knowledge and intellect so that knowledge can lead to positive outcomes.

The Indian view of cognition presented in philosophical traditions also involves the notion of *atman* (individual self) or *jiva* (the embodied person) that is seated within individuals and is destined not only with the capacity of knowing, but also with the capacity of acting and enjoying. The notion of *atman* or *jiva* as the "knower" in the Indian system of thought highlights the importance of the underlying structures and processes operating within an individual to account for cognitions or cognitive outcomes. Our beliefs, faiths, and opinions constitute the parts of the cognitive system as long as they help organize new information in understandable ways.

This conceptualization appears to be very close to the information processing viewpoint currently so popular in psychology. Various schemes of organization and their roles in cognitive processing represent a dominant theme in research on cognition today. In order to understand the known, a thorough understanding of the manner in which the knower operates is considered important in the Indian system of thought. Several practices are prescribed for the knower to guard against the biases and prejudices that often enter into the process of knowledge and color it with various shades. Pure knowledge is free from all kinds of biases. It has no boundaries of time, place, or person; it is universal in the true sense of the term.

COGNITIVE PROCESSES

Indian thinkers have attempted to conceptualize several cognitive processes. In the following discussion, the focus is particularly on consciousness, perception, memory, imagination, and thought processes.

Consciousness

As discussed earlier, Indian thinkers consider consciousness as the first stage of cognition. Since a lot of what follows later in cognitive terms is determined mainly by what happens to objects or events at this stage, a thorough understanding of this process is considered extremely important.

Rao (2001) presented a major review of consciousness studies. He clearly observed that "the importance of consciousness studies in the Indian context is not based on the strength of Indian psychological researches in this area but on the significance and heuristic value of classical Indian ideas to contemporary concerns in consciousness studies" (p. 19–20). *Consciousness* is often used as if it is synonymous with *awareness*. The process may be implicit or explicit. In its implicit form it refers to the underlying principle of all mental phenomena or the source of one's subjective experience. In its explicit form it refers to the awareness of specific objects and events whether they are real or imaginary. In this sense, consciousness always seems to be conscious of something.

Indian theories of consciousness try to answer three fundamental questions (Mohanty, 1993): (1) Does consciousness necessarily manifest itself as it manifests its objects, (2) is consciousness by its essential nature linked to an object, and (3) does consciousness have a form, structure, or content of its own? Yoga, Vedant, and Buddhist theories have particularly attempted to address these questions.

The theory of yoga proposes that there are essentially two principles that govern one's being. These are called *purusha* (consciousness) and *prakriti* (matter). *Purusha* is pure consciousness. It has no qualities or characteristics of its own. Hence, it cannot be perceived; its presence can only be inferred from the manifest purposefulness in the universe. On the other hand, *prakriti* is the material basis of a person's being, which is characterized by three fundamental features (*guna*), called *sattva* (essence), *rajas* (energy) and *tamas* (mass). Everything in this universe evolves from *prakriti*. In this process the incoherent, indeterminate, and undifferentiated *prakriti* manifests in a coherent, determinate, and differentiated form (Dasgupta, 1922/1988).

In yoga, the functional mind of an individual is called *chitta*. It comprises not only cognitive processes, but also instinctual tendencies inherited from previous lives including past experiences and their effects (called *vasanas* and *samskaras*). Yoga also prescribes an eightfold path to attain the highest state of consciousness in which the consciousness is realized as such without any phenomenal awareness. *Advait vedant* distinguishes between four states of consciousness; (a) the waking state, (2) the dream state, (3) the deep sleep state, and (4) the transcendental state. It is the first state in which the contents of consciousness are largely determined by external objects. On the other hand, Buddhists have identified some 121 states of consciousness based on a profound understanding of several cognitive, conative, and emotive factors that enter into the determination of consciousness at any given time.

Perception

Perception is another important cognitive process to which Indian thinkers have devoted substantial attention. In doing so, they generally recognize two distinct stages of perception: *nirvikalpa* (indeterminate) and *savikalpa* (determinate). The former refers to the immediate apprehension of the form of an object; the latter refers to the mediate perception of an object (recognition or naming) with its different properties and their relationship with each other. In modern psychological terminology, the former may be regarded as undifferentiated cognition, and the latter as differentiated cognition. Psychological differentiation theory (Witkin et al, 1962) proposes that cognitive development proceeds from an undifferentiated or less differentiated state to a more differentiated state of functioning. A number of indicators have been identified to assess the level of differentiation in different behavioral domains. Studies have presented the ecological, social, and cultural determinants of psychological differentiation (Berry, 1976; Berry, et al, 1986; Mishra et al, 1996).

The distinction between indeterminate and determinate perceptions has engaged the attention of Indian thinkers for centuries. In general, most schools of thought consider perception as indeterminate. This means that perception does not apprehend qualifications like generality, substantiality, quality, action, and the names of objects. These are supplied to the individual by other faculties of cognition, and form part of determinate perception. Thus, indeterminate perception is simple and common to everyone. On the other hand, determinate perception is complex and specific to individuals depending on how they apprehend and construct it. Only in the school of *Vedant* has the existence of indeterminate perception been denied by arguing that there can be no thought without language, and hence no nameless indeterminate perception. This position seems to be quite similar to the position exemplified in the theory of linguistic relativity (Gumperz & Levinson, 1996; Levinson, 2003; Whorf, 1956).

Some interpreters have argued that indeterminate perception does not necessarily imply the use of external sense organs. The cognition of such sentences as "This is an orange" (a fruit) does not lie in its sensuous origin. They are based on the identification of apprehending mode with the apprehended object, which is capable of being perceived and present at the time of cognition. In this case, the orange (the apprehended object) is present to the apprehending mental mode, which goes out to the object and identifies itself with the object. Thus, the cognition produced by the above-mentioned sentence satisfies all the conditions of perception, and hence it may be regarded as perceptual in nature.

The above discussion suggests that in the Indian system of thought, perception is taken much in the sense of cognition. While indeterminate perception involves immediacy (the criterion often used in psychology to distinguish between perception and cognition), determinate perception involves elaboration, active construction, and interpretation in physical or mental (image) forms of the information provided by sensory organs.

The foregoing discussion also suggests that indeterminate perception is a process that provides purely presentational knowledge of an object. On the other hand, determinate perception involves both the presentational and representational forms of knowledge. It deals not only with direct perception of an object, but also its relationship with and differentiation from other objects.

Some thinkers hold the view that perception involves an element of inference, which is a major characteristic of cognition. According to them, a complete perception takes place in the following five stages: (1) perceiving an object, e.g., a fruit (mango), (2) remembering the pleasure given by that fruit (mango) in the past, (3) knowing the relationship between the major and the minor terms (e.g., this "fruit" belongs to the class of "mango", called *paramarsajnana*), (4) inferring the pleasure-giving property of the fruit perceived as "mango" (called *sukhsadhanatva*), and (5) inferring the acceptability of the object (i.e., mango). The last two stages are akin to the processes of syllogistic reasoning studied by Luria (1976). For example, at the fourth stage, it would be something like this: "All mangoes are pleasure-giving; the perceived fruit is a mango; therefore, the perceived fruit must be pleasure-giving". At the fifth stage, the inference would be like this: "All things that give pleasure are acceptable (*upadeya*), the perceived mango gives pleasure; therefore, the perceived mango is acceptable." Thus, a complete act of perception involves recognition, memory, inference and acceptability. Many of these processes are not directly linked to sense organs; instead, they constitute the processes of mind, and represent the higher cognitive function of human beings.

In dealing with the process of perception, Indian thinkers have postulated several kinds of intercourse (*sannikarsa*) of the sense organs with their objects, which produce different kinds of effects (interpretations). As individuals we acquire most of our knowledge of the surrounding world through *laukik* (ordinary) or *alaukika* (extraordinary) intercourse of our sense organs with objects. The former forms the basis of perception within a given sense modality (e.g., knowledge of form or shape through visual sense modality). The latter forms the basis of perception across different sense modalities (e.g., knowledge of form or shape through tactual sense modality). This explains the interrelationship among different sense modalities, i.e., how a particular kind of knowledge acquired through one sense modality can be transferred to and accepted by another sense modality.

Supernormal Perception

Supernormal perception refers to those cognitions that transcend the categories of space, time, and causality. Indian thinkers generally believe that only through this process is the apprehension of the real nature of things possible. This perception involves higher level processes, and is beyond the ordinary or general laws and conditions of perception. It occurs through the powers of occult medicines, incantations, and the practice of austerities and intense meditation.

Indian and western scholars have tried to understand the processes of supernormal perceptions. While some of this work is mainly anecdotal (e.g., Chari, 1959; Thurston, 1993), other studies that focus on extra sensory perception (ESP, Rhine, 1934) are empirical in nature. A major finding of these studies is that ESP occurs mostly in the form of dreams and waking intuitive experiences. Studies (e.g., Grosso, 1990; Haraldsson, 1987) focusing on "miracle makers" have provided mixed results. Since these studies have not been carried out under controlled conditions, one still does not know what is true in this case or similar cases.

Some schools of thought deny the existence of supernormal perceptions. They argue that various practices can modify only the manifestation of natural capacities of the sense organs, which are limited to functioning in particular sphere(s). For example, the ear can never perceive color or taste even if it is extremely refined by the application of medicine or the practice of yoga or meditation. Hence, supernormal perceptions can, at best, refer to the recollection or memories of the past.

Much debate persists on the nature of yogic perception in the state of ecstasy (*samadhi*). In general, it is considered to be a kind of immediate intellectual intuition through which one can apprehend all objects of the world simultaneously. This is a supra-conscious stage that a person can reach in the highest stage of spiritual life after having conquered all desires and cravings of an ordinary worldly life. Such an intuitive cognition is also called "*arsa-jnana*" (seer's perception during ecstasy), which is produced by direct experience, not by inferential marks.

Studies carried out with respect to the effect of meditation on perception have demonstrated positive outcomes. Rao, Dukhan and Rao (1984) studied the ESP of a group of subjects who were practicing a standard form of meditation. A comparison of pre and post meditation ESP scores was attempted. The findings revealed that before the meditation session, the participants obtained very low hit proportions. The same participants obtained significantly higher hit scores immediately after meditation than they did before meditation, indicating the development of ESP as a result of participation in the meditation program. In a previous study also, Rao and Rao (1982) obtained somewhat similar results. In the first experiment of their study they examined the relationship between ESP and subliminal perception (SP), and found no evidence of relationship between the two measures. In the second experiment, they examined the same relationships again, but this time, one group of participants was allowed to practice Transcendental Meditation (TM), while the other group served as a control. The findings revealed a significantly positive correlation between the ESP and SP scores of the TM group, but not of the control group. Comparison of the ESP and SP scores of the TM and control groups revealed that the TM group performed better than the control on the SP task, but not on the ESP task. The findings also indicated that participants in the TM group who produced more SP hits than the mean hits of the group produced significantly more ESP hits than the high SP participants in the control group. These results suggested that the relationship between ESP and SP might depend on the strength of the subliminal signals and the state of the individual. It was argued that the ESP might be meaningfully related to other unconscious and subconscious phenomenon such as subliminal perception.

While these studies may appear to be quite impressive, it may be noted that the standard forms of meditation (e.g., TM) are not comparable with the state of ecstasy (*samadhi*). Hence, perceptual and other cognitive phenomena noted under the conditions of meditation and *samadhi* represent neither the same experience, nor do they convey the same meaning. The Indian notions of yoga and *samadhi* need a deeper level of operationalization and research using techniques other than those that are currently in practice in psychological science.

Memory

Memory has been a fascinating topic of discussion in Indian systems of thought. It is generally taken as a kind of recollection or recognition of previous experiences. This conceptualization is very similar to the way it is generally held by psychologists today. The most powerful exposition of memory is given in the *Nyaya* tradition of Indian thought. It is argued that recollection presupposes and implies a past apprehension of an object by the self, an impression (*samskara*) produced by the past apprehension of the same self, awakening (*udbodha*) of the impression by excitants, recognition of the recalled object as perceived in the past by the same self, temporal localization in the past and identity of the self (Sinha, 1958). The most important thing in this respect is the "identity of the self". This means that the self that recalls an object must be the same one that had perceived it in the past. If there were no identity of the self, there would either be no recollection, or there would be recollection of other's impressions. Such a viewpoint implies that retention (*dharana*) and recall (*smriti*) are the fundamental elements of memory that mutually define each other's existence.

Theorists have taken different stands on the definition of *recollection*. Some assert that recollection cognizes an object that was perceived in the past. Others define it as cognition that occurs either due to the revival of the impression generated by the perception of an object on a pervious occasion, or as merely due to the psychological presence of a particular cue. In this sense, it is a kind of representative cognition elicited by the physical or psychological availability of cues. This notion is basically one of "cue-dependent" memory, which fairly matches the current conceptualization of memory. It is also indicated that recollection is a mediate knowledge (*paroksa jnana*), because an object that was perceived in the past and is remembered at present can never be as vivid as an object being perceived in the present. Thus, there is always the chance of misrepresentation and distortion in memory.

A distinction is maintained between recollection and recognition. It is argued that recollection is concerned with cognizing objects experienced in the past, whereas recognition is concerned with cognizing objects qualified by both the past and the present. This means that recollection is based solely on impression; it does not require the presence of the object, whereas recognition involves sense-object intercourse, which is aided by impression. Thus, although they serve as measures of memory, recall and recognition differ in terms of their underlying processes. Indian thinkers believe that recalling is an internal process. However, this process is also expressed through a number of objective indicators such as shaking the head or turning the head upward, lowering or raising eyebrows, looking at the sky, gazing, or inhibition of body movements. Since these behaviors facilitate recall, they are generally considered "aids of recall". Memory aids are the most current topic of present day discussion and research on retention.

Indian thinkers also propose a distinction between two types of memory: *passive memory* and *active memory*. Passive memory is characterized by spontaneous recall of objects depending entirely on their impressions without involving any act of construction. Active memory depends largely on a person's will to remember. Hence, it involves certain acts of construction. A distinction is also made between valid recollection and invalid recollection. If the past apprehension is valid, recollection will also be valid. If it is invalid, the recollection will also be invalid. Thus, the validity of recollection depends on the degree of strength with which an object or event has been experienced in the past. This viewpoint is very similar to encoding theory in which the accuracy of recall is predicted by the strength of encoding.

In conceptualizing memory, Indian thinkers have given great emphasis to impressions (*samskara*), broadly defined as residua (*vasana*) of momentary cognitions. The intensity of impression may vary depending on a number of factors. This conceptualization is very close to the one proposed in trace theories of memory. The more frequent the perception of an object or event, the stronger and more durable the impression is likely to be.

Indian thought systems also present an elaborate discussion of the conditions of retention. One of these is the *healthy and vigorous condition of the body*. The *intensity* with which an object is attended to and perceived produces deep impressions (*samskaratisaya*) and results in better memory of that object. *Repeated experience or frequency of experience* of objects also produces deep impressions and stronger memory, and so does the *strange or interesting nature of objects*.

Things committed to memory cannot always be recollected automatically. Indian thought system discusses several conditions that may facilitate recall. The Buddhists enumerate 16 conditions of recall, which include not only the characteristics of stimuli, learning conditions, or learning cues, but also the characteristics of learners and the strategies they adopt. Recent research on recall memory also attempts to explain success or failure of recall in terms of these factors. These factors are classified as material causes (*samavai karan*), nonmaterial causes (*asamavayi karan*), and situational causes (*nimitta karan*) of retention and forgetting.

Other systems of Indian thought have also produced elaborate models of memory. For example, Gautam, a leading scholar of one of the thought systems, discusses 25 factors (e.g., attention, context, practice, need, etc.) that may influence learning of materials and their subsequent recall. However, these factors can be easily fitted into the same classificatory scheme as described with respect to Buddhist factors.

Does memory arise within individuals subjectively, or is it called upon by something outside the individual? Indian thinkers seemingly believe both. They deal with certain excitants (*udvodhaka*) of recall, some of which are located outside the individual such as associations (*sahacharya*) due to the similarity of objects, whereas others, such as reflection (*cinta*), are located within the individual.

Loss of memory is another important issue to which Indian thinkers have paid substantial attention. Since memory is largely explained in terms of impressions of past experiences, forgetting is often defined as the destruction of the impression of past experiences. This may take place for several reasons such as lapse of time, organic conditions (e.g., in physical and mental illness), obscuration or destruction of impressions, contrary cognitions, obliteration of impressions, emotional states, preoccupation of mind, and delusion or impairment of intellect. All of these factors have been implicated in western research on memory in one way or another; some of them have also served as the basis for the development of grand theories of memory.

Imagination

Although some recollections seem to involve imagination, Indian scholars propose a distinction between recollection and imagination. It is argued that recollection focuses on objects experienced in the past; it never goes beyond the limits of past experience. On the other hand, imagination generally transcends the limits of past experience, and in doing so it not only creates new order into the contents of past experience, but also adds some new dimensions to the objects or events. Thus, while in memory an individual is constrained by the subject matter experienced in the past, one is entirely free in imagination to reconstruct past experiences and to add some new elements to it that were not already there. Imagination belongs to the "territory of mind" (*manorajya*) in which one can exercise free will in given situations.

The mental process that deals with cognitions that are devoid of objects is called *vikalpa*. For example, when we speak of "sky flower", we have just a word (cognition) for something that does not correspond to a real object. Such cognitions are often referred to as *invalid cognitions*, because they are contained in words whose referent objects do not exist in reality. They have to be created by individuals using the faculties of the mind. In this sense, *vikalpa* seems to be linked to imagination.

Thinking

Thinking refers to a cognitive process that allows individuals to acquire assimilative and discriminative knowledge of the environment. This knowledge helps them in putting various objects into certain categories, and thereby reduces the range of stimuli. This reduction becomes possible through the process of assimilative knowledge (*anuvritta buddhi*), which allows for the extraction of common characteristics from various objects. This also calls in the process of discriminative knowledge (*vyavritta buddhi*), which allows individuals to consider those objects as different from other objects. The former is referred to as *concept*, and the latter as *percept*. It is argued that commonness is wider in extent than distinctiveness.

Indian thinkers believe in the existence of a genus (*jati*) or common characteristics among objects or individuals including their hierarchy. A distinction is made between summum genus (*para jati*) and subordinate genus (*apara jati*); the former is considered to be higher up in the hierarchy. Accordingly, concepts can be arranged from a higher to lower order. While acquisition of lower order concepts takes place through assimilation of individual entities, higher order concepts develop through assimilation of lower order concepts. The process through which such assimilations become possible is called *abstraction*. Recognition of the generic identity of various objects in terms of the discovery of their commonality and its expression through words is essential for the acquisition of concepts.

On the other hand, Buddhists do not believe in the doctrine of commonality. They argue that generality is only a cognitive construction (*kalpana*), which represents the cognition that is capable of being associated with a significant word. In this sense, the thought process seems to be intricately linked with language. When a substance or quality or action is known through the genus of substance or quality or action, it is referred to as qualified cognition (*visista jnana*).

Indian scholars also believe that thinking is carried out through inference by which the self passes from a set of given judgments to a new judgment. The process involves both inductive and deductive reasoning. Even unseen objects can be inferred through this process. The inference may be for oneself or for others. Inferential knowledge results from the invariable concomitance between a problem and a probandum. A common example is given about the relationship between smoke and fire. It requires the perception of a proban in the subject of inference (e.g., the hill has smoke), the recollection of uniform or pervasive relationship between them, called *vyaptismarana* (e.g., wherever there is smoke, there is fire), the knowledge of the existence of the probans is pervaded by the probandum in the subject of inference (e.g., the hill has smoke pervaded by fire). Such inferences are supported by evidence of concomitance. The more knowledge of these concomitances (e.g., uniform experience of smoke with fire in the kitchen, outside the house, in the forest, on the hill, etc.), the more precise and confident will be the inference about fire on the sight of smoke. Thus, knowledge of invariable concomitances is the principal cause of inferential knowledge. In Indian systems of thought, one finds a very detailed discussion of conditions of inference, validity of inferences, errors of inferences, and of impossible inferences. There is also exhaustive discussion about the role of language in concept learning and thinking.

CONCLUSIONS

The perspectives shared by Indian scholars on cognition and discussed in the foregoing pages are quite useful for the development of psychological science. There seems to be impressive psychological theorizing in classical systems of Indian thought, and it seems complementary to the psychological perspectives presented by western psychologists. With such a wealth of theoretical and experiential knowledge, one would normally expect Indian scholars to attempt to develop a psychology that would transcend the perspectives available from the western tradition. Unfortunately this has not happened in this country. Instead of carving out a psychology from Indian philosophical and socio-cultural traditions, psychologists in India have evidenced almost complete dependence on ideas, concepts, methods, and theories borrowed from the west.

Why has psychology in India not been able to exploit the richness of its traditional knowledge? One of the most frequently cited reasons is that classical psychological thoughts are metaphysical, and they do not allow empirical verification. However, as Rao (2001) argued, this should not automatically disqualify them from empirical testing since "what is considered to be metaphysical and speculative at one point in history has turned out to be empirically verifiable at a later time." (p. 61). There is a strong need to redefine and operationalize several concepts of psychology in order to render them open to empirical verification.

Some scholars have suggested ways and attempted to integrate Indian psychology with modern thought (Mishra, 1987; Paranjpe, 1984,1998; Rao, 1966, 2001; Sinha, 1965, 1981, 1997), but the effect has been fairly localized and marginal. The insignificant effect is clearly evidenced by almost complete absence of psychological research utilizing Indian ideas, conceptual schemes, and theoretical notions. At best, the evidence suggests only a sort of cultural tailoring of western psychological research in India

Reasons for the apathy of Indian psychologists towards rooting their research in their own cultural traditions may be numerous. In the first place, psychologists are generally not familiar with them. The textbooks and course contents of psychology contain nothing in them that may be called Indian. Having received their training in western psychological tradition, they fail to appreciate the value of classical Indian ideas.

The overall climate that prevails in the field of psychology is another important factor. The popularity of research and researchers is indicated by the number of their citations in the writings of fellow researchers. Since people are generally not interested in research on Indian concepts, the few studies produced in this domain hardly stand any scope for cross-referencing. This renders within the country a low academic status to those researchers who work on Indian concepts. At the international plane also, research on Indian concepts at the present time has seemingly failed to draw the attention of scholars, except in one or two selected areas (e.g., yoga or TM).

An important reason for this state of affairs is the lack of coherent models that may serve as the basis for evolving meaningful psychological research programs. The information is so scattered that a new researcher runs the risk of getting completely submerged. Systematization of Indian knowledge in diverse areas requires a strong national movement not only for making it researchable, but also for informing people of its academic and social value. The disciplinary and social values of knowledge are important factors in generating and sustaining people's interest in it. As Rao (2001) pointed out, "it is not a national pride that should prompt one to study traditional thought, but the possibilities it offers for an enhanced understanding of human nature, for progress of psychology in general, and for a better deal for psychology in the developmental process of the country in particular" (p. 66).

In the field of cognition, the situation is further complicated due to the recognition of cognitive processes as universal (Mishra, 1997, 2001), and the attendant belief that the concepts used in comprehending these processes have a pan-cultural appeal. Research reveals that these processes are adaptive to ecological and socio-cultural conditions of individuals and groups. Indian research in this respect is both innovative and productive. The interest has led to programmatic cross-cultural studies in which cognitive processes of people of different ecological, cultural, and linguistic backgrounds have been assessed using indigenous and standard methods (Mishra, 1997, Mishra, et al, 1996; Mishra, Dasen & Niraula, 2003). These studies do suggest substantial modification in the instantly employed theoretical models. On the other hand, several processes and mechanisms of cognition described in Indian systems of thought are not yet understood. We need to operationalize those processes, and design programmatic studies on them using such methods and technological innovations that grant scientific legitimacy to research.

The overall impression that one gets by making a journey into the domain of cognition from an Indian perspective is that except a little research in some areas, the wider domain is characterized by gross speculation and empirically unverified theoretical hunches. The present state of affairs in this domain seems to present a theoretical psychology whose concepts are frequently experienced, talked about, and shared as part of Indians' collective heritage. We look forward to a time when they would be dug out of the ground and become part of the larger scientific enterprise of psychology that is so strongly valued universally.

REFERENCES

Akhilanand, S. (1948). *Hindu psychology: Its meaning for the west*. London: George Allyn & Unwin.

Asthana, H. S. (1988). Personality. In J. Pandey (Ed.), *Psychology in India: The state-of-the-art, Vol. 1*, (pp. 153–190). New Delhi: Sage.

Berry, J. W. (1976). *Human ecology and cognitive style: Comparative studies in cultural and psychological adaptation*. New York: Sage/Halstead.

Berry, J. W., van de Koppel, J. M. H., Senechal, C., Annis, R. C., Bahuchet, S., Cavalli-Sforza, L. L., & Witkin, H. A. (1986). *On the edge of the forest: Cultural adaptation and cognitive development in Central Africa*. Lisse: Swets & Zeitlinger.

Berry, J. W., Mishra, R. C., & Tripathi, R. C. (2003). *Psychology in human and social development: Lessons from diverse cultures*. New Delhi: Sage.

Chari, C. T. K. (1959). Parapsychology studies and literature in India. *International Journal of Parapsychology, 2*, 24–32.

Dasgupta, S. N. (1988). *History of Indian philosophy, Vol 1–5*. Delhi: Motilal Banarasidass (original work published in 1922).

Datta, D. M. (1932). *The six ways of knowing: A critical study of the Advaita theory of knowledge*. Calcutta: University of Calcutta.

Dwivedi, C.B. (1987). On yogdarsana's *asampramosa* doctrine of memory. *Journal of Indian Psychology, 6*, 1–6.

Freud, S. (1915). The unconscious. In J. Strachey (Ed.), *Standard edition of the complete works of Sigmund Freud, Vol. 14*. London: Hogarth.

Gergen, K. (1985). The social constructionist movement in modern psychology. *American Psychologist, 40*, 266–275.

Grosso, M. (1990). Review of modern miracles: An investigative report on psychic phenomena associated with Sathya Sai Baba by E. Heraldsson. *Journal of Society for Psychical Research, 84*, 375–381.

Gumperz, J. J., & Levinson, S. (1996). *Linguistic relativity revisited*. New York: Cambridge University Press.

Haraldsson, E. (1987). *Modern miracles: An investigative report on psychic phenomena associated with Sathya Sai Baba*. New York: Fawcette Columbine.

Harré, R. (1986). *The social construction of emotions*. Oxford: Basil Blackwell.

Harré, R. (1987). The social construction of selves. In K. Yardley & T. Honess (Eds.), *Self and identity: Psychosocial perspectives* (pp. 41–52). New York: John Wiley & Sons.

Jung, C. G. (1958). Psychology and religion: West and the east. In H. Read, M. Fordham, & G. Adler (Eds.), *The collected works of C. G. Jung, Vol 2*. New York: Pantheon.

Krishnamurthy, J. (1998). *Shiksa samvad* (Dialogue on education). Varanasi: Krishnamurthy Foundation India.

Kuppuswamy, B. (1985). *Elements of ancient Indian psychology*. New Delhi: Vikas Publishing House.

Levinson, S. (2003). *Space in language and cognition*. Cambridge: Cambridge University Press.

Luria, A. R. (1976). *Cognitive development: Its cultural and social foundations*. Cambridge: Harvard University Press.

Mishra, R. C. (1981). Science of psychology: Challenge and necessity. *Prajna, 26*, 203–209.

Mishra, R. C. (1987). Towards a non-western perspective in psychology. *Research in Psychology, 5*, 73–85.

Mishra, R. C. (1997). Cognition and cognitive development. In J. W. Berry, P. R. Dasen, & T. S. Saraswathi (Eds.), *Handbook of cross-cultural psychology, Vol. 2* (pp. 147–179). Boston: Allyn & Bacon.

Mishra, R. C. (2001). Cognition across cultures. In D. Matsumoto (Ed.), *The handbook of culture and psychology* (pp. 119–135). New York: Oxford University Press.

Mishra, R. C., Dasen, P. R., & Niraula, S. (2003). Ecology, language and performance on spatial cognitive tasks. *International Journal of Psychology, 38*, 366–383.

Mishra, R. C., Sinha, D., & Berry, J. W. (1996). *Ecology, acculturation and psychological adaptation: A study of Adivasis in Bihar*. New Delhi: Sage.

Mohanty, J. N. (1993). *Essays on Indian philosophy: Traditional and modern*. Delhi: Oxford University Press.

Murphy, G., & Murphy, L. B. (1968). *Asian psychology*. New York: Basic Books.

Pandey, J. (1988). *Psychology in India: The state-of-the-art*. New Delhi: Sage.

Paranjpe, A. C. (1984). *Theoretical psychology: The meeting of east and west*. New York: Plenum Press.

Paranjpe, A. C. (1998). *Self and identity in modern psychology and Indian thought*. New York: Plenum Press.

Piaget, J. (1954). *The construction of reality in the child* (M. Cook Trans.) New York: Ballantine.

Ramachandra Rao, S. K. (1962). *Development of psychological thought in India*. Mysore: Kavlalaya Publishers.

Rao, K. R. (1966). *Experimental parapsychology: A review and interpretation.* Springfield: Charles C. Thomas.

Rao, K. R. (2001). Consciousness studies: A survey of perspectives and research, In J. Pandey (Ed.), *Psychology in India revisited: Developments in the discipline,* Vol. 2 (pp. 19–162). New Delhi: Sage.

Rao, K. R., Dukhan, H. & Rao, P. V. K., (1984). Yogoc meditation and psi scoring in forced choice and free response tests. In K. R. Rao (Ed.), *The basic experiments in parapsychology* (pp. 210–224). Jefferson, N. C. : Mcfarland.

Rao, P. V. K., & Rao, K. R. (1982). Two studies of EPS and subliminal perception. *Journal of Parapsychology, 46,* 185–208.

Rhine, J. B. (1934). *New world of the mind.* New York: William Sloane Associates.

Safaya, R. (1975). *Indian psychology.* New Delhi: Munshiram Manoharlal.

Sinha, D. (1965). Integration of modern psychology with Indian thought. *Journal of Humanistic Psychology, Spring,* 6–21.

Sinha, D. (1981). Non-western perspectives in psychology: Why, what and whither? *Journal of Indian psychology, 3,* 1–9.

Sinha, D. (1997). Indigenizing psychology. In J. W. Berry, Y. H. Poortinga & J. Pandey (Eds.), *Handbook of cross-cultural psychology, Vol. 1* (pp. 129–169). Boston: Allyn & Bacon.

Sinha, J. (1958). *Indian psychology, Vol. 1: Cognition.* Calcutta: Sinha Publishing House (Reprinted1986, Motilal Banarasidass, Varanasi).

Thurston, F. (1993). *Ghosts and poltergeists.* London: Burns, Oats, & Washbourne.

Watson, J. B. (1913). Psychology as the behaviorist views it. *Psychological review, 20,* 158–177.

Whorf, B. L. (1956). Langauge, thought and reality: Cambridge, MA: MIT Press.

Witkin, H. A., Dyk, R. B., Faterson, H. F., Goodenough, D. R., & Karp, S. (1962). *Psychological differentiation.* New York: John Wiley.

Part IV

Self and Personality

Chapter 13

Indigenous Personality Research
The Chinese Case

Kuo-Shu Yang[1]

After a comprehensive and systematic review of psychological studies on Chinese personality conducted before 1985, K. S. Yang (1986) characterized Chinese personality research as thoroughly Westernized, or, more precisely, Americanized, in the sense that nearly all of the studies uncritically borrowed theories, concepts, methods, and tools developed and standardized in Western historical, cultural, and social contexts specifically for use with Euro-American subjects. Under the influence of an academic movement labeled *psychological research indigenization,* since the mid-seventies increasing numbers of psychologists in Taiwan, Hong Kong, and China have been conducting research with an indigenized approach. This approach requires that the researchers' theories, concepts, methods, tools, and results sufficiently represent the natural structures, mechanisms, and processes of the studied psychological and behavioral phenomena as embedded in their original ecological, historical, cultural, and social contexts (C. F. Yang, 1993a, 1996; K. S. Yang, 1993b, 1997a, 1997b, 1999, 2000). Numerous indigenous psychological studies on Chinese behavior in various research areas of psychology have been published in domestic and international academic journals. K. S. Yang (1997a, 2000) has made selected reviews of the empirical, theoretical, and methodological accomplishments of indigenized research on Chinese psychological functioning. This chapter presents an additional review that specifically stresses the integrative analysis of indigenized studies on Chinese personality from the perspective of a particular conceptual system in terms of individual and social orientations.

[1] The author is deeply grateful to Professors Lawrence A. Pervin, A. Timothy Church, and Fanny M. Cheung for their critical and useful comments on an earlier version.

285

A FOUR-LEVEL CONCEPTUAL SCHEME FOR CLASSIFYING PERSONALITY ATTRIBUTES

Previous conceptual analyses and empirical evidence have repeatedly demonstrated that there are two cultural syndromes at the macro level (*cultural* collectivism and individualism), and two corresponding psychological syndromes at the micro level (*psychological* collectivism and individualism). These syndromes prevail in contemporary societies all over the world (e.g., Hofstede, 1980; Triandis, 1993, 1995; K. S. Yang, 2003). At each level, collectivism and individualism represent two generic categories, or, more appropriately, prototypes, although they both have specific, concrete variants in different cultures. Judging from its major characteristics (e.g., Ho, 1998; Ho & Chiu, 1994; King, 1991; Liang, 1974; K. S. Yang, 1995), Chinese culture is unequivocally collectivistic in nature. Specifically, it is a form of vertical collectivism in Triandis' (1995) sense. Associated with Chinese cultural collectivism is Chinese psychological collectivism, which is embodied in *Chinese social orientation* as systematically conceptualized by K. S. Yang (1986, 1995). As a collectivistic psychological syndrome, Chinese social orientation is mainly composed of four orientations: relationship orientation, authoritarian orientation, familistic (group) orientation, and (generalized) other orientation. Yang's conceptualization of each of the four orientations is partially based upon previous research on Chinese social psychological functioning conducted by Chinese psychologists, sociologists, and anthropologists.

According to K. S. Yang (1995), Chinese relationship orientation stresses relational fatalism, relational formalism, relational interdependence, relational harmony, and relational determinism (the Chinese form of particularism). Authoritarian orientation denotes an organized set of affects, cognitions, and behaviors toward social authorities (especially the head of the family), with authority sensitization (excessive sensitivity to authority), authority worship, and authority dependence (including psychological impotence before an authority) as its main features. Familistic orientation is a complex set of family-centered thoughts, attitudes, values, and behaviors that causes Chinese people to subordinate their personal goals, interests, and welfare for the sake of their families' existence, harmony, solidarity, glory, prosperity, and prolongation. Finally, other orientation is composed of such psychological characteristics as constant worry about non-specific or generalized (without individualized identities) others' opinions, strong conformity with non-specific others, deep concern about social norms, and high regard for face and reputation.

These four orientations represent the most important aspects of Chinese social psychological functioning whereby Chinese people attempt to fit themselves into and form harmonious unions with their social environments. Among the four, the relationship and authoritarian orientations both belong to the interpersonal level with the latter exclusively emphasizing relationships with an authority in a social milieu. These two may be combined for the sake of brevity to represent Chinese social psychological functioning at the interpersonal level. It may thus be said that Chinese social orientation is manifested at three levels: relationship (i.e., relationship and authoritarian orientations), group (e.g., familistic orientation), and non-specific others in the social environment at large (i.e., other orientation).

In contrast to social orientation, individual orientation, as defined by K. S. Yang (1986, 1995, 1996), comprises such core components as self orientation, autonomous orientation, independent orientation, and egalitarian orientation, all of which are especially prevalent among people in Euro-American societies. It is fair to say that individual orientation represents the major pattern of psychological individualism most prevalent in the Western world (especially North America). However, it must be pointed out that even people in social-oriented Chinese societies may manifest certain individual-oriented characteristics under some circumstances. This is increasingly true as Chinese people in Taiwan, Hong Kong, and China gradually become less social-oriented and more individual-oriented under the impact of social change induced by societal modernization (K. S. Yang, 1996). In order to have a conceptual framework complete enough for the systematic analysis of indigenized research on Chinese personality, individual orientation is combined with social orientation (three levels) to form a comprehensive four-level classificatory scheme.

This systematic scheme adopts a rather broad definition of personality, slightly modified from Pervin's (1996, p. 414) as "the complex organization of *aptitudes, temperaments, needs*, cognitions, affects, and behaviors that gives direction, *consistency*, and pattern (coherence), to the person's life" (italicized words added). Aptitudes, temperaments, needs, cognitions, affects, and behaviors are all rather enduring characteristics that result from being a person in a particular ecological, social, cultural, and historical milieu. It is assumed that culture and personality attributes (even aptitudes and temperaments) are more or less bidirectionally determined and mutually constituted (Kitayama, Markus, Matsumoto, & Norasakkunkit, 1997; Markus & Kitayama, 1998). With this broad definition, four varieties of personality attributes, viz., individual-, relationship-, group-, and other-oriented, may be meaningfully delineated in terms of K. S. Yang's conceptualization of individual and social orientation. Individual-oriented attributes are those formed mainly through one's interactions with one's own personal self, which functions with respect to the individualized aspects of daily life. Relationship-oriented attributes are those formed mainly through one's interactions with another person. Group-oriented attributes are those formed mainly through one's interactions with one's family and other groups. And other-oriented attributes are formed mainly through one's interactions with real or imagined non-specific unidentified others as the generalized audience in the social environment.

Among the four varieties of personality attributes, the individual-oriented ones include those personal traits (e.g., aptitudes and temperaments) that are predominantly genetically determined and those dispositions (e.g., self-oriented autonomy and independence) that are mainly formed in the milieu of an individualist culture. These personal propensities are embedded in the individual person or in the personal-oriented self. In contrast, social-oriented personality attributes are composed of relation-contextualized dispositions like harmoniousness and relational determinism, group-contextualized dispositions like familism and social identity, as well as other-contextualized ones like social desirability and face consciousness. These variously contextualized dispositions are deeply engraved, or even constituted with the social and cultural roles, norms, obligations, customs, and practices involving relationships, groups (especially the family), and generalized others.

Lay people may consider individual (personal)-oriented and social-oriented personality attributes to be either *fixed* or *malleable* in Dweck and his associates' (e.g., Chiu, Hong, & Dweck, 1997; Dweck & Leggett, 1988; Dweck, Hong, & Chiu, 1993) sense. Conceptually speaking, the origins or sources of attribute stability or changeability may be different for people from different cultures. In an individualist culture like that of the US, it should be the individual person or the personal-oriented self that acts as the major anchoring and stabilizing center of gravity for consistent and coherent personality functioning in everyday life. Sociocultural factors may be readily changed to suit the person's needs in an *alloplastic* way in Freud's (1924) sense. It is thus likely that Americans in particular and Westerners in general tend to view individual-oriented personality attributes as relatively fixed entities and social-oriented attributes as relatively malleable ones. In contrast, in a collectivist culture like the Chinese, it should be the sociocultural contexts, in terms of roles, norms, obligations, customs, and practices that act as the major anchoring and stabilizing center for consistent and coherent personality functioning in everyday life. However, the person's needs, cognitions, affects, and behaviors may be readily changed to adjust effectively to the sociocultural environment in an *autoplastic* way in Freud's (1924) sense. It may therefore be inferred that the Chinese and people in other East Asian countries within the Confucian cultural circle such as Japan and Korea tend to view social-oriented attributes as relatively fixed entities and individual-oriented attributes as relatively malleable. In each type of culture, some personality attributes may be relatively fixed and others relatively malleable, though in opposite patterns of relative fixedness and malleability.

This framework constitutes a comprehensive four-level scheme for the systematic analysis of personality characteristics (see Table 1).

Table 1. A Four-Level Conceptual Scheme for the Classification of Personality Attributes Based upon Individual Orientation and Social Orientation

Category of personality attributes	Corresponding psychological orientation(s) in terms of K. S. Yang's conceptual system	Major kind of experiences involved in attribute formation	Function of personality attributes
1. Individual-oriented attributes	Individual orientation	Experiences of interactions with one's personal or individualized self (in some cases, substantial genetic and maturational factors may be involved)	Facilitating one's psychological functioning as an independent, autonomous, and self-sufficient individual
2. Relationship-oriented attributes	Relationship orientation Authoritarian orientation	Experiences of culturally specific interactions with another person with whom one is acquainted	Facilitating one's harmonious integration with another person
3. Group-oriented attributes	Familistic orientation	Experiences of culturally specific interactions with one's family or some other group	Facilitating one's harmonious integration with one's family or some other group
4. Other-oriented attributes	Other orientation	Experiences of culturally specific interactions with real or imagined unidentified, non-specific others	Facilitating one's harmonious integration with the generalized other

In each of the four categories of personality attributes, the target of the actor's social interaction is progressively larger in the number of persons involved. It is thus possible to arrange the four levels of personality attributes into a system of concentric circles, with the individual-oriented dispositions in the innermost circle, the other-oriented dispositions in the outermost circle, and the relationship- and group-oriented ones in between. Such a conceptual scheme is useful not only for the analysis of Chinese personality, but also for the analysis of Chinese social behavior. This framework should be equally applicable to the study of personality and social behavior of people in other changing collectivistic-oriented cultures, especially East Asian ones. The scheme is also general enough in nature and scope to be potentially adoptable for analysis of personality and social behavior of people in individualistic-oriented societies.

The relative band widths of the concentric circles in the four-level conceptual scheme for the classification of personality attributes can represent the relative importance of the four kinds of personality traits in daily psychological functioning among people in a culture.[2] In the case of ordinary Chinese people, the relationship- and group-oriented traits tend to be more powerful, pervasive, and influential than the other-oriented ones, which in turn are more powerful than the individual-oriented ones, as shown in Figure 1a. In contrast, ordinary American people's individual-oriented traits tend to be more powerful, pervasive, and inferential than their relationship- and group-oriented ones, which in turn are more powerful than their other-oriented traits, as shown in Figure 1b. Generally speaking, the concentric pattern of the four kinds of traits in terms of relative importance in Figure 1a is basically for people in social-oriented cultures, whereas Figure 1b is basically for people in individual-oriented ones. As social-oriented cultures (like those in Taiwan, Hong Kong, China, Korea, and Japan) are becoming less social-oriented and more individual-oriented during the prolonged process of societal modernization, their concentric patterns will gradually transform from that in Figure 1a to that in Figure 1b within certain limits.

Most indigenous studies on Chinese behavior have been conducted in the field of personality and social psychology. There are far too many to comprehensively and thoroughly review them in this chapter. Findings and concepts from indigenized research on the Chinese self, the Chinese concept of justice, Chinese ways of thinking, and Chinese family socialization

---

[2] I would like to thank Professor Lawrence Pervin for reminding me to take care of this issue by saying that "the size of these circles can vary from culture to culture" in his enlightening comments on an earlier version of the paper.

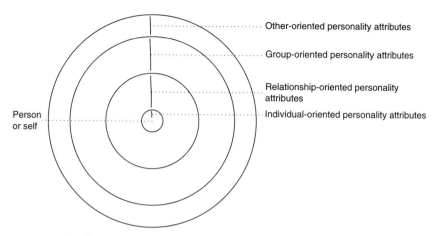

1a. The hypothesized relative band widths for the Chinese case

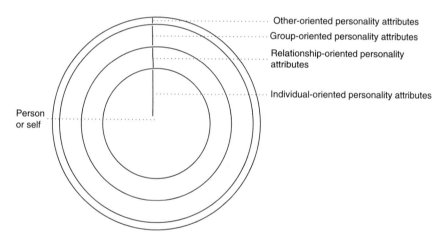

1b. The hypothesized relative band widths for the American case

Figure 1. The Relative Band Widths of the Concentric Circles Representing the Relative Importance of the Four Kinds of Personality Attributes for Chinese and American People

are reported and analyzed in other chapters of this volume. My goal in this chapter is to review selectively and critically the major indigenized studies on Chinese personality from a broad perspective, synthesizing both the dispositional and cultural psychological approaches[3] with the hope that a systematic picture will emerge.

---

[3] It is Church (2000) who first pointed out the possibility of integrating the trait psychology and cultural psychology approaches and first made an attempt to formulate an integrated cultural trait psychology.

SEARCH FOR BASIC CHINESE PERSONALITY
DIMENSIONS

Traditionally, the study of personality encompasses five major research areas, viz., personality genetics, personality development, personality structure (and assessment), personality dynamics, and personality change. Indigenized research on Chinese personality has focused on personality structure and dynamics. Some of the studies have adopted a multidimensional approach in identifying and measuring the basic dimensions of Chinese personality and others have preferred to construct a unidimensional scale with rather limited content coverage for the assessment of certain specific personality dispositions.

Until recently, psychologists in Taiwan, Hong Kong, and China have almost completely relied upon translated or adapted Chinese versions of Western-originated tests, inventories, questionnaires, and scales for practical as well as research purposes. In the case of Taiwan, nearly all the major American omnibus personality tests have been translated, (slightly) revised, and used over the last forty years under the dubious assumption that as human beings, Chinese and Americans have a similar, if not identical, personality structure.

In the last fifteen years or so, a few psychologists with an indigenous perspective from the three major culturally Chinese societies have begun to question the universality assumption seriously, and have embarked upon identification of basic Chinese indigenous personality dimensions and development of new indigenized tests and inventories to measure them. A number of researchers (e.g., F. M. Cheung, Leung, Fan, Song, Zhang, & Zhang, 1996; F.M. Cheung & Leung, 1998; P. C. Cheung, Conger, Hau, Lew, & Lau, 1992; Wang and Cui, 2003, 2004; K. S. Yang & Bond, 1990; K. S. Yang & Wang, 2000) have made a serious attempt with studies of basic dimensions. Almost all these studies began with a lexical or descriptive-term approach, but only two (i.e., F. M. Cheung et al., 1996; Wang & Cui, 2003, 2004) went a step further to develop a pool of complete-sentence items for construction of a multidimensional personality inventory. Among the trait-oriented studies on basic Chinese personality dimensions, the most representative are those conducted by F. M. Cheung et al. (1996), P. C. Cheung et al. (1992), and K. S. Yang and Wang (2000), in the sense that they are fairly indigenized and systematic in approach.

Major Studies on Basic Chinese Personality Dimensions

P. C. Cheung et al.'s (1992) research began with an initial pool of 191 bipolar trait descriptors (adjectives and phrases) collected by the late Professor William Lew (1998/2001) through a review of the literature on Chinese culture and personality as well as interviews with Chinese graduate students. From Lew's list, 178 bipolar descriptors were chosen and administered to 300 graduate students at the Chinese University of Hong Kong. Based upon the analysis of the Hong Kong data, the Multi-Trait Personality Inventory (MTPI) was constructed. It consisted of 122 bipolar descriptors tapping attitudes, beliefs, affective reactions, and typical behavior to be rated on a 6-step bipolar scale. About half of the final items reflected Confucian teachings and traditional values. The MTPI was administered to 2,617 adult Chinese (1,673 men and 944 women) from four Chinese populations (China, Taiwan, Hong Kong, and the United States) for the identification of measurable personality dimensions. Factor analysis of the obtained data generated five major bipolar factors, namely, Outgoing vs. Withdrawn, Self-Serving vs. Principled, Conforming vs. Noncomforming, Stable vs. Unstable, and Strict vs. Accepting. Comparisons of findings for the four groups revealed that all the Chinese groups internalized such Confucian values as moderation and self-discipline.

A much more serious attempt to identify major Chinese personality constructs and to develop an indigenized multidimensional personality assessment tool was made by F. M. Cheung, Leung, and their associates (1996, 1998). The instrument they finally constructed was the Chinese Personality Assessment Inventory (CPAI), which includes 22 normal personality scales and 12 clinical scales in the latest version. The development of the CPAI started with an initial pool of about 900 items written in simple Mandarin sentences in first-person format. "Items were selected from other personality tests including English-language personality scales or their translated Chinese versions, and locally developed Chinese scales" (F. M. Cheung et al., 1996, p. 187). About 120 items were chosen from statements about personality characteristics obtained during pilot studies to collect trait descriptions from Chinese novels, books on Chinese proverbs, self-descriptions, and descriptions of others' personalities made by students and professionals in Hong Kong and China. The researchers also wrote about 150 additional items to supplement the scales or to develop new scales. The 1991 trial and 1992 standardization versions of the CPAI were successively administered to large samples of respondents from Hong Kong and China for the purposes of item selection and scale standardization. The inventory consisted of 34 scales measuring various personality dimensions, 22 for the assessment of normal personality constructs, and 12 for the assessment of clinical constructs. The constructs measured by the 22 normal personality scales are as follows: Emotionality, Responsibility, Practical Mindedness, Inferiority vs. Self-Acceptance, Graciousness vs. Meanness, Optimism vs. Pessimism, Veraciousness vs. Slickness, External vs. Internal locus of Control, Face, Family Orientation, Meticulousness, Harmony, *Ren Qing* (exchangeable social favor) Orientation, Flexibility, Modernization, Thrift vs. Extravagance, Introversion vs. Extraversion, Leadership, Adventurousness, Self vs. Social Orientation, Logical vs. Affective Orientation, and Defensiveness (*Ah-Q* attitude). Factor analyses performed for the personality scales generated four second-order factors (i.e., Dependability, Chinese Tradition, Social Potency, and Individualism).

The third relevant research program for the investigation of basic Chinese personality dimensions was conducted by K. S. Yang and his associates (Yang & Bond, 1990; Yang & Wang, 2000; Hsu, Wang, & Yang, 2001). Yang and Bond's (1990) study, using Chinese personality adjectives, identified five bipolar factors, viz., Social Orientation vs. Self-Centeredness, Competence vs. Impotence, Expressiveness vs. Conservatism, Self-control vs. Impulsiveness, and Optimism vs. Neuroticism. These emic dimensions were correlated with the five imported or imposed-etic ones (i.e., Extraversion or Surgency, Agreeableness, Conscientiousness, Emotional Stability, and Culture), as empirically defined by Tupes and Christal (1958) and Norman (1961, 1963), revealing a one-to-one relation for only two (Social Orientation to Agreeableness and Optimism to Emotional Stability) of the five indigenous factors. The others were multiple-determined. While Yang and Bond's (1990) research had the merit of using multiple target persons, the external validity of the findings was limited by the fact that only Taiwanese students were used as subjects, and the number of personality adjectives actually employed was not large enough.

In order to do a better job of identifying basic Chinese personality dimensions and addressing the issue of cross-cultural universality of the American Big Five model, K. S. Yang and Wang (2000) initiated a second wave of research, starting from 1995, continuing to rely upon a trait lexicon of the Chinese language. This time they started with a pool of more than 4000 personality adjectives collected in Taiwan and mainland China from Chinese dictionaries, novels, newspapers, and personality descriptors generated by university students and adults. Chinese college students from both sides of the Taiwan Straits were asked to rate each of the 1520 descriptors chosen from the initial pool for meaningfulness, familiarity, social desirability, and modernity. The researchers carefully selected 410 descriptors (by excluding those with the lowest scale values on meaningfulness and familiarity, the highest values on modernity, and the highest and the lowest values on social desirability) as a representative sample of the 1520 adjectives, and administered them in a rating questionnaire format to four samples of Chinese participants (university students and adults from Taiwan and China). Participants rated their own personality on a five-point scale. Factor analysis of the correlational matrix for the total sample of 1441 respondents revealed seven bipolar factors, 5 major and 2 minor, in the decreasing order of the percentages of the total variance accounted for: Competence vs. Impotence, Industriousness vs. Unindustriousness, Other-Orientedness vs. Self-Centeredness, Agreeableness vs. Disagreeableness, Extraversion vs. Introversion, Large-Mindedness vs. Small-Mindedness, and Contentedness vs. Vaingloriousness. Separate factor analyses for the Taiwan and China samples (students and adults combined) indicated that the two combined samples differed only in the seventh factor: Optimism vs. Pessimism for the Taiwan sample and Contentedness vs. Boastfulness for the China sample. Intercorrelations among the adjectives with higher loadings on the same factor were computed and factor-analyzed to generate subfactors for each of the seven major factors. The first five factors were each composed of two or three related subfactors, but the last two could not be decomposed into subfactors.

Some of Yang and Wang's (2000) seven factors are quite similar to certain of Yang and Bond's (1990) five factors. For the combined *Taiwan* sample, Competence vs. Impotence, Other-Orientedness vs. Self-Centeredness, Extraversion vs. Introversion, and Optimism vs. Pessimism in the seven-factor model respectively corresponded to Competence vs. Impotence, Social Orientation vs. Self-Centeredness, Expressiveness vs. Conservatism, and Optimism vs. Neuroticism in the five factor model. Moreover, Competence vs. Impotence, Other-Orientedness vs. Self-Centeredness, and Extraversion vs. Introversion in the seven-factor model for the combined *mainland* sample also had counterparts in the 1990 Taiwan five-factor model.

The newly identified Chinese Big Seven were then correlated with the American Big Five as identified by Tupes and Christal (1958), Norman (1961, 1963), and Costa and McCrae (1985), viz., Neuroticism (or Emotional Stability), Extraversion (or Surgency), Openness (or Culture), Agreeableness, and Conscientiousness, with data collected by administering Norman's (translated), Costa and McCrae's (translated), and Yang and Wang's measuring instruments to the same Chinese samples. At least three of the five Tupes-Christal-Norman (TCN) factors were somewhat replicated in the Chinese seven-factor structure. Two Chinese factors (Competence vs. Impotence and Large-Mindedness vs. Small-Mindedness) were beyond the coverage of the TCN model. Three of the five Costa-McCrae (CM) factors had corresponding Chinese factors, and the Openness factor failed to substantially correlate with any of the seven Chinese ones. Three Chinese factors (Competence vs. Impotence; Other-Orientedness vs. Self-Centeredness, and Large-Mindedness vs. Small-Mindedness) were beyond the coverage of the CM model. These findings clearly revealed that while three of the basic personality factors of the American Big Five do have more or less corresponding factors in the Chinese Big Seven, three Chinese factors are beyond the coverage of the American models. Moreover, the first or largest Chinese factor, that is, Competence vs. Impotence, was one of the three not covered. These results indicate that there are both differences as well as similarities between Chinese and American basic personality dimensions. In other words, the American Big Five is not a complete cross-culturally universal model. The Culture factor in the TCN model did have a corresponding Chinese dimension, but the Openness factor in the CM model did not have one, which may evidence the possibility that these two personality constructs are not the same, at least for Chinese people.

K. S. Yang and Wang (2000) selected adjectives with the highest loadings on each of the seven factors along with their subfactors to construct a personality measuring tool, the Multidimensional Chinese Personality Inventory (MCPI), in the format of an adjective rating list for the assessment of indigenous Chinese personality dimensions and subdimensions. To go one step further, Wang and Cui (2003, 2004) constructed an omnibus personality inventory to measure the seven corresponding factors for Chinese, beginning with a large pool of more than 1600 items each in the form of a complete sentence describing a behavior or life experience for the concrete expression of the meaning of each chosen high-loading adjective (more than three items per adjective). The final 180-item Chinese personality inventory was made to measure not only the seven basic dimensions but also eighteen subdimensions.

Comparison of the Three Major Research Programs

Thus far, the three most representative large-scale research programs that have attempted to identify and measure Chinese basic personality dimensions using large samples of students and adults from China, Taiwan, and Hong Kong have been reviewed. Three obvious differences among the three programs deserve discussion here: degree of indigenousness, research strategy adopted, and the construct level tapped.

First, while all three used a more or less indigenized approach, they differed in the degree of indigenousness of the initial item pools. P. C. Cheung et al.'s (1992) study may be criticized for its insufficient indigenousness, or more technically, insufficient *indigenous compatibility* (K. S. Yang, 1997b, 1999, 2000), because the initial pool of trait terms included quite a number of descriptors directly chosen from R. B. Cattell's questionnaire (through personal communication with the late Professor Lew at the very early stage of his endeavor to construct an inventory for use in his research project on the personality development of Chinese intellectuals). F. M. Cheung et al.'s (1996) research might also suffer from insufficient indigenous compatibility due to the use of items of Western origin in constructing their personality scales. It is reasonable to believe that the items used in such culture-specific personality scales as Harmony, Face, *Ren Qing* Orientation, Family Orientation, Thrift vs. Extravagance, Responsibility, and Defensiveness (*Ah-Q* Attitude) were selected from available indigenized tests or scales or newly written on the basis of collected indigenous materials, but it is unknown how many items in the culture-general personality measures such as Introversion vs. Extraversion, Leadership, Flexibility, Logical vs. Affective Orientation, Emotionality, Adventurousness, and External vs. Internal Locus of Control were borrowed from Western tests or scales. As for K. S. Yang and Wang's (2000) research, its initial item pool included more than 4000 Chinese trait adjectives collected from widely used Chinese dictionaries, popular Chinese novels, leading Chinese newspapers, and personality descriptors provided by Chinese university students and adults. The 410 adjectives finally used in the factor analyses were carefully culled from the 1,520 descriptors chosen from such a highly indigenous and representative pool. Overall, P. C. Cheung et al.'s research has a lesser degree of indigenousness, and Yang and Wang's the greatest degree of indigenousness, with F. M. Cheung et al.'s in between.

Second, the three studies differed in the strategy used to identify and define basic personality dimensions. Yang and Wang (2000) typically adopted a lexical approach to identify and define basic Chinese personality constructs by factor-analyzing a representative sample of adjectives in the Chinese trait lexicon. P. C. Cheung et al. (1992) also used factor analysis to extract personality dimensions from a relatively small sample of adjectives and phrases that were not comprehensively and systematically drawn from a large pool of Chinese trait descriptors. Unlike the other two studies, F. M. Cheung et al. (1996) did not highly rely upon an empirical approach to systematically identify and define the Chinese personality dimensions for which all the final personality scales of their inventory are constructed. Instead, they conceptually selected the possible or potential scales that they thought were important to the understanding of Chinese personality, and then collected and wrote items they thought were conceptually appropriate for each scale. They refined each scale using an internal consistency procedure. The personality constructs of the CPAI were not systematically defined within the *same* coherent conceptual framework of personality structure, or through a systematic empirical analysis (e.g., factor analysis, latent structure analysis) of responses to a sample of representative items drawn from a comprehensive item pool for a well-conceived personality domain (e.g., temperamental, motivational, or evaluational). The personality constructs were separately and individually judged and chosen for inclusion in the inventory simply for the reason that each was seemingly important to the experiences of Chinese people in one way or another and therefore had been much discussed in the Chinese or American psychological literature.

A related problem with the CPAI is that, since the items for each personality scale were selected in terms of item-total correlations, rather than in terms of factor loadings obtained by a comprehensive, multidimensional factor analysis fulfilling the criterion of simple structure, certain individual scales may not be able to assess a well-integrated personality construct. This selection procedure may be why internal consistency reliabilities are quite low for some of the scales (for example, .55 and .58 on *Ren Qing* Orientation for the Hong Kong and China samples respectively), and why the four-factor solution obtained by factor-analyzing scores on all 22 personality scales did not display a good simple structure pattern (8 out of 22 scales each had considerable loadings on two or three factors).

The third major difference among the three studies lies in the content domain of the psychological entities tapped. The personality constructs assessed in both P. C. Cheung et al.'s (1992) and K. S. Yang and Wang's (2000) research properly belong to the *temperamental* modality of personality in Guilford's (1959) sense. According to Guilford, temperamental traits are basic dispositions that have to do with the *manner* in which one's actions occur. In contrast, what was assessed in F. M. Cheung et al.'s (1996) research may be classified into two groups: (a) temperamental constructs such as Emotionality, Responsibility, Inferiority vs. Self-Acceptance, Graciousness vs. Meanness, Optimism vs. Pessimism, Flexibility, Introversion vs. Extraversion, Adventurousness, Self vs. Social Orientation, and Logical vs. Affective Orientation, and (b) social psychological syndromes such as Face, Family Orientation, Harmony, *Ren Qing* Orientation, Modernization, Thrift vs. Extravagance, and Leadership. Social psychological syndromes are much broader in scope, more complex in structure, and more affected by culture than temperament. All in all, as pointed out earlier, the two groups of constructs simply are not psychological entities at the same level or in the same modality.

Traditionally, psychometrically oriented personality psychologists, especially those in Euro-American societies, have limited their search for basic personality dimensions to the domain of temperamental traits in a broad sense, usually excluding the domain of culture-specific, complex psychological syndromes. F. M. Cheung et al.'s (1996) effort to mix such syndromes with temperamental traits in measuring normal personality traits represents an important need for indigenous-oriented Chinese psychologists to study heavily culturally-colored social psychological characteristics from a psychometrical perspective. These rather culture-specific syndromes are "social psychological traits" in Matthews and Deary's (1998) sense. They are social-relational in nature and may thus be simply called social-oriented traits or dispositions from K. S. Yang's (1986, 1995) perspective of social orientation. Social-oriented syndromes tend to be multidimensional. The necessity of constructing tools for the measurement of these highly indigenous constructs is obvious, because once these tools are available (and accessible), it will be much easier for psychologists to conduct systematic indigenized studies on each by adopting a construct-validity or other research strategy. Since social-oriented and temperamental traits are conceptually not at the same level, these two groups of psychological dispositions should be assessed separately by different inventories, tests, or scales.

Furthermore, viewed from the four-level conceptual scheme in Table 1, most temperamental traits (e.g., Competence vs. Impotence, Extraversion vs. Introversion, Stable vs. Unstable) identified by one or more of the three

research programs in search for basic Chinese personality dimensions may
be classified as individual-oriented personality constructs. Among the
social-oriented constructs identified by F. M. Cheung et al. (1996), some (e.g.,
Harmony, *Ren Qing* Orientation) may be classified as *relationship-oriented* constructs, some (e.g., Family Orientation, Leadership) as group-oriented
constructs, and others (e.g., Face, *Ah-Q* Attitude) as other-oriented constructs.
In addition to F. M. Cheung and her associates, other indigenous-oriented
Chinese researchers have also made an effort to develop standardized scales
for the measurement of various social-oriented constructs and to conduct
research with them. The ideas, scales, and related studies of some of these
researchers are reviewed and discussed in the next section.

ATTEMPTS TO ASSESS SOCIAL-ORIENTED PERSONALITY ATTRIBUTES

While psychologists in individualist cultures have been more interested
in identifying and measuring personal-oriented personality attributes,
indigenous-oriented psychologists in collectivist cultures have been more
interested in identifying and measuring social-oriented ones. In the last
thirty years or so, an increasing number of Chinese psychologists have
endeavored to develop various indigenized scales and inventories to
assess social-oriented dispositions. In this section, a representative sample
of such personality constructs is reviewed in terms of three categories:
relationship-oriented, group-oriented, and other-oriented.

Relationship-Oriented Personality Attributes

Chinese culture has been repeatedly characterized as relation-based or
relation-centered by leading Chinese anthropologists and sociologists like
Chiao (1982), Fei (1980), and Liang (1974), and Chinese people have been
repeatedly described as relationship- or relational-oriented in their daily
functioning by Chinese psychologists like Ho (1991), Hwang (1987, 2000),
and K. S. Yang (1995). Chinese relationship orientation is so strong and
conspicuous even today that indigenous-oriented Chinese psychologists
have made considerable effort to assess relational-oriented personality
constructs. Indigenized scales and inventories have been developed for
the measurement of such constructs as interpersonal harmony, relational
determinism, *yuan* (predestined relational affinity), *xiaodao* (filial piety),
marital *enqing* (grateful love or affection).

According to K. S. Yang's (1995) conceptual analysis, Chinese relationship orientation comprises five major aspects, namely, relational formality,
relational reciprocity, relational fatalism, relational harmony, and relational
determinism. Chinese and Western psychologists have constructed
standardized scales for the measurement of relational fatalism, harmony,

and determinism. Chinese relational fatalism may be most adequately understood in terms of *yuan* beliefs. As a belief syndrome, *yuan* may be defined as a predestined relational affinity or the cause of such an affinity, which is believed to predetermine the occurrence, type, duration, and final outcome of an interpersonal relationship. Chinese people tend to attribute different types of relationships to different kinds of *yuan* as causal factors for those relationships. Chang and Holt (1991) and K. S. Yang and Ho (1988) made conceptual analyses of the meanings, kinds, and functions of *yuan* in traditional and contemporary Chinese societies. Yang and Ho (1988) contended that ascribing the formation and outcome of a relationship to *yuan* as an external and stable factor is an attributional process in Weiner's (1979) sense. In Chinese societies, external attributions to *yuan* have important social-defensive and ego-defensive functions that keep interpersonal relationships, especially those in the family, stable and harmonious in Chinese social life. Based on K. S. Yang and Ho's (1988) and Chang and Holt's (1991) conceptual analyses, Goodwin and Findlay (1997) constructed a *yuan* scale and used it to measure and compare British and Hong Kong university students' *yuan* beliefs.

Once a relationship is formed, it is extremely important to keep it stable and harmonious. Relational harmony is so important to the Chinese that they develop a strong propensity to pursue harmony for the sake of harmony and a strong fear of disharmony (the traditional Chinese term for conflict) (Huang, 1999; Leung & Wu, 1998; K. S. Yang, 1995). Zuo (2000) constructed a brief scale to assess the tendency towards harmony maintenance and disharmony avoidance. A more ambitious, systematic attempt at harmony assessment is being made by Huang, who is in the process of constructing a multidimensional scale for assessing the various kinds of harmony and conflict, based upon her comprehensive theory of interpersonal harmony and conflict (Huang, 1999).

Harmonious relationships are definitely useful. Chinese people have been characterized as particularistic, in Parsons' (1951) sense, in their thought and behavior (K. S. Yang, 1995). They tend to see standards, norms, regulations, and sometimes even laws as rough, abstract principles that are subject to modification when applied to practical, concrete cases. Exceptions are always possible when necessary, and the specific kind of relationship is the major factor according to which an exception is judged necessary or not. Chinese people are likely to give exceptional treatment or make special accommodation by relaxing or circumventing rules or principles as a favor for another person with whom they have an intimate or harmonious special relationship. It is the relationship with another person that *determines* what kind of exceptional favor that person will receive. Zuo (2000) constructed a short scale to measure this important aspect of Chinese relationship orientation.

The standardized scales constructed for assessing Chinese relational fatalism, harmony, and determinism are applicable to dyadic relationships in *all* domains of social life. Chinese psychologists have also developed scales for measuring relational-oriented personality attributes in *specific* domains of social life, of which the most important is family life. Typical examples of scales for the measurement and investigation of relational constructs in the family-life domain are those for *xiaodao* (filial piety) and *enqing* (marital grateful love or affection). Ho and associates (e.g., Ho, 1996; Ho & Lee, 1974) and K. S. Yang and associates (e.g., Yang, 1988; Yang, Yeh, & Huang, 1989) have conceptually and empirically analyzed Chinese filial piety. Ho and Lee (1974) constructed the first filiality scale. Sixteen years later, using K. S. Yang's (1988) definition of filial piety as a specific dispositional syndrome of cognitions, affects, intentions, and behaviors concerning being good to one's parents, K. S. Yang, Yeh, and Huang (1989) developed standardized multidimensional questionnaires to assess the four components of Chinese filiality: Reverence and Courteousness to Parents, Self-effacing Obedience to Parents, Attentiveness to Parents' Comforts and Worship of Parents after Death, and Protection and Glory for Parents. Four separate questionnaires were constructed to measure these four components at the cognitive, affective, intentional, and behavioral levels. Applying this set of tools, a large-scale study was conducted to investigate systematically the relationships between filial cognition, affection, intention, and behavior in terms of the four filiality components for each of the four relationships, viz., son to father, son to mother, daughter to father, and daughter to mother.

Another increasingly important relationship in the Chinese family is that between husband and wife. Attempts have been made to assess and investigate several matrimonial psychological constructs, of which Li's (1999, 2001) research on marital *enqing* (roughly meaning grateful love or affection) is the most indigenized and potentially useful. Li (1999) defined *enqing* as a kind of love, affection, and sentiment between husband and wife that is mainly based upon one party's feeling of indebtedness, gratitude, and appreciation for the other's kindness, consideration, favor, and tolerance during the history of the marital relationship. Based on qualitative data collected by depth interviews, she constructed the Multidimensional Marital Affection Scale for the assessment of *enqing*, which consisted of four subscales measuring the four affectional components identified by factor analysis, namely, Grateful Affection, Appreciative Affection, Intimate Affection, and Congenial Affection. Judged from these components, Chinese marital affection is apparently dominated by benevolence, forgiveness, forbearance, and unconditional care. It is interesting to note that not a single item with a sexual denotation can be found in the entire scale, vividly revealing Chinese couples' strong tendency to de-emphasize erotic love in their marital relationship. This nonerotic nature of Chinese marital affection seems to be different from American marital affection, which tends to carry more erotic sentiments.

Group-Oriented Personality Attributes

As repeatedly pointed out by C. F. Yang (1988) and M. H. Yeh and Yang (1998), the family is by far the most significant primary group in which Chinese people deeply and thoroughly function throughout their lives. The family is so important to the Chinese that a special sort of strong familism is formed through experiences of interaction with the family that emphasize the undeniable predominance of the family over its individual members in nearly all domains of life. At the core of Chinese familistic orientation, M. H. Yeh and Yang (1998) defined Chinese familism as a multifaceted system of cognitions, affects, intentions, and behaviors concerning the family that are held in common by the Chinese. They wrote separate pools of indigenized items and developed separate multidimensional scales to assess such components of Chinese familism as Family Harmony and Solidarity, Lineage Prolongation and Expansion, Family Prosperity, and Family Sentiments, as identified by factor analysis, for the measurement of familistic cognitions, affects, intentions, and behaviors. Of the four components, the first three are non-affective and the last affective.

Another group-oriented personality construct is paternalistic leadership. A series of such studies was conducted by the Cheng and Farh group, who used an indigenized perspective to conduct systematic research on leadership behavior in Chinese business organizations in Taiwan, Hong Kong, and China. Farh and Cheng (Farh & Cheng, 2000; Cheng, Chou, & Farh, 2001) developed a theoretical framework of Chinese paternalistic leadership, which proposed that paternalistic leadership is composed of three elements, leader morality, leader authoritarianism, and leader benevolence, which are respectively linked to three distinctive sets of subordinate responses: respect for and identification with the leader, dependence on and compliance with the leader, and indebtedness to and obligation to repay the leader. To test this three-element model, they constructed scales for measuring the three kinds of Chinese leadership (moral, authoritarian, and benevolent) and the three corresponding types of subordinate responses (identification, compliance, and gratitude) and obtained supportive results.

The third group-oriented personality construct is the social-oriented (S-O) achievement motivation, defined by K. S. Yang and Yu (1988) as the dynamic tendency to strive toward an *externally* determined goal in a *socially* chosen way with a certain amount of uncertainty in the outcome. In contrast, individual-oriented (I-O) achievement motivation refers to the dynamic tendency to strive toward an *internally* determined goal in a *personally* chosen way with a certain amount of uncertainty in the outcome. Using these definitions, Yu (1990) and Yu and Yang (1993) constructed two scales on the basis of a factor analytic study with a large set of theoretically derived items written in accordance with a conceptual scheme to compare systematically the two varieties of achievement motivation in terms of their achievement goal, achievement behavior, outcome evaluation, final consequences, and overall characteristics. They found that the two scales were negligibly negatively correlated. Empirical findings bearing on the construct validities of the scales for measuring the two independent achievement motives have been reported from a number of studies (for reviews, see K. S. Yang, 1999; Yu, 1996). For example, K. S. Yang (1982) theoretically predicted that the S-O achievement motive is an increasing function of parental dependence training, whereas the I-O achievement motive, an increasing function of independence training. Kuo, Zhang, and S. Z Yang's (1993) and Yu's (1990) studies confirmed Yang's prediction. Yu's (1990) study also found that the two types of achievement motivation were differently related to the same consequent (behavioral) variables. According to K. S. Yang and Yu's (1988, 1989), Yu's (1990, 1996), and Yu and Yang's (1993) definitional and conceptual analyses of the I-O achievement motivation, it is corresponding to the achievement motive in McClelland, Atkinson, Clark, and Lowell's (1953) sense.

Other-Oriented Personality Attributes

Other-oriented dispositions are mainly formed through past experiences of repeated interactions with non-specific, unidentified others in the social environment. These stable psychological and behavioral tendencies are particularly evident among people from collectivist cultures. In the case of Chinese people, the most pervasive and strong other-oriented dispositions are those related to face behavior. Many Chinese psychologists, anthropologists, and sociologists, notably Chen (1989), Chu (1983), Ho (1976), Hu (1944), Hwang (1987), and Zhai (1995), have advanced penetrating theoretical analyses of Chinese face psychology. A number of relevant empirical studies (e.g., Chen, 1989; Chou, 1995; Chu, 1983; Zuo, 1993) have been published since the early eighties. Chou's (1995) research on protective (P) and acquisitive (A) face orientations best represents those conducted on dispositional terms. She defined the P orientation as face behavior oriented towards protecting one's *lian* (moral face), and the A orientation as face behavior aimed at enhancing one's *mianzi* (social/positional face), which K. S. Yang and Yu (1989) and Yu (1996) termed *social-oriented self esteem*. Based on her conceptual comparison of the two face syndromes and materials collected from unstructured interviews, Chinese novels, daily newspapers, and common observations, she constructed the Protective and Acquisitive Face Orientation Scale to measure the two orientations, and standardized it on a large sample of working Chinese-Singaporeans. The total scores of the P and A subscales were found to be slightly negatively correlated with each other, revealing two fairly independent face constructs.

Another example of an other-oriented syndrome is Chinese social desirability (SD). The translated version of the Marlowe-Crowne Social Desirability Scale (Crowne & Marlowe, 1964) has long been used to provide a measure of SD as a response set control in many personality studies conducted in Taiwan. Using the perspective of self-presentation and impression management, C. F. Yang (1997) made a systematic conceptual analysis of the possible psychological processes behind Chinese people's responses to items on the SD scale. On the basis of this analysis, Lin and C. F. Yang (2001) wrote a large number of items from which 40 were empirically selected to construct an indigenized SD scale. Factor analysis identified two SD factors, one having high loadings on positive items, and the other on negative items, exactly like the two factors found in Paulhus's (1984, 1985, 1991) research. Paulhus (1991) interpreted the factor endorsing positive items as self-deception, and the factor endorsing negative items as impression management. In contrast, Lin and Yang (2001) made the opposite interpretation. That is, from the perspective of Chinese culture, the factor endorsing positive items should be labeled impression management, and that endorsing negative items, self-deception. Findings from subsequent research seem to be supportive of this interpretation. Lin and Yang's indigenized SD scale purported to be not only a measure of SD as a response set for control, but also a personality construct for research.

Future Research on Social-Oriented Personality Attributes

Among the social-oriented attributes reviewed in this section, most were found to be composed of two or more factorial components correlated with each other. This general finding indicates that a multidimensional social-oriented construct tends to be a psychological syndrome, rather than a simple unidimensional disposition. It may well occur because social-relational contexts in collectivist cultures are highly complicated, and a person functioning in such a culture tends to have highly complicated daily experiences that finally lead to the formation of complicated dispositional patterns for better adjustment in such a culture. It is also found that all the reviewed social-oriented constructs, unlike the individual-oriented ones, are apparently highly contextualized in interpersonal relationships, important groups, or non-specific others.

Personality psychologists in individualist cultures have devoted much of their time and energy to studying individual-oriented dispositions. Psychologists in collectivist cultures should put more effort into studying social-oriented syndromes, which have long been neglected by non-Western psychologists who conduct research from a Westernized perspective. To echo C. F. Yang's (1993a, 1993b) plea for more research on Chinese personality in its cultural, social, and historical contexts, Chinese psychologists should conduct more indigenized studies on relational-, group-, and other-oriented syndromes. Serious research is surely needed in many areas of social-oriented attributes, but four seem to be particularly worthy of special research attention, viz., self-related, affect-related, renqing-related, and zhongyong-related personality constructs. While the Chinese self may be markedly different from the Western self, as pointed out by C. F. Yang (1991) and K. S. Yang (2003), little indigenized empirical research has been done on Chinese people's self-related dispositional constructs. The two most important sets of such constructs are self-concept and self-esteem, on which K. S. Yang and associates (Yang, 2004; Yang & Cheng, 2002; Weng, Hsu, & Yang, 2004) have done theoretical analyses and empirical studies from a social-contextual perspective. They have developed indigenized multifaceted scales for the assessment of the individual-, relationship-, group-, and other-oriented modalities of the Chinese self-concept and self-esteem for use in further research.

Chinese affect is also a research topic long neglected by Chinese psychologists, indigenous and Westernized alike. Li's (1999, 2001) indigenized empirical study on the Chinese relational-oriented affection between husband and wife and Y. Y. Yang's (2001) on daughter-in-law and mother-in-law are all good starts. But more research of this kind by Chinese indigenous-oriented psychologists is badly needed. C. F. Yang (2001) recently made a systematic, penetrating indigenized conceptual analysis of Chinese affect that can definitely be relied upon as a theoretical guide for future personality research in this area.

Somewhat related to relational-oriented affection is *renqing* (exchangeable social favor), as conceptualized by Chu (1990), Hu (1944), Hwang (1987), King (1980), and Zhang and Yang (2001). While several useful conceptual analyses of *renqing* as a relationship-oriented social psychological phenomenon have been made, empirical research on the topic is rather meager. Hu (1944) and Zhang and Yang (2001) collected relevant empirical data by unstructured interviews and open-ended questions from small samples of people from China mainly for definitional purposes. K. H. Yeh (1989) conducted a more formal study by constructing the first *renqing* scale as a research tool. All these studies, however, are rather preliminary in nature. More systematic research is badly needed. Zhang and Yang (2001) have already provided a comprehensive conceptual framework for the analysis of *renqing* that is useful in deriving testable hypotheses for future personality research on this topic.

Finally, Chinese people are not the kind of people who interact or do things with others in a simplistic, straightforward, or linear way. Instead, they tend to live their lives in accordance with the way of *zhongyong* (*zhong* refers centrality, mean, and equilibrium and *yong* to ordinariness, universality, and harmoniousness), which is the Confucian Doctrine of the Mean. As a kind of meta-cognitive process, *zhongyong* is a Chinese way of dialectic thinking, the goal of which is to create and maintain interpersonal harmony (Chiu, 2000). This thinking style, still widely prevalent even among contemporary Chinese, "is characterized by holistic information processing, tolerance of apparent contradictions, and avoidance of extremities in implementation planning" (Chiu, 2000, p. 34). To assess this important mode of thinking, Chiu (2000) developed a unidimensional scale with satisfactory reliability and validity. With this scale, a new line of research may be conducted to explore the nature of *zhongyong* as a personality construct of cognitive style and to investigate the cognitive, affective, intentional, and behavioral processes and their interactions involved in the functioning of *zhongyong* in Chinese social life.

SOME GENERAL REMARKS

This chapter provides a review of a representative sample of empirical studies on Chinese personality conducted from an indigenized approach. As shown in Table 2, most of the reviewed personality attributes may

Table 2. A Classification of Selected Personality Constructs for Chinese People

Categories of Personality Attributes	Exemplary Personality Attributes
Individual-oriented Attributes	1. Competence vs. Impotence 2. Expressiveness vs. Conservatism 3. Self-control vs. Impulsiveness 4. Optimism vs. Neuroticism (1-4, *K. S. Yang & Bond, 1990*) 5. Outgoing vs. Withdrawn 6. Self-Serving vs. Principled 7. Stable vs. Unstable 8. Strict vs. Accepting (5-8, *P. C. Cheung et al., 1992*) 9. Emotionality 10. Responsibility 11. Practical Mindedness 12. Inferiority vs. Self-Acceptance 13. Optimism vs. Pessimism 14. Veraciousness vs. Slickness 15. External vs. Internal Locus of Control 16. Meticulousness 17. Flexibility 18. Thrift vs. Extravagance 19. Introversion vs. Extraversion 20. Adventurousness 21. Logical vs. Affective Orientation (9-21, *F. M. Cheung et al., 1996*)[a] 22. Competence vs. Impotence 23. Industriousness vs. Unindustriousness 24. Agreeableness vs. Disagreeableness 25. Extraversion vs. Introversion 26. Large-Mindedness vs. Small-Mindedness 27. Contentedness-Boastfulness

Continued

Table 2 (*cont.*)

Categories of Personality Attributes	Exemplary Personality Attributes
	28. Contentedness vs. Vaingloriousness (22-28, *K. S. Yang & Wang, 2000*)
	29. Individual-oriented achievement motivation (*Yu & Yang, 1997*)
Realtionship-oriented Attributes	30. Filial piety (*K. S. Yang, Yeh, & Huang, 1989*)
	31. Marital *Enqing* (grateful love or affection) (*Li, 1997*)
	32. Relational determinism (*Zuo, 2000*)
	33. Relational harmony (*F. M. Cheung et al., 1996; Zuo, 2000*)
	34. *Ren Qin* (exchangeable social favor) Orientation (*F. M. Cheung et al., 1996*)
	35. *Yuan* (predestined interpersonal affinity) (*Chang & Holt, 1991*)
Group-oriented Attributes	36. Familism (*M. H. Yeh & Yang, 1998*)
	37. Family orientation (*F. M. Cheung et al., 1992*)
	38. Leadership (*F. M. Cheung et al., 1996*)
	39. Paternalistic leadership (Farh & Cheung, 2000)
	40. Social-oriented achievement motivation (*Yu & Yang, 1997*)
Other-oriented Attributes	41. *Ah-Q* defensive mentality (*F. M. Cheung et al., 1996*)
	42. Conforming vs. Nonconforming (*P. C. Cheung et al., 1992*)
	43. Defensive and acquisitive face orientations (*Chou, 1995*)
	44. Face (*F. M. Cheung et al., 1992*)
	45. Other-Orientedness vs. Self-Centeredness (*K. S. Yang & Bond, 1990; K. S. Yang & Wang, 2000*)
	46. Social desirability (*Lin & Yang, 2001*)

[a] The test constructors did not provide evidence to indicate that all of the 13 individual-oriented attributes are sufficiently indigenous.

be classified into a four-level conceptual framework in terms of four categories of personality constructs, i.e., individual-, relationship-, group-, and other-oriented. Together, the last three are labeled social-oriented attributes. Individual-oriented constructs are devoid of substantial social contextual and social intentional components, whereas social-oriented ones are loaded with strong social contextual (relationship, group, and non-specific others) and social intentional considerations. While the four-level classificatory scheme as shown in Table 1 is useful for classifying Chinese personality constructs, it is also general enough to be more or less applicable to classification of personality characteristics of people in cultures all over the world. In individualist cultures, individual-oriented dispositions are more developed, differentiated, and influential in everyday life than social-oriented ones, and therefore more studied by local psychologists in these cultures. In contrast, in collectivist cultures, social-oriented dispositions are more developed, differentiated, and influential than individual-oriented ones, and therefore more studied by local psychologists in these cultures. Chinese psychologists adopting an indigenized approach are encouraged to do more research on social-oriented attributes. However, since Chinese people in Taiwan, Hong Kong, and China have been psychologically transforming from a social orientation to an individual orientation under the impact of societal modernization (K. S. Yang, 1986, 1996), they are gradually becoming less social-oriented and more individual-oriented in thoughts, attitudes, values, and behaviors than before. This change necessitates increased research on individual-oriented attributes even while Chinese psychologists continue to emphasize research on social-oriented attributes.

The term *personality* is used in this chapter in a rather broad sense to include not only individual-oriented constructs but also social-oriented ones. This usage is in dissonance with Hsu's (1971, 1985) argument that personality is an *individualistic* concept denoting a separate and *fixed* entity distinct from society and culture. Hsu argued that personality should be substituted by the interpersonal concept *jen* (or *ren* in pinyin, the Chinese word meaning personage), "because the Chinese conception...is based on the individual's transactions with his fellow human beings" (Hsu, 1985, p. 33). Hsu considered *jen* not as a fixed entity, but as something in a dynamic state seeking to maintain a satisfactory level of psychic and interpersonal equilibrium. He termed the process of maintaining this equilibrium *psychological homeostasis*.

Hsu set up personality as an individualistic concept as a strawman in order to argue that *jen* is better than personality as a basis for understanding human behavior with reference to sociocultural stability and change. As a matter of fact, personality is neither an individualistic concept nor a fixed entity. It is not individualistic for two reasons. First, the concept of personality is perfectly applicable to Shao Liu's classical theory of personality as fully expounded in his widely read book entitled *Renwu-ze* (*On Personages*) that appeared about 1,700 years ago in the Three Kingdoms Period (AD 220–280) of Chinese history. K. S. Yang (1993a, 1999) described and identified Shao Liu's full-fledged complex theoretical framework as a typical trait theory bearing all the basic characteristics of modern Western trait theories such as those of H. J. Eysenck, R. B. Cattell, J. P. Guilford, and R. R. McCrae and P. T. Costa. Liu's whole theory of personality is based upon five basic, intrapersonal traits of the temperamental nature conceptually derived from the Chinese doctrine of *yin* (passive, weak, and destructive) and *yang* (active, strong, and constructive) and the doctrine of *wuxing* (the Five Agents or Forces) (for a discussion of these doctrines, see Chan, 1963). Liu's theory provides clear evidence for the applicability of the concept of trait in particular and of personality in general, not only to people in a highly individualistic culture like the modern American one, but also to people in a highly collectivistic culture like that in ancient China. This wide applicability is one reason why personality should not be one-sidedly regarded as an individualistic concept.

Another reason against Hsu's (1971, 1985) conceptualization of personality as individualistic is that personality can be quite social-oriented in nature in people from collectivistic cultures. The relationship-, group-, and other-oriented personality attributes reviewed in the second section of this chapter are good examples of culture-specific social-oriented dispositions for Chinese people. All these attributes are formed through a person's transactions with fellow human beings in the social contexts of dyadic relationships, the family, and nonspecific others. The highly social nature of Chinese personality attests to the fact that personality may not be a separate or isolated entity, distinct from society or culture. Personality can be more individualistic or more collectivistic, depending upon whether it develops in an individualist or collectivist culture.

Moreover, personality is not a fixed entity as conceptualized by Hsu (1971, 1985). There are all sorts of existing entities with varying degrees of stability or changeability in the world and the universe as well. In the domain of psychology, there are different kinds of existing psychological and behavioral entities with varying degrees of stability or changeability. These entities should not be dichotomized into fixed and not fixed. We can only say that some of them are *relatively* stable and some *relatively* unstable or malleable. Personality can not be completely fixed; it is always changeable and changing, but normally at a slow pace and in a small way. Unusual change in personality may occur due to lasting drastic environmental change, natural or social. This is especially true of social-oriented personality attributes, which may change greatly with unusual changes in the social-relational environment, as those experienced by an immigrant in the process of rapid acculturation in the host country or by a non-Westerner in the process of societal modernization in the rapidly tranforming home country.

As a normally lasting but changeable entity, personality is a kind of structural system resulting from a person's continuous effort to maintain a uniform, stable, and beneficial psychological stability of dynamic equilibrium involving both personal-internal and social-relational factors in daily life. The social-relational aspects of personality, just as those of *jen*, are gradually structured through a person's transactions with other persons separately or collectively in his or her specific sociocultural environment. Once formed, the relatively stable personality is beneficial in three respects. First, a person's personality allows one's own thoughts and behavior to be understandable and predictable to *others* in daily social life. Second, a person's personality enables one's own thoughts and behavior to be understandable and predictable to *oneself* in daily social life. Third, and most important, a normal personality representing the most optimal level of psychic and social-relational equilibrium will allow the person to adjust to the sociocultural environment more easily and smoothly, without spending too much time and energy on trial-and-error.

Personality is not necessarily individualistic and definitely not fixed. As an important kind of structural and functional psychological entity, personality is composed of not only individual-oriented attributes but also social-oriented ones. As such, the concept of personality can be equally applicable to people in individualist and collectivist cultures in an indigenous way. The social-oriented aspects of personality should be able to effectively incorporate all kinds of experiences of social and relational transactions with fellow human beings in sociocultural contexts. There is no need to substitute the concept of personality with *jen*, which Hsu (1971, 1985) failed to define as a well-integrated concept in a clear way.

REFERENCES

Chan, W. T. (Translated and compiled) (1963). *A source book in Chinese philosophy*. Princeton, NJ: Princeton University Press.

Chang, H. C., & Holt, G. R. (1991). The concept of *yuan* and Chinese interpersonal relationship. In S. Ting-Toomey & F. Korzenny (Eds.), *Cross-cultural interpersonal communication* (pp. 28–57). Newburry Park, CA: Sage.

Chen, C. C. (1989). The psychology of face: Theoretical analysis and empirical research. In K. S. Yang (Ed.), *The Chinese mind* (pp.155–237). Taipei, Taiwan: Guiguan Book Co. (In Chinese).

Cheng, B. S., Chou, L. F., & Farh, J. L. (2001). Paternalistic leadership: The construction and assessment of the Three-element Model. *Indigenous Psychological Research in Chinese Societies, 14*, 3–64. (In Chinese).

Cheung, F. M., & Leung, K. (1998). Indigenous personality measures: Chinese examples. *Journal of Cross-Cultural Psychology, 29*, 233–248.

Cheung, F. M., Leung, K., Fan, R. M., Song, W. Z., Zhang, J. X., & Zhang, J. P. (1996). Development of the Chinese Personality Assessment Inventory. *Journal of Cross-Cultural Psychology, 24*(2), 181–199.

Cheung, P. C., Conger, A. J., Hau, K. T., Lew, W. J. F., & Lau, S. (1992). Development of the Multi-Trait Personality Inventory (MTPI): Comparison among four Chinese populations. *Journal of Personality Assessment, 59*, 528–551.

Chiao, C. (1982). *Guanxi* (relationship): A preliminary analysis. In K. S. Yang & C. I. Wen (Eds.), *The Sinicization of social and behavioral science research in China*. Taipei, Taiwan: Institute of Ethnology, Academia Sinica. (In Chinese).

Chiu, C. Y. (2000). Assessment of *zhong-yong* (dialectic) thinking: Preliminary findings from a cross-regional study. *Hong Kong Journal of Social Sciences, 18*, 33–55. (In Chinese).

Chiu, C. Y., Hong, Y., & Dweck, C. S. (1997). Lay dispositionism and implicit theories of personality. *Journal of Personality and Social Psychology, 73*, 19–30.

Chou, M. L. (1995). *The relationships of protective and acquisitive face needs with personality factors in self-presentation*. Unpublished manuscript, University of Hong Kong, Hong Kong.

Chu, R. L. (1983). *Empirical studies on the psychological and behavioral phenomena of face*. Unpublished doctoral dissertation, National Taiwan University, Taipei, Taiwan. (In Chinese).

Chu, R. L. (1990). Expressive and utilitarian *renqing*. In Teacher Chang Monthly (Ed.), *Chinese people's psychological games* (pp. 120–127). Taipei, Taiwan: Teacher Chang Monthly Editorial Board. (In Chinese).

Church, A. T. (2000). *Culture and personality: Toward an integrated cultural trait psychology.* Paper presented at the 25th International Congress of the International Association for Cross-Cultural Psychology, Pultusk, Poland.

Costa, P. T. Jr., & McCrae, R. R. (1985). *The NEO Personality Inventory Manual.* Odessa, FL: Psychological Assessment Resources.

Crowne, D. P., & Marlowe, D. (1964). *The approval motive: Studies in evaluative dependence.* New York: Wiley.

Dweck, C. S., & Leggett, E. L. (1988). A social-cognitive approach to motivation and personality. *Psychological Review, 95,* 256–273.

Dweck, C. S., Hong, Y., & Chiu, C. (1993). Implicit theories: Individual differences in the likelihood and meaning of dispositional inference. *Personality and Social Psychology Bulletin, 19,* 644–656.

Farh, J. L., & Cheng, B. S. (2000). A cultural analysis of paternalistic leadership in Chinese organizations. In J. T. Li, A. S. Tsui, & E. Weldon (Eds.), *Management and Organizations in the Chinese Context* (pp. 84–127). London: Macmillan.

Fei, H. T. (1980). *Rural China.* Hong Kong: Fenghuang Publishing Co. (In Chinese).

Freud, S. (1924). The loss of reality in neurosis and psychosis. In J. Stachey (Ed.), *The standard edition of the complete psychological works of Sigmund Freud, Vol. 19: The ego and the id and other works* (pp. 183–187). London: Hogarth Press.

Goodwin, R., & Findlay, C. (1997). "We were just fated together". Chinese love and the concept of *yuan* in England and Hong Kong. *Personal Relationship, 4,* 85–92.

Guildford, J. P. (1959). *Personality.* New York: McCraw-Hill.

Ho, D. Y. F. (1976). On the concept of face. *American Journal of Sociology, 81,* 867–884.

Ho, D. Y. F. (1991). Relational orientation and methodological relationalism. *Bulletin of the Hong Kong Psychological Society,* Nos. 26/27, 81–95.

Ho, D. Y. F. (1996). Filial piety and its psychological consequences. In M. H. Bond (Ed.), *The handbook of Chinese psychology* (pp.155–165). Hong Kong: Oxford University Press.

Ho, D. Y. F. (1998). Interpersonal relationships and relationship dominance: Analysis based on methodological relationalism. *Asian Journal of Social Psychology, 1,* 1–16.

Ho, D. Y. F., & Chiu, C. Y. (1994). Component idea of individualism, collectivism, and social organization: An application in the study of Chinese culture. In U. Kim, H. C. Triandis, C. Kagitcibasi, S. C. Choi, & G. Yoon (Eds.), *Individualism and collectivism: Theory, method, and applications* (pp.137–156). London: Sage.

Ho, D. Y. F., & Lee, L. Y. (1974). Authoritarianism and attitude toward filial piety in Chinese teachers. *Journal of Social Psychology, 92,* 305–306.

Hofstede, G. (1980). *Culture's consequences.* Beverly Hills, CA: Sage.

Hsu, F. L. K. (1971). Psychosocial homeostasis and *jen*: Conceptual tools for advancing psychological anthropology. *American Anthropologist, 73* (1), 23–44.

Hsu, F. L. K. (1985). The self in cross-cultural perspective. In A. J. Marsella, G. DeVos, & F. L. K. Hsu (Eds.), *Culture and Self: Asian and Western perspectives.* New York: Tavistock.

Hsu, K. Y., Wang, D. F., & Yang, K. S. (2001). Differences between Taiwanese and Mainland Chinese basic personality dimensions. *Indigenous Psychological Research in Chinese Societies, 16,* 185–224. (In Chinese).

Hu, H. C. (1944). The Chinese concept of "face". *American Anthropologist, 46,* 45–64.

Huang, L. L. (1999). *Interpersonal harmony and conflict: Indigenized theory and research.* Taipei, Taiwan: Guiguan Book Co. (In Chinese).

Hwang, K. K. (1987). Face and favor: Chinese power game. *American Journal of Sociology, 92,* 944–974.

Hwang, K. K. (2000). Chinese relationalism: Theoretical construction and methodological considerations. *Journal for the Theory of Social Behavior, 30,* 155–178.

King, A. Y. C. (1980). An analysis of *renqing* in interpersonal relationship. In Academia Sinica (Ed.), *Proceedings of the First International Conference on Sinology.* Taipei, Taiwan: Academia Sinica. (In Chinese).

King, A. Y. C. (1991) *Kuan-hsi* and network building: A sociological interpretation. DAEDALUS: *Journal of the American Academy of Arts and Science,* Spring, 63–84.

Kitayama, S., Markus, H. R., Matsumoto, H., & Norasakkunkit, V. (1997). Individual and collective processes in the construction of the self: Self-enhancement in the United States and self-criticism in Japan. *Journal of Personality and Social Psychology, 72* (6), 1245–1267.

Kuo, D. J., Zhang, G. L., & Yang, S. Z. (1993). Effects of parents' training style on the child's achievement motivation. *Journal of Beijing Normal University, 2,* 20–30. (In Chinese).

Leung, K., & Wu, P. G. (1998). The role of *he* (harmony) as a double-edged sword in management. In B. S. Cheng, K. L. Hwang, & J. Z. Kuo (Eds.), *Human resources management in Taiwan and Mainland China.* Taipei, Taiwan: Sinyi Cultural Foundation. (In Chinese).

Lew, W. J. F (1998/2001). *Understanding the Chinese personality.* Taipei, Taiwan: Yuanliu Publishing Co. (In Chinese).

Li, T. S. (1999). The content and measurement of marital intimate affection. *Chinese Journal of Mental Health, 12*(4), 197–216. (In Chinese).

Li, T. S. (2001). *The study of Chinese marital relationship from the perspective of enqing between husband and wife.* Unpublished manuscript, Fu Jen Catholic University, Taipei, Taiwan. (In Chinese).

Liang, S. M. (1974). *The essentials of Chinese culture.* Hong Kong: Chicheng Book Co. (In Chinese).

Lin, Y. C., & Yang, C. F. (2001). *The measurement and process of the tendency of social desirability: An indigenized approach.* Unpublished manuscript, National Taiwan University, Taipei, Taiwan. (In Chinese).

Markus, H. R., & Kitayama, S. (1998). The cultural psychology of personality. *Journal of Cross-Cultural Psychology, 29,* 63–87.

Matthews, G., & Deary, I. J. (1998). *Personality traits.* Cambridge: Cambridge University Press.

McClelland, D. C., Atkinson, J. W., Clark, R. A., & Lowell, E. L. (1953). *The achievement motive.* New York: Appleton-Century-Crofts.

Norman, W. T. (1961). *Development of self-report test to measure personality factors identified from peer nominations* (USAF ASD Technical Note No. 61–44). Lackland Air Force Base, TX: U.S. Air Force.

Norman, W. T. (1963). Toward an adequate taxonomy of personality attributes: Replicated factor structure in peer nomination personality ratings. *Journal of Abnormal and Social Psychology, 66,* 574–583.

Parsons, T. (1951). *The social system.* New York: The Free Press.

Paulhus, D. L. (1984). Two-component models of socially desirable responding. *Journal of Personality and Social Psychology, 46* (3), 598–609.

Paulhus, D. L. (1985). Self-deception and impression management in test responses. In A. Angletitner & J. S. Wiggins (Eds.), *Personality assessment via questionnaires.* New York: Springer-Verlag.

Paulhus, D. L. (1991). Measurement and control of response bias. *Measures of social psychological attitudes, Vol. 1* (pp.17–59). San Diego, CA: Academic Press.

Pervin, L. A. (1996). *The science of personality.* New York: Wiley.

Triandis, H. C. (1993). Collectivism and individualism as cultural syndromes. *Cross-cultural Research, 27,* 155–180.

Triandis, H. C. (1995). *Individualism and collectivism.* Boulder, CA: Westview Press.

Tupes, E. C., & Christal, R. E. (1958). *Stability of personality trait rating factors obtained under diverse conditions* (USAF WADC Technical Note No. 58–61). Lackland Air Force Base, TX: U.S. Air Force.

Wang, D. F., & Cui, H. (2003). Progress and preliminary results in the construction of the Chinese Personality Scale (OZPS). *Acta Psychologica Sinica, 35* (1), 127–136. (In Chinese).

Wang, D. F., & Cui, H. (2004). Reliabilities and validities of the Chinese Personality Scale. *Acta Psychologica Sinica, 36* (3), 347–358. (In Chinese).

Weiner, B. (1979). A theory of motivation for some classroom experiences. *Journal of Educational Psychology, 71,* 3–25.

Weng, C. Y., Hsu, Y., & Yang, K. S. (2004). Social-oriented and individual-oriented self-esteem: Conceptual analysis and empirical assessment. In K. S. Yang & K. Y. Hsu (Eds.),

Proceedings of the Conference in Chinese self process, concept, and evaluation. I-Lan County, Taiwan: Department of Psychology, Fu Guang College of Humanities and Social Sciences.

Yang, C. F. (1988). Familism and development: An examination of the role of family in contemporary China Mainland, Hong Kong, and Taiwan. In D. Sinha & H. S. R. Kao (Eds.), *Social values and development: Asian perspectives* (pp.93–123). New Delhi: Sage.

Yang, C. F. (1991). On the Chinese self: Theoretical analysis and research directions. In C. F. Yang & H. S. R. Kao (Eds.), *Chinese people, Chinese mind: Personality and social psychological processes* (pp. 15–92). Taipei, Taiwan: Yuanliu Publishing Co. (In Chinese).

Yang, C. F. (1993a). On ways to deepen the indigenization of psychological research in Chinese societies. *Indigenous Psychological Research in Chinese Societies, 1,* 122–183. (In Chinese).

Yang, C. F. (1993b). On how to study Chinese personality: Lessons from Western personality and social psychological research. In K. S. Yang & A. B. Yu (Eds.), *Chinese mind and behavior: Conceptual and methodological considerations* (pp. 319–439). Taipei, Taiwan: Guiguan Book Co. (In Chinese).

Yang, C. F. (1996). *How to study the Chinese people.* Taipei: Guiguan Book Co. (In Chinese).

Yang, C. F. (1997). *Study on underlying psychological processes of social desirability scores.* Unpublished manuscript, University of Hong Kong, Hong Kong.

Yang, C. F. (2001). The conceptualization of interpersonal relationship and interpersonal affection. In C. F. Yang (Ed.), *Chinese interpersonal relationship, affection, and trust: An interpersonal transactional viewpoint.* Taipei, Taiwan: Yuanliu Publishing Co. (In Chinese).

Yang, K. S. (1982). The Sinicization of psychological research: Levels and dirctions. In K. S. Yang & C. I. Wen (Eds.), *The Sinicization of social and behavioral research in China.* Taipei, Taiwan: Institute of Ethonology, Academia Sinica.

Yang, K. S. (1986). Chinese personality and its change. In M. H. Bond (Ed.), *The psychology of the Chinese people* (pp. 106–170). Hong Kong: Oxford University Press.

Yang, K. S. (1988). Chinese filial piety: A conceptual analysis. In K. S. Yang (Ed.), *The Chinese mind* (pp.39–73). Taipei, Taiwan: Guiguan Book Co. (In Chinese).

Yang, K. S. (1993a). Shao Liu's personality theory: Systematization and exegesis. In Y. K. Hwang (Ed.), *Person, meaning and society* (pp.89–127). Taipei, Taiwan: Institute of Ethnology, Academia Sinica. (In Chinese).

Yang, K. S. (1993b). Why do we need to develop an indigenized Chinese psychology? *Indigenous Psychological Research in Chinese Societies, 1,* 6–88. (In Chinese).

Yang, K. S. (1995). Chinese social orientation: An integrative analysis. In W. S. Tseng, T. Y. Lin, & Y. K. Yeh (Eds.), *Chinese societies and mental health* (pp.19–39). Hong Kong: Oxford University Press.

Yang, K. S. (1996). Psychological transformation of the Chinese people as a result of societal modernization. In M. H. Bond (Ed.), *The handbook of Chinese psychology* (pp. 479–498). New York: Oxford University Press.

Yang, K. S. (1997a). Indigenizing Westernized Chinese psychology. In M. H. Bond (Ed.), *Working at the interface of cultures: Eighteen lives in social science.* London: Routledge.

Yang, K. S. (1997b). Indigenous compatibility in psychological research and its related problems. *Indigenous Psychological Research in Chinese Societies, 8,* 75–120. (In Chinese).

Yang, K. S. (1999). Towards an indigenous Chinese psychology: A selective review of methodological, theoretical, and empirical accomplishments. *Chinese Journal of Psychology, 4,* 181–211.

Yang, K. S. (2000). Monocultural and cross-cultural indigenous approaches: The royal road to the development of a balanced global psychology. *Asian Journal of Social Psychology, 3,* 241–263.

Yang, K. S. (2003). Beyond Maslow's culture-bound linear theory: A preliminary statement of the double-Y model of basic human needs. In V. Murphy-Berman & J. J. Berman (Eds.), *Nebraska Symposium on Motivation, Vol. 49: Cross-cultural differences in perspectives on the self.* Lincoln, NE: University of Nebraska Press.

Yang, K. S. (2004). Toward a theory of the Chinese self: Conceptual analysis in terms of Social orientation and individual orientation. In K. S. Yang & K. Y. Hsu (Eds.), *Proceedings of the Conference on Chinese Self Process, Concept, and Evaluation*. I-Lan County, Taiwan: Department of Psychology, Fu Guang College of Humanities and Social Sciences.

Yang, K. S., & Bond, M. H. (1990). Exploring implicit personality theories with indigenous or imported constructs: The Chinese case. *Journal of Personality and Social Psychology, 58,* 1087–1095.

Yang, K. S., & Cheng, C. F. (2002). *Self-concept discrepancy and affect: An indigenized test of Higgins' theory* (Tech. Rep. No. 89-H-FA01-2-4). Taipei, Taiwan: National Taiwan University.

Yang, K. S., & Ho, Y. F. (1988). The role of *yuan* in Chinese social life: A conceptual and empirical analysis. In A. C. Paranjpe, D. H. F. Ho, & R. W. Rieber (Eds.), *Asian contributions to psychology* (pp. 263–281). New York: Praeger.

Yang, K. S., & Wang, D. F. (2000). *Basic Chinese personality dimensions and their relationships with the American big five.* Report of the 3-year Specially Appointed Research Project Financially Supported by the National Science Council of the Republic of China (NSC 86-2143-H002-026). Taipei, Taiwan: National Science Council. (In Chinese).

Yang, K. S., & Yu, A. B. (1988). *Social-oriented and individual-oriented achievement motivation: Conceptualization and measurement.* Paper presented at the 24th International Congress of Applied Psychology, Sydney.

Yang, K. S., & Yu, A. B. (1989). *Social-oriented and individual-oriented achievement motivation: An attributional analysis of their cognitive, affective, motivational, and behavioral consequences.* Paper presented at the 10th biennial meeting of the International Society for the Study of Behavioral Development, Jyävskylä, Finland.

Yang, K. S., Yeh, K. H., & Huang, L. K. (1989). Social psychological aspects of Chinese filial piety: Conceptualization and measurement. *Bulletin of the Institute of Ethnology, Academia Sinica, 65,* 171–227. (In Chinese).

Yang, Y. Y. (2001). Chinese affectional interaction pattern in the relationship between mother-in-law and daughter-in-law. In C. F. Yang (Ed.), *Chinese interpersonal relationship, affection, and trust: An interpersonal transactional viewpoint* (pp. 199–222). Taipei, Taiwan: Yuanliu Publishing Co. (In Chinese).

Yeh, K. H. (1989). *Renqing orientation, distributive equity, and performance.* Unpublished manuscript, National Taiwan University, Taipei, Taiwan. (In Chinese).

Yeh, M. H., & Yang, K. S. (1998). Chinese familism: Conceptualization and assessment. *Bulletin of the Institute of Ethnology, Academia Sinica, 83,* 169–225. (In Chinese).

Yu, A. B. (1990). *The construct validity of social-oriented and individual-oriented achievement motivation.* Unpublished doctoral dissertation, National Taiwan University, Taipei, Taiwan. (In Chinese).

Yu, A. B. (1996). Ultimate life concerns, self, and Chinese achievement motivation. In M. H. Bond (Ed.), *The handbook of Chinese psychology* (pp. 227–246). Hong Kong: Oxford University Press.

Yu, A. B., & Yang, K. S. (1993). The nature of achievement motivation in collectivistic societies. In U. Kim, H. C. Triandis, C. Kagitcibasi, S. C. Choi, & G. Yoon (Eds.), *Individualism and collectivism: Theory, method, and applications* (pp. 239–250). Thousand Oaks, CA: Sage.

Zhai, X. W. (1995). *Chinese views of lian and mian.* Taipei, Taiwan: Guiguan Book Co. (In Chinese).

Zhang, Z. X., & Yang, C. F. (2001). A study on the *renqing* concept. In C. F. Yang (Ed.), *Chinese interpersonal relationship, affection, and trust: An interpersonal transactional viewpoint* (pp. 223–246). Taipei, Taiwan: Yuanliu Publishing Co. (In Chinese).

Zuo, B. (1993). A social psychological study of Chinese students' cognitions of face events. In Q. S. Li (Ed.), *The social psychological study of Chinese people* (pp. 122–140). Hong Kong: Modern Culture Publishing Co. (In Chinese).

Zuo, B. (2000). *The measurement of Chinese relationship orientation: An indigenized approach.* Paper presented at the 5th Interdisciplinary Conference on Chinese Mind and Behavior: Family-Member Relationships and Psychological Processes Involved, held in the Institute of Ethnology, Academia Sinica, Taipei, Taiwan. (In Chinese).

Chapter 14

An Historic-Psycho-Socio-Cultural Look at the Self in Mexico

Rolando Diaz Loving

In 1901, Ezequiel A Chavez, an influential Mexican academic, wrote the following lines:

> Character varies across ethnic groups, and thus, the most relevant human endeavor is lodged in the study of the ethnic character of people. Not considering this cardinal rule has induced many to fall victim to the absurdity of attempting the direct transplant of educational, repressive, or political institutions, without even reflecting on the possible incompatibility of intellect, feelings, and will, of the people who they intend to improve, offering a beautiful, although inadequate reality . . . It is not enough for laws to satisfy intelligence in the abstract, it is indispensable that they concretely adapt to the special conditions of the people they were created for. Ideas and programs may seem very noble, however, a sad reality is lived to often in Latin American countries, when marvelous plans are traced on paper, harmonic constitutions are advanced, and like Plato's dreams, they crash against the crudeness of practice and reality.

This fragment offers at least two major considerations. On the one hand, it points out the cardinal role of culture in the construction of reality, on the other, it underscores the historic preoccupation of the Mexican people with the roots and reaches of their identity.

Before the Spanish arrived on the Mexican coasts in the 1500s, Mesoamerica was a thriving and culturally diverse region. Over one million Aztecs populated a bustling Tenochtitlan. They were a powerful warrior people who had many enemies. Among them, the Tlaxcaltecas contributed over 12,000 fighters to the Spanish attack on their city. Many other wonderful cultures developed in equally distinct geographical ecosystems of the area, such as the Mayans and the Olmecas. Each Pre-Columbian ethnic group contributed its biological and cultural heritage across three centuries of colonial rule. A priest, Bartolome de las Casas, wrote profusely in regard to the customs and rights of town and country during the colonial years. Extracting from his legacy, a vivid and distinct ethnic identity is conceivable for each group, and the depiction of integration of the races is full of clearly distinguishable paths. In the early 1800s, after a decade of war for independence, an army marched into Mexico City. Indigenous people, Mestizos and Criollos each led a contingent. However, Iturbide, a Spanish general also fighting for independence from Spain, arrived at the government palace first and established himself as the monarch of the newly free Mexican Empire. Questions arose as to whether the new nation's ethnic identity was akin to a European monarchy, or a multicultural republic led by the children of Spanish men and indigenous women, or to the indigenous peoples inhabiting the land before the Spanish ever came. Who did Mexicans identify with? Who were they? What was their character? The nineteenth century brought many new battles. After the independence movement, there was a French invasion, a reform movement to separate church and state, a military incursion of the United States into Mexican soil, and finally 40 years of dictatorship in the hands of Porfirio Diaz. Through out the 19th century, Mexican thinkers and philosophers quarreled over their European heritage, their indigenous roots, and our mixed reality. As a result, Mexicans grew for many years in the shadows of a comparison to the European philosophies and way of life.

The emergence of the twentieth century saw a civil revolution. At stake, aside from a power struggle, were the identity of a country and the emancipation of an indigenous Mestizo movement. In its aftermath, Jose Vasconcelos, a writer, politician, and thinker, promulgated the coming of a cosmic race that extracted its strength from its mixed past. The measuring stick for ethnic identity was now indigenous. No more comparisons were made to the European past. In essence, a time directly in line with the quote from Ezequiel Chavez had arrived.

However, as with any process of acculturation, stability only crystallized for a brief moment. A few years later, in the 1930s, Samuel Ramos, a Philosopher at the National Autonomous University of Mexico, avidly read Adler's depiction of the development of personality, and extracted the importance of autonomy and independence for the development of the self. With this new measuring tool in hand, he set out to the Mexican countryside and interviewed indigenous people in an attempt to describe the Mexican self. Over and over again he found depictions that focused on the importance of the community, of family, of the cardinal place that others have in the definition of the individual self. Ramos analyzed his data, and forgetting Chavez' admonition, took collective responses as a sign of a lack of independence. He arrived at the conclusion that the Mexican self was covered by an inferiority complex. The result was devastating to the ethnic identity of the Mexican people. Other writers and philosophers set out on a self-fulfilling prophecy that led them to verify the inferiority hypothesis with little or no data. It was as if the middle ages had returned. The only possibility of Renaissance was the development of serious and systematic psychological research.

The concept of *self* as a human endeavor has an ancient history. In the West, before Christ, inscriptions at the Oracle in Delphi dwelled on the importance of knowing thyself. Since, and before, all great philosophical writings cover its components and processes. In all cases, how we perceive ourselves, how we see ourselves through the eyes of others, if we behave differently or consistently according to the contingency and characteristics of the situations, how we see ourselves with the change of age and the expectations of others, and the way in which we explain the continuity of our lives, appears constantly as part of the basic human character. Without a doubt, the self-concept construct has been the reason for research and deliberation in different areas of knowledge.

However, in no place is this more evident than within Euro-American psychology, where the self functions as the core of every major theoretical inclination in the discipline, revealing its cardinal essence. In fact, the history of the self-concept as a psychological construct goes back to writings of several of the oldest theoreticians. William James (1890) considered not only the image that we have of ourselves, but the image that others have of us. His work opened a social conception of self and the promise to study the concept empirically. James distinguished three distinct components of the self. The material self, who worries about objects and places, the social self, who is concerned with relationships and interactions, and the spiritual self, who worries about immediate reality. Although James emphasized the unit and the continuity of the self-concept related to the continuity of the course of the individual's thought, he incorporated a plurality of selves derived from the social sphere. In his own right, and in the same period, Sigmund Freud (1967) rejected phenomenological positions, and thus had little use for a self-concept, but he left it implicit in the conceptual structure of the ego, the objective entity that gives a coherent organization to mental processes. Accordingly, Freud elected to speak of an *I* (ego) as one of the three basic structures that compose the personality of all individuals (id, ego, and super-ego). This *I* is the social mediator between consciousness, unconsciousness and reality. It controls all sensorial and perceptual functioning, dominates the motor responses, and is in charge of confronting information and pressures coming from outside and inside the organism.

Other influential authors of the past have focused on the processes related to the development of the self. In the late 1800s, Baldwin (1897) centered on how the self emerges and is constructed by the individual as a result of his/her interaction with others. Similarly, Cooley (1902) at the beginning of the 1900s postulated the self develops as a reflection that results from social interaction and the reactions those others have towards us. Later, in the 1930s, inscribed in his social interactionism theory, George Herbert Mead (1990) established the self as emerging from a process that uses symbols and develops with time from contact with others in a continuous deluge of social communication. This process initiates when people learn to see themselves as knowledge objects, which later will allow them to think about themselves. For Mead, the self is itself an object of knowledge that is not unitary, since it can be developed in multiple forms, creating many selves based on different social groups. Some will be closer to the individual self concept as in the case of traits, others to a social group as in the case of identity.

The path of the self as the principal topic in psychology has continued through out the twentieth century, as it influences all scopes of human behavior. According to Allport (1976) the self is implicated in all human conduct and influences the confidence, judgment, memory, reference frame, aptitude for learning and all other motivational aspects of behavior. In other words, because the self is so important in human life, it is defined as the unifying force of all habits, characteristics, attitudes, feelings, and tendencies of the human being. In summary, the self-concept is more than a simple phenomenon, and has been presented as the central construct of psychology, since it somehow rules human behavior, which is finally the primary object of study in psychology as a science. However, recognizing its importance was only a first step, the challenge became to delimit and define the concept suitably. With the need, came an endless number of sublime definitions and theories, which described it in terms of "I", consciousness, individualization, introspection, self-image, self-esteem and identity.

Given the attention the self has engaged, it seems fair to ask before continuing whether the self is a simple artifact of western psychology, or whether it can be rescued as a human phenomena if socio-cultural and eco-systemic effects are factored into the formula. The answer lies in a synthesis of the social psychological perspective of the self and the evident preoccupation with identity in the history of the dwellers of the Mexican territory. Adding these two theses, it seems clear that the phenomenon extends to this cultural group. Therefore, by paying close attention to Chavez's postulates and James's proclivity, it seems inevitable to study all selves from a socio-cultural perspective. True to this cross-cultural initiative, Diaz Guerrero (e.g. 1971, 1982, & 1994) has repeatedly shown that the interplay between biology (psychological structure) and culture (social) determine the development of personality. He further contended that each socio-culture offers a system of interrelated premises that provide norms for feelings and ideas, and hierarchy of interpersonal relationships. In other words, the socio-culture offers a system of interrelated premises that are internalized by individuals in such way that they provide norms for feelings, ideas, and behaviors by stipulating the types of social roles, the interaction of the individual in those roles, and the where, when, how, and with whom to play them. As result, the Mexican self is embedded in a social developmental process that relies on the socialization and enculturation practices of its people.

Based on this line of research, Diaz Guerrero (1977) proposed a typology of the Mexican prototype, in which 8 different personality structures would emerge. Given the strength an inclination of the socio-cultural premises in the development of personality, four of these types describe over 90% of the population. True to the emphasis destined in the Mexican socioculture to collective, social, and relational activities, the most widely spread character, over 75% of the population, was an affiliative obedient type who is affectionate, dependent, agreeable, controlled, and showed high need of social approval and support. A smaller percentage of the population would rebel against the dictates and norms of the society, producing an actively self-affirming orientation, which would translate into autonomous, independent, impulsive, dominant, rebellious, and intelligent characteristics, very similar to the typical profile found in instrumental hierarchical individualistic cultures. From the combination of the traditional premises and a moderate self-actualizing tendency, another small portion of the population would develop an active internal control, which would show through affectionate, thoughtful, rational, flexible, and capable traits. Finally, constructing from the negative emotional component of every bio-system and the traditional socio-emotive norms, a passive external control type would appear, engulfed in authoritarian, aggressive, corrupt, impulsive, pessimist, uncontrolled, and servile orientations.

The psycho-socio-cultural tracing of the Mexican self initiates with the research conducted by Diaz Guerrero (1982) using Osgood's Semantic Differential technique with Mexican adolescents in the 1960s. In a comparison of the evaluative, power, and dynamism scores of the self, Mexican teenagers consistently scored lower in evaluation and power than their cohorts from 16 other cultures. The activity scores set them at the median in relation to the other youths. In addition, when the scores for evaluation of the self were compared with other social and family stimuli, such as father, mother, sister, brother, grandparents, friends, and even strangers, the adolescents scored their self as less positive. This set of data replicate the findings Samuel Ramos gathered in the 1930s. However, the interpretation is different. Ramos instigated an inferiority complex as the culprit. Diaz-Guerrero proclaimed the deeply social character of the Mexican. In fact, in closer scrutiny of the data, the evaluation and power means for Mexican adolescents are above 1 (the scale goes form −3 to +3), indicating an absolute positive score, although relatively lower than adolescents from other cultures. Construing the Mexican self in a different light has definitely had an impact on the identity built for the group. A reanalysis of the events shows that when the Mexican philosophers have conceptualized the self relative to European norms, and when Ramos interpreted his results in congruence with Adler's position, the picture was dim. In contrast, when diversity was exalted by Vasconcelos in his cosmic race, or the social core of the self was brought up by Diaz-Guerrero, a collective, dependent, social, yet positive construal of the self is possible.

From a more deeply indigenous perspective, one which included method in its pursuit, La Rosa and Diaz-Loving (1991) set out to explore the idiosyncratic make up of the self concept of Mexicans. Starting with exploratory qualitative methodologies, they were able to discover social, emotional, ethical, physical, and instrumental dimensions of self concept. Brain storming and focus groups later led to free association sessions in the hunt for the precise attributes to describe each dimension. In a following step, adjective check lists and open-ended questions introduced the appropriate antonyms for each attribute. The resulting pairs of adjectives were set on a semantic differential with the stimulus *self* at its head. Factor analyses of the responses of over 3000 young Mexican males and females yielded conceptually clear, culturally congruent, and statistically robust dimensions. With out a doubt, the socio-emotional depiction of the self in Mexicans is accurate. The population describes itself as amiable and courteous in its social relationships, happy and optimistic in its outlook on life, expressive and communicative with close ones, romantic and sentimental with loved ones, and calm, conciliatory, and tranquil in all situations. As expected, the physical self is not a single dimension and does not form a factor, and the instrumental, individual, autonomous, and independent self, so prevalent in western psychological depictions of the self, appeared as a sixth factor, and even then was imbedded in a socio-emotional current, as it stressed social responsibility together with the more traditional industrious capabilities. In relation to the ethical dimension, attributes such as loyal and honest showed again the very social-emotional milieu of the Mexican self.

Concomitant attempts at describing the indigenous Mexican self have been carried out by Valdez (1994) and Lagunes (1996). Using semantic networks as a methodological tool and role depictions of the self, they asked participants to give words that best defined their selves as friends in different family member's positions. Their sampling included young, middle aged, and older people. Based on the results of the first phase, they constructed a psychophysical scale for each attribute and used self as the stimuli. Their results generally mimic those reported by La Rosa and Diaz Loving (1991). However, they report separate positive and negative evaluation factors, which is not the case in the previous studies. One possible explanation for the different pattern is that in the studies conducted with the semantic differential technique, the factors were bi-polar and included both positive and negative poles. Using bi-polar scales rather than independent scales seems to have masked some of the negative aspects of the self that can develop in the culture.

Aware of the ecosystem constraints of research conducted in Mexico City (the urban area has over 22 million inhabitants) and hoping to generalize to the Mexican population (90 million in 2000); Diaz Loving and Reyes-Lagunes (Diaz-Loving, Reyes-Lagunes & Rivera Aragon, in press) set out to test the indigenous measurement instruments in four distinct Mexican samples. Included were Mexico City and Toluca as representative of large and medium urban populations in the central mountains of the country, Hermosillo in the Northwestern cost, and Merida in the Southeastern Peninsula of Yucatan. Each of these sections boasts a unique group identity and evolved from distinct indigenous populations. Mexico City is a cosmopolitan melting pot, Toluca is a medium industrial city with an Aztec ancestry and a mestizo overtone, Hermosillo is Yaqui country combined with an individualistic outlook, which is congruent with its closeness to the United States of America, and Yucatan is deeply entrenched in its traditional Mayan heritage.

For the measuring instrument, an attempt was made to capture the strengths and avoid the weaknesses of the previous research enterprises. Attributes were selected to include all unique items form the instruments developed by La Rosa and Diaz-Loving and by Valdes and Reyes-Lagunes. A total of 104 items were included and set on seven point pictorial Likert-type scale. Participants were to select the square size that best indicated the amount that each attribute described them. The measures were distributed to participants in each ecosystem, ensuring equal size samples of males and females who were divided by age. One fourth were between 16 and 21 years old and represented the youth who are confronting the socio-culture in the development of their selves. A second group was aged between 22 and 26 and was cementing their newly acquired selves. The next group was between 27 and 35 and had young children who they were socializing into the socio-culture, and finally, the fourth group was between 36 and 44 and had adolescent offspring at home questioning them about the strengths and weaknesses of the socio culture.

Separate psychometric analysis by site, sex and age yielded generally congruent and similar factor structures. Analysis of the total set of participants, 800 in each location, is consistent with previous findings and adds theoretical and empirical robustness to ethnopsychological research. Congruent with the expectation of a social-emotional self, out of the seven highly significant factors, (Eigen values above three and factor weights over .40 for each item), six are clearly rooted in social interaction. On the socially desirable end of the spectrum, a first factor of normative affiliation grows out of the tendency to be accommodating, amiable, polite, courteous, decent, educated, honest, honorable, loyal, clean, straight, respectful, simple and sincere. The Cronback alpha for this scale is .97 and the scale mean is 5.5 on the seven-point continuum. The normative affiliation prototype is reminiscent of the Hispanic cultural script of *simpatia* advanced by Triandis, Marin, and Betancourt (1984), which bestows a general tendency that emphasizes positive and agreeable behaviors and the avoidance of interpersonal conflict. These authors indicated that *simpatia* is a need to behave with politeness and respect that discourages criticism, confrontation, and assertiveness. In addition to the *simpatia* script, the normative affiliation orientation resembles the self modifying coping style characteristic of people in the Mexican culture described by Diaz Guerrero (1994). According to this author, when confronted, the traditional Mexican will actively change to accommodate the needs and wishes of others. This abnegation behavior is so prevalent that Diaz Guerrero contends that it is a cardinal trait of the culture (Diaz Guerrero, 1993). In fact, further inspection of the normative affiliation factor clearly indicates that being courteous and polite is a moral imperative, given the normative ascendance that this factor has with the incorporation of loyalty, honesty and sincerity as part of the profile. However, it is not enough to have the good intention of being polite and loyal to become a truly abnegated member of this cultural group. The dwellers of this territory must also be patient in order to endure the strife of interpersonal relationships. This strength is extracted form the internalized emotional intelligence factor which covers the virtues of being calm, stable, obedient, peaceful, relaxed, serene, tolerant, and tranquil. A traditional Mexican saying asks, "Why are you jumping so much if the ground is flat?" The appearance of this dimension shows once more the impact of sociocultural premises built around enduring social interaction in a pleasant and constructive manner in the practice of interpersonal relationships. In fact, the strength of emotional self-control training, derived from the ever present affiliative obedience parenting strategies prevalent in the socialization of norms (which indicate that children should always respect and obey their parents who in turn should always love and protect their children), replicates the findings of an array of studies into the psychology of the Mexican.

The next two socially desirable socio emotional factors to appear stress the importance of good and happy interpersonal relationships with friends, family, and lovers. The first one, labeled *social affection*, explodes on the core of intimacy and closeness and is composed of items like affectionate, loving, caring, tender, romantic, generous, sentimental, noble, kindhearted, and considerate. The internal consistency for the scale was

Alpha .94 and the mean for all subjects was 5.3. The second dimension, coined Mexican style sociability and extroversion, is composed of traits like being a joker, jovial, sociable, friendly, talkative, fun, animated, pleasant, merry, and of course, *simpatico*. The internal consistency was .95 and the mean for all subjects was 5.2. These two factors replicated two of the factors reported by La Rosa and Diaz Loving (1991), and fill in the need of healthy and constructive social relationship with the spice of open communication and closeness. It is clear that the *simpatico* schema is not only about courteousness and a conciliatory demeanor; the self must also be happy and transmit this joy into its relationships. Furthermore, when these relationships enter the realm o f romance, they are intrinsically devoured by tenderness, flirting sentimentalism, and generosity. Self-modification and the pursuit of others' well-being encompasses acquaintances, friends, family, and intimate partners.

Social and emotional components of the self are not only "tamales and atole" (best semantic translation would be milk and cookies). There is also a dark ugly side to the emotional social interaction that occurs in a collective paradise. There are those who saddle others with their emotional weakness. There are those who impose their ways through their uncontrolled selfish and powerful behavior. The emotional vulnerability comes forth in the negative passive emotional external control depicted by attributes like corrupt, false, frustrated, undesirable, inept, pessimist, submissive, sad, lazy, slow, unreliable, inflexible. This factor had an alpha of .86 and a scale mean of 3.1. The negative emotional power is apparent in the external negative instrumental factor guided by aggressive, authoritarian, conflicting, hypercritical, dominant, egotistical, peevish, impulsive, stubborn, rebellious, rancorous, and temperamental tendencies. This factor had an internal consistency of .85 and a scale mean of 4.2. These two negative aspects of the social emotional self closely mirror the classic negative feminine expressive and masculine expressive-instrumental attributes disclosed in the gender literature (e.g. Diaz Loving, Diaz Guerrero, Helmreich & Spence, 1981). Imbedded in a constant expressive, social and emotional milieu, most children learn to control the negative edge of their self-indulging sentiments and graduate to the light side of socio emotional selves. However, the possibility is present of falling victim to bio-psychological personal needs and succumbing to the use of force or pretended weakness to influence others into one's whims.

There is also a time to produce and show agency and instrumental qualities. The Mexican self also contains a constructive inclination towards power, a positive instrumental internal control factor attests to this. Being active, intent, capable, efficient, studious, intelligent, zealous, laborious, punctual, orderly, and successful is also a part of the Mexican self. The internal consistency of .94 and the scale mean of 5.3 also show that it is coherent and quite common to identify with these characteristics.

For this culture, this is the only instrumental agentic dimension. It is definitely not absent, but it is only a fragment of a very differentiated and socio emotional laden self. And even here, where the individuals and their productions reign, they do it in harmony with their ecosystem, they do it through a humble persistence that is laborious and punctual, and that is efficient and active. It is true that the outer spheres reach all the way to intelligent and successful, but never come near the adventurous individuals willing to stake all on their wings. The socio emotional self comes through and works for the good of the group, not for personal expectations or gains.

The road is winds from a universal perspective. The straight line from conceptualization to measurement and conclusion has been lost. The coveted generalization of internally valid data seems forgotten. However, ethnopsychological approaches are also deeply rooted in methodology, theory and empiricism. They may not be as enamored with the straight lines of internal validity, but they are robust in their multi method approach. In addition, they are much better equipped to tangle with external validity issues. There is a goal. Part of it is the development of idiosyncratic theory and concepts. Part of it is the pledge of allegiance to the consideration of cultural end ecosystem variables, and part is the construction of a more vivid and mundane psychology. The first steps have been taken. Results show a consistent pattern of idiosyncratic and universal attributes. To follow the trend now requires further research that can complete the picture–what are the antecedents, correlates, and consequences of these selves?

REFERENCES

Allport, G. W. (1976). *Desarrollo y Cambio. Consideraciones básicas para una psicología de la personalidad*. Buenos Aires: Paidós.

Chávez, E. (1901). *Ensayo sobre los rasgos distintivos de la personalidad como factor del carácter del mexicano*. Revista Positiva, 3, 84–89.

Baldwin, J.M. (1897). *Social and ethical interpretations*. New York: Macmillan.

Cooley, C.H. (1902). *Human nature and the social order*. New York: Scribner's.

Díaz Guerrero, R. (1971). *Hacia una teoría histórico bio-psico socio-cultural del comportamiento humano*. Mexico City: Editorial Trillas.

Díaz Guerrero, R. (1977). Culture and personality revisited. *Annals of the New York Academy of Sciences, 285*, 119–130.

Díaz Guerrero, R. (1982). *Psicología del Mexicano*. Fourth Edition. México City: Editorial Trillas.

Díaz Guerrero, R. (1993). Un factor cardinal en la personalidad de los mexicanos. *Revista de Psicología Social y Personalidad, 9, 2*, 1–19.

Díaz Guerrero, R. (1994). *La psicología del mexicano: El descubrimiento de la etnopsicología*. Mexico City: Editorial Trillas.

Díaz-Loving, R., Díaz-Guerrero, R., Helmreich, R. and Spence, J. (1981). "Comparación Transcultural y análisis psicométrico de una medida de rasgos masculinos (instrumentales) y femeninos expresivos)". *Revista Latinoamericana de Psicología Social, 1, 1*, 3–37.

Díaz Loving, R., Reyes Lagunes, I. & Rivera Aragón, S. (unpublished manuscript). Auto concepto: Desarrollo y validación de un inventario etnopsicológico. (Self-concept: development and validity of an ethno psychological inventory). Universidad Nacional Autonoma de Mexico.

Freud, S. (1967). *Obras completas. Vols. I, II, y III*. España: Biblioteca Nueva.

James, W. (1890). *Principles of psychology*. New York: Henry Holt.

La Rosa, J. & Díaz-Loving, R. (1991). Evaluación del auto concepto: Una escala multidimensional. *Revista Latinoamericana de Psicología, 23, 1*, 15–34.

Mead, G. (1990) *Espíritu, persona y sociedad*. Buenos Aires: Paidós.

Reyes Lagunes, I. (1996). La medición de la personalidad en México. *Revista de Psicología Social y Personalidad. 12, 1–2*, 31–60.

Triandis, H.C. (1994). *Cultura and Social Behavior*. New York: Mc Graw Hill.

Triandis, H.C., Marin, G., & Betancourt, H., (1984). Simpatia as a cultural script of Hispanics. *Journal of Personality and Social Psychology, 47*, 1363–1375.

Valdez Medina, J. L. (1994). *El auto concepto del mexicano. Estudios de Validación*. Unpublished Doctoral Thesis. Facultad de Psicología. México: UNAM.

Chapter 15

The Chinese Conception of the Self
Towards a Person-Making (做人)
Perspective

Yang Chung-Fang

The indigenous approach I have adopted for the past fifteen years entails understanding the psychology of a people within their cultural/social/ historical context (C. F. Yang, 1991a; 1993). The way I have done this is to construct, based on local materials and observations, a set of commonly shared meaning systems with which the people under investigation make sense of their lives and their experiences, and give out and derive meanings while interacting with each other (C. F. Yang, 1991b; 2000a; 2000b; 2001). This set of systems also helps indigenous researchers understand and interpret the behaviors manifested by that people.

In the case of Chinese culture, this approach originated and an indigenization movement flourished from a general dissatisfaction among psychologists and other social scientists over employment of the cross-cultural approach for understanding non-western peoples (Li, K. S. Yang, & Wen, 1985). One of the problems encountered by non-western psychologists in adopting the cross-cultural approach illustrates why I chose the path I report here for investigation of the Chinese conception of self.

The problem involves the use of a common framework for comparison. As Geertz (1984) poignantly pointed out, differences are differences because they are viewed from the same perspective and measured using the same yardstick. Genuine understanding of another culture requires not differentiating it from others, but examining it from a native's point of view. In cross-cultural psychology, the perspective used for comparison has, almost without exception, been western. The cultures involved in the comparisons, even if both are non-western, are often juxtaposed using a western framework. The result is that the views of non-western cultures are often distorted to fit a comparative framework (see examples in the Chinese case in C. F. Yang, 1991c, 1996).

The indigenous approach advocates that non-local investigators put aside their past training and experience and their habitual way of thinking and understanding things in order to examine local people from the native's point of view. Local investigators need to put aside any western frameworks they adopted while receiving their social-science training in western countries, and examine their own cultures from within.

This alternative view-taking requires investigators to see and understand events and behaviors happening then and there. What is the thinking framework of the local people under study? Unfortunately, in pursuit of different thinking styles for different cultures, investigators have often returned to the cross-cultural approach. Consequently, western terminology permeates the discussions and debates even at this meta-cognitive level (see example in C. F. Yang, 2000b).

This paper has three goals: (1) to find a local thinking framework with which to develop an alternative perspective to the western one in order to discover new dimensions for future studies of the self, at least for studies of the Chinese self; (2) to explore the concept of the Chinese self at its formative stage, which was during the Pre-Qin (先秦) period in Chinese history (D. N. Zhang, 1989b; L. W. Zhang, 1989), and to use this deep-rooted conception to study the evolution of self-concept in the Chinese context and better understand the behaviors of modern Chinese people; (3) and, to suggest an alternative approach to the study of the self.

These goals are particularly worth pursuing in the case of Chinese culture for three unique reasons: (1) Scholars agree that mainstream Chinese thought about the self has not changed much since its formation in archaic times; (2) there are quite good written records preserved for such a pursuit, especially in recent years since many ancient tombs have been unearthed from which a number of books of important philosophical, social, and political thoughts have been recovered; (3) these writings mainly concern how to be a person and thus are about the self.

Before I go into the main theme, two more points need to be clarified to avoid misconceptions about the purpose of this paper. First, the purpose of this paper is not to find the ancient conception of the self and claim that modern Chinese are just copies of it. Employing a person-in-culture position, which I will elucidate shortly, I aim to find the model that modern Chinese people deal with and depart from. Understanding the archaic conception achieves only half of the goal that the indigenous approach sets. It lays out the foundation upon which the study of the modern Chinese self can begin.

The second point I would like to make clear entails answering a question often asked by readers of papers like this one. It is about whether there is only one Chinese conception of the self and whether it is too general and narrow-minded to think that there is only one model that shapes the modern Chinese mind. This question often leads to debate concerning the usefulness of the pursuit just outlined for this paper. Many people, especially those working closely with local people in the field, cast doubt on such an effort because representative models have often failed to help understand the everyday lives of local individuals.

My answer to this question is that there has been more than one competing model, especially before and during the formative stage of the Pre-Qin period. Political struggles at the time often determined which model prevailed (A. Wang, 2000). However, in the process of forming a dominating model, competitors learned and borrowed from each other as they consolidated their own models. Once the struggles in the social and political arenas ended and one model emerged as the official one, it had to incorporate rival thoughts in order to ensure survival. The mainstream model, the Confucian one in the Chinese case, actually absorbed many other thoughts prevailing at the time. It is fairly safe to say that, at least for the Chinese case, the official model has survived several serious challenges and emerged relatively unscathed as it evolved, which may not be true in other cultures.

There is, of course, local opposition to this mainstream ideology in China, but fully understanding the local scene requires examination of the official backdrop. Therefore, the usefulness of conducting a historical search for the main root is justified, whichever position researchers take concerning the relationship between culture and the individual.

ORGANIZATION OF THIS CHAPTER

In this paper, I first introduce the age-old Chinese yin/yang (陰陽) mode of thinking with the aim of replacing the western one for the study of the self. In my illustration of this mode, special attention is paid to its differences from the modern western mode usually employed by social sciences investigators. This comparison is made to demonstrate that the futile comparison of lower levels of cognitive processes, as often studied in cross-cultural research, could be the result of differences at the meta-cognitive level.

With this new mode of thinking, I then carry out a search, inspired by Wundt's approach to the study of folk psychology as elaborated by Jahoda (1992), for the root of the Chinese conception of the person and the self. This historical adventure provides good material from which a picture of the inception of the Chinese self can be reconstructed.

Based on this sketch, I then adopt the person in culture position to establish the link between culture and individual and to develop a new perspective for the study of the self. The person in culture position examines what types of problems the people under investigation living under and beyond the conditions and constraints of their cultural heritage face and how they come to solve these problems and hence demonstrate certain behaviors as a result. In other words, researchers can derive a set of meaning systems with which they can encode and interpret the manifest behaviors of a people.

Taking this position to study the Chinese self, I discuss the main problem with the Chinese conception of the self when applied to real-life situations, and briefly mention how a two-tier (large- and small-self) self meaning system solves this problem. With this meaning system, I suggest a new approach to the study of the Chinese self and some areas that are worth looking into.

THE YIN/YANG MODE OF THINKING

The basic Chinese mode of thinking has been discerned by many indigenous and outside scholars from various fields as being very different from the western mode used by mainstream social science and humanities (e.g., Meng & Kuang, 1993; R. B. Yang & Huang, 1996; L. W. Zhang, 1989). Many scholars characterize and call it the yin/yang mode of thinking. Adopting this mode of thinking, every phenomenon is viewed from a perspective that enables the perceiver to summarize and label it with a pair of terms, such as cold-hot, soft-hard, beautiful-ugly, etc. These terms are referential in the sense that they do not represent objects but describe states. They often seem as if they were contradictory or opposing, but they do not have to be so, as, for instance, in universe-human and country-family, both of which describe a relationship of inclusion.

The fact that yin describes a shady side of things and yang a bright side, has led many to think that these are not only logically incompatible concepts (and therefore can be called a contradiction), but also value-laden in the sense that yin denotes bad and yang good. This is not exactly the true picture; yin and yang are merely symbolic representing a relationship–any kind that makes sense to an observer.

In his attempt to distinguish the yin/yang mode of thinking from the western one, Choi (2000) argued that this Chinese mode, which on the surface resembles dialectical thinking, actually is fundamentally different from its western counterpart. The main terms of reference for the latter include concepts, substances, logical opposites, categories, dialectics, and compromises, which are all constituents of the philosophical thinking of essentialism and dualism.

Choi stated that the yin/yang mode of thinking is basically non-essentialist, and thus pays little attention and places little importance on concepts and concept formation. Therefore, whether yin and yang are opposites derived from formal logic is not relevant here. Yin and yang are not two objects relating to each other on the basis that they have internal qualities or reducible elements that are clearly definable so that they can be distinguished from one another.

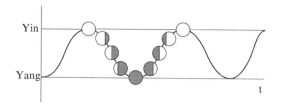

Figure 1. Yin/Yang Mode of Thinking

To Chinese philosophers, yin and yang are not objects; rather, they are terms or labels describing two possible states or statuses of events or situations that are developing along a time dimension. They do not mean anything when they are presented alone, but when they are put together, they represent a relationship of "one can be transformed to become the other," not that "one interacts with or influences the other". Figure 1 illustrates this unique dynamic relationship. Choi said that the relationship is like slow wavy movements that consist of ebbs and flows and that one state gradually transforms into the other state.

The crucial characteristic that connects movement between the two states is not the logical contradiction inherited in them, but the mobilizing force, and often comes from an actor whose actions direct the movements towards either of the two end-states represented by the two terms. So, yin and yang, even though they literally mean shadiness and brightness, are actually generic terms representing any relationship discerned to be the result of an actor's action. This mode of thinking can be considered an actor-centered perspective. (See Figure 2 for an illustration of this perspective.)

Since yin and yang are two possible end states or statuses involving a particular actor in a particular event or situation, the foci of attention of an investigation are naturally on: (1) detecting the possible actions taken by an actor that dominate (2) the underlying relationship or movement, and (3) finding the best action that achieves the most desirable result between the two end states. This mode of thinking can be considered an action-making perspective: finding the best action in a given event or situation.

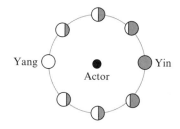

Figure 2. Actor-Centered Yin Yang Thinking Mode

After introducing this meta-cognitive framework, and before we discuss social-cognitive concerns regarding what the best action is and what action achieves the most desirable result, I need first to elaborate the historical roots from which this actor-centered and action-making mode of thinking came. This root lies in the way Chinese people conceive of the person and the self.

THE HISTORICAL ROOT OF THE CHINESE SELF

In my historical account of the origin and development of the Chinese self, I focused on the periods before the Qin dynasty (before 221 BC). Many Chinese historians take the view that many of the key terms that are still in use today were originated and formulated in those periods (e.g., Ding & Wu, 1993; Jiao, 1991), including the Huang Di (黃帝) period (Before 3000 BC), the Yin-Zhou Transition (殷周之交) period (around 1066 BC), the Spring/Autumn (秋春) period (770 – 476 BC) and the Warring States (戰國) period (475 – 221 BC).

Wo (我) as Autonomous and Powerful

The original meaning of *wo* (我), meaning *I* or *me*, is one's consciousness of oneself as a physically separate identity. Calling that awareness *I* or *me* was probably the source of the idea of the self.

Historically speaking, although there have been many Chinese characters denoting *I* and *me*, the main character that represents all of them and that modern Chinese people still use daily, is *wo*. *Wo* was first discovered on unearthed relics, like bone oracles and bronze wares, no later than around 3000 BCE at the period when Huang Di (黃帝) first defeated Chi You (蚩尤) and reigned China.

Wo is a pictograph that depicts a bronze weapon resembling a spear with an ornament hanging on the side (see Figure 3). Because pictographs are usually a reflection of the conscious image of the character, Jiao (1991) postulated that the idea of wo first came up into consciousness with people involved in a war. As the Huang Di/Chi You War was the first recorded war in Chinese history, this speculation sounds reasonable.

Jiao further stated that the *wo* inscribed on bone oracles and bronze wares often did not appear alone, but with another two characters

Figure 3. Evolution of the pictograph *wo* from left to right

meaning *I, alone* (我一人). Since a weapon with ornaments was probably owned or held by persons with power, Jiao asserted that *wo*, the character itself, originally may not have been used to refer to a single person, but to a class of persons who had power and were the masters of a country, an army, or a small community. This conclusion gains support from the fact that the oracles or wares were used mainly on ceremonial occasions and concerned the activities of emperors and kings.

Considering that only this group of people in the archaic times had the power to own land and slaves, which may have given them the feeling that they were their own masters and could do whatever they pleased, that the sense of being a separate entity started from these people should come as no surprise. According to Hori (1986), Chinese rulers allowed their citizens to own lands as early as the Spring-Autumn period (770–476 BC). Hori also stated that, no later than the Warring States period (475–221 BC), the rulers implemented the Even-Land Policy (井田或均田制度), which allowed eight families to own private lands surrounding a piece of public land (forming a territorial structure similar to the frame used to play the game of tic-tac-toe with the public land in the middle.) This distinction between private-owned land (私田) and public-owned land (公田) allowed ordinary people to have a sense of what belonged to them, the private, and what belongs to everyone, the public. The character *wo* became a symbol for anybody who had a sense of control and mastery as a separate entity.

THE CONCEPTION OF PERSON

Affirming the Embodied Person

R. B. Yang (2000) stated that the conception of *wo* in archaic China is hinted at through the mythological existence and descriptions of a type of person called *wu* (巫). According to the accounts of scholars from the Spring-Autumn Period, *wu* depicts a person who could be in two states of consciousness interchangeably: the embodied and the disembodied. In the latter state, the person was able to leave the body, sometimes with the help of mythical animals, to converse with mythical figures including the souls of deceased acquaintances.

R. B. Yang suspected that although according to these records, only very few people had the privilege of being a *wu*, the idea of a person having the possibility of disembodiment dominated the Chinese conception of person at the time and even now. Since these records were written in later times when Confucian ideology had already become the dominant ideology, R. B. Yang speculated that people during the Yin/Zhou Transition Period and even earlier, not just *wu*, often felt that they actually left their bodies behind with the help of alcohol. Meanwhile, people of that time also believed that souls could harm them once they left their familiar surroundings. Consequently, the person, as a separate entity, might have been conceived of as relatively weak and unstable at the time.

Historical records credited to Zhuan Xu (顓頊), the grandson of Huang Di, for putting an end to the idea of reaching souls in heaven and earth through disembodiment. Since then, the soul had been considered firmly grounded in the body. But R. B. Yang postulated that the practice of *wu* based on the belief that a person could become disembodied probably remained prevalent and was sometimes even done on a massive scale until the Xi Zhou (西周) Dynasty when new political, social, and religious orders were firmly established.

Situating the Person in Society

We can safely say that the Yin-Zhou Transition Period was the most crucial period in Chinese social history (Ding & Wu, 1993). During this period, people were trained to engage in institutionalized collective activities, namely, *li* (禮) and *yue* (樂). *Li* is a set of role expectations that guide people's behaviors and *yue*, literarily meaning music, is the vehicle used to arouse pleasant emotions to help people internalize and practice *li*. The Zhou (周) people who came from a remote western state, conquered and ruled the Yin (殷) people who resided in the center part of China at the time. The fact that they could overturn the Yin, indicates that the latter state was politically and socially in chaos. The new rulers had to establish everything anew not only to restore order, but also to assure their reign.

Claiming that they had the support of heaven, the Zhou rulers established *li* and *yue* as messages from heaven in order to stabilize and tame the Yin people. Positioning the Yin in a web of interconnected roles and encouraging them to participate in activities that gave them a sense of order and collectivity, presumably affirmed the importance and the strength of the person as an individual. However, this strength came from the tie between person and heaven, and between the person and society, not from the individuated self. During this period, people no longer needed to get help from spirits in heaven and earth to master the environment. According to historical writings from later periods about this period, this solution aimed at restoring social disorder worked very well and allowed the Xi Zhou (西周) rulers to rule the country for about 300 years.

Based on characters inscribed on the unearthed relics, some terms that described psychological states, like *de* (德), a feeling of accomplishment from practicing *li* and *yue*, and *jiang* (敬), a sense of fearfulness, humbleness, prudence, and alarm, began to appear at this time. The former is an internalization of *li* and *yue* and the latter a humble sentiment that allows the person to see room for improvement. Both seem to have served the function of consolidating individuals into persons with subjectivity and autonomy (Meng, 1993). Even more important, the person is conceived of as tied to society and as needing to be improved constantly.

Jiao (1991) pointed out that even as early as in the Spring-Autumn period of Chinese history many characters used *wo* as a definition or explanation, which indicates that these characters all conveyed the same meaning as *wo* and that *wo* was the generic term referring to one's physical self (施身自謂). These characters, such as 卬、吾、台、予、朕、身、甫、余、言 were used on different occasions by people with different statuses, and of different genders. This fact clearly indicates that the different *wo*s were considered differently depending on the social status of the person in society and the social occasion which required different *li*. One interesting example Jiao gave was the character, *zheng*, 朕. It was originally used by commoners, but later became the *I* reserved specially for emperors or empresses. This change happened after the Qin (秦) Dynasty united China and made it an autocratic state. After that, anyone other than the ruler, who called him/herself *zheng* would be put to death. This example demonstrates that a person is meaningful only as a member of society.

The Body/Mind Transformation

During this Yin/Zhou Transition Period, literature referred to people who had *de* and *jiang* as people with an air of *wei yi* (威儀), roughly translated as authority and integrity. This connection between internal cultivation and physical appearance precipitated the predominant Chinese conception of a close and dynamic relationship between body and mind.

Later when Confucius came into the picture during the Spring-Autumn period he further expanded the notion by saying that a person's moral cultivation(*li* and *yue*) was, in three dedicated ways, related to bodily changes and changes surrounding him via the presence of *qi* (氣, air): (1) inside a person's body, (2) on the person's appearance, and, (3) surrounding the person (R. B. Yang, 2000).

Becoming a Jun Zi (君子) or Xiao Ren (小人)

Confucius lived in the late Spring-Autumn Period after *li* and *yue* which had helped the Zhou Dynasty rule the country for three centuries, had shown signs of deterioration. Although he was a Yin offspring, he saw the value of the Zhou Dynasty's *li* and *yue* prescription in keeping up social order and keeping social calamity away. How to achieve order and harmony in a society preoccupied Confucius' school of thought and he believed that the rescue could only come from individuals living in that society (Cheung, 1989). In Confucian teachings, people were indispensable vehicles for achieving societal goals, valued in their ability to cultivate themselves and to take responsibility for maintaining social order and harmony.

With this belief, Confucius created a *ru* (儒) model, called *jun zi* (君子, literarily meaning *gentleman*), for his young followers to emulate. *Jun zi* was originally used to denote noblemen who ruled the states of the pre-Confucian Zhou Dynasty. The commoners under their rule were called *xiao ren* (小人, meaning *little people*). Gentlemen, the ruling class, were urged to observe a different set of rules of conduct from their subjects, the little people. Although the class undertone was not totally eradicated, Confucius took the symbolic meanings of these two terms and distinguished *jun zi* from *xiao ren* primarily based on the degree of self-cultivation. The difference between the two lies in the principle they adopted to guide their interactions with others. Gentlemen practiced the principle of yi (義, righteousness) and small men the principle of *li* (利, self-interest).

The terms no longer represent two classes of people, but refer to two possible models any person can emulate. The person, therefore, is conceived of in Confucian ideology as capable of cultivating himself or herself, as long as he or she chooses to do so, of becoming a moral being, and of having the virtue of *ren* (仁, benevolence). The way to become such a person, is to restrain oneself from behaving on impulse and to always practice *li* (克己復禮 in Chinese). The former implies that the person needs to overcome personal weaknesses and the latter emphasizes loving other people as one loves oneself, assuring social harmony and stability.

This gentleman/little people pair constituted the Confucian conception of person and a major part of the discussion recorded in the Confucian classics. The idea of achieving social order through self-cultivation not only further affirmed the importance of the person but also placed great faith on a person's ability to spread benefits to other people, and possibly to the rest of the world. This *ru* model was later revised by Mencius (孟子) and Xun Zi (荀子) during the late Warring States period, and went through several major modifications and reinterpretations when it faced challenges from other philosophical and religious schools. However, its status as the main conception of a person adopted by most of the rulers and their officials after the Han (漢) Dynasty remains largely unchanged to this day.

Due to the importance of the gentleman/little people pair, the *yi* (righteousness)/*li* (self-interest) relationship has been a major topic of debate for the past 2500 years. Even today modern Chinese people enter into this debate frequently and with a great passion. Zhang (1989a) contended that the debate on this relationship hinged mainly on the *gong* (公, public)/*si* (私, private) relationship which I will discuss later. Zhang concurred with Confucian scholars in the Sung (宋) Dynasty like Ju Xi (朱熹), that the *yi/li* pair was the most important subject for any Confucian scholar to study.

From External to Internal

In recently unearthed relics from Guo Dian (郭店) some hand-copied books written on bamboo pieces were found. They were authored by

Confucius' disciple Zi Si (子思) during the early Warring States period (Gao, 2001). Zi Si's and Mencius' later work combined to form one of the major schools that followed and consolidated Confucianism. The Si-Meng School (思孟學派), which emphasizes the internal cultivation of a person, became mainstream among Confucian scholars for thousands of years to come.

Although these books were written using the characters prevalent in a particular locality, Chu (楚), many of the terms used and the style in which they were written reflected not only their deep commitment to the Si-Meng School of teaching in that subculture, but also the conception of person of that school. In these books, many terms depicting the main teachings of Confucianism, and which modern Chinese people still use to denote the same meanings, were written in two versions. One was almost the same as the modern version (shown in the upper row of Figure 4), and the other was formed of compound characters: a radical plus another character. All of these compound words had a *xin* (心, literally meaning heart) as the radical (shown in the lower row of Figure 4). The pictograph *xin* resembles a heart, which is considered to be the most important organ. Because it takes charge of thinking and emoting it is often translated as *heart-mind* rather than just heart. That there were two versions for each of these characters, one with a heart and the other without, indicates that no later than just prior to when the Qin Dynasty united China, philosophers and scholars made the distinction between external teaching and learning and internalized psychological states.

The most revealing and interesting finding to psychologists from the uncovered Guo Dian relics is that the Confucian terms convey a general conception of a person as well as the process by which the person can approach the final goal of self-cultivation, i.e., sagehood. For instance, the second character from the left in the upper row of Figure 4, *ren* (仁, benevolence) consists of two parts: 身 and 心 with the latter as a radical. The two parts together literally mean *body* and *heart*–body and mind united. The third character, *yi* (義, conscience) is a combination of 我 and 心, meaning *I* and *heart*–heart coming from oneself. The fifth, *de* (德, morality) with 直 and 心, means *direct* and *heart*–directly coming from the heart. And the sixth, *zhi* (智, intellect) with 知 and 心, means *knowledge* and *heart*–knowledge in the mind.

愛仁義順德智敬憂
炁息惎慈悳智憼息

Figure 4. Moral Words (upper) with Their Internalized Counterparts (lower)

The character *de* (德), direct from the heart, indicates that humans are born good and moral in nature. To be a person, one needs to set up a goal or model to strive for through self-cultivation. The model can be a morally perfect sage or a common person; it is up to the individual to decide what to become. All one needs to do to reach the goal is to cultivate oneself from the bottom of one's heart. However, one's heart first has to be filled with knowledge (*zhi*, 智) and kindness (*ren*, 仁), which is a harmonious and benevolent state where body and heart (feeling and mind) unite. While *yi* (義) is the internalized thoughts and feelings that come from practicing *li* (禮, propriety), *wo* (我, I) guards the practice of those rituals in everyday life.

From Intention to Action

Many of these compound characters with heart (心, *xin*) as their radical, also had a corresponding version that replaced *xin* (心) with *thuo* (辵), literarily meaning walking or practicing. Examples are given in the lower row of Figure 5. The upper row shows their simplified counterparts. The process of self-cultivation does not stop at the distinction between external teaching and learning and internalized moral motivation, but extends to internalized intention and everyday practice (self-realization). The *de* (德) used later and up to the present, has another radical, *chi* (彳), which has the same meaning as *thuo*, added onto the earlier version, 直 心. It reaffirms the earlier observation that the conception of *de* later evolved as a self-realization or an externalization of internal virtue that directly comes from nature.

The Relationship of Tian (天, Heaven) and Ren (人, Human)

In the writings of Zhong Yong (中庸), the only analects on Confucian teachings that touched upon the metaphysical *tian* (天, the universe), a whole/part relationship was prescribed to exist between *tian* and *ren* (人). The universe was construed as ever-changing but following some cosmic order. The person, on the one hand, was an organic part of the universal; human nature corresponds with that of the universe. On the other hand, the person is a spiritual being situated at the center of the universe with the capacity to include the universe in the internal world through the process

Figure 5. Internalized Version (upper) and Behavioral Version (lower) of Some Words

of self-cultivation by which that person realizes morality or human nature (Tu, 1994). By doing so, the person and the universe become homogenized.

Summary

A historical review of the development of the conception of personhood during the formative Confucian/Mencius Era and sometime after, and an exploration of the yin/yang mode of thinking has allowed examination of the development and the relationships of several pairs of terms. From these relationships, a general picture of how ancient Chinese intellectuals envisioned the person and people's relationship with heaven and fellow citizens, society, and the world has been derived.

The person is construed as the center of the universe. People are not valued for what they are, but for what they can become. The person is born good and moral, but this nature is obscured by impulses and desires coming from association with undesirable people and imperfect environments. One can cultivate oneself to perfection (to become a sage) by exercising self-restraint and practicing rituals. The most important message is that people are their own master in deciding what kind of a person they want to become.

The gentlemen/little people pair gives a spectrum of moral possibilities from which a person can choose, as does the person/society pair. People can choose to keep to themselves or to unite with society and the environment through moral cultivation. Similarly, a person can choose to become a spiritual sage (內聖) or to participate in making the world a harmonious place for everyone by serving the country or society with moral teachings (外王). Even when one chooses to perfect oneself for oneself, the internal/external pair and the intention/action pair reveal that self-cultivation is a process that involves both deliberation and practice.

Finally, the body/heart (mind/feeling) pair inherited in the term *ren* (benevolence), sees the ideal of the person as an embodied actor who homogenizes bodily behavior and mind/feeling when dealing with fellow beings and/or serving society. One is gathering a formidable force, called *qi* (氣) inside that reflects on physical appearance and surrounds one while one continues with internal cultivating and the homogenizing.

All in all, the mainstream (Confucian) conception of person is not only individual -centered, but also action-oriented. It places great emphasis on the action of the person and the person's ability to improve on personal actions as a means to unite harmoniously with society. With this conception of the person, it is only natural that Chinese philosophers have spent much time on the individual and the self. The main ancient Chinese philosophical writings can be said to be inward-oriented, placing major emphasis on subjectivity and autonomy (Meng, 1993; Yu, 1993). They can be seen as schools devoted to the study of the psychology of the self.

However, a close examination of the conception of the self quickly reveals that the self as envisioned by Chinese scholars was not quite the same as that envisioned in western conceptions.

THE CONCEPTION OF *JI* (己), THE SELF

If one examines ancient Chinese texts, one will find discussions of all terms and issues that are normally included in any modern books Chinese or western, of the same nature, except one: the self. Nor can one find much discussion of the self in relation to another term representing a yin-yang type of relationship, as one finds in so many other Chinese discussions of ideas and thoughts. (A few exceptions are elucidated below.) However, if one reads these texts, one finds the word *JI* (己), the self, everywhere. In these texts, the individual was so much the center of everything that most discussions were about what *JI* (己), the self, was supposed to do or to improve. The few pairs of yin-yang relationships involving the self that were discussed in these texts were usually from the vantage point of the actor. The self was not viewed as an object to be studied and written about, but as an action-taker whose deliberation on "what to do" to become a worthy person was the main focus of attention.

The Meaning of *Ji* (己)

The character, *ji*, which came into existence later than *wo*, originally meant a centrally located house or place where consciousness and knowledge resided. According to a Han (漢) dictionary, *Shuo Wen Jie Zi* (說文解字), edited and interpreted by a Confucian scholar in the Qing (清) Dynasty, it is where *li* (理, principle or regularity) resides and it has to be understood with the term *ren* (人, person). It states that an individual speaks of *ji* to distinguish himself or herself from others and to describe a positional relationship between the self and others. The former is situated inside and in the middle, and the latter are on the outside and peripheral. However, the pictograph itself resembles something that bends forwards and backwards in order "to conceal or to conform" (See the left-most character in Figure 6). As in "human being", it resembles a person hunching his back and sticking out his stomach for the same reasons. This image depicts that the self is flexible and thus cultivatable or malleable.

The Ji (己) / Yi (已) Relationship

In the same dictionary, *ji* also is said to share the same root as another character *YI* (已), which means "past, done, used, practiced or executed". They share the same pictograph resembling a snake, which become uncoiled in the summer, but coiled in the winter. (See the two next to the left-most character in Figure 6). *Ji* resembles a moving snake that does not

Snake   Self   Past   Fear

Figure 6. Characters Related to *Self*

coil itself to the fullest; *yi* resembles one that coils more fully symbolizing something that has already been completed. The dictionary explains that the difference between *ji* and *yi* is that the former represents ideas or intentions whereas the latter solidity or reality. When one's ideas and intentions become solid and firm, one will take an action and make it a reality. This explanation clearly discloses that *ji* is a psychological counterpart of the physical *wo*. However, it does not refer to an entity, but a state of mind or a stage of a person when ideas or intentions have not been materialized into actions. So, it can be paired with outer behavior (externalized action) to represent a relationship: the latter is the reality of the former.

As stated earlier, in Confucian teachings the person is a vehicle and the self is a team player. The conception of person demands that the self keep the person hollow and humble, always finding room for improvement, and that the self is also the person's enemy when it becomes inflexible and insistent on acting according to raw impulses.

This conception of the self is further supported by the fact that the character for "fear, forbidden and dislike", is *ji* (忌), which is a compound character consisting a *ji* (己), the self, and a *xin* (心), the heart (see the right-most character in Figure 6). This compound word shows that the conception of the self is a complex one. As an isolated and close state, it is what the person needs to fear, to control, and to overcome. An open and inclusive state makes the person a social, natural, and moral being (Liu, 2000). As an open and inclusive state, its meaning can only be fully understood from writings concerning its relationship with another term, *ren* (人), human being.

Human Being (Ren, 人) / Self (Ji, 己)

Adopting the yin/yang mode of thinking, the term, *ji* becomes meaningful only when it is associated with another term, *ren* (人). According to Jiao (1991), *ren* (人) has four meanings: human being (人類), the public (眾人), a group of people based on ethnicity, or locality (族,中國人), others except oneself (他人). When one speaks of the *ren/ji* relationship, one is referring to a relationship between human beings and the self, which is a whole/part relationship.

In this whole/part relationship, human beings, including oneself, are considered to be born good and moral, as are all things in nature. However, they are also all different in the sense that people choose their own ways to realize their natures and each finds different ways to serve society. The relationship between *ren* and *ji* is an organic one in that all individuals are fundamentally the same, although they live their lives differently and contribute to the world differently. The similarity resides in that together they made the world function smoothly as a whole. In Chinese, this is described as "harmonious but not the same" (和而不同).

Group (*Cun*, 群) / Self (*Ji*, 己) Relationship

The same whole/part conception applies to the relationship between group and individual as well. Yu (1993), in a paper discussing the group/self relationship from a historical perspective, stated that both individualistic and collectivistic positions concerning the group/self relationship were brought up by pre-Qin scholars. For instance, Legalists' definitely emphasized the supremacy of the group, whereas mainstream Confucian scholars' did not emphasize either. Later, the evolution of Confucianism demonstrated oscillations between emphasizing group order and individual freedom.

In another article, Yu (1976) took a social/political perspective and enumerated that after the unification of China during the Qin dynasty, most of the emperors adopted the Legalist conception regarding how to run a country; i.e., totalitarianism. However, the Confucian influence was ever-present. Emperors often socialized their subjects with a modified version of Confucianism within which a lot of Legalistic ideas were incorporated. The modified Confucian ideology dispatched a *min gui* (民貴, people first) message to the emperors and their officials but downplayed individual citizens' right to overturn an emperor.

Due to this social/political development, Confucian scholars were no longer permitted by their totalitarian rulers to achieve self-realization externally through participating in the political arena. They gradually turned inward to become experts on self-cultivation adapting themselves to the external environment. This self-psychology entails how one can include others, society, and the universe in one's mind and action, regardless of what the real world is. The process of self-cultivation becomes a learning process for the self (de Bary, 1991).

Summary

The self is not construed as a solid thing, or even a concept, but a term paired with other collective terms to represent many whole/part relationships. The most important aspect of the self from this perspective is that the self is always at the center, as shown in Figure 7, and is surrounded by other people connected to one. The self-cultivation process involves the perforation of the boundary of the individuated self to include others, starting from those who are closest, such as family members. The process

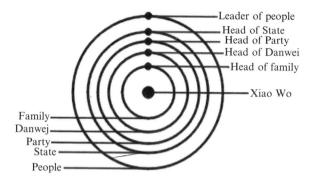

Figure 7. The Relationship between *Xiao wo* and the Different Levels of *Da wo*

can also be seen as an inclusive expansion of the self rather than a conquering expansion (F. Y. Wang, 2002).

The self is also seen as a process of action-taking by which the person improves relationships with the surroundings. The self-cultivation process makes the self an actor who uses observation, insight, and knowledge to link personal action with possible consequences that change the status of surrounding relationships. To achieve the goal of self-perfection, a person needs carefully to choose actions that can homogenize all these relationships. Through this process, people make themselves a participating member of the universe and live naturally and smoothly in their proper place. From this conception, it is clear that the self-cultivation process is a person-making process. The self creates a person as construed by the people of a particular culture.

THE PERSON-MAKING PERSPECTIVE OF THE SELF

The preceding discussion justifies a new way of looking at the self. I called this new way the person-making perspective because I think that, at least in the Chinese case, it is in the way one tries to become an all-around moral person that one sees the significance of the self.

This new perspective requires a new framework and relying on a culturally prescribed dimension of what is considered meaningful to the self and way of going about becoming a person who makes the self meaningful. Next, I use the Chinese case to illustrate the usefulness of this new perspective.

The Center in Yin/Yang Cosmology

The impetus in the yin/yang universe is the person, who is the observer and the actor. That is to say, the actor carefully discerns the various yin/yang relationships as the effects of personal actions in a given event or situation and acts in the best way possible to achieve the most desirable results.

Since yin and yang are related by the course of action taken by an actor, the pair actually represents many other possible states in between with different graduations of yin and yang, as shown in Figure 2. All of them represent the end-states the actor's different actions may lead to when dealing with a given situation. An acute observer/actor can not only detect the connection between possible actions and various possible states summarized by yin and yang, but also the minute progressive changes from one end-state to the other as the result of the choice of action. Based on this kind of observation and knowledge, a competent actor can then choose among these action options to arrive at the consequence that is considered most desirable for a given situation.

The *Zhong Yong* (中庸) Principle–A Way to Person-Making

What is the most appropriate action in a given event/situation? It depends on what kind of person one wants to become. It is related to one's person-making goal.

Person-making in the Chinese context refers to the process by which one returns to human nature, which is good and moral. It is the process of becoming through self-cultivation. The self-cultivation program of Confucian thought took shape mainly after Confucius' death and was recorded in two books entitled *Da Xue* (大學) and *Zhong Yong*. In these books, the proper route for self-cultivation was clearly prescribed: *xiu shen* (修身, cultivating oneself), *qi jia* (齊家, raising a good family), *zhi guo* (治國, running the country), *ping tian xia* (平天下, achieving world peace). On this route, the self is not a static object, but an evolving and expanding entity. Its final state is a unity of "the world and the self" and "heaven and person."

The *Zhong Yong* book, which many scholars consider to contain the quintessence of the Chinese spirit (e.g., Chan, 1963), deals with the cultural directive concerning what is the most appropriate action for the actor to take in dealing with a given situation. It outlined the principle that: (1) the most desirable decision goal is always to maintain inner and outer (interpersonal) harmony; (2) the most appropriate action leading to such a state always lies in-between those actions that lead to the two end-states dispatching a yin and yang relationship discerned by the observer/actor; and (3) one has to strike a balance among all the optimal actions each of which is the best action for a particular pair of end-state relationships (Cheung, et al, 2001; Yang & Chiu, 1997).

In-between does not necessary mean *a compromise* or *the mathematical average*. It means that the optimal course of action varies with the situation, with the people involved, and with time (Creel, 1987). What is considered optimal in a given situation involving a given group of people at a given time, may not be the same as that for another situation involving a different group of people at another time.

In addition, several crucial factors influencing the self's person-making process are related to the actor's personal experience and the level of self-cultivation already acquired. The quality and accuracy of the actor's perception regarding what action will lead to what consequence in a given context, depends very much on: (1) the person's knowledge and experience; (2) the skill in carrying out the chosen action; and, most important of all, (3) the actor's progress in his pursuit of moral perfection.

A NEW APPROACH TO UNDERSTANDING THE SELF

With this new person-making perspective, I propose that students of the self adopt a new approach for investigation. The approach entails deviating from existing approaches in the following seven aspects.

First of all, researchers have to give up construing the self as an abstract object or agent that always tries to exert influence or control over personal behavior and environment. They also need to give up the notion that a few key selves, past, present, or future, form the core of a person.

Second, the *self* is not a cause of a person's behavior. The action a person takes in a given situation *is* the self of that person, no matter what motives are behind the action. There are as many expressed selves as social situations.

Third, the self is not an object so it does not have motivational properties like self-consistency, self-enhancement, self-deception, etc. The self is the result of a person's strife for consistency, enhancement, and deception, all of which are strategic actions that may be employed to engage in person-making.

Fourth, the self is viewed as the center of a bundle of relationships that link a person's action with the environment and beyond. The self is a cobweb connected to many other people, each of whom is also a web. The cobweb is a dynamic field in which the person, as an action-taker pursuing everyday life and adjusting to the environment, has to think and do things affecting not only the self, but also those people linked to the web. Many actions may result in reshaping the web and all other webs associated with it. A person's deliberation and choice of action reflect that person's self.

Fifth, the process of person-making, i.e., the process of becoming the person in his natural and proper place in the society and the universe (安身立命, in Chinese), should therefore be the focus of attention in the study of the self. It involves the examination of the attempt to maintain harmonious relationships with the rest of the world through self-growth. The Confucian prescriptions for self-growth involve exercise of self-restraint and practice of moral teachings.

Sixth, researchers' main concern should be to understand how an actor derives what the most appropriate action in a given situation that leads to the desired goal of inner and outer harmony. The actor pays attention to relationships represented by various pairs of end-states and to the deliberation of decisions about how to act most appropriately in that given context. In his study of the Chinese political culture, Pye (1968), made the poignant observation that the Chinese know perfectly *what* to do; the problem always lies on the issue of *how*. His remark echoes the point made here.

Finally, sharing of observations and perceptions of the actor allows the researchers to derive the meanings of the actions taken by the former and thus to understand them properly.

UNDERSTANDING THE CHINESE SELF

Although adopting this new approach to the understanding of the Chinese self requires examination of an actor in a concrete, social, holistic, contextual, distributed, fluid, practical, and action-oriented manner due to the unique conceptions of the person and the self of a particular culture, it is still worth setting out some general guidelines with which researchers can achieve a better understanding of the Chinese self. The guidelines elucidated below are derived from the person-in-culture view described at the beginning of this paper. This view entails imagining what people living in a Chinese culture who are inculcated with the described conception of the person and self may do to run their lives. Taking this view, special attention is paid to the problems they share and the solutions they come up with to cope with these problems. These programs and solutions constitute the meaning system with which one can arrive at a general comprehension of the Chinese self.

What Preoccupies the Chinese Self?

Three pairs of relationships seem to preoccupy the Chinese mind in everyday interactions. All of them are derivatives of the Chinese people's shared conceptions of the person and self and all of them have moral implications.

The *Da Wo* (大我) / *Xiao Wo* (小我) Conception

In the Chinese conception, the individual is not valued in the same way as in modern western cultures. A person's value lies not in the fact of being an individual, but in the ability to develop human's innate social nature, i.e., to love other people and to live with them harmoniously (Bodde, 1953).

One means provided by the Confucian school of thought to realize this value is to have the person gradually relinquish the private and individuated self (called *xiao wo*, 小我, literally meaning the small self) and to embrace a larger collectivity to which one belongs as the operating self (called *da wo* 大我, the large self). The *operating self* refers the collectivity one identifies with and represents in a given situation. As shown in Figure 7, the person is encouraged to start off by including family members into the large self (loving and serving one's family), then gradually friends and associates, and then the community, the country, and finally the world.

By cultivating oneself through this route, one gradually sets the boundary of the individuated self to include all others. The ideal end state of the developing self was sagehood in which one was united with heaven and earth, which is represented in the middle of Figure 8 by the largest solid-line circle. The other smaller solid-line circles included in Figure 8 stand for other possible statuses of the self at various stages of self-inclusion or moral development. However, all of these solid circles encompass the small individuated self (the shaded area in the center of every solid-line circle).

Note here that the individuated small self is at the center of these concentric circles and that collectivities not only encompass it, but also include people belonging to the collectivity smaller in size and closer to the small self. In other words, these encompassing collectivities do not just overlap one another, they actually hold a whole/part relationship. Thus, the large selves do not represent the social groups to which a person belongs, rather they refer to the operating selves available to a person to choose from in dealing with a given event/situation. The more one's moral cultivation has advanced, the more large selves are available from which one can choose as an operating self for a given situation.

In addition, a person's self-cultivation requires placing the large selves in front of small self when interacting with others in family, social,

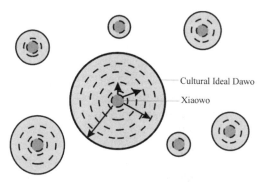

Figure 8. Different Levels of Moral Self Development (shown by different sizes of solid circles)

and political activities. When these goals conflict, the person needs to sacrifice the goal of the small self in order to accomplish those of the operating large self. When this sacrifice no longer represents a struggle, but is performed willingly, the actor is considered to have advanced in self-cultivation. Before then, people are constantly involved in and occupied with struggle and self-debate concerning how to choose between the large self and the small self, and among the large selves.

Public (*gong*, 公) / Private (*si*, 私)

Japanese scholar Mizoguchi (1994) compared the differences between the Japanese and the Chinese conceptions of the relationship between *gong* (公, public) and *si* (私, private) and gave a good historical account of the transformation of the Chinese conception. He stated that the Japanese *gong*, a word originally borrowed from the Chinese, refers strictly to a collective entity or the head or symbol representing such an entity. What is owned by oneself and one's family is called *si*. For the Japanese, both concepts are therefore territorial concepts that are mutually exclusive, value-neutral, and in no way opposing to each other in meaning.

However, he found that, as early as in the late Warring States Period, in China, *gong* had developed the meaning *for all and for everyone* in a collective entity, as in *a world for all (tian xia wei gong,* 天下為公); whereas *si*, for the private self, was more like *private property* (*si chan,* 私產). Consequently, the public and the private relationship became a whole/part relationship. One possible explanation is that the Confucian conception of the self had already taken shape then and the concentric circles had become the prevailing conception of the self.

Furthermore, at this time, both of these terms started to carry evaluative meanings. Anything associated with gong was deemed trustworthy and moral (like *gong ping,* 公平, fairness); anything with *si* was thought to be treacherous and amoral (like *si xin,* 私心, hidden agenda). This value imposition is a natural consequence of the transformation of meanings, which not only erased the territorial boundaries between the public and the private, but also made one contain the other. The conception of the self as a developing entity almost requires the private to be subservient to the public.

When a person was said to be working for the public (*wei gong,* 為公), or for a larger collectivity other than the individuated self, that person was expected to work solely for the collective entity. The person was supposed to work for the benefit of everyone in that entity without thinking about personal interests as the larger entity was owned by all and by thinking of the benefits of all one's own benefit was included. If the person did as expected, that person was said to be good and moral. However, if the person treated the collective entity as if it were personal property and did things for personal benefit, that person was considered *for oneself only* (*wei si*, 為私) and as amoral and bad. The way *gong* and *si* were used in *wei gong* and *wei si* demonstrates that the meanings of *gong* and *si* were more motivational than territorial.

The main distinction between working for the public and for private interests lies in whom one has in mind while working for a collective entity. This distinction, of course, is often very difficult to make by watching the expressed action of a person. It becomes even more difficult when a moral tone has been added making everyone want to show effort for public benefit. Before a person has been morally cultivated to the point of total selflessness, personal needs and desires must be addressed from time to time.

The person had to resort to either fulfilling those needs indirectly (through the help of others) or disguising them by pretending (C. F. Yang, 2000a; 2000b), especially for those who hold public positions and who on many public occasions have to declare that they work for a well-defined large self (the country or the community). The need to use such solutions is even stronger than for ordinary citizens since *for the public* has to be shown to people at all times. In the end, it becomes extremely difficult to tell which people are really for the public and which people are actually working for the private self. A set of attributional procedures are therefore developed to help solve the problem (C. F. Yang, 2000a).

Even in modern Chinese societies, there remains a plethora of phrases denoting how people handle this problematic issue of public vs. private: *Da gong wu si* (大公無私, being fair to all without self-serving biases), *ying gong wang si* (因公忘私, going all the way for the public and forgetting the self totally), *jia gong ji si* (假公濟私, seek self-interests in the name of public interests), *gong bao si chou* (公報私仇, revenge for private grudges with official excuses). This transformation of meanings of the public and the private and their operation in group/self interactions have led the Chinese to become very concerned about and constantly troubled by issues of sincerity, loyalty, and trust (C. F. Yang, 2000a).

Gentleman (Jun zi, 君子) / Hypocrite (Xiang yuan, 鄉愿)

The standards set to become a Confucian gentleman were apparently too high for common people to emulate even at the time Confucius was alive. Confucius knew most could not attain the standard and made many remarks about it. A lot of people exaggerated the rituals (*li*, 禮) prescribed for gentleman without actually internalizing them; i.e., without affiliating them with corresponding inner feelings (expressions of *ren*, 仁, benevolence). On several occasions recorded in *Lun Yu* (論語, Confucius Analects), Confucius showed his disgust for such insincere people. "The full observance of the rules of propriety in serving one's prince is accounted by people to be flattery." "Fine words and an insinuating appearance are seldom associated with true virtue."

The most hash words coming from him were: "*Xiang yuan* (鄉愿) are the thieves of virtue." *Xiang yuan* refers to people who live as if they were loyal and sincere, and behave as if they were honest and austere. Both characters in the word, *xiang yuan*, are compound characters containing the radical, *xin* (心) indicating they have to do with what is on a person's mind. *Xiang yuan* were considered hypocritical thieves because they confused and took advantage of others by pretending they were gentlemen, and therefore was deemed worse than those who claimed they were *xiao ren* (小人, commoners) in the first place.

There were many reasons for people however to want to falsely speak and act like gentlemen throughout Chinese history: (1) honor–many wanted to be labeled as learned gentlemen and as members of the desirable and respected ruling elite class; (2) instrumental value–speaking and acting like a gentleman often led to a good reputation and a better job; (3) habit–the tradition of practicing rituals prior to developing corresponding feelings and sentiments is ingrained in education, and breeds habits of feigned compliance.

The Study of Person-Making (做人)

Based on these problems preoccupying the Chinese mind, the direction of study of the self as a person-making process can be mapped out. In every event/situation, one is always faced with at least an operating *da wo*, large self, and a *xiao wo*, small self, each energizing and guiding one to act out a prescribed action. At times, there is no conflict between the actions prescribed for the large self and the small self, especially as one's self-cultivation, and thus self-expansion, progresses. At other times, there is a conflict between the two that requires the person to make a decision about what to do and how to act. The decision making and the resultant action taken form the person-making process. One's resolution of the conflict in a harmonious fashion makes the self grow to become a better person. In the Chinese case, a better person is one that approaches a moral and social being.

The person-making and the resulting action are not the same as *the self as process* discussed in western literature. The self is not the process by which one controls or influences a person's behavior. It is the meaning contained in the person's deliberation during the person-making process and the meanings of the action taken that reveal the person's self. These meanings often require a set of cultural meaning systems to decode.

In the study of the Chinese self, three aspects, at least, of the self need to be more closely examined. One is the conflict resolution process of the large self and the small self, especially their relationship with the development of a person's moral self; i.e., with the degree to which the person approaches the culturally ideal self. It is worthwhile for researchers to adopt the yin/yang mode of thinking and study how the *zhong yong* principle is used to solve this type of conflict.

The other area that is worth in-depth scrutiny is the social comparison process by which one learns about how well one does in the pursuit of the model self, *jun zi* (gentleman). As this Chinese model self is forever unreachable in real life, one's continuation of this pursuit as a cultural imperative becomes virtually standardless. One has to resort to real-life exemplars for comparison or to simply outperforming oneself. One's targets for social comparison are therefore not the abstract unreachable ideal self, but the human beings around one: past cultural role models or heroes and heroines, and oneself, the past or present. The aim of the comparison is always to surpass the target. The implications of this kind of social comparison on the social psychology of the Chinese people are complex but an interesting topic deserving further investigation.

Finally, the self-esteem derived from this kind of social comparison comes not from just that of any dimension or attribute, but mainly from the large self/small self resolution. A recent example illustrates this point. In 2001, a general who served a pivotal role in the history of modern China during the Sino-Japanese War, Zhang Xue Liang (張學良) died at the age of 101. Due to his significance, many of the newspapers in Hong Kong commemorated him in their editorials. The last few sentences in the editorial of the Ming Bao (明報), a newspaper read mostly by Hong Kong intellectuals represented the public sentiment:

> Zhang sacrificed his own freedom to help rekindle the determination to fight the Japanese, the big goal at the time for the country. From his personal perspective, he was mistreated by his country and its people. However, from a larger and collectivistic perspective, his words and actions helped save the country and its people, and set up an everlasting example for his countrymen to emulate. (October 16, 2001)

For a Chinese person, I think that no one would expect to get a better evaluation than that General Zhang received; i.e., as one who sacrifices small self for the larger self. One's self-esteem is built on the hope that after one's death one would receive similar words to those Zhang received. For the Chinese, history is recorded for future generations to emulate and surpass. One's self-regard, a better term than self-esteem, is derived from other's evaluations of oneself based on a shared cultural model of the person. The self and self-regard, however, do not motivate one to become a better person as some western theories claim (e.g., Sedikides & Strube, 1995). Rather, it is the goal (to become a better person) one sets for oneself that motivates him/her to choose to do good and moral deeds, thereby approaching the culturally ideal person.

Bridging with Western Self Psychology

Although I advocate studying the Chinese self using an indigenous approach, I do not think that there is an unbridgeable gap between what is obtained using indigenous and cross-cultural approaches or from indigenous and western studies. The influx of modern western ideology of individualism and its conception of the self as individuated and autonomous entity casts a long shadow on the Chinese mind in modern societies. The influence of my own western training must be quite obvious in this paper. Research on "becoming" (e.g., Allport, 1955; Rogers, 1961), the relational self (e.g., Andersen & Chen, 2002; Curtis, 1991), person/situation interaction in social psychology and personality theories (e.g., Mischel & Shoda, 1995), interactional psychology (e.g., Pervin & Lewis, 1978), action theory (e.g., Eckensberger, 1995; 2001), self-regulation (e.g., Carver & Scheier, 1990; Miller & Brown, 1991; Brown, 1998) and self-control (e.g., Logue, 1995), social comparison and self-evaluation (e.g., Festinger, 1954; Suls & Mullen, 1982; Wood, 1989), and self-presentation (e.g., Leary, 1995) can provide opportunities for dialogue after indigenous psychologists further refine these ideas.

   The psychologies developed in western countries have introduced psychology and helped train many Chinese psychologists in the past. What I hope to see in the future is that indigenous psychological research can enrich mainstream western psychology in return. What I outlined here allows me to see this possibility in areas like group identity and identification, self-evaluation and self-regard, self-deliberation before presentation, and the development of moral self. A further elaboration of these research possibilities definitely requires more discussion.

REFERENCES

Allport, G. W. (1955). *Becoming: Basic considerations for a psychology of personality*. New Haven: Yale University Press.

Andersen, S.M., & Chen, Serena (2002). The relational self: An interpersonal social-cognitive theory. *Psychological Review, 109*, 619–645.

Bodde, D. (1953). Harmony and conflict in Chinese philosophy. In A.F. Wright (Ed.), *Studies in Chinese thought* (pp. 19–75). Chicago: University of Chicago Press.

Brown, J. M. (1998). Self-regulation and the addictive behaviors. In W. R. Miller & N. Heather (Eds.), *Treating addictive behaviors* (2nd ed., pp. 61–73). New York: Plenum.

Carver, C. S., & Scheier, M. F. (1990). Principles of Self-regulation: Action and emotion. In R.M. Sorrentino & E.T. Higgins (Eds.), *Handbook of motivation and cognition* (Vol. 2, pp. 3–52). New York: The Guilford Press.

Chan, W. T. (1963). *A source book in Chinese philosophy*. Princeton: Princeton University.

Cheung, T. S. (1989). *Confucian ethics and order-complex: A sociological interpretation of Chinese thoughts*. Teipei: Ju Liou. (In Chinese.)

Cheung, T. S., King, A. Y. C., Chan, H. M., Chan, K. M., Yang, C. F., and Chiu, C. Y. (2001). *Zhong-yung rationality: Beyond instrumental, value, and communicative rationality*. A manuscript submitted for publication. (In Chinese.)

Choi, K. (2000). *Between Western dualism and Chinese Erh-chi (dual-element): Comparisons on categorization and thinking style*. A paper presented at the First Conference on "Social Sciences Concepts: Indigenous and Western", Taipei, Taiwan, April 1–2. (In Chinese.)

Creel, H. G. (1987). The role of compromise in Chinese culture. In C. Le Blanc, C. & S. Blader (Eds.), *Chinese ideas about nature and society*. Hong Kong: University of Hong Kong Press.

Curtis, R. C. (1991). *The relational self: Theoretical convergences in psychoanalysis and social psychology*. New York: Guilford.

de Bary, W. T. (1991). *Learning for one's: Essays on the individual in Neo-Confucian thought*. New York: Columbia University.

Ding, Z. Y., & Wu, J. D. (1993). *Changes in ideas and thinking style during the Spring-Autumn and the Warring-States Periods*. Changsha: Hunan Publishing Co. (In Chinese.)

Eckenberger, L. H. (1995). Activity or action: Two different roads towards an integration of culture into psychology? *Culture and Psychology, 1*, 67–80.

Eckenberger, L. H. (2001). Action Theory: Psychological. In N. J. Smelser & P. B. Baltes (Eds.), *International Encyclopedia of the Social & Behavioral Sciences* (Vol. 1, pp. 45–49). Oxford: Elsevier Science Ltd.

Festinger, L. A. (1954). A theory of social comparison processes. *Human Relations, 7*, 117–140.

Gao, Zheng (2001). The unearthed Guo Dan bamboo book and Si-Mencius School of Confucianism. *Cultural China, 8*, 36–43. (In Chinese.)

Geertz, C. (1984). From the native's point of view: On the nature of anthrological understanding. In R. S. Shweder & R. A. LeVine (Eds.), *Cultural theory: Essays on mind, self, and emotion* (pp. 123–136). Cambridge: Cambridge University Press.

Hori, B. I. (1986). *A study on the Even-Land Policy* (Chinese Translation Version). Taipei, Taiwan: Hung Wen Guan. (In Chinese.)

Hsieh, C. H. & Jen, W. (1991). "Great man" (Chun-tsu) and "small man" (hsiao-ren) in the Confucian Analects: A transformation approach. *Journal of Applied Behavioral Science, 27*, 425–443.

Jahoda, G. (1992). *Crossroads between Culture and Mind: Continuities and change in Theories of Human Nature*. New York: Harvester Wheatsheaf.

Jiao, G. C. (1991). *Thoughts on self-other relationship in ancient China*. Beijing: People's University Press. (In Chinese.)

Leary, M. R. (1995). *Self-presentation: Impression management and interpersonal behavior*. Boulder, CO: Westview Press.

Li, Y. Y., Yang, K. S., & Wen, C. I. (1985). *A collection of papers on modernization and indigenization*. Taipei: Gui Guan.

Liu, S. H. (2000). The openness of Confucianism. *Global Dialogue, Winter Issue*, 89–98.

Logue, A. W. (1995). *Self-control: Waiting until tomorrow for what you want today*. Englewood Cliffs, NJ: Prentice Hall.

Meng, P. Y (1993). *The subjectivistic thinking in Chinese philosophy*. Beijing: Orient Publishing Co. (In Chinese.)

Meng, P. Y. & Kuang, B. L. (1993). *The thinking style of traditional Chinese philosophies*. Hang Zhou: Zhejiang People's Publishing Co. (In Chinese.)

Miller, W. R., & Brown, J. M. (1991). Self-regulation as a conceptual basis for the prevention and treatment of addictive behaviors. In N. Heather & W. R. Miller & J. Greeley (Eds.), *Self-control and the addictive behaviors* (pp. 3–79). Sydney, Australia: Maxwell Macmillan.

Mischel, W., & Shoda, Y. (1995). A cognitive-affective system theory of personality: Reconceptualizing situations, dispositions, dynamics, and invariance in personality structure. *Psychological Review, 102*, 246–268.

Mizoguchi, Y. (1994). A comparison of the Chinese and Japanese conceptions of gong and si. *Twenty-one Century Bi-monthly, February Issue*, 85–97. (Chinese translation.)

Pervin, L. A., & Lewis, M. (1978). *Perspectives in interactional psychology*. New York: Plenum Press.

Pye, L.W. (1968). *The spirit of Chinese politics: The psychocultural study of the authority crisis in political development*. Cambridge, MA: MIT Press.

Rogers, C. R. (1961). *On becoming a person*. Boston: Houghton Mifflin.

Sedikides, C., & Strube, M. (1995). The multiply motivated self. *Personal and Social Psychology Bulletin, 21*, 1330–1335.

Suls, J. & Mullen, B. (1982). From the cradle to the grave: Comparison and self-evaluation across the life-span. In J. Suls (Ed.), *Psycyological perspectives of the self* (Vol. 1, pp. 97–128). Hillside, NJ: LEA.

Tu, W. M. (1994). Embodying the universe: A note on Confucian self-realization. In R. T. Ames, W. Dissanayake, & T. P. Kasulis (Eds.), *Self as person in Asian theory and practice* (pp. 177–186). Albany, NY: SUNY Press.

Wang, A. (2000). *Cosmology and political culture in early China*. Cambridge: Cambridge University Press.

Wang, F. Y. (2002). *The self in ancient Chinese mind: A cultural psychological interpretation*. An unpublished manuscript. (In Chinese.)

Wood, J. V. (1989). Theory and research concerning social comparison of personal attributes. *Psychological Bulletin, 106*, 231–248.

Yang, C. F. (1991a). Introduction. In H.S.R. Kao and C. F. Yang (Eds.), *The Chinese mind and the Chinese heart: Papers on indigenous Chinese psychology* (Vol. 1, pp. 9–60). Taipei: Yuan-Liou. (In Chinese.)

Yang, C. F. (1991b). A theory on the Chinese self. In C. F. Yang and H.S.R. Kao (Eds.), *The Chinese mind and the Chinese heart: Papers on indigenous Chinese psychology* (Vol. 2, pp. 19–93). Taipei: Yuan-Liou. (In Chinese.)

Yang, C. F. (1991c). A critical review of self and self-related research in Taiwan and Hong Kong. In C. F. Yang and H.S.R. Kao (Eds.), *The Chinese mind and the Chinese heart: Papers on indigenous Chinese psychology* (Vol. 2, pp. 93–145). Taipei: Yuan-Liou. (In Chinese.)

Yang, C. F. (1993). Toward a framework for the study of Chinese personality. In K.S. Yang & A.B. Yu (Eds.), *The mind and behavior of the Chinese* (pp. 319–441). Taipei: Guei-Guan. (In Chinese.)

Yang, C. F. (1996). *How to study the Chinese*. Taipei: Gui Guan. (In Chinese.)

Yang, C. F. (2000a). Psychocultural foundations of informal groups: The issues of loyalty, sincerity, and trust. In L. Dittmer, H. Fukui, & P.N.S. Lee (Eds.), *Informal Politics in East Asia* (pp. 225–244). New York: Cambridge University Press.

Yang, C. F. (2000b). *A conceptualization of the Chinese interpersonal emotion, qing*. Paper presented at The XVth Congress of the International Association for Cross-Cultural Psychology (IACCP), July 16–22, Pultusk, Poland.

Yang, C. F. (2001). Toward a new conceptualization of guanxi and renqing. In C. F. Yang (Ed.), *Chinese interpersonal relationship, affection, and trust: A interactional perspective* (pp. 337–370). Taipei: Yuan Liou. (In Chinese.)

Yang, C. F. & Chiu, C.Y. (1997). *A preliminary study of zhong-yong*. Paper presented at the Fourth Symposium on "The Psychology and Behavior of the Chinese", May 29–31, Taipei, Taiwan. (In Chinese.)

Yang, R. B. (2000). *Self and I and public opinion*. Paper presented at the First Conference on "Social Sciences Concepts: Indigenous and Western", Taipei, Taiwan, April 1–2. (In Chinese.)

Yang, R. B., & Huang, C. C. (1996). *The ancient Chinese thinking style: An exploration*. Taipei: Cheng Chung Publishing Co. (In Chinese.)

Yu, Y. S. (1976). The imperial power and the prime minister's power under "juen zuen chan bei". In Y. S. Yu (Ed.), *History and thoughts* (pp. 47–76). Taipei, Taiwan: Lien Jing.

Yu, Y. S. (1993). Between the self and the group. *Ming Bao Monthly, August Issue*, 106–108.

Zhang, D. N. (1989a). *Studies on Chinese Thoughts on Ethics*. Shanghai: Shanghai People's Publisher. (In Chinese.)

Zhang, D. N. (1989b). *The scope of classic Chinese philosophical concepts*. Beijing: Academy of Chinese Social Sciences Press. (In Chinese.)

Zhang, L. W. (1989). *The logical structure of Chinese philosophy*. Beijing: Academy of Chinese Social Sciences Press. (In Chinese.)

Zhu, Y. L. (1991). *Confucian model personality and Chinese culture*. Shanyang, PRC: Liouning Educational Books. (In Chinese.)

GLOSSARY

Chi You (蚩尤)

Even-Land Policy
   (井田或均田制度)

Guo Dian (郭店)

Han Dynasty (漢朝)

Huang Di (黃帝)

Ju Xi (朱熹)

Lun Yu (論語)

Mencius (孟子)

Person-Making (做人)

Pre-Qin (先秦時期) – before 221
   BCE

Private-owned lands (私田)

Public-owned lands (公田)

Qing Dynasty (清朝)

Spring-Autumn Period
   (秋春時期) – 770 BCE – 476
   BCE

Sung Dynasty (宋朝)

Warring States Period (戰國時期)
   – 475 BCE – 221 BCE

Xi Zhou (西周) Dynasty

Xunzi (荀子)

Yin-Zhou Transition (殷周之交)
   – around 1066 BCE

Yi Zhuan (易傳)

Zhong Yong (中庸)

Zhuan Xu (顓頊)

Zi Si (子思)

內聖 – to keep to himself aiming
   to become a sage

外王 – to participate in making
   the world a harmonious place
   for everyone by serving the
   country or society with moral
   teachings

段玉裁 – a Confucian scholar

chi (彳) – to do and to practice

cun (群) – the group

da gong wu si (大公無私) – being
   fair to all without self-serving
   biases

da wo (大我) – literally meaning
   the large self

de (德) – a feeling of accomplishment from practicing li and
   yue, morality

gong (公) – public

gong bao si chou (公報私仇) –
   revenge for private grudges
   with official excuses

gong ping (公平) – fairness

ji (己) – the self

ji (忌) – a character for fear,
   forbidden and dislike

jia gong ji si (假公濟私) – seek
   self-interests in the name of
   public interests

jiang (敬) – a sense of fear, humbleness, prudence, and alarm,
   a humble sentiment that allows
   the person to see rooms for
   improvement

jun zi (君子) – noblemen who
   ruled the states in pre-
   Confucian Zhou Dynasty

li (禮) – a set of role expectations
   that guide people's behaviors,
   propriety

li (利) – self-interest

li (理) – principles, regularities

min gui (民貴) – significance of
   people

ping tian zia (平天下) – make world peace

qi (氣) – air, formidable force

qi jia (齊家) – raise a family

ren (仁) – benevolence

ren (人) – human being

ru (儒) – Confucian model

si (私) – private

si chan (私產) – private property

Si-Meng School (思孟學派) – emphasizes the internal cultivation of a person, became the mainstream among Confucian scholars for thousands of years

si xien (私心) – hidden agenda

tian (天) – the universe

tian xa wai gong (天下為公) – a world for all

thuo (辵) – walking/practicing

wei yi (威儀) – authority and integrity

wei gong (為公) – for the public or a larger collectivity other than oneself

wei si (為私) – for oneself

wo (我) – meaning I or me

wu (巫) – a person who could be in two states of consciousness interchangeably, able to leave the body to converse with mythical figures

xiang yuan (鄉愿) – people who live as if they were loyal and sincere, and behaved as if they were honest and austere

xiao ren (小人) – the commoners under junzi rule

xiao wo (小我) – literally meaning the small self

xin (心) – literally meaning heart

xiu shen (修身) – self cultivation

yang (陽) – the bright side, denoted good

yi (義) – righteousness, conscience

yi (已) – means done, used, practiced or executed

yin (陰) – the shady side, denoted bad

ying gong wang si (因公忘私) – going all the way for the public and forgetting the self totally

yue (樂) – literally meaning music

zhe kuo (治國) – run the country

zheng (朕) – a *wo* preserved specially for emperors or empresses

zhi (智) – intellect, knowledge

Chapter **16**

Naïve Psychology of Koreans' Interpersonal Mind and Behavior in Close Relationships

Sang-Chin Choi[1] and Kibum Kim

For Koreans, forming close relationships with each other has special meanings to their interpersonal behavior. For example, quality of relationships between family members, close friends or colleagues is quite different from that of relationships between acquaintances or strangers (Cha, 1994; Choi, 1992, 1993, 1994, 1997, 1998, 1999, 2000; Choi & Choi, 1994; Choi & Kim, 1999a, 1999b, 2000; Choi, Kim, & Choi, 1993; Park, 1979; see also Gardner, Gabriel, & Lee, 1999). Categorization of *weness* (ingroup identity) is a mechanism, which underlies how Koreans interact with others. The former type of relationships, relationships with others within the category of *weness*, is characterized by the strong sense of our folks, private passion and emotion, interpersonal *jung*.[2] Recently, Korean goverment has changed the English spelling of Korean words. The words *jung* and *shimjung* have been previously written as *cheong* and *shimcheong*.[2] (牛, deep affection and attachment) and *uiri* (陰陽, loyalty) unconditioned friendship, mutual altruism and exclusive favoritism (Choi, 1998; Choi & Kim, 1999a). The latter type of relationships, relationships with others out of the *weness* category, however, is characterized by reason-based rationality, objective social norms, individual interests, social justice and equity. Like this, Koreans have different types of interactions with others depending on whether they are members of the *weness* category or not.

[1] This work was supported by grand No. 1999-1-521-001-3 from the Basic Research Program of the Korea Science & Engineering Foundation.
[2] Recently, the Korean government has changed the English spelling of Korean words. We have used the revised English spelling for Korean words.

Relationships between members of the *weness* category are based on *jung*, which is critical in understanding social behavior and interpersonal interactions of Koreans. The prototype of *jung*-based relationships can be found in the interactions among family members (Choi, 2000; Choi & Kim, 1999a; Choi, Kim, & Kim, 2000; Choi & Choi, 2001). The Korean family as a community historically and culturally bound together by common fate is characteristic of oneness, the sameness, self-sacrifice, mutual assistance, personal relationship, and *Jung*. Korean relationships with others on the basis of *weness* are a mere extension of psychology of within-family relationships to social settings. *Jung* is a central concept in the formation and maintenance of social relationships based on *weness*. The basic feature of *jung* is to care for others, as do siblings, which consists of behavior attentive, empathetic, helpful, and supportive.

Further, forming relationships based on *weness* imply that two minds of two persons are tied to one. For example, close friends are frequently rephrased as friends to share and understand their minds, or friends tied by their minds. This emphasis on mind in close relationships leads Koreans to be prone to evaluate behavior of their friends not by the behavior per se, but by the quality and magnitude of mind which the behavior conveys. Likewise, everyday discourses and narrations Koreans produce in the relational contexts rely heavily on references to their mind (refer to Harré & Gillett, 1994). For instance, the following expressions are quite common in everyday life of Korans: "Do not say anything that does not come from mind." "Do not hurt my mind", "I don't know how to show you my mind", "One must have a good mind", and so on. Moreover, the Korean dictionary contains a large number of words that include syllables meaning mind (New Korean Dictionary, 1974). This indicates that for Koreans mind is a very important concept and so the schema of mind is highly developed. Also, Korean concepts of self were found to be structured around their own minds (Choi & Kim, 1999a). All of these phenomena indicate that the main currency in Korean relationships is a mind exchange rather than a behavioral exchange.

Although Korean behavior is centered a round mind, invisible mind should be inferred from observations of behavior. This fact helps Koreans develop schema concerning the inferences of others' mind as well as one's own. However, those schemas may not always infallible, so that sometimes behavior can be interpreted in the wrong way. Possibility of misreading others' mind is especially high when there is a paucity of behavioral cues on their inner mind in ambiguous situations. This sort of situations likely engenders misunderstandings or even conflicts between those who are involved in the relationships. Under these circumstances, their *shimjung* (心情) is activated, which helps recognize their own and their partners' true mind (Choi & Kim, 1999a).

CHARACTERISTICS AND WORKING PROCESSES
OF *SHIMJUNG*

In the 88' Seoul Olympics, a Korean athlete would not come down the ring as a reaction against the unfair judgment when his loss was announced. This happening ended up with delayed processes of the remaining agenda of the day. Most of Western media criticized his behavior as illegitimate. However, Korean people expressed sympathies with the boxer. Headlines of Korean newspapers read like this: "Unfair judgment Kept a Korean boxer seated on the canvass", "The boxer's behavior understandable" or "The boxer's shimjung shared by Koreans."

In this case, Western people focus their point of view on social rules in evaluating the athlete's behavior and come up with judgment of the behavior as rule-breaking and so illegitimate. For Koreans, however, to take the boxer's personal feeling into account than to rely exclusively on social rules is more important in evaluating his behavior. Korean people frequently use such phrases as "treated unfairly", "too apathetic", "too inconsiderate" and "to hurt my mind" in everyday discourses about their relationships with close others (Choi, 1997; Choi & Kim, 1998; Choi & Kim, 1999a; Shon & Choi, 1999). Those phrases represent phenomena occurring inside the mind of persons involved in the close relationships. Koreans think much of being empathetic with what others experience in mind relating to their behavior and so of adjusting their behavior toward taking others into account. Thus Koreans are almost habitually sensitive to subjectifying inner experiences of others involved in close relationships based on *weness*. In this sense, Koreans share their inner experiences with each other as persons concerned, not as third persons (Choi, 1998).

Shimjung is a Korean word denoting personal experiences felt in mind. This term is so commonly used as to appear frequently on Korean newspapers and serial TV dramas. For instance, when a man of power is publicly disempowered, many articles titled such as "President Kim's *shimjung*", "President Chun's *shimjung*", "President Noh's *shimjung*" or even "*shimjung* of President Kim's wife" come forth on Korean newspapers. Expressions and discourses of *shimjung* may not be appropriate in formal interactions that require of rational thinking and reason-based discourses. However, they underlie a normative model of personal interactions based on *weness* or *jung*.

The term *shimjung* is constituted by two parts: *Shim* (心) meaning mind and *jung* (情) meaning affection (New Korean Dictionary, 1974). *Shimjung* means a state of aroused mind concerning a particular situation (Choi & Kim, 1999a, 1999b). The scope of usage of mind is much narrower for Koreans than for Western people. The English word mind carries with it both cognitive and emotional aspects of human activities (The Oxford Dictionary 2nd Ed.). However, the Korean word *shim* or *maum* (heart) equivalent to mind in English concerns emotion rather than cognition. For Koreans, mind corresponds to intentionality including interest, motivation, emotion, intention, determination and mood, as in "hurt mind", "mind in pain", "mind not in good mood", "motivated mind", "lenient mind", to have no mind to do", "determined mind", and so on (Choi & Kim, 1999a; see also Lillard, 1998).

For Koreans, mind is activated in conjunction to a wide range of objects: living things, impersonal materials, events, situations and even abstract concepts. Likewise, *shimjung* is activated in relation to specific behavior or events concerning others in close relationships within the weness category. The most frequently used expressions of *shimjung* are "disappointed *shimjung*", "rejected *shimjung*", "sad *shimjung*", "unfairly treated *shimjung*", "depressed *shimjung*", "despaired *shimjung*", etc (Choi, 1997; Choi & Kim, 1999a). Like this, *shimjung* Koreans express connotes their desires and motivations to pursue toward, hope for, avoid, and dislike something. *Shimjung* is engendered when expected or desired outcomes from close relationships are not achieved. So valence of *shimjung* is generally negative although it can be positive when desires or motivations are fulfilled in the relationships.

A variety of emotions and minds Koreans have toward their partners in close relationships can be experienced in the form of *shimjung* (refer to Gergen, 1994; Harré & Stearns, 1995). For example, emotional states such as jung, han (恨, lamentation), love, hatred and envy could be transformed into and experienced as *shimjung*. In this respect, *shimjung* can be considered an aroused state of emotion (Choi & Kim, 1999; 1999b). In addition to this, several other characteristics, which have been created culturally, are linked to *shimjung*: First, *shimjung* presupposes the existence of self-consciousness, which makes the person concerned aware of the arousal of emotion or mind. That is, both mind in action and conscious reading of that mind are all involved in shimjung (Choi & Kim, 1999b; see also Vygotsky, 1978; Wertsch, 1998). Secondly, on the side of the person concerned, *shimjung* is constituted by evaluative judgment of aroused emotion and explanation on psychological processes in which that emotion is evolved in relation to interpersonal and situational factors (Choi & Kim, 1999, 1999b; Stearns, 1995). That explanation takes a form of introspective narration of what makes one in a dyad feel such and such *shimjung* in relation to behavior of the other (Choi & Kim, 1999b). Given the two above-mentioned characteristics of shimjung, shimjung can be defined as "mind aware of content felt in mind" (Choi & Kim, 1999, 1999b). Also, the explanatory mode of shimjung has a sharp contrast to the reason-based explanatory mode of facts. Several differences between these two are presented in Table 1 (Choi, 1997, 1998; Choi & Kim, 1999, 1999b).

Third, *shimjung* of a person is evoked when the extent of considerate mind to which his or her partner expresses falls short of or exceeds the expectation held by that person (Choi & Kim, 1999, 1999b). That is, *shimjung* is not aroused until an expectation of considerate mind from the

Table 1. The Psycho-Logics of *Shimjung* and the Socio-Logics of Reason

The Logics of *Shimjung*	The Logics of Reason
Between us	Individual interactions
Private	Public
Exchange of mind	Social exchange of interests
Intersubjective	Objectivity
Cheong	Reason

partner is formed. This expectation is based on the psychological distance estimated between both in a dyad through reflective thinking of history of their dyadic interactions. Thus, the history of relationships between persons involved in *shimjung* or its arousal exercises important influence on interpretation and evaluation of behavior of their partner (Choi & Kim, 1999). For instance, when an old chum in a weness relationship refuses to offer a favor or rejects a personal request, Koreans express dissatisfaction with his or her relentless mind in the pour-out of *shimjung* such as "it is nonsense to refuse my asking in the light of our friendship of long standing". Like this, expressions of *shimjung* take a form of story-telling with reference to historical background of specific relationships.

Fourth, among most important characteristics which differentiate *shimjung* from other emotions is a perspective on one's own circumstances involved in the arousal of *shimjung* (Choi & Kim, 1999b). Generally, emotions such as hatred, love and jealousy are oriented toward external objects. Likewise, at the initial stage, *shimjung* is produced as a response to the behavior of a specific partner. That is, when considerate mind reflected in the behavior of the partner does not reach one's expectation, a negative *shimjung* is generated. *Shimjung* is developed onto another stage, however. *Shimjung* leads the person concerned to turn his or her attention to the self and then to evaluate negatively his or her own ability, characteristics and resources in relation to his or her circumstances. Negative self-evaluation driven by *shimjung* usually results in a self-pity and a self-handicapped feeling of humiliation, as expressed in the phrases of "my unfortunate lot", "my pitiful lot" and "my lot unappreciated by others" (Choi & Kim, 1999; Shon & Choi, 1999). So, the mode of pouring out *shimjung* is very similar to that of complaining about misfortunate circumstances.

An empirical study by Shon and Choi (1999) buttresses the idea that *shimjung* is a combination of initial emotion induced by the behavior of the partner and secondary emotion induced by negative evaluation of the self. They asked a group of Korean undergraduates to list occasions which hurt their *shimjung*. The following cases were high ranked in the rank order of frequencies: (1) When a truthful friend betrays me; (2) When my mind is misunderstood; (3) When others are not considerate and kind to me; (4) When I am not considered important; (5) when I feel myself terrible; (6) when I am treated unfairly. The first three responses concern experiences caused by one's own expectations unfulfilled by behavior of others, whereas the remaining three responses relate to the feelings of self-pity and self-humiliation derived from self-consciousness of not being acknowledged by others.

As mentioned earlier, *shimjung* is into operation in the contexts of *weness* relationships based on *jung*. However, *shimjung* can affect in turn the quality of those relationships. For example, when a negative *shimjung* occurs, this negativity drives a reconstruction of weness relationships in the way of under evaluating those relationships. In general, relational history of a dyad is important in the *weness* and Cheong-based relationships. Also, those relationships are constructed in the heads of the persons concerned by reflective thinking of that history. For example, Koreans construct their relationships in the form of predispositions such as "*jung* has emerged between us" by being aware reflectively of that they have shared their fortunes with each other over a long period of time.

However, *shimjung* is not a reflective evaluation of relational history of a dyad. Instead, it is an emotional state of "here-and-now" characteristic of a mixture of emotion caused by behavior of the partner and emotion related to self-evaluation. In this respect, *shimjung* is an immediate experience whereas the *Weness-* and *jung*-based relationship is a mediated experience (Choi, Kim, & Kim, 1999, 2000). Regardless of this difference, the relationship between these two experiences is like that of head and tail of a coin, so that they are intertwined with each other in a complementary way. That is, existence of one experience defines existence of the other. *Jung* which cannot be transformed into *shimjung* is not *Jung* any more and experience of *shimjung* evidence existence of *Jung* in the relationships. So, *shimjung* functions as a cue for identifying or conforming *weness-* and *jung*-based relationships (Choi & Kim, 1999b).

Finally, *Jung* and *shimjung* in close relationships are felt at a temporal point or moment and those feelings are ephemeral in that they are not persistent over a long period of interactions. Then, it is necessary to consider when Koreans feel *jung* and *shimjung* toward others in a stream of successive time. As noted earlier, *jung* and *shimjung* can be activated by specific behavior of others at a given moment of time. However, it is also possible without any apparent external stimulation. Recollection of the past behavior done by others can instigate *jung* and *shimjung* not only by providing cues for those emotions, but also by allowing reinterpretation and reconstruction of that behavior (Bruner, 1990, p. 39). In this respect, external stimuli are not indispensable to arousal of *shimjung*, although this does not mean that *shimjung* could be activated spontaneously. *shimjung* certainly requires either external or internal stimulations to be induced.

IMPORTANCE OF *SHIMJUNG* EXCHANGE IN THE *WENESS-* AND *JUNG*-BASED RELATIONSHIPS

The *weness-* and *jung*-based relationships are characteristic of exchange of mind with each other. Also, given that *shimjung* is a state of aroused mind, exchange of *shimjung* is the most dynamic among a variety of exchanges of mind. *Shimjung* exchange is not through verbal media and instead relies frequently on non-verbal cues for *shimjung*. The reason is that when *shimjung* is expressed verbally, it is often considered cognitive thinking rather than emotional mind or disguised rather than true mind. So, people in Confucian culture, including Koreans, regard as most ideal the exchange of mind based on "from one mind to another" in the *weness-* and *jung*-based relationships. Further, *shimjung* is a dynamic and active means quite suitable for this type of exchange of mind. One in a dyad experiences arousal of *shimjung* as an empathetic reaction to *shimjung* aroused in the mind of the other and then the other is empathetic to one's *shimjung* (Choi & Kim, 1999b).

Interactions based on "from one mind to another" occur most frequently between family members. Parents have developed the ability to read their children's mind and to act accordingly although those children do not unfold their true mind. Children also behave in the considerate ways of their parents' wishes and desires although they are not mentioned. Ability to read each other's *shimjung* unspoken outward and to react accordingly is well-developed in the parent-child relationships of Koreans (Choi & Kim, 1999, 1999b). In a serial Korean TV drama, when a son comes back home from a long leave, the son and his mother do not display blatant expressions of pleasure such as passionate hugging as typically shown in Western programs. It is because *shimjung* is a very special, private and secretive emotion so as not to be publicly displayed.

Let's take an example of *shimjung* discourse between son and mother.

> On a rainy day, a mother was waiting for her son back from school with an umbrella for him at a bus stop. Finally, the bus arrived and the son got angry on seeing his mother, "You shouldn't have come out here with the umbrella for me." The mother replied, "My baby, sorry about that."

Superficial contents of this discourse are constituted by a complaint made by the son about his mother and an apology made by the mother. However, *shimjung* of high strength is interchanged behind this discourse. The son must be grateful for the considerate behavior of his mother. Nonetheless, the son hides his real *shimjung* of gratitude by getting angry with his mother. The mother also conceals her true *shimjung* of being disappointed at her son just by apologizing to him. Often times the strength of *shimjung* in close relationships is reinforced by expressed emotions that are opposite to the real and hidden emotions. The parent-child relationship and in particular, the mother-son relationship is based on in-depth *shimjung*. To build up interpersonal relationships on deep *shimjung* means to become one in flesh and spirit. These relationships make one's *shimjung* dependent on the other's and finally make both feel identical *shimjung*.

Let's take another example of *shimjung* discourses. It has not been rare in Korea that a young man raises a hostage case. Every time, the police bring his mother to the spot and ask her to persuade her son to surrender himself. In most cases, the mother solicits her son to consider her painful *shimjung* and so to give up voluntarily. The man may be empathetic to his mother because strong *shimjung* is already established in their relationship. In the end, the man highly likely feels guilty at painful *shimjung* experienced by his mother and so intends to surrender himself for his mother's sake. This is a method of persuasion using *shimjung* transference.

Shimjung exchange does not always occur in the form of "from one mind to another." A long history of relationships, like that of relationships between family members, facilitates Koreans to read *shimjung* of others, although cues for their *shimjung* are not abundant and straightforward. However, some more specific behavior is required to exchange *shimjung* between common colleagues or friends. Patting a child in the head, grasping firmly hands of a close friend, sighing together with a friend in trouble, and so forth are all acts to convey one's own *shimjung* to the other. Interpretations of those acts in terms of *shimjung* are usually dependent on the situational contexts where they take place. Interpretative frames for *shimjung*-related behavior are well elaborated in Korean societies although they are not formalized explicitly (Choi & Kim, 1999, 1999b). Diary of Rural Life, a serial Korean TV drama of most long lasting, depicts delicately how Koreans exchange a variety of their subtle *Shimjung* with each other in diverse situations. Without well-developed *shimjung* and its schema, Koreans would not be attracted to that drama.

In the election culture of Korea, a sympathy vote is far from negligible. This sympathy vote indicates that a voter casts his or her vote for a candidate just because this candidate is miserable and poor. It is not rare at all in Korea that a candidate in prison wins the election. Being locked up in a prison often stirs *shimjung* of the public, which in turn stimulates them to vote for the candidate. Moreover, a candidate with history of several defeats in the past has higher probability of being elected. These anecdotal data demonstrate that Koreans are very sensitive and sympathetic to *Shimjung* of others.

Westerners often define Asian culture as characteristic of non-verbal communication. One reason that non-verbal communication is important to Asians is that the best way to convey true mind and *shimjung* to others is believed to be "from one mind and *shimjung* to another." Sowol Kim, one of the most distinguished poet in Korea, relies almost exclusively on paradoxical ways to express his own *shimjung*. For instance, sad *shimjung* caused by being deserted by the lover is expressed like this: "I will never shed a tear drop when your love to me dies away and so you leave me." Korean literature, Korean music, and Korean drama are all full of *shimjung* expressions to illustrate pains and agonies of life (Choi, 2000; Park, 1990). In short, *shimjung* is a central concept in the Korean culture and so reading *shimjung* of others is a direct path to understanding the Korean culture.

KOREAN MODES OF *SHIMJUNG* DISCOURSE

Given that *shimjung* is critical in the Korean culture, as mentioned earlier, Koreans develop elaborate schema of *shimjung* and interchange frequent communications based on *shimjung* with each other. That is, for Koreans *shimjung* plays a central role in their interpersonal interactions and discourses in the *weness* and *jung*-based relationships. Thus it is easy to conjecture that they should develop a variety of modes of *shimjung* discourse. The primary form of *shimjung* exchange is non-verbal as noted earlier. However, *shimjung* can not always be exchanged in non-verbal ways and instead, verbal communication is sometimes inevitable to deliver one's *shimjung* to others (Choi, 1997, 1998; Choi & Kim, 1999b). Even in that case, however, considering illocutionary functions of the words outspoken is more important than lexical meanings of the words per se (Choi & Kim, 1999, 1999b). For instance, Koreans often ask, "Where are you going?" or "Did you take a meal?" when they come across with a friend. In this type of discourses, what Koreans try to convey to the friend is their consideration of and care for him.

When *shimjung* is delivered verbally, it often takes the form of narration and discourse. As noted earlier, (1) a mode of discourse based on the logics of *shimjung*, (2) a mode of story-telling of what happened in inner mind, (3) a narrative mode of describing and interpreting on the side of a third person what already happened in mind (see Bruner, 1990, 1996; Crossley, 2000; Fontana & Frey, 1994), and (4) a mode of speaking out true inner mind straightforward are all available (Choi & Kim, 1999, 1999a). The Shon and Choi' study (1999) obtained results similar to those three modes (2, 3, and 4). Korean undergraduates watched one session of a serial Korean TV drama. Then the participants listed *shimjung*-related discourses or situations in the drama, along with reasons described for each. Top three reasons in the rank order of frequencies are: (1) because the person concerned tells his or her inner mind; (2) because the person concerned describes sore spots or shameful points generally hard to expose, and (3) because the person concerned speaks out his or her mind frankly.

When exposed to a wide range of modes of *shimjung* discourse from partners, Koreans perceive their behavior as a delivery or a pour-out of *shimjung* and also base their own behavior on the logics of *shimjung* rather than those of reason. The conceptual constructions of mind and *shimjung* are quite unique in the Korean culture. Koreans believe that mind and *shimjung* spring up spontaneously and yet cannot be induced artificially. Koreans have a pure view of mind and *shimjung* in that they regard these two phenomena as beyond intentional control exercised by the person concerned. Likewise, the person is not responsible for his or her *shimjung* and mind even though they comprise contents unfavorable to others involved in the close relationships (Choi & Kim, 1999, 1999b; Choi, Kim & Kim, 1999, 2000).

Thus when at odds with partners, Koreans tend to express their own feelings felt in inner mind to the partners through pour-out of *shimjung* or diverse modes of *shimjung* discourse. When those subjective feelings are not valid, behavior of the partners in the stream of *shimjung*-based discourse can correct those feelings. Also, their relationships can be made better through *shimjung*-based interactions. For instance, Koreans often invite close others in conflict with to bars and then interchange discourse based on *shimjung* over a glass of alcoholic drink. Misunderstanding and hard feelings between them are quickly dissipated in the shower of *shimjung* discourses. Of course, ahead *shimjung* expression is behavior reconfirming their *weness*- and *jung*-based relationship such as "We are quite old friends" (Choi, Kim & Kim, 1999). This helps close others understand that expression of *shimjung* is directed to improve their relationship.

Effectiveness of *shimjung* discourses in improvement of *weness*-based relationships concerns emphasis Koreans place on Jung in the relationships. *Jung* is a raw material for build up of *weness*-based relationships. The core quality of *jung* is feeling rather than thinking. That is, *jung* is more close to heart than head, to emotion than reason, to synthesis than analysis, and to mind than act. *Shimjung*, as a feeling of the mind of both one's own and close others, is a concept and phenomenon embedded in feeling-based relationships. Discourses between close persons are those reactive to *shimjung*, with feeling and considering *shimjung* of others. In this aspect, *shimjung* discourses function as most important cues for confirming Weness and Jung in interpersonal interactions (Choi, 2000).

Sometimes, however, Koreans pour out or narrate their *shimjung* in order to earn sympathy on their own difficulties and points of view from others rather than to improve their close relationships. In these cases, Koreans express their *shimjung* to a third person rather than to the other involved in the *Shimjung*. This sort of pour-out of *shimjung* is referred to as *hasoyeon* meaning an appeal to a person for his or her sympathy. The effect of hasoyon is thought of as next to catharsis of psychoanalysis. However, the basic purpose of hasoyon is to earn social support and sympathy from others.

In sum, for Koreans *shimjung* discourses can verify their *weness-* and *jung*-based relationships, build up intersubjectivity between them, conform their relationships as based on true mind, and help them reconstruct themselves in the relationship contexts. Also, *shimjung* discourses are constituted by words from heart, *weness-* and *jung*-related words, and words indicative of non-distance, decayed boundary, and oneness.

CONCLUSION

Observations of interpersonal interactions between Koreans uncover with ease that *shimjung* is a phenomenological reality, which has been shaped through the culture-bound history of longstanding and plays a pivotal role in everyday social behavior of Koreans. The fact that *shimjung*-related behavior is ubiquitous across a variety of situations and diverse modes of its expressions are developed in conjunction to social context demonstrates that *shimjung* is a very meaningful social product yielded by Korean culture. Also, arousal of *shimjung* is closely tied to cognitive judgment and interpretation of both one's own feeling and emotion experienced in mind and behavior of others concerned. In this respect, *shimjung* is far from a primitive emotion which is under control of biological mechanisms of survival.

Koreans are sensitive to *shimjung* of their own and others concerned in common situations. They also consider the quality and content of aroused *shimjung* significant in defining their relationships. One fundamental reason for this concerns Koreans' belief that *shimjung* is indicative clearly of how they are close to each other. That is, they believe that communications through *shimjung* underlie *weness-* and *jung*-based relationships. Ideally, Koreans thus try to co-experience intersubjectively *shimjung* aroused in the mind of all the persons involved in the relationships. When *shimjung*-based communication is available in spontaneous manners, Koreans evaluate their relationships as most desirable where self and others are all one.

Shimjung, as a psychological experience, may also exist in Western cultures. Western concepts as empathy, sympathy and confession may include the same aspects of *shimjung* as understood in the Korean culture. However, when *shimjung* is mentioned as an indigenous concept in Korean culture, it means: First, Koreans are exclusively sensitive to *shimjung* phenomena and weigh them in their relationships. Second, Koreans define, understand and evaluate relationships in terms of *shimjung*. Third, they have developed particular sets of communicative grammars and frameworks on the basis of *shimjung*. Fourth, communicative modes of *shimjung* such as discourses and pour-out of *shimjung* are developed and elaborated.

As a social entity alive in the Korean culture, *shimjung* always occupies the central point at the arena of communications between boss and subordinate, between teacher and student, between parent and child, and even between judge and the defended. *Shimjung* is seen as pure, candid, authentic and so beyond controversy in the eye of Koreans, and as such, the existence of *shimjung* of diversity conveys particular meanings to those Koreans who are involved in the *shimjung*. Finally, development of *shimjung* discourses accompanies developments of thinking and feeling based on *shimjung*. In this respect, a most important keyword is *Shimjung* in the close relationships between Koreans.

REFERENCES

Bruner, J. (1990). *Acts of meaning*. Cambridge, MA: Harvard University Press.

Bruner, J. (1996). *The culture of education*. Cambridge, MA: Harvard University Press.

Cha, J. H. (1994). Aspects of individualism and collectivism in Korea. In U. Kim, H. C. Triandis, C. Kagitcibasi, S. C. Choi, & G. Yoon (Eds.), *Individualism and collectivism: Theory, method, and applications* (pp. 157–174). Thousand Oaks: Sage Publications.

Choi, S. C. (1992). The Koreans' cultural and psychological self. *Human Science, 35*, 203–224.

Choi, S. C. (1993). The nature of Korean selfhood: A cultural psychological perspective. *The Korean Journal of Social Psychology, 7*(2), 24–33.

Choi, S. C. (1994). *Shimcheong* psychology: The indigenous Korean perspective. *Paper presented at the Asian Workshop: Asian Psychologies: Indigenous, Social and Cultural Perspectives, Seoul, June 10–11, Korea.*

Choi, S. C. (1997). The psychological characteristics of the Koreans. In The Korean Psychological Association (Ed.), *Understanding the modern psychology* (pp. 695–766). Seoul: Hak-Moon-Sa.

Choi, S. C. (1998). The third-person-psychology and the first-person psychology: Two perspectives on human relations. *Korean Social Science Journal, 25*, 239–264.

Choi, S. C. (1999). The Koreans' mind. In S. C., Choi, D-W., Han, H-K, Yun, G-H., Choi, & Lee S.W., (Eds) *The Oriental psychology* (pp. 377–479). Seoul: Ji-Sik-San-Up-Sa.

Choi, S. C. (2000). *Korean psychology*. Seoul: Chung-Ang University Press.

Choi, S. C., & Choi, S. H. (1994). Weness: A Korean discourse of collectivism. In G. Yoon, & S. C. Choi (Eds.), *Psychology of the Korean people* (pp. 57–84). Seoul: Dong-A Publishing & Printing Co., Ltd.

Choi, S. C., & Choi, S. H. (2001). *Cheong*: The socio-emotional grammar of Koreans. *International Journal of Group Tensions, 30*(1), 69–80.

Choi, S. C., & Kim, C. W. (1998). *Shimcheong* psychology as a cultural psychological approach to collective meaning construction. *The Korean Journal of Social and Personality Psychology, 12*(2), 79–96.

Choi, S. C., & Kim, J. Y., & Kim, K. (1999). Sweet *cheong* and hateful *cheong. Paper presented at the 3rd Conference of the Asian Association of Social Psychology, August 4–7, Taipei, Taiwan.*

Choi, S. C., & Kim, J. Y., & Kim, K. (2000). The structural relationship analysis among the psychological structure of Jung (sweet *cheong*, hateful *cheong*), its behaviors, and functions. *The Korean Journal of Social and Personality Psychology, 14*(1), 203–222.

Choi, S. C., & Kim, K. (1999). *Shimcheong*: The key concept for understanding Koreans' mind. *Paper presented at the Third Conference of the Asian Association of Social Psychology, August 4–7, Taipei, Taiwan.*

Choi, S. C., & Kim, K. (1999a). A conceptual exploration of the Korean self. *The Korean Journal of Social and Personality Psychology, 13*(2), 275–292.

Choi, S. C., & Kim, K. (1999b). The *Shimcheong* psychology: Psychological characteristics, interactions, and development of *shimjung*. *The Korean Journal of Psychology, 18(1)*, 1–16.

Choi, S. C., & Kim, K. (2000). A conceptual exploration of the Korean self. *Paper presented at the XVth Congress of International Association for Cross-Cultural Psychology, July 16–21, Pultusk, Poland.*

Choi, S. C., Kim, U., & Choi, S. H. (1993). Indigenous analysis of collective representations: A Korean perspective. In U. Kim, & J. W. Berry (Eds.), *Indigenous psychologies* (pp. 193–210). Newbury Park: Sage Publications.

Crossley, M. L. (2000). *Introducing narrative psychology: Self, trauma and the construction of meaning*. Buckingham: Open University Press.

Fontana, A., & Frey, J. H. (1994). Interviewing: The art of science. In N. K. Denzin, & Y. S. Lincoln (Eds.), *Handbook of qualitative research* (pp. 362–376). Thousand Oaks: Sage Publications.

Gardner, W. L., Gabriel, S., Lee, A. Y. (1999). I value freedom, but we value relationships: Self-construal priming mirrors cultural differences in judgment. *Psychological Science, 10(4)*, 321–326.

Gergen, K. J. (1994). *Realities and relationships: Soundings in social construction*. Cambridge, MA: Harvard University Press.

Harré, R., & Gillett, G. (1994). *The discursive mind*. Thousand Oaks: Sage Publications.

Harré, R., & Stearns, P. (1995). *Discursive psychology in practice*. London: Sage Publications.

Harré, R., & Stearns, P. (1995). Introduction: Psychology as discourse analysis. In R. Harré, & P. Stearns (Eds.), *Discursive psychology in practice* (pp. 1–8). London: Sage Publications.

Lillard, A. (1998). Ethnopsychologies: Cultural variations in theories of mind. *Psychological Bulletin, 123(1)*, 3–32.

Kim, M. S., & Hong, W. S. (1974). New Korean dictionary. Seoul: U-Mun-Gak.

Park, M. S. (1979). *Communication styles in two difference cultures: Korean and American*. Seoul: Han Shin Publishing Co.

Park, J. J. (1990). *Korean culture is Shimcheong culture*. Seoul: Mirae.

Shon, Y. M., & Choi, S. C. (1999). Shimcheong discourse mode in Korean soap opera. *Paper presented at the Korean Annual Conference, Seoul, August 18–19, Korea.*

Stearns, P. (1995). Emotion. In R. Harré, & P. Stearns (Eds.), *Discursive psychology in practice* (pp. 37–54). London: Sage Publications.

Vygotsky, L. S. (1978). *Mind in society: The development of higher psychological processes*. Cambridge: Harvard University Press.

Wertsch, J. V. (1998). *Mind as action*. New York: Oxford University Press.

Part V

Application

Chapter 17

Humanism-Materialism
Centuries-Long Polish Cultural Origins and 20 Years of Research in Cultural Psychology

Pawel Boski

In the paper that appeared in *Indigenous Psychologies* (Kim & Berry, 1993), I proposed the following formula for examining the emerging field of indigenous psychology:

$$I\Psi = IP * (CV + IS)$$

This formula reads: *indigenous psychology* (IΨ) is a function of *indigenous problems* (IP) typical for a given national/cultural/regional entity, and of *cultural values* (CV) plus *intellectual styles* (IS), which characterize the ways in which those problems are approached and solutions are sought. (The format of this statement does not suggest a literal mathematical function.)

The goal of this chapter is to outline some indigenous problems of Poland and values which remain in a reciprocal relationship to these problems. Humanism, which was the centerpiece of my conceptual analysis ten years ago, is now given a theoretical analysis and is supported with empirical evidence.

POLISH CULTURE AS SHAPED BY ITS HISTORY: A PSYCHOLOGICAL INTERPRETATION

Three elements of Polish culture are discussed from historical perspective as antecedents of people's mentality. They are: 1) Catholicism as a system of religious beliefs and practices, 2) village and farming life as opposed to city and business life, and 3) national sovereignty under threat and oppression.[1]

Catholicism: A System of Religious Beliefs and Practices

There is little doubt among social scientists that the type of dominant religion and religiosity over centuries exert profound impact on various domains of secular life. In Poland, Catholic Christianity has been such a religion for the last thousand years. I elaborate two of its effects: one is identity, and the other is socio-economic values (mentality).

Catholicism and Polish Identity

Poland has been labeled a *bulwark of Christianity*, which refers to Poland's position as a Western frontier state against the Eastern Islamic world of Turkey and the Tartars and also against Orthodox Russia. More specifically, the equation Polish = Catholic has been a strong identity symbol since the 17th century counter-reformation. In that context, Catholicism has also gradually became a contrasting feature against predominantly Lutheran neighbors at the northern and western borders: Prussia and Sweden.

A bulwark is, however, more of a defensive barricade than a crusader's fort; it serves more as a shelter of resistance against various invaders and occupants than as a fortress from which to launch religious wars (and from which the country was essentially spared). During the 200 years of foreign powers' domination (from the end of the 18th to the end of the 20th century), the Catholic church has played the crucial role in national identity and culture maintenance.

An important feature of Polish Catholicism over the centuries has been the cult of *Virgin Mary the Queen of Poland*. She has been a Goddess, a figure of a sensitive, compassionate, protective mother holding the country as a whole and each person separately as her child. Hence, femininity is an important psychological dimension of Polish Catholicism[2].

Social-emotional displays and rituals characterize this brand of religion. These displays serve as markers of social identity rather than symbolizing private spirituality. Since 1978 when John Paul II was elected, this kind of religiosity has often been manifested in spectacular gatherings with the Pope, drawing millions of people.

---

[1] For an account of the history of Poland, see Davies (1981, 1982).
[2] In line with Carl G. Jung, I consider Catholicism as feminine in its religious doctrine, when compared to the Protestant or Orthodox churches. This view is largely different from G. Hofstede's (1980/2001) interpretations, with his emphasis on the male-dominated hierarchy of the Catholic Church.

Catholicism and the Noneconomic Mind

The best example of religion causing economic activity is Weber's theory linking the rise and growth of capitalism to protestant ethics, especially with its strict Calvinist version (*Die Protestantische Ethik und das Geist des Kapitalismus*, 1904/1958). The theory was later elaborated by McClelland (1961) who found that in Europe and North America, need achievement was the psychological link between protestant culture and economic growth. According to the author of *Achieving society*, socialization in Protestant culture/religion (as compared to Catholic) facilitates higher levels of achievement striving in boys and prepares them psychologically for undertaking entrepreneurial challenges. Need achievement, or mastery (in terms of Schwartz's 1994 work on values), is also related to cultural masculinity.

The Catholic doctrine has always been strongly opposed to the essence of business on ethical grounds. In the writings of Medieval theologians (e.g. St. Thomas Aquinas), interest on loans and profit-making in general was incompatible with Christianity, or simply sinful. Human greed and lust for money (psychological ingredients of early capitalism and the modern market economy) are alien to the teachings of Roman Catholicism.

Cast against this background, the principles of the early capitalist economy did not influence Polish mentality of that time. The concepts of *profit, loans, interest,* and *banking* were foreign to Poles and regarded with disrespect on moral-religious grounds; if practiced, they could even lead to banishment. An honorable citizen could not give a loan with interest to another nobleman, nor could he get directly involved in any business venture.

Though I am referring here to the historic past, Pope John-Paul II's encyclicals provide ample testimony to the church's reservation towards a market economy, which continues up to the present day. His teachings emphasize human rights for living and working in dignity and appeal for compassionate solidarity around the world. Since the Pope has been considered the most important moral authority in his native land, the impact of his words is hard to deny.

If Protestant culture can be psychologically translated into need achievement and individualism, what then could be the psychological consequences of Catholicism? The official doctrine of the church and the number of terms referring to humanism and its derivatives: human face, human dignity, human rights, and being human (and the opposite, *inhuman*) justifies humanism as the most appropriate concept in response to this question. Interestingly, socialist humanism became the central philosophical concept in official Marxist doctrine during the decades of communist regime.

Farming and Village Life vs. Business Economy and City Life

Until well into the second half of 19th century, Polish society was comprised mainly of two social classes: 1) nobility or free citizens and 2) serf-peasants. Although the former enjoyed freedoms and privileges while the latter belonged to their landlords, both classes were paradoxically similar in some important characteristics of their socio-economic existence; they were settlers in the rural world of agriculture. One could say that landlords and peasants belonged to their land, rather than that they owned or cultivated it. Land has not been treated as a market commodity, nor as a means for profit-oriented farm production. Land meant an identity and life-style for which people stood and fought. Excellent documentation of this orientation is offered in Thomas and Znaniecki's *The Polish Peasant in Europe and in America* (1918/1927, vol.1). In Znaniecki's account, land cultivation was for Polish peasants far more than an economic activity; it was a way of being, where *naturalist, spiritual*, and *communal* sentiments prevailed.

Townships were underdeveloped and economic activities typical of town dwellers, such as trading or manufacturing, were foreign to ethnic Poles for the reasons already discussed. The trading of grain and other agricultural products was predominantly in Jewish hands while crafts and manufacturing were organized by people of German origin. Town-dwellers and Jews were long-deprived of citizens' rights (until the end of the 18th century). Later, if successful, they were regarded as exploiters in terms of class conflict or nationalist ideology.

The core elements of this traditional social structure lasted until WW II. Poland remained a predominantly agricultural country of small peasant farms and large nobility estates. Jewish and German minorities held to their enclaves of private industrial and commercial enterprises. Since the end of the 19th century, an important newcomer to the social structure has been the intelligentsia whose roots lay in nobility and whose mentality reflected the same distance to practicality of earthly undertakings. Noble landlords became noble intelligentsia as documented in the classics of the 19th and 20th centuries. Novels of that time testify to the power of the noble's mentality of resistance to the challenges of the changing world and to the plight of those who were trying to substitute pragmatic (positivist) calculations for romantic lofty ideals.

Polish society of the 20th century lacked sizeable cities with an indigenous middle class population to carry on economic growth. World War II eliminated the most economically active groups: Jews perished as victims of the Holocaust, while Germans –the perpetrators–were forced to leave the country as members of the defeated nation or as guilty of Nazi crimes. After social classes associated with the capitalist mode of production had disappeared, Poland was ideally suited to enter the era of the communist command economy, which froze the spirit of entrepreneurship for another half century.

Today when the main national task is catching up and a successful integration with the European Union, the devastation brought by communism can be seen better than ever. Poland's inefficient industrial sector has been gradually collapsing since the transformation began in the early 1990s. Agriculture, which stayed underdeveloped during the communist freeze, is facing inevitable restructuring as 30% of the population is still involved in family farming.

In conclusion, favorable conditions to instill the standards of work ethics, systematic effort, and accountability, did never occur in the history of Poland.

National-Political Issues: Between Internal Anarchy and External Aggression

For the last 300 years Poland has been the stage of numerous foreign aggressions, internal uprisings, heroic defeats, and short days of triumph. Historians debate what portion of blame should be attributed to internal vs. external causes.

It may seem to be a semantic contradiction, but the name for the Kingdom of Poland, which lasted until the end of 18th century, was the First Republic. The reason for this name is that kings were elected as presidents for life and efficiently controlled by the nobility against any attempt to seize absolute power or to establish a dynasty. The privileged ten percent, the nobility, basked in their *golden freedoms* or *Nobles' Democracy*. Democracy operated according to a procedural rule called *liberum veto*, which meant that all bills had to be passed unanimously–an impossible task. Increasingly, *liberum veto* was abused by corrupt politicians and gradually the country had neither effective executive nor legislative power.

Individual golden freedoms contributed to internal anarchy so that the country fell prey to stronger neighbors (Russia, Prussia, Austria), who had been ruled by absolutist monarchs. Gradual partitioning took place in late 18th century. After a brief period of 20 years of independence regained after World War I, independence was lost again in 1939.

Each time loss of independence came as a blow, reawakening patriotic feelings and solidarity in resistance. Poles staged a large number of national uprisings in the 19th and 20th centuries, most of them were defeated and the toll of ultimate sacrifices was high. Heroes were eulogized in national literature, poetry, fine arts, and in music. Romanticism has been the prototypical artistic expression in Poland, largely instrumental to the national cause. Fed by heroic struggle against the forces of oppression, romanticism created a national mythology, which instigated the next generation to fight for just causes against the odds.

Well rooted in the 19th century, the tradition of insurrections continued until recent times. Of all countries belonging to the Soviet block,

Poland had by far the strongest anti-communism movement. *Solidarity* during the 1980s was the last of the national efforts directed against that system. It was characterized by the same romantic idealism as earlier uprisings.

Anarchy during the periods of independence and heroism during foreign dominance had similar psychological underpinnings: the bottom line was a low level of reality-testing and of pragmatic cost-benefit assessment. While anarchy could be interpreted as extreme egocentrism (my rights above anybody else's), heroism meant a selfless sacrifice. If the former reflected a hedonistic principle, the latter was an expression of a moral principle. *Liberum veto* used to be justified by the supreme value of freedom; *gloria victis* was the moral tribute paid to those who fell fighting for a just cause. In both cases the proper act rather than its outcome and consequences was what really mattered.

POLISH CULTURE: INDIVIDUALISM/COLLECTIVISM OR HUMANISM-MATERIALISM?

Based on this historical analysis, a number of psychological themes stand out to characterize Polish culture. The list below has a hypothetical status and the research reported later serves to verify some of these assumptions.

1. *Close personalized human relations.* This should be the consequence of strong family ties on one hand and of a poorly-developed inefficient administration system and civil society on the other. Individual survival depends on solid networks of loyal friends.
2. *Non-utilitarian, non-pragmatic approach to daily activities; low priority of business mentality.* A consequence of the inhibitory impact that Catholicism and subsistence farming had on the development of a market mentality and competences.
3. *Romantic orientation in national-political matters.* Legacy of centuries long history and modeling principles: "fight for the right cause whatever the outcome," "measure your strengths against your strivings" (rather than the reverse order).
4. *Low priority of legal matters and procedures, low trust in state authorities.* Legacy of anarchistic tendencies and laws treated as repressive instruments, serving alien outgroup interests.
5. *Low priority given to work conceived of as a hard, systematic, and efficient effort.* This view is a consequence of work being treated as either a mixture of extrinsically enforced duty and ritual (peasants' farming) or as a spontaneous, intrinsically rewarding pastime (among intelligentsia).

6. *High status of women and femininity.* This value is a consequence of the unique cult and worship practices accorded to the Virgin Mary, the Queen of Poland. Also, there have been equal inheritance laws for descendants of both sexes, and widespread norms of chivalry and courtesy displayed by men toward women. At the same time, cultural models for men emphasize heroism but, more often than not, for a lost cause. Machismo was unknown.

A question arises as to whether these psycho-cultural characteristics could be subsumed under any of broad pan-cultural *etic* dimensions, or whether social scientists face a more complex, indigenous *emic* constellation. The first part of this question draws researchers' attention to collectivism/individualism. Does the picture provided above suggest a definite tilt of Polish culture toward collectivism or towards individualism?

Pro-collectivist arguments might be: Catholicism (as compared with reformed Christianity), a rural-agricultural (rather than urban-entrepreneurial) way of living, familism, and a preoccupation with national sovereignty. Pro-individualist tendencies are also clearly seen in the following: the nobility's *golden freedoms* bordering on anarchy and their subsequent evolution in the intelligentsia's ethos where intellectual freedom and spontaneity of the mind were considered key values. Deficits in group-organized and coordinated productive efforts point in the same direction. Finally, romantic patriotism (as immortalized in national literature and arts) is more about individual experience and action (lonely soul suffering for the nation) than organized group behavior. With this type of mixed and contradictory evidence, I do not see the collectivism/individualism construct as offering a sufficient explanatory model fit to account for the psychological phenomena of Polish culture.

Humanism and Collectivism/Individualism

When one reads the literature on collectivism/individualism that does not abstain from axiological comments (Triandis, 1990; Kagitcibasi, 1997), it is easy to find both those who criticize and others who eulogize one end point of the construct or the other. But authors who give individualism contrastingly different evaluations do not speak about the same issues. For those who define individualism in positive way, this mode of culture is associated with freedom, self-direction, active agency, and progress in all domains. Critics do not question these values but point to selfishness (egoism) and damage to the web of social connections, and depletion of social responsibility, all of which characterize advances of individualism.

It is possible then, to differentiate between two axes which remain theoretically confounded in the concept of individualism and which feed the

Table 1. A Taxonomy of Value Orientations: Humanism and Its Alternatives

	Agency, Direction	
Interest, Orientations	I-as-Subject	I-as-Object
Social	Humanism	Collectivism
Self	Individualsim	Alienation

endless debates: 1) agency and self-direction vs. subjugation, and 2) self interest vs. social interest. By deconfounding the sense of agency, *I* or *not-l*, from the type of interest (value orientation), *me* or *others*, we have conceptual space for four separate mentality types. This new theoretical framework results in the taxonomy displayed in Table 1.

The framework presented here is partly derived from Greenwald (1982), particularly from his observations that *deindividuation* phenomenon can assume a pattern of alienation in an anonymous crowd or a format of "melting" within group uniformity. A similar argument can be extended to *individuation*, where a self-directed person may strive either for predominantly individual interests or be motivated by concerns for other people's (community) well-being. Thus, for instance, humanism shares some elements common with collectivism and some with individualism. With the former it is the social embeddedness of value-orientation, with the latter it is self-directedness in pursuing these goals.

An even closer reference to our theorizing can be found in Kagitcibasi's twofold taxonomy of self in family context: 1) agency as autonomy vs. heteronomy, and 2) interpersonal distance as relatedness vs. separation (Kagitcibasi, 1996a, 1996b, pp. 52-71). Her argument has been that these two conceptual axes should be viewed as independent, rather than equating autonomy with separation and relatedness with heteronomy. Thus, humanism is very close to autonomous relatedness.

Schwartz (1990) raised similar arguments in his critique of collectivism/individualism. In Schwartz's own theory of value structure, elements of collectivism and individualism are split into a number of separate value types. Collectivistic values, for instance, are found: 1) in *self-transcendence* and in *conservatism* at the individual level of analysis (Schwartz, 1992), and 2) in *embeddedness* and in *hierarchy* at the cultural level of analysis (Schwartz, 2004).

Finally, a concept and a measurement scale of *Humane Orientation* appear in the GLOBE project (House, Hanges, Javidan, Dorfman, and Gupta, eds., 2004). "Five questionnaire items in the GLOBE study were used to operationalize the societal Humane Orientation: Being concerned, sensitive toward others, friendly, tolerant of mistakes, and generous". (Kabasakal, Bodur, 2004, p. 571). They are similar to my operationalization of humanism.

PSYCHOLOGICAL STUDIES ON HUMANISM-MATERIALISM VALUES

Although they have provided a major breakthrough in cross-cultural psychology, studies of universal value dimensions are not the only and last word in the progress of this discipline. Even if researchers endeavor to measure individualism/collectivism, masculinity/femininity, power and a host of other value dimensions worldwide, and the result is useful for some broad comparisons (similar to macro-economic indices, like GNP), the sense and understanding of cultural specificity will still be missed.

Paradoxically, the universalist approach does not assume any prior cultural knowledge of the phenomena studied. This is clearly seen in the study of values. Terms denoting values in the Rokeach-Schwartz survey, such as *pleasure, wealth, health, wisdom,* etc., are as free from any cultural context as a person from the Euro-American tradition can think of. In contrast, the essence of cultural psychology consists of *emic* or indigenous values (syndromes) extraction, which can only be done with intimate knowledge of the culture of origin. Syndromes like *Greek philotimo (Triandis,* & Vassiliou, 1972; Georgas, 1993); Mexican-Hispanic *simpatia* (Triandis, Marin, Lisansky & Betancourt, 1984; Marin, 1994) or Chinese *Confucian dynamism,* and *filial piety* (Chinese Culture Connection, 1987; Hofstede, 2001) would not be discovered without this kind of expertise.

Cultural Identity and Immigrants' Acculturation

The first set of studies, where humanism-materialism emerged as a value dimension was conducted in the late 1980s and early 1990s as part of a research project on the cultural identity of Polish immigrants in North America. A research instrument called the Emic Culture Value and Script Questionnaire (ECVSQ) was designed for these studies. The ECVSQ consists of 66 items, which were formulated in terms of specific and context-loaded cultural values, Polish and American, and in two languages simultaneously. Since cultural identity was theoretically conceived of as the distance (similarity) between self and perception of culture (or cultural prototype) on important values, two levels of measurement were implied: individual and cultural[3]. Accordingly, participants attempted self-reports and constructed their representations of American and Polish cultures (culture prototypes). The answering format of the questionnaire assumed a Q-sort distribution.

I present here the results from four studies, comparing HUMAT at both levels, among various categories of Poles, Americans, and Polish

---

[3] The reader should be reminded that the term "culture level of analysis" is understood differently than in works on value dimensions by Hofstede or Schwartz. Here it is not a mean of individual scores constituting a country sample, but a prototype or another cultural target of description and evaluation.

immigrants from three generations. These studies stretch over the period of ten years (1986–1995), the details of locations and charactersitics of participants follow:

1. Warsaw, Poland [1989–90, n = 100];
2. Kingston (Ontario), Canada [1986, n = 66]. Participants were: new [Immig.CAN(a)] and old [Immig.CAN(b)]. Polish immigrants; and Polish-Canadians of first generation [POL-CAN 1stgen.];
3. Passaic-Bergen, New Jersey, USA [1989, n = 59]. Participants were direct immigrants from Poland; Passaic-Bergen, New Jersey (1990, n = 77). Participants were again immigrants, 1st and 2nd generation Polish-Americans;
4. Jacksonville, Florida (1995, n = 155). Participants were Euro-Americans (not of Polish descent); foreign students from a large numbers of countries were also included. Most of subjects were UNF students.

The total number of participants was N = 456; they were at least high school graduates (according to Polish, Canadian, or American criteria). Females and males were equally represented, while age distribution was from mid 20s (in all samples) to mid 60s (in Canadian, New Jersey, and Warsaw samples).

As the studies progressed, Q-sort data of self and prototype constructions were gradually factor-analyzed. Table 2 presents the factor dimension of HUM-MAT, based on all measures from four studies (due to

Table 2. Humanism–Materialism Scale

Humanism-materialism [HUMAT]	Loading
01. Selfless sympathy and helpful hand	.669
02. Care for long lasting friendships	.565
03. Principles of Christianity-guidance in life	.558
04. Happiness and harmony in family	.524
05. The well-being of own children	.514
06. Having and valuing a sense of humor	.418
07. Gentleman towards women	.406
08. Kindness and politeness	.405
09. People of all races equal	.510
10. Public affairs of interest only if affect personal well-being	−.462
11. Watching TV programs hours and hours	−.490
12. Happy to see bank account grow	−.530
13. With others -business-like	−.553
14. Cunning and law evasion	−.560
15. To become a successful business person	−.563
16. Buy a house, sell it, buy a better one	−.573
17. Always tease out profit or advantage	−.609

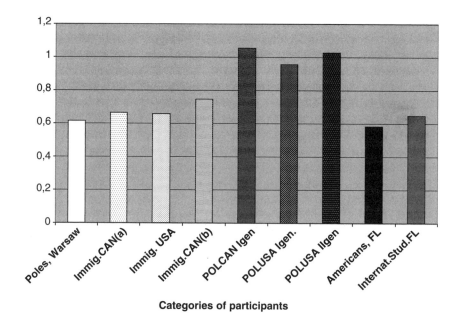

Categories of participants

Figure 1. Humanism as self-value in a range of Polish-American categories

repeated measures of self and cultural prototypes, the number of observations was 1,274, exceeding the sample size by three).

The scale is based on the 17 items (9 humanistic and 8 materialistic, with negative loadings) that emerged as the first component with oblim rotation, explaining 12.95% of the total variance with high reliability, Cronbach α = .855.

It can be clearly seen that the bipolar scale constrasts two domains of concerns: people and relations vs. things and pecuniary matters. At the humanist pole, other people are imbued with autotelic value by a subject who shows genuine prosocial concern for them. In contrast, the importance of money and profit define the materialist end of the scale, while fellow human beings are reduced to instrumental means.

The self-related measures of HUM-MAT were compared in 9 cohorts.

Though the omnibus ANOVA yielded a significant result $F_{(8,446)}$ = 5.13, p <.001, eta^2 = .084, the differences appear slim. Indeed, *post hoc* comparisons (Tukey's HSD) confirmed that the only significant differences were those between Americans from Florida (lower results) and 1st generation Polish-Canadians or 2nd generation Polish-Americans; the same two immigrant categories differ from the Warsaw sample, taken as control (Dunnet's test).

It appears clear, though puzzling, that humanism reached its highest levels among those participants whose ancestors came from Poland. I am

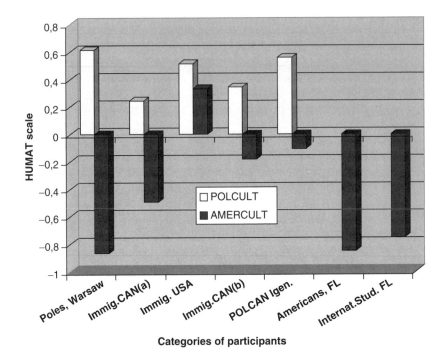

Figure 2. Humanism-Materialism in Polish and American cultures

inclined to interpret this result in terms of a freezing effect that immigration exerts on transmission of ancestral culture, which lags behind the flux of change that continuously takes place in the home country. Other supporting evidence for the reported findings comes from the observation that Polish immigration in North America has been noted for lack of entrepreneurial spirit or spectacular business success.

A very different picture is obtained when we compare humanism at the level of culture representations. Among the five cohorts in which the two types of measures were taken (excluded are Americans and foreign residents in Florida who did not construe their image of Polish culture), Polish culture is perceived as humanist, while American (or Canadian) as materialist, $F_{(1, 219)} = 177.59$, $p < .001$, eta^2 = .360. Of no less interest is the fact that American culture appears equally materialist for Poles who never lived there as for Americans who never migrated from their country. As the interaction effect of participant category and culture shows, it is again among the immigrants that a more benevolent image of American culture is kept; $F_{(4,219)} = 24.28$, $p < .001$.

It also follows, that levels of humanism in self and own culture are much closer among Poles and Polish immigrants than among Americans. When Warsaw and Florida residents were compared, the magnitude of this difference was striking: $F_{(1,217)} = 156.68$, $p < .001$, eta^2 = .42. Poles seem to come very close to their cultural ideal in humanism, while Americans who are not lower in personal humanist values appear alienated from their materialist culture in this respect.

Humanism-Materialism and Other Value Dimensions

The four value-type taxonomy (Table 1), which differentiates humanism from collectivism/individualism on theoretical grounds, needed a validity test of its own. This was done within the framework of a broader research project on the understanding and evaluation of political democracy in Poland.[4] The project was a longitudinal study conducted in five waves between 1992 and 1995 on a convenience sample of 160 teachers, bank employees, city councilors, and skilled laborers from public and private industrial sectors of Warsaw and Lodz, the two largest cities in Poland.

Humanism was measured at culture and individual levels with the items reported earlier. Sample *collectivism* items include: "I am at distance with others until we have decided to call each other by our first names." "I feel comfortable with others only if I have come to know them as the palm of my hand."

Individualism was measured with items like: "I think of myself as being an individualist." "During a travel to another city, I would stay at a hotel rather than with my relatives."

Political alienation was measured after Korzeniowski (1995) with items such as the following: "One can never be sure whether the decisions made by political authorities are correct and appropriate or not." "Ordinary people have no influence on decisions made by politicians."

The measures of humanism were found to be negatively correlated with all three remaining normative dimensions, while alienation correlated positively both with measures of collectivism and individualism.

Since alienation is symptomatic for being a misfit and feeling estranged in one's socio-cultural environment, the pattern of results suggests that neither collectivism nor individualism could be considered the normative core of Polish culture; this role is better represented by humanism.

Table 3. Project on Democracy: Correlations between Humanism and Other Mentality Scales

	Alienation	Collectivism	Individualism
Humanism	−.235**	−.047	−.410***
Alienation		.404***	.234**

Note: *** p<.001; ** p<.01, * p<.05

[4] The project was directed by Janusz Reykowski at the Polish Academy of Sciences (Reykowski, 1995) and funded by the Committee for Scientific Research (KBN) of the Polish Government.

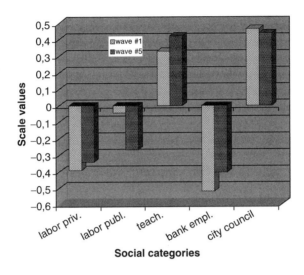

Figure 3. Humanism in five social categories at initial (1) and final (5) waves of measurement

Another test of discriminant validity for humanism is provided by comparing the levels of its measures derived from five social categories of our research Ss, $F(4,127) = 7.97$, $p < .001$, $eta^2 = .201$. As Figure 3 shows, humanism was consistently high (from wave 1 to 5) among the social categories *working with people*, i.e., city councilors and teachers, while those employed in the private sector of economy, i.e., physical laborers or educated bank employees, had significantly lower scores on measures of humanism.

A different picture emerges with measures of collectivism and individualism (see Figure 4). Here, more educated city councilors and bank

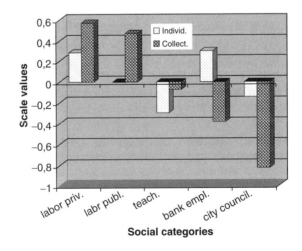

Figure 4. Individualism and collectivism in five social categories

employees had the lowest scores on collectivism, in contrast to less educated laborers, whatever their job sector, $F(4,118) = 12.64$, $p < .001$, $eta^2 = .300$. Finally, and predictably, bank employees had the highest scores on individualism, $F(4,118) = 3.27$, $p < .05$, $eta^2 = .100$; and they differed from teachers and city councilors again.

All of these empirical results convincingly demonstrate the discriminant validity of humanism as a theoretical construct separate from collectivism as well as from individualism. Most revealing in this respect is the contrast between city counsilors who have lowest scores on collectivism, while remaining highest on humanism, and bank employees who score low on both these measures but are high on individualism.

Humanism-Materialism in Political and Economic Domains

The results reported in the above paragraph come from the study whose main goal was to establish the psychological predictors of political democracy emerging in Poland in the last decade of the 20th century. The measure of political democracy was designed by Reykowski (1995). It consists of a set of normative markers constitutive for the concept (e.g. free elections, freedom of expression, equality in law, protection of minority rights) and of unrelated though politically sensitive buffer items (e.g., market full of goods affordable to everyone, safety on our streets and in communities, full employment). Participants are instructed to sort the pool of 54 items into descriptive categories that are essential, more or less important, or irrelevant to democracy. Another task is to elicit evaluative characteristics of all these items.

The four mentality dimensions discussed in the taxonomic model (Table 1) were employed as predictors of understanding and preferences for political democracy. As argued by Reykowski (1994), individualism should be positively related to the principles of political democracy, while collectivism (considered as a communist legacy) should be an impediment to democracy in the post-communist transformation. Humanism, which characterized Polish positive cultural prototypes, personalized by "Solidarity" activists opposing the communist totalitarian regime in the 1980s, should also be a predictor of preferences for democratic political system.

We used a hierarchical regression model to predict understanding and preferences for democracy from mentality variables among the five categories of participants. In the final wave #5 we obtained five predictors that contributed to $R^2 = .468$, $F(5,117) = 22.49$, $p < .0001$. Table 4 summarizes results of the regression analysis.

As the results demostrate, indices of humanism at both personal (self-endorsed values) and cultural (societal representation) levels are positive antecedents of democratic thinking, while alienation and collectivism are negative predictors of democracy. Of all social categories, being a bank employee brings also an independent positive contribution.

Table 4. Understanding democracy: Summary of regression analysis

	Beta	R² change	F change
Alienation	−.435***	.373	71.98***
Humanism (Individual)	.212**	.028	5.69*
Collectivism	−.133*	.025	5.20*
Humanism (Cultural)	.154*	.024	5.20*
Bank employees (*dummy*)	.216**	.039	9.05**

Note: *** p<.001; ** p<.01, * p<.05

It might be argued that humanism should be under pressure and declining during the period or rapid economic transformation from communism command to market economy, which characterized the past decade of Polish history. Having the 1989 baseline measures (reported in the first set of studies), we were in a fortunate position to check this possibility. Comparative results came from two convenience samples run in 1996 and 1997. Participants were students from a business school in Warsaw and their acquaintences from the entrepreunerial sector. This sampling decision served to select people who might represent the least humanist approach to life and to give our cultural hypothesis the toughest test. Participants filled out the ECVSQ three times: 1) their self-reported

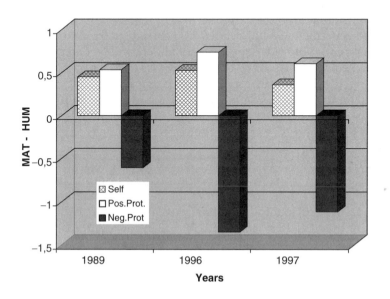

Figure 5. Humanism-materialism during the first decade of Polish transformation

value priorities, 2) in reference to a person considered as a positive Polish prototype, and 3) in reference to a person considered as a negative Polish prototype. Results from these three studies are presented in Figure 5.

The findings reveal with consistency that humanism characterizes the self and positive (idealized) image of Polish culture, while materialism is attributed to its negative prototype, $F_{(2,384)} = 478.63$, $p < .0001$. Yet, this pattern also shows changes over the period of 7–8 years, $F_{int.(2,770)} = 11.79$, $p < .001$. Admittedly, it is the change in materialism, accentuated in the negative prototype, that has been the main consequence of market economy reforms in Poland, and even at the heart of business elites of the country!

By its intensity and dynamism, the equation: materialism = negative social evaluation, prevails in the Polish cultural landscape. Only the targets labeled with this stigma have changed: from communist leaders in 1980s to business people ten years later. Another conclusion, heavy in political consequences, should to be drawn from these results: As much as it promotes democracy in government and social life, humanism inhibits and devalues the private business mentality in the economy.

Humanism and the European Union

On May 1, 2004, Poland became a member state of the European Union. Integration with the EU has been an extended process since the country reached the status of associate member in 1997, and will continue in the years to come. EU membership has been the main challenge for external negotiations, internal adaptation, and an important topic of public discourse. Much of the debate for vs. against integration has concentrated on cultural identity–its maintenance, threat, or need for modification. In this context, a large survey study has been conducted to determine the psychological factors responsible for favorable and unfavorable orientations to the process of unification.

Research was conducted on a country representative sample of 1,092 participants (from 1999 to 2001). Values were the prime object of investigation. The study implemented a conceptual distinction between *descriptive* and *evaluative* aspects of cultural values. *Descriptive* refers to representation of cultural reality of a given country, organization, or group. Here the question is whether a value is or is not entrenched in a (perceived) lifestyle of that social entity. The *evaluative* aspect has to do with the desirability of that value, ranging from *rejection, ambivalence*, through *maintenance*, to *acquisition* (importation) or outside *expansion* (exportation).[5] Common to *acquisition* and *expansion* is the high desirability of the values, but while the first reflects the

---

[5] Expansion was not considered as one of the alternatives in this study.

Table 5. Polish and European Union Values: Crossing Descriptive and Evaluative Classifications (in percentages)

			Evaluation		
Description	Acquire	Preserve	Ambivalent	Reject	Total rows
PL ˙ EU	5.84	9.49	2.86	3.13	21.32
PL ˙ ~ EU	2.02	11.83	3.90	9.90	27.64
~ PL ˙ EU	17.10	2.52	4.26	4.68	28.5
~ PL ˙ ~ EU	8.20	2.57	7.99	3.72	22.48
Total	33.15	26.41	19.01	21.43	100%

Note: Figures in cells, rows, and columns represent mean percent points. The total (100%) is based on 66 items of ECVSQ or on lower number of valid answers, when missing values appeared. PL = Poland; EU = Europeon Union;* = and; ~ = non.

state of deficit and inferiority, the other indicates a mission of those who feel themselves to be culturally superior.

Accordingly, respondents were asked to complete two separate tasks on the questionnaire items (ECVSQ): 1) to sort the items in a descriptive manner, whether they represented (i) Polish, (ii) European Union, (iii) combined, or (iv) neither way of life; 2) to perform an evaluative sorting, i.e. to decide whether each item should be: (i) acquired (assimilated), (ii) preserved, (iii) rejected, or (iv) considered as ambivalent. Presented below are the findings that jointly characterize Polish and European values in their descriptive and evaluative (preferential) modes.

Both distributions are highly uneven (see Figure 5). The mean scores in rows demonstrate that disjoint values attributed to the EU (28.56%) and to Poland (27.64%) prevail over common cultural elements (21.32%) and those considered to be alien (22.48%), $F_{(3,3105)} = 101.05$, $p < 0.001$, eta^2 = 0.09. This suggests a sense of relative separatedness between the two cultural entities. Results aggregated in columns, $F_{(3,3105)} = 258.63$, $p < 0.001$, eta^2 = 0.20, show that well over 50% of the total pool of cultural items are deemed to be changing or need changing. Of them, the ones to be acquired (33.15%) are greater than those that should be rejected (21.43%). Barely over one fourth (26.41%) of the current cultural reality is regarded as worthy of preservation, leading to another conclusion: Poles are determined to overhaul the profile of their present culture radically. This inclination for a *cultural revolution* can be best appreciated when one considers the three value categories (descriptive * evaluative cells) of largest capacity: *European* to be acquired (17.10%), *Polish* to be preserved (11.83%), and *Polish* to be rejected (9.90%). Among European values, virtues strongly prevail over vices. In Polish cultural heritage the balance is tilted towards vices.

Table 6. Polish and European Union values (vices and virtues) of highest consensus in the research sample

Polish values			
Reject (vices)	%	Preserve (virtues)	%
Heated political debates	68	Memories for deceased	61
Uneasy at someone's success	60	Strong family bonds	42
Make the ends meet	53	Patriotism	42
Don't compromise easily	49	Courtesy for women	39
Be smart and sly	46	Three generation family	39
Take it east, things will turn out OK, somehow	43	Life long friendships	39
Enjoy your life, you live once!	42	Fantasy, romanticism	35

European (Union) values			
Reject (vices)	%	Acquire (virtues)	%
Human relations business like	30	Youths taught independence	57
Human value=material worth	28	Solid work	56
Catching up with pace of life	25	Being on time	54
Profit is everything	23	Harmony with nature	49
		Tolerance for alternative styles	48
		Smiling face	41
		Secular public life	40
		Business mentality	39
		Politic.-economic freedom	38
		Meet other cultures	38
		Respect for laws	38
		Professionalism	37
		Optimistic outlook	37
		Stylish outlook	37

The question arises how do the humanist values stand this critical historical test: do they belong to the core domain that needs to be preserved or should they be overhauled? I will answer this question in several steps, starting with simple frequency statistics of virtues and vices (Table 6) within the three largest categories mentioned above.

Poles wish to preserve their interpersonal, family-related bonds and national attachments, often buried in the historical past. They would equally like to get rid of other also interpersonal ways of being or excesses: propensity for contentiousness, nonchalance towards observing laws, and fulfilling obligations. These vices have been noticed for centuries and appear not less grounded in culture than the virtues. Both aspects of culture are consequences of values dominating the interpersonal world: while virtues are their positive occurrences, reinforced externally and internally, vices indicate controversial satisfactions in other contexts of social life.

In terms of preferences, European values are not evenly split like Polish values. Most of them are located in the positive category "to be acquired (assimilated)." Of most interest is the fact that these positive European values belong to different domains than the Polish virtues and vices. European values form a cluster of more impersonal and professionally efficient lifestyles. They represent a culture of less intensive personal involvements and are more fit for smooth, goal-oriented interaction with variety of partners.

Principal component analysis with oblique rotation was performed on the ECVSQ evaluative data. Four factors emerged as reported in Table 7.

Table 7. Four Value Dimensions (Factorial Scales)

Item in ECVSQ	Humanism	Liberalism	Materialism	Sarmatism
Selfless help	.550			
Generosity for charity	.514			
Life-long friendships	.480			
High culture cultivation	.479			
Patriotism	.476			
Broad intellectual horizons	.449			
Happiness, harmony in family	.439			
Forgiveness and mercy	.434			
People of all races equal	.395			
Remembrance of those who passed away	.394			
Love without format commitment		.580		
Grown-up children living with parents		−.572		
Standing by the teachings of the church		−.570		
Tolerance for alternative life-styles		.487		
Grandparents with children		−.423		
Taking life with `grain of salt'		.422		
Sacrifice and hardship		−.407		
Secular public life		.386		
Business-like with people			.579	
Catching up with modern world			.554	
Tough competition			.529	
Always calculating profit			.470	
Improving housing conditions			.468	
Work, always hard work...			.458	
Business-entrepreneurial values			.453	
Well planned, organized life			.423	
'Your worth is what you own'			.395	
'Mind your life, leave others'			.393	
'Enjoy! – you live once!'				.636
'Take it easy, things will turn out somehow'				.539
Hospitality, big parties				.514
Laid back life, not to die of overwork				.472
Be smart and sly				.424
'Hold to your positions, don't look for compromise'				.362

The four factors explained 22.20% of the total variance. Their respective contributions were: HUM = 7.86%, LIB = 5.59%, MAT = 4.80%, and SARM = 3.96%. Much of the variance was left unaccounted for due to the fact that evaluative item scales were reduced to three points: positive (acquire or preserve), ambivalent, and negative (reject). This led to scores highly deviating from a normal distribution.

As with the earlier studies, humanism emerged as the central cultural dimension, but materialism was a separate factor. A bipolar HUMAT dimension in the first set of studies may have been due to the fact that the analyses were performed on data pooled from repeated measures containing self and cultural prototype construals, which were highly polarized evaluatively. *Sarmatism* is an indigenous label given to values and lifestyles characterized in the introduction as anarchic personal freedoms, impulsive self-assertion, and social hedonism. Finally, *liberalism* is an expression of (post-)modern individualism: autonomy and non-coercive relations with other people. Humanism was by far the most positively endorsed orientation, while sarmatism had the lowest acceptance rate. Also, and similar to the earlier reported study (see Figure 3), the highest net humanism (HUM minus MATerialism) was found among the intelligentsia, while lowest was in the private business sector.

To find out how these four value dimensions matched the preferences for preservation vs. change in culture patterns, the two sets of variables were correlated as shown in Table 8.

Humanism is built on values of traditional Polish culture and is considered as the locus of the virtues that must be preserved and continued into the future. Sarmatism, on the other hand, represents the negative side of past heritage, and, being negatively correlated with the rejection of cultural vices, manifests a retreat to a defensive orientation. Readiness to overhaul Polish traditions is strongly associated with a low appreciation for sarmatism.

Endorsement of work-materialistic values was related to low rejection of EU values. Finally, liberalism was negatively related to Polish heritage and positively related to European values. Consequently, liberalism was the strongest predictor of *Euroenthusiasm*, an aggregate measure of pro-EU attitudes, ($\beta = .178$, $p < .001$), followed by materialism ($\beta = .100$, $p < .001$) (Boski, 2004).

Table 8. Correlations between Category Capacity of Polish and EU Virtues (+) / Vices (–) and Four Factorial Value Dimensions (n=1037)

	Humanism	Sarmatism	Work-Material	Liberalism
POL. (+) preserve (+)	.553	.315	0	−.365
POL. reject (−)	−.189	−.629	.136	.329
EU acquire (+)	0	−.248	.132	.310
EU reject (−)	.145	0	−.459	−.316

Liberalism in the Polish context appears destructive to indigenous culture, it tries to eradicate Poland's positive heritage as much as its vices. Most public ideological debates in Poland today are a contest between liberalism and humanism as contrasting visions of the country's future.

Two More Culture Constrasts within a Four Value-Dimensions Framework

The four value dimensions structure discussed above was recently used in several research projects of my students. Studies by Rymek (2002) and Nosarzewska (2004) are briefly reported.

Rymek set her study within an acculturation context. Her aim was to compare inter-generational culture transmission among Poles in Warsaw and Polish immigrants to the U.S. Parents performed a descriptive task of Polish and American culture perception on ECVSQ. Next, both parents and their young adult children performed the evaluation task on the same value items: "How important are these values in my family and in my personal life?" Figure 6 summarizes the descriptive part of Rymek's results for parents from the two countries, Poland and the U.S.

The numbers of items in each of the four value categories: (HUM), (SARM), (MAT), and (LIB) refer to their frequencies allocated in Polish, Polish-American (joint), and American cultures, respectively.

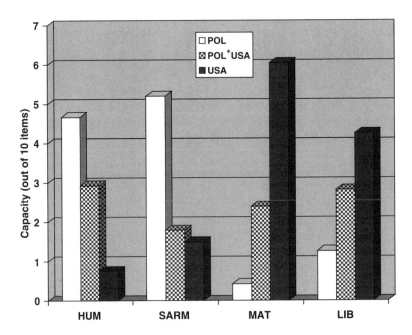

Figure 6. Capacity of four value dimensions in Polish and American cultures

The interaction between the four value types and their cultural distribution was highly significant, $F(6, 660) = 241.15$, $p < .000$, eta^2 = 0.62. Humanism and Sarmatism were considered charactersitic of Polish culture, while materialism and liberalism belonged to American culture. Moreover, on each of the four dimensions the two national cultures occupied extreme high or low positions, with the hybrid Polish-American category always in the middle.

Next, the evaluative aspects of dimensions and of cultures as wholes were examined. Their respective results are presented in Figure 7.

On the left side, mean evaluation scores for the four dimensions appear. They differ substantially, $F(3,160) = 151.08$, $p < .000$, eta^2 = 0.36. Humanism was the most prefered, with liberalism second, while evaluations of sarmatism and materialism were much lower. Thus, each culture had a positive and a darker (shadow) side. For Poland, there was a contrast between humanism and sarmatism. For the U.S., it was the opposition of liberalism and materialism. Consequently, the level of general evaluation for the two national cultures (Figure 7B) was similar. The Polish-American hybrid entity and the remaining neither categorgy, had much lower appeal, $F(3,160) = 108.37$, $p < .000$, eta^2 = 0.31. It is particularly interesting that the integrated (Polish * American) culture received the lowest evaluation. This result runs against the well established preference for integration among other acculturation strategies (Berry & Sam, 1997).

Nosarzewska (2004) ran her project with a group of French expatriates residing in Warsaw and with Polish controls matching for sociodemographics. The context of her study was acculturation of the French.

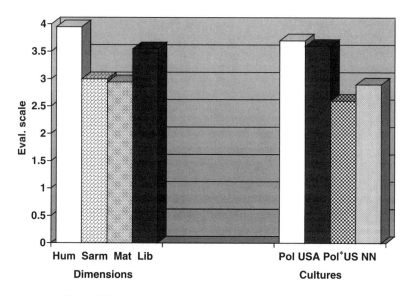

Figure 7. Evaluation of value dimensions [A] and cultures [B]

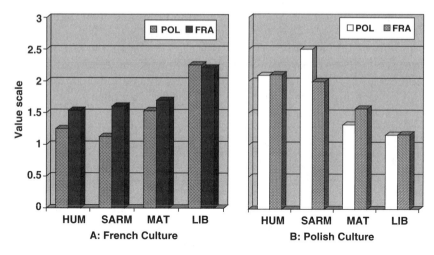

Figure 8. French [A] and Polish [B] cultures judged on four dimensions by participants from both countries

Descriptive measures of both cultures on four value dimensions were taken from French and Poles, followed by their personal value endorsements. Figure 8 shows the descriptive data.

Both cultures differed profoundly in their value profiles, $_{Fint.}(3,273) =$ 115.90, eta^2 = .56. LIBeralism is essentially a French value system, perceived this way by expatriates and by Polish hosts. Similarly, HUManism and SARMatism are Polish, with much consensus again. The only significant interaction in culture perception occured for Sarmatism, where each national group construed its own culture as more sarmatic than the other.

HUM had the highest personal endorsement among both nationalities, and it was the only value appreciated more by Poles than by French, $_{Fint.}$ (3,270) = 14.40, eta^2 =.138 (Figure 9). In contrast to their culture level judgements, Poles appreciated SARM considerably less, and also gave higher ratings to LIB.

In conclusion, the two studies by Rymek (2002) and Nosarzewska (2004) showed similar contrasts between values characterizng Polish culture on one side and American or French on the other. These findings are also convergent with earlier reported results in the context of European integration. Poland appears to be a place where humanist sentiments prevail, to the extent that liberalism dominates Western culture. This picture is complemented by two secondary dimensions of sarmatism and materialism, which are regarded as vices rather than virtues.

Humanism–Materialism and Ingroup/Outgroup Orientations

The last set of empirical results to be reported in this paper comes from a number of studies where the consequences of humanism on intergroup relations were investigated.

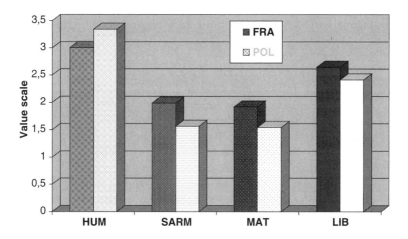

Figure 9. Personal acceptance of 4 value types among French expatriates and Poles

1. *Immigrants' feelings towards Poland and the host country (Canada).* As part of a research program on immigrants' acculturation (see section 1), Poles' feelings toward their homeland and toward their host country were measured. As usual, feelings were polarized into negative (*humiliation, grievance, shame, despair*, etc.) and positive (*happiness, gratitude, hope, pride*, etc.) affects. In a regression model analysis, humanism emerged as the strongest predictor of positive affect for Poland ($\beta = .276, p < .01$) and for Canada ($\beta = .336, p < .01$).

2. *Americans' outgroup evaluation.* In a study conducted in the USA, the research question was to investigate relationships between personal values, identities, and outgroup evaluations (Boski, 1998). American students answered the ECVSQ and responded to videorecorded episodes featuring gender role interactions within the context of Polish culture. Results showed that humanism was a strong positive predictor of the foreign culture's approval ratings ($\beta = .423, p < .001$) and a negative predictor of prejudice against that culture ($\beta = -.335, p < .001$).

3. *Own vs. foreign cultures in the multicultural landscape of Warsaw.* Warsaw residents reacted to a number of cultural stimuli (mainly temples of various denominations and ethnic restaurants) located in the capital of Poland. We were interested to find out how the syndrome of multicultural orientation (knowledge, competence and attitudes) related to Polish cultural orientation and whether the two could be predicted by humanism–materialism (Boski, 2002a). Our results showed that multicultural and Polish cultural orientations were unrelated. Each orientation formed two clusters (individuals high vs. low in multiculturalism, and high vs. low in Polishness). The two classifications differed significantly along the

humanism-materialism dimension. Higher levels of materialism characterized people who had a low appreciation of any culture: their own or foreign. A net positive HUM-MAT score promoted appreciation of foreign cultures.

4. *Humanism, patriotism, and nationalism.* Patriotism and nationalism are often differentiated in the literature as alternative manifestations of attachment to one's country-state (Staub, 1997). While patriotic attachment is a sentiment without prejudice of other countries or ethnic communities, nationalism is founded on superiority/inferiority comparisons (nationalism thrives on animosities). In several studies reported earlier, we were interested in finding the roots of these orientations in values. It was predicted, in particular, that humanism should be the precursor of patriotic feelings. Confirming results were reported in the study on psychological antecedents of preferences for democracy. Not only was humanism a predictor of patriotism ($\beta = .207, p < .05$) but its negative relationship with nationalism was even stronger ($\beta = -.350, p < .001$). Individualism, on the other hand, was a negative correlate of patriotism ($\beta = -.263, p < .01$). The later survey study on *Values and Identity in the Context of European Integration* extended these results. Humanism again correlated positively with patriotism ($r = .250, p < .001$), while liberalism correlated negatively ($r = -.133, p < .01$). Also, while patriotic feelings assumed selective attachment to the values of cultural heritage, nationalistic feelings were linked to uncritical approval of that heritage.

The overall pattern of results is consistent: Humanism promotes positive feelings to the home country and to the host country among immigrants. It was related to positive appreciation of foreign cultures among Poles as well as Americans. Humanism strengthened patriotic, non-antagonistic attachment to the homeland.

CONCLUSION

With the help of historical analysis, several psychological themes were postulated as characteristic of Polish culture. Humanism was suggested as its core element. This approach resembles some other works in the field of indigenous psychology (e.g. Diaz-Guerrero, 1982, 1993). But humanism as a value dimension (or type) was also derived theoretically from the analysis of ambiguities concerning collectivism/individualism. Thus, the emic (bottom-up) and etic (top down) strategies converged in what Berry has called *derived etic* (Berry *et al.*, 1992, p. 234).

An empirical measure of humanism–materialism (HUMAT) emerged some 20 years ago with the use of Emic Culture Values and Scripts Questionnaire (ECVSQ), in the context of research on acculturation of

Polish immigrants in Northern America. HUMAT showed deep contrasts between Polish and North American cultures. Similar differences were later found in Polish-West European (EU) comparisons. These constrasts turned out to be of lesser (though still consistent) scope at the level of personal value endorsements. To date, we have accumulated cross-cultural evidence confirming humanism as a Polish value priority in comparison with data from England (Lewandowska, 2003), France (Nosarzewska, 2004), Lithuania (Kaminska, 2002), Austria and Sweden (Aleksandrowska, 2003), Italy (Chojnowska, 2003), Pakistan (Soomro & Boski, 2002), Canada and the United States (Boski, 1992; Rymek, 2002) and the European Union (Boski, 2004).

Humanism is conceptually and empirically separate from collectivism/individualism. It differentiates various sectors of Polish society, being high among inteligentsia, teachers, and local politicians, but relatively low among business people and bank employees.

Durings the years of political transformation in Poland, humanism has shown stability in self and positive prototypes. Materialism has largely increased in negative Polish prototypes, reflecting culturally embedded mistrust against business activities and their outcomes. This tradition has been further reinforced by current media reports and personally witnessed pathological aspects of the indigenous market economy such as "becoming rich overnight" by fraudulent or corrupt practices.

While humanism should be seen as an inhibitor of a business orientation, it facilitates political democracy, constructive patriotism, and appreciation of other cultures. Humanism is part of the cultural heritage that Poles wish to preserve, and our empirical evidence strongly suggests that cultural identity maintenance largely depends on the continuity of humanist values. Moreover, the growing neccessity of openness to the ouside world within the European Union and beyond is accepted by the vast majority of Poles and remains compatible with humanist acceptance of outgroups, as long as these ingroup traditions are not denied.

My final note concerns potential challenges to the claim for the indigenous status of humanism construct. Indeed, some of the reported findings show that it has similar consequences beyond the context of Polish culture (eg. outgroup appreciation among Poles and Americans). The problem is more general and relevant for discussion of any indigenous concept: Is *amae*, for instance, uniquely Japanese? Studies by Yamaguchi (2005) demonstrate the fruitfulness of crossing the borders with investigations on concepts originally conceived as indigenous.

Indigenous themes, along the proposed line of reasoning, belong to broader families of pancultural concepts but profiled in a unique way. A recent study by Kaminska (2002) suggests that humanism may be a mixture of conservation and self-transcendence (or benevolence) in Schwartz's scheme of universal value types. But as benevolence is not equivalent to collectivism (in Schwartz's own terms), so humanism is not

equivalent to benevolence either. Both have separate theoretical foundations and different modes of expression. What is particularly important is
that Poland has a relatively low position on benevolence and on egalitar-
ianism, to which benevolence subsumes at culture level of analysis.
Poland ranks well below Sweden, Italy, France, or Austria (Schwartz,
1994, 2004); each and all of which have been shown to score considerably
lower than Poland on humanism!

How can we reconcile such contradictions? Perhaps the similarity of
the constructs is more apparent than real. Unlike a pancultural scheme,
which takes general snapshots of world's cultures, the indigenous
approach focuses on in-depth analysis of a single culture, and its recurrent
themes that have molded the lives of subsequent generations. As Schwartz
recently found, even cross-cultural psychologists, experts in the field, are
not very good at making valid learned guesses in a task where seven cultural value types are hidden behind 'blind' country rank orders (Schwartz,
2003). It is very difficult to distinguish not only between the adjacent value
types (e.g. hierarchy and embeddedness) but even between opposites, like
harmony and mastery. Consequently, such pancultural hierarchies are perhaps not the best tools for orientation and understanding of a given culture. The indigenous approach is a better choice.

The indigenous approach may be theoretically less ambitious than the
pancultural wholistic view. It is about the psychology of a local people and
their relations (wars and peaceful exchanges) with neighbors whose collective software of the mind has been shaped by different environmental conditions and events. Still, it is a psychology of direct interest for millions of
people and indirectly for many more who may want to learn about diversity within humankind. Individualism has been an indigenous Anglosaxon
construct, which drew world-wide interest, even from those who do not
share this cultural orientation, or are opposed to it. Similarly, humanism
(and its opposites materialism and sarmatism) offers interpretation of the
collective fate of Poles and expands understanding of human nature.

REFERENCES

Aleksandrowska, K. (2003). Macro-cultural and individual level determinants of European
    Union enlargement: Findings from 15 member states and samples of Austrians, Poles,
    and Swedes. *Unpublished M.A. thesis*, Warsaw: Warsaw School of Social Psychology.
Berry, J. W., and Sam, D. (1997). Acculturation and adaptation. In Berry, J. W. Segall, M. H.,
    and Kagitcibasi, C. (Eds.), *Handbook of cross-cultural psychology, Second Edition, Volume III*
    (pp. 291–326). Boston: Allyn and Bacon.
Berry, J. W., Poortinga, Y. H., Segall, M. H., and Dasen, P. R. (1992). *Cross-cultural psychology:
    Research and applications*. Cambrdige: Cambridge University Press.
Boski, P. (1992). O byciu Polakiem w ojczyznie i zmianach tozsamosci na obczyznie [Being
    Pole in homeland and changing identity in immigration – *in Polish*]. In Boski, P.,
    Jarymowicz, M., and Malewska-Peyre, H. *Tozsamosc a odmiennosc kulturowa [Identity and*

cultural distinctiveness -in Polish] (pp. 77–211). Warsaw: Wydawnictwo Instytutu Psychologii PAN.

Boski, P. (1993). Between West and East: Humanistic values and concerns in Polish psychology. In Kim, U., and Berry, J. W. (eds.), *Indigenous psychologies: Research and experience in cultural context* (pp. 79–103). Newbury Park: Sage.

Boski, P. (1994). Psychological analysis of a culture: Stability of core values among Poles in the motherland and Polish immigrants. *Polish Psychological Bulletin, 25(4)*, 257–282.

Boski, P. (1998). Cultural identity, subjective well-being and outgroup evaluation. Paper presented at the XIV IACCP Congress, Bellingham.

Boski, P. (2002a). Humanism-materialism: Polish cultural origins and cross-cultural comparisons. In Lonner, W. J., Dinnel, D. L., Hayes, S. A., and Sattler, D. N., (Eds.), *Online readings in psychology and culture. www.wwu.edu/culture.*

Boski, P. (2004). Czy wyraza Pan/Pani zgode na przystapienie Rzeczypospolitej Polskiej do Unii Europejskiej?" -Wartosci kulturowe euro-entuzjastów i euro-sceptyków. [Do you agree for Poland to become an EU member state? – Cultural values of euroenthusiasts and euroscptics – *in Polish.*] In Skarzynska, K, and Jakubowska, U. (Eds.), *Psychologiczne wyjasnienia aktualnych wydarzen politycznych [Psychological explanations of current political events].* Warsaw: Academica.

Chinese Cultural Connection. (1987). Chinese values and the search for culture-free dimensions of culture. *Journal of Cross-Cultural Psychology, 18*, 143–164.

Chojnowska, M. (2003). Cultural masculinity in Italy and femininity in Poland. *Unpublished M.A. thesis*, Warsaw: Warsaw School of Social Psychology.

Davies, N. (1981). God's playground: A history of Poland, Volume 2: 1795 to the present. Oxford: Oxford University Press.

Davies, N. (1982). God's playground: A history of Poland. Vol.1: The origin to 1795. Columbia University Press, New York.

Diaz-Guerrero, R. (1982). The psychology of socio-cultural premises. *Spanish Language Psychology, 2*, 383–410.

Diaz-Guerrero, R. (1993). Mexican ethnopsychology. In U. Kim, & J.W. Berry (Eds.), *Indigenous psychologies: Research and experience in cultural context* (pp. 44–55). Newbury Park: Sage.

Georgas, J. (1993). An ecological-social model for indigenous psychology: The example of Greece. In Kim, U., and Berry, J. W. (Eds.), *Indigenous psychologies: Experience and research in cultural context* (pp. 56–78). Sage, Newbury Park,

Greenwald, A. G. (1982). Is anyone in charge? Personalysis versus the principle of personal unity. In Suls, J. (Ed.), *Psychological prspectives on the self, vol.1*, (pp.151–184), Hillsdale: Lawrence Erlbaum.

Hofstede, G. (2001). *Culture's consequences, Second edition.* Thousand Oaks: Sage.

Hofstede, G. (1991). *Culture and organizations.* London: McGraw-Hill.

House, R. J., Hanges, P. J., Javidan, M., Dorfman, P. W., Gupta, V. (Eds.) (2004). *Culture, leadership, and organizations. The GLOBE study of 62 nations.* Thousand Oaks: Sage.

Kabasakal, H., Bodur, M. (2004). Humane orientation in societies, organizations, and leader attributes. In House, R. J., Hanges, P. J., Javidan, M., Dorfman, P. W., Gupta, V. (Eds.). *Culture, leadership, and organizations. The GLOBE study of 62 nations* (pp. 564 – 601). Thousand Oaks: Sage.

Kagitcibasi, C. (1996a). The autonomous – relational self: A new synthesis. *European Psychologist, 1(3)*, 180–186.

Kagitcibasi, C. (1996b). *Family and human development across cultures.* Mahwah, NJ: Lawrence Erlbaum

Kagitcibasi, C. (1997). Individualism and collectivism. In Berry, J. W., Segall, M. H., and Kagitcibasi, C. (Eds.), *Handbook of Cross-Cultural Psychology. Volume 3, Social Behavior and Applications* (pp. 1–50). Boston: Allyn and Bacon.

Kaminska, S. (2002). Values and mutual ethnocentrism in Polish-Lithuanian relations. *Unpublished M.A. thesis*, Warsaw: Warsaw School of Social Psychology.

Kim, U., and Berry, J. W. (Eds.), *Indigenous psychologies: Research and experience in cultural context*. Newbury Park: Sage.

Korzeniowski, K. (1995). (1995). Alienacja polityczna a demokracja [Political alienation and democracy – *in Polish*]. In Reykowski, J. (Ed.). *Potoczne wyobrazenia o demokracji demokracji [Popular understanding of democracy – in Polish]*. Wydawnictwo IP PAN, Warszawa, pp. 187–206.

Lewandowska, E. (2003). More Polish or British? -Cultural identity of first generation Polish immigrants born in United Kingdom. *Unpublished M.A. thesis*, Warsaw: Warsaw School of Social Psychology.

Marin, G. (1994). The experience of being a Hispanic in the United States. In Lonner, W. J., and Malpass, R. S. (Eds.), *Psychology and Culture*, pp. 23 – 27.

McClelland, D.C. (1961). *The achieving society*. Van Nostrand, Princeton.

Nosarzewska, Z. (2004). French expatriates in Poland: Culture comparisons and psychological adaptation. Unpublished M.A. thesis. Warsaw: Warsaw School of Social Psychology.

Reykowski, J. (1994). Collectivism and Individualism asdimensions of social change. In Kim, U., Triandis, H. C., Kagitcibasi, C., Choi, S. C., and Yoon, G. (Eds), *Individualism and collectivism: Theory, method and applications* (pp. 276–292). Thousand Oaks: Sage.

Reykowski, J. (Ed.). (1995). *Potoczne wyobrazenia o demokracji [Popular understanding of democracy – in Polish]*. Wydawnictwo IP PAN, Warszawa.

Rymek, M. (2002). Values and inter-generational value transmission among Poles in the country and immigrants in America. *Unpublished M.A. thesis*, Warsaw: Warsaw School of Social Psychology.

Schwartz, S. H. (1990). Individualism and collectivism: Critique and proposed refinements. *Journal of Cross-Cultural Psychology, 21*, 139–157.

Schwartz, S. H. (1992). Universals in the content and structure of values: Theoretical advances and empirical tests in 20 countries. In Zanna, M. P. (Ed.), *Advances in experimental social psychology, Vol.25* (pp.1–65). Orlando: Academic Press.

Schwartz, S. H. (1994). Cultural dimensions of values; Toward an understanding of national differences. In Kim, U., Triandis, H. C., Kagitcibasi, C., Choi, S. C., and Yoon, G. (Eds), *Individualism and collectivism: Theory, method and application* (pp. 85–122). Thousand Oaks: Sage.

Schwartz, S. H. (2003). "Expert" ratings of cultural value dimensions. Unpublished manuscript.

Schwartz, S. H. (2004). Mapping and interpreting cultural differences around the world. In Vinken, H, Soeters, J., and Ester, P. (Eds.), *Comparing cultures, Dimensions of cultures in a comparative perspective*. Leiden: Brill.

Soomro, N. H., and Boski, P. (2002). Individualism – Collectivism and related value dimensions: A comparative study of Pakistani and Polish students. Paper presented at XVI IACCP Conference, Yogyakarta, Indonesia, July 15–19.

Staub. E. (1997). Blind vs. constructive patriotism: Moving from embeddedness in the group to critical loyalty and action. In Bar-Tal, D., and Staub, E. (Eds.), *Patriotism in the lives of individuals and nations* (pp. 213–228). Chicago: Nelson Hall.

Thomas, W. I., Znaniecki, F. (1918/1927). *The Polish peasant in Europe and in America, vol 1.* New York.

Triandis, H. C. (1990). Cross-cultural studies of individualism and collectivism. In Berman, J. (Ed.), *Nebraska Symposium on Motivation, 1989* (pp.41–133). Lincoln: University of Nebraska Press.

Triandis, H.C., Marin, G., Lisansky, J., and Betancourt, H. (1984). *Simpatia* as a cultural script of Hispanics. *Journal of Personality and Social Psychology, 47*, 1363–1374.

Triandis, H. C., and Vassiliou, V. (1972). A comparative analysis of subjective culture. In Triandis, H. C. (Ed.), *The analysis of subjective culture* (pp. 299–338). New York: Wiley.

Weber, M. (1904/1958). *The Protestant ethic and the spirit of capitalism*. New York: Ch.Scribner's Sons.

Yamaguchi, S & Ariizumi, Y. (2005). Chapter 7 in this volume.

Chapter 18

Chinese Conceptions of Justice and Reward Allocation

Zhi-Xue Zhang

Questions about justice arise whenever decisions are made about how resources should be allocated among people. Justice takes an important role in human social life, ensuring that people receive what they are due. Researchers from several fields have explored this question. In this chapter, justice will be examined from a social psychological perspective.

The study of social justice has focused on two issues: distributive justice and procedural justice. In this chapter, I focus on distributive justice, which is also the first form of justice to capture the attention of justice researchers, although procedural justice has received somewhat more attention in the past decade (Cropanzana & Greenberg, 1997). Distributive justice concerns whether resource allocation is fair in terms of the outcome people receive. As the outcome always results from a specific set of processes or procedures, people are very concerned about whether the procedures themselves are fair (Leventhal, 1980; Lind & Tyler, 1988).

Distributive justice theorists generally hold two perspectives on the justice norm that allocators use to distribute rewards. Equity theorists assume that the equity principle, which dictates that one's obtained reward is in proportion to one's contribution, is the only way to achieve the goal of "being fair to all" (Adams, 1965; Walster, Berscheid, & Walster, 1973). In contrast, multi-principle advocates have highlighted the importance of context in which the resource allocation occurs, and argue that principles other than equity, such as equality and need, may be more appropriate in some situations (Deutsch, 1975; Lerner, 1975; Leventhal, 1980).

Empirical studies have indicated that the choice of allocation norms is subject to the influence of many factors, including social interactive factors such as the relationship between the participants, the goals of social interactions, and the anticipated social interactions (for a review see Tornblom, 1992). A theory is needed to integrate these factors and explain the nature of distributive justice.

Cross-cultural studies have revealed that cultural background substantially influences either people's conception of justice or their choice of distribution principle. For example, it has been found that Americans are more likely to distribute resources according to the equity norm than Europeans (e.g., Gergen, Morse, & Gergen, 1980). All of these augments and findings suggest that an individual's fairness perception is culture-specific rather than universal.

Individuals in different cultures define fairness differently. Gudykunst and Ting-Toomey (1988) maintained that fairness in individualistic cultures is viewed from a self-oriented and short-term perspective, which implies that people should get what they deserve on the basis of their inputs and commitment level. In contrast, in collectivistic cultures fairness is typically interpreted from an other-oriented and long-term perspective, which implies people should be rewarded evenly regardless of their contributions. Both Sampson (1975) and Deutsch (1975) criticized that the preference for equity, which stresses agency, individualism, and competition, epitomizes the particular historical and cultural pattern dominant in Western culture, and results from the pervasiveness of economic values over other concerns in Western societies. They posited that equality and need may be more relevant to the question of justice in societies where communion, collectivism, and cooperation are valued.

Chinese people characterized by social orientation treat others differently depending on their relationship with others (Yang, 1995). Such a tendency is also reflected in reward allocation. Due to cultural differences, Chinese people and their Western counterparts may follow different distribution principles in the same situation. Western theories of justice are not adequate to fully explain the Chinese conception and behavior of social justice.

In this chapter, I first review justice research in Chinese societies. Empirical studies conducted in a Chinese context as well as conceptual thinking on Chinese justice are examined. Following this, I propose a social interactional perspective on reward allocation, in which allocation decision or behavior is interpreted as a social act governed by the prevalent social norm. Subsequently, I report several empirical studies demonstrating the social interactional nature of reward allocation. While past researchers have considered reward allocation or fairness judgments as a simple process of determining whether the outcome benefits the individuals, these studies examined the distribution of rewards in social interactional contexts. Finally, based on existing research, I draw some conclusions on the conception of Chinese justice.

JUSTICE RESEARCH IN THE CHINESE CONTEXT

In the past two decades, social psychologists from Hong Kong and Taiwan have examined the justice issue in Chinese societies. Some of them replicated studies originally conducted in the West using Chinese samples, and others engaged in cross-cultural studies. These studies found differences between Chinese and Western people in fairness perception.

In an early study on reward allocation, Chu and Yang (1976) found Taiwanese participants did not distribute rewards according to relative contribution. When their performance was lower than their coworker's, they allocated the reward according to the equity norm; however, when their performance was greater, they divided the reward according to the equality norm. This study revealed that Chinese allocation decisions are not based only on self-interest concerns.

Cross-cultural research findings have indicated two differences between Chinese individuals and their Western counterparts in the distribution of rewards. First, compared with Western individuals, Chinese individuals seem generally to prefer the equality norm to the equity norm. Second, Chinese people are more likely to follow the allocation norms that are to their counterpart's advantage. Hui, Triandis, and Yee (1991) found Chinese participants are more generous and other-serving than American participants when dividing a fixed amount of reward with their counterpart, especially with friends, and they are more egalitarian when there is no constraint on the total amount of reward to be distributed.

Yang and Hui (1986) found that the more university students in Hong Kong regard their work team as a group, the more they judge an equal distribution to be fair. Leung and Bond (1984) revealed that Chinese and American allocators followed different norms for different coworkers. The Chinese employed the equity principle more closely than Americans for a stranger, but were more likely to use the equality principle for a friend. If a participant's input was higher than a friend's, they followed the equality norm more closely than American participants. In addition, Leung and Bond found that Chinese participants like an allocator who divides the group rewards equally with a friend more than one who divides equitably, but American participants like an allocator who allocates equitably with a friend more than the one who allocates equally. These findings suggest that the relationship between people has a bearing on the perceived fairness of a distribution. More recently, Li (1993) found as compared to their American counterparts, Chinese participants' judgment of the fairness of an act was more dependent on the person who did the act.

Cross-cultural researchers have attributed the difference between Chinese and American fairness perception to the difference in cultural value of Individualism-Collectivism (I-C), assuming that the Chinese are collectivists, whereas the American individualists (Hui, Triandis, and Yee,

1991; Leung & Bond, 1984). However, Chen, Meindl, and Hunt (1997) commented that the conceptualization of I-C alone is weak and needs to be refined. They distinguished vertical and horizontal collectivism, where vertical collectivism means that individuals subordinate their personal goals to those of the collective and horizontal collectivism indicates interpersonal harmony among group members. Chen, Meindl and Hunt pointed out, previous cross-cultural justice studies have only investigated the horizontal dimension of I-C, ignoring the vertical dimension.

Many scholars have attempted to pinpoint the nature of Chinese justice, and these perspectives are helpful for our understanding of the aforementioned differences between Chinese and Westerners in fairness perceptions or justice behavior.

Hwang (1991) claimed that social justice in Confucian thought is based on the concept of benevolence (*ren*), which demands that one always convey affection (*qing*) for others. One way of showing feeling for others is to offer the resources in one's possession to others. However, people only have a limited amount of resources, and thus can not give something to everyone. They have to show different levels of feeling to the different people with whom they maintain relationships. This feeling is not always expressed spontaneously, but is expressed in the form of fulfilling one's relational obligations. According to Hwang (1987), in a distribution situation, allocators first judge their relationship (*guanxi*) with others before making a decision. If the relationship is perceived to be an instrumental tie, the equity norm is employed. If it is an expressive tie, the need norm will be used. In a mixed tie, allocators employ the *renqing* (affective) norm to distribute resources to others in a beneficial way.

Chiu (1991a) advanced the idea that the Chinese conception of justice is based on the concept of righteousness (*yi*), which calls for doing the right thing at the right time and in the right context. *Yi* prescribes different obligatory requirements for various role relationships and requires one to fulfill the functions of one's position and observe the prescriptive rules implied in one's social role. In one multidimensional scaling study, Chiu found that *yi* shares the same semantic meaning with fulfillment of role expectations, and both *yi* and fulfillment of role expectations are good predictors of Chinese judgments of justice. Chiu's (1991b, 1991c) studies also indicated that Chinese people have different justice standards for different social relations, and that the dominant justice standard in a particular relationship can be predicted from the specific behavioral expectations attached to that relationship.

Chiu (1991a) concluded that both roles and imposed obligations are essential parts of the Chinese conception of social justice, and are where the differences between Western and Chinese conceptions of justice conception lie. While the former implies the use of distributive principles applicable to everyone concerned, the latter suggests the incorporation of obligatory considerations that are context-specific and relation-bound. Chiu (1991a) further postulated that the Chinese notion of justice seems to have a bearing on *renqing*–the norm that governs an individual's social interactions with others in Chinese culture. Unfortunately, he did not elaborate this seminal idea.

More recently, Chiu and Hong (1997) linked the Chinese notion of justice with the fundamental principles of social regulation in Chinese societies. They claimed that four principles of social regulation are closely relevant to Chinese justice judgments, they are: enforcement of role behavior, sharing of group responsibility and outcome, regulation of individual motivation and morality, and conflict containment. Chiu and Hong tried to integrate extant research findings in this framework. However, such a post hoc theory is not cogent given that they did not provide convincing arguments for the proposed four social regulation principles.

In sum, research has indicated that Chinese individuals have different ideas about fairness, and thus make different reward allocations or show different behavior from their Western counterparts. Underlying the difference is the Chinese individuals' motivation to fulfill their obligatory requirement in their relationships and to express affection towards others. Based on these findings and thoughts, I advanced a new perspective on reward allocation to integrate the essential factors underlying Chinese distribution decisions.

A SOCIAL INTERACTIONAL PERSPECTIVE ON REWARD ALLOCATION

The distribution of rewards or outcome is a social action in which individuals communicate feelings with each other. A distribution decision is not just a calculation-and-allocation act motivated by self-interest concerns, but an interpersonal-oriented act with symbolic meanings. From this exchange, individuals consider their counterpart's personal characteristics, attitudes, and motives, based on which they estimate the possibility of their further interaction with that person. In this regard, how an allocator distributes a reward is inevitably influenced by social interactive factors such as the relationship between the participants and the nature of their previous social interactions. Therefore, *guanxi* (interpersonal relationship) matters in making allocation decisions.

Moreover, human behavior is regulated by a society's fundamental principles (Chiu & Hong, 1997; Deutsch, 1985). Since the distribution of a reward always occurs in social situations, the allocator has to follow the social norms governing people's conduct, one of which is the Chinese relational norm—*renqing*. As both *guanxi* and *renqing* have roles in allocation decision and behavior, I shall briefly describe the two concepts before we proceed.

Guanxi refers to the status of the ties between two parties. It is construed to contain ascribed and interactive components (Yang, 2000). The former, which has also been called "*guanxi* base" (Jacobs, 1979), represents a collection of institutionally ascribed relationships shared by the interacting dyad (such as locality, kinship, colleague, etc.). Each of these relationships prescribes mutual obligations for relational partners. According to Yang (2000), the interactive component of *guanxi* refers to the experience accumulated through two or more parties' direct interaction. Ascribed relations differ in the pressure for relational partners to fulfill obligations. The pressure is usually the strongest in family relationships. Once *guanxi* evolves to a close tie due to the change of affective feelings involved, for example, from "casual friends" to "good friends," the obligations lodged in the relationship change accordingly and so does the obligatory pressure.

Guanxi is more obligation-bound than the Western conception of social relationships. Chinese people's behavior is based on *guanxi* (Jacobs, 1979), and they treat others differentially according to the type of *guanxi* they have with a particular individual (Hwang, 1987). Theorists have characterized Chinese culture as a relation-oriented culture because Chinese people are very much concerned about interpersonal harmony, group solidarity, and the fulfillment of social obligations (Ho, Chan, & Chiu, 1991; Yang, 1995). Having described *guanxi* and its function, let us look at another indigenous Chinese concept—*renqing*.

Literally, *renqing* means "affection," "human sentiment" or "human emotion". *Renqing* refers to either human emotion (Hu, 1949) or a relational norm. When *renqing* refers to a relational norm, it requires people to perform proper behaviors in various interpersonal situations, and to show good feelings in front of others. The expression of *renqing* could be practiced by helping others, caring for others, and showing sympathy to others (Zhang & Yang, 2001). *Renqing* functions in every sphere of Chinese people's social life. As a social norm, *renqing* is shared by most Chinese individuals, governs their social interaction, and regulates all kinds of *guanxi* among individuals (King, 1980; Zhang & Yang, 1998).

Zhang and Yang (1998) argued that, in general, Chinese people adopt three norms by which to treat others: the *renqing* norm, the reasonableness (*he qing he li*) norm, and the fairness (*he li*) norm. Their major distinction lies in the degree to which individuals emphasize affection (*qing*) and reason (*li*) in making social decisions. The *renqing* norm requires individuals to convey good feelings to others so as to maintain interpersonal harmony. People sometimes are required to be concerned about the matter of fairness (*he li*) and they have to make a rational judgment or decision in order to achieve instrumental ends. Sometimes people may strive for a balance between the affective and rational aspects so as to make a reasonable (*he qing he li*) decision. The reasonableness norm requires people to integrate their considerations of both affection (*qing*) and reason (*li*) in making a decision.

Guanxi and *renqing* interact to influence Chinese social behavior in general and reward allocation in particular. As the *renqing* norm is prevalent in Chinese culture, it is quite likely that, in making allocations, people would also observe it besides the fairness concern. Moreover, they decide who should be given what kind of affection and how much affection based on their *guanxi* with others.

Chinese individuals' offering *renqing* to others does not mean they are ignorant of fairness. In distribution situations, if allocators exactly know a participant's relative contribution to the task, they are required to make the distribution relevant to the person's actual contribution. As a consequence, allocators usually face two conflicting demands from *renqing* considerations and fairness concerns. To accommodate the two demands, they may make a compromise by taking both *renqing* and fairness into consideration. Consistent with this notion are studies demonstrating that Chinese people tend to exercise dialectical thinking or a moderate style of thinking by seeking the golden mean (a middle way) (Peng, 1999; Tu, 1976).

REWARD ALLOCATION STUDIES IN THE CONTEXT OF SOCIAL INTERACTION

Following a social interactional perspective, this author conducted a series of empirical studies to examine Chinese individuals' allocation decisions under different social situations.

Influences of *Guanxi* and *Renqing* on Allocation Decisions

As discussed, to solve the conflicting demands from *renqing* and fairness, Chinese allocators make a compromise by following the reasonableness norm by taking both the rational and affective aspects of reward allocation. Results of one study (Zhang & Yang, 1998) supported this prediction.

In this study, adult participants were divided into six groups and each of them was asked first to read a scenario and then to answer some questions. The scenario was described as follows: Two individuals collaborate on a task for a company and obtained a bonus of 100 yuan (US$12) after they finished it. Their contributions to the task are 70% and 30% respectively. Each participant was instructed to act as the high performer and to divide the bonus six times, each time assuming the coworker was a different relational partner. The six imagined partners included a parent (father/mother), a sibling (brother/sister), a friend, a colleague, a casual acquaintance, and a stranger. Each participant in five groups was instructed to allocate the reward to each of the six coworkers according to one of the following norms: the fairness (*he li*), reasonableness (*he qing he li*), *renqing*, "should" (*ying gai*), and equity (*gong zheng*) norms. Participants in another group were asked to make the distribution under no specific instructions (the "would" condition).

The findings indicated that, allocations under the "would," "reasonable," and "should" conditions did not differ. This suggests that what Chinese individuals would do is consistent with what they should do, and what they should do is to deal with others in a reasonable way by accommodating the affective and rational aspects. Further statistical analysis revealed interesting results. For parents and siblings, the reasonable allocations did not differ from the *renqing* allocation, but were more than the rational allocations. For friends, the reasonable allocations were less than the *renqing* allocations, and were marginally different from the rational ones. For colleagues, acquaintances, and strangers, the reasonable allocations were much less than the allocations with *renqing* considerations, but were not different from the rational ones. These results suggest that the reasonableness norm is flexible under different interpersonal contexts.

In sum, this study (Zhang & Yang, 1998) indicated that the distribution of reward is influenced by the *guanxi* between the participants, and the results also echo previous findings that Chinese people make different allocations depending on their relationship with the coworker (Chu & Yang, 1976; Hui, Triandis, & Yee, 1991; Leung & Bond, 1984; Li, 1993).

The Effect of Interactional Experience

Relationships are characterized by both ascribed and interactive components (Yang, 2000), but researchers who look at the relationship's influence on reward allocation have not distinguished the two components. The study just described indicated the influences of the ascribed component of *guanxi* on reward allocation. How can we learn the impact of the interactive component?

Research has shown that when future interaction is anticipated, the allocator tends to make a distribution beneficial to the other and less beneficial to himself or herself (Shapiro, 1975). Likewise, the individuals' interaction in the past also influences reward allocation. Taking the interaction between person A and person B as an example, A tends to evaluate B's attitude and personality during their interaction. If A feels B is a nice partner, he/she will show kindness or help. In turn, B will hold a positive attitude of A, and initiate more agreeable contacts with him/her. They become closer and closer through the reciprocal exchange. However, if A perceives B is not a good partner for some reasons, he/she will discontinue their social exchange.

Consequently, the affective quality of a relationship is reflected in the frequency of the two sides' interaction. The frequency of past interaction is predicative of future interaction, as people who have maintained frequent interaction are likely to continue more interaction. The frequency of past interaction is predicted to influence allocation decisions like the expectation of future interaction.

The relationship between colleagues may be used as an example. It is common to almost all people. The relationship is established because the individuals work at the same organization. However, interaction between two colleagues varies. People may maintain a distant or a very intimate connection with their colleagues.

Zhang (2001) asked four groups of participants to read a scenario similar to that in the study reported above, but the two partners were described as colleagues. The scenario presented to each group differed in the two coworkers' interactions. Their past interaction was described as frequent or infrequent, and the anticipated interaction was manipulated in terms of whether one person was described to leave the current organization very soon. Four conditions were created. Participants were asked to act as the high-input coworker and to allocate the bonus. They were also required to indicate their attitude and behavioral responses to the low-input partner.

Results indicated that past interaction proved to have a significant effect on allocation decisions. Participants in the two "frequent past interaction" conditions not only made more allocations than in the two "infrequent past interaction", but also scored higher on the frequency of two colleagues' future interaction, the likeability of the partner, and their willingness to cooperate with the partner. The four conditions share the same type of relationship but differ in the affective quality, which led to the allocation difference.

This study also involved additional conditions, in which the relationship between the two partners was described as strangers, good friends, and casual acquaintances. Allocations in the four "colleague" conditions and those in other conditions were compared. It was found that the allocation for a colleague with whom one has kept frequent interaction was not different from that given to a good friend. However, the allocation for a colleague with whom one seldom interacted was close to that for a stranger or an acquaintance. Although the type of relationship is the same, the interacting experience exerts an effect on the allocation decision. As Yang (2000) claimed, the interactive component of a relationship takes a more and more important part than the ascribed component as people continue their interaction.

Social Treatment and Allocation Decisions

Distributive justice researchers have usually ignored the symbolic message conveyed in distribution decisions. They usually adopt the minimum interaction paradigm in their studies, in which participants know nothing about the coworker except their relative contribution to the task. They have generally found that participants divide the reward based on relative contribution. I suspect these participants have to use the availability heuristic to make the allocation decision (Tversky & Kahneman, 1974) as contribution is the only information available.

In reality, when individuals are working together, they are concerned about how they are treated by others. They judge the coworker's personality, attitude, and motive according to how he/she behaves. In allocating the rewarded bonus, they take into account these pieces of information in addition to the relative contribution. On the other hand, since an allocation decision is deemed to communicate how an individual is treated (Lind & Tyler, 1988), the allocator recognizes that the coworker judges him/her according to the decision itself. The allocator thus manages his/her impression in front of the coworker. One strategy the allocator uses is to follow a general social norm to deal with the coworker (Chiu & Hong, 1997; Deutsch, 1985). The minimal interaction paradigm adopted by previous researchers just captures the one snapshot of an individual's fairness judgment, filters these pieces of relevant information, and over-simplifies the nature of people's social interactions. It fails to see the effect of social interactional factors.

When the two coworkers have a chance to interact during their work, they will try to reach interpersonal harmony by generating and maintaining a positive social-emotional atmosphere. If one participant acts accommodatingly and behaves in an agreeable manner, the other will be pleased and form a positive impression of the individual. When the latter is asked to divide the obtained bonus, he/she will consider not only the partner's contribution but also how the partner behaves during their interaction.

Zhang (2000) examined the reward distribution between two strangers who have neither past interactive experience nor future interaction. Participants were asked to read a scenario regarding two strangers' collaboration on a task, which is similar to that adopted in the previous two studies. The high performer would act as the allocator. The behavior of the low performer during the work was detailed differently in the three groups. In the first condition, the stranger does not greet the allocator when arriving at the office, and then totally concentrates on the job. This stranger goes out for a break, and never talks with the high performer during the work ("no talk" group). In the second condition, the stranger warmly greets the other when arriving at the office, and chats with him/her during the break ("chat" group). The stranger in the third condition warmly greets his/her partner allocator when arriving at the office, talks with the coworker during the break, and offers him/her a better ball-pen to complete the task ("do favor" group).

Having read the scenario, each participant in the three conditions was instructed to be in the high performer's position and to divide the bonus. Participants were also asked to assess the stranger's personal characteristics such as whether he/she is warm, helpful, and friendly, and whether this person has a feeling of *renqing* as well as their behavioral responses to the partner including whether they like him/her and whether they would like to have further interactions with the stranger.

Participants' allocations, their judgments of the stranger's personal attributes, as well as their behavioral responses to him/her, were quite different in the three conditions. Participants in the "no talk" and "chat" groups differed in ratings of all six items, and participants in the "chat" and "do favor" groups significantly differed in ratings on five items except "friendliness." The three groups of participants differed in their perception of whether the stranger was helpful, friendly, and warm.

Zhang and Yang (2001) reported that the Chinese conception of *renqing* implies an individual's good nature including being helpful, friendly, and warm. It was shown that participants in the "chat" and "do favor" groups perceived the stranger has the feeling of *renqing* to a greater degree than the "no talk" group. The different person perceptions of the coworkers in the three conditions confirm Zhang and Yang's (2001) findings on *renqing*.

The coworker's behavior also affects the allocator's decision. In the "no talk" group, the allocation was nearly in proportion to the stranger's contribution. The coworker in the "chat" group was depicted as a friendly person, and in the "do favor" group as one willing to do favors for the allocator as well as having a friendly nature. Our study showed that Chinese individuals generally have a positive attitude to people who show *renqing* (Zhang & Yang, 2001). Participants in the "chat" and "do favor" groups judged that the stranger had more *renqing* than the "no talk" group and they made greater allocations than for the "no talk" group. The coworker in the "do favor" group did a favor for the allocator, and the allocator reciprocated with greater allocations. In Chinese culture, *renqing* requires a person to reciprocate another's help or favor (Zhang & Yang, 2001). In this sense, *renqing* implies the norm of reciprocity (Goulder, 1960).

The allocation decision is made according to the coworker's social characteristics instead of contributions. The finding suggests that individuals are sensitive to social interactional cues, based on which they judge whether their partners have desirable personality traits and attitudes. The perception in turn influences their decisions toward the partner. Past reward allocation researchers who employed the minimal interaction paradigm have failed to consider the influence of social interaction. Some justice theorists have used interactional justice (Bies & Moag, 1986) and interpersonal justice (Colquitt, 2001) to refer to the fairness of the interpersonal treatment received during the enactment of decision-making procedures. However, most empirical studies on interactional justice or interpersonal justice have focused on people's perception of fairness when they are treated in a certain way. However, our study shows that the reward decision-makers tend to consider how they are treated socially by the other and vary their treatment of the other accordingly.

The Judgment of *Guanxi* and Reward Allocation

Outsiders can judge the type or the nature of the relationship between two persons from their interaction. This judgment also influences the outsider's distribution of rewards between the two parties. Zhang's (2000) study confirmed this prediction.

This study used the scenario-based experiment in which participants were exposed to hypothetical situations. There were two experimental groups and one control group. The experimental groups were presented with two scenarios, with the first concerning a gift exchange between two colleagues, and the second regarding the two colleagues' collectively working on a job. The control group was only presented with the second scenario.

The gift exchange scenario described person A giving a present to person B, after which B either reciprocated with a gift of equivalent value a few days later ("short interval" condition), or gave A a gift a few months later on A's birthday ("long interval" condition). In this scenario, three variables were manipulated: (a) the time between receiving and return, (b) the comparability of the benefit returned to that received, and (c) the occasion on which the benefit was returned. After they read the scenario, participants were required to judge of the quality of the *guanxi* between the two colleagues.

Participants in all the three conditions were asked to read the second scenario. This scenario delineated that the above two individuals do a job for their organization and get a joint reward of 100. A's contribution to the task was 70%, and B's 30%. Person A was asked to divide the reward. Participants were asked to estimate the amount of money person A would give person B.

The two parties' relationship was judged to be closer in the "long interval" condition than the "short interval" condition. Participants in the "long interval" condition not only judged that A liked B more, but also inferred that the frequencies of their past contacts and future interactions were much higher than the "short interval" condition. The result is consistent with previous theories. Researchers have suggested that, the greater correspondence in the type and value of the gifts received and returned, the less affective component exists in the relationship (Roloff, 1987; Schwartz, 1967), and the noncomparability of the benefits given and taken as well as the flexibility of the time gap between receiving and return are two salient cues to the existence of friendship (Clark, 1981; Roloff, 1987).

Allocations under the two experiment groups differed significantly, and the allocation in the "short interval" condition was much less than that in the control group. The allocation in the "long interval" condition was much more than that in the control group. Chinese people hold a heuristic theory on the closeness of relationships between individuals, and they make their judgments based on their interactions with particular partners. They also believe that individuals who have engaged in a certain type of relationship will treat each other in a particular manner, for example, showing generosity towards others with whom one has a close relationship. People understand the relational norms and predict individuals' behavior in general and allocation decisions in particular according to the social norms. This study once again demonstrated that an individual's reward allocation is greatly influenced by how individuals interact with each other in distributive situations.

In conclusion, the four studies reported above show that an individual's distribution of rewards is not just motivated by the maximization of self-interest. Allocation decisions are affected by many social-contextual factors, including the affective quality of the coworkers' relationship, their interactions, the social-emotional climate in the situation, and even the general norms governing social exchange. In particular, individuals are concerned with their relationship with others and how others treat them. Underlying these concerns are people's motivations to fulfill the obligations inherent in a social relationship and to maintain interpersonal harmony with others.

In these studies, participants were provided with the information regarding the coworkers' relationship or interaction in addition to the two parties' relative contribution to a task. Such a rich-context research paradigm can capture the dynamic nature of an individual's allocation decision-making process and the interpersonal facet of distributive justice.

PRELIMINARY CONCLUSIONS ON CHINESE
CONCEPTION OF JUSTICE

The findings reported above indicate that Chinese people have a different conception of justice or have different perceptions of fairness from Westerners. Based on these findings and that of previous research, some conclusions on Chinese conceptions of justice may be drawn.

Buchanan and Mathieu (1986) suggested that different views of human beings will lead to different conceptions of justice. Western theories and research on justice have resulted from the American culture's economic socialization practices that emphasize agency, individualism, and competition (Sampson, 1975). As most of the individuals are motivated by a need or desire to maximize their own outcomes, allocation behavior or decision is considered as an instrumental and rational act.

Chinese individuals are characterized by relational or social orientation (Ho, Chen, & Chiu, 1991; Yang, 1995), and they are more concerned about how others look at them and are very sensitive to the way they are treated by others. In distributive situations, how allocators make allocations is considered a signal indicating their attitude and treatment. Some theorists have noted that fairness judgments communicate symbolic messages for the individuals who are involved, such as whether they are treated with respect and sensitivity (Bies & Moag, 1986; Lind & Tyler, 1988). However, these scholars have considered this aspect as international justice or procedural justice rather than a facet of distributive justice[1].

In Zhang and Yang's (1998) study, when two groups of participants were asked to make allocation under the instruction of "to be fair" (*he li*) and "to be equitable" (*gong zheng*), it was found that the two allocations were not different. However, the "equitable" and "fair" allocations for each of the six relational partners were much higher than the average allocation based on the equity norm reported in Western literature.

Zhang and Yang's (1998) study shows that *guanxi* considerably influences the distribution of rewards. Allocations for the six partners correspond to the closeness of an individual's *guanxi* with them. The close *guanxi* with family members or close friends either brings with it a strong obligation or implies a good interactive experience between them. Allocators are obligated to offer more rewards to them and make the distribution to their advantage. In contrast, the *guanxi* with acquaintances and strangers implies weak obligations, and an allocator who has made the higher contribution to the task makes the distribution of rewards according to contributions, which is beneficial to himself/herself. These results are very robust and have been consistently found in previous studies (Chu & Yang, 1976; Hui, Triandis, and Yee, 1991; Leung & Bond, 1984).

Based on these findings, this author suspects that the Chinese conception of justice may consist of two components: one is the Western conception of equity and the other is the obligation prescribed by *guanxi*. While the former guarantees that allocations are made at least according to the participants' contributions (30% in Zhang & Yang's study), the latter assures that allocators grant an additional allocation to represent their fulfillment of obligations to close relational partners. In other words, Chinese conceptions of justice require individuals to fulfill the obligations implied

---

[1] Recently, Greenberg (1993) suggested that the respect and sensitivity aspects of interactional justice might be considered as interpersonal facets of distributive justice because they alter reactions to decision outcomes.

in their social roles or relationships. Similarly, Chiu and Hong (1997) proposed that Chinese conceptions of justice are closely tied to an individual's role requirements as well as their group membership. Hwang (1991) also related Confucian justice to the fulfillment of social obligations. One of Chiu's studies revealed that fulfillment of role expectation is a good predictor of Chinese justice judgments (see Chiu, 1991a). In Chinese societies, people have to fulfill their obligations and meet the expectations imposed on them. Therefore, a person's judgment of fairness is not based on purely rational calculations, but is influenced by the prescribed rules which dictate what social members should and should not do.

On the other hand, Chinese conceptions of justice are also related to *renqing*. As Chinese people expect to maintain interpersonal harmony with others, they tend to express *renqing* for others by caring for their welfare, fulfilling relational obligations, and expressing positive emotions. In a distributive situation, individuals who rigidly follow the equity norm in dealing with close *guanxi* partners are regarded as a "cold-blooded" without a feeling for *renqing*. As a kind of emotion, *renqing* refers to Hu's (1949) assumed emotion. It is similar to what Markus and Kitayama (1991) labeled other-focused emotion. As an other-focus emotion, *renqing* represents a feeling of interpersonal communion that has other persons as the primary referent, and results from one's being sensitive to others. Expressing *renqing* helps Chinese individuals to facilitate the reciprocal exchanges and to reinforce them to be bound with others. It is almost compulsory for Chinese people to express *renqing* in order to operate effectively in social interactions.

Previous scholars have linked Chinese conceptions of justice with *renqing* (Chiu, 1991a; Hwang, 1991). While Western conceptions of justice emphasize rationality and self-interest, Chinese conceptions of justice are inseparable from *renqing*. In this regard, Chinese justice implies interpersonal responsiveness. As Miller (1994) claimed, interpersonal responsiveness and caring hold different moral status from justice obligations. Justice concerns are general and rationally grounded, but interpersonal expectations are particularistic and affectively based. This may be the greatest difference between Chinese and Western conceptions of justice.

In conclusion, our research findings clearly demonstrate that Chinese reward allocation decisions are influenced by the relationship between the partners, by their past interactions and anticipated social interactions, and by the present experience of the interaction. The role of *guanxi* (interpersonal connections) and *renqing* (human emotion) in reward allocation decisions suggest that Chinese conceptions of justice are related to the obligation in relationships and social norms requiring people to treat others in a proper way. These conclusions are preliminary, and await systematic empirical investigation.

AUTHOR'S NOTE

The author wishes to thank Chung-fang Yang for her supervision of the research described here, and Chi-yue Chiu and David F. Y. Ho for their helpful suggestions.

REFERENCES

Adams, J. S. (1965). Inequity in social exchange. In L. Berkowitz (Ed.), *Advances in experimental social psychology, Vol. 2* (pp. 267–299). New York: Academia Press.

Bies, R. J., & Moag, J. F. (1986). Interactional justice: Communication criteria of fairness. In R. J. Lewicki, B. H. Sheppard, & M. H. Bazerman (Eds.), *Research on negotiations in organizations Vol. 1*, (pp. 43–55). Greenwich, CT: JAI Press.

Buchanan, A. & Mathieu, D. (1986). Philosophy and justice. In R. L. Cohen (Ed.), *Justice: Views from the social sciences* (pp. 11–45). New York: Plenum Press.

Chen, C. C., Meindl, J. R., & Hunt, R. G. (1997). Testing the effects of vertical and horizontal collectivism: A study of reward allocation preferences in China. *Journal of Cross-cultural Psychology, 28*, 44–70.

Chiu, C. (1991a). Righteousness: The notion of justice in Chinese societies. In C. F. Yang & H. S. R. Kao (Eds.), *Chinese people and Chinese mind: The cultural tradition* (pp. 261–285). Taipei, Taiwan: Yuan-Liu Publishing Co. (in Chinese)

Chiu, C. (1991b). Role expectation as the principal criterion used in justice judgment among Hong Kong college students. *Journal of Psychology, 125*, 557–565.

Chiu, C. (1991c). Hierarchical social relations and justice judgment among Hong Kong Chinese college students. *Journal of Social Psychology, 131*, 885–887.

Chiu, C., & Hong, Y. (1997). Justice from a Chinese perspective. In H. S. R. Kao & D. Sinha (Eds.), *Asian perspectives on psychology* (pp. 164–184). New Delhi, India: Sage Publications.

Chu, J. L., & Yang, K. S. (1976). The effect of relative performance and individual modernity on distributive behavior among Chinese students. *Bulletin of the Institute of Ethnology, Academia Sinica, 41*, 79–95. (in Chinese)

Clark, M. S. (1981). Noncomparability of benefits given and received: A cue to the existence of friendship. *Social Psychology Quarterly, 44*, 375–381.

Colquitt, J. A. (2001). On the dimensionality of organizational justice: A construct validation of a measure. *Journal of Applied Psychology, 86*, 386–400.

Cropanzana, R., & Greenberg, J. (1997). Progress in organizational justice: Tunneling through the maze. *International Review of Industrial and Organizational Psychology, 12*, 317–372.

Deutsch, M. (1975). Equity, equality, and need: What determines which values will be used as the basis of distributive justice? *Journal of Social Issues, 31*, 137–149.

Deutsch, M. (1985). *Distributive justice: A social-psychological perspective.* New Haven: Yale University Press.

Gergen, K. J., Morse, S. J., & Gergen, M. M. (1980). Behavior exchange in a cross-cultural perspective. In H. C. Triandis, & R. W. Brislin (Eds.), *Handbook of cross-cultural psychology*, Vol.5 (pp. 121–154). Boston, MA: Allyn & Bacon.

Gouldner, A. W. (1960). The norm of reciprocity: A preliminary statement. *American Sociological Review, 25*, 161–178.

Greenberg, J. (1993). The social side of fairness: Interpersonal and informational classes of organizational justice. In R. Cropanzano (Ed.), *Justice in the workplace: Approaching fairness in human resource management* (pp. 79–103). Hillsdale, NJ: Erlbaum.

Gudykunst, W. B., & Ting-Toomey, S. (1988). *Culture and interpersonal communication.* Newbury Park, CA: Sage Publications.

Ho, D. Y. F., Chan, S. J., & Chiu, C. (1991). Relational orientation: An inquiry on the methodology of Chinese social psychology. In K. S. Yang & K. K. Hwang (Eds.), *Chinese psychology and behavior* (pp.49–66). Taipei, Taiwan: Kuei-Kuan Publishing Co. (in Chinese)

Hu, H. C. (1949). *Emotions, real and assumed, in Chinese society.* Unpublished manuscript. New York: Columbia University.

Hui, C. H., Triandis, H. C., & Yee, C (1991). Cultural differences in reward allocation: Is collectivism the explanation? *British Journal of Social Psychology, 30,* 145–157.

Hwang, K. K. (1987). Face and favor: The Chinese power game. *American Journal of Sociology, 92,* 944–974.

Hwang, K. K. (1991). The Confucian conception of justice. In K. S. Yang & K. K. Hwang (Eds.), *The psychology and behavior of the Chinese (1989)* (pp. 67–93). Taipei, Taiwan: Kuei-Kuan Press. (in Chinese)

Jacobs, B. J. (1979). A preliminary model of particularistic tie in Chinese political alliance: "*Renqing*" and "*guanxi*" in a rural Taiwanese Township. *China Quarterly, 78,* 237–273.

King, A. Y. C. (1980). An analysis of "*renqing*" in interpersonal relationships: A preliminary inquiry. In *Proceedings of the International Conference on Sinology.* Taipei, Taiwan: Academia Sinica. (in Chinese).

Lerner, M. J. (1975). The justice motive in social behavior: An introduction. *Journal of Social Issues, 31,* 1–20.

Leung, K., & Bond, M. H. (1984). The impact of cultural collectivism on reward allocation. *Journal of Personality and Social Psychology, 47,* 793–804.

Leventhal, G. S. (1980). What should be done with equity theory? New approaches to the study of fairness in social relationships. In K. J. Gergen, M. S. Greenberg, & R. H. Willis (Eds.), *Social exchange: Advances in theory and research* (pp. 27–55). New York: Plenum.

Li, M. C. (1993). The cultural difference of in-group favoritism: A comparison between Chinese and American undergraduates. In K. S. Yang & A. B. Yue (Eds.), *The psychology and behavior of the Chinese (1992)* (pp. 121–164). Taipei, Taiwan: Kuei-Kuan Publishing Co. (in Chinese)

Lind, E. A., & Tyler, T. R. (1988). *The social psychology of procedural justice.* New York: Plenum Press.

Markus, H., & Kitayama, S. (1991). Culture and the self: Implications for cognition, emotion, and motivation. *Psychological Review, 98,* 224–253.

Miller, J. G. (1994). Cultural diversity in the morality of caring: Individually oriented versus duty-based interpersonal moral code. *Cross-Cultural Research, 28,* 3–39.

Peng, K. (1999). Culture, dialectics, and reasoning about contradiction. *American Psychologist, 54,* 741–754.

Roloff, M. E. (1987). Communication and reciprocity within intimate relationships. In M. E. Roloff & G. R. Miller (Eds.), *Interpersonal process: New directions in communication research* (pp. 11–38). Beverly Hills, CA: Sage Publications.

Sampson, E. E. (1975). On justice as equality. *Journal of Social Issues, 31,* 45–64.

Schwartz, B. (1967). The social psychology of the gift. *American Journal of Sociology, 73,* 1–11.

Shapiro, E. G. (1975). Effect of expectations of future interaction on reward allocations in dyads: Equity or equality. *Journal of Personality and Social Psychology, 31,* 873–880.

Tornblom, K. Y. (1992). The social psychology of distributive justice. In K. Scherer (Ed.), *Justice: interdisciplinary perspectives* (pp. 177–285). Cambridge: University Press.

Tu, W. M. (1976). *Centrality and commonality: An essay on cheung-yung.* University of Hawaii Press.

Tversky, A., & Kahneman, D. (1974). Judgement under uncertainty: Heuristics and biases. *Science, 185,* 1124–31.

Walster, E., Berscheid, E., & Walster, G. W. (1973). New directions in equity research. *Journal of Personality and Social Psychology, 25,* 151–176.

Yang, C. F. (2000). Psychocultural foundation of informal groups: The issues of loyalty, sincerity, and trust. In L. Dittmer, H. Fukui, & P. N. S. Lee (Eds.), *Informal politics in East Asia* (pp.85–105). New York: Cambridge University Press.

Yang, C. F. & Hui, C. H. (1986). Reward allocation behavior and feeling of unfairness. *Chinese Journal of Psychology, 28,* 61–71. (in Chinese).

Yang, K. S. (1995). Chinese social orientation: An integrative analysis. In T. Y. Lin, W. S. Tseng, & E. K. Yeh (Eds.), *Chinese societies and mental health* (pp. 19–39). Hong Kong: Oxford University Press.

Zhang, Z. X. (2001). The effects of frequency of social interaction and relationship closeness on reward allocation. *Journal of Psychology, 135,* 154–164.

Zhang, Z. X. (2000). *Sensing contextual cues in reward allocation: The effect of situational factors.* Paper presented at the 15th Annual Conference of the Society of Industrial and Organizational Psychology, April, 2000. New Orleans, Louisiana.

Zhang, Z., & Yang, C. F. (1998). Beyond distributive justice: The reasonableness norm in Chinese reward allocation. *Asian Journal of Social Psychology, 1,* 253–269.

Zhang, Z. X., & Yang, C. F. (2001). An investigation of the concept of renqing. In C. F. Yang (Ed.), *Interpersonal relationship, trust, and affect* (pp. 223–246). Taipei: Yuan Liu. (in Chinese)

Chapter 19

Family, Parent-Child Relationship, and Academic Achievement in Korea
Indigenous, Cultural, and Psychological Analysis

Young-Shin Park and Uichol Kim

During the past century, South Korea (abbreviated as Korea) experienced dramatic social and cultural changes. After 35 years of oppressive Japanese colonial rule (1910–1945), Korea was arbitrarily divided along the ideological line by the Soviet Union and the United States (abbreviated as U.S.) in 1945. The devastating Korean War broke out in 1950 in which more than a million people lost their lives and millions more were dislocated and separated from their family members. It was followed by a decade of economic, social, and political turmoil (Kim, 2001a).

In 1960, Korea had all the problems of a resource-poor, low-income, illiterate, and under-developed nation (Kim, 2001a; Park & Kim, 2004a). Korea was one of the poorest nations in the world, with per capita GNP at a meagre $82. The vast majority of people were dependent on agricultural products produced on scarce farmland. The infant mortality rate was one of the highest in the world: 124/1,000 live births for children under the age of five. From 1965, however, the Korean society has been dramatically transformed, with the economy growing at an average annual rate of over 8%. The per capita GNP increased to $1,640 in 1981 and to $14,100 in 2004. By 2002, the infant mortality rate was dramatically reduced to nine.

The phenomenal economic growth and social change in Korea have been spurred by educational transformations (Park & Kim, 2004b). In 1965, only 54% of elementary school continued to the middle school. The school enrollment reached 99% for middle school in 1985 and for high school in 1995 (Korea Educational Development Institute, 2003). By 1983, Korea had the highest percentage of adolescents wishing to obtain a university degree (85%), followed by the U.S. (81%), Thailand (69%), Japan (62%), England (50%), and France (38%) (Korea Educational Development Institute, 1983).

In 1998, 98% of Korean parents wanted their children to obtain at least a college degree (Im, 1998). Korean parents wanted to educate their children for the following reasons: Education provides access to obtaining a desirable job (37%); it is a method of cultivating a moral character (35%); it helps children to improve their natural talent and interests (14%); it increases their chances of finding a good marriage partner (9%); and it can compensate for their own low educational status (6%) (Korea Educational Development Institute, 1995). Currently, adult literacy rate stands at 98%, youth literacy rate is 100%, and more than 80% of students enroll in a college or university (Korea National Statistics Bureau, 2005).

The purpose of this chapter is to examine factors that influence academic achievement of Korean children and adolescents. In the first part section, the authors review the results of international studies of academic achievement. In the second section, the authors trace the changes in the traditional parent-child relationship. Although the structural features of the family have changed, the basic features of parental socialization that emphasize sacrifice, devotion and educational aspirations remain strong. This type of socialization practices instills a sense of indebtedness, respect, and emotional closeness in their children and it is responsible for high academic aspirations and achievement. In the third section of this chapter, the influence of Confucianism and educational system is reviewed. In the fourth section, a series of empirical studies that used indigenous methodology to examine the relationship between parent-child relationship and academic achievement is reviewed. These results challenge traditional psychological and educational theories emphasize biology (i.e., innate ability, intelligence), individualistic values (e.g., intrinsic motivation, ability attribution and self-esteem) and structural features (e.g., high educational spending, small class size and individualized instruction). Indigenous psychological analyses can provide a powerful and rigorous understanding of parent-child relationship and academic achievement in Korea.

INTERNATIONAL STUDIES OF ACADEMIC ACHIEVEMENT

In international studies of academic achievement of middle-school students (39-nation study of Grade 8 students, National Center for Educational Statistics, 2000, abbreviated as TIMSS) and in the 31-nation study of Grade 9 students (Organisation for Economic Cooperation and Development, 2003, abbreviated as PISA), Korean students are top achievers in mathematics, science, and reading literacy. In TIMSS (2000), Korean students are ranked second in mathematics and fifth in sciences. In PISA (2003), Korean students are ranked first in sciences, second in mathematics, and sixth in reading literacy.

Students from the U.S. perform far below their Korean counterparts. They are ranked 19th in mathematics and 18th in sciences (TIMSS, 2000). In PISA (2003), they are ranked 15th in reading literacy, 19th in mathematical literacy, and 14th in scientific literacy. Follow-up studies conducted in 2003 indicated a similar pattern of results (PISA, 2004; TIMSS, 2004).

These results baffle many psychologists and educators since they are inconsistent with existing psychological and educational theories. Traditional psychological and educational theories that emphasize biology (e.g., innate ability, I.Q.), individualistic values (e.g., intrinsic motivation, ability attribution, self-esteem), and structural features (e.g., high educational spending, small classes, and individualized instruction) cannot explain the relatively poor performance of American students and high performance of Korean students.

First, although the U.S. government spends more than twice the amount per student than Korean government and the class size of U.S. schools are much smaller, Korean students perform much better than American students. Second, although American students perform relatively poorly in mathematics and science, they have high self-esteem for these subjects. They are ranked first in self-esteem for science and fourth for mathematics (TIMSS, 2000). By contrast, Korean students had relatively low self-esteem: 32nd in self-esteem for mathematics and 21st for self-esteem in sciences. Similar pattern of results has been found in subsequent studies (PISA, 2004; TIMSS, 2004) forcing researchers to question the validity of self-esteem measures and theories.

Third, as to the motivation for studying math, 41% of U.S. students strongly endorsed the personal motivation (i.e., it is "to get the desired job") (TIMSS, 2000). However, only 10% of Korean students strongly endorsed the personal motivation. For Korean students, 85% agreed that it is to "enter a desired university" (social motivation) and 62% agreed that it is "to please their parents" (relational motivation). For Korean students, relational and social motivations outweighed the personal motivation.

Fourth, in developmental psychology, Freudian, Piagetian, behavioral, and humanistic theories do not systematically examine the role played by parents. Although attachment theory examines the role of parents, it affirms individualistic values by asserting that separation and individuation are necessary for healthy human development (Bowlby, 1969). In Korea, parents play a central role in child development by defining the goals of socialization, teaching children the necessary cognitive, linguistic, relational, and social skills, and providing them with a supportive family environment (Park & Kim, 2004a). Parents play a central role throughout a child's life, even through adulthood, and the maintenance of strong familial relationships is the key to understanding the educational and success and maintaining a high quality of life (Kim & Park, 2004; Park & Kim, 2004b).

Fifth, concepts such as guilt have a very different connotation in Korea (Kim & Park, Chapter 2; Park & Kim, 2004a). In many Western psychological theories, guilt is presumed to reflect irrational beliefs, neurotic fears, or forbidden wishes. The extensive experience of guilt is believed to cause developmental problems in adolescence and adulthood. In Korea, it is considered appropriate that children feel guilty and indebted toward their parents for all the devotion, indulgence, sacrifice, and love that they have received (Park & Kim, 2004a). Children feel indebted to their parents because they cannot return the love and care that they have received. Guilt in Korea has a positive aspect and it is viewed as an important interpersonal emotion that promotes filial piety, achievement motivation, and relational closeness.

KOREAN CULTURE, FAMILY, AND SOCIAL CHANGE

In contrast to Western philosophy that emphasizes the individual uniqueness, separateness, and abstracted identities, Confucian worldview focuses on relations and emotions that bind individuals and family members together (Kim, 2001b). The Korean word for human being is *ingan* (人間, "human between"). In other words, the human essence is basically relational and it can be defined in terms of what happens between individuals and not solely within an individual. Mencius stated that: "If you see a child drowning and you don't feel compassion, you are not a human being." It is compassion that helps us to relate to the child and propels us to take the necessary risks to save the child's life. It is the *in* (仁, "human-heartedness") that binds parent and children and becomes the basis of all human relationships (Kim & Park, Chapter 2). Maintenance of human relationship is considered basic, moral, and imperative.

Confucianism has influenced all facets of Korean society: Conception of self, family relationship, education, and organizational life (Kim, 2001b; Kim & Park, Chapter 2). Relationships and not individuals are considered to be a basic unit and parent-child relationship provides the basis of the development of the self. Parental devotion and indulgence are two important features of the traditional socialization practice which still remain in modern Korea (Kim & Choi, 1994; Park & Kim, 2004a). In Korea, parents view unselfish devotion and sacrifice to their children as their basic role and duty.

For many Korean women, motherhood is their single most important role (Kim & Choi, 1994; Park & Kim, 2004a). A Korean mother's self is not abandoned, but extended to that of her children. It is not a case of self-denial, but of self-transformation, becoming one with their children. The life-goal for Korean mothers become closely and intrinsically attached to their children (Park & Kim, 2004a). Korean mothers see their children as extensions of themselves. Children's accomplishments become their own and children vicariously fulfill their dreams and goals. For Korean mothers, attaining this vicarious gratification is one of the most important personal goals (Gallup Korea, 1985; Park & Kim, 2004a). The relational orientation of Korean mothers is best evidenced by their persistent and enduring support for their children throughout their lives. Even adults report that their parents provide strong emotional support and they are important figures enabling them to succeed in life (Kim & Park, 2003; Park, Kim & Tak, 2002).

Traditional Family Structure and Relationship

In traditional Korean society, socialization begins from the onset of pregnancy, with the umbilical cord symbolizing the connectedness between the mother and the child. During pregnancy, a mother is taught to think, feel, and act on behalf of the baby in the womb. When the child is born, the physical bond is transformed into psychological and relational bonds. To maintain and cultivate the close mother-child relationship, a mother remains close to the child to make the child feel secure, to make the boundary between herself and the child minimal, and to meet all of the needs of the child. Children's strong dependency needs, both emotional and physical, are satisfied by their mother's indulgent devotion, even if it means a tremendous sacrifice on her own part.

A child's psychological and physical well-being is considered the prime responsibility of the mother. It is the role of the mother to indulge the child and gratify children's wishes as much as possible. In weaning, toilet training, and bedtime, a tremendous degree of flexibility is exercised (Kim & Choi, 1994; Park & Kim, 2004a). Children are not forced to eat by themselves until the age of three. Even at this age, if children do not show any intention to do so, they are not pressured. Bedtime is not strictly enforced and is usually determined by the child. Emotional relatedness, not independence, is emphasized during infancy.

As children mature, they sense that it is through the mother that they obtain gratification, security, and love. As such, children become motivated to maintain the close relationship. They do so by gradually taking a more active role by attempting to please their mothers and behaving according to their mothers' wishes. The feeling of relational dependence helps children to incorporate their mothers' values and beliefs as their own. They learn to develop a strong sense of *proxy* control (Bandura, 1997) in which children learn that it is through their mothers their physical and psychological needs can be satisfied.

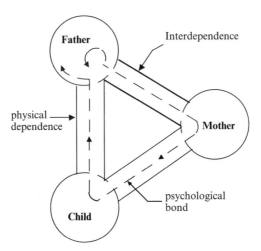

Figure 1. Triadic relationship

The mother uses her strong emotional bond to encourage the child to extend himself or herself to others, such as the father, siblings, and teachers. The role of the father is to educate the child for society and he becomes an active socializing agent when the child is about four or five years old. A mother represents the inner world of acceptance and indulgence and the father represents the outside world of strictness, rules, and responsibility (Park & Kim, 2004a). The role that a father and mother plays is differentiated and complementary and it is best summarized in a popular Korean phrase *umbu jamo* (嚴父慈母, "strict father, benevolent mother"). In a mother-child relationship, a mother shows her devotion to her child through sacrifice and indulgence (i.e., it flows downward, from a mother to a child). (See Figure 1). In a father-child relationship, children are required to display their devotion to their father through obedience, respect, and compliance (i.e., it flows upward, from a child to a father).

Figure 2 depicts a prototypical extended family structure in the traditional agricultural communities. The three-generations-in-one-roof was considered as the basic family unit. Although Confucius considered the father-son relationship to be primary, it is the relationship between the husband and wife that is basic. Through the union of husband and wife children are born and the family is maintained. In the traditional extended family, the role of each family member is defined and prescribed.

As the symbolic head of the household, the father represents the family and makes decision concerning the family. The father represents a link between the family and the outside the world. Through the father, children are linked across time (i.e., through his lineage) and across space (i.e., through his position in the community). It is the responsibility of the father to maintain, propagate, and elevate the position of the family. When

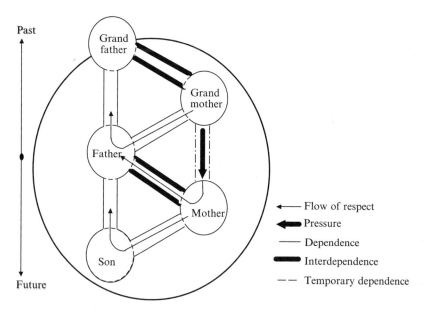

Figure 2. Extended family

making a decision, he must consider implication of his decision on the particular individual, family, lineage, and community. Wisdom and foresight are essential ingredients of the decision-making process in order to maintain harmony. Children are considered not capable of understanding such a complex process and they are required obey, respect, and abide by fathers' decision. From children's perspective, it often means sacrificing personal interests for the benefit of the family.

One of the prime responsibilities of the father is to give birth of a son, who can continue the family line. Without a son, the lineage of the family can come to a stop. The other main responsibility is to educate his son so that he will be able carry on the family name and to represent the family. As the symbolic head of the household, he holds the authority to represent the family, to speak and act on behalf of the family, but not against the family. For example, property was the communal possession of a family, and not the father (Kim & Lee, 1994). Although he had the right to dispose of the property for the benefit of the family, the other family members also had rights to the property (Kim & Lee, 1994). An arbitrary decision by the father against the family was considered uncustomary and an illegitimate act (Kim & Lee, 1994). A father had the authority, duty, and responsibility of handling family property on behalf of the family and not for himself.

Mother is responsible for raising children, ensuring that children respect and obey their father, taking care of elderly parents and extended family members, and managing the household affairs. She socializes her sons and daughters differently. The son is taught to be a leader and to become a breadwinner and the daughter is taught to follow and to support her future husband and family. Once the daughter is married, she is considered a member of her husband's family and no longer a member of her birth family. The mother is responsible for managing the household affairs, including household finance, maintaining social relationships, and ensuring that the children are properly socialized. She is also responsible for ensuring that the daughter-in-law is respectful to her son and actively participates in the socialization of the grandchildren. While the father represents the outside world, mother represents the inside world of family and she is responsible for maintaining harmony in interpersonal relationships.

The age of 60 represents a full cycle in one's life: It represents a second birth. At this age, the father typically passes his property and power to his eldest son and the son becomes responsible for managing the family affairs. He takes on the role of the grandfather. Similarly, the mother passes her role and responsibility to the eldest daughter-in-law and takes on the role of the grandmother. They no longer hold major responsibilities and they are to be taken care of and indulged like children.

In Korea, the conception of past and future are relationally based. Ancestors represent the past and children represent the future. It is important to pay respect to the ancestors since it is through one's ancestor one has come into being. Even in modern Korea, people pay respect to their ancestors by bowing to them in their grave and symbolically sharing a meal with them. Grandparents are a living testimony and linkage to the past. Children, on the other hand, represent the future of the family and as such tremendous emotional, financial, and social investments are made for them and in them.

Social and Cultural Change

With modernization, urbanization, and industrialization, the traditional extended families have virtually disappeared. Currently, less than one in ten families have three generations living under one roof (Korean National Statistics Bureau, 2005). In 1975, the average size of household was more than five, but this number was reduced to three in 2004, even in rural areas (Korean National Statistics Bureau, 2005). While the economy has rapidly grown, fertility rate has seen a dramatic decrease. The fertility rate of 6.0 in 1960 has been reduced to 1.17 in 2004 (Kim, Park, Kwon & Koo, 2005).

With modernization, urbanization, and industrialization, the nuclear family structure has replaced the traditional extended family. Although grandparents no longer play a significant role in family life, the core family structure has remained the same (Kim et al., 2005). (See Figure 3). In the modern nuclear family, the role of educating children has transferred

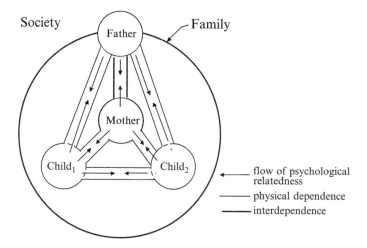

Figure 3. Nuclear family

to the mother. It is the responsibility of the mother to educate the children and to ensure they succeed academically. She serves as a mediator between her children and the school and it is her primary role to ensure that the children succeed academically (Park & Kim, 2004b). In addition, mothers are financial managers at home, responsible for handling and investing household income. In some case, mothers are also required to work outside the home to increase the family income. In this situation, her workload has doubled, being responsible for the family and her career.

Although many people assume that Korea has simply adopted Western values, this is not the case. Although capitalism, industrialization, urbanization, science and technology have been adopted, the underlying cultural values that emphasize human-relatedness remain strong. Western commerce, industries, and institutions became modified to fit underlying Korean values that emphasize human-relatedness and collective solidarity (Kim, 2001a). The main change that occurred is a shift from status quo, conservatism, and harmony with nature to change, progress, and control of the environment. (See Table 1). Traditionally, learning has been linked to Confucian Classics and literature. Currently, success is defined in terms of acquiring scientific and technological knowledge. The primary role of the parents is to educate their children in a highly competitive world. Traditionally, women did not receive a formal education, but currently both men and women have to be educated to succeed in life. Sex-role differentiation and discrimination have diminished significantly in the family and schools, and to some extent in the workplace.

Family and inheritance laws have been changed to give greater equality to women. In 1990 Korean Civil Law Article 837 gave greater equality to

Table 1. Changes in values

Rural	Urban
Agricultural	Industrial
Past-oriented	Future-oriented
Extended-family	Nuclear family
Ancestor	Children
Status quo	Change
Conservatism	Progress
Harmony with nature	Control environment
Formalism	Pragmatism
Cooperation	Competition
Wisdom	Analytical skills
Sex differentiation	Equality

women (Kim et al., 2005). The Korean inheritance law guarantees rights of the wife, sons, and daughters as being basic and inalienable. Although the eldest son is allowed to receive a higher inheritance to perform ancestor ceremonies, the Supreme Court of Korea upheld a decision that the wife and other children have a basic right to the inheritance, even if it is denied in the will left by the deceased father (Kim et al., 2005). Also, the wife and children are responsible for the debt left by the deceased father. A mother has the same right to custody of the child as the father. From 2008, a child will have the right to take on the family name of the mother or the father.

Educational System

With the adoption of Confucianism about 2,000 years ago, individuals of merit were selected through regional and national examinations. During the Three Kingdom period, the Goguryo Kingdom (37 B.C. – 668 A.D.) established the National Confucian Academy in 373 (Kim & Park, 2000). The curriculum consisted of learning Confucian and Chinese classics. The National Examination system was established in 788 that allowed youths from aristocratic class to compete for a government position.

Successful candidates in the national examination were given a position as a government official (Kim & Park, 2000). In return for their services, they were given a large track of land from which they could acquire a stable income for three generation. Passing the national examination was considered to be one of the most important filial duties of a son. Educational success benefited the individual, family, and the lineage and it became the primary avenue to success.

The Confucian educational system was maintained until Japanese colonization in 1910. Highly centralized, bureaucratic, and authoritarian educational system that was modeled after German *völk* school was instituted in Korea. With the liberation of Korea from Japan in 1945, the U.S. educational system was adopted. The current educational system is thus a blend of Confucian, German and U.S. educational systems.

In modern Korea, mothers play a mediating role between the home and school environment. With the competitive academic environment, children spend most of their time preparing for their schoolwork and the entrance examination. It is the role of the mother to take care of their children's emotional, physical, relational, and financial needs. A mother's job is to use her close relationship with her child to encourage their children to expand their relationships and to succeed in life. She becomes a mediator between the home environment and the outside environment by socializing appropriate values and norm. As children grow up, they are expected to transfer their identification and loyalty from their mothers to teachers.

A typical climate of Korean schools affirms the strong relational bond, pressures the student to strive for excellence, and encourages students to cooperate in a group. Children are taught to please the teacher and their attention is focused on the teacher. Even in a class size that is as large as 50, Korean students are attentive, devoted to doing their schoolwork, and motivated to do well (Park & Kim, 2004b). There is a high degree agreement among adolescents, parents, and teachers about the value of academic achievement and how to attain it (Park & Kim, 2004b).

EMPIRICAL STUDIES

Qualitative Studies

A series of empirical studies were conducted from 1996 to examine factors that influence academic achievement of Korean students using the indigenous methodology. In 1996, focus group interviews were conducted with a sample of Korean students, teachers, and parents to explore the factors that influence academic achievement of children and adolescents (Ahn, Hwang, Kim & Park, 1997). In addition, ecological analysis of the school environment and the surrounding areas were conducted. These qualitative analyses indicated the important role played by parents, teachers, and friends and social support that they provided (Ahn et al., 1997).

Based on the above studies, an open-ended questionnaire was developed and administered to a cross-section of Korean students and adults (Kim & Park, 2003). A total of 1,157 respondents participated in the study, consisting of 730 students and 427 adults. Participants were asked to write down their important accomplishments, achievements, or successes in their lives. They are then asked to list the people who supported them and the type of support they received from them. They are asked to specify what

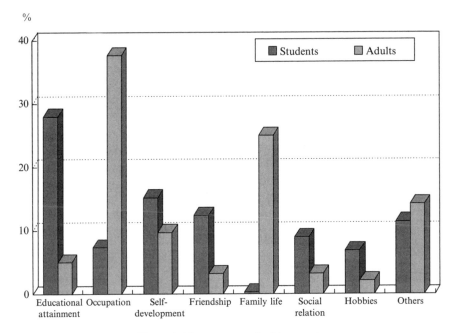

Figure 4. The most proud achievement

they consider to be the most important factor contributing to their success. A similar set of questions were asked about their failure experiences.

For the most proud achievement, students mentioned educational attainment, followed by self-development, friendship, and human relations. (See Figure 4). For the adult sample, occupational success was mentioned most frequently, followed by family life, self-development, and educational attainment.

When respondents were asked to list the person who provided social support, both students and adults mentioned their parents most frequently (students=35%, adults=27%). For the student sample, it was followed by friends (26%), teachers (15%), and other family members (6%). For the adult sample, it was followed by other family members (23%), colleagues (8%), and friends (8%). As for the type of social support received, both groups reported emotional support (students=35%, adults=34%), followed by advice (students=32%, adults=25%).

As for the most important factor that contributed to their success, for both groups self-regulation was listed as being the most important. (See Figure 5). The self-regulation category consisted of items such as effort, will, persistence, patience, and endurance. For the student sample, it was followed by family environment, social support, positive thinking, personality, and friends. For the adult sample, personality was the second

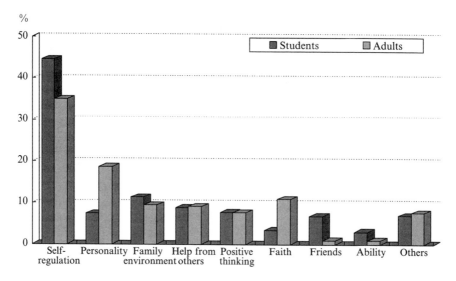

Figure 5. Most important reason for success

most frequent response, followed by religious faith, family environment, social support, and positive thinking.

As for their failure experiences, both groups listed academic failure as being the most painful failure experience (students=45%, adults=30%). In the student sample, it was followed by human relationship (22%), lack of self-management (20%), and problems in family life (5%). For the adult sample, it was followed by problems in family life (20%), lack of self-management (17%), human relationship (14%), and occupation (11%). In terms of the people who contributed most to the failure the student sample listed no one (25%), followed by friends (23%), myself (20%), and parents (8%). For the adults sample, other family members were listed most frequently (23%), followed by myself (18%), no one (14%), friends (14%), and parents (11%).

In terms of the most important factor that led to their failure, the student sample listed a lack of self-regulation, followed by personality problem, bad surrounding, myself, and a lack of ability. For the adult sample, the most important factor was personality problem, followed by a lack of self-regulation, bad surrounding, and a lack of ability.

In 2001, a follow-up study was conducted using a matched sample of Korean students and their parents (Park, Kim & Tak, 2002, 2005).[1] A total 481 students and 507 parents completed the same open-ended questionnaire as in the 1997 study. The results of the 2001 study paralleled the results of the 1997 study. The importance of educational success, social

---

[1] In 1998, the per capita GNP contracted by 32% and recovered to the 1997 level in 2001.

support received from parents, and self-regulation become more pronounced in 2001.

These results indicate Korean students view academic achievement and adults view occupational success as the most important accomplishment in their life. For the failure experience, both groups listed academic failure as being the most painful. In order to succeed in Korea, whether it is academic or occupational success, people believe that self-regulation is the most effective strategy. If they work hard and try their best, they believe that they can accomplish their desired goal. In contrast, a lack of self-regulation is responsible for their failures. The second most important factor for success was the social support received from parents. Even adults considered social support received from their parents as being very important. Thirdly, the type of support they received was affective in nature.

In contrast to the importance in self-regulation and social support, ability and environment factors were considered to be less important. Although personality was listed, the items in the category reveal that good personality was necessary for maintaining harmonious social relationship in school and at work. Overall, it appears that Korean respondents believe that success is contingent on self-regulation and maintaining harmonious interpersonal relationship, and they play down the role of ability and environmental factors.

The Role of Parents

The qualitative studies have revealed the importance that parents play in children's development and academic achievement. A series of studies have been conducted to examine the parent-child relationship as perceived by children and adolescents (Park & Kim, 2004a). Previous studies indicated that Korean and American adolescents view parental control very differently (Kim & Choi, 1994). Although American adolescents viewed parental control negatively, Korean adolescents viewed parental control as a sign of warmth and low neglect (Kim & Choi, 1994). This has been replicated with a sample of elementary, middle, and high school students in Korea (Park & Kim, 2000). In addition, parental achievement pressure was positively correlated with academic achievement and low delinquency among Korean students (Park & Kim, 2004b).

An opened-ended questionnaire was distributed to elementary, middle, and high school students in Korea and they were asked to write down what came into their mind when they thought about their mothers and fathers (Park & Kim, 2004a). The most frequent response was that they felt gratitude towards their parents, followed by respect, indebtedness, closeness, conflict and distance. In a follow-up study, a sample of Korean students (elementary school = 212, middle school = 267, high school = 284) were asked how much they felt respect, indebtedness, close, conflict and

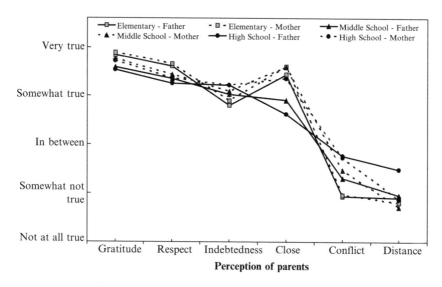

Figure 6. How Korean children perceive their parents

distance toward their mother and father on a 5-point scale and the reasons why they felt that way (Park, Kim & Han, 2003).

The results of the study are presented in Figure 6. (See Figure 6). Students are most likely feel gratitude, respect, indebtedness and closeness to their parents and much less likely to feel conflict or distance. The feeling of gratitude and respect is slightly higher among elementary school students, and the feeling of indebtedness is higher among middle school and high school students. The feeling of closeness is lower for middle and high school students, especially for fathers. Feeling of conflict is highest among high school students, followed by middle school students. The feeling of distance is highest for fathers among high school students, but differences for mothers were not found.

Students were then asked, in an open-ended format, the reasons behind their feeling gratitude, respect, indebtedness, close, conflict, and distance toward their parents. As for the reason for feeling gratitude towards their parents, the most frequent response was their sacrifice (father = 26%, mother = 50%), followed by their suffering for the family (father = 41%, mother = 22%), and by emotional support (father = 20%, mother = 17%). As for the reasons for respecting their parents, the most frequent response was their sacrifice (father = 35%, mother = 39%), sincerity (31%, mother = 27%), consanguinity (father = 12%, mother = 13%), and benevolence (father = 10%, mother = 11%).

As for the reason for feeling indebtedness to their parents, the most frequent response was failing to meet their expectations (father = 31%, mother

= 43%), followed by failing to obey them (father = 27%, mother = 43%), failing to be diligent in schoolwork (father = 19%, mother = 19%), and not being filial (father = 16%, mother = 14%). As for the reason for feeling close to their parents, the most frequent response was that parents understood them (father = 20%, mother = 27%), followed by feeling comfortable (father = 21%, mother = 22%), and consanguinity (father = 21%, mother = 17%).

As for the reason for having conflict with their parents, around a third of the students reported not having any conflicts (father = 37%, mother = 31%). For those students who reported having conflict with their parents, it was due to generational gap (father = 25%, mother = 28%) and academic achievement (father = 15%, mother = 18%). As for the reason for feeling distance with their parents, more than half of the students reported that they did not feel distance (father = 50%, mother = 63%). For those students who reported feeling distance with their parents, it was due a lack of communication (father = 16%, mother = 11%), followed by interpersonal difficulties (father = 11%, mother = 18%), and by generational gap (father = 8%, mother = 9%).

These results indicate that Korean adolescents have close parent-child relationship into their adulthood. They felt gratitude, respect, indebtedness, and close to their parents and they were much less likely to feel conflict or distance, regardless of their age. Although the feeling of gratitude and respect were lower for middle and high school students, the feeling of indebtedness was the highest among the high school students. Majority of the students did not feel distant to their parents and a third of the students reported not having any conflicts with their parents. This pattern of results has been found in a series of studies examining parent-child relationship in Korea (Kim et al., 2005; Kim, Park, Kim, Lee, & Yu, 2000; Park & Kim, 2000, 2004a, 2004b; Park, Kim & Chung, 2004).

Cross-Sectional and Longitudinal Studies

A cross-sectional study was conducted in 1998 to examine the factors that influence academic achievement of Korean students (Park & Kim, 2003a). A total of 961 elementary school, 898 middle school and 1,236 high school students completed a structured questionnaire. Approximately equal number of male and female students participated in the study. The questionnaire included the social support received from their father, mother, friends and teachers (developed by the present researcher), life-satisfaction scale (developed by Taft, 1986) and the self-efficacy scales developed by Bandura (1995). In addition, relational efficacy and efficacy for promoting social harmony developed by the presented researchers, have been included.

The results of the structural equation model for high school students are presented in Figure 7. The goodness-of-fit for all three models were at

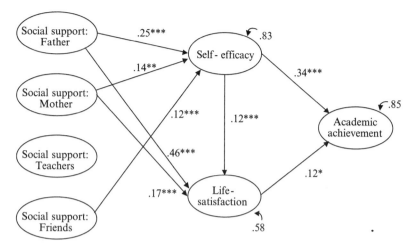

Note: * p<.05, ** p<.01, *** p<.001
Adapted from Park, Kim, Chung, Lee, Kwon and Yang (2000)

Figure 7. Predictors of academic achievement and life-satisfaction

the acceptable level (Park & Kim, 2003a). (See Figure 7). The results indicated that self-efficacy has a direct and positive influence life-satisfaction and academic achievement. Life-satisfaction has a positive influence on academic achievement. Support received from parents and friends has a direct and positive influence on self-efficacy, while support received from teachers is not significant. Support received from parents has a direct positive influence on life-satisfaction.

For middle school students, a similar pattern of results has been obtained. Self-efficacy has a direct and positive influence life-satisfaction and academic achievement. Life-satisfaction has a positive influence on academic achievement. Support received from parents and friends has a direct and positive influence on self-efficacy. Support received from mother and teachers has a direct positive influence on life-satisfaction.

For elementary school students, a similar pattern of results has been obtained, with teachers playing a more important role. Self-efficacy has a direct and positive influence life-satisfaction and academic achievement. Support received from parents, teachers and friends has a direct and positive influence on self-efficacy. Support received from teachers has a direct positive influence on life-satisfaction.

These results document the important mediating role self-efficacy play in positively influencing life-satisfaction and academic achievement. Second, social support received from significant others help to raises the self-efficacy beliefs for children and adolescents. Parents play an important role in raising their children's self-efficacy in all three samples and life-satisfaction for the high school sample. Social support received from friends increase the self-efficacy of adolescents in all three samples. The role of teachers is important for elementary students, but the influence is non-significant for high school students.

Finally, a six-year longitudinal study has been conducted to examine the factors that influence academic achievement of Korean students. Park, Kim and Chung (2004) examined longitudinally influences that parents have on their children's academic achievement and the mediating role of self-efficacy and achievement motivation. In the first phase of the longitudinal study, a total of 961 Grade 6 students participated in the study. When they became Grade 9, 830 students participated in the study and 694 when they became Grade 11. The present chapter reports on the results of the critical transition from middle school (Grade 9) to high school (Grade 11).

In terms of parents-child relationship, the following variables as perceived by adolescents are included: Social support received from parents, a sense of indebtedness to parents, and parental pressure for academic achievement. In addition, the following variables are assessed: self-efficacy, achievement motivation, studying time and academic achievement. The achievement motivation scale is developed by Yu and Yang (1994).

The results of the path analysis are presented in Figure 8. (See Figure 8). Efficacy for self-regulated learning, achievement motivation and studying time have a direct and positive influence on academic achievement for Grade 9. Efficacy for self-regulated learning has a direct positive influence

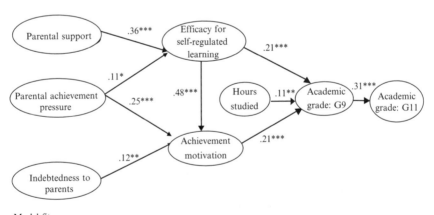

Model fit

x^2	df	x^2/df	Significance	GFI	AGFI	NFI	RMR
30.14	10	3.14	P<.001	.99	.95	.98	.03

Note: * p<.05, ** p<.01, *** p<.001
Adapted from Park, Kim and Chung (2004)

Figure 8. Longitudinal analysis of academic achievement

on achievement motivation. Parental support and parental achievement pressure have a direct positive influence on efficacy for self-regulated learning. Parental achievement pressure and a sense of indebtedness to parents have a direct positive influence on achievement motivation. Mastery experience in term of academic achievement in Grade 9 predicts adolescents' academic grade in Grade 11.

The results of the path analysis indicate that parental factor (i.e. pressure and social support) and relational factor (i.e. a sense of indebtedness to parents) increase academic achievement through efficacy for self-regulated learning and achievement motivation. In other words, close parent-child relationship and social support are important factors in elevating adolescents' self-efficacy and achievement motivation, which in turn increased their academic achievement.

DISCUSSION

Consistent with Confucian values, Korean students and adults view education as an important life goal and persistent effort and discipline as the means to the goal. The sacrifice and support received from parents are viewed as essential ingredients for success. Emotional support in the form of encouragement, praise, security and understanding are valued. Koreans believe that ability can be acquired and personality can be polished through persistent effort and the support of significant others.

The results from the series of empirical studies conducted in Korea affirm the important mediating role that self-efficacy play in influencing academic achievement and life-satisfaction (Kim & Park, Chapter 2). Social support received from parents, achievement pressure and a sense of indebtedness raise self-efficacy, which in turn raise students' academic achievement and life-satisfaction. These results are consistent with the results obtained in Europe and U.S. (Bandura, 1997).

Results from a series of indigenous psychological analyses in Korea point to the limitation in the traditional psychological theories. First, very few Koreans emphasize innate ability. Instead they believe in self-regulation as being the most important factor that can lead to success and failure. Second, most developmental theories do not examine the influence of parents on child or adolescent development. The series of studies clearly indicate the central role parents play in children's development and achievements. In Korea, parental support and influence are strong during childhood, adolescence and they persist even in adulthood. Fourth, close ingroup members are highly influential, while professional relationships are less important. The support from teachers is important when children are young, but their influence decreases when they become older. Fifth, emotional support rather than informational support is found to be the most influential factor. Sixth, self-serving bias has not been found in Korea. Koreans attribute their success to persistent effort and failure to a lack of effort. Finally, although Western theories have assumed guilt to be negative, it is considered appropriate that children feel indebted toward their parents in Korea for all the devotion, sacrifice, support and affection they have received. A sense of indebtedness has been found to be a positive interpersonal affect that promotes achievement motivation.

Korean students are able to become high achievers since they live in a culture in which education is valued and self, proxy and collective efficacy for academic achievement is high (Kim & Park, 2005). Children are taught to discipline themselves to become high achievers. Many high school students study up to 14-16 hours a day focused on their academic work. Parents play a key role in providing emotional, informational and financial support to ensure that they children succeed in school. They set high goals for their children and pressure their children to excel in school. They provide a good studying environment so that their children can focus their attention on academic work. Their peers also view educational success as the most important life goal. Schools and teachers complete the picture by providing adolescents in developing the necessary academic skills. It is the concerted effort of the adolescents, parents, teachers and administrators that is responsible for promoting high self, relational and collective efficacy for academic achievement (Kim & Park, 2005).

The ingredients necessary for academic success is not limited to Korea. Similar patterns of results have been found in other East Asian countries (Stevenson, Azuma, & Hakuta, 1986; Stevenson & Lee, 1990). The main factor that is responsible for high academic performance lies in socialization practices that promote and maintain a strong relational and emotional bond between parents and children (Azuma, 1986; Ho, 1986, Park & Kim, 2004b). This type of socialization promotes the development of proxy control. A second major factor is the emphasis on self-regulation, especially the belief in the importance of persistent effort. The third major factor is the compatibility of values between the family and school environment that promotes collective efficacy.

The importance of self-regulations, parental support, and collective control is not unique to East Asia. In the U.S., Asian American students are high achievers since they possess the above characteristics (Farkas, Grobe, Sheehan, & Shuan, 1990; Hsia, 1988; Kim & Chun, 1994; Kim & Park, 2005). Similarly, socialization practices and emphasis on education in Finland closely parallel those values found in East Asia, which may be partially responsible for the high level of educational achievement of Finnish students (Helgesen & Kim, 2002; PISA, 2004).

Although Korean students are high achievers, they are costs. In 1996, when students were asked to describe the most stressful aspect of their lives, 28% report pressure to achieve academically, followed by human relationship (20%) and family life (15%; Kim & Park, 1997). During the economic crisis in 1999, 44% reported pressure to achieve academically as being the most stressful (Park, Kim & Kim, 2002). Even with the pressure and stress, when students succeed academically they are given social, relational and economic rewards and they feel that it is worth the investment (Park et al., 2002).

Korean society, however, is not prepared to deal with those students who cannot adjust to the rigid school system, cope with the pressure to achieve, fail to do well academically, and adolescents who engage in delinquent behavior (Park & Kim, 2003b). The rates of students who refuse to attend school, the level of delinquency and school violence have been increasing in recent years (Park, Kim, & Tak, 2004). Nearly half of the teachers and students feel that teachers and administrator have lost some of the leadership and authority to teach and regulate students and around half of the elementary, middle and high school students report experiencing school violence (Park et al., 2003b).

Students, teachers and parents have low efficacy in dealing with school violence and they are unable to stem the rising tide (Park & Kim, 2004b). Korean society has been able to foster the development of self, proxy and collective control in promoting high academic achievement. But it has yet to develop the necessary control in stemming the rising dropout rate, delinquency and school violence. This is the next important challenge for Korean society in the 21st century.

REFERENCES

Ahn, K. D., Hwang, J. K., Kim, U., & Park, Y. S. (1997). *Adolescent culture of Korea: Psycho-social structure and dynamics* [in Korean]. Seoul: Academy of Korean Studies.

Azuma, H. (1986). Why study child development in Japan? In H. Stevenson, H. Azuma, & K. Hakuta (Eds.), *Child development and education in Japan* (pp. 3–12). New York: W. H. Freeman.

Bandura, A. (1995). *Self-efficacy scales.* Unpublished manuscript, Dept. of Psychology, Stanford University, USA.

Bandura, A. (1997). *Self-efficacy: The exercise of control.* New York: Freeman.

Bowlby, J. (1969). *Attachment and loss: Vol. 1. Attachment.* New York: Basic Books.

Farkas, G., Grobe, R. P., Sheehan, D., & Shuan, Y. (1990). Cultural resources and school success: Gender, ethnicity and poverty groups within an urban school district. *American Sociological Review, 55,* 127–142.

Gallup Korea (1985). *The Korean children and mothers* [in Korean]. Seoul: Korea survey Gallup polls.

Helgesen, G. & Kim, U. (2002). *Good government: Nordic and East Asian perspectives.* Copenhagen: NIAS Press.

Ho, D. Y. F. (1986). Chinese patterns of socialization: A critical review. In M. H. Bond (Ed.), *The psychology of the Chinese people* (pp. 1–37). Oxford: Oxford University Press.

Hsia, J. (1988). *Asian Americans in higher education and work.* Hillsdale, NJ: Lawrence Erlbaum Associates.

Im, Y. K. (1998). *National study of attitudes toward education* [in Korean]. Seoul: KEDI.

Kim, U. (2001a). Analysis of democracy and human rights in cultural context: Psychological and comparative perspectives. In H. S. Aasen, U. Kim, & G. Helgesen (Eds.), *Democracy, human rights, and peace in Korea; Psychological, political, and cultural Perspectives* (pp. 53–94). Seoul: Kyoyook Kwahasa.

Kim, U. (2001b). Culture, science and indigenous psychologies: An integrated analysis. In D. Matsumoto (Ed.), *Handbook of culture and psychology* (pp. 51–76). Oxford: Oxford University Press.

Kim, U., & Choi, S. H. (1994). Individualism, collectivism and child development: A Korean perspective. In P. Greenfield & R. Cocking (Eds.), *Cross-cultural roots of minority child development* (pp. 227–258). Hillsdale, NJ: Lawrence Erlbaum.

Kim, U., & Chun, M. (1994). Education "success" of Asian Americans: An indigenous perspective. *Applied Behavioral Development, 15*, 329–341.

Kim, U., & Lee, S. W. (1994). The Confucian model of morality, justice, selfhood, and society: Implications for modern society. In Academy of Korean Studies (Ed.), *The universal and particular natures of Confucianism* (pp. 167–210). Seoul: Academy of Korean Studies.

Kim, U., & Park, Y. S. (1997). Stress, appraisal and coping: An indigenous analysis. K*orean Journal of Health Psychology, 2*, 96–126. [in Korean]

Kim, U., & Park, Y. S. (2000). Confucian and family values: Their impact of educational achievement in Korea. *Zeitshrift fur Erziehungswissenschaft (Journal of Educational Science), 3*, 229–249.

Kim, U., & Park, Y. S. (2003). An indigenous analysis of success attribution: Comparison of Korean students and adults. In K. S. Yang, K. K. Hwang, P.B. Pedersen, I. Daibo (Eds.), *Progress in Asian social psychology: Conceptual and empirical contributions* (pp. 171–195). New York: Preager.

Kim, U., & Park, Y. S. (2004). Factors influencing the quality of life for Korean adolescents and adults at home, school, work and leisure settings: Indigenous psychological analysis. *Korean Journal of Health Psychology, 9*, 973–1002. [in Korean]

Kim, U., & Park, Y. S. (2005). Integrated analysis of indigenous psychologies: Comments and extensions of ideas presented by Shams, Jackson, Hwang and Kashima. *Asian Journal of Social Psychology, 8*, 75–95.

Kim, U., Park, Y. S., Kim, M. U., Lee, K. W., & Yu, S. H. (2000). Intergenerational differences and life-satisfaction: Comparative analysis of adolescents, adults, and the elderly. *Korean Journal of Health Psychology, 5*, 119–145. [in Korean]

Kim, U., Park, Y. S., Kwon, Y. U., & Koo, J. S. (2005). Values of children, parent-child relationship, and social change in Korea: Indigenous, psychological, and cultural analysis. *Applied Psychololgy: International Review, 54*, 338–354.

Korea Educational Development Institute (1983). *Analysis of educational aspiration* [in Korean]. Seoul: KEDI.

Korea Educational Development Institute (1995). *Educational index* [in Korean]. Seoul: KEDI.

Korea Educational Development Institute (2003). *Social indicators in Korea* [in Korean]. Seoul: KEDI.

Korean National Statistics Bureau (2005). *Annual statistics* [in Korean]. Seoul: Government of Korea.

National Center for Educational Statistics (2000). *Mathematics and science in eighth grade: Findings from the Third International Mathematics and Science Study*. Washington, DC: U.S. Department of Education.

National Center for Educational Statistics (2004). *Highlights from trends in mathematics and science study (TIMSS 2003)*. Washington, DC: U.S. Department of Education.

Organisation for Economic Co-operation and Development (2003). *Education at a glance: OECD indicators*. Paris: OECD.

Organisation for Economic Cooperation and Development (2004). *Learning for tomorrow's world: First results from PISA 2003*. Paris: OECD.

Park, Y. S., & Kim, U. (2000). The impact of changing parent-child relationship on adolescents' functioning: Comparison of primary, junior high, senior high, and university students. *Korean Journal of Educational Research, 38,* 109–147. [in Korean]

Park, Y. S., & Kim, U. (2003a). The nature of educational achievement in Korea: Psychological, indigenous, and cultural Perspectives. *Korean Journal of Educational Psychology, 16,* 37–54. [in Korean]

Park, Y. S., & Kim, U. (2003b). The formation and change of adolescents' delinquent behavior. *Korean Journal of Psychological and Social Issues, 9,* 81–114. [in Korean]

Park, Y. S., & Kim, U. (2004a). *Parent-child relationship in Korea: Indigenous psychological analysis of self-concept and family role* [in Korean]. Seoul: Kyoyook Kwahaksa.

Park, Y. S., & Kim, U. (2004b). *Adolescent culture and parent-child relationship in Korea: Indigenous psychological analysis* [in Korean]. Seoul: Kyoyook Kwahaksa.

Park, Y. S., Kim, U., & Chung, K. (2004). Longitudinal analysis of the influence of parent-child relationship on adolescents' academic achievement: With specific focus on the mediating role of self-efficacy and achievement motivation. *Korean Journal of Psychological and Social Issues, 10,* 37–59. [in Korean]

Park, Y. S., Kim, U., Chung, K. S., Lee, S.M., Kwon, H. H., & Yang, K. M. (2000). Causes and consequences of life-satisfaction among primary, junior high, and senior high school students. *Korean Journal of Health Psychology, 5,* 94–118.[in Korean]

Park, Y. S., Kim, U., & Han, K. H. (2003). How Korean children and adolescents perceive their parents: Indigenous psychological analysis. *Korean Journal of Psychological and Social Issues, 9,* 127–164. [in Korean]

Park, Y. S., Kim, U., & Kim, M. S. (2002). The experience of stress, coping, and social support of students and parents after the economic crisis: The indigenous psychology approach. *Korean Journal of Psychological and Social Issues, 8,* 105–135. [in Korean]

Park, Y. S., Kim, U. J., & Tak, S. Y. (2002). The effect of economic crisis on success attribution among Korean students and adults: An indigenous psychological analysis. *Korean Journal of Psychological and Social Issues, 8,* 103–139. [in Korean]

Park, Y. S., Kim, U., & Tak. S. Y. (2004). Indigenous psychological analysis of delinquency among Korean adolescents: Comparison of adolescents under probation and high school students. *Korean Journal of Psychological and Social Issues, 10, Special Issue,* 107–145. [in Korean]

Park, Y. S., Kim, U., & Tak, S. Y. (2005). Failure experience and aspirations for the future: Indigenous psychological analysis of Korean adolescents and their parents. *Korean Journal of Psychological and Social Issues, 11,* 109–142. [in Korean]

Stevenson, H., Azuma, H., & Hakuta. K. (Eds.) (1986). *Child development and education in Japan.* New York: W. H. Freeman.

Stevenson, H., & Lee, S. Y. (1990). Context of achievement: A study of American, Chinese and Japanese children. *Monographs of the Society for Research in Child Development, 55,* 1–75.

Taft, R. (1986). The psychological study of the adjustment and adaptation of immigrants to Australia. In N. T. Feather (Ed.), *Survey of Australian psychology: Trend for research.* Sydney: George Allen and Unwin.

Yu, A. B., & Yang, K. S. (1994). The nature of achievement motivation in collectivistic societies. In U. Kim, H. C. Triandis, C. Kagitcibasi, S. C. Choi, & G. Yoon. (Eds.), *Individualism and collectivism: Theory, method and applications* (pp. 239–250). Thousand Oaks, CA: Sage Publication.

Chapter 20

Paternalism
Towards Conceptual Refinement and Operationalization

Zeynep Aycan

Few constructs in the management literature are as intriguing, complex and controversial as "paternalism." The nature of paternalism is hard to capture, and yet almost every discussion about it (scholarly or otherwise) is loaded with controversy as well as ideological and moral overtones. This is reflected in metaphors, descriptions, and titles of books or papers on paternalism, such as "benevolent dictatorship" (Northouse, 1997, p.39), "legitimated authority" (Padavic & Earnest, 1994, p.391), "noncoercive exploitation" (Goodell, 1985, p.252), "the sweetest persuasion" (Jackman, 1994, p.9), "strategic flexibility" (Padavic & Earnest, 1994, p.397), "the velvet glove" (Jackman's book title, 1994, implying an "iron fist in a velvet glove"), "remoralization of the workplace" (Warren, 1999, p.51), "role-transcending concern of an employer" (Padavic & Earnest, 1994, p.396), "from paternalism to partnership" (Fitzsimons, 1991, paper title), "the *business* of benevolence" (Tone, 1997, book title), "cradle to grave management" (Fitzsimons, 1991, p.48), "paternalism *vs.* autonomy" (Cohen, 1985), "paternalism *vs.* benevolence" (Jackman, 1994, p.11). Is paternalism "something" to endorse or avoid; moral or immoral; effective or ineffective; empowering or repressing; exploitative or benevolent? These controversies make paternalism an interesting construct to investigate.

There are other unique features of paternalism that make it important. First, while, paternalism is rooted in indigenous psychologies of Pacific Asian, Middle-Eastern, and Latin American cultures as a salient cultural characteristic, it is perceived negatively in Western developed and industrialized societies. Despite the negative attitudes, however, Western societies now consider it as a viable solution to some societal and organizational problems. Paternalism now goes beyond its indigenous boundaries and is considered as a tool to contribute to societal development in both the East and West.[1] Second, paternalism remains as an issue that evokes opinions in almost opposite directions in Eastern and Western cultures, which suggests that it is a construct that has potential to yield substantial variation in cross-cultural organizational research. Third, it can be construed at individual (e.g., paternalistic leadership), organizational (e.g., paternalistic organizational culture and practices), and socio-cultural levels (e.g., paternalism as a cultural dimension). This enables cross-cultural researchers to utilize it at different levels of analysis. The focus of discussion in this chapter is on paternalistic leadership at the individual level.

Despite significant scientific and practical implications, paternalism remains a topic that has received little attention from contemporary scholars of management and psychological sciences (cf. Jackman, 1994; Mead, 1997). This chapter aims to fill this void by providing a conceptual refinement. It also presents preliminary findings of research to validate the conceptual framework and operationalize the construct of paternalism.

PATERNALISM: A HISTORICAL PERSPECTIVE

Jackman's (1994) assertion that "paternalism is a time-worn term that has had indefinite meaning in common usage" (p. 10) reflects its complexity. Whilst the context may determine its meaning, being paternalistic, as the name denotes, refers to acting in a manner similar to the way a father behaves toward his children. Webster's (1975) defines it as "the principle or system of governing or controlling a country, group of employees, etc. in a manner suggesting a father's relationship with his children." This definition implies that paternalism occurs in a dyadic and hierarchical relationship between a superior and subordinate, and that there is a role differentiation in this relationship. In the organizational context, the role of the superior is to provide care, protection, and guidance to the subordinate both in work and non-work domains, while the subordinate, in return, is expected to be loyal and deferential to the superior.

Paternalism is one of the most salient cultural characteristics of Pacific Asian cultures (Dorfman & Howell, 1988; Pye, 1986) such as those in China, Japan, Korea, Taiwan, and India. The literature also suggests that paternalism is prevalent in countries of the Middle-East (Ali, 1993; Aycan, Kanungo, et al., 2000; Ayman & Chemers, 1991) and Latin America (Osland, Franco, & Osland, 1999). The underpinning of paternalism in Asian cultures is the traditional value of familisim with a strong emphasis on patriarchal, patrilocal, and patrilineal relationships within the family unit (Kim, 1994).

---

[1] The terms 'East' and 'West' are used loosely to denote traditional, hierarchical, collectivistic cultures of Asia, Latin America, and the Middle-East, and egalitarian, industrialized, individualistic cultures of North America, Western and Northern Europe, respectively. The author acknowledges the limitations of the overgeneralization in grouping countries in such ways, but uses these terms for communication convenience only.

In time, paternalistic relationships went beyond family boundaries, and vertical relationships in the family were extended to those based on seniority and gender in workplace and social life (Kim, 1994, Redding & Hsiao, 1990). Chao (1990) links paternalism to one of the fundamental principles of Confucian ideology that balances an employer's authority and guidance in exchange for loyalty and deference from subordinates.

Paternalism has assumed a significant role in society. In the past, maintenance of hierarchy and social order was ensured through the power of paternalistic families or dynasties (Redding & Hsiao, 1990). In the absence of social control regulated by laws, paternalism served an important function in the feudalistic system where protection of the less powerful was ensured in exchange for their loyalty and submission. However, with the establishment of formalistic control and structure in society and its organizations, a tendency to move away from paternalistic norms emerged, as in the case of China (Kao, Sek-Hong, & Kwan, 1990). Kim (1994) argues that the establishment of trade unions and collective bargaining provided the necessary protection to all workers, and hence resulted in the demise of occupational welfare in the West.

Although through a different root, paternalism has enjoyed a long reign also in American and European industrial history (Tone, 1997). Weber (1958) traces the nexus of paternalism back to nineteenth century philanthropy, religious ideologies, and early industrialization. The American mill owners of the nineteenth century and the bourgeois entrepreneurs of the twentieth century were concerned with the physical, moral and spiritual well-being of their workers, and promoted social and moral welfare of workers based on the principle of "industrial betterment" (Kerfoot & Knights, 1993). However, the positive sentiments soon turned into severe criticisms against paternalism due to their association with racism in labor relations (e.g., Black Detroit workers of the Ford Motor Company between 1937–1941, Meier & Rudwick, 1979), worker exploitation (e.g., Blumer, 1951; van den Berghe, 1967), slavery in the American South (e.g., Genovese, 1972), and rural labor relations in Britain (e.g., Newby, 1977). As will be reviewed in the next section, many scholars attack paternalism on ideological and philosophical grounds (e.g., Carter, 1977; Drowkin, 1971; Kleining, 1983; Mill, 1950 [1859], Van DeVeer, 1979). Increased public awareness of alternative ways of democratic relationships through the mass media, educational, and political institutions and a decline in individualized interactions in the workplace, such as market determinism pushing for large-scale lay-offs, unionization, and national welfare policies resulted in the demise of paternalism (Padavic & Earnest, 1994). The Weberian (1966) analysis of modernization theory purported that paternalism would be superseded by the rational-bureaucratic, modern industrial authority.

In recent years, however, paternalism seems to have been resurrected in the West in national welfare programs and organizational contexts. State welfare programs are now becoming more paternalistic mainly due to political and economic pressures. According to recent polls about welfare and poverty, paternalism is the social policy that is preferred by the majority of Americans (Mead, 1997, p.13). In the "new paternalism," as it is now called (e.g., Mead, 1997), there is increased governmental intervention and interference with the lives of the poor and deviant who are not able or willing to assume responsibility for their own well-being. The new approach now questions the assumption of individual accountability, efficacy, and autonomy; ironically such questioning constituted the basis for attacks against paternalism.

In the organizational context, new paternalism is developed to humanize and remoralize the workplace as well as establish more flexible management systems instead of rigid and contractual relationships between employers and workers. Padavic and Earnest (1994) attributed the rise of paternalism to the pressures of labor exploitation and declining union power. Anthony (1986, p. 77) put it well by stating that paternalism "mediates between humanity and economic exploitation. Between the awfulness of one alternative and the ineffectiveness of the other, paternalism is a model that is worth re-examining". Warren (1999) asserted that "the new paternalism [is implemented] in HRM policies to elicit employee commitment and team based productivity" (p. 51). In the new paternalism, companies are more involved in the non-work lives of their employees by assisting them in their social and family problems. According to Gordon (1998), "companies are helping themselves by helping their employees" (p. 68), because such programs ease personal burdens, and promote performance and commitment.

Despite the recent resurgence of interest in paternalism in Western industrialized societies, it remains controversial. The next section will compare the ideological underpinnings of paternalism in Western and Eastern cultures to be able to capture its complex nature.

"IS PATERNALISM 'GOOD' OR 'BAD'?": ISSUES OF CONTROVERSY

In its broadest sense, the organizational context of paternalism denotes treating employees as if they are part of the extended family. In interpersonal relationships, the paternalistic superior behaves in a fatherly manner towards his subordinates.[2] We must first understand what this relationship entails in order to analyze the reasons behind the controversies surrounding paternalism. It is possible to outline paternalistic leadership behavior as follows (e.g., Aycan, Kanungo, et. al, 2000; Kim, 1994; Padavic & Earnest, 1994; Redding & Hsiao, 1990; Sinha, 1990):

---

[2] The gender terminology that is used in this article to describe superiors in paternalistic relationships is in favor of males. This bias is only for communication convenience.

- *Creating a family atmosphere in the workplace*: behaving like a father to subordinates, giving fatherly advice to subordinates in their professional *as well as* personal lives.
- *Establishing close and individualized relationships with subordinates*: establishing close relations with every subordinate individually, knowing every subordinate in person (personal problems, family life, etc.), is genuinely concerned with their welfare, takes a close interest in subordinates' professional as well as personal life.
- *Getting involved in the non-work domain*: attending important events (e.g., wedding and funeral ceremonies, graduations, etc.) of his subordinates as well as their immediate family members, providing help and assistance (e.g., financial) to subordinates if they need it, acting as a mediator between an employee and their spouse if there is a marital problem.
- *Expecting loyalty*: expecting loyalty and commitment from subordinates, expecting employees to immediately attend to an emergency in the company even if this requires employees to do so at the expense of their private lives.
- *Maintaining authority/status*: giving importance to status differences (position ranks), and expecting employees to behave accordingly; believing that he knows what is good for subordinates and their careers; not wanting anyone to doubt his authority.

Employee reactions and behaviors in a paternalistic relationship have not been systematically investigated in the literature, but anecdotal evidence and qualitative studies (e.g., Aycan, 1999; Fikret-Pasa, 2001; Padavic & Earnest, 1994) suggest that employee loyalty and deference are manifested in various forms as follows.

- *Considering the workplace as a family*: accepting the workplace as his/her own family, feeling that there is emotional bonding with the paternalistic leader, feeling proud to be associated with him, seeking his advice on personal and professional matters because they genuinely trust his/her opinions.
- *Being loyal and deferential*: protecting the leader from criticisms inside and outside the company, working hard to reciprocate the managers' favors and not lose face in front of him, showing loyalty and deference towards the leader out of respect, leaving the organization with the manager if he quits, doing voluntary overtime if needed.
- *Getting involved in non-work domains*: going out of one's way to help the leader in his personal life if needed (e.g., helping him to paint his house).
- *Accepting authority*: willingly accepting the leader's authority, genuinely believing that the leader knows what is good for the employee.

These are some of the sample behaviors of subordinates and superiors in a paternalistic relationship. When I give public presentations on such behavior manifestations of paternalism, I observe two main reactions from audiences. One reaction (mainly from Asian audiences), is members nodding their head indicating an approval of paternalistic behavior, while the other reaction (mainly from audiences of North Americans) is of shaking their heads indicating a strong disapproval. What is right in this picture for the first group that is so wrong for the second group? I argue that the disagreements between Eastern and Western scholars arise for two reasons. First, the socio-cultural context determines whether or not the paternalistic relationship is perceived as appropriate. As will be discussed in the next section, paternalism is congruent with characteristics of collectivistic and high power distant cultures. In addition, levels of affectivity, particularism, and diffuseness affect the acceptance of paternalism as an appropriate leadership style. Second, the controversy may arise because there might be various types of paternalism that yield different outcomes. I will argue that benevolent paternalism is more effective than exploitative paternalism to elicit higher employee satisfaction and higher organizational commitment.

The Socio-Cultural Context

Individualism vs. collectivism: Paternalism seems to be a valued characteristic in collectivistic cultures compared to individualistic ones. Ho and Chiu (1994) discussed five main components of the individualism-collectivism construct, and three of them have direct implications for paternalism: autonomy/conformity (including privacy expectations), responsibility, and self-reliance/interdependence. In collectivistic cultures where there is high conformity, more responsibility-taking for others, and more interdependence, paternalism is viewed positively. In contrast, in individualistic societies where autonomy, self-reliance, and self-determination are of pivotal importance, paternalism is undesirable. A paternalistic leader's involvement in an employee's personal and family life can be perceived as a violation of privacy in individualistic cultures, whereas it is desired and expected in collectivistic ones.

In a paternalistic relationship, compliance to the paternalistic leader is on a voluntary basis. Singh and Bhandarker (1990) summarized the paternalistic relationship in the following way:

> A person looks for a father-figure (symbolically speaking) in the work place for empowering, protection, grooming, and development. In return, the individual develops respect for his superior and demonstrates willingness to accept his authority. (p. 134)

Similarly, Kao, Sek-Hong, and Kwan (1990) summarize the paternalistic leader-subordinate relationship based on Confucian logic where "personalized obligations and loyalty [of the leader] leading to subordinates' willingness to comply and conform with the wishes of the 'surrogate' parents in their leadership roles" (p. 105). Because compliance and conformity with authority cannot be perceived as something to be done voluntarily, paternalism has always been equated with authoritarianism in the Western literature.

Paternalism also implies a voluntary dependency on the paternalistic leader. Protection, guidance, and various benefits provided to employees and their families create a dependent relationship. Kim (1994) observed that "Westerners are usually surprised when they see that this dependency is not resented, but usually appreciated by employees. This willingness to welcome dependency, however, is more explicable to Westerners if they understand Korean familism and paternalism" (p. 257).

Because conformity and dependency are contradictory to individualistic values such as autonomy, self-reliance and self-determination, paternalistic practices have been criticized in the context of elderly care (e.g., Cicirelli, 1990; Cohen, 1985; Gordon & Tomita, 1990), child protection programs (Calder, 1995), health care (e.g., Backlar, 1995; Beisecker & Beisecker, 1993; Christensen, 1997; Kjellin & Nilstun, 1993; Mesler, 1994), and academia (e.g., Callahan, 1988). In all these studies, the ethical dimension of paternalism was discussed. The emphasis was on the extent to which experts (e.g., leaders, social workers, doctors, teachers, etc.) should have the right to act in a paternalistic way (i.e., claiming that they know what is best for the ones under their care) despite the wishes of those who seek their advice or treatment. Therefore, paternalism is viewed as a practice that restricts individual rights to exercise autonomy and choice (Blokland, 1997).

Power Distance: Paternalism is endorsed in hierarchical societies. The paternalistic relationship is based on the assumption of power inequality between the paternalistic leader and his subordinates. In high power distance cultures, inequality in the distribution of power is approved and not resented. Paternalism is criticized in Western societies because of this unquestioned power inequality and its implications. One of the major implications is that the paternalistic leader assumes that he has superiority over his subordinate with respect to key competencies (knowledge, skills, and experience) as well as moral standards. Van de Veer (1986), in his provocative book *Paternalistic intervention: The moral bounds of benevolence* defines paternalism as a relationship "in which one person, A, interferes with another person, S, in order to promote S's own good" (p. 12). Underlying this definition is an implicit assumption that the superior "knows what is best for the subordinate." The assumption of the manager's superiority and of the employee's inferiority maybe invalid, but it is nevertheless unquestioned and unchallenged. The paternalistic leader's status is ascribed by the virtue of his position, age and experience, and therefore his power and authority is legitimated. Van den Berghe (1985) criticized paternalism for this particular aspect: "Paternalism should be regarded as a legitimating ideology characteristic of agrarian societies and as the model of all relationships of inequality within such societies" (p. 262).

The power inequality is manifested in many ways, but two of them are particularly important: being in a position to *determine* employee wants and needs, and not allowing reciprocity. Luke described the process of defining a subordinate's wants and needs sharply:

> A may exercise power over B...by influencing, shaping or determining his very wants... Is it not the supreme and most insidious exercise of power to prevent people, to whatever degree, from having grievances by shaping their perceptions, cognitions, and preferences in such a way that they accept their role in the existing order of things, either because they can see or imagine no alternative to it, or because they see it as natural and unchangeable, or because they value it as divinely ordained and beneficial? (1974, pp. 23–24)

In this description, Luke argues that the power and influence process is so strong that the subordinate is not even aware of the fact that he is being manipulated. This represents one of the most fundamental and intriguing criticisms against paternalism.

The power inequality is also manifested in the rules of reciprocity. In paternalistic relationship, the dominant party makes sure that he is the provider while the beneficiary is the receiver. Goodell (1985) asserts that the power inequality "guarantees that the beneficiary cannot get back, answer back, question, help himself, . . .reciprocate, or repay, in short, regain his autonomy" (p. 254). This is the ideology of paternalism that rests on the denial of reciprocity in similar terms and in the short-run. The generosity of the giver, according to Levi-Strauss (1969, p. 53), aims at crushing the receiver. In this sense, Goodell (1985) argued, paternalism resembles patronage and potlatch (a ceremonial giveaway to perpetuate the power establishment).

Affectivity, particularism, and diffuseness: Paternalism is most likely to occur in cultures also high on affectivity (vs. emotional neutrality, cf. Trompenaars, 1993), particularism (vs. universalism, cf. Trompenaars, 1993), and diffuseness (vs. specificity, cf. Trompenaars, 1993). The relationship between the paternalistic superior and loyal subordinate is a heavily emotional one. The emotional bonding is so strong that often times both parties go beyond their role boundaries to help and nurture one another. Their happiness and sorrow are lived together as a joint experience (cf. Kim, 1994). The affectionate nature of the relationship is another controversial aspect of paternalism. Jackman (1994), for example, argues that the friendship offered in a paternalistic relationship is a "potent *weapon* with which to extract compliance" (p. 273, emphasis added) from those who depend on the superior for emotional and social needs. It has even been compared with an intimate love relationship with sexual overtones (e.g., Jackman, 1994; Kerfoot & Knight, 1993). In this context, the emotional nature of the paternalistic relationship is contrasted with Western professionalism (cf. Gupta, 1999). In strictly professional business relationships, emotions have no place; what matters is job performance and goal achievement. Care, protection, and affection in the paternalistic relationship may easily create an organizational culture in which low performers are protected and tolerated (e.g., Osland, et al., 1999).

Rules in the paternalistic relationships may also vary depending on the situation and person. Padavic and Earnest (1994) promote paternalism in Western cultures now simply because *universalistic* practices are too costly and rigid. Instead, the new paternalism brings a *strategic flexibility*, so that there is no guarantee of getting benefits from the employer: "The system of impersonal, legalistic system of mutual rights and obligations [is replaced] by employer's enactments of his role-transcending concern which is situationalized and subject to his criteria" (Padavic & Earnest, 1994, p. 395). Paternalistic leaders may not be able or willing to meet the needs of every employee to the same degree. Organizations in many developing countries suffer from the lack of institutionalization because of the established paternalistic pattern of *differential treatment*. Sinha (1995) attributes this to the increasing size of the organization as well as the employer's liking of some members more than others:

> The differential love and care [of the paternal boss] are generally reciprocated by similar feelings and acts. The loved and cared ones get increasingly close to the father [the paternal figure] while others are distanced...The leader indeed starts believing that so-and-so is really bright and dynamic and therefore, in good faith, tends to extend favors to him." (p. 78)

In such cases, paternalism may pave the way to nepotism and favoritism. That is why it is sometimes referred to as "discrimination without the expression of hostility" (Jackman, 1994, p. 10).

Finally, paternalism transcends boundaries. In diffuse cultures, role-boundaries are permeable, and this is exactly the case in a paternalistic relationship. The superior is more than an employer or a manager in his role. At times, he is like a father, a close friend, a brother, and so on. He is involved in employees' personal lives, and he has the right to expect personal favors from them. This raises the issue of invasions of privacy, where the extent and justification of boundary-crossing is constantly questioned.

The Nature of Paternalism

Duality between control and care: Duality between control and care, which is inherent in paternalism, may be difficult to comprehend and reconcile for Western scholars. In order to appreciate this duality, it might be necessary to examine the relationships within the family as the idea of paternalism in work and social life derives from the relationships between parents and children.

In the family, parents assume a dual role of both control and care. These roles have been juxtaposed in the Western literature. Control has been equated with authoritarianism and therefore rejected. However, Lau and Cheung (1987) challenged this position by arguing that there are two types of parental control: dominating (restrictive) and order keeping (caring), and that the latter is associated with parental affection and love. Similarly, Kagitcibasi (1970, 1996) provided evidence for the independence of parental affection and control, and showed that both can coexist in child-rearing practices. Another example of this coexistence comes from one of the predominant Indian values pertaining to the role of karta, the father figure "who is nurturant, caring, dependable, sacrificing and yet demanding, authoritative, and a strict disciplinarian" (Sinha, 1990, p. 68).

A similar duality in managerial roles can also be observed. Western scholars (e.g., Likert, 1961; Vroom & Yetton, 1973) drew a clear distinction between task- and people-oriented management styles. Strictly task-oriented managers are portrayed as authoritarian who emphasize inequality in power distributions, whereas people-oriented managers are portrayed as participative who emphasize equality among all. However, based on his research on Indian organizations, Sinha (1980) proposed that both task and people concerns can coexist even in a relationship where there is a power hierarchy. He labeled such leaders as *nurturant-task leaders*. Similarly, Misumi (1985) proposed a PM leadership theory in which he also reconciled managerial concerns with control of performance (P) as well as maintenance of harmonious relationships among workers (M). These seemingly conflicting and yet coexisting roles that parents and managers assume are at the root of paternalism. In addition to benevolence, care, and generosity, there are elements of authoritarianism and obedience in paternalism. Because such conflicting values are not easy to reconcile for western scholars, their perception of paternalism is not favorable.

The issue of Intent and types of Paternalism: Perhaps the strongest criticism of paternalism is related to its agenda. Why do employers take a close interest in the personal and professional lives of their workers? Is it really for employees' own good or does it serve different strategic purposes? Goodell (1985) concludes that most studies credit the paternalist with benevolent rather than Machiavellian intentions. However, not all scholars agree with this conclusion. Jackman (1994, p. 13) ponders two critical questions: "Is the paternalist capable of assessing the best interest of others, and separate this from his or her own interests? ...How is the observer to distinguish acts that are altruistically or benevolently motivated from malevolent acts that merely purport to be benevolent?"

What is the hidden agenda (if any) of the paternalistic leader? The literature discusses possible beneficial outcomes of paternalism for the organization, including reduced cost (Padavic & Earnest, 1994; Kim, 1994), increased flexibility (Kerfoot & Knight, 1993; Padavic & Earnest, 1994), decreased turnover (Kim, 1994), and improved commitment, loyalty and teamwork (Gordon, 1998; Kim, 1999; Sinha, 1990). Paternalistic organizations save costs because the allocation of various resources and benefits are done on an individual basis, rather than for the entire workforce as it would be in more institutionalized systems. Such flexibility reduces employers' liability. As one manager puts "there is no warranty on the stuff you give and that's good. You don't want to guarantee these little benefits" (cited in Padavic & Earnest, 1994, p. 395). Moreover, paternalistic systems reduce the control costs. Kim (1994) found that managers in Korean organizations favored in-kind benefits because this enables them to exercise control over employees.

Loyalty and commitment are perhaps the most important benefits of paternalism for employers. Especially in the context of developing countries, loyalty is more valued in a worker than his/her job performance and competencies. (see, Cheng, 1999, for an excellent discussion). Employees give their best to the job not to lose face for their beloved managers. This is almost the only possible way of reciprocating the benefactor's care, protection, and nurture. Employees derive their sense of identity as members of "one big family" (cf. Warren, 1999), and teamwork flourishes in this environment.

The issue of intent is the key to distinguish among various forms of paternalism. Two types of paternalism that are most frequently discussed in literature are exploitative vs. benevolent paternalism (cf. Kim, 1994). The most distinguishing factor is the motivating force behind (a) employer generosity and care, and (b) employee loyalty. In exploitative paternalism, the emphasis is almost exclusively on organizational outcomes, whereas in benevolent paternalism there is more emphasis on and genuine concern for employee welfare. From the employee perspective, loyalty towards the paternalistic leader is a way to reciprocate his/her sincere generosity and care in benevolent-type paternalism. In contrast, in exploitative paternalism, employees show loyalty and deference mainly because they know that the leader is capable of fulfilling their needs or depriving them of critical resources.

Figure 1 depicts the proposed conceptual framework where the two types of paternalism are contrasted with authoritarian and authoritative management styles. Accordingly, *benevolent paternalism* occurs when the main emphasis is on the employee's welfare by the employer. In return, the employee shows loyalty and deference out of respect and appreciation for employer's benevolence. In *exploitative paternalism* the overt behavior is also care and nurturance, but for a different reason, which is to elicit employee

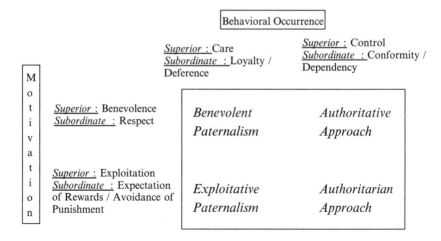

Figure 1. The conceptual framework contrasting benevolent and exploitative paternalism with two other management styles.

compliance to achieve organizational objectives. *Authoritarian management* relies on control and exploitation on the part of the superior, where the subordinate shows conformity and dependence in order to receive rewards or avoid punishment. *Authoritative management* also exercises control, but the underlying reason is to promote a subordinate's welfare. The subordinate, in return, respects the superior's decisions and complies with the rules, knowing that this is for his/her own benefit. The distinction between authoritative and authoritarian parenting has been drawn in the literature (e.g., Kochanska, Kuczynski, & Radke-Yarrow, 1989), but there are few studies dealing with this issue in the organizational context.

MODEL VALIDATION AND SCALE CONSTRUCTION

This section describes three empirical field studies testing the proposed model to operationalize the construct. It should be noted that the scale that was developed captured paternalism in the work context only, and did not aim at measuring different types of paternalism (i.e., benevolent vs. exploitative).

First Phase: Verification of the Conceptual Model of Paternalism

The purpose of this research was to test the relationship among the four types of management/leadership styles that were described in Figure 1. It was hypothesized that benevolent paternalism would have a significant negative correlation with exploitative paternalism and authoritarian management, whereas it would be positively correlated with authoritative management. Exploitative paternalism, on the other hand was expected to correlate positively with authoritarian management, and negatively with authoritative management.

Participants: A total of 60 employees were randomly drawn from various private (90 %) and public sector (10 %) organizations in Turkey. Slightly more than half of the sample was comprised of females (55%), and the mean age for the overall sample was 28.08 years. The sample had high educational attainments: 46.7 % were university graduates, and the rest were high school or vocational school graduates.

Measurement: The questionnaire designed for this research had two parts. The first part assesses the perceived status difference (i.e., power distance) in eight dyadic relationships (e.g., employer-employee, doctor-patient, parent-child, etc.). Participants rated the perceived status difference in each relationship using a 7-point Likert scale (0 = no status difference; 4 = of equal status; 6 = very large status difference). In addition, participants were presented with four possible sources/reasons of the status difference (e.g., knowledge, experience, tradition, other resources), and were asked to indicate to which they attributed the status difference. For each relationship, participants evaluated the extent to which each reason influences the existing status difference by using a 7-point scale (0 = is of no influence; 6 = is of great influence).

The second part included 62 phrases that included descriptions of the roles of superiors and subordinates in our culture as per the four types depicted in the proposed model. For example, the following eight phrases were developed for the employer-employee relationship.

- Employers genuinely care for their employees to promote their well-being (*benevolent paternalism*)
- Employers care for their employees because they are exploitative (*exploitative paternalism*)
- Employers control their employees to get them to work harder (*authoritarian management*)
- Employers control their employees to promote their well-being (*authoritative management*)
- Subordinates show loyalty and deference towards their superiors out of respect (*benevolent paternalism*)
- Subordinates show loyalty and deference towards their superiors to get benefits or avoid punishment (*exploitative paternalism*)
- Subordinates show conformity and dependence to their superiors to get benefits or avoid punishment (*authoritarian management*)
- Subordinates show conformity and dependence to their superiors out of respect (*authoritative management*)

Similar phrases were developed for all other dyadic relationships. The 64 phrases were presented in a random order, and participants were asked to rate their level of agreement by using a 5-point Likert scale (1 = strongly disagree; 5 = strongly agree).

Results. Descriptive findings showed that the maximum status difference occurred in teacher-student relationship, whereas almost none existed among colleagues, married couples, and friends. Therefore, these relationships were not included in the subsequent analyses. The power distance between student-teacher and patient-doctor who have status/level differences were reported due to differences in knowledge and experience levels. The difference between parent-child was due to traditions and cultural norms as well as knowledge and experience (see, Table 1). Among the remaining four relationships that had high power distance, benevolent paternalism and authoritative approaches were observed mostly in parent-child relationships, whereas exploitative paternalism and authoritarian approaches were mostly observed in leader-follower and employer-employee relationships.

In order to examine the validity of the conceptual model, the relationships among four types of management/leadership behaviors were examined. Pearson Product Moment correlations showed that benevolent paternalism was negatively correlated with exploitative paternalism and authoritarianism ($r = -.25$ and $r = -.21$, $p < .05$, respectively), and positively correlated with authoritative approaches ($r = .53$, $p < .01$). Exploitative paternalism was positively and significantly correlated with authoritarianism ($r = .50$, $p < .01$), and negatively but not significantly correlated with an authoritative approach ($r = -.12$, $p < .10$). The results confirmed the hypotheses.

Additionally, the relations among these four types of superior and subordinate behaviors were also examined. As expected, a high score on benevolent care on the part of the superior was correlated positively with *respect-based* loyalty and deference as well as conformity and dependence on the part of the subordinate ($r = .43$, $r = .40$, $p < .001$, respectively). Similarly, a high score on exploitative paternalism was positively correlated with subordinate loyalty ($r = .24$, $p < .05$) and conformity ($r = .36$, $p < .01$) due to the expectations of rewards and avoidance of punishment. This further provided preliminary evidence in support of the model.

Second Phase: Scale Development

Participants: A total of 177 employees participated in this phase. Among the 23 employees who participated in the pilot study, 82.6 % were women, 95.2 % were private sector employees and 65 % were university graduates. The mean age for this sample was 25.34 years and the average tenure was 15.13 months. Among the 154 employees who participated in the

Table 1. Level and Sources of Power Difference in Eight Dyadic Relationships, and Descriptive Statistics on the Four Management Styles

	Power/Status Difference[a]		Knowledge[a]		Experience[a]		Tradition/Norms[a]		Benevolent Paternalism[b]		Exploitative Paternalism[b]		Authoritative Management[b]		Authoritarian Management[b]	
	M	SD	M	SD	M	SD	M	SD	M	SD	M	SD	M	SD	M	SD
Parent-Child	3.02	0.52	3.38	0.73	4.02	0.81	2.93	0.24	4.07	0.72	2.38	0.56	4.20	0.45	1.83	0.45
Teacher-Student	3.92	0.48	4.72	0.52	4.88	0.29	2.45	0.70	3.62	0.65	2.00	0.64	2.83	0.63	2.43	0.78
Doctor-Patient	3.50	0.85	4.93	0.73	4.55	0.82	2.25	0.95	3.62	0.82	2.72	0.82	3.37	0.43	2.78	0.56
Leader-follower	3.50	0.50	3.73	0.79	3.80	0.70	2.05	0.80	2.57	0.75	3.83	0.24	3.10	0.78	3.85	0.55
Employer-Employee	3.63	0.33	3.93	0.34	3.58	0.43	2.07	0.65	2.55	0.66	3.43	0.45	2.73	0.45	3.6	0.45
Friends[c]	1.55	0.40														
Married Couples[c]	1.77	0.41														
Colleagues[c]	2.52	0.35														

Note: a. Maximum score is 6; b. Maximum score is 5; c. These relationships were not included in the subsequent analyses due to low power distance.

main study, 84.4 % were males; the mean age was 24.36 years; 59.1 % were high school graduates and 27.3% were university graduates; the average tenure in the organization was 3.03 years.

Results: Twenty-six items were initially generated to assess paternalism. After the pilot study, participants reported that all but 2 items were easy to understand and respond to. These two items were dropped from the subsequent analyses. Furthermore, participants were asked to guess what the items were trying to assess, 84 % claimed that the items were about behaviors of managers who try to create a family environment in the workplace.

In the main study, the internal consistency coefficient was found to be $\alpha = .81$ for the 24-item scale. The item-total correlation ranged. 30 to .64. For three items, item-total correlations were low, and these items were removed after which Cronbach's alpha increased to $\alpha = .85$. The mean score of the 21-item scale was 3.79 (SD = .55), the lowest score was 1.65 and the highest score is 5.00. Items as well as overall scores distributed normally (for scale score, skewness = −0.31; kurtosis = 0.62).

Principle Components Analysis was conducted to investigate the dimensions of the construct. Table 2 presents the 5-factor solution after Varimax Rotation. Five factors explained 62.70 % of the total variance. Kaiser-Meyer Olkin measure of sampling adequacy test (KMO =.82) and Bartlett's test of sphericity (Chi-Square (136) = 846.58, $p < .001$) estimates were acceptable. The first factor, which explained 18.42 % of variance, was entitled "Family atmosphere at work". The factor consisted of five items. The second factor, which explains 16.30 % of variance, consisted of four items that expressed the superior's relationships with each of employees. The factor was named as "Individialized relationships". The third factor was named as "Involvement in employeess" non-work lives. This factor had four items and explained 10.41 % of variance. The fourth factor was "Loyalty expectation" included three items and explained 9.72 % of variance. The last factor consists of five items that concerned "Status hierarchy & authority". The factor explained 7.85 % of variance. The factor structure closely resembled the aspects of paternalistic leadership behaviors outlined in the Introduction. However, further research with larger samples is required to test the stability of this factor structure.

Third Phase: Validity Study

In this last phase, the validation study of the paternalism scale was conducted. The Nurturant-Task Leadership Scale (NT), developed by Sinha (1990) was used to test the convergent validity. As for the divergent validity test, the Authoritarian Leadership scale was used (Sinha, 1995). Finally,

Table 2. Principle Component Analysis with Varimax Rotation

Factor / Item	Factor Loadings				
	1	2	3	4	5
FACTOR 1: Family atmosphere at work					
• Behaves like a family member (father/mother or elder brother/sister) towards his / her employees.	0.72				
• Provides advice to employees like a senior family member.	0.70				
• Creates a family environment in the workplace.	0.67				
• Feels responsible from employees as if they are his or her own children.	0.66				
• Protects employees from outside criticisms.	0.60				
FACTOR 2: Individualized relationships					
• Places importance to establishing one-to-one relationship with every employee.		0.74			
• Places importance to knowing every employee in person (e.g. personal problems, family life etc.).		0.70			
• Shows emotional reactions, such as joy, sorrow, anger, in his or her relationships with employees.		0.68			
• Closely monitors the development and progress of his or her employees.		0.66			
FACTOR 3: Involvement in employees' non-work lives					
• Does not hesitate to take action in the name of his or her employees, whenever necessary.			0.83		
• Is ready to help employees with their non-work problems (e.g. housing, education of the children, health etc.) whenever they need it.			0.80		
• Attends special events of employees (e.g. weddings and funeral ceremonies, graduations etc.)			0.78		
• Is prepared to act as a mediator whenever an employee has problem in his or her private life (e.g. marital problems).			0.67		
FACTOR 4: Loyalty expectation					
• Expects loyalty and deference in exchange for his or her care and nurturance.				0.79	
• Does not consider performance as the most important criterion while making a decision about employees (e.g. promotion, lay-off).				0.77	
• Places more importance to loyalty than performance in evaluating employees				0.65	
FACTOR 5: Status hierarchy and authority					
• Is disciplinarian and at the same time nurturant (sweet & bitter).					0.79
• Believes that s / he knows what is best for his or her employees.					0.77
• Asks opinions of employees about work-related issues, however, makes the last decision himself or herself.					0.66
• Wants to control or to be informed about every work-related activity.					0.65
• Despite establishing close relationships with employees, keeps his or her distance.					0.63
Explained variance	18.42	16.30	10.41	9.72	7.85

concurrent validity was tested using the Organizational Commitment scale (Mowday, Porter, & Steers, 1982).

Participants: Participants of the validation study were 100 employees of a large privately-owned rubber factory. The majority of the participants (91 %) were males; 54 % were university graduates and 27% were high school graduates. The mean age was 28.2 years, and the tenure was 3.03 years on average.

Results: As expected, the paternalism scale was positively and significantly correlated with the Nurturant-Task leadership ($r =.69$, $p <.001$), and the Organizational Commitment scales ($r =.25$, $p <.05$), whereas it was negatively correlated with the Authoritarian Leadership scale ($r = -.27$, $p <.05$). This provided initial support to the validity of the scale.

Further evidence for the validity of the scale comes from a large-scale cross-cultural research (including the 10 countries of the USA, Canada, China, Romania, Germany, Israel, Turkey, Pakistan, India, and Russia) on the impact of socio-cultural context on work culture and human resource management practices (Aycan, Kanungo, et al., 2000). In this study, a short version of the questionnaire was used. Paternalism as a socio-cultural dimension yielded the largest variance among countries (omega-square: 0.27). According to the findings, India, Turkey, China and Pakistan scored the highest on paternalism, Russia, Romania, the USA and Canada scored in the middle, and Israel and Germany scored the lowest. Paternalism was positively correlated with the work culture dimension that emphasized the importance of fulfilling obligations towards one another in the workplace. However, paternalism was negatively correlated with the work culture that promotes proactivity and initiative taking. It was also negatively correlated with job enrichment in HRM practices which involved work design in a manner where workers have more autonomy, use various skills, receive more feedback, and comprehend the importance of what they do for the company and for others' lives. Paternalism positively correlated with empowerment and participation.

CONCLUSIONS AND FUTURE RESEARCH DIRECTIONS

Paternalism is a salient and powerful construct that has many faces. It is an effective leadership style in the socio-cultural contexts where it originated. However, when taken out of its original context and applied in Western organizations, paternalism loses its meaning and has become the object of criticism and controversy. Even in its appropriate cultural context, social scientists need to understand the personal and situational contingencies under which its efficiency is maximized. There are a number of fruitful research avenues. First, future studies should investigate the characteristics of employees who are most and least likely to prefer paternalism and benefit from it. Included in these characteristics are demographic attributes such as education, gender, age, profession, and position, as well as personality- or socialization-related variables (e.g., attachment style). Similarly, the personal attributes of superiors should be investigated to find out the differences between benevolent and exploitative paternalists. Such research projects have been initiated by the present author. Finally, institutional paternalism as well as organizational attributes such as size, age, industry, ownership, and developmental stage that are more prone to the occurrence and effectiveness of paternalistic leadership should be studied.

Second, research should explore the outcomes of paternalism for the organization as well as its employees. Especially important is the empowerment of the subordinates. Aycan, Kanungo, et al. (2000) found a positive relationship between paternalism and empowerment. However, the literature suggests that the loss of autonomy and high dependency are contrary to empowering practices. Third, examining the relationship of paternalism to other relevant constructs such as mentoring, coaching, charismatic leadership, participative leadership, and nurturant-task leadership will help refine the conceptualization. Fourth, the empirical studies presented in this chapter are based on Turkish samples. Future cross-cultural research should investigate whether or not the characteristics of paternalism identified here are similar in other cultural contexts. Fifth, in order to test the conceptual model fully (Figure 1), future studies should develop measures to assess employee reactions and behaviors in the paternalistic relationship. Finally, the dynamics of paternalism should be investigated in other dyadic relationships including teacher-student, doctor-patient, and husband-wife.

REFERENCES

Ali, A.J. (1993). Decision-making style, individualism, and attitudes toward risk of Arab executives. *International Studies of Management and Organization, 23*, 53–73.

Anthony, P.D. (1986). *The Foundation of Management*. London: Tavistock.

Aycan, Z. (1999). *Anadolu Kaplanlari: Insan Kaynaklari Uygulamalari ve Yönetim Sistemleri (Management Systems and HRM practices in Anatolian Tigers)*. Paper presented at the VII. National Congress of Management and Organization, May, Istanbul.

Aycan, Z. & Fikret-Pasa, S. (2000). *Leadership preferences, career choice and workmotivation in Turkey: A national profile and regional differences*. Paper presented at the Fifteenth International Congress of the International Association for Cross-Cultural Psychology. July, Poland.

Aycan, Z. & Kanungo, R.N., Mendonca, M.; Yu, K., Deller, J.; Stahl, G.; Khursid, A. (2000). Impact of culture on human resource management practices: A ten country comparison. *Applied Psychology: An International Review, 49(1)*, 192–220.

Ayman, R., & Chemers, M.M. (1991). The effect of leadership match on subordinate satisfaction in Mexican organizations: Some moderating influences of self-monitoring. *Applied Psychology: An International Review, 40*, 299–314.

Backlar, P. (1995). Will the "Age of Bureaucracy" Silence the Rights Versus Needs debate? Special Section: Ethics in Community mental Health Care. *Community Mental Health Journal, 31(3)*, 201–206.

Beisecker, A.E., & Beisecker, T.D. (1993). Using Metaphors to Characterize Doctor-Patient Relationships: Paternalism versus Consumerism. *Health Communication, 5(1)*, 41–58.

Blokland, H. (1997). *Freedom and culture in western society*. London: Routledge.

Blumer, H. (1951). Paternalism in Industry. *Social Process in Hawaii, 15*, 26–31.

Calder, M.C. (1995). Child Protection. *British Journal of Social Work, 25(6)*, 749–766.

Callahan, J.C. (1988). Academic Paternalism. In J.C. Callahan (Ed.), *Ethical Issues in Professional Life (pp.105–113)*. New York: Oxford University Press.

Carter, R. (1977). Justifying Paternalism. *Canadian Journal of Philosophy, 7(1)*.

Chao, Y.T. (1990). Culture and Work Organization: The Chinese Case. *International Journal of Psychology, 25(4)*, 583–592.

Cheng, B. (1999). Chinese chief executive officers' employee categorization and managerial behaviour. In H. S. R. Kao, D. Sinha, & B. Wilpert (Eds.), *Management and cultural values: The indigenization of organizations in Asia* (pp.233–251). New Delhi, India: Sage Publications India Pvt Ltd.

Christensen, R.C. (1997). Ethical Issues in Community Mental Health: Cases and Conflicts. *Community Mental Health Journal, 33(1)*, 5–11.

Cicirelli, V.G. (1990). Relationship of Personal-Social Variables to Belief in Paternalism in Parent Caregiving Situations. *Psychology and Aging, 5(3)*, 458–466.

Cohen, E. S. (1985). Autonomy and paternalism: Two goals in conflict. *Law, Medicine and Health Care, 13(4)*, 145–150.

Dorfman, P.W., Howell, J.P. (1988). Dimensions of national culture and effective leadership processes across cultures. *Leadership Quarterly*.

Dworkin, G. (1971). Paternalism. In R. A. Wasserstrom (ed.), *Morality and the Law*. Belmont CA:Wadsworth.

Fikret-Pasa, S., Kabasakal, H., & Bodur, M. (2001). Society, organizations and leadership in Turkey. *Applied Psychology: An International Review, 50*, 559–589.

Fitzsimons, D. J. (1991). From paternalism to partnership. *Journal of Compensation and Benefits, 6(5)*, 48–52.

Genovese, E. D. (1972). *Roll, Jordan, roll: The world the slaves made*. New York: Vintage.

Goodell, G. E. (1985). Paternalism, patronage, and potlatch: The dynamics of giving and being given to. *Current Anthropology, 26(2)*, 247–257.

Gordon, R.M., & Tomita, S. (1990). The reporting of Elder Abuse and Neglect: Mandatory or Voluntary? *Canada's Mental Health, 38(4)*, 1–6.

Gordon, J. (1998). The new paternalism. *Forbes, 162 (10)*, 68–70.

Gupta, R. K. (1999). The truly familial work organization: Extending the organizational boundary to include employees' families in the Indian context. In H. S. R. Kao, D. Sinha, & B. Wilpert (Eds.), *Management and cultural values: The indigenization of organizations in Asia* (pp.102–120). New Delhi, India: Sage Publications India Pvt Ltd.

Ho, D. Y. & Chiu, C. (1994). Component ideas of individualism, collectivism and social organizations: An application in the study of Chinese culture. In U. Kim, H. C. Triandis, C. Kagitcibasi, S. Choi, & G. Yoon (Eds.), *Cross-Cultural research and methodology series: Vol.18. Individualism and collectivism: Theory, method and applications* (pp.251–266) California, USA: Sage Publications, Inc.

Ho, D.Y.-F., Hong, Y.Y., & Chiu, C.-Y. (1989). *Filial Piety and Family-Matrimonial Traditionalism in Chinese Society*. Paper presented at the International Conference on Moral Values and Moral Reasoning in Chinese Societies, Academia Sinica Conference Center, May, Taipei.

Jackman, M. R. (1994). *The velvet glove: Paternalism and conflict in gender, class, and race relations*. California: University of California Press.

Kao, H. S. R., Sek-Hong, N. & Kwan, C. (1990). Cultural adaptations and diffusion for managerial strategies and responses in Hong Kong. *International Journal of Psychology, 25(5/6)*, 657–674.

Kagitcibasi, Ç. (1996). Family and Human Development Across Cultures: A view From the Other Side. New Jersey: Lawrence Erlbaum Associates, Publishers.

Kâğitçibaşi, Ç. (1996). *Family and Human Development Across Cultures: A View From the Other Side*. New Jersey: Lawrence Erlbaum Associates, Publishers.

Kao, H.S.R., Sinha, D., & Sek-Hong, Ng. (Eds.) (1994). *Effective Organizations and Social Values*. New Delhi: Sage.

Kerfoot, D., & Knights, D. (1993). Management, masculinity and manipulation: From paternalism to corporate strategy in financial services in Britain. *Journal of Management Studies, 30(4)*, 659–677.

Kim, S. (1999). Determinants and characteristics of the corporate culture of Korean enterprises. In H. S. R. Kao, D. Sinha, & B. Wilpert (Eds.), *Management and cultural values: The indigenization of organizations in Asia* (pp.86–101). New Delhi, India: Sage Publications India Pvt Ltd.

Kim, U. M. (1994). Significance of paternalism and communalism in the occupational welfare system of Korean firms. In U. Kim, H. C. Triandis, Ç. Kâğitçibaşi, S. Choi, & G. Yoon (Eds.), *Cross-Cultural research and methodology series: Vol.18. Individualism and collectivism: Theory, method and applications* (pp.251–266) California, USA: Sage Publications, Inc.

Kjellin, L.,& Nilstun, T. (1993). Medical and Social Paternalism: Regulation of and Attitudes towards Compulsory Psychiatric Care. *Acta Psychiatrica Scandinavica, 88(6)*, 415–419.

Kleining, J. (1983). *Paternalism*. Manchester: Manchester University press.

Kochanska, G., & Kuczynski, L., & Radke-Yarrow, M. (1989). Correspondence Between Mothers' Self-Reported and Observed Child-Rearing Practices. *Child Development, 60(1)*, 56–63.

Lau, S., & Cheung, P.C. (1987). Relations Between Chinese Adolescents' Perception of Parental Control and Organization and Their Perception of Parental Warmth. *Developmental Psychology, 23*, 726–729.

Levi-Strauss, C. (1969). *The Elementary Structures of Kinship*, rev. ed. Boston: Beacon Press.

Likert, R. (1961). *New patterns of management*. New York: McGraw-Hill.

Lukes, S. (1974). *Power: A Radical View*. London:Macmillan.

Mead, L. M. (1997). *The new paternalism: Supervisory approaches to paternity*. Washington, D.C.: Brookings Institution Press

Meier, A., and Rudwick, E. (1979). *Black Detroit and the Rise of the UAW*. New York: Oxford University Press.

Mesler, M.A. (1994). The Philosophy and Practice Control in Hospice: The Dynamics of Autonomy Versus Paternalism. *Omega Journal of Death and Dying, 30(3)*, 173–189.

Mill, J.S. (1859). On liberty. In *Utilitarianism*. London: Fontana, 1986.

Misumi, J. (1985). *The Behavioural Science of Leadership: An Interdisciplinary Japanese Research*. Ann Arbor: The University of Michigan Press.

Mowday, R. T., Porter, L. W., & Steers, R. M. (1982). *Employee-Organizational Linkages: The Psychology of Commitment, Absenteeism, and Turnover*. New York: Academic press.

Newby, H. (1977). *The Deferential Worker: A study of Farm Workers in East Anglia*. London: Allen Lane.

Northouse, P. G. (1997). *Leadership: Theory and Practice*. Thousand Oaks: Sage Publications.

Osland, J. S., Franco, S., & Osland, A. (1999). Organizational implications of Latin American culture: Lessons for the expatriate manager. *Journal of Management Inquiry, 8(2)*, 219–234.

Padavic, I., & Earnest, W. R. (1994). Paternalism as a component of managerial strategy. *Social Science Journal, 31(4)*, 389–356.

Pye, L. W. (1986). The China trade: Making the deal. *Harvard Business Review, 64 (4)*, 74–80.

Redding, S. G., & Hsiao, M. (1990). An empirical study of overseas Chinese managerial ideology. *International Journal of Psychology, 25*, 629–641.

Singh, P., & Bhandarker, A. (1990). *Corporate Success and Transformational Leadership*. New Delhi: Wiley Eastern.

Sinha, J.B.P. (1980). *The nurturant task leader*. New Delhi: Concept.

Sinha, J.B.P. (1990). *Work Culture in Indian Context.* New Delhi: Sage.

Sinha, J. B. P. (1995). *The Cultural Context of Leadership and Power.* New Delhi: Sage Publications.

Tone, A. (1997). *The business of benevolence: Industrial paternalism in progressive America.* New York: Cornell University Press.

Trompenaars, F. (1993). *Riding the waves of culture.* London: Brealey.

van den Berghe, P.L. (1967). *Race and Racism: A comparative Perspective.* New York: John Wiley & Sons.

Van den Berghe, P.L. (1985). Paternalism, Patronage, and Potlach: The Dynamics of Giving and Being Given to. *Current Anthropology, 26(2),* 262–263.

VanDeVeer, D. (1979). Paternalism and Subsequent Consent. *Canadian Journal of Philosophy, 9(4).*

VanDeVeer, D. (1986). *Paternalistic Intervention: The Moral Bounds of Benevolence.* Princeton: Princeton University Press.

Vroom, V. H., & Yetton P. (1973). *Leadership and Decision Making.* Pittsburgh, PA: University of Pittsburgh Press.

Warren, R. C. (1999). Against paternalism in human resource management. *Business Ethics: A European Review, 8(1),* 50–59.

Weber, M. (1958). *The Protestant Ethic and the Spirit of Capitalism.* New York: Wiley.

Weber, M. (1966). *The Theory of Social and Economic Organization.* New York: Free Press.

Webster (1975). *Webster's dictionary.* Springfield, MA: Merriam-Webster

Chapter 21

Creating Indigenous Psychologies
Insights from Empirical Social Studies of the Science of Psychology

John G. Adair

About 20 years ago I was introduced to the concept of indigenous psychology by a young graduate student in Canada, Uichol Kim. Intrigued by the concept he was presenting, I posed the question, "How do you know when the goal is achieved — when a non-indigenous psychology within a country has become an indigenous psychology?" Uichol responded with examples of indigenous concepts, that only made me puzzle more about the dynamics of the process called indigenization. My question had been posed from my social studies of science perspective rather than from my perspective as a cross-cultural psychologist. I was interested in operationalizing and studying how the indigenization process worked.

My work over subsequent years has applied social science research methods, e.g., bibliometric and content analyses, interviews, surveys, and database analyses, to the study of the science of psychology — in this case how it develops and is made culturally appropriate in countries around the world. Social studies of science are not common within psychology, and particularly uncommon in the study of indigenous psychologies. Aside from occasional empirical data collections on the state of development of a subfield or of the discipline within a country, Gabrenya's (2004) research on the indigenous psychology movement within Taiwan represents the only other systematic program of research on the topic from this perspective. His research has focused on understanding the individual, interpersonal and organizational dynamics, and contextual factors influencing the community of psychologists engaged in indigenising psychology within a single country, Taiwan. In contrast, my research has focused on the indigenization process across several countries. My approach is to empirically describe the course of change in research over time with the goal of determining the factors that facilitate and impede the ways in which an imported discipline is made more culturally sensitive and appropriate and of identifying the variables that impact on this process. My approach is primarily descriptive and analytical of what has occurred rather than prescriptive or normative of what should occur. In this paper I review some of the insights that have emerged as a result of these studies.

HOW THIS APPROACH DIFFERS

A social studies of science approach differs in many ways from those that pursue the identification and promotion of indigenous research accomplishments. For example, rather than culturally unique findings as the goal for this research, indigenous psychologies and the way they develop are the objects of study. This different perspective hopefully will challenge and inform thinking about indigenous psychologies.

Indigenous contributions vs. Indigenous Psychologies

The first difference may be the distinction between indigenous contributions and indigenous psychologies. Research is conducted in discrete projects. Research projects that attempt to explain thoughts and behaviors that are unique to a culture with concepts and measures developed within the culture may make identifiable indigenous contributions. Such contributions are important to the society and to the development of its indigenous psychology. They may better represent the culture, identify differences from so-called Western mainstream psychology, and serve as stimulants and models for indigenous research by others. But we should resist the temptation to equate indigenous contributions with an indigenous psychology. Indigenous contributions are like anecdotes — they serve a useful purpose, but are an inadequate means of assessing discipline progress. For example, it is safe to say that many of the research projects that proceeded in the fashion described at the opening of this paragraph would not make significant contributions, yet such research by any definition would be regarded as that found in an indigenous psychology.

Moreover, it should not be assumed that merely increasing the number of such indigenous contributions will, like building blocks, ultimately lead to an emerging indigenous psychology. Such a perspective confuses indigenization as a goal with its function as a process to develop an "appropriate" psychology for the culture. Much more is involved. The creation of an appropriate psychology for any country is not solely dependent upon its indigenization. Other factors, such as a basic core of researchers, supportive research environments, established research training programs, and good quality national journals have received less attention than indigenization of the discipline. Yet general development of the discipline is an essential adjunct to the process of indigenization. My empirical research seeks to study and inform these broader processes by which indigenous psychologies develop. Before turning to this research and reviewing its findings, two additional general observations are in order.

Source of the Problem

Psychology has its roots in Europe, however, it is the modern discipline developed in the United States, which was generally an acultural, positivistic, experimental psychology that has been imported into countries around the world. Often it took some time to notice that this imported psychology did not always work and that there was a need to indigenize the imported discipline and to adapt it to the local culture and problems. But often the blame for the ill fit of the imported discipline has been placed on the model, or, less constructively, politicized by pejorative references to U.S. colonialism or imperialism. Without denying some of these concerns, this negative perspective unnecessarily externalizes a problem that must be seen as a problem of the country importing the discipline.

The alternative perspective is to internalize the problem. It was the local psychologists who returned from their Western graduate training and uncritically attempted to apply to their own culture the psychology that seemed to work in graduate school. Whereas it is true that they were not trained to recognize the role of culture or context as variables to consider, acceptance of responsibility for the challenge provides a constructive context and attitude for the psychologist who must now cope with the problem. This perspective replaces the need to belittle or denigrate U.S. psychology with an emphasis on the need to modify, build upon, and shape the imported psychology to the needs of one's own culture. Psychology seemed at one time to be worthy of being imported; there may be much to be gained by recognizing the amount of the imported psychology to be retained and the amount to be modified or indigenized.

Indigenization: Need Is Universal, but Unequal across Countries

An important point to understand is that although the need for indigenous psychology development is universal (outside of the United States), the extent of that need and the degree of transformation of the discipline that is required is not uniform throughout the world. For example, differences between European and American social psychology have been observed on numerous occasions (Jaspars, 1986; Rijsman, 1990). These differences are obviously not as large as those between psychology in the U.S. and in Taiwan, but the need for indigenization of the discipline is present for developed world countries as well as for those in the majority world. This is true because (a) psychology has been imported from the U.S. into every country in the world, and (b) psychology was developed earlier and is more established in the U.S. There will be differences between sets of countries in the extent of transformation required. The extent of change required will vary largely as function of (a) the extent of the difference with U.S. culture, and (b) the stage of development of the discipline. The greater the cultural difference and the less developed the discipline, the greater the degree of indigenization of the discipline required. Based on this analysis, the need for indigenization of psychology will be greatest in Asia and Africa, much less in Latin America, even less in Europe, and probably least in Canada. Although the logic of this hierarchy is obvious now, it was not so apparent when I first began this research.

Empirical Study of Indigenization

My research began as a study of the indigenization process. Within the limited early literature most analyses (Atal, 1981; Azuma, 1984; Sinha, D.,1986; Sinha, J.B.P., 1984) contended that indigenization was a transformative process of gradual stages through which the discipline moved toward the goal of creating an indigenous psychology. The problem was that these analyses were conceptual, often anecdotally-based, and without empirical documentation of the discipline's movement toward culturally appropriate psychological research within any country. It seemed to me that it should be possible to operationalize and measure the process to reveal more about indigenization than we could discern from citable indigenous contributions.

I adopted an operational definition of indigenous psychology as reflecting the extent to which the theories, concepts, research problems, hypotheses, methods, and measures emanate from, adequately represent, and for which the results reflect back upon the cultural context in which the behavior is observed, rather than coming from and addressing a foreign research literature. Assuming that indigenization develops by degrees, increasing sensitivity to the local culture should appear in the studies of a widening circle of native researchers. These changes would be reported and archived within their published research. Because journals are the universally accepted outlet for empirical work, they provided a uniform database for assessing the discipline at each stage of its development. Indigenization within a country, therefore, could be empirically measurable over time by content analysis of the research published in representative journals. Because indigenous theories, concepts and methods occur infrequently in any new discipline, measures of the indigenization of a discipline had to be sensitive to modest changes in degree of general concern with culturally-relevant variables and focus on the process rather than on indigenous accomplishments.

I devised 65 different measures of research change that could be recorded within research reports. Because so much research in developing countries emulates research from the developed world, I regarded *any* attention to the local culture as a movement toward indigenization. For example, reference to the culture within the Introduction and Discussion were separately rated on seven-point scales as containing no, slight, or modest references to culture or culture reference equal to prior literature or mostly or solely local culture. The rationale or justification for conducting the research was rated according to whether it was because of the absence of any prior research on the topic within the culture, because of some unique cultural relevance to the culture, or because of some universal rationale. The source of the research problem was rated as arising from social norms, social traditions, religion, or exclusively from the prior literature. Tests were rated according to their origins in developed world countries or locally constructed or adapted. Research subjects were coded as reflecting the traditional society or the ubiquitous undergraduate.

Ratings of these elements of research over an extended period of time enabled a quantification and measurement of discipline change, particularly of its maturation and indigenization. These measures were applied in content analyses of psychological research published in international and national journals within India (Adair, Puhan, & Vohra, 1993), and national journals in Bangladesh (Shirin & Adair, 1989) and Canada (Adair, 1999a; 1999b) during the period between 1972 and 1987. Articles were selected from among those journals in which culture would be expected to play a role, e.g., in social psychology, or broad band journals from the soft side of the discipline, e.g., developmental, personality, organizational behavior. Although limited to this time period, content analyses across the three countries provided a composite picture of the indigenization process. Rather than update content analyses to the present, I have recently completed much broader assessments by country of research presented at international congresses and in PsycLIT entries (Adair, Coêlho, & Luna, 2002) to document the international visibility of research in each country.

THE INDIGENIZATION PROCESS

Indigenization is the process by which an imported psychology is transformed into a discipline that is more appropriate to the culture, i.e., into an indigenous psychology. Indigenous psychology develops and evolves

Table 1. Stages and Activities in the Spread of Psychology around the World

1. Importation
   a. Discipline is introduced to a country,
   b. becomes part of the university curriculum, and
   c. scholars are sent abroad to be trained.
2. Implantation
   a. Returning scholars begin functioning as psychologists,
   b. conduct research emulating Western training model,
   c. research topics selected from journals,
   d. use textbook application of methods to guide research, and
   e. teach discipline as it was taught in graduate school.
3. Indigenization
   a. Scholars criticize Western models and methods as inappropriate,
   b. adapt tests and methods to language and culture,
   c. research topics in the national interest, and
   d. identify culturally unique behaviors/thoughts for study.
4. Autochthonization
   a. Establish graduate training programs to self-perpetuate discipline.
   b. Locally-authored/edited textbooks published and used.
   c. National association promotes journals, discipline, and
   d. standards for research ethics and professional practice.
   e. National funding reliably available for research, and
   f. critical mass of mature, established scholars focus on research problems that are culturally appropriate and nationally important.

through a series of stages. Importation, implantation, indigenization, and autochthonization are the four stages that I have identified through my research and analysis. Autochthonization refers to the processes leading to the emergence of a self-perpetuating discipline independent of its imported source, the culmination of the indigenization process. These stages are outlined and elements within each are detailed in Table 1. I will elaborate on these in the course of the ensuing discussion of findings from studies of the indigenization process in Bangladesh, India, and Canada, countries that varied in the nature and focus of their national disciplines and in their responses to the need for indigenization over the years of my content-analysis study. Coming from three well-placed locations on the indigenization continuum, a look at each provides a composite of the indigenization process.

Toward Indigenization: The Bangladesh Example

Bangladesh is a heavily populated, economically poor country that had a small psychological discipline just emerging from the early stages of importation in the early 1970s. Most faculty had been recently trained in the U.K., or Canada, and subsequently a few more trained in the U.S. and India. Some were trained within Bangladesh, but most of these were employed as teachers with lesser expectations for research activity. The stronger academics with expectations for research were trained abroad.

Our content analyses of Bangladeshi publications (Shirin & Adair, 1989) during this earliest period indicated an unexpectedly high degree of research sophistication in design and statistical methodology, higher even than that found in Indian psychological research some years later. However, closer examination revealed that most of these earliest publications were simply reports of dissertations and other research conducted abroad while the new faculty had been graduate students. This pattern of an apparent regression of research sophistication is likely duplicated in other countries at this early stage of discipline development. Subsequent Bangladeshi research fell into a more typical pattern of replications of previously published research. Moreover, these studies appeared often to be presented as if replication of a Western finding within Bangladesh was evidence of the researcher's investigatory ability.

Unpublished interviews of faculty conducted in 1987 indicated that most were unaware of the concept of indigenization and not broadly sensitive to the ill fit of Western psychology to their cultural context. Survey responses of Bangladesh psychologists similarly indicated a lesser need for research to become more sensitive to their culture. These facts provided strong evidence for the discipline positioned at a pre-indigenization stage. Moreover, the numbers of psychologists working on similar topics were insufficient to provide a critical mass for the stimulation of ideas and feedback or to create a complete, broad-based discipline, thus precluding conditions necessary for rapid progress toward the indigenization stage of development.

Indigenization of Psychology: The Indian Example

Indian psychology, on the other hand, provides a classic example of a discipline at the indigenization stage of development. Although it has had a long history and large numbers of research-trained scholars, psychology in India has continued for many years to manifest a discipline that has engaged in what Mohanty (1988) called Yankee Doodling (i.e., replication of Western psychological research). This led Durganand Sinha to issue several calls for changes in Indian psychology: a call for psychology to become more relevant to Indian society through attention to national social problems (1973) and a companion call for indigenization (1984), i.e., for developing a psychology that was more culturally appropriate.

Empirical assessment of progress. Our content analysis of published Indian psychological research over 16 years (Adair, et al., 1993) provided evidence of a slow but increasing response to Sinha's calls. Rather than a compilation of indigenous contributions such as those that are reported in this collection of papers, these measures provided evidence of subtle changes in the sensitivity and changing nature of Indian psychological research and insights into the manner in which the indigenization process evolves. Although these data and interpretations come from only one country, the following summary of enumerated conclusions from this research likely reflects the manner in which the indigenization process unfolds in many countries. Overall the response to calls for indigenization and the progress toward indigenization has been manifest in several distinctive ways.

(1) The starting point, of course, was the universal orientation of virtually all Indian research. Ratings indicated that the vast majority of research emanated from the previous literature and analysis of references indicated substantial dependency upon Western psychology in 1972–74, with only gradual improvement over subsequent time periods.

(2) In early research reports, cultural sensitivity was displayed typically by passing references in the Introduction sections of research articles — an initial almost ritualistic response or need to pay homage to the culture — followed by its noticeable absence later in the article. One is tempted to interpret that researchers had some inclination to direct their attention toward their own culture, maybe in response to Sinha's calls, but either lacked understanding of how to do this, or were distracted by their attention to statistical methodology that led to universalistic interpretations of their data. Over time this pattern was gradually replaced by more balanced expressions of cultural sensitivity throughout some articles. In spite of these averaged increases, there still was not any evidence of increased sensitivity to the Indian context among a broad base of Indian scholars.

(3) The third noticeable pattern was for greater cultural sensitivity to be expressed in non-empirical analyses and theoretical reviews rather than within research articles. This was most evident within the more recent time periods of the study where references to the culture within non-empirical articles were much greater than those found within both the Introduction and Discussion sections of empirical articles. These trends suggested the importance of some conceptual level analysis and psychological understanding of the culture as a precursor to its appearance in the empirical literature.

(4) The nature of empirical indigenous developments, although infrequent, also changed over time from the identification of simple differences between India and the West or within India to more complex explanations of Indian problems and behaviors. More substantial increases occurred in the most recent time period in the combined frequencies of the two most indigenous categories — attempts to explain

typical behaviors of Indians and references to indigenous theories. The nature and timing of these observations, however, suggests they could have resulted as much from the maturation of the discipline as from its indigenization.

(5) The infrequency of applied research on national social problems precluded the discipline in India making obvious indigenous contributions to their resolution. Because several of the journals we surveyed included reports of applied research this observation was not due to a sampling bias. Rather, it seems as if there was a lesser response to Sinha's call for socially relevant research than to his call for indigenization. An applied approach and contributions should be an important component of an indigenous discipline. Applied research focuses investigators on their own culture, provides local perspectives and solutions to social problems, and generates new research questions within the culture. But to achieve an applied approach requires new perspectives and skills — in addition to understanding of the culture and problem, the researcher must have an understanding of the nature and difficulties of applied research. It seems as if the difficulties due to the lack of perspective and experience that the Indian researchers had in initiating indigenous research, similarly impeded their development of applied contributions. Possibly at a later stage in the indigenization process as the numbers of experienced researchers increased, applied research could be an effective device for further indigenizing the discipline. Encouraged to solve problems, experienced researchers should find that problem-oriented research frees them from the shackles of methodology (which is Western) to focus on what can solve the (indigenous) problem. It might also engage a larger number of psychologists within the country to look at problems within their own culture.

(6) The attraction to publish in better quality foreign journals common among psychologists in many countries was also found to be true of Indian psychologists (Adair, Pandey, Begum, Puhan, & Vohra, 1995). Indeed, content analyses revealed that Indian research published abroad was generally more culturally sensitive than the research published in India. The fact that research that contains culturally unique elements is more readily publishable in foreign or international journals encourages leading scholars to publish their indigenous research there rather than in their own country. High quality, indigenous research that could serve as the model and stimulus for similar research within the country is at least initially directed to the wrong audience, a problem that is not uncommon among developing countries (see Öngel & Smith, 1999).

(7) Truly indigenous developments were least evident within research methodologies, a finding that has been general across countries. Indigenous test constructions were uniformly rare across the duration of the study, and overall indigenous methodology was much less advanced than progress

toward increasing cultural sensitivity and indigenous conceptualizations. This finding may be disconcerting given the strong criticism of Western methodology, but not unexpected given the challenging task of devising new methods. Researchers need considerable experience with the imported discipline before they are in a position to alter Western methods or develop indigenous methodologies. Similarly, experience is necessary for the development of indigenous concepts and contributions and this relationship suggests the importance of discipline development to the indigenization process.

Within a newly imported discipline, the vast majority are either newly graduated psychologists or young researchers still in training. Most are just beginning to establish themselves as independent investigators. To these scholars, previous research serves as a model for how research should be conducted and topics to research are readily selected from the journals. As researchers become more experienced they more confidently begin to identify problems arising from within their own culture that their research methods can address. With increasing numbers of seasoned researchers a critical mass is reached whereby researchers begin to stimulate and guide one another to increasing levels of indigenous research. This intertwining of indigenization and discipline development is integral to defining autochthonization as the next and final stage in the indigenization process to which Indian psychology aspires.

Contextual Influences on Indigenization of Psychology in India. In addition to the general role of discipline development, factors specific to India have been instrumental in shaping the unique character of its indigenous psychology movement. Most influential were Durganand Sinha's calls for indigenization of Indian psychology. In contrast to the leading proponents in other countries, i.e., Yang (Taiwan), Enriquez (Philippines), and Diaz-Guerrero (Mexico), each of whom focused on cultural aspects of the problem in their native language, Sinha's (1973) initial call was for increased relevance — for application of psychology to informing and resolving national social problems. His subsequent appeals for indigenization (e.g., 1984; 1986; 1994) were always made in the English language, and emphasized relevance and the importance of looking at research from the Indian context or perspective. He regarded research based on cultural traditions or early Vedic writings as acceptable modes for indigenising the discipline, but seemed more inclined to promote the full transformation of the discipline into an indigenous psychology applicable to Indian thought and behavior, rather than a cultural psychology of the Indian subcontinent, an ethnopsychology, or a subspecialty of Indian psychology.

The result has been to make Indian indigenous psychology somewhat different from that found in other countries. There is not a specific journal or forum in which indigenous contributions are collated, nor is there a single accepted format or model for indigenous research.

According to Sinha (1994), even some locally-conducted, Western-based research has yielded indigenous contributions by virtue of findings interpreted and researched from the perspective of the Indian context. Achievement motivation (Agarwal & Misra, 1986), for example, has been demonstrated to be based by Indian participants upon familial and social goals rather than on personal achievement. Similarly, J.B.P. Sinha's (1980) organizational research has led him to postulate a theory of a nurturant-task leader as a better fit than Western leadership models for the Indian context. Other indigenous contributions to Indian psychology have been derived from concepts identified within ancient Indian religio-philosophical writings, such as Pande & Naidu's (1992) study on detachment as a means of stress relief, or Chakraborty's (1987) conceptualizations of work motivation as an almost spiritual personal duty rather than a contractual obligation. Viewed positively, J. Sinha (2000) has labeled this process of accepting indigenous insights from all manner of sources as integrative indigenization. On the other hand, because these diverse indigenous contributions are scattered and loosely connected if at all, they problematically give the impression of indigenization of psychology in India as lacking focus and integration, and as proceeding quite slowly.

Another consideration is the effect of English as a national language on the indigenization process in India. Although it is unclear whether it has diminished progress, it is obvious that the widespread use of English has fostered Indian participation in the larger world of psychology. For example, among all of the countries around the world (Adair, et al, 2002), Indian psychologists were found to have a greater presence at international congresses and their research more frequently included within PsycLIT than any other majority-world country and even more than many developed-world countries. But has this external presence of Indian research diminished its indigenous thrust within? These interesting questions reinforce the view that indigenization of psychology within a country is a complex, multi-determined process, and not a matter of simply increasing sensitivity toward one's own culture.

At the same time that Indian research has been gradually becoming more culturally sensitive, psychology in India has made significant strides toward autochthonization of its discipline. The Indian Council of Social Science Research (ICSSR) has not only provided a national source of funding for research, it has promoted and financed several infrastructure developments that would be the envy of the discipline in most countries. Recognizing the difficulties of researchers maintaining awareness and gaining access to the vast amount of psychological research conducted within the country, ICSSR has sponsored the regular publication of a journal, *Indian Psychological Abstracts and Reviews*, each issue of which contains a feature review article together with indexed abstracts of recent Indian research. ICSSR has also sponsored a series of edited books compiling and reviewing the accumulated Indian research since the last publication. Although published less frequently than the *Annual Reviews*, the format is similar. The impressive three-volume series *Psychology in India: The state of the art* (1988), was followed by another set of volumes *Psychology in India Revisited: Developments in the Discipline* (2001). Both series, under the general editorship of Janak Pandey, are important for taking stock and for the promotion of further research within the discipline. These exceptional infrastructure developments strengthened by additional high-quality journals, a strong national association, and other professional developments within the country will be useful in moving Indian psychology toward that final stage of an autochthonous discipline.

Indigenization and Autochthonization of Psychology: The Canadian Example

Development of the discipline and its independence from its foreign origins is ultimately necessary for the realization of an indigenous psychology. Although it is listed as the final stage, the need for autochthonization emerges much earlier with the perceived needs for local graduate training and other resources. The processes of indigenization and autochthonization are thus continuously intertwined, until an autochthonous, indigenous psychology is ultimately realized.

Need for a Canadian psychology: Canadians and Americans may seem similar in appearance and behaviors, but their cultures differ in a number of important ways: Canada is a multicultural society with a national policy that promotes maintenance of an immigrant's ethnic heritage and customs, which leads to a society that is characterized as an ethnic/cultural mosaic, not a melting pot. The country is officially bilingual. Its aboriginal population is proportionally much greater than that of the U.S., whereas its black population is proportionally much less. Canada has a more socialized system of health care and other social services, different laws, sports, and life style. As a discipline, psychology in Canada is considerably smaller and was much later in its development than in the U.S. The importation of a large number of foreign-trained psychologists in the late 1960s and early 1970s deterred development of a national indigenous psychology although in some ways it facilitated the development of the national discipline.

Unlike European psychology, Canadians have had an additional obstacle to autochthonous development: It is so close to the United States that it is difficult to carve out a distinctive identity. I have argued through previous research and writing (Adair, 1999a) that the development of the Canadian national discipline had to undergo a degree of both indigenization and autochthonization. I next summarize and underscore the parallels of the Canadian experience with those of psychologists in other cultures. I contend that the Canadian example that follows serves as a prototype of the processes that every country experiences. Readers may have difficulty accepting that indigenization or autochthonization of psychology in Canada has any relevance or applicability to the indigenization process in majority-world cultures. I would simply urge the reader to substitute the name of their country, e.g., Taiwan, for the name of my country, Canada, and to substitute Chinese or Taiwanese for example, wherever I have used the word Canadian. Such a substitution is an effective device for realizing that the experiences of Canadian psychologists have been prototypical of those within majority-world countries. Just as in many of the countries of Asia and elsewhere, psychology in Canada has been heavily influenced by the United States. We had grants in the early years from the Rockefeller and Ford Foundations that were designed to help us get started. For several additional years Canadian researchers were able to hold grants from U.S. agencies. Canadian funds were seldom available. For our fledgling discipline, it was expedient to adopt the APA Code of Ethics and APA clinical accreditation standards. Our classrooms were dominated by U.S.-produced textbooks and Canadians who had gone abroad (to the U.S.) for graduate training and returned to teach a universal psychology with examples from their U.S. experience. No more than one or two Canadian textbooks had been written. The parallel with conditions within developing countries at about this same stage is striking. We even added obstacles to our own indigenization.

But from the mid-1960s to about the late 1970s, Canadian higher education underwent enormous expansion. My own department grew from about 10 persons to over 40 in just over five years; in a single year we hired 12 new faculty members! Canada had few established doctoral training programs to produce the quantities of new Ph.D.s that were required. As a consequence Canada imported large numbers of new faculty, some from Europe, but primarily from the U.S. These U.S.-born and certainly U.S.-trained psychologists began teaching a universalistic (mostly U.S.-based) psychology to Canadian students. U.S.-trained faculty typically did not understand that there were Canadian issues and there was relatively little research on topics of national interest to Canadians. The excellent Canadian research that was conducted (e.g., Lambert's work on bilingualism) was not widely known among many faculty who exclusively read U.S. journals and belonged to the APA rather than becoming members of the Canadian Psychological Association (CPA).

Although calls for Canadianization of the social sciences became common, in psychology primarily from John Berry (1974), it was difficult for many of us to know how to respond. Just as in India, content analysis of Canadian publications revealed them to be largely universalistic in orientation, stimulated by and largely only extensions of the prior literature, and relatively devoid of cultural sensitivity. It was comparable in many ways to the situation that prevails in many majority-world countries and in many respects the resolution or indigenization of Canadian psychology can be regarded as an analogue of the indigenization process in these countries. Slowly, measures of cultural sensitivity began to reflect changes in Canadian research.

The process took about 20 years in spite of great financial resources made available to Canadian Universities and to Canadian psychology. A number of developments and policies were helpful in bringing about this change. These elements that would be necessary across most countries are listed in Table 2. The first step, probably unique to the Canadian context, was to make "Canadian First" the instruction to all hiring committees. The task of hiring Canadians was made possible in large part by the graduation of increasing numbers of high-quality Ph.D.s trained within newly established graduate programs.

As large numbers of new faculty established their research programs and became more seasoned scholars, the amount, quality, and cultural sensitivity of their research began to increase. Critical masses of scholars emerged within many research areas and increasingly their work began to focus and have impact on Canadian national issues -an aging population, family, and women at work – and on topics that were of uniquely Canadian concern: multiculturalism, immigration, acculturation, bilingualism, stereotypes and prejudice. This shift was facilitated by the national granting agency targeting funding on some of these topics.

As a first step in addressing the need for Canadian textbooks, edited books of readings were produced that brought together examples of Canadian research on culturally-relevant issues. Concurrently, the infrastructure for the discipline was developed and enhanced: Two new journals were added, a code of ethics was drafted and adopted, CPA began to assess and accredit its own clinical training programs, ultimately in joint

Table 2. Necessary Elements in the Creation of an Autochthonous Indigenous Psychology

---

   i. A critical mass of researchers,

  ii. who are seasoned scholars capable of independent problem-centered research

 iii. and are aware of or sensitive to thoughts and behaviors unique to their culture and who

 iv. include culturally-appropriate variables in their research and

  v. research topics of importance to society.

 vi. make a number of original research contributions to understanding local thought and behavior and national social issues (as well as universal knowledge).

 vii. This research may then be compiled and described in locally edited/authored textbooks,

viii. utilized in more culturally-relevant curricula and classroom teaching, and

 xi. developed into graduate training programs to make the discipline self-sustaining and no longer dependent upon foreign training.

  x. A developed discipline infrastructure sustains accomplishments.

---

site visits and accreditations with the APA were set up, and an independent national office for the Canadian Psychological Association was established with a full-time executive director.

I marked the culmination of the Canadianization process with the publication of a Canadian-authored textbook (Alcock, Carment, & Sadava, 1988) that highlighted Canadian research as part of the world literature in social psychology. The significance of this publication was the realization that enough Canadian research had been accumulated as the basis for a textbook and for classroom instruction. Moreover, the number of researchers and the quality of their research had increased greatly over the previous three decades. They have contributed much to the understanding of Canadian society, as well as to the universal understanding of behavior. That there was a distinctively Canadian psychology to market commercially affirmed the vitality and relevance of the discipline and its status as an indigenous and autochthonous psychology.

The indigenization process was much broader than merely becoming aware of Canadian issues and shifting research to culturally appropriate topics. Discipline development was as important as the cultural sensitivity of the researcher to the need for indigenization. Although government money and other resources were available, the indigenization process was gradual and extended over a long period of time. To many of us it was slower than we would have anticipated. But that may have reflected the complexity of the process and the many elements that had to fall into place before Canadian psychology could achieve its current status.

In conclusion, the goal of developing a culturally appropriate psychology of Canada was achieved through the dual processes of making the research more culturally sensitive and relevant, and developing the discipline into a mature, autochthonous psychology. These processes were intertwined. Culturally sensitive contributions were necessary for stimulating investigators' indigenous research and for providing models of what and how it could be achieved. Discipline development, on the other hand, strengthened the base of researchers who would conduct this research. Both processes were essential for the indigenization of Canadian psychology. Similar processes and stages will likely need to be followed by disciplines in other countries seeking to develop indigenous psychologies.

Dilemmas Confronting Indigenous Psychologies

The process of creating indigenous psychologies is complex and the different variables that come into play are far greater than this summary description has covered or that my research has so far examined. But in these closing paragraphs I conceptually present several variables and processes that pose dilemmas confronting the creation of indigenous psychologies.

Languages of science and of the culture. A dilemma for indigenous psychologies arises from the language in which research must be conducted, in which the science is taught, and in which the science must be written. The language of science is English; the language of culture may be Hindi, Mandarin, Spanish or German. This dilemma for psychologists attempting to promote an indigenous psychology was vividly articulated for me by a psychologist I interviewed during my research in India. She said, "As a psychologist I think in English; but as a person I feel in Hindi." In other words, although writing and publication must be in the language of science, indigenous research is likely to be more successful if it is conceptualized and the data are collected in the native language.

English is the language of science because its use is intended to facilitate international communication. Unfortunately for psychologists from the majority world, this communication is largely uni-directional and less is achieved than is hoped for in absolute terms. International scientific communication occurs through both publications that are internationally accessible and presentations at international congresses. In recent research (Adair, et al., 2002) we empirically researched this question by examining the country affiliation of first authors in PsycLIT as an international database of the psychological research literature, and in a database of the presentations at the International Congresses of Applied Psychology. We documented that majority-world psychologists have a proportionally much greater share of the presentations at international congresses, whereas within PsycLIT that share is discouragingly small. Although we were surprised to find that an impressive 45% of the entries in PsycLIT were for research by psychologists from outside the United States, non-English entries, which were once about 12% of the database, have substantially declined to only about 6% on average in recent years. Finally, only about 3% of PsycLIT entries were for research by persons from majority-world countries. These figures discourage psychologists from these countries from attempting to communicate with the broader world of psychology. Yet, as I argue next, it is important to the indigenous discipline to make that effort.

Communicating Indigenous Research Within the Country or to the Larger World of Psychology. An important dilemma confronting indigenous psychologies is where to communicate its research results. There is always value in communicating research to broader audiences. They provide you with feedback, criticism, and advice. Such communication can also provide opportunities for cross-indigenous comparisons within other cultures and countries. And, lastly, it provides the important opportunity for indigenous psychologies to contribute to a new universal psychology. On the other hand, communicating research to others who are also researching indigenous concepts may stimulate the work of others. Some balance has to be reached.

Uniqueness vs. relevance. An early concern I expressed about indigenous psychology was the danger of an investigator, accepting the need to indigenise psychological research, researching culturally-unique traits or concepts, without regard to how commonly they occur, how they conceptually integrate, or how behaviorally-meaningful they are to contemporary society (Adair, 1996). Following indigenous contributions as the model for their "culturally-appropriate" research, some have been led to equate indigenous research narrowly with a search for either (a) uniquely native traits or concepts, (b) early religious or philosophical writings, or (c) linguistically-defined constructs. Each of these meet the major criterion of cultural uniqueness, yet if they are to have a place in a larger indigenous psychology of the country, the criterion of relevance to explaining contemporary behaviors and cognitions must also be met. In particular some attention must be given to the theoretical integration of these contributions into a larger meaningful indigenous psychology with contemporary relevance.

How much of a national discipline of psychology needs to be indigenous? This question raises all sorts of concerns to which attention must be directed. What portion of behavior and cognition is not determined or substantially influenced by culture, and hence does not need to be indigenized? What portion of social, developmental, and clinical psychology, i.e., areas substantially influenced by culture are likely to result in derived *etics* or universals, and hence supplant the need for indigenous findings? Our study of Canadian psychology offers some insight into this by substantial yet relatively modest levels of culturally sensitive research contained in its broad band social/developmental/applied journal *Canadian Journal of Behavioral Science* over 15 years of study. Some of our measures indicated a degree of cultural sensitivity in as much as 20% to 30% of published research, but this seems to have reached an upper limit. Whereas it is unlikely that such percentages will rise much higher, future research might examine the types of studies that do not reflect the cultural sensitivity our measures were designed to assess.

Conclusion

This analysis of indigenous psychologies has shown how an empirical study of discipline indigenization offers a different view of the process that can inform the thinking of researchers engaged in indigenous work. At the same time, it can be used to provide an objective assessment of where the discipline is as a counterbalance to hopes of where it might be or of negativism regarding its lack of development. Empirical data also provide a baseline against which to judge the impact of calls for indigenization or other historical events within each country. It is particularly helpful for providing insights into the variables that influence the indigenization process and its development within a country. In summary, a rigorous, empirical social study of the science can be used to assist psychologists in majority-world countries to realize their goal of creating an effective indigenous discipline.

REFERENCES

Adair, J. G. (1996). The Indigenous psychology bandwagon: Cautions and considerations. In J. Pandey, D. Sinha, & D. P. S. Bhawak (Eds.), *Asian contributions to cross-cultural psychology* (pp. 50–58). New Delhi: Sage.

Adair, J. G. (1999a). Indigenization of Psychology: The concept and its practical implementation. *Applied Psychology: An International Review, 48,* 403–418.

Adair, J. G. (1999b, May). The Indigenous Psychology Movement in Developing Countries: Its Goals and Implications for Canadian Psychology. Paper presented to the Section on International and Cross-Cultural Psychology, Canadian Psychological Association, Halifax.

Adair, J. G., Coêlho, A., & Luna, J. R. (2002). How International is International Psychology? *International Journal of Psychology, 37,* 160–170.

Adair, J. G., Pandey, J., Begum, H. A., Puhan, B. N., & Vohra, N. (1995). Indigenization and Development of the Discipline: Perceptions and Opinions of Indian and Bangladeshi Psychologists. *Journal of Cross-Cultural Psychology, 26,* 392–407.

Adair, J. G., Puhan, B. N., & Vohra, N. (1993). Indigenization of psychology: Empirical assessment of progress in Indian research. *International Journal of Psychology, 28,* 149–169.

Agarwal, R., & Misra, G. (1986). A factor analytic study of achievement goals and means: An Indian view. *International Journal of Psychology, 21,* 717–731.

Alcock, J. E., Carment, D. W., & Sadava, S. W. (1988). A textbook of social psychology. Scarborough, Canada: Prentice-Hall.

Atal, Y. (1981). Call for indigenization. *International Social Science Journal, 33,* 189–197.

Azuma, H. (1984). Psychology in a non-Western country. *International Journal of Psychology, 19,* 45–56.

Berry, J. W. (1974). Canadian psychology: Some social and applied emphases. Canadian Psychologist, 15, 132–139.

Chakraborty, S. K. (1987). Managerial effectiveness and quality of work life: Indian insights. New Delhi: McGraw-Hill.

Gabrenya, W. K. (2004). Understanding the Taiwan Indigenous Psychology Movement: A Sociology of Science Approach. Unpublished manuscript, Florida Institute of Technology, Melbourne, FL.

Jaspars, J. (1986). Forum and focus: A personal view of European social psychology. *European Journal of Social Psychology, 16,* 3–15.

Mohanty, A. K. (1988). Beyond the horizon of Indian Psychology-The Yankee doodler. In F. M. Sahoo (Eds.), *Psychology in Indian Context* (pp. 1–8). Agra: National Psychological Corporation.

Öngel, Ü, & Smith, P. B. (1999). The search for indigenous psychologies: Data from Turkey and the former USSR. *Applied Psychology: An International Review, 48,* 465–479.

Pande, N, & Naidu, R. K. (1992). Anasakti and health: A study of non-attachment. *Psychology and Developing Societies, 4,* 89–104.

Rijsman, J. B. (1990). How European is social psychology in Europe? In P. J. D. Drenth, J. A. Sergeant, & R. J. Takens (Eds.). *European perspectives in psychology, Vol. 3: Work and organizational, social and economic, cross-cultural* (pp. 169–181). New York: Wiley.

Sinha, D. (1973). Priorities and programmes of research in the field of psychology. *Journal of Psychological Researches, 17,* 22–27.

Sinha, D. (1986). *Psychology in a Third World country: The Indian experience*. New York: Sage.

Sinha, D. (1994). Indigenization of Psychology in India. *Indian Psychological Abstracts and Reviews, 1,* 179–214.

Sinha, J. B. P. (1980). *The nurturant task leader*. New Delhi: Concept.

Sinha, J. B. P. (1984). Towards partnership for relevant research in the Third World. *International Journal of Psychology, 19,* 169–178.

Sinha, J. B. P. (2000). Towards indigenization of psychology in India. *Psychological Studies, 45,* 3–13.

Shirin, S. & Adair, J. G. (1989, June). Psychology in Bangladesh: The First Twenty Years. Paper presented at the annual meeting of the Canadian Psychological Association.

About the Editors

Uichol Kim is Inha Fellow professor, Inha University, Incheon Korea. He has taught at Chung-Ang University and the University of Hawaii at Manoa (1988-1994). He has specialized in the area of indigenous and cultural psychology and published over 100 articles and 12 books. His publications include *Indigenous psychologies* (Sage, 1993), *Individualism and collectivism* (Sage, 1994), *Progress in Asian social psychology* (Wiley, 1997), *Good government* (NIAS Press, 2002) and *Democracy, human right and Islam in Modern Iran* (Fagbokforlaget, 2003). He has conducted research in the area of family and parent-child relationship, education attainment and school violence, organizational culture and change, health and subjective well-being, and democracy, human rights, and political culture. He has taught at University of Tokyo, Japan, the University of Stockholm, Sweden, the Nordic Institute for Asian Studies, Denmark, the University of Konstanz, Germany, the Warsaw School of Advanced Social Psychology, Poland, and the University of Bergen, Norway. He has provided consulting services for governmental agencies and multi-national companies in Canada, Denmark, Hong Kong, India, Korea, Malaysia, Singapore, Thailand, and the United States. He is the founding editor of *Asian Journal of Social Psychology* and currently the president of Division of Psychology and National Development, International Association of Applied Psychology. *E-mail*: *uicholk@chol.com*.

Kuo-Shu Yang is currently the Chair and Professor in the Department of Psychology at Fo Guang College of Humanities and Social Sciences. He received his Ph.D. in personality and social psychology from the University of Illinois in Urbana, after which he became an Associate and then Full Professor in the Department of Psychology at National Taiwan University and was jointly appointed as Associate Research Fellow and Research Fellow at the Research Institute of Ethnology, Academia Sinica in Taiwan. He went on to serve as the Vice President of AS for four years. His research interests include the indigenized, systematic study of Chinese personality and social behavior and their changes due to societal modernization, especially Chinese familism, filial piety, psychological traditionality and modernity, individual- and social-oriented achievement motivation, and individual- and social-oriented self. He has orchestrated a group of Chinese psychologists in Taiwan, Hong Kong, and mainland China to promote an academic movement for the indigenization of psychological research in Chinese societies. He has authored and edited more than 20 books and published more than 150 academic papers in Chinese and English. He was elected as an Academician in the 1998 biennial meeting of domestic and overseas academicians of Academia Sinica. Address correspondence to Department of Psychology, National Taiwan University, Taipei, Taiwan. Fax: (886-2) 2362-9909. E-mail: *kuoshu@ntu.edu.tw.*

Kwang-Kuo Hwang obtained his Ph.D. in social psychology at the University of Hawaii. He is currently a National Chair Professor awarded by Taiwan's Ministry of Education at National Taiwan University. He has endeavored to promote the indigenization movement of psychology and social science in Chinese society since the early 1980s, and has published eight books and more than one hundred articles on related issues in both Chinese and English. He is currently President of the Asian Association of Social Psychology. E-mail: *kkhwang@ccms.ntu.edu.tw.*

Name Index

Subject Index